ARGUMEN

Drawing from the study of human reasoning, *Argumentation* describes different types of arguments and explains how they influence beliefs and behavior. Raymond S. Nickerson identifies many of the fallacies, biases, and other flaws often found in arguments as well as "stratagems" (schemes, illogical and alogical tactics) that people regularly use to persuade others (or themselves). Much attention is given to the evaluation of arguments. As a source for understanding and evaluating arguments in decision-making, it is ideal for courses on cognition, reasoning, and psychology.

RAYMOND S. NICKERSON is retired from Bolt Beraneck and Newman Inc (BBN Systems and Technologies) where he was a senior vice president. He was the founding editor of the *Journal of Experimental Psychology: Applied.* He is now a Visiting Scientist at Tufts University, Massachusetts. He is a recipient of the Franklin V. Taylor Award from the American Psychological Association's Division of Applied Experimental and Engineering Psychology, and an Outstanding Career Achievement Award from Tufts Graduate School of Arts and Sciences and School of Engineering. The American Psychological Association established the Raymond S. Nickerson Best Paper Award, to be given annually, in his honor. *Argumentation* is his tenth book.

Books by the Author

The Teaching of Thinking (with David N. Perkins and Edward E. Smith) - 1985
Using Computers: Human Factors in Information Systems - 1986
Reflections on Reasoning - 1986
Looking Ahead: Human Factors Challenges in a Changing World - 1992
Psychology and Environmental Change - 2003
Cognition and Chance: The Psychology of Probabilistic Reasoning - 2004
Aspects of Rationality: Reflections on What it Means to be Rational and Whether We Are - 2008
Mathematical Reasoning: Patterns, Problems, Conjectures and Proofs - 2010
Conditional Reasoning: The Unruly Syntactics, Semantics, Thematics and Pragmatics of "If" - 2015

ARGUMENTATION

The Art of Persuasion

RAYMOND S. NICKERSON

Tufts University

CAMBRIDGE
UNIVERSITY PRESS

University Printing House, Cambridge CB2 8BS, United Kingdom

One Liberty Plaza, 20th Floor, New York, NY 10006, USA

477 Williamstown Road, Port Melbourne, VIC 3207, Australia

314–321, 3rd Floor, Plot 3, Splendor Forum, Jasola District Centre, New Delhi – 110025, India

79 Anson Road, #06–04/06, Singapore 079906

Cambridge University Press is part of the University of Cambridge.

It furthers the University's mission by disseminating knowledge in the pursuit of education, learning, and research at the highest international levels of excellence.

www.cambridge.org
Information on this title: www.cambridge.org/9781108835268
DOI: 10.1017/9781108892032

First published 2021

A catalogue record for this publication is available from the British Library.

ISBN 978-1-108-83526-8 Hardback
ISBN 978-1-108-79987-4 Paperback

For Mia, Asher, Emmett, Ray, and their generation.

Contents

Figure

Tables

Preface

Argument has many connotations as the term is used in the psychological literature. While respecting this diversity, in this book I use the term to mean an effort to modify beliefs or behavior. The focus is primarily, though not exclusively, on verbal arguments. Two questions about verbal arguments are emphasized: what makes an argument persuasive, and what makes an assertion (e.g., a premise of an argument) plausible?

The ability and propensity to argue – with oneself and others – are distinctively human traits, and traits on which we daily depend. The prototypical argument is a set of claims (premises) that are intended to support another claim (a conclusion). Arguments vary with respect to the degree to which they are persuasive. An argument may be said to be *strong* if its premises strongly support its conclusion in the sense that if its premises are known (or believed) to be true, its conclusion is likely to be accepted as true as well. It may be said to be *sound* if it is strong *and* its premises are known (or believed) to be true.

For practical purposes, we want to be able to tell the difference between arguments that are sound and those that are not. This requires being able to judge whether the premises strongly support the conclusion *and* whether they are true. With this conception of argumentation in mind, I attempt in this book to review what the literature has to say on the questions of what makes an argument *persuasive* and what makes a claim *plausible.*

Any attempt to address these questions is bound to raise a plethora of related questions: What is an argument? How might arguments be classified? What purpose(s) do arguments serve? How are arguments enabled or constrained by human capabilities and limitations? What strategies or stratagems do people use in attempts to win arguments? Or to judge the persuasiveness of arguments? What role(s) does logic play in argumentation? What is the basis of the authority of logic? Why do we feel obliged to try to be logical? How does argumentation relate to reasoning? What is a fallacy? Are there fallacies that are common in arguments? What other types of problems (unjustified assumptions, biases, foibles) affect argumentation? Do people treat assertions as true or false, or do they accept them to varying degrees. If the latter, what determines the amount of credence they give to specific assertions? Why do different people draw different conclusions from the same evidence? The questions multiply.

I make no claim that this book offers answers to all of these questions, but I hope it stimulates productive thinking about a nontrivial subset of them and provides useful pointers to relevant sources.

- Chapter 1 addresses the questions of what an argument is, for purposes of this book, and what purposes arguments serve. It also relates argumentation to reasoning.
- Chapter 2 discusses differences among various types of argument: deductive, inductive (abductive, conductive), postulational, analogical.
- Chapter 3 focuses on the important task of evaluating arguments, both formal and informal, distinguishing the roles of form (e.g., rules of logic) and substance (empirical truth).
- Chapter 4 deals explicitly with one of the two major questions that motivate this book: What makes an argument persuasive? Attention is given both to properties of arguments and properties of arguers.
- Chapter 5 focuses on the second major question dealt with in the book: What makes a claim plausible? Factors are noted that determine whether an assertion will be believed, or the degree of credibility it will be given.
- Chapters 6, 7, and 8 identify and discuss numerous types of reasoning problems – fallacies, biases, and assorted other foibles – that plague argumentation, often making arguments invalid and/or unsound.
- Chapter 9 focuses on *stratagems*, a term borrowed from Schopenhauer (undated/1896) to whom it connoted an alogical ploy that is used for the purpose of winning debates or disputes or for shaping or molding beliefs or behavior by methods other than appeal to relevant information and cogent reasoning.
- Chapter 10 considers the question of how argumentation may be taught, and the position is taken that teaching argumentation requires teaching reasoning, and conversely.

I note, with gratitude, the support of grant N00014-14–1-0529 from the US Office of Naval Research – in particular Program Director Harold Hawkins – for much of the time this book was in preparation. It is a pleasure too to acknowledge many stimulating discussions with colleagues including, especially during this time, Daniel Barch, Susan Butler, Mike Carlin, Rich Chechile, Ruma Falk, and helpful comments from several anonymous reviewers of the manuscript, or parts thereof, while it was in preparation. I am grateful to the Psychology Department of Tufts University for letting me, a nonacademic, maintain an affiliation since I retired from industry (BBN Systems and Technologies) thirty years ago.

I would be remiss if I did not acknowledge the role that George Miller played in establishing my interest in the relationship between reasoning and argumentation. About thirty-five years ago, at his invitation, I wrote a paper titled *Reasoning in Argument Evaluation*. It was one of forty-six papers commissioned by The Study Group on the National Assessment of Student Achievement. It was included in a report to the National Assessment of Educational Progress, prepared by Miller (1986), but was otherwise never published. I have incorporated parts of that paper, to the extent that they are still relevant, in several places, especially in Chapter 3. The invitation from Miller to write the paper for that project unquestionably stoked my interest in the subject, and it has lasted these many years.

In previous books, I have acknowledged the constant and invaluable loving support of my wife, Doris. She died peacefully at home while this book was in preparation. The loss was profound, but her legacy continues.

It gives me special pleasure to dedicate this book to the first few arrivals of the next generation (great-grandchildren) in my family: Mia, Asher, Emmett, and Ray.

1

Argumentation

> The domain of argumentation is that of the credible, the plausible, the probable, to the degree that the latter eludes the certainty of calculations
>
> (Perelman & Olbrechts-Tyteca, 1969, p. 1).

> In philosophy, we spend half our time arguing that our opponent's arguments are fallacious. No philosophers admit to being equivocators, but all philosophers agree that the *other* philosophers are equivocating. Exactly where the equivocations are is part of what everybody argues about"
>
> (Powers, 1995, p. 300).

It would be difficult to overstate the importance of the role that argumentation has played in the history of humankind. Arguments are used to determine who will rule a nation and how a nation will be ruled. They are used to decide on the guilt or innocence of people accused of criminal behavior. Philosophers use them to justify or challenge world views. Academics use them to shape the thinking of their students regarding whatever they are teaching. Merchants use them to influence people's purchasing behavior. Parents use them to convince their offspring to behave, or not, in certain ways, and the offspring use them in the hope of showing their parents' arguments to be flawed.

What is an Argument?

In everyday language *argument* often connotes a verbal dispute or quarrel and arguing successfully is likely to be equated with getting the better of one's opponents in such interactions. The winning of verbal disputes requires ability in case building, which sometimes means marshaling evidence favoring a particular position while ignoring, discounting, or contesting evidence that opposes it. A more philosophical or idealistic connotation of the term would be an impartially reasoned support of a conclusion; from this perspective, to reason well argumentatively means to judge evidence on its merits and to reach conclusions that unbiased inferential use of evidence supports. Both connotations are of interest in this book.

One can find many definitions of argument or argumentation in the literature, the following among them.

- Argumentation . . . is made up primarily of reasoning together with facts for your belief. It is designed to convince and to persuade others to subscribe to your facts and principles and to the conclusions warranted by these premises and evidence (Baird, 1950, p. 7).
- Arguments are more than mere inference-steps and may have a structure with different elements in them. Nevertheless there are clear cases of arguments that are non-deductive: inductive arguments, arguments from authority, and arguments which rely on one or another kind of emotive appeal (Hamblin, 1970, p. 249).
- a mode of conveying to readers or listeners organized evidence and reasons that tend to prove or disprove a proposition (Thompson, 1971, p. 6).
- a sentence or sequence of sentences containing statements some of which are set forth as supporting, making probable, or explaining others . . . a discourse in which certain claims or alleged facts are given as justification or explanation for others (Thomas, 1973, p. 2).
- Argumentation is the process of advancing, supporting, and criticizing claims (Rieke & Sillars, 1975, p. 6).
- a statement with the proper support for it (Ehninger & Brockriede, 1963, p. 48).
- an attempt to get someone to believe something, whether he wants to believe it or not (Nozick, 1993, p. 4).
- a conclusion supported by reasoning and evidence (Keefe, Harte, & Norton, 1982, p. 379).
- a claim and its associated rationale, either of which may be implicit (Benoit, 1986, p. 299).
- any statement, accompanied with reasons or evidence (Buchanan, 1986, p. 131).
- a speech act complex consisting of a constellation of statements designed to justify or refute an opinion and which is aimed at convincing a rational judge, who reacts reasonably, of the acceptability or unacceptability of that point of view (van Eemeren, 1986, p. 202).

- By the term "argument" I mean a set of natural-language declarative sentences, one of which is the *conclusion*, the remainder of which are the *premises*. Arguments, on this view, are products: they are artefacts, collections of text (Godden, 2003, p. 1).
- We define an *argument* to be a non-empty collection of sentences in the formal language, one of which is designated to be the conclusion. The other sentences (if any) in an argument are its premises (Shapiro & Kouri Kissel, 2018).
- The word "argument" can be used to designate a dispute or a fight, or it can be used more technically. The focus of this article is on understanding an argument as a collection of truth bearers (that is, the things that bear truth and falsity, or are true and false) some of which are offered as reasons for one of them, the conclusion (McKeon, undated).

Some definitions are very broad. Richard Rieke and Malcolm Sillars (1975), for example, describe argumentation as a process, and say that what they mean by it is "an ongoing transaction of advancing claims, supporting them with reasons, and the advancing of competing claims with appropriate support, the mutual criticism of them, and the granting of adherence to one" (p. 6). These writers contend that any claim is an argument to the extent that it is capable of being supported by other claims. Sally Jackson (1986) similarly holds that "*Any* conversational act is potentially arguable" (p. 218). Viveka Adelswärd (1986) says "all human interaction can be studied from a perspective of argumentation" (p. 327).

Sometimes a definition is given in terms of a function, or functions, that arguments may serve. "[A]rguments serve in finding a rational fulfillment of disputable claims of validity and as such serve in mastering crises or problem-situations in which the requirements or conditions for a possible understanding about something in the world have become problematic" (Kopperschmidt, 1986, p. 180). "Typically, conversationalists offer arguments only if they encounter disagreement or if they have some reason to expect disagreement; when arguments are offered, they are typically limited to just what is needed to satisfy expressed or expected disagreements" (Jackson, 1986, p. 218). "Conversational argument is a realization of general conversational principles adapted to the demands of a particular function – that of disagreement management" (Jacobs, 1986, p. 229). Charles Hamblin (1970) cautions against equating argument with implication. "There may be an argument where there is *no* implication: I may argue from *P* to *Q* when *P* does not, in fact, imply *Q*. 'Argument' is not synonymous with 'valid argument'" (p. 229).

Kristiane Zappel (1986) makes the point that argumentation has been studied from many different perspectives over the years, but notes in particular Chaim Perelman and Lucie Olbrechts-Tyteca's (1969) *The New Rhetoric: A Treatise on Argumentation*, published first in French in 1958, and Stephen Toulmin's *The Uses of Argument*, also first published in 1958, as influential in setting the course for subsequent work. She describes the "salient feature" of more recent work as "the consideration of argumentation in practical and pragmatic terms, placing it between the poles of consensus and controversy" (p. 218).

Jos Hornikx and Ulrike Hahn (2012) distinguish three meanings of the word *argument* as one finds it in the scientific literature: "argument as a reason, argument as a structured sequence of reasons and claims, and argument as a social exchange" (p. 225). Several writers make a distinction between two types of argument. James Blair (1986), for example, distinguishes between a "set of reasons adduced to support a claim" and a "dispute" (p. 189). He stresses the importance of recognizing two very different types of interaction, both of which are referred to as arguments. (More regarding this distinction presently.) Blair, like Perelman and Olbrechts-Tyteca, also recognizes the possibilities of arguments with oneself regarding the acceptability of some point of view, as well as arguments involving disagreements between two or more people; he refers to the former as *inquiries* and to the latter as *disputes*.

Deanna Kuhn (1991) distinguishes between rhetorical arguments and dialogical arguments. "An argument in its first, more restricted [rhetorical] sense, can be defined simply as an assertion with accompanying justification," or, as the *American Heritage Dictionary* has it, "a course of reasoning aimed at demonstrating the truth or falsity of something." According to the more common [dialogical] connotation, "we think of an argument as a dialog between two people who hold opposing views. Each offers justification for his or her own view; in addition (at least in skilled argument), each rebuts the other's view by means of counterargument" (p. 12). Kuhn contends that the two kinds of argument are closely related with respect to the types of thinking they entail.

Citing Sally Jackson (1983), Scott Jacobs (1986) makes a related distinction in contending that American studies of argumentation have been in two major traditions, which he refers to as methodological individualism and methodological socialism. "The former tradition has tended to equate argument with those reasoning processes whereby a single individual privately arrives at a conclusion. The structure and process of argument is taken to mirror the structure and process of human cognition. The latter tradition has tended to equate argument with those social procedures whereby two or more individuals publicly arrive at a consensus" (p. 236).

That what is considered an argument can be a matter of perspective is illustrated by Maurice Finocchiaro's (1986) discussion of Galileo's (1632) *Dialogue*:

> By one count there are seventeen main arguments that Galileo gives in support of conclusions he favors, and twenty-nine critiques of arguments he opposes. And I am referring here to main arguments and main subdivisions of the book, and not to the various subarguments that are parts of these; counting the latter would yield a much greater number. Moreover, it is possible to show that all these forty-six main discussions can be integrated into a single argument, since the seventeen main positive conclusions are all part of or steps toward the single cosmological thesis that the earth moves, while the twenty-nine critiques support the negative conclusions that undermine the opposite thesis that the earth stands still at the center of the universe (p. 84).

"When the text of Galileo's *Dialogue* is studied in accordance with these principles [just specified], the forty-six main arguments mentioned earlier generate several hundred reconstructed subarguments, each of which may to some extent be examined by itself" (p. 85).

Maarten Henket (1986) distinguishes two modes of rationality as that concept pertains to argumentation – two goals, we might say, that arguments can have: that of *solving* conflicts of opinion, and that of *settling* such conflicts. The first of these goals, Henket contends, is realized when an argument ends in agreement between the protagonists. The second goal – settling a conflict – is typically the operational one for courtroom argumentation. "Given this aim, it is perfectly rational to ensure the finality of the discussion, whether the parties reach an agreement or not" (p. 129).

Citing Toulmin, Rieke and Janik (1984), Manfred Kienpointner (1986) distinguishes between *arguments* and *warrants*: "'Arguments' are propositions stated to support or attack a controversial opinion; 'warrants' are propositions stated – or more often presupposed implicitly – to guarantee the step from arguments to conclusion. Warrants must establish an *appropriate* sense relation between arguments and conclusion to fulfill their function as 'step-authorizing statements'" (p. 276). (More regarding warrants in Chapter 3.)

Some writers make a distinction between an argument and an inference. Ralph Johnson (1986), borrowing an example from Karel Lambert and William Ulrich (1980), notes that from "Boston is a city and Boston is in the United States," one may legitimately infer that Boston is a city in the

United States, but such an inference would probably not be considered an argument.

For some, the concept of argument necessarily carries the notion of conflict or controversy. Johnson (1986), for example, rejects "a set of reasons leading to a conclusion" as an appropriate definition of argument. "That which is argued about must be controversial, contentious, really in doubt, and for this to occur, there must be contrary views" (p. 48).

For present purposes, it seems appropriate to give argument a sufficiently broad connotation to include any effort to influence one's beliefs or behavior. We argue with ourselves when we are trying to decide what to believe or do. We argue with others when it is their beliefs and behavior that we wish to affect. Underlying the use of arguments to influence the behavior of others is the assumption, sometimes referred to as the principle of consequentialism (Bonnefon & Hilton, 2004), that generally people will engage in behavior if they believe that doing so will have desirable consequences; so arguments aimed at influencing behavior are likely to note the desirable consequences the proposed behavior will have.

Arguments vary greatly in complexity. At one extreme is a simple three-term syllogism – All A are B; all B are C; therefore, all A are C – at the other is a lengthy contention of why one should believe X or do Y. Often a lengthy argument can be viewed as a series of abbreviated syllogisms. "The conclusion of one syllogism becomes the premise for the next one, so that the result is a chain of reasoning. The problem is to organize the assertions into full syllogisms and to test each one separately" (Baird, 1950, p. 153).

Explicit verbal efforts to persuade are readily recognized as such. There are many other, more subtle, ways to attempt to influence beliefs or behavior, however, and while these may go unrecognized as arguments, the ability to see them for what they are and to react to them in a rational way is an immensely important one, especially in a media-rich society. A thorough assessment of reasoning ability as it pertains to argumentation would have to pay attention to the evaluation of both direct, and indirect arguments of various types.

The stereotypical argument is composed of claims, usually expressed in words. But if argument is defined as an effort to influence others' beliefs or behavior, this can be done in ways other than by verbally laying out a set of premises in support of a stated conclusion. R. C. Manning (1986) gives compelling illustrations of how films can be used for this purpose. "[W]hen the BBC began distributing films of people starving in Ethiopia, no arguments accompanied them. The faces told the story. One might begin at the obvious 'conclusion,' viz., that something ought to be done, and argue about just what that something was, but the pictures needed no supporting arguments" (p. 171). Manning contends that at least in the case of moral issues, there is more to reasoning than the construction, analysis, and critique of verbal arguments, if it is to be effective in motivating behavior. "[M]oral reasoning is more than principle applied to situation yielding conclusion. A persuasive moral case must be made personal. If the people involved are not known to us, we must come to know them in some way, through pictures or films or newspaper accounts. The faceless suffering hordes must become persons, must have names or faces" (p. 172).

The ability to reason effectively about arguments of all types is an immensely important one in daily life, simply because arguments – attempts to persuade – confront us all more or less continuously. Without the ability to evaluate arguments effectively, we would be at a loss to know which of the numerous claims that we encounter daily to accept and which to reject.

The list of comments regarding arguments at the beginning of this chapter illustrates the fact that scholars define the concept in many different ways, but it also shows that the definitions – or most of them – have much in common. In the simplest form of argument, we can identify two types of assertion: one *conclusion* or key assertion and one or more *premises* or supporting assertions. The conclusion or key assertion is what the originator of the argument really wants us to believe or do; the other assertions are offered in support of it – to implicate it in the case of formal deductive arguments, or to make it highly plausible or probable in that of informal ones. In extended arguments, the same assertion may play the role of conclusion or key assertion with respect to one part of the argument and that of premise or supporting assertion with respect to another.

Purposes That Arguments Serve

Noting that "Argumentation Theory is a relatively young scientific field," Jérôme Jacquin (2018) describes it as "one of the verbal underpinnings of *reasoning* and *decision-making* .... In much the same way as classical Rhetoric, argumentation is viewed as the skeleton of democracy, where citizens are expected not only to *hold* an opinion, but also to *support* it with arguments" (p. 285).

Citing Ulrike Hahn and Michael Oaksford (2012) and Hugo Mercier and Dan Sperber (2011), Hahn and Hornikx (2016) contend that reasoning and argumentation are essential "for humans to learn, make decisions, and interact with others" (p. 1833). In short, according to this view, without the ability to reason and argue, humans could not function as humans. Arguments serve many specific purposes, but as already suggested, effecting changes in beliefs or behavior is paramount among them. A. Craig Baird (1950) puts it this way:

> The elementary principle behind all argumentative thinking and speaking is this: Whenever you make an assertion or advance any proposition which you wish others to accept, couple that idea with evidence sufficiently complete to convince "beyond a reasonable doubt." Because people have their prejudices and individual points of view, it is often necessary to justify to others what to you seems obvious. (p. 90).

The goal of all argumentation according to Perelman and Olbrechts-Tyteca (1969) "is to create or increase the adherence of minds to the theses presented for their assent" (p. 45). This definition is sufficiently broad to include arguments that support conclusions that few people are likely to challenge – arguments that are intended to reinforce feelings of patriotism, of camaraderie, of commitment to a moral principle. Such arguments are sometimes referred to as *epideictic*. Perelman and Olbrechts-Tyteca describe their purpose as that of increasing "the intensity of adherence to values held in common by the audience and the speaker" (p. 52). The same authors describe the purpose of a theory of argumentation as "the study of the discursive techniques allowing us *to induce or to increase the mind's adherence to the theses presented for its assent*" (p. 4).

Here we shall focus on arguments that are intended to persuade people to believe something they do not already believe or to behave in a way in which they had not been inclined to behave – which is to say arguments intended to effect some kind of change. "One of the purposes of argument, whether we like it or not, is to convince, and our criteria would be less than adequate if they had nothing to say about how well an argument may meet this purpose" (Hamblin, 1970, p. 240). Hamblin gives a pessimistic appraisal of the likelihood of arguments changing the minds of participants: "no argument, even when willful sophistry is set aside, ever *settles* a dispute once and for all, beyond the possibility of being reopened" (p. 251).

Developers of the argumentative theory of reasoning contend that the primary function of reasoning is not to form accurate beliefs, but to evaluate and produce arguments to convince others (Mercier, 2016; Mercier & Sperber, 2017, 2019). From this perspective, the prevalence of a confirmation bias is neither surprising nor objectionable because if one's primary purpose in reasoning is to produce compelling arguments, one should, and naturally does, seek evidence that supports that goal, and shun evidence that tells against it.

A testable implication of the theory, noted by Mercier and Sperber (2019), is that one should not be able to find any instances of the confirmation bias (or closely related my-side bias) in contexts other than human reasoning (e.g., human perception or animal cognition).

Regarding reasons for studying argumentation, Baird (1950) identifies six: "to (1) educate you for active and responsible participation in democratic government, (2) assure you more efficiency in your occupation or profession, (3) strengthen your self-confidence and enable you to make more satisfactory social adjustments, (4) provide you with defenses against 'bad' propaganda, and (5) widen your general influence in social movements" (p. 4). One may be dubious as to whether training in argumentation will always have all these effects, and yet still appreciate the practical value of rhetorical skill. The art of persuasive speaking or writing has been recognized for a long time: training in this art has long been considered especially important in certain fields of endeavor, such as law and politics (Hamblin, 1970), but it is of unquestioned value too for coping with the challenges of daily life.

If there is one distinction that is more important than all the others that could be made regarding purposes that arguments can serve, it is, in my view, the distinction between *consensus seeking* (or *dispute resolving*) and *competing*. In consensus seeking, an attempt is made to come to a conclusion, through argumentation, on some question for which incompatible answers have been proposed. The goal of such arguments is to arrive at a consensus as to which of the considered answers is correct or most likely to be so. In competing, the goal of each party to the argument is to "win," to force the conclusion that one's opponent's position is wrong.

This distinction, or something close to it, has been recognized by many others, though not always in the same terms. Perelman and Olbrechts-Tyteca (1969), for example, describe the distinction this way:

> When successfully carried out, discussion should lead to an inevitable and unanimously accepted conclusion, if the arguments, which are presumed to weigh equally with everyone, have, as it were, been distributed in the pans of a balance. In a debate, on the other hand, each interlocutor advances only arguments favorable to his own thesis, and his sole concern with arguments unfavorable to him is for the purpose of refuting them or limiting their impact. The man with a settled position is thus one-sided, and because of his bias and the consequent restriction of his effort to those pertinent arguments

> which are favorable to him, the others remain frozen, as it were, and only appear in the debate if his opponent puts them forward. And as the latter is presumed to adopt the same attitude, one sees how discussion came to be considered as a sincere quest for the truth, whereas the protagonists of a debate are chiefly concerned with the triumph of their own viewpoint (p. 38).

Perelman and Olbrechts-Tyteca note that the line between the two types of argument is not a sharp one and is often hard to draw. They contend further that whether one sees an argument as a discussion or a debate is likely to depend on the intentions one ascribes to the participants, which may change as the dialog proceeds.

Blair (1986) also discusses the distinction:

> [I]f argumentation to resolve disputes involves a confrontation between two sides, in which each tries to defeat the other without making concessions, it does not seem that there is really going to be any resolution of their disagreement. On the other hand, for argumentation to deliver on its promise to be morally superior to force, it must be possible for people actually to change their minds as a result of it (p. 190).

Again,

> To the extent that opposing parties are determined not to change their minds, their argumentation has to be a charade if it is conceived as directed against an opponent. The intrinsic goal of the argumentation being to convince someone, if neither side has any intention of being convinced, they are either wasting their time, or else using the practice of argumentation for some ulterior purpose (p. 196).

Blair notes that among arguers' purposes may be the intention of one or both to convince some audience – not the arguers themselves – of the merits of their positions. Surely, this is descriptive of many of the arguments one sees on television between spokespersons for different positions on politically controversial issues. It is descriptive too of formal debates in which participants defend opposing views, and of courtroom arguments for which the audience is the judge and/or the jury. In none of these instances do the arguers expect, or intend, to change the minds of their opponents – or to change their own – although they undoubtedly hope to influence the beliefs of observers.

The courtroom scenario illustrates a distinction articulated by Douglas Ehninger and Wayne Brockriede (1963), who noted that the outcome of some debates is judged by witnesses to it, whereas the outcome of others is judged by the debaters themselves. In the presentation of evidence, the debaters are the prosecutors and the defense attorneys, and the goal of each side is to convince the jury of its case; in the jury room, the debaters are the jurors and their goal is to converge on a verdict – to convince themselves that they have it right.

Blair stresses the importance of disposition as a determinant of people's willingness to consider critically the merits of their own positions on controversial issues, which he sees as a defining characteristic of a critically reflective thinker. "Critically reflective thinkers should analyze and evaluate the arguments they can find or construct on behalf of – and also, perhaps especially, against – their own beliefs, rejecting the ones that do not stand up to such scrutiny no less firmly than they reject indefensible arguments and claims asserted by others in support of other beliefs" (p. 190). This is an ideal with which many people undoubtedly will agree; whether it is a realistic aspiration is another question.

G. B. Walker (1986) makes a distinction between negotiations and arguments in the context of a discussion of international negotiations. "International bargainers, while not oblivious to the needs of their adversaries, rely on argument to gain or maintain an advantage or control. Negotiators use arguments to support their own positions, interests, and offers, but arguments are intended primarily to modify the other party's perceptions and expectations concerning preferences and outcomes" (p. 239).

In a discussion of argumentative, as contrasted with nonargumentative, approaches to decision-making, Rieke and Sillars (1975) divide the former into three categories, not always identified by these names: *conferences*, *debates*, and *negotiations*. It is easy to imagine the first and second of these categories marking the ends of a continuum representing the degree to which the goal of interactions is to arrive at a compromise solution that takes all parties' preferences into account, and the third approach (negotiations) somewhere between the extremes.

Contending that the question of *how* humans reason has received a lot of attention, whereas that of *why* they reason has not, Mercier (2011a, 2011b, 2011c, 2017) contend that the answer to the why question is that people reason in order to produce and evaluate arguments. They, with colleagues, have proposed a theory of reasoning –"the argumentative theory of reasoning" – that explicitly combines reasoning and argumentation. According to this theory "the main function of reasoning is to exchange arguments in dialogic contexts in order to improve communication" (Mercier et al., 2016, p. 1; see also Mercier & Landemore, 2012). From the perspective of this theory, argumentation is considered a social phenomenon: "the public exchange of reasons meant to convince" (Mercier et al., 2016, p. 2). Reasoning, which Mercier et al. (2016) define as "a mechanism that deals with the relation between reasons and their conclusion" (p. 12), has two main tasks: "to produce arguments in order to convince others, and to evaluate others' arguments in order to determine whether we should be convinced" (p. 2). As to how well reasoning generally does on these tasks, Mercier et al. give an uncharitable assessment: "It is biased in that people mostly find reasons that support their own point of view, it is lazy in that people do not examine these reasons critically, and it is inefficient in that reasoning typically fails to correct mistaken beliefs" (p. 12).

Mercier and Sperber (2011) maintain that as the term *reasoning* is commonly understood, it refers to a form of inference in which both a conclusion and the previously held beliefs that warrant it are consciously entertained. "The premises are seen as providing *reasons* to accept the conclusion" (p. 57). Taking exception to this view, they make a distinction between reasoning and intuitive inference, and defend the idea that "the arguments used in reasoning are the output of a mechanism of intuitive inference" (p. 58).

By *intuitive inference*, they mean, as I understand it, inference that is made unconsciously; one is aware of the conclusion of such an inference, but not of the premises that justify it or the process of making it. Intuitive inferences generate *intuitive beliefs* – beliefs that people hold without being aware of reasons for holding them. Reasoning that is done with respect to one's beliefs or actions is not done for the purpose of forming those beliefs or selecting those actions, but to justify those beliefs or actions after they have been formed or done. People reason (i.e., find reasons), Mercier and Sperber (2011) contend, primarily to construct arguments that can be used to explain or defend their beliefs or actions to others, or to convince others to believe or act as they themselves do. "The main function of reasoning, we claim, is *argumentative*" (p. 60).

Notable Arguments in History

History is replete with arguments that have made a difference. I have already mentioned Galileo's *Dialogue.* Darwin's *Origin of Species* has been referred to, by Darwin himself, among others, as "one long argument" (Mayr, 1991). In American history, one thinks of the Federalist Papers – eighty-five essays in which Alexander Hamilton, James Madison, and John Jay laid out, and argued for, many of the principles on which the United States was founded.

One thinks too of the marathon debate between Stephen Douglas and Abraham Lincoln – seven three-hour debates over a period of two months in 1858. Contested elections in the United States and other democracies are invariably preceded by a period of intense argumentation during which each candidate presents arguments why he/she should be elected, and his/her opponent(s) should not be.

Argumentation as Reasoning and Conversely

Argumentation and reasoning are closely related concepts. Some would contend that they are the same thing, or very nearly so (Amgoud & Cayrol, 2002; Kuhn, 1991; Mercier, 2017; Mercier et al., 2016; Perelman & Olbrechts-Tyteca, 1969). There is the view that much of the reasoning we do is best described as arguing with oneself. In trying to decide what (or whom) to believe on a controversial issue, how to approach a problem that requires a solution, or, more generally, which action to take among several possibilities, one debates with oneself, as it were, hoping for the issue to be resolved.

Perelman and Olbrechts-Tyteca (1969) explicitly espouse this view, promoting the desirability of considering self-deliberation a kind of argumentation. They quote approvingly Isocrates (*To Nicocles*) on the matter: "The arguments by which we convince others when we speak to them are the same as those we use when we engage in reflection. We call those able to speak to the multitudes orators, and we regard as persons of sagacity those who are able to talk things over within themselves with discernment" (p. 41).

Michael Billig (1991/1987) also promotes this view and contends that psychologists have failed to see the correspondence between thinking and argumentation. "[P]sychologists have overlooked the extent to which our inner deliberations are silent arguments conducted within a single self. If deliberation is a form or argument, then our thought processes, far from being inherently mysterious events, are modeled upon public debate. In consequence, the rhetorical handbooks, which provide guides to debate, can also be considered as guides to thought" (p. 35).

Kuhn (1991), citing Billig (1991), promotes this view as well. "[T]o engage in reasoned argument lies at the heart of what one does as a thinking human being" (p. 11). "Interiorized dialogic argument . . . is a way of conceptualizing informal reasoning" (p. 13).

While the equating of reasoning with arguing with oneself has much to recommend it, it also deserves a caveat. A considerable body of research has revealed that people are capable of talking themselves into accepting something as true simply by focusing on the possibility that it is so. Derek Koehler (1991) describes the phenomenon this way:

> A person asked to provide an argument supporting a given hypothesis usually finds this hypothesis more plausible as a result. People who first give reasons why a theory might be correct or why an event might occur tend to express greater confidence that the theory *is* true or that the event *will* occur, as compared with people who are asked to give reasons for an opposite theory or event (p. 500).

Another word of caution regarding the equating of argumentation with reasoning: reasoning itself is a complex concept, so equating argumentation with reasoning does not necessarily simplify the former concept. The complexity is illustrated by a definition of reasoning, prompted by a review by Kathleen Galotti (1989) of experimental approaches to the study of reasoning:

> mental activity that consists of transforming given information (called the set of premises) in order to reach conclusions. This activity must be focused on at least one goal (but may be focused on more than one). The activity must not be inconsistent with systems of logic when all the premises are fully specified, although there may not always be an applicable system of logic to govern specific instances of reasoning. The activity may or may not be self-contained; that is, people may implicitly or explicitly add to, subtract from, or otherwise modify any or all of the premises supplied. When original premises are modified, the final conclusion may be consistent with the modified premises. The activity may, but need not, involve the breaking of mental set. The conclusions may, but need not, be startling or non-obvious at the outset of the activity. The conclusion may, but need not, be deductively valid (p. 333).

Complexities and the limitations of definitions notwithstanding, the assumption underlying this book is that if argumentation and reasoning are not equivalent, they are closely related concepts and one cannot get far in the study of either without dealing with the other.

Why Another Book on Argumentation?

Argumentation, often under the rubric of rhetoric, has been a topic of discussion, debate – and yes argumentation – for millennia. It has been the subject of numerous books, many of which are referenced in this one. Extensive overviews include *Argumentation: Across the Lines of Discipline* (van Eemeren, Grootendorst, Blair, & Willard, 1986). *Argumentation:*

Analysis and Practices (van Eemeren et al., 1986), *Fallacies: Classical and Contemporary Readings* (Hansen & Pinto, 1995). *Exploring Argumentative Contexts* (van Eemeren & Garssen, 2012), the *Handbook of Argumentation Theory* (van Eemeren et al., 2014). Do we really need another book on the subject? Is there anything left to say that has not already been said countless times?

My excuse for writing on argumentation is that I find the subject fascinating and assume that many others do so as well. My intention is to focus primarily on empirical work – especially relatively recent work – that relates more or less directly to questions of what makes arguments persuasive and assertions plausible. My hope is that a review of that work, even if incomplete, will give interested readers a better understanding of the many ways in which people construct, evaluate, and use arguments, and will provide them with points of departure from which they can explore specific regions of this sprawling domain.

2
Types of Argument

> In strict reasoning the principal thing is to distinguish a proof from a guess, a valid demonstration from an invalid attempt. In plausible reasoning the principal thing is to distinguish a guess from a guess, a more reasonable guess from a less reasonable guess
>
> (Polya, 1954a, p. vi).

> All reasoning may be divided into two kinds, namely demonstrative reasoning, or that concerning relations of ideas, and moral reasoning, or that concerning matter of fact and existence
>
> (Hume, 1939/1748, p. 604).

Scholars have long contended that there are many types of argument and have produced a variety of proposals regarding how they might be classified (Fohr, 1980; Govier, 1999; Kienpointner, 1986; Skyrms, 1975; Visser et al., 2018; Wagemans, 2016, 2019; Woods & Walton, 1979). Many typologies have been proposed, nearly all (if not all) of which recognize a difference between deductive and inductive arguments. Some writers argue that these two types exhaust the possibilities – if an argument is not deductive it must be inductive, and conversely. Some treat these two types as super categories and make distinctions within each of them. Others do not accept the idea that all arguments are either deductive or inductive but contend that there are categories that lie outside of both. It is clear already that much depends on how relevant terms are defined. It is clear too, however, that, of all the distinctions regarding argument types that have been made since the days of Aristotle, the oldest and most durable of them is the distinction between deductive and inductive types, which contrasts conclusions that are logically implicit in the claims from which they are drawn with those that go beyond what is given (Copi, Cohen, & McMahon, 2010; Moore & Parker, 1993; Rescher, 1964a, 1964b; Salmon, 1963; Weddle, 1986).

Deductive versus Inductive Arguments

Deductive arguments adhere to one or another canonical logical form and typically involve proceeding from claims of fact (premises) to conclusions that can be drawn from (are implicit in) them. Inductive arguments do not adhere strictly to specific forms and typically involve arguing from particular to more general assertions. Sometimes the term inductive has served to connote any type of argument that is not wholly deductive. Extended arguments are likely to contain both deductive and inductive components.

According to some scholars, deduction involves arguing from generalities to particulars, whereas induction typically involves arguing from particulars to generalities (Creighton, 1922; Mill, 1843). Nicholas Rescher (1964b) makes the distinction this way: "An argument that attempts (or is claimed) to provide conclusive evidence for its conclusion is called a deductive argument. In contrast, an inductive argument attempts (or is claimed) simply to provide some grounds for the conclusion – that is, to furnish good reasons for accepting the conclusion without providing conclusive evidence for it" (p. 60).

The conclusion of a deductive argument is contained implicitly in the premises from which the conclusion is drawn, assuming the argument is valid. "An argument is a valid deductive argument if all that it does is to reach a conclusion tacitly contained in the premises, that is a conclusion such that it would be self-contradictory to assert the premises but to deny the conclusion" (Swinburne, 1974, p. 1). This fact has been noted as a severe limitation of deductive reasoning. John Stuart Mill (1843), for example, claimed that syllogisms invariably beg the question. Consider the argument that has been used countless times to illustrate syllogistic reasoning: All men are mortal; Socrates is a man; therefore, Socrates is mortal. That Socrates is mortal is presupposed in the major premise – All men are mortal. So, what has one learned from the argument? In contrast, a conclusion arrived at by induction asserts something more than what is contained implicitly in the evidence evoked in its support. Induction goes beyond the "givens," one may say, but the conclusions it yields are never certain, although they may be sufficiently reliable for practical purposes.

That deductive reasoning makes explicit only knowledge already contained implicitly in the premises from which the deductions are made does not mean that deductive arguments can never produce surprises. Carl Hempel (1945) points out that while it is true that the conclusion of a valid deductive argument asserts nothing that is *theoretically new* – nothing that is not contained implicitly in the argument's premises – it may well contain something that is *psychologically new*, which is to say some truth of which one was not aware before.

Induction leads to conclusions that state more than is contained implicitly in the claims on which those conclusions are based. When, on the basis of noticing that all the members that one has seen of a specific class of things has a particular attribute (all the crows I have seen are black), one concludes that *all* – or more safely *most* – of the members of that class (including all those not seen) have that attribute, one is generalizing, which is one form of induction. In doing this, one is going beyond the data in hand and asserting something that cannot be deduced from them.

Deduction lends itself to formalization and there are many formal constructs and tools to facilitate construction and assessment of deductive arguments. These include syllogistic forms, calculi of classes and propositions, Boolean algebra, and a variety of diagrammatic aids to analysis such as truth tables, Euler diagrams, and Venn diagrams.

Inductive arguments are not readily formalized and indeed, except in the case of mathematical induction, which has a special meaning, inductive reasoning is almost synonymous with informal reasoning. It has to do with weighing evidence, judging plausibility, and arriving at uncertain conclusions or beliefs that one can hold with varying degrees of confidence. Deductive arguments can be determined to be valid or invalid. The most one can say about an inductive argument is that it is more or less persuasive or convincing.

Just a word about mathematical induction, which is not a focus of this book. Mathematical induction is a method of argument that makes it possible to demonstrate that something holds for all – infinitely many – natural numbers. The form of the argument is as follows:

If R is true for n, it is true for $n+1$
R is true for n
Therefore, R is true for $n+1$.

If one can be sure that if R is true for n it is true for $n+1$, and knows that it is true for, say, 1 then one can be sure that it is true for 2; and if it is true for 2, it is true for 3, and so on indefinitely.

This type of argument is to be distinguished from simple generalization, which works well in science, but is not reliable in mathematics; the fact that a mathematical relationship is true in many cases is not compelling evidence that it is true in all cases. As Dan Silver (2016) points out, there are many examples in the history of mathematics of "proofs" of infinite number series that turned out to be false. Silver gives an example noted by

Leonard Euler and later cited by Charles Babbage: for n equals 1 through 39, the function n^2+n+41 yields a prime number; however, for $n = 40$, the solution, 1681, is not prime, but is divisible by 41. For values of n between 41 and 79 inclusive, n^2+n+41 yields 34 prime numbers and 6 composites; the composites (1763, 2021, 2491, 3233, 4331, and 5893) are for n = 41, 44, 49, 56, 65, and 76 respectively: $1763 = 41 \times 43$; $2021 = 43 \times 47$; $2491 = 47 \times 53$; $3233 = 53 \times 61$; $4331 = 61 \times 71$; $5893 = 71 \times 83$.) The observant reader will note interesting progressions here.

The function $n^2-79n+1601$ produces nothing but primes for n equals 1 through 79, but for $n = 80$, it yields a composite number. In a curious coincidence, the first composite number it yields is 1681, the same as the first composite yielded by n^2+n+41. Further, the prime numbers produced by $n^2-79n+1601$ for $1 \leq n < 80$ are the same as those produced by n^2+n+41 for $1 \leq n < 40$ (though not produced in the same order), with all but one of those produced by $n^2-79n+1601$ occurring twice. Thus, for example, 971 is produced by n^2+n+41 with $n = 30$, and it is produced by $n^2-79n+1601$ with $n = 9$ and with $n = 70$. There is no value of n for which n^2+n+41 and $n^2-79n+1601$ yield the same result. I leave it to the reader to ponder why such apparently disparate functions behave so similarly in their production of prime numbers. I note in passing that for $80 < n \leq 120$, n^2+n+41 yields 11 composite numbers and $n^2-79n+1601$ yields 6. Thus, ends our tiny detour into the world of mathematical induction.

Deductive arguments are generally associated with logic and inductive arguments with probability theory. E. J. Lowe (1993) makes the distinction this way: "In its broadest sense, logic is the science of consequence relations: entailment relations in the case of deductive logic, probabilistic support relations in the case of inductive logic" (p. 212). Zeno Swijtink (1987) describes the associations in similar terms:

> An argument is a piece of discourse, consisting of a set of premises, and a single conclusion. Premises and conclusion express propositions; that is, what they say is true or false. An argument is deductively valid if its conclusion follows strictly from its premises, in the sense that its premises could not be true and its conclusion false. Logic tries to find tools with which one can establish deductive validity, and the philosophy of logic tries to explain what could possibly be meant by the "could not." Similarly, an argument is inductively strong if it is improbable, given that the premises are true, that the conclusion is false (p. 274).

To this point, the distinction between deductive and inductive arguments has been relatively clear and stark; the distinguishing features of the one type are distinctly different from those of the other. Alfred Sidgwick

(1884) cautions, however, that the distinction can sometimes be blurred and many arguments may be difficult to fit in this dichotomy: "in a large number of cases we have no means of deciding whether the argument may best be classified as empirical [inductive], or deductive, or both" (p. 217). Moreover, although the distinction between deductive and inductive arguments is almost universally recognized – and held to be basic – in the literature on reasoning (Creigton, 1922; Whewell, 1858), there is the contrary view that the distinction is not viable, or not enlightening (Ennis, 2001; Govier, 1987; Johnson & Blair, 1983; Weddle, 1980, 1986). Robert Ennis (2001), for example, contends that dealing effectively with arguments does not require classifying them with respect to some typology and that, in fact, doing so is not possible, in part, because "the distinction between deductive and inductive arguments is not viable" (p. 98). He gives an extensive exposition of problems with the deductive–inductive distinction and declares that he can think of no account of it that does not suffer from one or more of them (see p. 112). He rejects the contention of some theorists (Fohr, 1980; Govier, 1999; Woods & Walton, 1979) that evaluating an argument requires that one determines what the argument is and classifies it as to type (deductive, inductive, etc.).

Ennis (2001) contends that "many arguments appear to come close to satisfying deductive standards (usually after reasonable assumptions are added) they include implicit or explicit qualifying terms like 'generally', 'probably', '*ceteris paribus*', and 'prima facie', which usually render them deductively invalid" (p. 98). However, despite such worrisome criticisms, the distinction between deduction and induction has been widely accepted for a long time and continues to be so today.

As used here and in most texts on logic, *validity*, or *invalidity*, is a property of the *form* of an argument, and has nothing to do with an argument's content. It is a binary concept: an argument is either valid or invalid; there is no middle ground. And it applies only to deductive arguments; an inductive argument can be classified in many ways, but it cannot be said to be valid or invalid. Monroe Beardsley (1975) uses the appropriateness of application of the concept of validity to an argument as the feature that distinguishes between deductive and inductive arguments: "A deductive argument is an argument that either is or claims to be valid. All other arguments are inductive" (p. 23). However, as used in everyday discourse, and often as defined in standard dictionaries, the term has much more nuanced meanings. Ennis (2001), among others, points out that it often appears to be used to mean well-grounded, sound, or very persuasive. A definition of deductive argument that makes no reference to validity, but focuses on the argument's author's beliefs, has been proposed by Mark Vorobej (1992): "An argument is deductive if, and only if, the author of the argument believes that the truth of the premises necessitates (guarantees) the truth of the conclusion. In other words, in a deductive argument the author of the argument believes that it is not logically possible for all the premises to be true and the conclusion to be false" (p. 105).

A distinction that is very similar to – some might say essentially the same as – that between deductive and inductive arguments is one between formal and informal arguments. As the name suggests, informal arguments typically lack the precise sequential structure that formal arguments have. In a formal argument, one lays out a sequence of premises from which a conclusion presumably follows. D. S. Clarke, Jr. (1985) sees this form of argument as the essence of reasoning: "To reason is to derive one sentence as conclusion from others as premises" (p. 155). In an informal argument, what one is more likely to do is present a set of assertions that are believed to provide evidence in favor of the conclusion. Weight of evidence is an important, although typically undefined, concept in this context.

Both formal and informal arguments can vary in length and complexity. Sometimes what is referred to as a lengthy argument might better be considered a collection of shorter arguments that support the same ultimate conclusion. The Constitutional Convention that occurred over several months (May through September) in Philadelphia 1787, and produced the US Constitution, is an especially interesting and historically important illustration of how people with some common – and some conflicting – interests can, through argumentation, arrive at a conclusion that all can accept, if not all enthusiastically.

The questions with which the delegates struggled were many and contentious. How should government be structured, and the functions of governments be distributed? Should the executive be one person, possibly a king, or several, perhaps a committee of three? Should the legislature have two houses – like the British – or only one? What should determine the amount of influence the individual states would have in governing the nation (via the number of delegates to the legislature, say)? How should the "sizes" of the states be determined: By land area? By population? Should slaves be counted? What authority should specific branches of government have – or, possibly, more importantly, not have? Where should the funds come from that will be required to run the federal government? And so on.

If there was a single issue that was more contentious than all the rest, it was perhaps the question of how the powers and obligations of the state governments would relate to those of the federal government. On the one hand were delegates (federalists) who wished power to be concentrated primarily in the central government, and on the other were delegates (anti-federalists) who wished the nation to function as a federation of sovereign states. The resolution was not to everyone's liking and the "states' rights" issue continues to be debated to this day.

In the end, a constitution was produced. No one liked every aspect of it. Getting it to a point at which nearly all (thirty-eight of forty-one) of the delegates could accept it, if not love it, required many compromises among delegates with different points of view and different vested interests. Often, in the countless debates that occurred, participants warned that the nation could not survive adoption of one or another policy that had been proposed. In fact, many such policies were adopted, and the nation did survive.

We have here a striking example – in fact many such examples – of the use of prefactual conditionals in arguments aimed at influencing others' beliefs or behavior (see Nickerson, 2015, chapter 7). These examples include many predictions that the adoption of some proposal would be beneficial to the body politic as well as many predictions that the consequences of adoption of some proposal would be dire. An engaging and sobering account of the proceedings of the Convention – the arguments and counterarguments that occurred regarding specific issues – has been produced as a recorded book by Allen Guelzo (2017) in collaboration with the Smithsonian Museum.

Immediately following the Constitutional Convention, the Federalist Papers, authored by Alexander Hamilton, James Madison, and John Jay (Hamilton and Madison were delegates to the Convention) began to appear and were published serially between October 1787, and August 1788. These papers were also an example of a prolonged argument containing many component arguments. In this case, the prolonged argument had a specific purpose, which was to support the ratification of the new US Constitution, which occurred state-by-state until the ninth state to ratify, New Hampshire, did so in June 1788. (It was not to become the law of the land until ratified by nine of the existing thirteen states.) Its ratification was followed by the adoption of twelve amendments – the Bill of Rights – in September 1789, to assure recognition by the government of certain principles that were not adequately addressed by the constitution.

A more recent example of a prolonged argument composed of numerous component arguments of considerable national interest was the rash of reactions to the Warren Commission Report following its publication in

1964. The Warren Commission was established by President Lyndon Johnson in November 1963, with a mandate to investigate the details of the assassination of President John F. Kennedy, which had occurred about two months earlier. The report of the commission's findings, which included the conclusion that Lee Harvey Oswald acted alone and was solely responsible for the president's death, was presented to President Johnson in September 1964, and made public shortly thereafter. Many people refused to accept the conclusion that Oswald acted alone, and numerous contrary explanations, most suggesting a conspiracy of one sort or another were proposed, some of which live on to this day.

There are many other examples in history of prolonged arguments composed of numerous shorter arguments. One such is the famous debate between Stephen Douglas and Abraham Lincoln, which lasted for twenty-one hours – seven occasions on which each debater held forth for an hour and a half – in 1858. The central issue was slavery. Douglas argued that the individual states and territories had the right to decide for themselves – without the interference of the federal government – whether they would be "slave" or "free." Lincoln adamantly insisted that in claiming in the Declaration of Independence that "all men are created equal," the forefathers intended that "all men" here meant "all men," whatever the color of their skin, and that sooner or later slavery should become a thing of the past in the United States of America. Not surprisingly the position of neither debater was much affected by the argument of the other. Of course, presumably neither expected to change the other's mind; what each hoped was to influence the beliefs, and voting behavior, of the audiences who listened to the debates.

Another lengthy debate of historical significance concerned the question of what to do with fifty-three African slaves who seized control of a ship – the *Amistad* – on which they were being transported from Havana, Cuba, to Puerto Principe, Cuba, killing its captain and cook in the process. The debate went on for about two years, during which time many arguments were made, some to condemn the actions of the Africans and some to justify them. Advocates of slavery generally argued that the Africans should be considered guilty of piracy and murder, or at least be returned as property to their owners; abolitionists argued that they had a legal and moral right to escape by whatever means possible from the bondage in which they found themselves. The issue was resolved in 1841 by the Supreme Court of the United States, which found the defendants to be free men guilty of no crime. The case for the Africans was argued by former US president John Quincy Adams; that for the prosecution was argued by

Attorney General Henry D. Gilpin. It would be hard to find a more compelling illustration of how perspectives, beliefs, and vested interests can shape the arguments people make.

An instructive imaginary argument among three students regarding the dropping of atomic bombs on Hiroshima and Nagasaki to force the surrender of Japan at the end of World War II has been provided by Bruce Reed (2018). Issues that emerge and are debated include the problem of estimating the number of deaths and casualties that would result from alternative ways to bring the war to an end, the question of how to decide which (if any) of the conflicting estimates to believe, whether the decision to use atomic bombs (or not) should be made on moral grounds, and so on. As is the case in many, if not most, lengthy arguments about complicated subjects, the end is not a conclusion with which all the participants can readily agree; and the issues that are raised remain largely unresolved. However, articulation of the issues should, presumably, broaden the perspectives of the participants and give them a better appreciation of the complexities involved. The question of whether the atomic bomb should have been used continues to be argued (Freeman, 2006; Hasegawa, 2007), and one suspects that it will be a contentious matter for a long time to come.

In the United States and other democracies, one can expect to be bombarded with components of extended arguments every few years, aimed at convincing citizens to vote for this or that candidate for public office. Such component arguments may give reasons why one should or should not vote for specific candidates, why one should or should not support specified policies, and so on. Recipients of such arguments have the nontrivial problem of judging the plausibility of the many claims contained in them and determining whether those they find plausible collectively convince them how to vote.

The term *form* as applied to arguments sometimes has the fairly narrow connotation of linguistic structure, but it also is used to connote structure in a more schematic, less literal, sense. *Reductio ad absurdum*, for example, might be considered a form of argument in the latter sense. In such an argument one shows that a specified supposition leads to a false or contradictory conclusion and therefore cannot be true. Or, one may use the form to demonstrate that a statement is true: assume the statement you wish to prove, S, is false; if, on this assumption, you can deduce from S a contradiction, this shows S to be true. If it can be shown that a supposition, when combined with propositions that have been proved or are granted, implies both a conclusion (C) and its negation (not-C), the supposition is said to have been reduced to an absurdity.

A famous example of the use of this kind of argument is Galileo's (1967/1632) logical demonstration of the absurdity of the assumption that heavier bodies fall faster than lighter ones. Salvatio, who represents Galileo's views in the dialog is speaking.

> If we then take two bodies whose natural speeds are different, it is clear that on uniting the two, the more rapid one will be partly retarded by the slower, and the slower one will be somewhat hastened by the swifter . . .. But if this is true, and if a large stone moves with a speed of, say, eight while a smaller moves with a speed of four, then when they are united, the system will move with a speed less than eight; but the two stones when tied together make a stone larger than that which before moved with a speed of eight. Hence the heavier body moves with less speed than the lighter; an effect which is contrary to your supposition. Thus, you see how from your assumption that the heavier body moves more rapidly than the lighter one, I infer that the heavier body moves more slowly (Fisher, 2004, p. 91).

The importance of recognizing that the type of reasoning that is often required to solve structured problems for purposes of experimentation in the laboratory does not always adequately represent the reasoning that is required to deal with the problems that present themselves outside the laboratory. This has been noted by many investigators and is reflected in contrasts that have been drawn: between pure, or theoretical, and practical thinking (Scribner, 1986; Wason & Johnson-Laird, 1972), between academic and practical intelligence (Sternberg & Wagner, 1986), between school-based and out-of-school-based learning (Resnick, 1986), between formal and everyday reasoning (Galotti, 1989), between contextualized and decontextualized reasoning (Thompson, Evans, & Handley, 2005), between reasoning about well-structured problems (which have single and well-defined solutions) and about ill-structured problems (which lack definite solutions) (Kuhn, 1991), and others of a similar nature.

Valerie Thompson et al. (2005) note that most experimentation on reasoning has focused on decontextualized inference tasks. Allen Garnham and Jane Oakhill (1994) similarly contend that everyday reasoning has not been studied very much and attribute this neglect to everyday reasoning being much harder to study.

> One explanation for [the comparatively little work that has been done on everyday reasoning] is that, in contrast to formal reasoning, there is no well-defined methodology. Another is that it is difficult for an experimenter to be sure how subjects will interpret a problem – they can apply world knowledge and personal biases in an uncontrolled manner. In addition, there is often no "correct" answer to a practical reasoning problem, so standard

> techniques of assessing subjects' performance, such as number of problems correctly solved, cannot be used (p. 259).

Increasingly in recent years, researchers and theorists have focused on how people deal with arguments with premises or supporting assertions that are not known, or assumed, to be true (Hadjichristidis, Sloman, & Over, 2014; Murphy, Chen, & Ross, 2012; Murphy & Ross, 2010). Recognition that many, if not most, of the arguments one encounters in everyday life contain claims the truth of which is not certain, has prompted the treatment of conditional assertions – *If A then C*[1] – as probabilistic statements – *the probability of C on the assumption of A*, that is, $p(C|A)$. Treating conditionals in this fashion and applying probability theory to the analysis of conditional reasoning have been described as the "new paradigm" in cognitive psychology or the "new psychology of reasoning" (Chater & Oaksford, 2009; Evans, 2012; Gilio & Over, 2012; Manktelow, 2012; Over, 2009; Pfeifer, 2013). Much of the relevant literature is reviewed in Nickerson (2015).

An aspect of the new paradigm that has received considerable attention is the question of how beliefs may change as a consequence of the receipt of relevant new information over time. New information can reveal that a component of an argument (premise or conclusion), the truth of which was unknown, is definitely true or definitely false. Or it can be a basis for one to change one's estimate of the probability that it is true. Bayesian-based rules for applying new information to the updating of beliefs have been proposed (Jeffrey, 1983; Oaksford, Chater, & Larkin, 2000), but their generality has been challenged (Hadjichristidis et al., 2014; Zhao & Osherson, 2010).

Galotti (1989) distinguishes between the kind of reasoning that is often studied in psychological experiments, in which people are given well-structured problems to solve and all the information that is needed to solve them, and the kind of reasoning that is more typical of what is required in everyday life. He refers to the former as *formal* reasoning and to the latter as *informal* or *everyday* reasoning.

My purpose in what follows is to develop the relationship between deductive and inductive arguments or reasoning more fully.

Deductive Arguments

> Deductive reasoning . . . consists of those ways of deriving new statements from accepted facts that compel the acceptance of the derived statements
>
> (Kline, 1953, p. 26).

> At the heart of rationality is the capacity to make valid deductions
> (Johnson-Laird, 1993, p. 2).

Fundamental to the idea of deductive reasoning are the concepts of implication and inference. Implication is a logical relationship; inference is a cognitive act. Statements imply; people infer. B is said to be implied logically by A if it is impossible for B to be false if A is true. People are said to make an inference when they justify one claim (conclusion) by appeal to others (premises). Implications either exist or they do not, independently of whether inferences are made that relate to them. Inferences are made or they are not made; they can be based on valid arguments or invalid arguments, but they are inferences in either case.

Matthew Lipman (1991) distinguishes between implication and inference this way:

> [R]easoning can ... be thought of in one sense as being composed of symbolic *operations* and in another sense as being composed of the cognitive *moves* by which those operations are performed. Thus, *implication* is a logical operation in which, in a valid argument, the premises can be said to imply the conclusion. Inference, however, is a cognitive *move* in which someone actually *draws* the conclusion from the premises. Thus, in reading, we may fail to infer what is being implied in one paragraph, just as we may incorrectly infer what is not implied in another (p. 75).

The distinction between implication and inference is an important one, and failure to keep it in mind can make for confusion. When discussing reasoning as something that people do, we are focusing on inference. People are sometimes said to imply when they make statements with the intention that their hearers will see the implications of those statements and make the appropriate inferences, but to be precise in our use of language we would have to say not that people imply but that they make statements that imply.

Harold Fawcett (1938) describes how individuals who understand the nature of deduction will deal with a deductive argument: They will select the significant words and phrases in any statement that is important to them and ask that they be carefully defined; require evidence in support of any conclusion they are pressed to accept; analyze that evidence and distinguish fact from assumption; recognize stated and unstated assumptions essential to the conclusion; evaluate these assumptions, accepting some and rejecting others; evaluate the argument, accepting or rejecting the conclusions; and constantly reexamine the assumptions that are behind their beliefs and which guide their actions (p. 11, paraphrased). It is a formidable list of actions, and I find it easy to believe that Fawcett intended it to represent what people should do, ideally, rather than what they actually do.

Jonathan St. B. T. Evans (1982) defines the deductive reasoning task as a task "that involves making an inference from information which is *given*. If a task requires access to memory of things which are not presented, then it is not simply a reasoning task" (p. 5). Evans's definition does not preclude the operation of reasoning in the performance of memory-dependent tasks; it merely specifies that a task that requires the use of memory is more than a reasoning task. One could quibble with this distinction and argue that any reasoning without the use of memory would be impossible – simply understanding the information given is a memory-dependent process – but I take the point to be that we should distinguish between tasks that require nothing more of memory than what is necessary to understand the information given and those that require the retrieval of additional knowledge of real-world relationships.

The preeminent name in the history of deductive logic is Aristotle, whose codification of implicative relationships provided the foundation for the work of many generations of logicians and epistemologists. Should we think of the patterns of valid deductive inference that he identified as discoveries or as inventions? In either case, what kind of thinking led to their codification? Was it a sort of induction? What else, we might ask with George Polya (1954b), could it have been?

Aristotle analyzed the various ways in which valid inferences can be drawn with the structure we refer to as a *categorical syllogism*, which is a form of argument involving three assertions, the third of which (the conclusion) follows from the first two (the major and minor premises). A syllogism is said to be valid if the conclusion does indeed follow from (is implied by) the premises and to be invalid otherwise. Aristotle identified many valid forms and related them to each other in terms of certain properties that we refer to as *figure* and *mood*. Figure relates to the position of the middle term – the term that is common to both premises – and mood to the types of premises involved. More will be said later about syllogisms in the context of a discussion of findings of empirical research on people's ability to deal with syllogistic arguments (Chapter 3). An explanation of the system Aristotle used to classify syllogistic forms can be found in any introductory text on first-order predicate logic and need not be reviewed here.

To Aristotle, the syllogism represented reasoning at its best. For centuries the challenge to Aristotelian logicians in evaluating any line of reasoning was first to reduce it to syllogistic form. All valid reasoning was believed to be reducible in this way; the ability to effect such a reduction was taken as a test of an argument's validity. Medieval logicians developed several rules of thumb for judging the validity of syllogisms, among which are the following four from N. E. Wetherick (1993):

1. If there is a negative premise then the conclusion, if valid, will be negative. (A syllogism with a negative premise cannot yield a valid positive conclusion.)
2. If there is a particular premise then the conclusion, if valid, will be particular. (A syllogism with a particular premise cannot yield a valid universal conclusion.)
3. Any pair of premises yielding a valid conclusion distributes the middle term (the term common to both premises) in at least one premise.
4. No term can be distributed in a valid conclusion unless it is distributed in one of the premises.

The concept of distribution, which appears in the third and fourth rules of thumb, has to do with whether a term refers to every member of the designated class. In the statement *All men are mortal*, for example, *men* is said to be distributed, because the claim covers all members of the class of men, but *mortal* is said not to be distributed, because the claim does not cover all mortal beings.

Application of these rules of thumb suffices to identify as invalid all the invalid syllogisms that can be constructed within Aristotle's classification system, but as Wetherick (1993) points out, they are empirical rules that were discovered by logicians over an extended period of time, and they are useful because they work, but they were not derived from a theory of the syllogism and they do not constitute an explanation of why valid syllogisms are valid and the others are not.

I think it fair to say that the syllogism does not now have the revered status among logicians or students of reasoning that it once had. Baird (1950) describes its limitations this way:

> What practical applications, then, shall we make of deduction as framed in syllogistic forms, to argumentation, discussion, and debate? The syllogism, as a pure demonstration of logical formula, is of doubtful value to students of discussion. Formal logic apparently assumes that the premises are "either true or false." The syllogistic methodology puts down conditions under which the conclusion inevitably follows. The assumption is that of "*absolute truth and certainty*." Argument, on the contrary, concerns itself with the *probability* of a given proposition (p. 158).

Second, perhaps only to Aristotle in importance in the history of deductive thought is Euclid, whose *Elements*, in which he applied the axiomatic-deductive approach not only to mathematics but to all of science as it existed in his day, remained the preeminent treatment of the subject for over 2,000 years. Morris Kline (1980) characterizes Euclid's *Elements* as the vehicle through which "the notion of a logical organization of all physical knowledge based on mathematics entered the intellectual world" (p. 29).

George Boole, the nineteenth century self-taught mathematician who is remembered today as the founder of symbolic logic, did not reject the syllogism, but he did remove it from the place of prominence that it held for more than two millennia in the Aristotelian scheme. In particular he rejected the idea that all valid argumentation can be reduced to syllogistic form. Subsequent logicians have agreed with Boole on this point.

We have already noted that for traditional (Aristotelian) logicians the chief problem was to reduce all available forms of argument to the syllogism. William Bartley (1977) contends that for post Booleans, the central problem of logic became that of determining the total amount of information contained about a given term in a set of propositions. This task is illustrated with the following problem, which is typical of those found in logic textbooks of the time.

Six children, A, B, C, D, E, and F are required to obey the following rules:

(1) On Monday and Tuesday, no four can go out;
(2) On Thursday, Friday, and Saturday, no three can stay in;
(3) On Tuesday, Wednesday, and Saturday, if B and C are together (i.e., if both go out, or both stay in), then A, D, E, and F must be together;
(4) On Monday and Saturday, B cannot go out, unless either D stays in or A, C, and E stay in.

A and B are the first to decide what they will do; and C makes his decision before the other three. Find:

(1) When C must go out;
(2) When he must stay in; and
(3) When he may do as he pleases (Bartley, 1977, p. 23).

Contemporary logicians, in Bartley's words,

> are preoccupied with questions having to do with the foundations of mathematics, consistency proofs, proof construction, axiomatization, decision procedures, and the limitations of all these. The questions set for

> students in the textbooks that they write rarely require the deduction of a conclusion from a set of premises. Rather both premises and conclusion are given, and the student is asked to examine the argument as a whole for validity, usually by means of a consistency test similar to the kind [Lewis] Carroll uses in Book XII (p. 25).

Bartley argues that something of value has been lost to logic in this shift of emphasis from the importance of facility in deduction to the mathematical foundations of logic and claims that one sees the consequences in the commonness of elementary logical mistakes in contemporary work in philosophy.

For a long time in the history of logic, theorems were derived from ordinary language, more recently the tendency has been first to construct a purely formal system and to look later for an interpretation in everyday speech (Boyer & Merzbach, 1991). This trend of increasing abstractness has its counterpart in mathematics, and perhaps also in science, especially physics.

The Force of Logic

> Reason commands us far more imperiously than a master; for in disobeying the one we are unfortunate, and in disobeying the other we are fools
>
> (Pascal, 1947/1670, p. 226).

Logic has force; we feel compelled to be logical, to the extent that we can. So much is widely acknowledged, but why that is so is something of a mystery. We would like to know, with Nathan Court (1961/1935), "How and where have they [the 'inviolate laws of logic'] acquired their infallibility? On what is based their tyrannical power over the mind of man?" (p. 58). One view has it that there is no answer to this question. David Stove (1986) states that view this way: "There are *no* explanations in logic . . .. The greatest logician in the world cannot explain, any more than the layman can, why "All swans are black, and Abe is a swan" entails "Abe is black" (p. 130).

Aristotle saw the rules of logic as intuitively compelling to any rational mind. The law of contradiction – that a proposition cannot be both true and false at the same time and place – for example, was considered to be too obvious to require defense. The codification of these rules was simply a matter of making explicit what every mentally competent person would acknowledge, upon reflection, to be true. This point of view prevailed until relatively modern times. Even George Boole, who took the syllogism off the pedestal on which Aristotle had placed it, considered logic to be a representation of the way the mind worked when it functioned at its best. Eric Temple Bell (1991/1946) describes the long-prevailing attitude of "some of the more philosophical mathematicians" as follows: "logic is a necessity, an eternal fate, imposed upon the human mind from without. It is not an invention of men but a timeless gift to mankind from the immortal gods" (p. 41). In one form or another this belief persisted, Bell contends, for more than 2000 years.

More recently, the idea that logic might better be considered an invention than a discovery has been expressed and a debate on the question has ensued. Bell (1991/1946) likened this debate to that about the same question with respect to numbers. In both cases, he sees the opposing views as irreconcilable and equally defensible: "Each may choose the answer which best accords with his temperament. Great minds have disagreed" (p. 41).

Deductive arguments are generally considered to be considerably more straightforward and easier to understand than inductive ones. Unlike induction, deduction has widely agreed upon rules of inference that have been codified and are readily available to anyone with an interest in knowing them. However, as Lance Rips (1995) points out, deduction has its own set of problems that belie its apparent simplicity. Some deductive inferences seem to be sufficiently obvious to all that they require no justification and, in fact, seem to defy reduction to simpler concepts from which they might be derived. On the other hand, some inferences that also appear to be simple give people trouble. Rips sees reconciliation of these facts as the central problem in the psychology of deductive reasoning.

Nathan Court (1961/1935) argues that logic is based on, and gets its force from, the way things are in the physical world as we perceive it.

> [T]he common sense of logic and its intuitive rules are seen to be the outcome of a schematization that is based upon our experience in the world of common objects. Furthermore, since the abstract laws that logic formulates have their origin and realization in the domain of concrete objects, those laws take on the significance of very primitive natural laws and are therefore practically infallible. That is what accounts for their usefulness, on the one hand, and for their irresistible power over us, on the other hand (p. 68).

The idea that logic is an invention gets some support from the fact that several different systems of logic have been developed, including a number of three-valued logics that allow for statements that are *undecided* as well as for those that are determined to be either true or false. Also, even within traditional two-valued logic, some implicative relationships are more intuitively compelling than others. Consider, for example, the material conditional, "If A then C," or "A implies C." In conditional logic, this proposition is defined to be false when A is true and C false, and true otherwise. People are likely to have little trouble seeing why the proposition should be considered true when both A and C are true, and false when A is true and C false, but they often have difficulty understanding why it should be considered true in the two remaining cases (when A is false and C true, and when A is false and C false). (See Nickerson, 2015, chapter 4.)

In some cases, what should be considered intuitively compelling is not clear. Does "All A are B" entail "Some A are B" and does "No A are B" entail "Some A are not B?" According to one view, the answer in both cases is yes, while according to another it is not. In the latter case, the universal statements are considered true even if the set of As is empty – there are no As – whereas the particular statements are not. When asked, many people (typically a majority) say that the answer, especially in the first case (All entails Some), is yes (Begg & Harris, 1982; Newstead & Griggs, 1983).

The question of whether logic is better viewed as a discovery or as an invention is not likely to be resolved to everyone's satisfaction any time soon. Resolution of this issue is not essential to a recognition that logic, whatever its origin, makes a strong claim to our allegiance as thinking beings. And we have to ask why that is so. Why do we feel obliged to try to be logical, at least insofar as we understand what that means? Why do we feel compelled to try to make only valid inferences? Why do we think it wrong knowingly to espouse contradictory views for the sake of convenience? Why does the discovery of logical inconsistencies among our beliefs make us uncomfortable and motivate us to resolve them?

These are difficult questions, and I do not pretend to know the answers. The fact that the questions themselves have some force, however, seems to me to be strong evidence that if logic is an invention, and not a discovery, it is not an arbitrary invention. Its parameters are limited both by the way our minds work and by the nature of reality, whatever that is. I believe we have an innate sense of logic, similar in principle, perhaps, to the innate "universal grammar" that linguists have hypothesized to account for the "paradox of language acquisition" – the fact that normal children master spoken language with ease during the first few years of life, despite the inability of professional linguists to sort out completely the complex rules of language use (Chomsky, 1968; Jackendoff, 1994).

This is not to deny that we are capable of reasoning illogically, but to suggest that we are unlikely to do so deliberately. When convinced that a particular line of reasoning violates logic, we see the situation as undesirable and are motivated to correct it. Moreover, as a general rule, upon reflection people are highly likely to agree as to what constitutes valid and invalid deductive arguments in specific instances; in other words, when probed deeply enough, our intuitions with respect to what logic demands show a great deal of consistency. None of this is to deny that people can, and sometimes do, intentionally use faulty arguments against adversaries who might be expected not to recognize them as faulty.

Logic and Truth

The validity of a logical argument does not guarantee the truth of the argument's conclusion. If at least one of the premises of the argument is false, the conclusion also may be false, although it is not necessarily so. However, if all the argument's premises are true and its form is valid, the conclusion must be true. A false conclusion cannot follow from true premises. This is a powerful fact. Truth is consistent: to the extent that a collection of true premises implies anything at all, what it implies must be true. It follows that if one knows the conclusion to a valid argument is false, one can be sure that at least one of the argument's premises is false.

Inductive Arguments

> There is indeed an infinity of inductive rules, any one of which can be arbitrarily picked to assess the others
>
> (Lenz, 1974/1958, p. 99).

> The sense of "reasonable" as applied to belief in inductive conclusions is different from the sense of "reasonable" as applied to belief in logically necessary propositions
>
> (Braithwaite, 1974/1953, p. 107).

Induction is a form of generalization. It proceeds from the specific to the general. It starts with observation and ends with theory. Having seen many white swans and none of any other color, one induces that all swans are white – that the next swan that one sees will be white; or if one is more conservative, one induces that most swans are white – that the next swan one sees will, with high probability, be white. If one happens to be Isaac Newton, one observes a certain regularity in the motions of objects both on the earth and in the heavens and induces (some would say abduces) the theory of universal gravitation.

Types of Induction

Different types of induction – or, more accurately, non-deductive argumentation – have sometimes been distinguished. Ulrike Hahn and Jos Hornikz (2016), for example, list a variety of types of argument identified by several writers (Garssen, 1997; Hastings, 1962; Kienpointner, 1992; Perelman & Olbrechts-Tyteca, 1969; Schellens, 1985). For present purposes, it will suffice to recognize two examples, both of which, I believe, have not received the attention they deserve. The first of these two types of argument is *abductive* and the second is *conductive.*

Abductive Arguments

Charles Sanders Peirce described a type of thinking that he contrasted with both *deduction* and *induction* and called it *abduction*. Abduction has received considerably less attention in the literature than has either deduction or induction. However, it is a very important type of reasoning and often used in science. It is what is done when one reasons from an unexplained observation to a hypothesis that, if true, would account for the observation. The rate of rotation of the Andromeda Galaxy, and of most other spiral galaxies, exceeds what can be attributed to the gravitational effects of the visible matter they contain. Their rates of rotation would be accounted for if they contained, in addition to the visible matter they are known to contain, invisible matter in the right quantities. Thus, we hypothesize that the universe contains "dark" matter, because in doing so we "explain" why the galaxies are rotating as fast as they are. The prevailing view among particle physicists appears to be that the hypothesis is correct, and that dark matter accounts for perhaps as much as 20 to 25 percent of the universe's mass. Belief in the existence of dark matter gains credence from the fact that it helps explain properties of the universe in addition to the rates of rotation of galaxies. However, despite much effort to identify the particles that contribute the mass, they remained a mystery as of 2015 (Dobrescu & Lincoln, 2015).

As a type of argument, abduction has the liability that it imposes no constraints on the hypotheses that can be offered to explain otherwise unexplained phenomena. One can imagine many hypothetical explanations of the rates of rotation of galaxies other than that of the existence of dark matter. Perhaps the techniques for estimating the mass of visible matter produce numbers that are systematically too low. Perhaps the galaxies are not rotating as fast as they appear to be. Possibly the theory that relates a galaxy's rotation rate to its mass is incorrect. Maybe spiral galaxies are all occupied by creatures with technologies that are eons more advanced than ours, the use of which makes the galaxies they occupy rotate faster. Of course, for any proposed hypothesis to be taken seriously, it will have to be consistent with what is already known, or believed, to be true, and it must have implications that can be tested. Perhaps this is enough to ensure reasonable restraint on hypothesizing, although it is not uncommon for hypotheses to be advanced (e.g., in high-energy physics) for which empirical testing is not (yet?) possible.

We should note that the existence of dark matter could be *deduced* from the conventional conditional syllogism:

> If spiral galaxies are rotating at a rate that is greater than their visible matter can account for, they must contain some invisible matter.
>
> Spiral galaxies are rotating at a rate that is greater than their visible matter can account for.
>
> Therefore, they must contain some invisible matter.

But to accept the conclusion of this argument as true, one must believe the premises to be true, and if the only reason for accepting the major premise as true is that doing so helps explain certain properties of the universe, such as the fact that the galaxies are rotating faster than their visible matter accounts for, the reasoning appears to be abductive after all.

The construction and testing of theories, when done in accordance with principles that have traditionally defined the scientific method, have been more likely to be seen as involving the stating of hypotheses by generalizing specific observations, deducing testable consequences of those hypotheses, and determining by research whether their predictions prove to be true. However, Peirce's idea, and perhaps even his term, have been gaining in popularity recently, especially among researchers on artificial intelligence. William Rozeboom (1997) makes this point and argues that good science is abductive – not hypothetico-deductive. His own term for the concept is *explanatory induction*. Rozeboom, and Garnham and Oakhill (1994) give as an example of abduction the inference

q
if p then q, therefore
p,

which, as they point out, in deductive logic would be considered an invalid argument known as affirming the consequent. As noted, however, it is nevertheless a form of argument that is common in science. One observes a phenomenon, q, and realizing that q would result if p were the case, one surmises that p is the case. In this scenario, p is not a firm conclusion, as q would be if the form were the deductively valid

p
if p then q, therefore
q.

It is rather a tentative conclusion and its tenability depends on the extent to which it is supported by other evidence.

Rozeboom (1997) defends the claim that good science is abductive and not hypothetico-deductive by reference to examples of explanatory induction in the history of science.

> Early chemists did not learn about acids and alkalis by first speculating that such theoretical properties might exist, next deducing observable consequences of this hypothesis, and finally confirming those predictions as a triumph of hypothetico-deductive science. Rather, the alkali/salt/acid notions and their eventual refinement into a continuum of *pH* levels were an explanatory induction from observed patterns of reaction such as collated by Boyle. Or so I submit (p. 375).

Rozeboom stresses the provisional nature of explanatory abductions and notes the likelihood of their becoming "revised, expanded, or superseded altogether by more intricate configurations of factors, hidden or manifest, as more of the total pattern enters our ken" (p. 382). Although, one might argue that the same comment about their provisional nature could be made about hypotheses, Rozeboom's definition emphasizes the dynamic and evolving nature of explanatory abductions and distinguishes them from hypotheses that are set up for the sake of being shown conclusively to be either true or false.

In this book, abduction is treated as a form of induction in the sense that comments about induction usually pertain to abduction as well as to induction more generally. For present purposes, perhaps it is enough to recognize that abduction is more useful for proposing hypotheses than for testing them.

Conductive Arguments

The term "conductive argument" has more than one connotation in the philosophical and psychological literature. The *Internet Encyclopedia of Philosophy* gives the definition: "an argument whose premises are convergent; the premises count separately in support of the conclusion. If one or more premises were removed from the argument, the degree of support offered by the remaining premises would stay the same." This appears to be the connotation that Trudy Govier (1986) had in mind when writing:

> As I use the term, "conductive" applies to those arguments in which the connection between premises and conclusion is based solely on the relation of relevance. Premises are put forward as being relevant – either conceptually or normatively – to the conclusion and not as being sufficient for it – either deductively or inductively. Characteristically, conductive arguments have several premises which support the conclusion quite separately. That is to say, premises are not linked. If one were to turn out to be false, the others would still be relevant and would still give some support to the conclusion (p. 60).

A different connotation of conductive argument is credited by its proponents to Carl Wellman (1971). In fact, Wellman had much to say about conductive argument, but most of the attention his ideas have received has been on one particular type of argument (Blair & Johnson, 2013). Yun Xie (2017) describes this type of conductive argument this way:

> in many occasions when we argue for a view on issues that are controversial, besides providing reasons to support our conclusion, we also try to introduce some reasons that go against it. This common phenomenon is now to be captured by the concept of conductive argument. The beauty of conductive argument, then, lies in the fact that there is no other type of argument that explicitly collects both affirmative and negative reasons bearing on the conclusion into a single structure, and thereby indicates that the conclusion is reached in a way of *weighing* and *balancing* (p. 4).

Dean Goorden and Thomas Fischer (2011) describe a conductive argument, "as described by Wellman, as something which is neither inductive nor deductive, as well as something that takes into consideration the pros and cons. A conductive argument, simply put, is an argument that can take the form of a balance of considerations argument" (p. 3). Goorden and Fischer make a case for conductive argumentation being the method used by scientists in making inferences to the best explanations.

In another description of conductive arguments, Govier (1986) likened the reasoning involved as the kind in which pros and cons regarding some claim are considered and a judgment is made of their aggregate significance. "They typically involve specification of several factors, and the statement of a conclusion on the basis of what the arguer takes to be their collective force" (p. 61). Assuming the several factors include some that are supportive of a specific conclusion and some that are supportive of its antithesis, this makes this representation close to what Wellman had in mind, as described by Xie. Conductive arguments, thus defined, are arguments that one presumably is likely to have with oneself when trying to decide between, or among, possible courses of action: which car to buy, which job to take, where to spend a vacation.

Such arguments may also play important roles in deciding what to conclude about controversial social issues. When definitive answers prove to be illusive, one may have no reasonable alternative to believing, or acting on, whatever is supported by the "preponderance of evidence." Whether human behavior is a significant driver of global warming is a case in point. Whether the banning of DDT caused more good than harm is perhaps another. The relative fallibility of conductive argumentation is recognized in the distinction that is made between criminal and civil litigation: a guilty verdict in a criminal trial requires that the evidence must support that verdict "beyond a reasonable doubt;" a guilty verdict in a civil case requires only that the verdict be supported by "the preponderance of evidence." In evaluating conductive arguments, it is well to bear in mind that often – perhaps more often than not – the various ways in which one can be wrong are not equally unpalatable, so building a bias into the decision process may be desirable.

In a letter to Joseph Priestly, dated September 19, 1772, in response to a request from Priestly for advice, Benjamin Franklin (1907) described his now famous method of selecting between two courses of action – of weighing evidence – when the choice involves many factors and is not easy to make. What makes such choices difficult, in Franklin's view, is that the factors relevant to the selection cannot all be held in the mind at once.

> To get over this, my Way is, to divide half a Sheet of Paper by a Line into two Columns, writing over the one Pro, and over the other Con. Then during three or four Days Consideration I put down under the different Heads short Hints of the different Motives that at different Times occur to me for or against the Measure. When I have thus got them all together in one View, I endeavour to estimate their respective Weights; and where I find two, one on each side, that seem equal, I strike them both out: If I find a Reason pro equal to some two Reasons con, I strike out the three. If I judge some two Reasons con equal to some three Reasons pro, I strike out the five; and thus proceeding I find at length where the Ballance lies; and if after a Day or two of farther Consideration nothing new that is of Importance occurs on either side, I come to a Determination accordingly.

Wellman's connotation of conductive argument has proved to be controversial (Govier, 2011; Possin, 2016). Jonathan Adler (2013), for example, contends that such arguments are not possible, while J. Anthony Blair (2013) contends that they are. Kevin Possin (2016) challenges the idea that conductive arguments are sufficiently different from other arguments to justify treating them as a class of argument: "Some of what are deemed conductive arguments are simply inductive arguments, and some are best construed as subsets of the constituents of what is commonly called a position paper" (p. 563). Despite, perhaps because of, decades of debate, Possin contends, the very concept of conductive argument "the nature of conductive arguments has become progressively less clear" (p. 564).

Xie (2017) notes that the negative reasons for an argument may be clothed in somewhat apologetic terms such as an "even though," "although," or "notwithstanding" clause. One may be excused for doubting that people would be as good at finding reasons against a favored conclusion as they are at finding reasons supporting it. Nevertheless, the obligation to come up with reasons against a favored conclusion at least assures that some consideration will be given to them. Whether one accepts conductive argument as a form of argument different from, and on a par with, deduction and induction, or not, the ideal of weighing evidence, pro and con impartially, is an ideal to which we can aspire.

Justification of Induction

Much has been written about deduction and much is known about it. Much has been written about induction also, but it has given philosophers a rather bad time. As Bertrand Russell (1967/1912) put it, "all knowledge which, on a basis of experience, tells us something about what is not experienced, is based upon a belief which experience can neither confirm nor confute;" the existence of such a belief, he contends, "raises some of the most difficult and most debated problems of philosophy" (p. 48).

Some philosophers have argued that induction is irrational. In the middle of the seventeenth century, Thomas Hobbes (1919/1651) pointed out the limitations of induction the following way: "though a man have always seen the day and night to follow one another hitherto, yet can he not hence conclude they shall do so, or that they have done so eternally: *experience concludeth nothing universally*" (p. 10). About 100 years later, David Hume (1939/1748), made essentially the same point:

> For all inferences from experience suppose, as their foundation, that the future will resemble the past, and similar powers will be conjoined with similar sensible qualities. If there be any suspicion that the course of nature may change, and the past be no rule for the future, all experience becomes useless and can give rise to no inference or conclusion. It is impossible, therefore, that any argument from experience can prove this resemblance of the past to the future, since all arguments are founded on the supposition of that resemblance (p. 606).

Wesley Salmon (1974) describes the circular bind posed by Hume: "inductive inference may fail completely to establish knowledge of the unobserved if nature is not uniform. We cannot validly show, either *a priori* or *a posteriori*, that nature is uniform, prior to a justification of induction. Therefore, we cannot justify induction" (p. 86). A century and a half or so after Hume stated his position, Russell (1967/1912) questioned the rationality of induction in similar terms: "Do *any* number of cases of a law being fulfilled in the past afford evidence that it will be fulfilled in the future?" (p. 43). "Have we any reason, assuming that they [laws like the law of gravitation] have always held in the past to suppose that these laws will hold in the future?" (pp. 44, 45). Karl Popper (1981/1962) answers Russell's question in the negative: "no rule can ever guarantee that a generalization inferred from true observations, however often repeated, is true" (p. 76). We have already noted that the fact that a mathematical relationship is true in many cases is not compelling evidence that it is true in all cases.

That the generalizations to which induction leads are not guaranteed to be true is colorfully illustrated by G. K. Chesterton. The world, he suggests is neither totally reasonable nor totally unreasonable, and our understanding of it is hindered by the fact that it is nearly reasonable, but not quite:

> It looks just a little more mathematical and regular than it is; its exactitude is obvious, but its inexactitude is hidden; its wildness lies in wait. I give one coarse instance of what I mean. Suppose some mathematical creature from the moon were to reckon up the human body; he would at once see that it was duplicate. A man is two men, he of the right exactly resembling him on the left. Having noted that there was an arm on the right and one on the left, a leg on the right and one on the left, he might go further and still find on each side the same number of fingers, the same number of toes, twin eyes, twin ears, twin nostrils, even twin lobes of the brain. At last he would take it as a law; and then where he found a heart on one side, would deduce that there was another heart on the other. And just, then, where he most felt he was right, he would be wrong (Chesterton, 1959/1908, p. 81).

Such considerations have led to much discussion of the problem of justifying induction. In the minds of many, the problem has not yet been resolved; the question of "why in a particular instance we should act on the most probable or believe the most probable will occur" is one, some would say, that has yet to be answered satisfactorily (Nozick, 1993, p. 123). But the very notion of justifying induction is itself a controversial one. Stove (1986) contends that this turn of phrase is misleading, and states flatly "There is no such thing as the problem of justifying induction" (p. 31). The idea that proving that induction *is* justified makes sense, he argues, but not the idea of *justifying* induction. Induction either is justified, or it is not; the challenge is to determine which is the case. Perhaps it can be assumed that people who have spoken of the need to justify induction have usually had in mind the need to convince themselves that induction *is* justified.

The problem is not that of convincing ourselves that induction is *ever* justified; the problem is that of convincing ourselves that induction is justified as a *type* of reasoning that can be applied generally with the confidence that, given true premises, it is likely to yield true conclusions. The claim that *no* inductive generalization is justified is self-contradictory; inasmuch as the claim itself is such a generalization, it rules out its own acceptance. It is for this reason that it has been held that a "general, unrestricted denial of the propriety of induction cannot coherently be made" (Campbell, 1974/1963, p. 148).

One approach to resolving the problem of induction is to give induction a deductive basis:

> Whenever one is aware of a large number of positive instances of a phenomenon and of no negative instances, one may legitimately infer that the next instance of the phenomenon one encounters will be positive (principle of induction, and major premise).
>
> I am aware of a large number of positive (black) instances and no negative (nonblack) instances of a phenomenon (crows).
>
> Therefore, I may assume that the next instance of the phenomenon (crow) I see will be positive (black).

This gives induction a deductive foundation, but it is not a satisfactory one because it assumes the very principle one wants to establish. In the view of many philosophers, there is no way to avoid this circularity, so it appears that one must accept the disquieting conclusion that induction is not justified.

One may be tempted by common sense to justify induction on the grounds that it has always worked in the past. The argument would be that inasmuch as inductive inferences have been effective in the past, it is reasonable to assume that they will be effective in the future. But to make this a complete deductive argument, we need the major premise: If something has worked effectively in the past, it is reasonable to assume that it will work effectively in the future. The argument is circular in that the justification of the principle of inference the argument is intended to justify rests on the truth of the major premise of the argument, which, as in the preceding example, is the very principle that is in need of justification.

What are we to say to compelling discreditations of inductive reasoning? We seem to be left in a hapless situation. If the observation of order and regularity in nature in the past provides no assurance that it will continue in the future, how are we to make sense of anything at all? Reflection on the lack of justification of induction led Hume (1854/1739) to the despairing observation:

> The intense view of these manifold contradictions and imperfections in human reason has so wrought upon me, and heated my brain, that I am ready to reject all belief and reasoning and can look upon no opinion as more probable or likely than another. Where am I, or what? From what causes do I derive my existence, and to what condition shall I return? Whose favor shall I court, and whose anger must I dread? What beings surround me? And on whom have I any influence, or who have influence on me? I am confounded with all these questions and begin to fancy myself in the most deplorable condition imaginable, environed with the deepest darkness, and utterly deprived of the use of every member and faculty (p. 331).

Hume reported relieving himself of such "philosophical melancholy and delirium" by dining, playing a game of backgammon or conversing, presumably not about philosophy, with friends.

What we are forced to acknowledge is that inductive reasoning – generalizing, extrapolating, predicting – rests solidly on the *assumption* that we live in a lawful universe and that the laws that have governed its behavior in the past will continue to do so in the future. The assumption that is required involves more than this, because one can conceive of a set of laws that would permit the kinds of discontinuities that would make induction unreliable, or laws that are beyond human discovery. We must assume also that the kinds of regularities that have been observed in the past are trustworthy clues to the laws by which the world works and that these laws are unchanging and, to some degree at least, comprehensible by human minds. If we are to have any confidence in this kind of reasoning, we must believe, as Einstein (1961/1916) put it that "God is subtle, but not malicious."

Harold Himsworth (1986) makes a similar argument in replying to Hume's dismissal of induction. He notes that Hume's position itself rests on a presupposition and, in the spirit of William James's (1979/1896) *Will to Believe*, points out that the contrary presupposition is equally defensible and may be preferred on other grounds. "If we can suppose that the course of nature might change, we can equally well suppose that it might not" (p. 10). And if we wish to make the latter supposition, we could replace Hume's second and third sentences (above) with "If there be no suspicion the course of nature may change and the past may not continue to be the rule for the future, therefore, inferences and conclusions can properly be drawn from past experience as to the course of future events" (p. 11).

So, we are brought to different conclusions depending on whether we start with the proposition that the course of nature might change or the proposition that it will not. Himsworth (1986) goes on to argue that it makes more sense for us to assume that the course of nature will not change, because if it does, we will, as a consequence, not be around to observe the fact. In his words, "As long as human beings exist, they can count on a future resembling the past and, hence, can justifiably infer the course of future events from past experience" (p.13). Himsworth's argument here involves an unstated assumption that one might wish to challenge, namely that any change in the course of nature would be fatal to humankind; but this assumption is not essential to a recognition that the belief that nature will continue to obey the laws it has in the past is at least as tenable as the belief that the laws of nature will change. The whole scientific enterprise, not to mention the planning that is done in every walk of life, rests squarely on the belief that the laws will not change; it is hard to imagine how it could be otherwise.

Hans Reichenbach (1938) argues that we really have no feasible alternative to induction, because if induction is assumed to fail, no other method of learning about nature can be assumed to succeed. Here is an account of Reichenbach's argument given by Salmon (1967):

> [N]ature may or may not be uniform – if she is, induction works; if she is not, induction fails. Even in the face of our ignorance about the uniformity of nature, we can ask what would happen if we adopted some radically different method of inference. Consider, for instance, the method of the crystal gazer. Since we do not know whether nature is uniform or not, we must consider both possibilities. If nature is uniform, the method of crystal gazing might work successfully, or it might fail. We cannot prove a priori that it will not work. At the same time, we cannot prove a priori that it will

> work, even if nature exhibits a high degree of uniformity. Thus, in case nature is reasonably uniform, the standard inductive method *must* work while the alternative method of crystal gazing *may or may not work*. In this case, the superiority of the standard inductive method is evident. Now, suppose nature lacks uniformity to such a degree that the standard inductive method is a complete failure. In this case, Reichenbach argues, the alternative method must likewise fail. Suppose it did not fail – suppose, for instance, that the method of crystal gazing worked consistently. This would constitute an important relevant uniformity that could be exploited inductively. If a crystal gazer had consistently predicted future occurrences, we could infer inductively that he has a method of prediction that will enjoy continued success. The inductive method would, in this way, share the success of the method of crystal gazing, and would therefore be, contrary to hypothesis, successful. Hence, Reichenbach concludes, the standard inductive method will be successful *if any other method could succeed*. As a result, we have everything to gain and nothing to lose by adopting the inductive method. If any method works, induction works (pp. 52, 53).

Variants of the argument that if induction does not work, nothing else does either, have been given by others as well. Richard Braithwaite (1974/1953), for example, notes that "[t]here is no general policy other than an inductive policy which there is good reason to believe has been effective in the past" (p. 102), and again, "[t]he justification for the use of an inductive policy in terms of its effectiveness must be read in the context of other predictive policies being known to be ineffective" (p. 103).

Another response that has been given to the kinds of objections to inductive reasoning raised by Hume, Russell, and others is that they are based on a narrow and somewhat esoteric meaning of reasoning. Paul Edwards (1952) contends that the questions asked by Russell can be answered affirmatively without appealing to any nonempirical principles, and suggests that when Russell took the position that observed instances are not by themselves a reason for an inductive conclusion, he attached such a narrow meaning to "reason" as to make the position uninteresting. When Russell used the term in the context of discussions of the legitimacy of induction, he, like Hume and others, meant "*logically conclusive* reason." In this sense, it must be admitted, Edwards argues, that past observations do not provide a basis for predictions, but "reason" is given a much broader meaning in science and in ordinary discourse. "Russell's assertion that the premises of an inductive argument never by themselves constitute a *logically conclusive* reason for an inductive conclusion in no way contradicts the common sense assertion that they frequently constitute a reason *in the ordinary sense of the word*" (p. 68).

Stephen Toulmin (1958) contends that the problem that philosophers have had with induction stems from their misguided insistence on applying to it criteria that are appropriate only for analytical arguments.

> In the case of substantial arguments [as distinct from analytical or abstract formal arguments] there is no question of data and backing taken together entailing [logically forcing] the conclusion, or failing to entail it: just because the steps involved are substantial ones, it is no use either looking for entailments or being disappointed if we do not find them. Their absence does not spring from a lamentable weakness in the arguments, but from the nature of the problem with which they are designed to deal. When we have to set about assessing the real merits of any substantial argument, analytic criteria such as entailment are, accordingly, simply irrelevant (p. 168).

Such terms as "logically possible," "logically necessary," and "logically impossible," Toulmin argues, are misnomers.

> To say that a conclusion is possible, impossible, or necessary is to say that, bearing in mind the nature of our problem and data, the conclusion must be admitted to consideration, ruled out, or accepted as forced on us. The "logical" criteria of possibility, impossibility and necessity, on the other hand, do nothing to show us that any conclusion we shall be concerned with in practice is genuinely possible, impossible, or necessary – at any rate so long as the problem with which we are concerned involves us in the use of *substantial* arguments. This is why I claim that "logical" modalities are misnamed (p. 170).

In short, grounding induction on deduction is neither possible nor desirable. Induction serves a different purpose from that of deduction and it should not be surprising that it functions in a qualitatively different way.

Let us return for a moment to the distinction made by Stove (1986) between the goal of justifying induction and that of demonstrating that induction is justified. On this distinction, induction either is or is not justified, independently of anything we say about it, and the challenge is to determine which is the case. Suppose we assume, for the sake of discussion, that we are unable to prove that induction is justified. It does not follow that it is *not* justified. Inasmuch as we have little choice but to use it, we may perhaps take some comfort in this thought. Moreover, as Max Black (1974/1958) has pointed out, "If we were never entitled to *use* a correct rule of inference before we had formally argued in support of that rule, the process of inference could never get started" (p. 133).

Perhaps the most telling counter to arguments against the utility of induction is the recognition that all critics of the method themselves demonstrate by their behavior that they use it just like everyone else. They behave as though they believe the laws of physics that have been in force up to a given point in time are likely to remain in force beyond that point; one does not expect to see them jumping off tall buildings on the rationale that there is no reason to expect the law of gravity to continue to hold just because it has always held in the past. They write books, expecting people to be around to read them. They plan for the future in the usual ways. They are in very much the same position as people who deny the government's right to collect taxes, but pay them all the same, just in case. "[I]t simply is a fact," as Edwards (1952) points out, "that, given certain sets of observations, human beings can make true predictions" (p. 77), and skeptics benefit from that fact every bit as much as do true believers. As S. F. Barker (1974) puts it, "The man who expects for the future the opposite of what he has observed in the past is a paradigm case of irrationality: we point to him when we teach children the meaning of the term 'irrational'" (p. 61).

Induction is so basic to our thinking that it is doubtful if we could think at all, in any meaningful sense, without it. Whenever we engage in generalization, which we do constantly in treating things as members of classes or categories – chairs, houses, vehicles, plants, people – we are using inductively established concepts. The debate about whether it is justified, or whether it can be shown to be justified, is likely to continue; in the meantime all of us – including those who argue most strongly against its legitimacy – will continue to use it, as we always have, simply because we cannot get along without it, and to attempt to do so would be to commit intellectual suicide.

To say that induction is a justified form of reasoning is not, of course, to say that all inductions are justified, any more than to say that deduction is a justified form of reasoning is to say that all deductions are valid. People can, and often do, draw conclusions inductively that prove to be wrong. As Alan Sokal and Jean Bricmont (1998) put it,

> some inductions are justified, and others are not; or, to be more precise, some inductions are more reasonable and others less so. Everything depends on the case at hand: to take a classic philosophical example, the fact that we have seen the Sun rise every day, together with all our astronomical knowledge, gives us good reasons to believe that it will rise tomorrow. But this does not imply that it will rise ten billion years from now (indeed, current astrophysical theories predict that it will exhaust its fuel before then) (p. 59).

Whatever one's position regarding the justification of induction, there is no denying that people use it constantly. One focus of much inductive thinking is the future – thinking about how things are likely to be sometime beyond now. Interest among researchers in such thinking, sometimes referred to as *prospection* (Gilbert & Wilson, 2007), appears to have been increasing in recent years (Baumeister & Vohs, 2016). Pragmatic prospection has been defined as "thinking about the future in ways that will have practical utility, which is to say ways that will guide action… in ways that will assist the process of producing future desired outcomes and avoiding undesired ones" (Baumeister, Vohs, & Oettingen, 2016, p. 4). Clearly such thinking is unlikely to go far without the assumption that the laws of nature will continue to operate as they do now and as they have in the past.

Scholars have found it much easier to deal with deductive arguments than with inductive arguments, but the importance of the latter is universally recognized. Alfred North Whitehead (1956/1925) noted the incongruity between the importance of induction and its status in philosophy: "The theory of Induction is the despair of philosophy – and yet all our activities are based upon it" (p. 405).

Polya on Induction

> A conjecture becomes more credible by the verification of any new consequence
>
> (Polya, 1954a, p. 22).

George Polya is one of a small minority of mathematicians who have written about the process of doing mathematics, and, in his case, about problem solving more generally. His two-volume set on plausible reasoning in mathematics (Polya, 1954a, 1954b) is widely recognized as a definitive treatment of the subject, and his *How to Solve It* (1957/1945) as a seminal work on problem-solving heuristics.

Polya (1954a) considered the need for inductive reasoning to be ubiquitous: "In dealing with problems of any kind we need inductive reasoning of some kind" (p. 76). He characterizes the inductive investigation of a conjecture as "confronting its consequences with the facts" and calls the following form of argument the *fundamental inductive pattern*:

A implies C
C true
A more credible

Recall that in deductive logic

A implies C
C <u>true</u>
A true

is an invalid argument known as affirmation of the consequent. Polya argues that the fundamental inductive pattern is much more indicative of the kind of reasoning that people actually do than is deductive logic. It expresses a belief, as Polya (1954b) puts it, which no reasonable person seems to doubt, namely that "*the verification of a consequence renders a conjecture more credible*" (p. 5); it is important to note however that the pattern says something only about the direction of change in belief and nothing about the magnitude.

Polya notes that people may agree that if A implies B, the discovery that B is true should increase the credibility of A, but have different opinions as to the amount by which it should do so. Such differences of opinion may have their roots in the different backgrounds – including different prior assessments of the likelihood that A is true, or different attitudes regarding the desirability of A being true – that people bring to the judgment.

Close to the distinction between deductive and inductive reasoning, perhaps identical to it, is the distinction that Polya (1954a) makes between what he refers to as *demonstrative* reasoning, on the one hand, and *plausible* reasoning on the other. Demonstrative reasoning, in Polya's view, is the kind of reasoning by which mathematical knowledge is secured; plausible reasoning is what we use to support our conjectures; all knowledge outside mathematics, Polya suggests, consists of conjectures. "A mathematical proof is demonstrative reasoning, but the inductive evidence of the physicist, the circumstantial evidence of the lawyer, the documentary evidence of the historian, and the statistical evidence of the economist belong to plausible reasoning" (p. v). This is very close to the distinction made by C. S. Peirce (1869) between a demonstrative argument, in which the conclusion is true whenever the premises are true (assuming the argument is valid in form), and a probabilistic argument, in which the conclusion is usually true whenever the premises are true.

The contrast Polya draws between the two types of reasoning is stark. Demonstrative reasoning is "safe, beyond controversy, and final;" it has rigid codified standards, but by itself demonstrative reasoning is incapable of giving us new knowledge about the world. In contrast, plausible reasoning is "hazardous, controversial, and provisional;" its standards are fluid and not explicated in any widely accepted theory. It is only by means of plausible reasoning, however, that we learn anything new about the world. Mathematics provides a means of learning demonstrative reasoning in school. There is no comparable vehicle for learning plausible reasoning.

Plausible reasoning does not have rules of the kind that demonstrative reasoning has. This is not to say it has no rules at all, but only that the rules it has are of a different sort; they are, in Polya's (1954a) words, "rules of admissibility." The patterns of plausible inference that he describes are characterized as "rules of admissibility in scientific discussion." One is not obliged to give a certain degree of credence to a conjecture if some of its consequences have been verified, but such verifications are admissible in scientific discussion and one is only being fair and reasonable to be influenced by them.

Herein lies one of the major differences between demonstrative reasoning, as represented in the deductive syllogisms of Aristotle, and plausible reasoning, as represented by forms showing a conjecture to be strengthened by the verification of a consequence. In the former case, there is no room for differences of opinion regarding the nature of the inference, whereas in the latter there is: "When we raise the question 'How much is the conjecture strengthened by the verification of this consequence?' we open the door to personal differences" (Polya, 1954a, p. 114). Again, "In opposition to demonstrative inference, plausible inference leaves indeterminate a highly relevant point: the 'strength' or the 'weight' of the conclusion. This weight may depend not only on clarified grounds such as those expressed in the premises, but also on unclarified unexpressed grounds somewhere in the background of the person who draws the conclusion" (p. 115).

Using the fundamental inductive pattern as a point of departure, Polya (1954b) develops many variations on it to make the point that the verification of some consequences of a conjecture strengthen our belief in that conjecture more than does the verification of others. He makes several suggestions as to the sorts of variables that should affect the strength of a plausible inference:

- *The verification of a new consequence counts more or less according as the new consequence differs more or less from the formerly verified consequences* (p. 7).
- *The verification of a consequence counts more or less according as the consequence is more or less improbable in itself* (p. 9).
- *The more confidence we placed in a possible ground of our conjecture the greater will be the loss of faith in our conjecture when that possible ground is refuted* (p. 123).

- *The more confidence we placed in an incompatible rival of our conjecture the greater will be the faith in our conjecture when that rival is refuted* (p. 124).
- *The less credible a circumstance appears without a certain conjecture, the more will the proof of that circumstance enhance the credibility of that conjecture* (p. 127).

Thus, although the fundamental inductive pattern says nothing about the strength of the conclusion, the pattern can be elaborated in ways that do have implications for strength. If it is the case that B is believed to be almost certain, whether or not A is true, then the discovery that A is true adds little credibility to B. On the other hand, if one finds it hard to imagine a way that B could be true without A (B without A is hardly credible) then the determination that B is true adds greatly to the credibility of A.

Other heuristic inferences discussed by Polya (1954b) include:

- *Our confidence in a conjecture can only diminish when a possible ground for the conjecture is exploded* (p. 20).
- *Our confidence in a conjecture can only increase when an incompatible rival conjecture is exploded* (p. 20).
- *Our confidence in a conjecture is influenced by our confidence in one of its consequences and varies in the same direction* (p. 25).

Polya (1954b) compares and contrasts the ways in which the scientist (naturalist), the jurist, and the individual who has an immediate practical problem to solve make use of verifying evidence in evaluating conjectures:

> If, in spite of much work, the naturalist succeeds in verifying only a few not-too-surprising consequences of his conjecture, he may be moved to drop it. If too little evidence is submitted against the defendant, the court may drop the case. If, after a long and strenuous effort, only a few weak indications in favor of his plan have occurred to the problem-solver, he may be moved to modify his plan radically, or even drop it altogether .... On the other hand, if several consequences are verified, several pieces of evidence against the defendant submitted, several indications observed, the case for the naturalist's conjecture, for the prosecution, or for the problem-solver's plan may be greatly strengthened. Yet even more important than the number may be the variety. Consequences that are very different from each other, witnesses who are obviously independent, indications that come from different sides, count more heavily (p. 157).

Polya makes it clear that he does not intend to suggest that the situations faced by the naturalist, the court, and the everyday problem-solver call for identical treatments of verifying information.

> The naturalist's task is to gather as much evidence as he can for or against his conjecture. The court's task is to examine all the relevant evidence submitted. Yet it is not the problem-solver's task to collect as much evidence as he can for or against his plan of the solution, or to debate such evidence to the bitter end: his task is to solve the problem, by any means, in following this plan of the solution, or any other plan, or no plan (p. 157).

In short, Polya presents induction as a form of reasoning that proceeds in accordance with certain identifiable principles. These principles have to do with the formation and modification of beliefs. And they pertain to how evidence should affect the strength with which beliefs are held. Polya stops short of developing a calculus of belief revision, but he provides many examples of how observations should increase or diminish the strengths of beliefs by greater or lesser amounts.

Rule-Based Approaches to Induction

Richard Nisbett and colleagues have discussed a variety of aspects of induction. Paul Thagard and Nisbett (1982) consider the role of variability in generalization and argue that the degree to which an instance (say observation of an A that is a B) confirms, or increases one's confidence in, a generalization (say All As are Bs) depends on one's knowledge of how variable the entities of which A is a kind tend to be with respect to entities of which B is a kind. In particular, confirmation increases with number of confirmatory observations, but at a rate that is inversely proportional to variability. Because people have different types and amounts of background knowledge of As and Bs and the classes to which they belong, the same observation can be confirmatory for different observers to different degrees. More generally, in Thagard and Nisbett's view, when people differ markedly in their background knowledge on any given topic, it should not be surprising to find that they differ also in the inductive generalizations they make from an observation relating to that topic.

Nisbett et al. (1983) describe inductive reasoning as encompassing concept formation, generalization from instances, and prediction. They propose the following statistical rules that these variants of inductive reasoning must satisfy to be correct:

> Concepts should be discerned and applied with more confidence when they apply to a narrow range of clearly defined objects than when they apply to a broad range of diverse and loosely defined objects that can be confused with objects to which the concept does not apply. Generalizations should be more confident when they are based on a larger number of instances, when the instances are an unbiased sample, and when the instances in question concern events of low variability rather than high variability. Predictions should be more confident when there is high correlation between the dimensions for which information is available and the dimensions about which the prediction is made, and, failing such a correlation, prediction should rely on a base rate or prior distribution for the events to be predicted (p. 339).

John Holland et al. (1986) take induction "to encompass all inferential processes that expand knowledge in the face of uncertainty" (p. 1). "The study of induction . . . is the study of how knowledge is modified through its use" (p. 5). Holland et al. give a dim appraisal of the progress that has been made in understanding such processes, in spite of the fact that philosophy, psychology, and artificial intelligence are all concerned with understanding them.

> Philosophers have spent hundreds of years attempting to characterize inductive inference, yet the current research most concerned with the topic – on formal inductive logics and Bayesian decision theories – bears little relation to how people actually think. Behaviorist psychologists spent decades developing learning theories that were not fully adequate as descriptions of the inferential and learning capacities of rats and fell very far short of the mark for humans. Researchers in artificial intelligence are able to build sophisticated game players and powerful expert systems but have been largely stymied in attempts to program these systems to improve themselves . . . . Induction, which has been called "the scandal of philosophy," has become the scandal of psychology and artificial intelligence as well (p. 1).

Holland et al. (1986) present a framework – which they are careful to note is not a theory – for understanding induction. Their intent is to identify principles of thought processes that are computationally feasible and appropriate for describing induction as carried out by both machines and animals including mice and men. By computationally feasible principles they mean principles that can be represented as computational procedures on computers.

The central problem of induction, in their view, "is to specify processing constraints that will ensure that the inferences drawn by a cognitive system will tend to be plausible and relevant to the system's goals" (p. 5). The key assumptions underlying their conception of an inductive processing system are "that induction is (a) directed by problem-solving activity and (b) based on feedback regarding the success or failure of predictions generated by the system" (p. 9). Various kinds of induction are recognized, each of which is triggered by specific contextual conditions. Examples of a triggering condition would be failure of a prediction and occurrence of an unusual event.

Holland et al. (1986) see induction as goal-directed activity. "The fundamental use of induction is to generate models of the environment that the cognitive system can use in selecting actions that will lead to environmental states with positive value" (p. 39). "[Induction is a problem-directed activity, executed in response to specific system objectives such as seeking plausible explanations for an unexpected outcome" (p. 68).

Although inductive arguments are usually thought of as being less strictly guided by rules than are deductive arguments, the model that Holland et al. develop is a rule-based system; its behavior is controlled by a set of rules expressed as condition-action pairs. Two fundamental types of inductive change for such a system are recognized: the refinement of existing rules and the generation of new ones. Rules gain or lose strength as a consequence of feedback from correct or incorrect predictions. The ability to generate new rules is seen as essential for any inductive system. Because the space of possible rules is always effectively infinite, any rule-generating process that is to have practical value must generate rules that are plausible.

Unlike the case with deductive inference, in which one tends to think in terms of arguments being either valid or invalid, the rules for inductive reasoning are all matters of degree. The view put forth by Nisbett and colleagues is reminiscent of that expounded by Polya in its specification of a variety of factors that should influence the strength of the inductive inferences drawn; one should, according to this view, have more or less confidence in one's classifications, generalizations, or predictions depending on the considerations indicated.

The distinction between deductive and inductive arguments, or reasoning more generally, is a time-honored one. Over several decades, however, scholars have been pointing out its limitations and the problems that arise when all reasoning, or argumentation, is considered to fit in one or the other of these categories. In other words, there has been increasing unwillingness to consider these categories to be exclusive and exhaustive (Fisher, 2004; Perelman & Olbrechts-Tyteca, 1969; Toulmin, 1958; Wisdom & Barker, 1991). As Govier (1986) puts it, "It is well known that many naturally occurring arguments are not easily classified as inductive or deductive. In addition, there are many problems about just how the inductive–deductive distinction is to be defined" (p. 57). The only way to make the distinction exhaustive, Govier contends, is to define inductive as nondeductive, which would effectively make induction a grab bag category. In their extensive treatment of argumentation – rhetoric in their terms – Perelman and Olbrechts-Tyteca (1969) identify numerous types of arguments and illustrate them with copious examples taken primarily from the philosophical literature.

Despite the limitations of this dichotomy, it remains useful for expository purposes; but it is important to recognize that the boundary between the types is fuzzy and that there are arguments that are not easily classified with respect to it.

Postulational Reasoning and Empirical Reasoning

Cassius Keyser (1926), a prominent American mathematician during the early part of the twentieth century, published a little book in 1926, entitled *Thinking about Thinking*, in which he distinguished between postulational thinking and empirical thinking. The distinction is similar to the distinction between deductive and inductive reasoning, but Keyser went beyond that distinction in emphasizing the role of a set of postulates from which deductions in postulational thinking are to be made and in promoting postulational thinking as a goal in all fields of intellectual endeavor. Postulational thinking, as he conceived it, takes the form of *if-then* propositions.

Keyser argued that any doctrine must employ some undefined terms and some unproven propositions but that these should be held to a minimum: "a doctrine can have maximum clarity and cogency when and only when it has the minimum of undefined terms and undemonstrated propositions." From this point of departure, he goes on to characterize postulational thinking in the following way.

> If, knowing these things, you begin the work of construction by deliberately selecting (1) a few terms or ideas which you intend to employ without defining them, (2) a small set of compatible propositions which must, of course, connect the terms already chosen and which you intend to employ as a basis without demonstrating them; and if, having performed that initial task of selecting what we may call your undefined terms and undemonstrated propositions, you proceed with the task of definition and proof, defining all other terms as you have occasion to use them, and demonstrating the propositions that are logically implied by, and deducible from, the

> undemonstrated ones: If you do that, if in the work of building your doctrine you proceed in the manner I have indicated, then and only then you are engaged in autonomous or postulational thinking in the full sense of the term. I call such thinking postulational because the propositions that are taken for granted in a reasoned discourse, though they are sometimes called assumptions or primitive propositions or axioms, are most commonly called postulates; and I call it autonomous thinking because a doctrine constructed by it is an autonomous doctrine, one, I mean, that is independent in the sense of being a logically organized whole containing as an integral part of itself the foundation on which it stands (p. 20).

Postulational thinking, Keyser suggests, is done "in some small measure, in a haphazard and rudimentary way, probably unconsciously," by everyone and always has been, but "as a full-grown procedure deliberately and systematically employed in the construction and criticism of doctrine" it is of relatively recent origin and rarely used. The most famous historical example of such thinking, in Keyser's view, was Euclid's *Elements*. More recent examples of significant attempts to use this type of thinking to construct a doctrine include Baruch Spinoza's abortive effort to develop a system of ethics, Giovanni Saccheri's successful, though largely unrecognized, construction of a non-Euclidean geometry and the non-Euclidean geometries subsequently created independently by János Bolyai and Nikolai Lobachevski. In the twentieth century, scores of postulational systems were developed, many but not all in mathematics. Keyser held that the method of postulational thinking is available for and highly important to all fields of thought.

Empirical thinking, as Keyser characterizes it, is distinguished by two facts: "(1) in any specimen of it, there is present some ingredient or process of logic; (2) the occurrence of the logical factor, however frequent or important, is always subordinate, its presence being that of a servant, not that of a sovereign" (p. 42). Empirical thinking yields empirical knowledge and is more common than is postulational thinking. It involves

> observation ... experimentation, collection of facts or data, formation of concepts, manipulation of these in some incomplete measure by the processes of logic, making of guesses or hypotheses respecting causes and orders of events, testing of such conjectures by various devices for verification: all motivated partly by curiosity, partly and mainly by the felt needs of life. It is thus evident that empirical thinking is universal in the sense that it occurs in the lives of all human beings, whatever their gifts, interests, or occupations (p. 46).

Empirical thinking is seen to be a practically useful form of thinking because of the knowledge it produces. However, in Keyser's view, having acquired knowledge empirically, the goal should be to systematize that knowledge in a postulational form. Knowledge is expressed in various ways: in institutions, customs, habits, and procedures, but most importantly in propositions. Sets of such propositions constitute the bodies of knowledge of various disciplines. If one accepts a postulational system as the goal of any particular discipline, what one hopes to do is to organize these propositions in such a way that the logical relationships among them are clear and to find eventually a relatively small set that can be taken as postulates from which all the others can be logically deduced. The motivation for organizing knowledge as postulational systems is in part practical, but also in part aesthetic. "An autonomous doctrine is indeed a work of art of the highest order" (p. 54). Keyser argues that "the autonomous form is the ideal to which every scientific branch . . . consciously or unconsciously aspires" (p. 61).

Postulational and empirical thinking were seen by Keyser as mutually beneficial in science. Empirical thinking produces the knowledge represented in the postulates of the system and implicitly in the propositions derived from them. Postulational thinking is responsible for the derivation of the secondary propositions many of which pose challenges for empirical research. "And so. it is seen that the two great types of human thinking, far from being mutually antagonistic, serve to stimulate and to direct one another, thus cooperating to advance human knowledge whether of the actual world or of the vaster world of possibility" (p. 66).

I have discussed Keyser's view at some length because I believe the distinction it makes between postulational and empirical thinking to be indicative of a distinction that many scientists make, though not necessarily in precisely the same terms. Einstein (1961/1916), for example, articulated a view very similar to Keyser's. He too saw the postulates, or axioms, of a theory that would account for many observational data as the goal of the scientific enterprise.

> From a systematic theoretical point of view, we may imagine the process of evolution of an empirical science to be a continuous process of induction. Theories are evolved and are expressed in short compass as statements of a large number of individual observations in the form of empirical laws, from which the general laws can be ascertained by comparison. Regarded in this way, the development of a science bears some resemblance to the compilation of a classified catalog. It is, as it were, a purely empirical enterprise.
>
> But this point of view by no means embraces the whole of the actual process; for it slurs over the important part played by intuition and deductive thought in

> the development of an exact science. As soon as a science has emerged from its initial stages, theoretical advances are no longer achieved merely by a process of arrangement. Guided by empirical data, the investigator rather develops the system of thought which, in general, is built up logically from a small number of fundamental assumptions, the so-called axioms. We call such a system of thought a *theory*. The theory finds the justification for its existence in the fact that it correlates a large number of single observations, and it is just here that the "truth" of the theory lies (p. 123).

Numerous other dichotomous distinctions have been made by scholars that are similar in spirit, though not perhaps identical, to the distinction between postulational and empirical reasoning. These include the distinctions between closed and adventurous thinking (Frederic Bartlett, 1958), right-handed and left-handed thinking (Jerome Bruner, 1962), convergent thinking and divergent thinking (Joy Paul Guilford, 1967), and problem solving and problem finding (Norman Mackworth, 1965). Much could be said about these distinctions and their roles in mathematical, scientific, and everyday thinking. For now, it suffices to note the necessity of two types of thought: of demonstrative and plausible reasoning in Polya's terms, of postulational and empirical thinking in Keyser's, of deductive and inductive argumentation more generally. Neither type by itself is an adequate basis for a rational existence; it is difficult to imagine that an organism as complex and as vulnerable as a human being would be viable without the ability to argue both from the general to the specific and from the specific to the more general, even if only imperfectly.

Another Major Distinction

There is another distinction between two types of reasoning that I consider to be as important as any of the others that have been made. The first type, which I have referred to as *exploratory* (or investigative) reasoning, is what one does when trying to decide what to believe on some subject or what to do at some choice point. The second type, which I have called *justificatory* (or confirmative) reasoning, is what one does when one explains why one has come to a particular conclusion or decided on a specific course of action: "I have concluded X or done Y and here is my reasoning for doing so" (Nickerson, 2004).

The distinction is apparent in mathematical reasoning, or accounts of same. Mathematics texts are likely to devote much more space to justifying theorems and explaining the specifics of proofs than to reporting the often, messy details of how mathematicians come to believe that a theorem is worth proving. Polya (1957/1945) captures this distinction in noting the difference between mathematics when presented with rigor as a systematic deductive science, and mathematics in the making, which he describes as an experimental inductive science. Roger Penrose (1989) makes a similar distinction in noting that a rigorous argument typically is the last step in the mathematician's reasoning and that generally many guesses – albeit presumably constrained by known facts and logic – precede it.

G. H. Hardy (1989/1940) famously not only makes a distinction between doing mathematics and explaining how it is done, but shows his esteem for the first activity and disdain for the second: "There is no scorn more profound, or on the whole more justifiable, than that of the men who make for the men who explain. Exposition, criticism, appreciation, is work for second-rate minds" (Hardy, 1989/1940, p. 61). His excuse for engaging in expository writing (*A Mathematician's Apology*) in his later years was his conviction that he was then too old to *do* mathematics.

> If then I find myself writing, not mathematics, but "about" mathematics, it is a confession of weakness, for which I may rightly be scorned or pitied by younger and more vigorous mathematicians. I write about mathematics because, like any other mathematician who has passed sixty, I have no longer the freshness of mind, the energy, or the patience to carry on effectively with my proper job (p. 63).

While there undoubtedly are mathematicians who have done creative work well into their later years – Paul Erdős comes immediately to mind – creative mathematics is still widely considered to be pretty much a young person's game.

The distinction between exploratory and justificatory reasoning is stark in mathematics (Nickerson, 2010), but it pertains in other areas as well. In general terms, we may think of exploratory reasoning as reasoning that goes into the development and refinement of an argument, and justificatory reasoning as the argument in its final – dressed-up – form.

Probative Logic

Probative logic, as defined and discussed by Michael Scriven (1986, 2009), is an approach to the evaluation of practical arguments that relies on neither the rules of deductive logic nor the conventions of inductive reasoning. Scriven (2009) explains that the term *probative* is taken from jurisprudence "where it means 'having the quality or function of proving or demonstrating' a conclusion" (p.1). He contrasts probative logic "with two other established processes for doing the same task, notably deduction, and induction in a special sense of the latter" (p. 1). The need for its development is the assumed inadequacy of the "classic duo" of deduction and induction to encompass all the types of reasoning by which people legitimately arrive at conclusions. "[G]iven the preponderance of cases of empirical inference which are neither deductions from true generalizations nor statistical inferences from samples, it seems plausible to conclude that much, perhaps even most, of our commonplace inferences, in everyday life and in science, are probative inferences" (p. 2).

Scriven (1986) argues that classical models of reasoning – deductive and inductive – are inadequate to account for how people reason in everyday situations.

> The classical models of reasoning provide inadequate and in fact seriously misleading accounts of most practical and academic reasoning – the reasoning of the kitchen, surgery and workshop, the law courts, paddock, office and battlefield; and of the disciplines. Most reasoning is not the deductive reasoning of the mathematician or pure logician, nor is it best interpreted as an incomplete version of deductive reasoning. Neither is it the reasoning of the pollster using inferential statistics, or of the gambler using probability theory – although, like these, it often leads to probabilistic conclusions. Nor is it the reasoning modeled by any of the attempts at a formal inductive logic, attempts which are doomed by their definition. The kind of reasoning that is most common but poorly served by the logicians will be referred to here as *probative inference*, and we will say that it is 'governed by' *probative logic* (p.7).

Scriven's assessment of the practical value of formal logic for practical reasoning is harsh: "Formal logic is, as far as we know, simply an intellectual chess game with no payoff for either practical argumentation or, more sadly, for other pure and applied disciplines" (p. 18). Similar assessments of the practical usefulness of formal logic are not hard to find.

> Is it not sad that a hundred years after its justly acclaimed modernization, modern logic still has nothing to offer to human political life, and nothing to offer to students of political life? I take it to be a fact, and a recognized one, that logic, in its usual form, has still virtually nothing to offer in this direction and does not even try (Barth, 1986, p. 33).

Probative logic, Scriven (1986) says, is not a system of rules, but an approach or point of view, based on a number of principles that spawn a set of procedures. He does not contend that reasoning of the types that are identified by the classical models does not occur; they appear as components in common reasoning; "the problem is that they are *only* components, and a completely distorted picture of the nature of reasoning results from supposing that these neat pieces are what reasoning, inference, and hence logic, is all about" (p. 7). There are inferences and arguments, Scriven holds, that are neither deductive nor probabilistic but that thoughtful people find strongly persuasive. It is with such arguments that probative logic is intended to deal.

> The patterns which are important to probative inference are ones often dismissed or crudely misrepresented by formal logics; they are far from the exceptionless exactitude of the universally quantified statement. Indeed, they are often not expressible at all; but one of the clues to the presence of probative inference is the use of terms like "typically," "ideally," "essentially," "naturally," and in some uses, "approximately," and "generally" or its informal counterparts "most" or "mostly" .... Thus, probative logic is partly defined as dealing with much that formal logic rejects as makeshift or illicit (p. 9).

Scriven stresses the role of what is not said in practical arguments but maintains that making everything explicit is wearisome and seldom worth the effort.

> The thrust and parry of discussion and debate makes sense only because of what is not mentioned at all, and there is far more of this that is relevant, indeed crucial, to the significance of what is actually said than the transcript includes. Trying to formulate the "missing premises" ... is not getting on with the job of discussion and debate unless there is just cause for doing so. If just cause of this kind were common, conclusions would be rare; we would never have time to get to them (p. 10).

Similarly, Scriven stresses that what is *said* in an argument is not necessarily what is *meant*. "From the probative point of view, what is *said* is only a first indication of what is *meant*, and the first tools to teach the student are the tools of inquiry to pin down meaning before we get to the tools of reconstructive surgery, or those used in classifying an argument as valid or invalid" (p. 25). Scott Jacobs (1986) makes a closely related point in noting that "there are no ironclad guarantees that communicative intentions will correspond to communicative interpretations" (p. 235).

Probative inferences or arguments seldom, if ever, prove conclusions to be true, but they do provide conclusions that can be considered true beyond reasonable doubt – as arguments in criminal trials typically are intended to do. Probative inferences can be challenged, as can other inferences or generalizations, by the noting of counterexamples. Scriven (2009) describes what he refers to as the General Elimination Method (GEM) – and expressly calls a heuristic as distinct from an algorithm – which, he contends, underlies whole sciences such as epidemiology, forensic medicine, criminalistics, and geology. As the term suggests, GEM produces probative conclusions by a process of eliminating alternatives that might be considered.

Probative logic is a logic of plausibility, not a logic of proof. It recognizes degrees of plausibility, and the defeasibility of arguments and their conclusions. It represents what is intended to be a guide to practical reasoning, a heuristic approach to argumentation and argument evaluation that offers no assurance of infallibility but that is expected to get it right most of the time without overtaxing limited cognitive resources. Whether "logic" is an appropriate label for the approach is debatable.

Analogical Arguments

> Analogy seems to have a share in all discoveries, but in some it has the lion's share
>
> (Polya, 1954a, p. 17).

Analogical reasoning is sometimes described as a type of inductive reasoning, but even if that is an accurate description, it is sufficiently important to warrant special attention. (For a claim that analogy making should not be considered a *type* of reasoning, but essentially the whole ball of wax – the "core of cognition" – see Douglas Hofstadter (2000). A concept, Hofstadter contends, "is a package of analogies" [p. 123].) One of the principles of plausible reasoning promoted by Polya (1954a) is that a conjecture becomes more credible if an analogous conjecture becomes more credible, or turns out to be true.

Govier (1986) describes case-by-case reasoning, as presented by John Wisdom in his 1957 *Virginia Lectures* (Wisdom & Barker, 1991), as a form of analogical reasoning. She illustrates case-by-case reasoning with arguments like the following:

1. Case x has features a, b, c.
2. Case y has features a, b, c.
3. Case x is of type e.

Therefore,

4. Case y is of type e (p. 59).

Some people might argue that the term "analogical reasoning" is a misnomer, that the drawing of an analogy is not an instance of reasoning but something else. David Gelernter (1994), for example, makes a distinction between reasoning and the drawing of analogies.

> Reasoning is one big part of human thought and thought science has reasoning decently under control. Philosophers and psychologists understand it, and computers, up to a point, can fake it. But there is one other big piece of the picture, which goes by many names: creativity, intuition, insight, metaphoric thinking, "holistic thinking;" all these tricks boil down at base to *drawing analogies* (p. 2).

How analogical thinking works, Gelernter contends, is not known. "Today the logical or analytical component of human thought is understood, at least to some extent. But analogy is not. Until we glimpse a solution, thinking can't possibly be more than – at most – half-understood" (p. 84).

Analogies can be used to advantage for a variety of purposes. They can be very useful in teaching, for example. A time-honored way of explaining an unfamiliar principle or process is to point out its similarity to some other principle or process with which one can be assumed to be familiar. A heuristic that people who are good at problem-solving often use when dealing with unfamiliar problems is to look for familiar analogs to problems they are having difficulty solving and to use these analogs as sources of ideas for how to approach the problems to be solved (Clement, 1983, 1991).

René Descartes believed analogies to be indispensable to scientific explanation. "I claim that they [analogies] are the most appropriate way available to the human mind for explaining the truth about questions in physics; to such an extent that, if one assumes something about nature which cannot be explained by an analogy, I think that I have conclusively shown that it is false" (quoted in Barrow, 1990, p. 97).

Specific analogies have sometimes become very widely adopted by scientists and laypeople alike to represent nature in whole or in part. Musical analogies were common in early scientific thinking. The "music of the spheres," the Pythagorean idea that the structure of the universe reflected ratios and proportions analogous to those that made for harmony in music, motivated Johannes Kepler's search for harmonic proportions in the movements of the planets. Writing about a half century before Kepler's birth, Francesco Giorgio, in his *Harmonia Mundi*, described the world order in musical terms. "By using the metaphors of 'consonance' and 'accord,' and by linking these disparate universes of discourse by the bonds of the numbers they mention, he [Kepler] produces a unified system, whose main aim is to show how beautiful and proportioned and harmonious everything is" (Butler, 1970, p. 56). Others also made much of musical analogies; as Butler points out, the musical-cosmic parallel was one of the basic metaphors used by many medieval writers in their reflections on the beauty of the universe. By way of illustration, he quotes the sixteenth/seventeenth century cleric and poet, John Donne: "God made this whole world in such a uniformity, such a correspondency, such a concinnity of parts, as that it was an instrument perfectly in tune" (p. 122).

The mechanistic view of the universe, which likened nature to a clock or other complex mechanism that operates according to deterministic laws and whose behavior is, in principle, totally predictable given sufficient knowledge of the details of the works, was popular for a long time. This analogy began to lose favor, in large part as a consequence of the emergence of the theory of the quantum. In recent years, the clock has given way to the digital computer as the instrument of choice among analogizers. The computer has been used as an analog of the brain for some time – or is it that the brain has been used as an analog of the computer? Information-processing analogies have become increasingly common in biology since the discovery that the genetic construction manual for every life-form is written with the same four-letter alphabet. And more and more, one sees the cosmos itself likened to a colossal computational system (Bostrom, 2003; Toffoli, 1982; Wright, 1988a, 1988b).

Many researchers have noted the important role that analogies and metaphors play in the thinking of individual scientists, especially during early phases of the discovery process (Bronowski, 1965; Gentner & Grudin, 1985; Tweney & Doherty, 1983). Jacob Bronowski (1965) illustrates the point with a reference to Kepler's use of his knowledge of certain relationships in music and geometry in his attempt to understand planetary motion.

> Kepler's mind, we know, was filled with . . . fanciful analogies; and we know what they were. Kepler wanted to relate the speeds of the planets to the musical intervals. He tried to fit the five regular solids into their orbits. None of these likenesses worked, and they have been forgotten; yet they have been and remain the stepping-stones of every creative mind. Kepler felt for his laws by way of metaphors, he searched mystically for likenesses with what he knew in every strange corner of nature and when among these guesses he hit upon his laws, he did not think of their numbers as the balancing of a cosmic bank account, but as a revelation of the unity in all nature. To us, the analogies by which Kepler listened for the movement of the planets and the

> music of the spheres are farfetched. Yet are they more so than the wild leap by which Rutherford and Bohr in our own century found a model for the atom in, of all places, the planetary system? (p. 12).

Another characterization of Kepler's willingness to look far afield for ideas that might be applied to his investigations of the heavens is given by Herbert Turnbull (1956/1929). Speaking of Kepler's *Harmonices Mundi*, in which he describes the third of his planetary laws, Turnbull says:

> In it he makes a systematic search into the theory of musical intervals, and their relations to the distances between the planets and the sun: he discusses the significance of the five Platonic solids for interplanetary space: he elaborates the properties of the thirteen semi-regular solids of Archimedes: he philosophizes on the place of harmonic and other algebraic progressions in civil life, drawing his illustrations from the dress of Cyrus as a small boy, and the equity of Roman marriage laws (p. 127).

Although there probably have been very few scientists or natural philosophers who outdid Kepler in this regard, it is not difficult to find instances in scientific writing of concepts being borrowed from one field to be applied in another, often deliberately and sometimes perhaps unwittingly. The hierarchical universe of Aristotle and the medieval schoolmen, for example, reflected the hierarchical class organization of the societies of their day, whereas today's conception of the universe is more egalitarian than hierarchical with, for example, the cosmological principle whereby the universe is assumed to appear the same to any observer independently of the observer's location in it.

To facilitate reasoning about – and presentation of – his theory of electrodynamics, James Maxwell made use of physical models involving cogwheels and pulleys, as well as rotating tubes and ethereal vortices; he also based his kinetic theory of gas on an analogy between the behavior of molecules and that of people, both of which are predictable in the aggregate but not individually (Maxwell, 1873/1890). Ludwig Boltzmann (1974/1886) too drew parallels between the statistical regularities involving "voluntary actions" such as marriages, crimes, and suicides and the behavior of interacting gas molecules. Lord Kelvin claimed never to be satisfied that he understood something until he had made a mechanical model of it.

The nineteenth century saw rapid increase in the use of statistics in various sciences. Theodore Porter (1986) makes the remarkably strong claim: "Seemingly without exception, those who applied statistical thinking to any of the sciences during the second half of the nineteenth century thought in terms of analogies with the social science of statistics" (p. 136). No one showed a stronger tendency in this regard than did Francis Galton in his work on the statistics of heredity. He defended the use of similes because of their ability to facilitate understanding and used them extensively, often attempting to elucidate biological processes by likening them to political ones.

Erwin Ackerknecht (1981) sees in the writing of Rudolph Virchow, whom I. B. Cohen (1985) credits with revolutionizing the biological basis of medicine, a mutual reinforcement of political and biological opinions:

> Cellular pathology showed the body to be a free state of equal individuals, a federation of cells, a democratic cell state. It showed it as a social unit composed of equals, while an undemocratic oligarchy of tissues was assumed in humoral, or solidistic (neuro) pathology. Just as Virchow fought in politics for the rights of the "third estate," thus in cellular pathology he fought for a "third estate" of cells (connective tissue) not duly recognized in their value and function (quoted in Cohen, 1985, p. 317).

In comparing the information revolution to the industrial revolution, James Meindl (1987) likens the importance of silicon in the former case to that of iron in the latter. Silicon doped with impurity atoms is likened to iron combined with other elements to yield steel alloys. At the device level a transistor is likened to a piston, at the circuit level an integrated circuit is likened to an internal combustion engine, and at the system level a computer network to a transportation system.

Analogies are often used by scientists as instruments of explanation or to facilitate understanding. Chet Raymo (1998), for example, uses the following analogy to illustrate relative distances within and beyond the Milky Way.

> Think of the Milky Way Galaxy as a dinner plate. The next spiral galaxy – the Great Andromeda Galaxy – is another dinner plate across the room. At this same scale, the nearest galaxies in the Hubble Deep Field photograph are dinner plates about a mile away. The faintest are dinner plates more than twenty miles away, at the very edge of space and time (p. 242).

Amo Penzias (1992) uses an analogy based on dust particles in a room.

> When I try to depict the universe for non-technical people, I often ask them to think of a large room . . . and to imagine all the little invisible particles of dust floating in the air within it. If you could imagine that each one of the billions of dust particles in this room were itself a galaxy of a hundred billion suns, you would begin to appreciate the vastness of just a small corner of the universe (p. 80).

There can be little doubt that analogies and metaphors have been used to great advantage by scientists and other thinkers. It is also the case however that analogies can be misleading and that sometimes they must be given up if further progress is to be made. Moreover, all analogies are imperfect and often they can be manipulated to serve the purposes of the analogizer.

> Because all things are different, except for the similarities, and are the same except for the differences, any analogy (however apt) can be rejected by those who find it a sufficient objection that the things being analogized are not "really" the same. By the same token, any analogies favored (however strained) can be defended on grounds that those things analogized involve the same "underlying" or "essential" principle (Sowell, 1995, p. 93).

A major advance in medical science was marked by abandonment, as a consequence of William Harvey's work, of the metaphor of the heart as a furnace in favor of the idea that it is better thought of as a pump. Sometimes analogies persist after they have been shown to be inappropriate. The Rutherford-Bohr planetary model of the atom, for example, is dying hard, although the fact that it is a misleading representation of atomic structure has been known for a considerable time. John Barrow (1990) characterizes false analogy – "the mistaken belief that an entire body of ideas that apply successfully to one phenomenon can be taken over and used to describe another quite different one" – as "the major source of erroneous scientific reasoning" (p. 51). An analogy is like a map – if one may be permitted to define analogy with an analogy – it represents some aspects of the terrain but not all of them.

Even the simplest metaphors can have problems "at the edges." A balloon model is often used to explain the idea of an expanding universe and to illustrate specific aspects of it, such as why any point can be seen as the center and why the rate at which any two points recede from each other increases with the distance between them. A weakness of the model is that when a balloon is blown up, *everything* on the surface expands, not only the space between points, but the points as well. This aspect of the model would be misleading if applied to the universe, because in that case the distances between entities are assumed to be growing, but not the entities themselves. (It is not assumed, for example, that the distances between atoms are expanding so that you and I are increasing in size as parts of the expanding universe; of course if we were, we would not be able to detect the fact because our measuring instruments would be increasing as well.) Indeed, it is not even the case that all inter-object distances are believed to be increasing: the distances between objects in the solar system, for example, are not increasing, nor are those between stars in the same galaxy, or perhaps even between galaxies in a cluster; the expansion, according to the theory, as I understand it, is due to the increasing distances between galaxy clusters.

Analogies can be, and often are, misused in argumentation. The fact that two entities, X and Y, are alike with respect to certain properties, say A, B, and C is not an adequate basis for inferring that they must be alike with respect to specific other properties, say D and E, as well. Nevertheless, such inferences are often made. There is nothing wrong with using the fact that X and Y are alike with respect to A, B, and C as the basis for entertaining the *hypothesis* that they are also alike with respect to D and E, but such a hypothesis requires empirical confirmation before it can be considered a fact.

The distinction between hypothesis and conclusion is not always maintained very sharply. Sometimes the argument from analogy is taken, even in science, to be relatively conclusive. Raymond Nogar (1966) points out, for example, that an argument from analogy is often made to fill gaps in the evidentiary trail of the evolution of species. He argues that when the less complete of two evolutionary histories parallels a more complete one in those respects that are known, "then it is sound to fill in the gaps in the less complete case by analogy to the more complete" (p. 107). But using analogy in this way can hardly be considered to demonstrate the correspondence between the histories involved, because it is the assumption of correspondence that gives the application of analogy its justification.

In short, analogical reasoning is an important form of reasoning, and argument by analogy is an important form of argumentation. It is an effective tool with many uses. However, it must be used with care and with an understanding of its limitations.

Summary Comments

As we have seen, arguments come in many shapes and sizes. It is customary to divide them into two major types: deductive and inductive. In principle, this distinction is easy to make and to illustrate, but when dealing with real arguments – especially long and complicated arguments – the boundary between the two major types is often hard to find. Real arguments are likely to contain both deductive and inductive elements, as well as elements that are not easy to classify with respect to this distinction. Arguments from analogy – generally inductive – are sufficiently commonly used to warrant special attention.

Arguments serve many purposes; however, one stands out as definitive: that of influencing beliefs or behavior. Given this purpose, the question of practical interest is generally not whether an argument is logically valid, but whether it has the intended cognitive or behavioral effect. Whether it is likely – or how likely it is – to have the desired effect depends on many factors; to these we will turn subsequently, especially in Chapters 3 and 4.

A variety of argument types and purposes has been distinguished to this point, and many more could be added to the list. However, I think it would be difficult to identify a distinction that is more important than that between: (1) exploratory or investigative reasoning and (2) justificatory or confirmative reasoning. In the first case, the goal is to determine – to the extent that one can do so – what one should believe or do. In the second, the goal is to try to justify, to oneself or others, a belief already held, or action already taken. In the first case, one's mind is open to wherever the evidence takes one; in the second, one's mind is made up and counter-indicative evidence is likely to be given short shrift.

3

Evaluating Arguments

In view of the large number of shapes and sizes that arguments can take, it should come as no surprise that evaluating them can be a challenging task. On the other hand, if one accepts the claim that the main purpose of most arguments is to influence beliefs and/or behavior, the practical challenge becomes that of identifying variables that determine the effectiveness with which arguments serve that function. This chapter and the following two represent an attempt to do that.

Until relatively recently, studies of argumentation dealt primarily with formal logic and deductive reasoning. Robert Trapp, Julie Yingling, and James Wanner (1986) describe an expansion of the subject in more recent times to make it relevant to the everyday activities of ordinary people. They note that one of the consequences of this expansion was to complicate the task of argument evaluation. "When formal logic was *the* standard against which to judge the validity of arguments, argumentative competence was non-problematic. A competent arguer was one who produced arguments that conformed to formal logic" (p. 253). Trapp et al. point out that rejecting formal logic as the sole standard for judging arguments necessitates the development of a new standard for judging argumentative competence.

There appears to be a growing awareness that there is much more to being an effective reasoner in everyday life than being able to distinguish between valid and invalid logical forms. Many, if not most, of the arguments one encounters do not fit any canonical pattern. They tend to be extended and to include deductive and inductive (including abductive) components, to depend on unstated assumptions, to assume – wittingly or not – a particular knowledge base on the part of the listener or reader, to contain ambiguities and obscurities, and to make use of various alogical stratagems, about which more will be said later.

Evaluating Formal Arguments

> In logic what is needed is to mortify, not to inflame, the passion for high generality
>
> (Stove, 1986, p. 130).

In most of the practical reasoning situations that we encounter in our daily lives, we are likely to be more interested in forming an opinion about the truth or falsity of the conclusion an argument is intended to support than about the logical validity of the argument. Before one should feel compelled, on the strength of a deductive argument, to accept its conclusion as *true*, one should be convinced *both* of the validity of the argument's form and of the truth of its premises. Thus, evaluating a deductive argument for practical purposes involves more than logic; it requires also judging the plausibility of claims.

It may also sometimes require that arguers agree on how to interpret ambiguous terms or conflicting claims that cannot be resolved by consideration of objective facts. The point is illustrated by an argument between Galileo and Tolomeo Nozzolini regarding whose estimate of the worth of a horse, which was really worth 100 crowns, was most in error: that of one who estimated 1,000 crowns or that of one who estimated ten.

Sometimes a distinction is made between validity and soundness. A deductive argument is valid if it has a correct form; it is said to be sound if it has a correct form *and* its premises (and hence its conclusion) are true. In everyday reasoning, soundness is generally of greater concern than validity; what one wants to know is whether to believe an argument's conclusion and knowing only that the argument is valid does not ensure that its conclusion is true. As Manfred Kienpointner (1986) puts it, "the soundness of argumentation can't be judged independently of semantic and pragmatic standards underlying the argumentation" (p. 279).

The top-level rules for evaluating deductive arguments are simple to state: if the form of the argument is valid and the premises are true, the conclusion must be true. If either the form is invalid or at least one of the premises is false, the truth value of the conclusion is undetermined. In evaluating such arguments, therefore one has to consider questions of both form and content. The following arguments illustrate possible combinations of valid and invalid forms with true and false premises and conclusions.

- Valid argument with false major premise and false conclusion: "If tigers eat meat, they are herbivores. Tigers eat meat. Therefore, they are herbivores."
- Valid argument with false premises and true conclusion: "If tigers are herbivores, they eat meat. Tigers are herbivores. Therefore, they eat meat."
- Invalid argument with false minor premise and false conclusion: "If tigers are herbivores, they eat grass. Tigers eat grass. Therefore, they are herbivores."
- Invalid argument with false premises and true conclusion: "If tigers are carnivores, they eat grass. Tigers eat grass. Therefore, they are carnivores."
- Invalid argument with true premises and true conclusion: "If tigers are carnivores, they eat meat. Tigers eat meat. Therefore, they are carnivores."

The Role of Form

The question of the logical validity of a deductive argument is a question of form. If and only if the form is valid, the conclusion follows from the premises. In judging a deductive argument to be valid, one is not guaranteeing the truth of its conclusion, one is guaranteeing only that the conclusion is true *if* the premises are true – which is not to say that the conclusion *necessarily* is false if one or more of the premises are false, although it may be. Charles Hamblin (1970) contends that the claim, which one finds in textbooks on logic, that a valid argument may be built on false premises and may thus have a false conclusion, is a "complete misrepresentation of the nature of argument" (p. 232). As I understand his contention, the objection is to the idea that any argument with false premises should be considered a good argument, even if the argument's conclusion follows from its premises; "whatever the textbooks say, *in practice* we like our premises to be true, and we do not describe an argument as a good one if the premises are false" (p. 232).

Hamblin (1970) reminds us that in assessing an argument, one does so from some point of view – possibly that of the arguer, or that of the one(s) to whom the argument is addressed, or one's own as a spectator, or some mixed point of view. "[A] logically-minded onlooker who judges 'That argument is valid' will frequently mean 'If I accepted those premises and did not accept that conclusion, that argument would persuade me'" (p. 245).

We may sum up the relationship between validity and truth of formal arguments thus: If the form is valid and the premises are true, the conclusion must be true. If the form is valid and one or more of the premises are false, the conclusion could be true or false. The only thing that is ruled out is an argument with a valid form having true premises and a conclusion that is false. "The simplest of all demonstrations that an argument is invalid – and hence, perhaps, equivocal – is the demonstration that its premises are true and its conclusion false" (Hamblin, 1970, p. 293).

A person's ability to distinguish between valid and invalid deductive forms can be tested by using arguments that are devoid of semantic content. Consider the following arguments:

All bletes are crogs
All crogs are trons
Therefore, all bletes are trons.

No bletes are crogs
No crogs are trons
Therefore, no bletes are trons.

We need not know anything about bletes, crogs, or trons to recognize that the first argument is logically valid, and therefore if its premises are true then its conclusion must be true also, whereas the second one is invalid, so being assured that its premises are true would not let one conclude that its conclusion is true.

I suspect that most people will find it easier to acknowledge that the first argument is valid than to agree that the second one is not. Perhaps if we substitute for bletes, crogs, and trons, respectively, Scandinavians, Chinese, and Swedes, we will find the invalidity easier to see.

No Scandinavians are Chinese
No Chinese are Swedes
Therefore, no Scandinavians are Swedes.

In neither of the invalid cases does the conclusion follow from the premises. In evaluating the argument regarding bletes, crogs, and trons, one can easily be misled by the fact that it has the structure of "All As are Bs and all Bs are Cs; therefore, all As are Cs," which is a valid argument. However, "No As are Bs and no Bs are Cs; therefore no As are Cs" may look valid, but it is not, which is shown by the fact that it is possible to construct an argument in this form (e.g., No Scandinavians are Chinese . . .) that has true premises but a false conclusion.

The following is an example of a formal deductive argument taken from a logic textbook (Searles, 1948):

Nothing intelligible ever puzzles me
Logic puzzles me
Therefore, logic is unintelligible.

This is the *modus tollens* form of the conditional syllogism:

If A then B
Not B
Therefore not A.

Expressed in canonical *modus tollens* form, Searles's example, which came originally from Lewis Carroll, could be stated:

If it is intelligible, it does not puzzle me
It (logic) puzzles me
Therefore, it (logic) is not intelligible.

The following argument has the same form:

If he were really sympathetic to the demands of the coal miners, he would have voted for the XYZ bill

He voted against the bill
So, he is not sympathetic to the miners' demands.

Much of the empirical literature on argument evaluation focuses on properties of arguments that make them more or less difficult for people to evaluate. Difficulty is generally measured in terms of the percentage of participants in an experiment who correctly judge an argument to be valid or invalid, the time required to make such judgments, and difficulty ratings on the judgments made (Rips, 1995). Models of human reasoning that assume people reason deductively by applying rules tend to predict argument difficulty will depend on the number and complexity of the rules that must be applied in specific instances (Braine, Reiser, & Rumain, 1984; Rips, 1994). Lance Rips (1994) notes too that "attributing errors to subjects can be a delicate matter that depends on how we justify the logical systems themselves" (p. 378). A distinction may be made between the need to apply a given rule several times and the need to apply several different rules, and the latter is generally seen to make for greater difficulty than the former.

In general, *modus ponens* inferences – *If A then C; A; therefore C* – have been shown to be easier for people to make than *modus tollens* inferences – *If A then C; not C; therefore not A* (Marcus & Rips, 1979; O'Brien, 1973; Rips & Marcus, 1977; Rumain, Connell, & Braine, 1983; Wason & Johnson-Laird, 1972). People have even greater difficulty with *modus tollens* arguments when the antecedent in the conditional proposition is negative (*If not A then C; If not A then not C*) (Evans 1977a; Pollard & Evans, 1980; Roberge, 1978). Evans (1982) concludes from a review of relevant research that people are competent to reason from antecedents to consequents but not vice versa, and that "abstract conditional reasoning performance indicates no more than a superficial understanding of the sentence *If P then Q*, and little evidence of any depth of reasoning" (p. 231).

That people find it easier to deal with the *modus ponens* than with the *modus tollens* form of argument is true when the conditional premise is expressed in the form *If A then C*. The difference diminishes or disappears, however, when it is expressed in the logically equivalent form *A only if C* (Evans, 1977a; Roberge, 1978). With this form, *modus ponens* and *modus tollens* arguments are about equally difficult, and both are more difficult than *modus ponens* when expressed in the conventional *If A then C* form. Philip Johnson-Laird and Ruth Byrne (1991) interpret this difficulty pattern as supportive of the assumption that people solve deductive reasoning problems by constructing mental models of the premises, because the *A only if C* form prompts the development of two models for either a *modus ponens* or *modus tollens* argument, whereas, the *modus ponens* argument with *If A then C* requires only that a single model be used.

A variety of representational systems, including truth tables, Euler diagrams, Venn diagrams, and mental-model diagrams, can often be helpful in evaluating the formal validity of arguments (Garnham & Oakhill, 1994; Johnson-Laird & Byrne, 1991; Nickerson, 1986b), although their effective use is not trivially straightforward.

The Role of Content

> [I]f you want the truth rather than merely something to say, you will have a good deal less to say
>
> (Nagel, 1986, p. 9).

The importance of content in the evaluation of deductive arguments is sometimes overlooked. The emphasis typically is on form, which is appropriate but not to the exclusion of substance if the question is whether the argument's conclusion should be accepted. But results from a considerable body of research indicate that when deductive arguments have semantic content, people typically find it difficult to ignore that content in judging whether they are formally valid (Nickerson, Butler, & Barch, in press; Staudenmayer, 1975; Wason & Johnson-Laird, 1972). To be sure, one can evaluate the logical validity of a deductive argument without reference to its substance, but because of the ambiguous nature of language, logical validity, by itself, is not enough to compel one to believe the conclusion to an argument. Hamblin (1970) makes this point and punctuates it with a quote from the third century philosopher Sextus Empiricus:

> For just as we refuse our assent to the truth of the tricks performed by jugglers and know that they are deluding us, even if we do not know how they do it, so likewise we refuse to believe arguments which, though seemingly plausible, are false, even when we do not know how they are fallacious . . . if there should be an argument which leads us to a confessedly absurd conclusion, we shall not assent to the absurdity just because of the argument but avoid the argument just because of the absurdity (p. 96).

Consider the following deductive argument:

Nothing is better than eternal bliss.
Cold soup is better than nothing.
Therefore, cold soup is better than eternal bliss.

It clearly is valid; but equally clearly unpersuasive. What is wrong with it? The answer is that "nothing" is ambiguous and can take on different meanings in different contexts. In this argument, it has a meaning in the first premise that differs from the meaning it has in the second one. The difference is easily illustrated: I ask you, what would you like to talk about. You say "nothing." Are you telling me that you would like to talk about the concept *nothing*? Or that you would like not to talk?

Nothing is illustrative of concepts that can have more than one meaning depending on the context in which they occur and can wreak havoc if the effect of context is not recognized. (See fallacy of equivocation in Chapter 8.) Anthony Flew (1968) considered the fact that such expressions exist to have been a major discovery.

> We might say that "This is past" and "This is red," "It goes on to London" and "It goes on to infinity," and "Nobody came" and "Somebody came" are pairs of grammatically similar expressions. But the members of all these pairs of grammatically similar expressions are logically very different. That is to say, that nothing but nonsense and paradox will result if we ask questions

> about one assertion which are only appropriate and significant when asked about the other. It would be absurd, but it would also be easy, to be misled by the grammatical similarity of "It goes on to London" to "It goes on to infinity" into the misconception that "Infinity" like "London" refers to a place, albeit a very queer and very inaccessible place. It is absurd, but to some people it is also easy, to be misled by the grammatical similarity of "Somebody came" to "Nobody came" into the misconception that "Nobody" refers to a person as does "Somebody" (p. 7).

Although most writers emphasize the importance of form in evaluating deductive arguments, Stove (1986) insists that the validity, or invalidity, of arguments cannot be judged on purely formal grounds. He does not deny that some formal arguments are valid, and others are not, but he makes a distinction between "being valid" and "being able to be *proved* valid." Proving the validity of a form is tricky business, in his view. "Purely formal judgments of validity, if they employ a predicate variable or a propositional variable to pick out the class of arguments in question, are all or almost all exposed to counter-examples, direct or indirect, or they generate paradoxes" (p. 124). Conversely, it does not follow from the fact that a form of argument cannot be proved to be valid that it is necessarily invalid, that it is impossible to find valid instances of it. "There are few or no logical forms," Stove claims, "above a low level of generality, of which every instance is valid: nearly every such supposed form has invalid cases or paradoxical cases. The natural conclusion to draw is that formal logic is a myth, and that over validity, as well as over invalidity, forms do *not* rule: cases do" (p. 127).

The point that Stove is making is illustrated by the syllogistic form: *A x'd B. B is a C. Therefore, A x'd a C.* This seems a perfectly valid form, but consider the following variation on an instantiation of it offered by Willard Quine (1960): Jack married Jill. Jill is dead. Therefore, Jack married a dead woman. One might argue that the abstract form obviously is valid only on certain assumptions about the nature of the entities that the symbols (A, B and C) can represent. But was this obvious before it was made so by the nonsensical concrete illustration? And who is to say that the presumed validity of other (presumably valid) abstract forms does not similarly rest on unstated assumptions the necessity of which remains to be revealed through the discovery of concrete instantiations that make no sense?

Stove does not deny that it is possible to make true judgments of logical validity and invalidity; he denies that such judgments can be made on the basis of the formal properties of arguments alone. One is entitled, he claims, to judge a particular argument to be valid (or invalid) without being obliged to judge the next argument of the same form that one encounters to be valid (or invalid) as well. This is not, in his view, cause for concern: "to despair of the possibility of formal logical knowledge does not at all require that we despair of the possibility of logical knowledge" (p. 129).

In the foregoing, I have made the common distinction between validity and truth and associated validity with logical form and truth with factual reality. The two concepts are linked in deductive logic by the claim that if the form of a deductive argument is valid *and* the premises of the argument are true, the argument's conclusion must be true. If either of the conditions is not met – the form is invalid or one or more of the premises is untrue – the truth of the conclusion is not assured. I have now made explicit an additional requirement that must be met in order to assure that a deductive argument in a valid form yields a conclusion that is true. That is, that the same words appearing in the premises must have the same meaning in both cases. My sense is that people generally assume this to be the case and, to the extent that they think about it at all, considerate it to be sufficiently obvious to not require comment.

Consider again the argument:

All bletes are crogs
All crogs are trons
Therefore, all bletes are trons.

Suppose I discover that there are such things as bletes, crogs, and trons. Suppose further that I discover a blete that is not a tron, which is to say I discover that the conclusion of the above syllogism is false, that it is not a true description of nature. I then *know* that at least one of the premises of the argument is also false. But what gives me the right to say I know this? Note that I am claiming to know something about nature, not just about logic. What gives me this right is the assumption – deep conviction – that nature is logically consistent, that empirical truth harbors no logical contradictions.

That true premises cannot yield a false conclusion in a valid deductive argument is a thought-provoking fact, telling us, as it does, something about the nature of truth and reality. A related thought-provoking thought, expressed by William James (1983/1890) in the chapter on reasoning in *Principles of Psychology*, is that reasoning would probably be impossible if the world did not behave lawfully. As already noted, the constraint that the conclusion must be true if the premises are true is the only one that holds. We cannot say, for example, that if at least one of the premises is false the conclusion is necessarily false, or that if the conclusion is true, all the premises are necessarily true. Henry may well be a stuffed shirt, even if one or both of the premises of the following argument is false.

All logicians are stuffed shirts.
Henry is a logician.
So, Henry is a stuffed shirt.

The question of which is the more fundamental concept – validity or truth – is an interesting one, but one we are not likely to be able to answer in an unequivocal way, although it seems safe to say, as already noted, that people generally are likely to be more concerned about whether a particular assertion is true than whether it is the conclusion of a logically valid argument. Whether, upon discovering that the conclusion of an argument that one believed to be valid in form and with true premises turned out to be false, one would be more likely to question the validity of the form or the truth status of premises is an interesting question. My guess is that one would be more likely to do the latter, but perhaps it would depend on specifics: the logical form involved and the nature of the premises.

To argue that validity or invalidity cannot be judged on purely formal grounds is not to say that all logical truths are empirically based. Following Rudolf Carnap, Stove (1986) argues that deductive logic, no less than inductive logic, rests ultimately on intuition. Consider the assertion "'Abe is black and Bob is black' entails 'Abe is black'" or the syllogistic claim "'Abe is a raven and all ravens are black' entails 'Abe is black'." If one does not simply see the truth of these claims, Stove argues, there is nothing that can be done to convince one of it; if one does not know these truths a priori, one cannot learn them from experience.

This view is contrasted by Stove (1982) with that of Bernard Bolzano and Carl Popper, both of whom defended the idea that deductive logic has an empirical basis. One discovers the invalidity of a faulty deductive argument, according to these writers, by finding a counterexample to it – an instance of the argument with true premises and a false conclusion. The validity of a deductive argument is established as a consequence of no counterexamples having been found despite concerted efforts to find one. Stove (1986) holds that every normal human being has an immense amount of knowledge of what does and what does not follow from what: "every normal human being is, in the extent of his knowledge of such truths, a millionaire" (p. 128). As to how much of this knowledge could have been gained from experience, Stove argues that relatively little of it could.

Consider first the case of invalid arguments. We could learn from experience that an argument was invalid if we knew its premises to be true and we discovered its conclusion to be false, but there are countless arguments that we know to be invalid that have both true premises and true conclusions. Stove uses the example:

All men are mortal
Socrates is mortal
Socrates is a man.

The reader will undoubtedly agree that this is an invalid argument. But suppose that someone insists that it is valid. How could that person be shown *empirically* that it is *not*. One may become convinced that this argument is invalid – say by seeing formally similar arguments with true premises and false conclusions – but not by researching the empirical claims of the specific argument in question. Nor can we learn from experience the invalidity of an argument with a false premise and true conclusion. In short, Stove argues, "[s]carcely any of the vast fund of knowledge of invalidity which every human being possesses can be acquired from experience" (p. 156).

With respect to our knowledge of validity, Stove makes a like claim. "No singular judgment of validity ... can be learnt from experience. And *a fortiori* no general one can" (p. 158). He argues that the attempt to rest our confidence in the validity of a particular schema, say the classical *Barbara* form,

All A are B
All B are C
All A are C,

on observations of only truth-preserving instances of it involves one in an infinite regress like that described by Lewis Carroll in his fable of the tortoise and the hare. The use of an observation of an instance (I) of a schema as a confirmation of the validity of that schema (S) assumes a metaschema according to which I confirms S. And if all logic is to have an empirical basis, the validity of the metaschema must itself be established observationally, and so on ad infinitum.

Stove (1986) makes a further interesting observation about logicians' stress on the importance of logical form. Logicians tend, he suggests, to account for validity in terms of schemas or logical forms, whereas their own arguments about validity typically are "constant free," which is to say they are arguments about what is or is not empirically true, composed of assertions whose subjects and predicates have real-world referents and not abstractions. This being the case, he claims, their arguments cannot satisfy their own requirements for validity.

> The class of constant-free arguments may perhaps seem odd or unimportant. For this reason, I should point out that it includes most of the arguments that philosophers and logicians *employ*, as distinct from those which they have principally *studied*. A superficial reader might suppose that philosophers and logicians are interested, and even interested to an inexplicable degree, in Socrates, or in his humanity or mortality, or in the mortality of all men. But in fact, of course, they are not in the least interested in any of these things. What they are interested in is, rather, individuals, properties, existence, universality, necessity, possibility – and probability and relative-truth-frequency! It is these things which their arguments are really about (p. 173).

I have devoted considerable space to Stove's treatment of formal arguments as it pertains to the problem of evaluation because it represents what strikes me as a relatively unorthodox view and makes a thought-provoking case regarding the role of content in the evaluation of formal, or deductive, arguments. I leave it to the reader to judge the persuasiveness of Stove's claims of the importance of content in the evaluation of deductive arguments.

In any case, understanding the difference between logical validity and empirical truth is critical to effective evaluation of formal arguments, because such arguments can be evaluated from both perspectives. While such an understanding is not enough to guarantee that one will always avoid reasoning errors that stem from insensitivity to this distinction, it should make such errors less likely and increase one's ability to modify one's thinking appropriately when they are pointed out.

The great advantage of formal logic is its lack of ambiguity, for the most part. It is a system of rules of inference that can be stated in relatively straightforward ways. Whether a specific argument is consistent with the rules, and is therefore valid, or violates them, and is therefore invalid, can usually be determined, if not unequivocally at least adequately for practical purposes.

A limitation of formal logic is that it works unambiguously only at the level of form, which can best be represented by abstract symbols. As soon as one attempts to replace the abstract symbols of a formal argument with words, one necessarily must deal with semantics and things become much less crisp. In order to evaluate a substantive argument – in the sense of deciding whether to believe its conclusion – one must consider not only the validity of the argument's structure but what the premises *mean*. If a more than passing acquaintance with the rules of formal logic is essential to good reasoning, it must be considered only a necessary condition and not a sufficient one.

Ensuring that the words used in an argument have the same meaning for both, or all, of the arguers is a formidable undertaking. Most words have many meanings, and even when the dictionary gives only a single meaning for a word, how that word is interpreted may differ subtly with the context in which it is used, and with the intentions of its user. The futility of trying to ensure that there is no possibility that two evaluators of the same statement (e.g., a premise of an argument) will interpret it in precisely the same way was noted by Sidgwick (1884) this way.

> It is obvious, further, that if there is to be an absolutely clear mutual understanding between speaker and audience as to the meaning of every separate word employed, and also of the assertion as a whole, a large part of every speaker's life would be occupied in the process of defining, or explaining his statements, than could well be spared from his other occupations; and that long before the meaning of most assertions could be settled, their value as practical information would have passed away (p.187).

This dilemma is generally avoided by simply assuming that most of the time different people will give sufficiently close interpretations to the same words to let meaningful communication occur, and insisting on, and bickering about, definitions only in relatively rare cases.

On the other hand, there is the view that the importance of definitions is generally not appreciated, and to our detriment. F. Max Müller (1887) made the point: "Definition is the only panacea for all our philosophical misery" (Appendix, p. 24). Müller (1887) maintained that all the words in the English lexicon can be traced to about 800 roots, which, in turn, can be reduced to about 120 concepts. "These one hundred and twenty concepts are really the rivers that feed the whole ocean of thought and speech. There is no thought that passes through our mind, or that has passed through the minds of the greatest poets and prophets of old, that cannot directly or indirectly be derived from one of these fundamental concepts" (p. 32). Müller insisted that most of the misunderstandings among people are the direct result of careless use of language: "All difficulties which visit us in the various spheres of thought, whether scientific, historical, philosophical, or religious, vanish as soon as we carefully examine the words in which we think" (Müller, p. 78).

As to the question of whether human reasoning is consistent with the rules of deductive logic, one can only say that sometimes it is and sometimes it isn't. Johnson-Laird and Byrne (1991) put it this way: "Our view of logical competence is that people are rational in principle, but fallible in practice. They are able to make valid deductions, and moreover they sometimes *know* that they have made a valid deduction. They also make invalid deductions in certain circumstances" (p. 19).

We know from a considerable body of research that when arguments have semantic content, people often find it difficult to ignore that content in judging whether they are formally valid (Evans, Barston, & Pollard, 1983; Evans, Newstead, & Byrne, 1993; Marcus & Rips, 1979; Markovits & Nantel, 1989; Newstead et al., 1992; Oakhill & Johnson-Laird, 1985; Quayle & Ball, 2000; Staudenmayer, 1975; Wason & Johnson-Laird, 1972). Judging an argument to be valid simply because its conclusion is believed to be true is sometimes called the *belief bias* effect (Brisson et al., 2014; Klauer, Musch, & Naumer, 2000) and has been defined as a tendency of people "to rate an argument as valid if they think that the conclusion is empirically true, and vice versa" (Markovits & Nantel, 1989, p. 11), or "to accept or reject a conclusion on the basis of its consistency with everyday knowledge, regardless of its logical status" (Dube, Rotello, & Heit, 2010).

Although discussions of reasoning in argumentation are likely to emphasize the importance of the concept of logical validity – it is easy to show that whether an argument is valid is not the sole determinant of whether it is persuasive. Nickerson et al. (in press) had college students evaluate arguments with respect to both validity and persuasiveness. Invalid arguments that were judged to be persuasive were almost three times as likely to be considered to be valid as were invalid arguments that were considered not to be persuasive. Here is an example of an invalid argument that was considered by 85 percent of the subjects to be persuasive:

If John is in France, he is in Paris.
John is in Paris.
Therefore, he is in France.

The argument is invalid by virtue of *affirming the consequent.* The following argument was considered by 80 percent of the subjects to be persuasive, despite being invalid, in this case by virtue of *denying the antecedent*:

If Jane has any pets, she has a dog.
Jane doesn't have any pets.
Therefore, she doesn't have a dog.

The degree to which formal logic is descriptive of normal untutored human thought is a matter of long-standing controversy within psychology and philosophy. Investigators have compiled long lists of how thinking often is illogical. Some theorists have argued that thought is not greatly constrained by principles of logic (Cheng & Holyoak, 1985; Evans, 1989; Harman, 1986) or that even when it produces results that are consistent with logic, those results may be based on operations other than logical ones (Johnson-Laird, 1983). Others have taken the position that thinking is basically logical and that what appears to be evidence of illogicality can usually be traced to linguistic confusions or misinterpretations (e.g., Cohen, 1981; Henle, 1962).

Evaluating Informal Arguments

> [U]nfortunately, there is no precise agreed use for the expression "inductive argument," nor any pair of adjectives similar to "valid" and "invalid" for assessing inductive arguments
>
> (Swinburne, 1974, p. 2).

> In establishing the structure of an argument, we must interpret the words of the speaker, supply the missing links, which is always very risky
>
> (Perelman & Olbrechts-Tyteca, 1969, p. 187).

> Induction can only be defended by appeal to it
>
> (Polkinghorne, 1989, p. 30).

As Alvin Goldman (1986) points out, not all the rules of belief justification can be derived from deductive logic. "Where nondeductive inferences are appropriate – and such cases are certainly legion – truths of deductive logic are of little or no help" (p. 67). Whether the breach might be filled by truths of inductive logic, Goldman sees as "very dubious." "Many epistemologists and philosophers of science now question whether there is a body of truths we can call 'inductive logic'" (p. 67). However, inductive arguments are ubiquitous, and we have to deal with them.

Despite their formality and the rules that determine their validity, formal arguments can be difficult to evaluate. Informal arguments can be doubly so. The time-honored binary distinction between valid and invalid arguments is widely considered to be too course to be very helpful in evaluating informal arguments (Grennan, 1986; Rescher, 1976). One is more likely to encounter argument evaluations in terms of their *strength* (Hoeken, Šorm, & Schellens, 2014; Hoeken, Timmers, & Schellens, 2012), *quality* (Hahn & Hornikx, 2016; Park et al., 2007) *persuasiveness* (O'Keefe, 2013), or some other property that admits off degrees. But, as Hahn and Hornikx (2016) point out, "Despite its importance, and considerable research effort aimed at the issue, a comprehensive theory of argument quality has remained elusive" (p. 1834).

Stephen Thomas (1973) proposed that arguments be evaluated in terms of levels of strength – *weak, moderate, strong* – marked at the extremes by *nil* and *deductively valid.* Others have recognized, at least implicitly, that inductive arguments seldom prove their conclusions to be true beyond doubt. Scriven (1986) makes the point this way: "Argument will rarely result in the discovery of the absolute truth; this is clear in science, and it should be clearer in non-scientific discourse" (p. 13). From this perspective, he promotes the need to seek a process that will produce the best conclusions. "To this end, it is important to look beyond the content of the arguments to the process whereby arguments are generated, developed and evaluated" (p. 13).

Rieke and Sillars (1975), who offer advice on how to compose, evaluate, and refute arguments in a variety of contexts, describe how what they refer to as an "audience-centered" theory of argumentation would be evaluated: "The ultimate test of argument is whether or not people give their adherence to claims made by the arguer by stating concurrence or behaving accordingly. This understanding of why we advance claims and give reasons for them dictates a distinctive understanding of argumentation" (p. 2). The focus of this kind of theory is on "those arguments that win adherents, and not on those that are 'correct' or 'true' or that ought to have been selected" (p. 24).

Richard Swinburne (1974) suggests that although the terms "valid" and "invalid" are not applicable to informal, or inductive, arguments, the qualifications "correct" and "incorrect" are. In his view, a correct inductive argument is one in which the premises "make it reasonable" for us to accept the conclusion whereas an incorrect inductive argument is one in which the premises do not make it reasonable for us to accept the conclusion, but it is falsely claimed that they do. Stated in probabilistic terms, a correct inductive argument is said to be one in which the premises "make the conclusion more probable than any equally detailed rival, although the argument is not deductively valid" (p. 5).

Max Black (1974/1958) draws a similar contrast between deductive and inductive arguments, and contends that inductive arguments vary in strength, whereas deductive arguments do not. "If a deductive argument is not valid it must be *in*valid, no intermediate cases being conceivable . . .. Appraisal of an inductive argument admits of degrees" (p. 129). Unfortunately, if one accepts this position, one does not thereby free oneself of conceptual difficulties, because philosophers can find much to argue about around such concepts as reasonableness and probability.

Most "everyday" arguments are neither exclusively deductive nor expressed in a canonical logical form. However, they typically do have certain identifiable components. These include a conclusion and one or more assertions that are offered, directly or indirectly, as support for it – as reasons for believing it to be true. Informal arguments can be complex and confusing, especially when several conclusions and supporting assertions are run together in a random fashion. A complex argument may contain assertions that are intended to support certain conclusions and that are themselves conclusions supported by other parts of the argument.

Sometimes a distinction is made between an argument and the language in which it is expressed. Ronald Fisher (2004/1988), for example, gives his objective in *The Logic of Real Arguments*, as describing and demonstrating "a systematic method for extracting an argument from its written context and for evaluating it" (p. 128). Whether one finds this distinction a compelling one, there can be little doubt that often the most challenging aspect of evaluating an informal argument is figuring out exactly what its various components are and what they are intended to mean.

The following, excerpted from Nickerson (1986a), are two informal arguments taken from *The Boston Globe* published in 1982 in anticipation of a referendum on a Massachusetts law requiring that a refundable deposit be paid for certain beverage containers sold in the state. (A bottle bill – the *Beverage Container Recovery* Law – had been enacted by the legislature overriding the governor's veto in 1981.) The first argument is from a proponent of the bill; the second is from an opponent. A "yes" vote on the referendum would keep the law in place; a "no" vote would do away with it. The arguments were restricted in length.

Argument For:

The bottle bill was passed by two-thirds vote of the Legislature last year in order to clean up the litter cluttering our lawns, streets, and parks. This sensible legislation will put a stop to an enormous waste of money and resources.

> Similar laws have proven popular and successful in achieving those aims in states much as Maine, Vermont, Connecticut, and Michigan. New York has passed a bottle bill which will take effect next July.
>
> Among the benefits of the Massachusetts bottle bill:
>
> An 80 percent decrease in beverage container litter, the most prevalent and dangerous type;
>
> Lower prices: A 5 percent reduction of beverage prices; Tax savings: Millions of tax dollars saved due to reduced garbage collection and disposal costs;
>
> More jobs: A net increase of more than 2,000 skilled and unskilled jobs for Massachusetts residents;
>
> Less waste: 33 percent less energy consumed by the beverage industry.
>
> *Argument Against*:
>
> In this age of limited resources, it is understandable that Massachusetts voters said "no" to forced deposit containers the only time they had an opportunity to vote on the issue. They knew that requiring return of cans, plastic bottles, and other containers would create many problems, and were concerned about the need to:
>
> Save town and private recycling operations; Save the state's water supply during a declared emergency;
>
> Save local separation programs because landfill space is rapidly disappearing;
>
> But most importantly, save money for already over-burdened consumers.
>
> Further, our position is that the will of the electorate is better served by people voting in free elections than legislators acting in a highly political environment. A "no" vote is a vote for an industry-funded litter control and recycling law – which will give money to communities for cleanup and recycling projects and anti-litter education programs.

The referendum was on the ballot in 1982 and the bottle bill survived by a 60 percent to 40 percent margin. It would be interesting to know which, if any, of the predictions offered in the pro and con arguments proved to be true, but inasmuch as the bill has been modified more than once over the years, it is unlikely that could be determined. It seems more likely that each side would be able to argue that its position had been justified.

Here is another example of an informal argument, this one in support of the further development and use of nuclear power in the United States:

> That there is nothing inherently unworkable about nuclear power is borne out by the success of nuclear projects overseas and indeed of many projects in the U.S. Moreover, although a variety of alternative sources of energy are available to utilities, and several promising new non-nuclear technologies are under development, abandoning nuclear power might well render the nation's electricity supply substantially less efficient and environmentally

> benign. Oil and gas, albeit currently plentiful, will eventually grow scarcer and costlier. Coal is difficult to burn cleanly: acid rain and other by-products of coal combustion are causing serious damage to the environment and will be expensive to control, and in the future, the carbon dioxide released by the combustion of fossil fuels may have a severe effect on global climate. The potential of solar electric technology to compete economically outside a fairly narrow range of favorable sites or specialized uses has not yet been demonstrated (Lester, 1986, p. 31).

While informal, these arguments are still much neater than many of those one encounters in daily life. The people who constructed them were motivated to make them concise and compelling. Even so, they are not nearly as easy to evaluate as are formal deductive arguments; and, as already noted, there are no widely agreed-upon rules for doing the evaluation. To assess such arguments one must, at least, recognize the claims that are being made, decide how much credence to give to each of these claims, judge how much support each of them – if true – gives to the conclusion or position the argument is intended to substantiate, and somehow aggregate the results of these considerations into an overall assessment of the persuasiveness of the argument as a whole. In short, evaluation of informal arguments of any substance and complexity involves at least the following components: analysis, judgments of relevance and weight, and aggregation or synthesis.

Analysis

Figuring out what the essence of the argument is often requires analysis. Informal natural-language arguments can be buried in an excess of verbiage and the first challenge in evaluating them is to determine what they are – to discover precisely what the argument is (Copi, Cohen, & McMahon, 2010). This is made the more difficult – and the more necessary – when the argument is expressed poorly or its originator's intentions are camouflaged by a superfluity of words, but in order to evaluate an argument one must know, or make an assumption about, what the argument is. This means, at least, identifying the conclusion(s) one is intended to draw and what is being asserted in its (their) support.

Figuring out the essence of an argument, even when it is well stated, can be a considerable challenge. This observation holds for short deductive arguments as well as for long inductive ones. Consider the argument that the second law of thermodynamics (essentially that in any closed system randomness increases) implies a beginning for the universe. One statement of it is as follows: "the universe cannot have existed forever, otherwise it would have reached its equilibrium endstate an infinite time ago. Conclusion: The universe did not always exist" (Davies, 1983, p. 11).

Is the argument sound? Is the claim that if the universe had always existed it would have reached its endstate (equilibrium, total randomness) an infinite time ago true? Does the claim imply that the universe *never* could have been in a state of disequilibrium (less-than-maximum-randomness)? If it does imply that, then the second law of thermodynamics does seem to entail a beginning. On the other hand, if it does not have that implication – if the notion that the equilibrium endstate would have been reached an infinite time ago is compatible with the idea that at *some* time the universe contained some structure, it is not clear what rules out the possibility that we are now living in that period. And so on.

Cassius Keyser (1926) notes the importance of "postulate detection" to good thinking, not only by scientists or philosophers but by all people in everyday life. This is because much of daily thinking has to do with the acceptance or rejection of propositions. Arguments in defense of, or in opposition to, a given proposition invariably make use of other propositions, some of which may be taken for granted and given the status of postulates. Only by recognizing explicitly what are being taken as postulates do we have the opportunity to decide whether we consider them to be true or false. Unfortunately, the identification of arguments' postulates is often complicated by the existence of ambiguities and unstated assumptions (Nickerson, 1996).

Fisher (2004/1988) suggests that analyzing informal arguments can be facilitated by learning to recognize certain words or phrases that typically signal a conclusion (therefore, so, hence, thus, . . .) or a reason given in support of a conclusion (because, for, since, follows from, . . .). He refers to the first group as "conclusion indicators," to the second as "reason indicators," and to the combination as "inference indicators" or "argument indicators." Fisher describes a procedure for evaluating written formal arguments that begins with the identification of such indicator words and includes identifying any conclusions that are drawn (perhaps flagged by indicator words), identifying "reasons" that are given why one should believe those conclusions, and so on.

So, there is much advice on record regarding how to go about analyzing inductive arguments. Undoubtedly some, perhaps most, of that advice is helpful; at the least it provides food for thought. But whereas there appears to be general agreement that analysis is an important aspect of argument evaluation, there is no algorithm that is universally – or nearly universally – accepted as *the best* way to do it.

Judgments of Relevance and Weight

To determine how much credence to give to the conclusion of an argument, one must be able to judge the assertions that are made in its support as to their relevance and, given that an assertion is considered relevant, one must decide how much weight to attach to it (Campbell, 1986; Pham, 1998; Skovgaard-Olsen, Singmann, & Klaur, 2016). How much weight to attach to an assertion depends in part on what one believes to be the likelihood that it is true; if one believes the assertion to be false, one will give it no weight. In both cases the judgment is one of degree, relevance can vary continuously as can weight. The same types of considerations must be given also to counterarguments that one may construct, inasmuch as the assertions comprising them can also be more or less relevant and can vary in the degree to which they increase the credibility of the counter conclusion.

Judgments of Truth or Falsity

A claim may be judged to be relevant to a conclusion and to give the conclusion considerable support – assuming it is true. The assumption here is critical. A false claim provides no support. So, a major task in evaluating an informal argument is to judge whether to accept the claims made in its support as true. In many cases that is likely to be the most difficult of the evaluations that must be made. Often it will be impossible to judge with certainty either that a claim is true or that it is false; the best one can do is to make a judgment of the amount of credence to give to a claim that is somewhere between certainly true and certainly false. This is where probability theory becomes a useful tool in argument evaluation.

Aggregation or Synthesis

Having considered the argument's parts, one must assess its persuasiveness as a whole. One must decide how convincing it is relative to the most compelling counterarguments one is able to construct, and on this basis accept or reject its conclusion(s), perhaps with qualifications or provisos, and probably at some level of surety less than absolute.

In some instances, one may feel justified in being very confident that a conclusion is true on the grounds that one can imagine no way that the supporting statements (which one believes to be true) could be true if the conclusion were false. This comes very close to the situation one has with a formal deductive argument, except that in the informal case, what is lacking is the authority of the formal rules of inference. More often, the conclusion is likely to be accepted at something less than certainty. (Of course, this is true also when formal logic is applied to real-life situations. In this case, one can be certain the conclusion of a valid inference is true *if* the premises that imply it are true, but if the premises are meaningful assertions about the real world, one's certainty of their truth is likely often to be less than complete.)

I do not mean to suggest that one always does each of the noted aspects of evaluation in a conscious and deliberate fashion, but the effective evaluation of informal arguments involves them, at least implicitly. Further, these activities draw upon other capabilities such as the following.

- *Assessment of own knowledge.* If one knows a lot about the topic of an argument, one is in a better position to evaluate the argument than if one knows only a little. Equally as important as one's knowledge of a topic, however, is one's awareness of the extent and limitations of that knowledge. Especially vulnerable is the person who believes his/her knowledge to be extensive when, in reality, it is very limited. This consideration becomes important in certain types of plausibility judgments. Suppose, for example, that I judge a particular assertion to be highly implausible on the grounds that it declares to be a fact something of which I am unaware. My tacit assumption must be that if that which is declared to be a fact really were a fact, I would be aware of it, and since I am not aware of it, it must not be a fact. Such a basis for judging plausibility is justified only to the degree that I am highly knowledgeable with respect to the subject. If my knowledge of the subject is very limited and I am aware that it is, then the fact that I do not know some assertion pertaining to that subject to be true should give me very little reason to conclude that it is false.
- *Information seeking and selection.* It may be desirable to obtain additional information to supplement what one has in one's head, especially if one's knowledge of the domain is limited. Skill in the finding of information is a useful one not only in the context of argument evaluation, but much more generally. "Poor arguments are not necessarily poor because they are illogical, but because they ignore some relevant possibility or piece of evidence" (Garnham & Oakhill, 1994, p. 262). At least some aspects of this skill should be relatively easy to address through training, namely those pertaining to the use of formal information-finding resources such as encyclopedias, atlases, almanacs, indexes, and a variety of computer-based search engines. Instruction in

the effective use of such resources should, I believe, receive considerable emphasis throughout the educational system. This is not to suggest that students should be led to adopt the idea that answers to all questions can be found or should be sought in books or other repositories of information, but it is to their advantage to know how to find those that are to be found there.

- *Estimation and approximation.* Many arguments have quantitative components: assertions about populations, incidence, costs, distances, rates of change, probabilities. In order to evaluate such arguments, it is necessary to judge the plausibility of their component assertions, and inasmuch as the quantities involved are often – perhaps typically – unknown to the evaluator, such judgments must be based on the ability to estimate or approximate them. Skills of estimation and approximation appear to be grossly undervalued by society and their development is strangely neglected by many educational systems.
- *Detection of inconsistencies.* Inconsistencies can occur within an argument or between an argument's assertions and known or assumed facts. Such inconsistencies, when recognized, weaken an argument, so the ability to detect them is important. This is a knowledge-based ability; one cannot detect inconsistencies between assertions and facts unless one knows the facts.

To assess an individual's competence with respect to argumentation probably requires explicit attention to each of these aspects and several more. It is not safe to assume that an individual who is competent at detecting fallacies in deductive arguments posed in syllogistic form will be equally competent at judging the amount of credence that should be given to assertions offered in support of informal inductions.

An important aspect of the evaluation of informal arguments involves going beyond the information comprising the argument itself. The most compelling reasons for rejecting an argument are often found in what could have been said but was not. A general strategy that is useful in evaluating arguments is to attempt to make explicit those relevant facts that were left unstated. It may be especially useful to attempt to explicate any facts that are inconsistent with the conclusion drawn. That is to say, it may be especially useful to attempt to construct a counterargument. The ability to do so will depend heavily, of course, on one's knowledge of the domain.

It is perhaps here, in the realm of counterargument construction, that reasoning in argument evaluation is most heavily knowledge dependent. It is here too that one's metaknowledge – one's awareness of the extent and limitations of one's own knowledge of a domain – is especially important. If I know a lot about a domain, and realize it, and am unable to construct a compelling counter to a given argument, I am likely to give more credence to the argument's conclusion than if I am aware that I know too little about a topic to be able to construct a counterargument even if there were a simple but compelling one to be constructed.

Enthymemes

In everyday reasoning arguments are often stated incompletely; such arguments are known as *enthymemes*.

> The contract is signed by both parties, so it is binding.
> The contract is not signed by both parties, so it is not binding.

What is missing in the first case is:

> If the contract is signed by both parties, it is binding,

and in the second:

> If the contract is not signed by both parties, it is not binding,

Some might want to claim that if one concludes that a contract is not binding upon being told that it was not signed by both parties may not be reasoning at all, but simply recalling from memory the fact that to be binding a contract must be signed by both parties. However, even if memory is implicated in this fashion, it is a missing assertion that justifies the conclusion; and what memory can supply is the knowledge that for *any* contract to be binding it must be signed by both parties, and to get from contracts in general to the particular contract in question requires an inference.

Other enthymemes:

> She does not speak French, so she did not grow up in Paris.

Missing premise:

> If she does not speak French, she did not grow up in Paris,

or

> If she grew up in Paris, she speaks French.
> The percolator light is not on, so the coffee is not ready.

Missing premise:

If the percolator light is not on, the coffee is not ready,

or

If the coffee is ready, the percolator light is on.

Enthymemes are very common in everyday discourse (Hitchcock, 1986); undoubtedly, they are more common than fully expressed arguments in which all premises and the conclusion are explicitly identified. Baird (1950) makes the point in contending that arguments are usually stated as enthymemes: "One premise at least is usually taken for granted or may be considered too obvious for statement as a formal proposition" (p. 155). Baird recognizes three orders of enthymeme depending on whether what is absent is the major premise, the minor premise, or the conclusion. To illustrate the expression of an argument as an enthymeme, the missing middle term of which may be supplied by the context, Baird uses the following: "The United States will go bankrupt, for it is headed toward a debt of more than 500 billion dollars" (p. 156). (As of January 2019, the US national debt stood at approximately 22 trillion dollars, and was increasing at the rate of about 3.8 billion dollars a day. What a difference sixty-six years can make!)

The observation that people often state arguments incompletely is not a criticism. Sometimes stating a premise may amount to wasting words because it can be safely assumed that the information that would have been conveyed by the missing premise is well known to the argument's participants. Sometimes what is missing is one or more premises; sometimes it is a conclusion. (A conclusion may go unstated because the originator of the argument considers it too obvious to require being stated.) Of course, when participants in an enthymematic argument are having difficulty agreeing on whether it is persuasive – that its conclusion should be accepted – they may find it helpful to make the missing part(s) of the argument explicit.

Models of Argument Evaluation

Attempts to provide prescriptive models of how arguments – especially informal arguments – should be evaluated typically state a set of principles by which the process should be guided. The following case in point is from John Hoagland (1986).

> First the structure of the argument must be established: the conclusion must be identified, the premises including tacitly assumed ones must be stated, and the argument scanned for formal patterns like *modus ponens*. Then ambiguity and equivocation must be removed. Internal criticism must focus on the relation of premises to conclusion: do the premises, if true, establish the conclusion? External criticism asks whether the premises are true, then tests the strength of the argument with counterarguments. Finally, an overall evaluation must be given: is the argument strong or weak? Some writers recommend diagramming the premises relative to the conclusion to reveal argument structure (p. 392).

Here is another set of rules for evaluating arguments (Table 3.1), this one offered by Evert Vedung (1986). (Rules 2a and 2b have been modified to correct typing errors in Vedung's table).

Table 3.1 *Rules of assessment in argumentative inquiry (from Vedung, 1986, p. 357)*

1. The rule of support: Claims should be supported by reasons.
2. The rule of clarity: The content should be clear.
   a. Claims and reasons must not be tacit and so give rise to obscurity.
   b. Words must not be used in an unclear way.
   c. The presentation should be arranged so as not to cause obscurity.
3. The rule of relevance: The content should be relevant.
   a. Pronouncement should be relevant.
   b. Relevant aspects of the case should be acknowledged and presented.
4. The rule of consistency: The content should be consistent.
   a. Inferences from reasons to claims should be derived in a logically valid way.
   b. Claims should be consistent with other claims, reasons with other reasons.
5. The rule of truth: The content should be true.

William Benoit (1986) contends that there are two important phases to argument evaluation, the first of which is to identify the argument in its entirety. "Since most arguments are enthymematic, the argument critic must identify the premises that the auditor is willing to supply in order to complete it .... Once the entire argument is displayed, the critic can proceed to the second phase, evaluation" (p. 302).

Ennis (2001) offers an approach to argument evaluation that recognizes five "phases" (as paraphrased):

(1) Identification of argument parts (conclusions and supporting reasons).

(2) Deciding to what extent (unstated) assumptions should be added.
(3) Abandonment of attempts to classify arguments into types.
(4) Successive application of sets of argument standards "usually in conjunction with assumption ascription, stopping only when the argument satisfies a set of standards (in which case the argument is deemed a good argument), or when the set of sets of standards is exhausted without any set being satisfied (in which case it is deemed a weak or poor argument)" (p. 120).
(5) Qualified reasoning tempered by flexibility toward the degree of precision needed in the situation. (Listed on pages 120, 121, and again, slightly modified, on page 134.)

Ennis (2001) expands on each of these phases in a thoughtful and thought-provoking way. Using actual court proceedings in a murder trial to illustrate how they may play out, he judges an argument to be inductively valid by virtue of satisfying the following "best-explanation" standards, the first three of which, he contends, are necessary conditions, while the fourth is desirable.

(1) The conclusion should explain facts.
(2) Plausible alternative hypotheses should be ruled out.
(3) The conclusion should be consistent with known facts, and a reasonable effort should have been made to uncover facts inconsistent with the conclusion.
(4) The conclusion should be plausible (p. 123).

Ennis treats this set of standards as one among others that might be used, and the selection of an appropriate set as itself a decision that an argument evaluator must make.

> There are different sets of standards, including, in my view, soundness standards, inductive standards (including best-explanation standards and standards for generalizing from instances), and value judging standards, all of which are subject to qualified-reasoning adjustments. Using the sets-of-standards approach, we are not required to classify an argument before evaluating it. Instead we successively apply sets of standards. We then accept the conclusion if, in the context, it satisfies any set of standards – remembering the set of standards that it satisfies, and showing this, if need be, in appropriate qualifications to the acceptance of the argument or the conclusion. If the argument satisfies no set of standards, the argument is deemed defective (p. 125).

How one is to judge the adequacy of any particular set of standards to apply to any particular argument is not clear. Failure to get agreement on the answer to this question leaves open the possibility of different evaluators coming to different opinions regarding the quality (validity, strength, soundness) of any specific argument. Ennis effectively acknowledges this in noting that the standards in terms of which an evaluator will assess an argument will depend on his or her goals.

In a highly influential book (*Uses of Argument*), cited in Chapter 2, Stephen Toulmin (1958) likens an argument – an extended argument I should say – to an organism and notes that its structure can be examined at more than one level. He considers the traditional distinction between deductive (conclusive, demonstrative) and inductive (inconclusive, non-demonstrative) arguments to be an unfortunate one and one that has led to an increasingly wide gap between the work of logicians and the reasoning required by everyday life. However, the distinction between deductive and inductive arguments, for better or worse, is a widely accepted one, and in my view we do well to pay it some mind.

Toulmin contends that logicians have focused on deductive reasoning, and in particular on the analytic syllogism, because it is tractable, but it is not very usefully applied to problems of reasoning with practical import. The distinction between deductive and inductive reasoning, as it has been made historically, Toulmin suggests, conflates all of the following distinctions: arguments with necessary conclusions versus arguments with probable conclusions, formally valid arguments versus arguments that cannot be formally valid, arguments that rely on a warrant the adequacy and applicability of which have already been established versus arguments that are intended to establish the adequacy of a warrant, arguments that are expressed in terms of logical connectives or quantifiers (all, some, or) versus those expressed in other terms (most, few, but), and analytic (abstract) arguments versus substantive ones.

Toulmin presents a structured approach to argument evaluation that distinguishes several components of an argument other than the traditional premises and conclusion. There is first the *claim* (C) that is being made and that the entire argument is intended to support. Then there are the *data* (D), the facts that provide the foundation for the claim. *Warrants* (W) are the kinds of propositions that justify arguing from data to claims. These are the basic components that all arguments contain, implicitly if not explicitly. Consider, for example, the argument: Harry is a British subject, because he was born in Bermuda. The claim is that Harry is a British subject; the datum is that Harry was born in Bermuda; the warrant, unstated, is that anyone born in Bermuda is a British subject. In this simple case, we could easily have analyzed the argument in terms of a (supplemented) major premise (Anyone born in Bermuda is a British subject), minor premise (Harry was born in Bermuda), and conclusion (Harry is a British subject).

In this example, the warrant was not explicitly stated in the argument. In Toulmin's conceptualization, this is a distinguishing difference between data and warrants: data are stated explicitly, warrants are not. Analyzed in traditional terms as a deductive argument involving premises and a conclusion, the example would be considered an enthymeme and, in particular, an enthymeme of the first order, which is to say an argument missing the major premise.

Toulmin's approach is intended to be able to deal with arguments much more complex than the above example, but additional concepts are necessary for the more complex cases. *Modal qualifiers* (Q), such as "necessarily," "probably," and "presumably," and *conditions of exception or rebuttal* (R) (unless . . .) are used to indicate the degree of force that a warrant carries and conditions under which it may not hold. The force of the argument in ensuring the truth of the claim, even as qualified and delimited by provisos, depends on the truth of the datum and the warrant, both of which are claims themselves. The situation is analogous to that of a conventionally structured deductive argument, in which the guarantee of the truth of the conclusion rests on the truth of the argument's premises. The question of the truth of the data in such an argument is likely to be less problematic than the question of the truth of the warrant, because the former will tend to involve particular verifiable facts, whereas the latter are more likely to be general claims that may not be verifiable empirically in practice or even in principle.

Toulmin recognizes the need for support for warrants and provides for it in his representation of an argument with a component that he calls *backing* (B). "Standing behind our warrants . . . there will normally be other assurances, without which the backing themselves would possess neither authority nor currency" (p. 103).

We see here the possibility of an infinite regress – an endless stack of turtles standing on the backs of turtles – but this does not distinguish Toulmin's approach to argument evaluation from any other serious approach of which I am aware. All involve justifying certain claims in terms of certain other claims. In all cases, the claims that are used for justification require justification themselves. Invariably one can be pushed back to a point at which one must say, I take thus-and-so as given, and that is the end of it. Toulmin recognizes this problem and acknowledges the need to take something for granted.

> Some warrants must be accepted provisionally without further challenge, if argument is to be open to us in the field in question; we should not even know what sort of data were of the slightest relevance to a conclusion, if we had not at least a provisional idea of the warrants acceptable in the situation confronting us. The existence of considerations such as would establish the acceptability of the most reliable warrants, is something we are entitled to take for granted (p. 106).

Toulmin emphasizes the distinction between a warrant and its backing. It is critically important, he argues, to keep clear the difference between the force of warrants and the backing on which their authority depends. The *force* of a statement of a given type, say a universal statement, when used as a warrant is the same in all fields of argument, in Toulmin's view, but the *backing* for a warrant of a given sort is likely to vary from field to field. In this sense the criteria for argument evaluation are field-dependent. Toulmin sees the fact that his representation of the structure of arguments makes the distinction between *warrant* and *backing* explicit as one of its major benefits and what most sharply differentiates his representation of the structure of arguments from the more traditional representation in terms of premises and conclusions.

> [I]f we pay closer attention to the differences between warrants and backing, and between different sorts of backing for one and the same warrant, and between the backing for warrants of different sorts, and if we refuse to focus our attention hypnotically on the traditional form "All A's are B's," we can not only come to see *that* sometimes "All A's are B's" does have existential implications and sometimes not, but furthermore begin to understand *why* this should be so (p. 116).

Again, "[o]nce we bring into the open the backing on which (in the last resort) the soundness of our arguments depends, the suggestion that validity is to be explained in terms of 'formal properties,' in any geometrical sense, loses its plausibility" (p. 120).

In addition to the distinction between analytical and substantial arguments, a key aspect of Toulmin's approach is his insistence that substantial arguments are field- or context-dependent and the criteria by which arguments should be judged can differ across fields. "Arguments within any field can be judged by standards appropriate within that field, and some will fall short; but it must be expected that the standards will be field-dependent, and that the merits to be demanded of an argument in one field will be found to be absent (in the nature of things) from entirely meritorious arguments in another" (p. 255). "If we ask about the validity, necessity, rigour, or impossibility of arguments or conclusions, we must ask these questions within the limits of a given field, and avoid, as it were, condemning an ape for not being a man or a pig for not being a porcupine" (p. 256).

The field-dependence of argumentation is reflected in the fact that different sorts of problems require different types of warrants, backing and criteria of necessity, and probability. It is critical, in Toulmin's view, that people who wish to make progress on the evaluation of arguments in a given field agree on how to test the adequacy of warrants for arguments pertaining to that field. "Two people who accept common procedures for testing warrants in any field can begin comparing the merits of arguments in that field: only where this condition is lacking, so that they have no common ground on which to argue, will rational assessment no longer be open to them" (p. 176).

It is the field- or context-dependency of substantive arguments that ensures the limited applicability of abstract logic – which does not recognize inter-field differences – to them. Toulmin's assessment of the relevance of symbolic logic to practical arguments is severe: "By now, mathematical logic has become a frozen calculus, having no functional connection with the canons for assessing the strength and cogency of arguments" (p. 186). "In logic, as in morals, the real problem of rational assessment – telling sound arguments from untrustworthy ones, rather than consistent from inconsistent ones – requires experience, insight and judgment, and mathematical calculations (in the form of statistics and the like) can never be more than one tool among others of use in this task" (p. 188).

Toulmin's *Uses of Argument* was (is) a very influential (and accessible) book – in effect an extended argument regarding the inadequacy of formal logic for understanding and evaluating the kinds of arguments encountered in daily life. First published more than a half century ago, it (an updated edition published in 2003) is still in print, and much cited. In my view, no treatment of argumentation would be adequate that did not give it substantial space. However, despite my admiration for Toulmin's work, I have elected to stay with the conventional distinction between deductive and inductive (formal and informal) arguments. The several new concepts that Toulmin introduced in his work on argument evaluation – warrant, backing, field- or context-dependency are of unquestioned interest and importance to researchers who study argumentation; how much they add to our understanding of how people actually evaluate arguments in daily life is debatable.

Evaluating arguments involves two kinds of judgment: (1) whether the argument's conclusion or key assertion follows logically from, or is made highly likely by, its premises or supporting assertions, and (2) whether to accept the premises or supporting assertions as true or very probably so. Reflection prompts two further questions: What makes an argument persuasive and what makes an assertion plausible?

These questions are of considerable interest in many contexts: education, debating, diplomacy, marketing/advertising, diagnostic reasoning, military planning, crime investigations, judicial proceedings, among numerous others. They are considered in Chapters 4 and 5.

4

Persuasiveness

A valid argument form is one in which the conclusion follows from the premises. Colloquially, of course, a valid argument is one that is pertinent and persuasive

(Hacking, 1975, p. 64).

What is gratuitously asserted may be gratuitously denied

(Nogar, 1966, p. 312).

To be effective, an argument must be persuasive. It need not be logical, or well-formed or even coherent; to be effective, it need only accomplish the goal of influencing beliefs or behavior as intended by its originator. As we shall see, persuasiveness is a function of many variables, logicality, good form, and coherence being only a subset of them.

What Makes an Argument Persuasive?

It is a small comfort to know that an argument is entirely logical, that it validly derives its conclusion from its premises, and that all the rules of the syllogism, or whatever, are observed to a nicety, *if* it turns out that the premises are frauds, snares, delusions

(Fearnside & Holther, 1959, p. 2).

It must be noted at the outset of the discussion of what makes an argument persuasive that some scholars have explicitly rejected persuasiveness as a proper criterion for judging the quality of arguments. Douglas Ehninger (1966) and Dale Hample (1981) are cases in point. It is easy to understand why one might hold this view, because, as we shall see, persuasiveness can be affected by many variables, including some that would seem to have little to do with whether an argument is valid or sound. But in this book the focus is on the practical question of what determines an argument's persuasiveness, or more generally, on what people find to be persuasive; the question of quality, as judged by other criteria, is a very important one, but not the focus here.

In contrast to the idea that persuasiveness is not a proper criterion for judging the quality of arguments is the assumption that a major, if not the primary, purpose of arguments is to persuade others to accept some claim as true or to behave in a certain way. In the preceding chapters it was noted that arguments take many forms and evaluating them can be a nontrivial task. However, for practical purposes, the overriding concern about any argument is the question of whether it is persuasive, or, recognizing that persuasiveness is not a binary concept, the question becomes how persuasive is it?

Sometimes a distinction is made between persuasion and conviction. "If a judgment is valid for every rational being, then its ground is objectively sufficient, and it is termed a *conviction*. If, on the other hand, it has its ground in the particular character of the subject, it is termed a *persuasion*" (Kant, 2003/1781, p. 460). Others have also made this distinction. It will not concern us here; for present purposes, it will not hurt to consider persuasion and conviction as synonyms.

The question of what makes an argument persuasive – convincing – is not new. Aristotle addressed it in his *Art of Rhetoric* (circa 325 BC) and suggested three ways in which one might be convinced of the truth of an argument's conclusion: by the argument's source (ethos), by feelings it evokes (pathos), and by logic (logos). Many philosophers since Aristotle's time have similarly offered opinions regarding how people are, or are not, persuaded by arguments. A notable case in point is the nineteenth-century philosopher Arthur Schopenhauer, whose ruminations on the subject we will note in due course. Psychologists also have shown interest in the question for some time (Hovland, Janis, & Kelley, 1953), and especially in recent decades (Bonnefon & Hilton, 2004; Evans et al., 2007; Grosset & Barrouillet, 2003; Hoeken, Timmers, & Schellens, 2012; Nickerson, 2015; Thompson, Evans, & Handley, 2005).

Sometimes a distinction is made between persuasive and dissuasive arguments. A persuasive conditional argument may be described as one in which the antecedent of the major premise identifies a means of realizing a desirable consequent, and a dissuasive argument as one in which the antecedent identifies a means of preventing an undesirable consequent (Green, 2008; Thompson et al., 2005). Here "persuasive" is used to characterize an argument that persuades, whether it persuades one to believe or do something or to refrain from believing or doing something.

As already noted, according to the standard rules of logic, *If A then C; A; therefore, C* and *If A then C; not C; therefore, not A* are both valid arguments, the first by *modus ponens* and the second by *modus tollens. If A then C; not A; therefore, not C* and *If A then C; C; therefore, A* are both invalid arguments; the first commits the fallacy of *denying the antecedent* and the second the fallacy of *affirming the consequent.* These rules specify what does or does not follow, logically, from the premises of an argument, but they do not tell us whether an argument is persuasive.

If a formal argument is valid and its premises are true, then its logically implied conclusion must be true. So, if one believes a formal argument to be valid and its premises to be true, one *should* find it to be persuasive – one should accept its conclusion as true. In the case of informal arguments, there is no comparably simple rule. Even in the case of formal arguments, the rule is limited in explanatory power, inasmuch as it does not tell us what determines the persuasiveness of arguments, whether valid or invalid in form. That an invalid argument may or may not be persuasive is readily illustrated by the following two arguments.

- If the car is John's, it's a Ford. The car is not John's. Therefore, it's not a Ford.
- If Jane has any pets, she has a dog. Jane has no pets. Therefore, she does not have a dog.

Both of these arguments are invalid. Both illustrate the fallacy of denying the antecedent. However, I venture the guess that while most readers will find the first one unpersuasive, many will consider the second one to be compelling. Or consider the following two arguments, both of which illustrate the fallacy of affirming the consequent.

- If he was born in New York, he is a US citizen. He is a US citizen. Therefore, he was born in New York.
- If he's alive, he's breathing. He's breathing. Therefore, he's alive.

Again, I suspect that people generally are likely to find the second argument more persuasive than the first.

Of course, it is not difficult to construct arguments that are valid in form and persuasive.

- If it's a whale, it is a mammal. It's a whale. Therefore, it's a mammal.

What may be less obvious is that it is also easy to construct arguments that are valid in form but are not persuasive.

- If the Amazon is the longest river in the world, boron is a chemical element with atomic number 5. The Amazon is the longest river in the world. Therefore, boron is a chemical element with atomic number 5.
- If $2 + 2 = 4$, dogs are marsupials. Dogs are not marsupials. Therefore, $2 + 2 \neq 4$.

The first of these arguments is valid and its conclusion is true, but it is hardly persuasive; that the Amazon is the longest river in the world has no obvious connection with the fact that boron is an element. We will return to this example in the context of a discussion of relevance. With regard to the second argument, it is valid, but its major premise and conclusion are false, so it is not persuasive, at least to people who know something about dogs and numbers.

Any satisfactory answer to the question of what makes an argument persuasive will have to take into account both the content of the argument and properties of the persons who are or are not persuaded by it, because arguments that some people find persuasive may be highly unpersuasive to others. Moreover, typically, persuasiveness is not an either-or state; it can vary in degree over the whole gamut from total lack of persuasiveness to persuasiveness bordering on proof.

Generally, one expects valid arguments with true premises to be more persuasive than invalid arguments, but it is easy to find exceptions to this rule.

- If John is in Europe, he is in Paris; John is not in Europe; therefore, he is not in Paris.

This is another example of the fallacy of *denying the antecedent* and, strictly speaking, the conclusion of the argument does not follow logically from the premises. Nevertheless, most people would, I surmise, find the argument to be persuasive and – assuming the second premise to be true – would take the conclusion to be true. Perhaps many would also consider it to be logically valid. The argument is an example of what we might call pragmatic inference, the rules of which are not clear. What is clear is that whether an argument that is composed of meaningful components is persuasive, or how persuasive it is, is likely to be greatly influenced by extralogical knowledge and beliefs that one brings to the task.

In this example, one might well accept the conclusion of the argument as true by means of a denial-of-the-antecedent error; but one also might accept it on the basis of the minor premise coupled with knowledge of a little geography, without reference to the major premise at all. If one knows that Paris is in Europe and is told that John is not in Europe, one can infer that John is not in Paris.

So, what makes an argument persuasive? When some people find an argument to be persuasive while others do not, it is not always easy – perhaps even possible – to tell who is in the right in such instances. A moment's reflection on the behavior of the United States Supreme Court makes the point. The Court hears about 130 cases a year; 80 with arguments and another 50 without. From 1995 to 2013 inclusive, the decision was unanimous on approximately 44 percent of the cases heard and split 5-to-4 on about 22 percent. Eric Posner (2014) discusses the interesting question of why the majority of decisions fall in one or the other of these categories, leaving only about one-third to be accounted for by the other six possibilities (8–1, 7–2, etc.) Why the court does not always reach a unanimous decision is an interesting question. All the justices are highly intelligent. All have had many years of experience with legal matters. All are intimately familiar with constitutional law. All have sworn to support and defend the US Constitution and to administer justice without respect to persons. Most importantly, considering only the cases that are heard, all the justices hear precisely the same arguments, pro and con, for each case.

What differs among justices is what they bring to the cases. Each comes with a unique life history, a particular interpretation of the constitution and its implications, a personal perspective on matters of justice, his/her own understanding of the relationship of the court to the other branches of government, and a political orientation, among other individuating characteristics. That the justices differ, sometimes heatedly, in their assessments of the arguments they hear is compelling evidence that the persuasiveness of an argument is as much a function of its hearer as of its substance.

If further evidence on this point is needed, other examples are easy to find, and perhaps nowhere easier than in reactions to arguments on opposite sides of controversial issues with political relevance. The ability of partisans to defend arguments with conclusions they like and to find flaws in those with conclusions they dislike is nothing short of phenomenal. Of course, one might say, this is neither surprising nor objectionable; presumably people hold the positions they do on controversial issues *because* they find the arguments that support them to be persuasive. But the fact that many intelligent people find arguments convincing that many other equally, intelligent people consider to be faulty is impressive and worthy of study.

Recognizing that people differ with respect to what they find to be persuasive does not abrogate the need to identify and understand the various factors that can be influential in determining whether an argument is likely to be persuasive at least to some substantive subset of the people to whom it is addressed. Some of the variables that appear likely to affect the persuasiveness of arguments to many people are noted in what follows. The variables fall roughly into two categories: properties of arguments and properties of arguers. Arguers include both persuaders and persuadees in Susan Kline's (1986) terms, or agents and targets in those of Marian Friestad and Peter Wright (1994).

Properties of Arguments

Validity of Form

As should be clear from the foregoing, logical validity does not ensure the persuasiveness of an argument, and logical invalidity does not preclude it, but it seems reasonable to expect valid arguments, other things equal, to be more persuasive than invalid arguments. However, judging the validity of an argument's form is often less straightforward than one might assume.

All A are B; all B are C; therefore, all A are C

is unquestionably a valid argument; if the premises are true, the conclusion is necessarily true, no matter what *A*, *B* and *C* represent.

Some A are B; some B are C; therefore, some A are C

may appear to be valid, but it is not. Although the premises and conclusion may all be true.

Some pets are dogs; some dogs shed hair; therefore, some pets shed hair.

It is easy to think of cases in which the premises are true and the conclusion is false.

Some cars are green; some green things are cucumbers; therefore, some cars are cucumbers.

But consider the argument

Most A are B; most B are C; therefore, most A are C.

By most definitions of validity as it pertains to deductive arguments, this argument would be considered invalid. But it is considerably more difficult to come up with meaningful examples of arguments in this form in which the premises are true and the conclusion is false. So, we should perhaps not be surprised to learn that people are likely to find arguments in this form, or the closely related form

Many A are B; many B are C; therefore, many A are C

to be relatively persuasive.

My sense is that arguments with indeterminate qualifiers – *some, many, most* – have not been studied very much. How people use them in argumentation – how they draw conclusions from premises containing them – is not, to my knowledge, well known. There is an opportunity for some interesting and useful research.

Relevance

Arne Naess (1966) contends that the evaluation of reasons that are given for accepting or rejecting a claim or point of view requires the consideration of two questions regarding each such reason: (1) is it tenable? and (2) is it relevant? Chapter 5 is addressed to the question of how people determine the plausibility – tenability to use Naess's term – of claims, such as those that comprise premises and conclusions of arguments. Of course, if a claim is considered untenable, the question of its relevance is moot. But the question of relevance is very much at issue for claims that are tenable, as is illustrated by the argument already noted involving the Amazon river and boron. The argument is perfectly valid, and its components – major premise, minor premise, and conclusion – are all true. If one accepts the premises as true, one is obliged to accept the conclusion, which follows from them, as true. But there is something radically wrong with the argument as a whole, and the problem is not hard to spot: there is no meaningful relationship between the antecedent and consequent of the major premise, and no clue as to what sanctions the premise's use as a reason for accepting the argument's conclusion. It seems to be irrelevant.

Relevance, like plausibility, is a matter of degree. It is apparent and strong in many cases, and – like the example just considered – obviously nonexistent in others. Perhaps in most instances of natural language arguments, it lies somewhere between these extremes.

Complexity

We should not be surprised to discover that how difficult it is to evaluate an argument depends in part on its complexity. Expressed opinions regarding what determines complexity have focused on such variables as the direction of inference (from antecedent to consequent vs. from consequent to antecedent), whether the argument contains negations, the argument's form (*modus ponens* versus *modus tollens*), among other considerations (Grosset & Barrouillet, 2003; Johnson-Laird & Byrne, 1991; Ormerod, Manktelow, & Jones, 1993). Arguments can vary greatly too in length and structure. Short simple arguments are likely to be easier to evaluate than long complicated arguments. We might expect too that, in general, formal arguments are likely to be easier to evaluate than informal ones, not only because they tend to be shorter, but also because the rules for evaluating them are better known and they have been more extensively studied for a longer time.

Associations

Advertisers understand that opinions and attitudes are molded, and behavior influenced, effectively by a great variety of techniques other than explicit argumentation regarding the merits of products. Such techniques include associating a product with the good life, glamorous people, adventure, health (seldom done by means of explicit claims but rather by showing products pictorially in settings that convey these associations), endorsements by celebrities or other well-known personalities, humor, memorable images, jingles, slogans, drama, human interest episodes – psychology has served advertising exceedingly well.

The effectiveness of promotion by association is attested to by the willingness of major corporations to sponsor popular events even when their ability to promote their products explicitly is severely limited by regulations. Cigarette advertising on electronic media has been prohibited by law in the United States since 1971. The prohibition does not preclude sponsorship of televised events by cigarette manufacturers. According to Carl Bartecchi, Thomas MacKenzie, and Robert Schrier (1995), "during the 93-minute broadcast of the 1989 Marlboro Grand Prix, the Marlboro name flashed on the screen or was mentioned by the announcers 5,933 times, for a total of 46 minutes. For 18 of those minutes, the Marlboro name was clear and in focus, which represents an estimated $1 million of commercial airtime" (p. 47).

Neal Postman (1985) also points out that modern advertising relies very little on the use of propositions, which is to say, it makes little use of assertions the truth, falsity, or plausibility of which can be evaluated.

> The truth or falsity of their [advertisers'] claims is simply not an issue. A MacDonald's commercial, for example, is not a series of testable, logically ordered assertions. It is a drama, a mythology, if you will, of handsome people selling, buying, and eating hamburgers, and being driven to near ecstasy by their good fortune. Is this a claim? Is this true or false? I submit that such questions do not apply to the world of visual images. One can like or dislike a television advertisement, but one cannot refute it (p. 5).

Postman makes similar observations regarding the use of visual media for political purposes. "In the age of TV, the ideas of political leaders are not, for the most part, expressed in the form of subjects and predicates and therefore are not susceptible either to refutation or logical analysis, any more than are MacDonald's commercials" (p. 5). Again,

> what I am saying is that exposition, explanation, and argument – the instruments of rational discourse – are less and less used as a means of expressing political ideas, and therefore the traditional means of educating people in critical thinking are less and less relevant .... In the political domain, as well as in other arenas of public discourse – religion and commerce, for example – Americans no longer talk to each other; they entertain each other. They do not exchange ideas; they exchange images (p. 5.)

The emergence and pervasive influence of visual media, especially television, represents a formidable challenge, in Postman's view, to educators who are concerned with critical thinking.

> We are no longer talking about providing students with technical apparatus with which they can uncover the unwarranted assumption, the carelessly expressed fact, the logical mishap, or even the demographic generalization. We are talking about how to help students protect themselves and their culture from a new kind of epistemology, a new kind of discourse – indeed, from a culture on the verge of amusing itself to death (p 8).

As one way of meeting this challenge, Postman recommends efforts to help students understand how media control the form, distribution, and direction of information and how this affects people's cognitive habits, beliefs, and social relations. The suggestion, in other words, is that an important objective of education should be to make students aware of the various ways in which media are used to mold opinions and influence behavior, many, if not most, of which have little to do with argument in the conventional sense, but, like argument, are aimed at influencing beliefs and behavior.

It has been more than thirty years since Postman made these observations; my sense is that, with the arrival of social media and other developments in communication technology, they are probably more relevant today than when he made them. I believe the importance of Postman's point regarding education would be difficult to overstate, and that the need for a better understanding of how beliefs and behavior can be, and are, influenced by mass media applies not only to students but to all of us. Although given evidence that, as of 1990, the average American eighth grader spent more than three hours a day watching commercial television (Hafner et al., 1990), the importance of the question of the effect of this medium on the thinking of school children is obvious. Attitudes, opinions, perspectives, values, ambitions are shaped in countless ways. Styles and fashions are set. We are told, or shown, what we should want, or what we must have, if we are to view ourselves as experiencing the good life. What is presented as normal becomes the norm. I am not suggesting that the influence of the media is all bad; the question of whether, on balance, we are better or worse as a consequence of this influence is independent of the point I am making. My point is simply that the influence is great and that we are, for the most part, oblivious to it. The emergence of social media has only complicated the picture.

In an engaging account of the beginnings of electric communication technologies in the late nineteenth century, Carolyn Marvin (1988) argues that "the early history of electric media is less the evolution of technical efficiencies in communication than a series of arenas for negotiating issues crucial to the conduct of social life; among them, who is inside and outside, who may speak, who may not, and who has authority and may be believed" (p. 4). Access to, and control of, communication media provide the power to influence the thinking and behavior of masses of people in both obvious and not-so-obvious ways. In my view it is essential to the survival of democracy that such access and control be widely distributed and not concentrated in a few hands and that thinking people pay attention to how the media shape opinions, attitudes, and behavior.

Cosmetics/Appearances

The persuasiveness of an argument may depend not only on its content and logical form, but on more cosmetic aspects of the language in which it is expressed. "[W]e are naturally led to believe that a man is in the right when he speaks with grace, with ease, with gravity, with moderation, and with gentleness; and, on the contrary, that a man is in the wrong when he speaks harshly, or manifests anything of passion, acrimony, or presumption, in his actions and words" (Arnauld & Nicole, 1995, p. 52).

Dressing up an argument so it has the appearance of being scientific by using technical terms – what Jenifer Haard, Michael Slater, and Marilee Long (2004) refer to as "scientese" – or unnecessary images, or by claiming a scientific basis for assertions without citing specific evidence, can enhance its persuasiveness (Greene & Cahill, 2012; McCabe & Castel, 2008; Weisberg et al., 2008). Aner Tal and Brian Wansink (2014; see also Tal, 2015) found that even what they considered to be trivial cues to scientific status – inclusion of graphs or a chemical formula – were effective in increasing the persuasiveness of ads.

Many, if not most, words have synonyms, but seldom are synonyms interchangeable everywhere. Subtle, and not so subtle, differences in meaning and/or emotive effect can become apparent in different contexts. Perelman and Olbrechts-Tyteca (1969) stress the importance of an arguer's choice of terms as a determinant of the persuasiveness of arguments in which they appear. They give many examples of how a particular choice of words would get one reaction from one audience and a different one from another. They note too that the same point may be made in an approving, disapproving, or neutral way, and they illustrate many linguistic subtleties that can affect the persuasiveness of arguments. Even the use and placement of conjunctives may play some role.

> [S]uch expressions as "although," "in spite of," and "doubtless" indicate that one is making certain concessions, but their main function, depending particularly on their position in the phrase, is to show the degree of importance attached to what is conceded. With the help of these techniques [just described], the speaker can very effectively guide the hearer toward what he wants to get him to admit (p. 157).

Whether one uses a single or plural noun where either would be acceptable – the politician versus politicians; the doctor versus doctors – can make a difference.

Narrative

Melanie Green and Timothy Brock (2000) contend that many years of scholarship on persuasion have focused almost exclusively on advocacy and neglected narrative as a vehicle of persuasion, despite the fact – they claim it is a fact – that "in the experience of people everywhere, public narrative predominates over public advocacy: Novels, films, soap operas, music lyrics, stories in newspapers, magazines, TV, and radio command far more waking attention than do advertisements, sermons, editorials, billboards, and so forth. The power of narratives to change beliefs has never been doubted and has always been feared" (p. 701). The fear is seen in attempts to control public exposure to some narratives – incidents of book banning and other forms of censorship.

In discussing the role of narrative, some writers (Green & Brock, 2000) use the metaphor of transportation. The reader of (listener to, viewer of) a narrative (story) is said to be transported from his/her real world to the fictitious world of the narrative. According to transportation theory, while in the world of the narrative one's attitudes, beliefs, preferences, and so on may be influenced by events and experiences in that world, and the effects may be retained, to some degree, when one returns to the real world. Green and Brock's claim is that the persuasive power of narrative has been neglected as a focus of research despite that it is greater than that of advocacy (direct and explicit efforts to persuade) by far.

Green and Brock (2000) distinguish their Transportation Model from two other models of the persuasive effects of narrative: the Elaboration Likelihood Model (Petty & Cacioppo, 1981) and the Heuristic-Systematic Model (Chaiken, 1980). Cognitive elaboration, they contend, "leads to attitude change via logical consideration and evaluation of arguments, whereas transportation may lead to persuasion through other mechanisms" (p. 702).

Closely related to the suggested role of narrative in persuasion is that of causal models in efforts to predict future events. The idea is that, in trying to select among possible actions in a choice situation, people naturally consider what they see as likely outcomes of the various possibilities before them. This they do by constructing causal models of their options – imagining the unfolding of the consequences of specific choices (Green 2007; Green & McCloy, 2003; Sloman & Lagnado, 2005). Such models are said to be "run" mentally much like a video tape or CD is run in reality.

Explicit versus Implicit Conclusions

In making an argument for the purpose of influencing beliefs or behavior, one may state the argument in full, explicitly providing the argument's premises and its conclusion, or one may state only the premises, leaving it for the hearer to make the inference to the conclusion. Whether one of these approaches is generally more effective than the other and, if so, which is the more effective are questions that have received some attention from researchers. Carl Hovland and Wallace Mandell (1952), for example, found that explicitly providing the conclusion was considerably more effective in producing changes of opinion than leaving it for the hearer to infer.

In discussing this finding, Hovland et al. (1953) identify three factors that might help determine which approach is the more effective: kind of communicator, kind of audience (recipients), and kind of issue. Regarding the first factor, the idea is that explicit provision of a conclusion may be less effective if the argument's source is suspect in some way than if it is not. Regarding the audience, Hovland et al. surmise that its degree of sophistication with respect to the issue, as well as the personalities of its members (whether highly suggestible and prone to accept conclusions drawn by others, or the opposite), is likely to modulate the effect. As for the kind of issue, they suggest that the effect would also depend in part on the degree to which it is of primary concern to recipients, and on its complexity. "If it is easy to see the implications, it is not to be expected that the communicator's drawing the conclusion will make much difference. If, on the other hand, the issue is quite involved and the steps in drawing the conclusion from the premises are difficult, the advantage of having the conclusion drawn explicitly may be quite pronounced" (p. 104).

Many experiments have been done since those of Hovland and colleagues. Daniel O'Keefe (1997) did a meta-analytic review of several studies, each of which had people compare the persuasiveness of arguments that made their conclusions explicit with the same arguments that left their conclusions unstated. Although the results of individual studies were not entirely consistent, in the aggregate, subjects judged the arguments with explicit conclusions to be more persuasive than those whose conclusions were not stated.

O'Keefe (1997) points out that whereas explicitness is generally considered to be a desirable property of an argument, there is a perspective from which it can be seen as undesirable. It "enlarges the 'disagreement space,' in the sense that it puts more claims on the table for discussion – claims to which objections might be raised . . .. Each further articulation of an advocate's viewpoint invites closer scrutiny, counterargument, objection, rejection. Failing to be fully explicit might minimize the space for disagreement and thereby enhance persuasion" (p. 2). In short, whether explicitness is considered to be a desirable property of an argument depends on one's hopes for it to be accepted or to be rejected.

Plausibility of Premises

A time-honored and effective way to undermine an argument is to challenge the premises that imply, or support, its conclusion. Not surprisingly, experimentation has shown that reducing one's confidence that the grounds for a conclusion are true reduces one's confidence in the truth of the conclusion as well (Cummins, 1995; Politzer, 2005; Politzer & Carles, 2001). There is considerable evidence that how readily or strongly one will believe the conclusion of a causal conditional argument depends in part on the extent to which one is aware of possible alternative causes that would bring the conclusion about or of potential inhibitors or disablers that would prevent it (Beller & Kuhnmünch, 2007; Cummins, 1995; Cummins et al., 1991; De Neys, Schaeken, & d'Ydewalle, 2003a; Markovits & Potvin, 2001; Politzer, 2003). (For a brief review, see Nickerson, 2015, chapter 5). This being so, it may suffice in many cases simply to inform or remind one of the existence of inhibitors of an argument's conclusion to put its truth in doubt.

If the only reason one has for accepting the conclusion of a valid argument as true is the support for the conclusion that is provided by the argument's premises, then the extent to which one accepts the conclusion should depend on how plausible one finds the premises to be. If one is certain that the premises are true, one should accept the implied conclusion without reservation. If one is sure that one or more of the premises is false, one does well to be skeptical of the conclusion; however, as we have already noted, it is possible for an argument to have one or more false premises and nevertheless have a true conclusion.

> If 2 is an odd number, 9 is divisible by 3; 2 is an odd number; therefore 9 is divisible by 3.

The conclusion of this argument is true, despite the fact that (at least) one of the premises is false. If one is uncertain whether the premises are true or false, but gives them some degree of credence, one should consider the truth or falsity of the conclusion to be undetermined, and give it an amount of credence that is consistent with one's judgment of the likelihood that the premises are true. According to Rescher's (1976) plausibility theory – about which more in Chapter 5 – one of the principles used in evaluating arguments is that the plausibility of a conclusion should be determined by that of the argument's least plausible premise. The extent to which this, or similar, rules of thumb are descriptive of people's reasoning is not, to my knowledge, known. The question of what determines the plausibility of a claim – whether the conclusion of an argument or not – is the focus of Chapter 5.

Properties of Arguers

Originator/Source

Most arguments involve at least two people (although who can doubt that one can carry on an argument with oneself), who may alternately take the role of speaker and listener, writer and reader, or, more generally, originator or source and recipient or audience. It is not surprising that what one knows about the source of an argument is likely to affect the argument's persuasiveness.

Arguments made by people who are believed to be knowledgeable with respect to the subject at issue and trustworthy are more likely to be persuasive than are arguments made by people who are not believed to be knowledgeable or that are not considered to be trustworthy. The phenomenon is sometimes referred to as the *prestige effect* (Kulp, 1934; Lewis, 1941). However there is some evidence that skepticism regarding a source of information tends to subside over time so that originally untrusted information can become accepted and remembered as factual (Hovland & Weiss, 1951/1952).

People tend to be more easily persuaded by people to whom they are attracted than by people they dislike. Both attractiveness and persuasiveness appear to vary with the degree to which people perceive others to be similar to themselves (Brock, 1965). Francesca Gino, Jen Shang, and Rachel Croson (2009) found that people gave greater weight to advice from people who were similar to themselves than to advice from people who were dissimilar to themselves when the advice was for themselves but not when it was for others.

H. B. Lewis (1941) found that people were more likely to change an opinion in response to an argument if they initially agreed with the arguer's intentions than if they disagreed with them. Douglas Oxley, Arnold Vedlitz, and B. Dan Wood (2014) found that a persuasive negative message from a credible source can change attitudes about socially significant issues, such as global warming, the amount of the change depending on how credible the message's source is, the negativity of the message and the message recipient's political predisposition. Hovland et al. (1953) describe implications of some findings by T. N. Ewing this way. "In general, Ewing's results support the hypothesis that when a communication comes from an unknown or ambiguous source, acceptance will be increased if, at the beginning, the communicator explicitly claims that his own position is in accord with that held by the audience" (p. 27).

Recipient/Audience

The importance of the character of the audience, and of the proposer's knowledge of that character, as a determinant of an argument's persuasiveness has been emphasized by some writers. Perelman and Olbrechts-Tyteca (1969) stress the importance of an arguer's knowledge of whomever he or she wishes to persuade. "In argumentation, the important thing is not knowing what the speaker regards as true or important but knowing the views of those he is addressing" (p. 23). When one's audience is a collection of diverse people, the challenge is to express an argument so as to appeal to many views; Perelman and Olbrechts-Tyteca define a great orator as "one who possesses the art of taking into consideration, in his argumentation, the composite nature of his audience" (p. 21).

Perelman and Olbrechts-Tyteca (1969) distinguish three kinds of audience that play normative roles in determining the "convincing character" of arguments: the *universal audience* (all of humankind), a single *interlocutor* addressed in a dialog, and *oneself*. Inclusion of oneself as the third kind of audience illustrates a point stressed by these writers that much thinking, especially thinking about what to believe or how to act, is properly considered to be arguing with oneself. Presumably, in addressing the universal audience, one speaks to what one considers to be an average or typical person of normal intelligence and need not worry about individual differences. In arguing with a single person – or group that is distinctive in some way – individual differences become very important. It is harder to have a productive argument with some people – cynics, dogmatists, fanatics – than with others. Perelman and Olbrechts-Tyteca define a fanatic as "a person who adheres to a disputed thesis for which no unquestionable proof can be furnished, but who nevertheless refuses to consider the possibility of submitting it for free discussion and, consequently, rejects the preliminary conditions which would make it possible to engage in argumentation on this topic" (p. 62).

Relationship between Originator and Recipient

The relationship between the originator and recipient of an argument can vary in many ways: strength, polarity (friendliness, antagonism), rank (subordinate, superior), importance (great, little or none), and so on. Perceived power of the originator relative to that of the recipient has long been recognized as an important contributor to the persuasiveness of an argument (Briñol & Petty, 2012), although exactly how the relationship works is a matter of continuing research and debate (Briñol et al., 2007; Briñol et al., 2018; Galinsky, Rucker, & Magee, 2015; Guinote & Vescio, 2010). The problem is that the effect of power on persuasiveness is usually, but not always, positive (increasing persuasiveness); it sometimes has a negative effect (Briñol et al., 2007; Dubois, Rucker, & Galinsky, 2016). The question of how power relates to persuasiveness has been a focus of research for some time (Petty & Cacioppo, 1984, 1986), and continues to be so (Briñol et al., 2018; Dubois et al., 2016; Guinote & Vescio, 2010).

Domain Knowledge and General Intelligence

An important aspect of the understanding of informal arguments is the need to go beyond the information contained in the argument itself. It is often the case that the most compelling reasons for rejecting an argument are found in what could have been said but was not. For this reason, it is useful in analyzing arguments to attempt to make explicit those relevant facts that were left unstated. It may be especially useful to attempt to explicate any facts that are inconsistent with the conclusion drawn, which is to say, to attempt to construct a counterargument. The ability to do this will depend greatly on one's knowledge of the domain. It is perhaps here, in the realm of counterargument construction, that reasoning in argumentation is most knowledge dependent. It is here too that one's metaknowledge – one's awareness of the extent and limitations of one's own knowledge of a domain – is especially important.

Kuhn (1991) did a study of argumentation "to examine how people reason about real, complex issues of genuine importance, issues they are likely to have occasion to think and talk about in their own everyday experience" (p. 264). Her method was to ask domain experts their beliefs/opinions about the causes of three socially significant problem areas: criminal recidivism (What causes prisoners to return to crime, after they're released?), failure in school (What causes children to fail in school?), and unemployment (What causes unemployment?).

Regarding the role of domain knowledge in determining one's ability to judge the quality of domain-specific arguments, Kuhn concludes from the data collected from domain experts and non-experts that "small but consistent differences have appeared in performance across topics, with subjects showing slightly better argumentative reasoning to the degree that they have personal experience related to the topic. Still the variation, in both the degree of personal experience and resulting performance is not great" (p. 240). How much, if at all, familiarity with the topic affected people's performance varied somewhat with the topic and the area of subjects' expertise. Parole officers, for example, showed no superiority in reasoning about crime recidivism relative to their reasoning about topics other than crime, and a similar finding was obtained with teachers when reasoning about causes of failure in schools and other topics. The conclusion: "expertise with respect to a content area may expand the amount of knowledge that is available, but it does not necessarily enhance the forms of reasoning that are used" (p. 262). Kuhn concludes also, however, on the basis of the same data, that "there are forms of reasoning that transcend the particular content and context in which they are manifested" (p. 263). In short, Kuhn recognizes the roles of both domain-specific knowledge and domain-independent reasoning as determinants of effectiveness of argumentation.

Kuhn notes, too, that participants in her study generally expressed higher levels of certainty with their causal explanations than the explanations justified. "[P]eople confidently 'know' the answers to our questions, but in the naïve sense of never having contemplated that the answers could be otherwise" (p. 265). The receipt of new information, including information that was inconsistent with participants' explanations, seldom changed their views.

> In our examination of how people interpret new information related to their theories, we find a prevalent, and disturbing, tendency to assimilate any new information to existing theories. Whether the information is meager and nonsuggestive as to causal explanation or points to an overdetermining set of causes, people tend to assimilate it in terms of the "this pretty much goes along with my own view" reaction .... Moreover, just as they report a high degree of certainty regarding the correctness of their own causal theories, they express considerable certainty that new evidence they are asked to evaluate supports these theories (p. 268).

All very much in keeping with the idea of a prevailing confirmation bias (Nickerson, 1998). Kuhn reports also that people in her study generally were more adept at generating counterarguments to others' causal theories than at generating counterarguments to their own.

People who are relatively well informed on a subject are likely to find two-sided arguments regarding that subject more persuasive than one-sided arguments (McCroskey, Young, & Scott, 1972; McGuire, 1964). People who are knowledgeable on the subject are likely to be able to think of counterarguments, and the presenter of an argument who fails to acknowledge that such counterarguments exist risks being seen either as lacking relevant knowledge or as being disingenuous.

Hovland, Arther Lumsdaine, and Fred Sheffield (1949) found the degree to which a two-sided argument was more effective than a one-sided argument in modifying recipients' opinions in the direction of the argument's conclusion to be greater for better-educated than for less-well-educated people. They also found change of opinion in the direction of an argument's conclusion to be greater when the conclusion was consistent with their preexisting beliefs than when it was not. Hovland et al. summarize their findings regarding the relative effectiveness of one- and two-sided arguments in changing of opinions as follows:

1. A two-sided presentation is *more* effective in the long run than a one-sided one *a*) when, regardless of initial opinion, the audience is *exposed* to subsequent counterpropaganda, or *b*) when, regardless of subsequent exposure to counterpropaganda, the audience initially *disagrees* with the commentator's position.
2. A two-sided presentation is *less* effective than a one-sided one if the audience initially *agrees* with the commentator's position and *is not exposed* to later counterpropaganda (p. 110).

O'Keefe (1999), citing Hovland et al. (1949), Cornelia Pechmann (1990), and Robert Settle and Linda Golden (1974) notes that "It is commonly speculated . . . that acknowledging opposing arguments may, by suggesting the communicator's honesty and lack of bias, boost the communicator's credibility and thereby the message's effectiveness" (p. 210). Of course, there is the possibility that, at least in some instances, the appearance of honesty and lack of bias is appearance only, as when opposing arguments are intentionally misrepresented.

With respect to two-sided arguments, O'Keefe (1999) makes a distinction between refutational and non-refutational cases.

> A *refutational* two-sided message attempts to refute opposing arguments in some fashion; this might involve attacking the plausibility of opposing claims, criticizing the reasoning underlying opposing arguments, offering evidence that is shown to undermine opposing claims, and so forth. A *non-refutational* two-sided message acknowledges the opposing considerations but does not attempt to refute them directly; it might suggest that the positive supporting arguments outweigh the opposing ones, but it does not directly refute the opposing arguments (p. 211).

Citing Mike Allen (1991, 1994), Ayn Crowley and Wayne Hoyer (1994), and Sally Jackson and Allen (1987), O'Keefe reports that previous discussions of the relationship between sidedness and refutation have tended to support the view that "sidedness effects may vary significantly depending upon whether the opposing arguments are refuted" (p. 211). More specifically, the suggestion is that two-sided arguments are more persuasive than one-sided arguments if they are refutational, but not necessarily so if they are not.

O'Keefe (1999) did another meta-analytic review, this time of studies of the effects of one- and two-sided arguments. The results supported the view that "Refutational two-sided messages do appear to enjoy a persuasive advantage (over one-sided messages) that non-refutational two-sided messages do not" (p. 231). O'Keefe's analysis did not show effects of several variables – "initial audience attitude, audience education, counterargument availability, and order of arguments" – that had been mentioned in attempts to account for effects of sidedness on the persuasiveness of arguments.

Knowledge can affect argument evaluation also by influencing the amount of effort one puts into the evaluation. People appear to be likely to devote more time to evaluate conclusions that are inconsistent with their beliefs than to evaluate conclusions that are consistent with them (Edwards & Smith, 1996). This is in keeping with the idea that people are likely to be less critical of arguments that yield conclusions they believe to be true than of arguments that yield conclusions they believe to be false (Henle & Michael, 1956; Janis & Frick, 1943; Klaczynski & Robinson, 2000; Morgan & Morton, 1944). Kevin Barton, Jonathan Fugelsang, and Daniel Smilek (2009) have presented evidence that people's processing of statistical data is likely to differ depending on whether the data pertain to content about which they are knowledgeable.

How susceptibility to opinion change from argumentation relates to general intelligence is not clear. In a review of the literature up to the time of their writing, Gardner Murphy, Lois Murphy, and Theodore Newcomb (1937) reported little or no correlation between intelligence and susceptibility to propaganda. Later, Hovland et al. (1953) noted that subsequent investigations "indicate that there are positive correlations for some persuasive communications and negative correlations for others, depending upon the types of arguments and appeals that are used" (p. 181). Hovland et al. mention studies by Henry Wegrocki (1934) and Hovland et al. (1949) as finding negative and positive correlations, respectively, between intelligence and susceptibility to persuasion. They summarize what can be inferred from these studies as two hypotheses:

1. Persons with high intelligence will tend – mainly because of their ability to draw valid inferences – to be *more* influenced than those with low intellectual ability when exposed to persuasive communications which rely primarily on impressive logical arguments.
2. Persons with high intelligence will tend – mainly because of their superior critical ability – to be *less* influenced than those with low intelligence when exposed to persuasive communications which rely primarily on unsupported generalities or false, illogical, irrelevant argumentation (p. 183).

Citing Nico Voigtländer and Hans-Joachim Voth (2015) among others, Hugo Mercier (2017) contends that a major determinant of the success of propaganda is the extent to which its content fits the target's preexisting beliefs. "[I]t can be argued that when propaganda efforts do succeed, it is because propagandists have tailored their messages to the beliefs and preferences of the population" (p. 112).

The role of general intelligence as a determinant of performance on inference tasks remains a topic of considerable interest. Perhaps the safest conclusion coming from experimental work on the question is that performance correlates with intelligence on some inference tasks and not on others. Nina Attridge and Mathews Inglis (2014), for example, found positive (though small) correlations between intelligence and performance on conditional reasoning tasks involving denial of the antecedent or affirmation of the consequent, but not on tasks involving *modus tollens*. They note that this result replicates those of Newstead et al. (2004).

Feelings/Mood/Attitude

Who can doubt that one's mood can affect one's thinking, and that one's thinking can affect one's mood? If scientific evidence of the fact is needed, there is plenty of it. Research on consumer behavior has shown that the weight consumers attach to information about a product is greater if that information is consistent with their mood when it is received than if it is not (Clore, Schwarz, & Conway, 1994; Cohen & Areni, 1991; Gorn, Goldberg, & Basu, 1993). Rashmi Adaval (2001) attributes the phenomenon to an affect-confirmation process: "consumers might give a piece of information more weight when its evaluative implications are similar in valence to affect they are experiencing for other reasons" (p. 1).

Adaval presents data from a series of experiments in support of the hypothesis and offers a model of how the process works. She argues that the model not only accounts for data on consumer behavior but provides an alternative to memory-based explanations of affect effects on judgment in other contexts studied by Gordon Bower (1981), Joseph Forgas (1995) and Alice Isen et al. (1978) as well. Memory-based explanations of affect effects hold that mood facilitates the retrieval of memories that evoke the same mood as do the immediate circumstances.

Joseph Cesario and colleagues provide evidence that nonverbal cues about a message source can enhance the persuasiveness of a message if they reveal the source's perspective to be similar to that of the recipient (Cesario, 2006; Cesario, Grant, & Higgins, 2004; Cesario & Higgins, 2008; Cesario, Higgins, & Scholer, 2008). "We propose that when the nonverbal cues of a message source sustain the motivational orientation of the recipient, the recipient experiences regulatory fit and feels right, and that this experience influences the message's effectiveness" (Cesario & Higgins, 2008, p. 415).

There is considerable evidence that people often make judgments or decisions largely on the basis of their feelings about a situation (Avnet, Pham, & Stephen, 2012: Cohen, Pham, & Andrade, 2008; Greifeneder, Bless, & Pham, 2011; Schwarz, 2007), especially if they have little else to guide them, or they lack the time or ability to process other relevant information (Albarracin & Kumkale, 2003; Albarracin & Wyer, 2001). Avnet et al. (2012) suggest that the extent to which people base judgments or decisions on feelings depends on three factors, the first two of which are well documented and the third of which they propose on the basis of their own recent findings.

The first two factors are the degree to which feelings are believed to be representative of the target of evaluation – "when they are perceived to emanate from the target and reflect its essential characteristics (Pham, 2009)" – and the degree to which they are considered to be relevant to the judgment being made (Pham, 1998). When these factors pertain, feelings are said to be more reliable indicators of the judgments or decisions that should be made than when they do not (Schwarz & Clore, 1983, 2007).

The third factor that Avnet et al. identify, and for which they present experimental data, is the amount of trust that people have in the general reliability of their feelings. Unlike the first two factors, which might be considered invariant across people, the third one would be expected to differ from individual to individual. As they put it, "Some individuals may believe that their feelings are generally 'trustworthy' in that their feelings usually point in the 'right' direction in judgments and decisions (resulting in better outcomes or higher judgment satisfaction); other individuals may believe that their feelings are generally 'untrustworthy'" (p. 722). As to why people would be expected to differ with respect to how trustworthy they consider their feelings to be, Avnet et al. suggest that this could be due, in part, to differences in their personal histories of success or failure when relying on their feelings and, in part, on differences in the social and cultural environments in which people find themselves. They emphasize that the concept of trust in feelings they have in mind is not a function of the representativeness and relevance of those feelings, but independent of them; it is a property of individuals and not of situations.

Emilie Falk et al. (2010) report findings from an MRI study that they believe to be the first of its kind in showing the activation of neurocognitive processes at the moment that persuasion occurs. Their summary, in brief: "Neural activations associated with feeling persuaded were almost exclusively, and repeatedly, associated with a neural network involved in mentalizing and perspective taking" (p. 2458). Essentially the same results were obtained whether the arguments were presented as text or as video-based commercials, and with participants from different cultural backgrounds.

That attitudes – toward sources, content, contexts – can affect the persuasiveness of arguments has been noted several times in the foregoing. We should note too that the cause-effect relationship can go in the other direction as well: persuasive arguments can affect attitudes.

Expectations

There is much evidence that expectations can influence the persuasiveness of arguments. On the basis of research they reviewed, Hovland et al. (1953) identified three types of expectations that could increase or decrease the acceptance of an argument: "1) expectations of being 'right' or 'wrong;' 2) expectations of being impartially advised, or of being manipulated by the communicator; 3) expectations of being approved or disapproved by others" (p. 293).

Some of the more recent evidence of the influence of expectations on persuasiveness of arguments comes from studies of interrogation techniques that are often used in criminal investigations. The findings of these studies are very important, in view of the well-established fact that interrogations have sometimes elicited confessions from innocent parties (Gudjonsson, 2003; Kassin & Gudjonsson, 2004; Leo & Ofshe, 1998; Scheck, Neufeld, & Dwyer, 2000; White, 2003). Especially troublesome is the frequency of false confessions by adolescent suspects during interrogation (Kassin et al., 2010; Malloy, Schulman, & Cauffman, 2014).

Wrongful convictions have occurred many times, even in capital cases resulting in the death penalty (Radelet, Bedau, & Putnam, 1992; Rattner, 1988; Servick, 2016; Starr, 2016). Death penalties have been decided solely on the basis of confessions that proved later to be false (Drizin & Leo, 2004).

Saul Kassin, Cristine Goldstein, and Kenneth Savitsky (2003) describe an interrogation as "a theory-driven social interaction led by an authority figure who holds a strong a priori belief about the target and who measures success by his or her ability to extract an admission from that target" (p. 189). Acknowledging the belief "that police interrogations are persuasive, and at times too persuasive, in part because they are theory-driven social interactions founded upon a presumption of guilt" (p. 188), these investigators demonstrated the importance of expectations and the ease with which they can be influenced. They manipulated the expectations of student interrogators in a mock criminal interrogation by telling them either that four out of five (guilty expectation) or one out of five (innocent expectation) suspects actually committed the crime. Kassin et al. also gave participants two conflicting goals: "(1) to secure a confession, and (2) to make an accurate determination of the suspect's guilt or innocence" (p. 191). They had student interrogators select six questions from a list of twelve possibilities that they would elect to ask a suspect. Six of the twelve were guilt presumptive and six were not. In another manipulation, they had participants select six from thirteen possible interrogation techniques.

> Among the techniques included were making repeated accusations, exposing inconsistencies in the suspect's story, threatening to involve others, appealing to the suspect's self-interest, promising an end to questioning or leniency in consequences, appealing to the suspect's religious or moral character, offering sympathy and understanding, presenting false evidence, overplaying the seriousness of the offense, and minimizing the seriousness of the offense (e.g., by suggesting it was accidental, spontaneous, or provoked) (p. 191).

The participants' task was to determine, by interrogating suspects, whether they had committed a mock crime. Half of the suspects had done so and the other half had not (and did not know the specifics of it). Interrogators who had been prompted to assume guilt selected more guilt-presumptive questions than did interrogators who had been prompted to assume innocence. In general, interrogators were not effective in distinguishing between innocence and guilt, but interrogators prompted to assume guilt made somewhat more guilty judgments than did those prompted to assume innocence.

Kassin et al. (2003) tape recorded the interrogation sessions and had observers listen either to the interrogators' questions or the suspects' answers (not both) and to make judgments regarding each suspect: whether he/she was guilty or innocent, whether the interrogator had judged him/her to be guilty or innocent, the degree to which the interrogator presumed the suspect's guilt at the outset, how hard the interrogator had tried to get a confession, and so on. In brief, the results generally supported the hypothesis that presumption of guilt affected interrogations and in ways that were observable in the behavior of both interrogators and suspects. Kassin et al. (2003) summarize their findings this way.

> Interrogators with guilty expectations chose more guilt-presumptive questions, used more techniques in their interrogation (including the presentation of false evidence and promises of leniency) and were more likely to see suspects in incriminating terms, exhibiting a 23% increase in guilty judgments relative to those with innocence expectations. The suspect's actual guilt or innocence had a paradoxical and particularly disturbing effect on interrogators, leading them to exert the most pressure on innocent suspects. A presumption of guilt triggered aggressive interrogations, which constrained the behavior of suspects and led others to infer their guilt – thus confirming the initial presumption (p. 199).

Worthy of special notice among their results is the finding that guilt-presumptive interrogators were especially hard on innocent suspects. It appears that guilt-presumptive interrogators interpreted plausible denials from innocent suspects as "proof of a guilty person's resistance" and this caused them to increase their efforts to get a confession. In short, advice regarding how to obtain confessions from suspects in criminal cases sometimes promotes techniques that may increase the likelihood of obtaining confessions not only from guilty parties but from innocent ones as well (Kassin et al., 2003; Meissner & Kassin, 2002). This is especially worrisome in view of the persuasive power of confessions, sometimes even if coerced or retracted (Greitemeyer, 2014; Kassin & Sukel, 1997; Wallace & Kassin, 2012).

Fred Inbau et al. (2001) note that a criminal interrogation is conducted only if the investigator is reasonably certain that the suspect is guilty. The reasonable certainty may be based on a suspect's demeanor and interaction during a preliminary interview. It is not difficult to imagine that an interrogator, working on the assumption of guilt, is likely to seek evidence to corroborate the assumption, and not evidence that would prove the assumption to be false. Further, by virtue of conducting an interrogation, an investigator is making his/her assumption known to colleagues and thereby acquires an additional incentive to prove the assumption to be correct – to safeguard or bolster his/her reputation as an astute law-enforcement official.

It seems reasonable to expect that the ability to detect deception would increase with experience; however, evidence that this is the case appears to be lacking in the relevant literature. Bella DePaulo and Roger Pfeifer (1986) investigated the relationship between amount of on-the-job experience and skill at detecting deception. They compared the performance on deception detection tests of undergraduates with no experience, recruits in a law-enforcement training program with limited on-the-job experience, and law-enforcement officers with years of experience. Experienced officers expressed more confidence in their judgments than did the students, but their judgments were no more accurate. In a subsequent review of the literature, Ray Bull (1989) found no evidence of a positive effect of training on the ability to detect deception, despite claims or insinuations in police recruitment ads or training books to the contrary.

More recently, Kassin and Christina Fong (1999) had students, some of whom had been trained in the analysis of verbal and nonverbal deception cues and others of whom had not, make judgments of suspects in mock crimes. Detection performance was generally low. Participants who had received the training expressed more confidence in their judgments, and gave more reasons for them, than did those who had not received it, but they actually did more poorly in detecting deception by perpetrators. Kassin and Fong point to DePaulo et al. (1997) as further evidence that people are not very good at evaluating their own lie-detector skills.

Contending that there is little hard evidence to support the assumption that investigators can make accurate judgments of truth and deception on the basis of verbal and nonverbal behavioral cues, Christian Meissner and Saul Kassin (2002) did an experiment similar to that of Kassin and Fong (1999), but with veteran investigators rather than college students. Students (in Kassin and Fong's experiment) were less confident of their guilty/innocent judgments than were the bona fide investigators (in Meissner and Kassin's), but the two groups did not differ in overall accuracy in identifying truthful and deceitful suspects (of committing a mock crime).

Meissner and Kassin (2002) noted that very few studies had compared deception detection with both truthful and deceitful target persons, and none had explicitly applied signal-detection analyses. The point of this observation is that without knowing both the hit rate (detection of deception) and false alarm rate (judging truthfulness as deception), the effectiveness of interrogations cannot be determined. Meissner and Kassin (2002) subjected data from six experiments to a signal-detection analysis. Four of the experiments examined the influence of experience and two the influence of training. They summarized the results of the analysis as follows. "[A]cross studies, both training and prior experience engendered a more liberal response criterion (i.e., a bias toward responding 'deceitful') when compared to participants in the no-training and no-experience control conditions. In contrast to what might have been expected, however, training and experience had no significant effect on participants' ability to accurately discriminate truth from deceit" (p. 472). Investigators produced both more hits and more false alarms than did the students. Correlation analyses revealed no relation between years in law enforcement and accuracy of guilt-innocent judgments, but a significant correlation between amount of prior experience and both false alarm responses and likelihood of responding "deceit." Meissner and Kassin express concern that "if investigators are truly biased toward deception (or guilt) in their initial judgments, then preinterrogation interviews could prompt the subsequent use of strong, pressure-filled methods of interrogation that, in turn, could increase the risk of coerced false confessions" (p. 473).

Preferences

Fisher (2004) takes the position that in order to evaluate an argument in support of a particular conclusion, one should be able to say, in advance of seeing the argument, what would provide good support for that conclusion. One should start any attempt at argument evaluation, he suggests, with the Assertibility Question: "What argument or evidence would justify me in asserting the conclusion? (What would I have to know or believe to be justified in accepting it?)" (p. 27). The philosophical justification for the use of this question, which should be especially helpful whenever one has difficulty seeing clearly the arguer's intentions, is the assumption: "If you understand a proposition you must be able to give at least some account of how you could decide whether it was true or false, what argument would show it to be true or false (otherwise you don't understand it at all)" (p. 23).

The suggestion seems apt. However, it needs to be tempered with realization that one's ability to specify reasonable criteria for acceptance of a conclusion may be severely constrained by one's limited knowledge of the subject to which the conclusion pertains. Moreover, what one decides would provide good support for a conclusion could be subject to bias of one sort or another; in particular, what I will consider necessary to justify a conclusion may be less demanding if the conclusion is one I like than if it is one I dislike. Given the role that people's preferences have been shown to play in determining the plausibility of claims (Lefford, 1946; Matlin & Stang, 1978; McGuire, 1960; Weinstein, 1989), it would be remarkable if they were not instrumental determinants of the persuasiveness of arguments as well.

Personalities/Predispositions

Undoubtedly, people's personalities differ in many respects that have implications for how they evaluate arguments. People who are inherently inquisitive and critical are likely to demand more from an argument before accepting it than people who are less critical and more trusting. Some studies have supported the idea of a causal connection between susceptibility to persuasion and such negative personality traits as feelings of social inadequacy and depression (Janis, 1954; Robinson, 1941).

More than sixty years ago, Hovland et al. (1953) suggested that there probably are personality traits that make uncritical acceptance of arguments more likely and others that make them less so. "Persons who are relatively low in ability to engage in critical thinking, to discern fallacious arguments, and to discount propagandistic devices would tend to be highly gullible, readily accepting conclusions that others with a higher level of critical ability would tend to reject" (p. 289). In contrast, "a variety of personality tendencies, such as generalized suspiciousness, might be found to have an inhibiting effect on acceptance" (p. 289). More recently, the concept of personality signatures has emerged according to which the ways in which people react to specific situations are indicated by sets of *if-then* rules that reflect personality traits (Bonnefon, 2010; Mischel, 2004).

Omar Shehryar and David Hunt (2005) found evidence that how people reacted to messages regarding drinking and driving depended on both their preexisting attitude about drinking and the specifics of the messages involved. Participants who were committed to a worldview of drinking alcohol rejected messages projecting socially acceptable attitudes toward drinking and driving when the messages appealed to fear of death but not when they appealed to fear of arrest or serious injury.

Maferima Touré-Tillery and Ann McGill (2015) found that whether advertisements read by people were preferred to those delivered by "anthropomorphized agents" – talking products – depended in part on the listeners' trustfulness. People low in level of interpersonal trust were more persuaded by talking products than by spokespeople, whereas people high in interpersonal trust were indifferent to the two sources. The investigators argue that people with low interpersonal trust are generally more attentive to the source than are those with high interpersonal trust and tend to suspect that humans are more lacking in goodwill than anthropomorphized agents. When induced to be attentive, people with high interpersonal trust tended to find human-delivered messages to be more persuasive than those delivered by non-human agents. When conditions were such as to encourage low attentiveness by all participants, the source of the messages was moot.

Psychological Factors and Individual Differences

As noted several times in the foregoing, the purpose of persuasion generally is to change the status quo in some fashion – to convince someone to believe or do something that, in the absence of the attempt to persuade, one typically would not be inclined to believe or do. It is to be expected that how difficult it will be to effect a desired change will depend, in part, on how committed one is to an existing belief that is the target for modification or how resistant one's habitual behavior is to modification. There are many other psychological factors that are likely to play significant roles in determining what different individuals will find to be persuasive.

Susan Kline (1986) identifies several variables that she describes as related to the identities – self-images – of the arguers that can hinder the resolution of disputes. These include lack of respect shown for, or by, one's opponent, concern about appearing to be inconsistent if one changes one's view, competing tendencies for competition and cooperation, lack of knowledge of one's opponent's beliefs and other attributes, and inability to get an opponent to grant one's position even if the argument has shown it to be justified.

Citing work of Erving Goffman (1967), Bert Brown (1968, 1970), and Penelopy Brown and Stephen Levinson (1978), Kline points out the importance that people attach to being liked and well thought of by others and the role that face-saving can play in interactions among people. She contends that maintaining one's image can be difficult in argumentation, "because disagreeing and defending one's views are intrinsically face-threatening" (p. 244). People cope with the threat of losing face in a variety of ways, Kline suggests: "Arguers may decide to avoid disagreeing entirely, and thereby prevent any face loss, they may decide to argue for their views directly, to maximize clarity and efficiency, or they may present their views indirectly, or with specific politeness strategies to redress their opponent's face loss" (p. 244). Successful persuaders, Kline contends, are aware of the psychological hindrances to effective argumentation and have ways of addressing them: "Successful persuaders also argue that their proposal is consistent with the persuadee's values, is socially pleasant, and easy for the persuadee to do" (p. 244).

People may treat arguments differently depending on whether they are made by members of groups to which they themselves belong. Diane Mackie and colleagues, for example, found that people are likely to be persuaded by strong arguments made by in-group members although not by weak arguments made by in-group members, but to be relatively unmoved by arguments made by people outside the group, independently of their strength (Mackie, Gastardo-Conaco, & Skelly, 1992; Mackie, Worth, & Asuncion, 1990).

Hovland et al. (1953) suggest that the pressure for conformity that one is likely to experience as a member of a group depends on the importance one attaches to one's membership in the group and the level of esteem one attributes to other members.

> The more highly esteemed the other members, the greater are the satisfactions derived from adopting their opinions and values. The more important is the group as a refuge from external dangers, the more powerful become any threats of exclusion and, other things being equal, the closer the conformity. Thus, the more strongly the person is motivated to maintain membership in a group, the greater will be his behavioral conformity to its norms, and, at least under some circumstances, the more conforming will be his *opinions* (p. 138).

Hovland et al. cite Leon Festinger, Stanley Schacter, and Kurt Back (1950) and Back (1951) as evidence of effects of group membership on members' beliefs and opinions and of the importance of members' valuation of their membership as a determinant of degree of compliance.

> [T]he available evidence seems to indicate that the more highly a person values his membership in a group the more closely will his opinions and attitudes conform to the consensus within the group. The implication of this phenomenon is that the person who places high value on the group is highly influenced by communications from other members, particularly with respect to issues about which he believes the group to have norms (p. 149).

Hovland et al. also note evidence that people who highly value their group membership are less likely to be influenced by opinions that are contrary to group norms than are those whose group membership is not so highly valued. They cite Herbert Barry, Jr. (1931) as a source of evidence that susceptibility to social influence may be inversely correlated with aggressiveness toward others.

Persuasion Knowledge

As we have noted, there are many factors that contribute to the persuasiveness of arguments; it would be surprising if people did not learn from experience what at least some of them are and how they work. However, Friestad and Wright (1994) note that, surprisingly, theories of persuasion have neglected what they call *persuasion knowledge.* They propose a model – the Persuasion Knowledge Model (PKM) – of how such knowledge influences people's responses to efforts to persuade them to believe or do something. They contend that for a theory of persuasion to be complete, it must explain "how people develop persuasion knowledge, how persuasion knowledge is used in various types of persuasion episodes, and how changes in that knowledge alter what occurs" (p. 1). They refer to persons to whom persuasion is directed as targets and to those who are doing the persuading (which could be individuals or corporate entities) as agents. The PKM recognizes three types of knowledge that, from a target's perspective, are topic knowledge, persuasion knowledge, and agent knowledge; from an agent's perspective, the three types of knowledge are topic knowledge, persuasion knowledge, and target knowledge. Of course, agents use their knowledge to try to persuade, and targets use theirs to cope with such attempts – to resist them if they wish to do so. A person can be a target on some occasions and an agent on others and can switch between roles even in the course of a single argumentative encounter.

Friestad and Wright suggest that persuasion knowledge is acquired via personal experience throughout one's lifetime, and increases during childhood and adolescence in synchrony with increases in information-processing capabilities and awareness of the possibility of persuasion, which they describe as "the strategic presentation of information so as to influence people's beliefs and thereby their behavior" (p. 6). The motivation to learn how to cope with persuasion attempts (e.g., by marketers among others) should increase, they argue, throughout life, "because the variety of everyday tasks in which persuasion knowledge is valuable increases" (p. 6).

Friestad and Wright discuss at length several aspects and implications of their PKM model and compare it to other theoretical accounts of persuasion, notably the Elaboration Likelihood Model of Richard Petty and John Cacioppo (1986) and the Heuristic-Systematic Model of Shelly Chaiken (1987). They contend that past theorizing about persuasion knowledge has focused primarily on the connection between the *persuasion episode* (an incidence of attempt to persuade) and topic knowledge or attitude: "the existing theories have tried to explain how what happens in a single episode, or repeated episodes in which message content is held constant, influence audience members' topic beliefs and feelings" (p. 26). They argue that their PKM shows that the potential for empirical research and theory development is broader than that, and that the perspective of their model should be of special interest to consumer researchers "because coping with marketers' influence attempts is a central part of being a consumer. After all, the marketer is a known persuasion agent, so that among all types of social interactions the marketplace is a context in which people are apt to be using persuasion knowledge" (p. 26).

Promoted Reflection

The ability, and willingness, to see things from different perspectives is an asset in argumentation, as it is in thinking more generally. Hovland et al. (1953) identify several studies that support the idea that people are more likely to be persuaded to change beliefs, preferences, and attitudes by role-playing or by participating in discussions than by gaining knowledge of the issues in a more passive way, such as by reading about them. Relevant studies noted include those of Irving Janis and Bert King (1949), J. E. Hadley (1936) and Leslie Zeleny (1940). Among possible explanations of this effect is that people find it easier to read without paying attention than to participate in a conversation without doing so. The effect of role-playing appears to be due to people coming to accept, or at least to be more receptive of, the beliefs and attitudes of those whose roles they are playing.

David Green, Ronit Applebaum, and Simon Tong (2006) have studied the effects on people's attitudes on controversial issues of prompting them to consider what the consequences might be if specified actions were or were not taken. They found that such prompts could affect opinions in different ways depending on how they were worded. Prompts in the form of "if only action X were to be taken" tended to increase favorability of a proposed policy more than did prompts in the form of "even if action X were to be taken." Green (2008) describes the difference in terms of distinctions between counterfactual and semi-factual assertions and between persuasive and dissuasive arguments.

David Broockman and Joshua Kalla (2016) report data from a door-to-door canvassing study showing that a ten-minute face-to-face conversation in which one is encouraged to take the perspective of others – members of a shunned group – can reduce prejudice, at least temporarily. The positive result was obtained when the canvassers were members of the shunned group as well as when they were not.

While the question of what makes an argument persuasive is easy to ask, the foregoing should make it clear that it does not have a simple answer. Persuasiveness is a function of many variables and interactions among them. Much has been learned from experimentation, but much remains unknown and a challenge for continuing research.

5

Plausibility

> When people must make a plausibility judgment, they examine how well a particular scenario conceptually coheres with what they know about the world
>
> (Connell & Keane, 2006, p. 98).

To decide how much credence to give to the conclusion of a valid argument, deductive or inductive, on the strength of the argument's premises, one must know how much credence to give to those premises. Hence, an essential aspect of argumentation – the making and analyzing of arguments – is the ability to judge the plausibility of assertions (Stevenson & Over, 1995).

Every day each of us encounters numerous assertions, claims, alleged statements of fact. They come from many sources: news media, advertisers, government officials, doctors, employers, employees, automobile mechanics, teachers, friends, strangers. Some assertions are important to us because they relate to matters of personal concern; others are of little or no interest. Those in the latter category we may ignore, or process too superficially to worry about their truth or falsity. Among the assertions that matter, some we accept as true; others we reject as false, and some give us trouble on this dimension – we do not quite know whether to believe them or not.

What determines what people believe? Why do some people acquire beliefs that most people would consider unfounded, and perhaps odd? Christopher Evans (1973) points out that within a couple of decades of the publication of L. Ron Hubbard's *Dianetics: The Modern Science of Mental Health*, tens of thousands of people were reporting sightings of "mysterious flying objects in the skies, and some even reporting mental and physical contact with their occupants" (p. 139). It would be easy to produce a long list of things that subsets of humanity believe that the nonbelievers consider untrue, if not absurd. Regarding what should determine what one believes, Charles Sanders Peirce (1956/1878) argued that one's state of belief should depend not only on probability as determined by evidence, but on the amount of evidence on which the probability is based, although he saw uncertainty and doubt as states of mind that people find uncomfortable and attempt to avoid. The assumption that people are uncomfortable with uncertainty and attempt to avoid it has much support from research conducted over more than a century since Peirce first expressed it.

The idea that the strength with which beliefs are held should depend on the amount and/or strength of evidence that supports them seems an eminently reasonable one. Happily, research has shown that claims supported by evidence are more readily accepted than are claims that lack evidentiary support (Hample, 1979; Levasseur & Dean, 1996; Stiff, 1986). The same evidence can be represented in different ways. From this fact the question arises as to whether the way in which evidence is represented affects its effectiveness as evidentiary support.

It should not be assumed that we always can give, or even know, reasons for specific beliefs that we hold. As Alfred Sidgwick (1884) put it more than 130 years ago: "in very many instances the causes of a belief are too numerous or too shadowy to be remembered in detail, or even to be summed up in any concise expression" (p. 33). Somewhat more recently Rieke and Sillars (1975) made a similar observation:

> The process by which human beings come to believe, think, or feel what they do may be different from the public process that they employ to justify those beliefs and the behaviors to which they lead. This is a necessary distinction because we often may not know ourselves why we behave in a certain way; we often may be unable to communicate satisfactorily to others what we truly believe to be so; we often may find that society is unwilling to put sufficient stock in our belief to act on that basis alone. In each of these instances, we must be able to communicate some basis for justifying our behavior that will serve the others involved (p. 6).

Most empirical studies of argument evaluation take the factuality of the assertions comprising an argument as given. Attention typically is focused on the question of the legitimacy – validity – of the reasoning process that gets one from various assertions to the conclusion they are intended to support. This is an important question, but for life outside the laboratory, it represents only half of the problem. What one wants to know is whether to accept an argument's conclusion as true, and this involves making judgments about whether to believe its premises or supporting assertions.

Paul Pollard (1979, 1982) goes so far as to question the usefulness of an understanding of validity. If, as he assumes, we are more interested in the truth or falsity of conclusions drawn than in the question of the validity of inferences involved, why worry about the latter. Moreover, it is not clear that judging the truth or falsity of premises is easier in general than judging directly the truth or falsity of a conclusion drawn from them. A counterargument to this position is that there may be cases in which one is sure of the truth of premises, but not sure of the conclusion except by inference.

William Lycan (1988) gives an analysis of deduction that ends up with much the same point as that made by Pollard, namely that the evaluations of deductive arguments come down to explicit or implicit comparisons of plausibility. His explication goes as follows. Every deductive argument can be represented by a set of assertions {P, Q, R} where R represents a conclusion that follows from the assertions P and Q. The situation can be represented equally well by noting that the set {P, Q, and not-R} is inconsistent, which is to say that P, Q and not-R cannot all be true, or, equivalently, that a commitment to the truth of P and Q is a commitment also to the affirmation of R. But how does one know, Lycan asks, that P and Q are true? Whatever basis one has for believing P and Q would be accepted only if it were found to be more plausible than any basis there might be for believing not-R. So, the situation reduces to deciding which of the alternatives is the more plausible.

But what determines the plausibility of an assertion? This question subsumes numerous others of considerable practical significance:

- What determines whether specific instances of propaganda will be believed?
- Why are brainwashing and other types of efforts to indoctrinate sometimes effective and sometimes not?
- What gives rise to extremist views of various types?
- Why do some people readily espouse such views while others do not?
- How do superstitions gain credence?
- What establishes the plausibility of scientific hypotheses before they have been put to rigorous test?

The importance of such questions is obvious, and some of them have been subjects of considerable research. Louise Connell and Mark Keane (2006) note the many contexts in which plausibility has been studied:

> In memory research, plausibility is used as a kind of cognitive shortcut in place of direct retrieval from long-term memory, especially when verbatim memory has faded (e.g., Reder, 1982; Reder & Ross, 1983; Reder, Wible, &

> Martin, 1986). In comprehension, it has been proposed to speed the interpretation of ambiguous sentences (Pickering & Traxler, 1998; Speer & Clifton, 1998; Traxler & Pickering, 1996) and constrain the understanding of novel compounds (Costello & Keane, 2000, 2001). In thinking, it has been shown to support commonsense reasoning (Collins & Michalski, 1989), induction (Smith, Shafir, & Osherson, 1993), and the solution of arithmetic problem solving (e.g., Lemaire & Fayol, 1995) (p. 95).

The immediate focus of this chapter is the question of what determines the plausibility, or lack thereof, of the types of assertions that ordinary people are likely to encounter in their daily lives. Not surprisingly, people find some assertions more plausible than others, and the same assertion may be more plausible to one person than to another. We seek an understanding of what makes an assertion more or less plausible, and it seems reasonable to assume that just as with the question of what makes an argument persuasive, the answer will necessarily involve properties of the assertion, properties of the asserter, and properties of the listener/reader who must assess it. What follows are some findings, and some conjectures, regarding variables that are, or that are hypothesized to be, among the determinants of plausibility.

Knowledge and Metaknowledge

The more one knows about a topic the better basis one has for making judgments of the probable truth of assertions pertaining to that topic. Assertions that follow from what one knows, or believes, to be true will be seen as true. Assertions that contradict what one knows, or believes, to be true will be judged to be false. Of special interest are assertions that fall between these extremes, those that neither follow from nor contradict what one knows, or believes, to be true. Such assertions might be said to be consistent with one's knowledge, but consistency is a much weaker relationship than implication or contradiction. Two assertions may be consistent with each other (the truth of either does not establish the falsity of the other); if they are viewed as unrelated, the truth of one will be no help in determining the truth value of the other. On the other hand, if the assertions are considered to be closely related, knowledge of the truth value of one may well be used as a basis for judging the probable truth value of the other.

Inasmuch as most of the arguments encountered in daily life are neither complete and well-formed nor strictly deductive, the practical question that must be decided when evaluating an argument is less likely to be whether the conclusion follows logically from the premises than how much credence to give to the conclusion in view of the claims that have been made in its support. Even for strictly deductive (say syllogistic) arguments that are encountered in daily life, evaluation involves more than judging formal validity. If one is trying to determine whether to accept the conclusion as true on the basis of the argument that is advanced, one must be satisfied that not only is the form of the argument valid, but that its premises are true. (Of course, one might have good reasons to believe the conclusion is true other than the argument in question.)

Not only does the ability to judge the truth or falsity of assertions, or their degree of plausibility, require knowledge of the domain to which those assertions pertain, it requires also the ability to judge the adequacy of one's own knowledge as it relates to that domain: one must be able to judge how one's knowledge of a domain compares to what there is to know about the domain and, in particular, whether one knows enough to have confidence in one's assessment or needs to seek further information.

Evidence that people often are willing to make judgments regarding the plausibility of assertions, or implied assertions, in the absence of relevant knowledge is not hard to find. Jeff Jacoby (2015) describes results from several polls that make the case. In one instance Public Policy Polling asked a national sample of voters: "Would you support or oppose bombing Agrabah?" Thirty percent of Republican respondents and 19 percent of Democrats favored bombing. (Agrabah is the fictional city in the 1992 Disney film "Aladdin.") Other examples noted by Jacoby include an Oklahoma State University survey that found that about 80 percent of respondents favored mandatory labeling foods containing DNA, apparently oblivious to the fact that all foods contain DNA.

I have used the term *knowledge* in the foregoing as though its meaning is clear, and the same to everybody. It is perhaps time to try to say what it means for someone to *know* something. Like many common words or concepts, it is easy for one to assume its meaning is clear, until one tries to make it so. Israel Scheffler (1965) argues that one can legitimately be said to know something, say *Q*, only if one believes *Q* to be true, has adequate evidence of its truth, and *Q* is indeed true. This is a demanding definition; undoubtedly, we all believe things – believe we know things – for which we have inadequate evidence of their truth. It would seem to follow from Scheffler's definition that we are unlikely to know as much as we think we do.

Kuhn (1991) makes a distinction between two kinds of knowledge but notes that they mark the two poles of a continuum: "At one pole, knowing prevails in the comfortable ignorance of the knower's never having considered that things could be otherwise. At the other pole, knowing is an ongoing, effortful process of evaluating possibilities, one that the ever-present possibility of new evidence and new arguments leaves never completed" (p. 267). This view appears to rule out the possibility of knowing anything in the sense of being certain that something one believes could not be shown by new evidence to be false. For present purposes, it will suffice to give knowledge a somewhat fuzzy connotation and to consider it to be beliefs that correspond to what is generally considered to be true, leaving open the possibility that what is deemed to be knowledge today may turn out to be erroneous tomorrow.

Presumably we all have had the experience of suddenly seeing a relationship or a solution to a problem that had eluded us before. We call such instances of sudden illumination insight. A question of considerable interest is whether insight is a distinctive form of knowing. One bit of evidence that it is comes from studies of people's introspections regarding their efforts to solve problems. Often when people are unable to answer a general-knowledge question or to solve a problem that is assumed to require an insight, they are able to report the strength of their "feeling of knowing" (Nelson, Gerler, & Narens, 1984), or the strength of their "feeling of not knowing" (Liu et al., 2007) – their belief that they will or will not eventually be able to provide the answer or solution. Janet Metcalfe (1986a, 1986b) and Metcalfe and David Weibe (1987) have shown that the relationship between expressed feelings of knowing and the probability of eventual success differs for cases in which insight is required and those in which it is not. In particular, the relationship is stronger and more regular for problems that do not require insight than for those that do; it seems that until one actually has an insight, one has little foreknowledge of whether it is likely to occur.

The most interesting questions about plausibility relate to situations in which one does not have adequate knowledge on which to base a judgment. What is it, in these instances, that determines the credence one will give to an assertion? The remaining variables to be considered relate to this question.

Believed/Assumed Relationship between Antecedent and Consequent

This may be considered a type of knowledge, but it seems sufficiently important to deserve special attention. By definition, an indicative

Table 5.1 *Illustrating the difference between* p*(A|C) and* p*(C|A)*

p(A|C)	p(C|A)	A	C
high	high	*knows who Hank Aaron is*	*baseball fan*
high	low	*US citizen*	*lives in Wisconsin*
low	high	*US senator*	*male*
low	low	*poet*	*plumber*

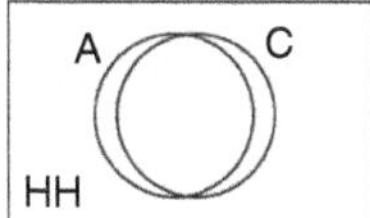

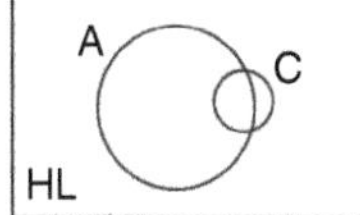

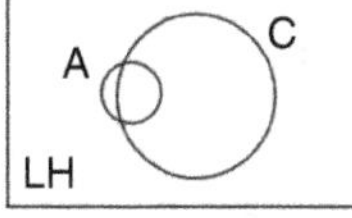

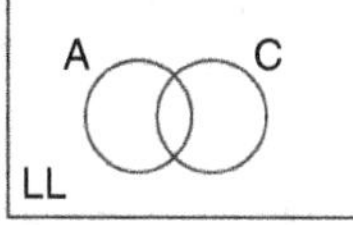

Figure 5.1 Illustrating possible relationships between *p*(A|C) and *p*(C|A)

conditional assertion is composed of two statements: *If A* (*statement 1*) *then C* (*statement 2*). The component statements bear some relationship to each other; *A* specifies a condition under which *C* holds. The relationship may be expressed in conditional probabilistic terms and can be viewed from both directions, the probability of *C* conditional on *A* – *p*(*C*|*A*) – and the probability of *A* conditional on *C* – *p*(*A*|*C*). If the relationship is causal, *p* (*C*|*A*) may be seen as an indication of the *sufficiency* of *A* as a cause of *C*, while *p*(*A*|*C*) may be taken as an indication of the *necessity* of *A* as a cause of *C*. The value of one of these conditional probabilities does not constrain the value of the other. Table 5.1 illustrates the possible combinations of high and low *p*(*A*|*C*) and *p*(*C*|*A*).

The first row in the table illustrates a case in which we presume both *p*(*A*|*C*) – the probability that one knows who Hank Aaron is, given that one is a baseball fan – and *p*(*C*|*A*) – the probability that one is a baseball fan if one knows who Hank Aaron is – are high. The second row illustrates a case in which we presume that *p*(*A*|*C*) – the probability that one is a US citizen if one lives in Wisconsin – is high, and *p*(*C*|*A*) – the probability that one lives in Wisconsin, given that one is a US citizen is low. And so on.

The following figure illustrates the same relationships graphically. *p*(*A*|*C*) and *p*(*C*|*A*) are both high when their areas are both relatively large and nearly overlap (left-most representation); *p*(*A*|*C*) is high and

$p(C|A)$ is low when most of *C* overlaps *A* but little of *A* overlaps *C* (second from left representation), and so on.

In many cases, the condition is causal – *A* is seen as a cause of *C* – but other types of relationship can hold as well. In any case, the condition may be necessary, sufficient, necessary and sufficient, or contributing (but neither necessary nor sufficient). Examples follow:

- If one is a US senator, one is at least thirty years old. (necessary, not sufficient)
- If Pete was born in Nebraska, he is a US citizen. (sufficient, not necessary)
- If a number is divisible only by itself and 1, it is prime. (necessary and sufficient)
- If he was 6'8" in high school, he probably played basketball. (contributing)

The perceived or assumed relationship between antecedent and consequent may be especially important in judging the plausibility of counterfactual assertions. Although precisely what constitutes a counterfactual assertion and at what age children begin to demonstrate the ability to engage in counterfactual reasoning are questions that still motivate research (Beck, Riggs, & Gorniak, 2009; Byrne, 2016; Gutting & Ferrell, 2004; Rafetseder & Perner, 2010, 2014; Riggs et al., 1998; Robinson & Beck, 2000). For present purposes we will consider a counterfactual assertion to be an assertion of something that presumably might have happened but did not. Some might argue that plausibility may not be the most appropriate property with respect to which to judge counterfactuals, and that something like assertibility would be more appropriate. Consider the following counterfactuals:

- If Hitler had not declared war on the Soviet Union in 1941, he would have conquered all of Europe.
- If the earth's atmosphere were 78 percent oxygen and 21 percent nitrogen instead of 78 percent nitrogen and 21 percent oxygen, fires would be impossible to control.

One can readily imagine contexts in which either of these counterfactuals could be meaningfully asserted. It is more difficult to imagine contexts (books like this one aside) in which the following counterfactuals would be expressed:

- If the earth were a pumpkin, its core would be composed of seeds.

- If triangles had four sides, they would not be triangles.

The question of what triggers counterfactual thoughts has been the subject of much research, as has the question of the kinds of counterfactual thoughts that are triggered (Nickerson, 2015, chapters 7, 8). Prominent among triggers of counterfactual thinking are events (e.g., accidents or illnesses) that have undesirable effects – events that leave one wishing they had not occurred and imagining how much better things would be if they had not (Davis et al., 1996; Epstude & Roese, 2008; Leithy, Brown, & Robins, 2006). Such counterfactuals are referred to as "upward" – as distinct from "downward" – counterfactuals, because the imagined counterfactual event or condition is preferable to the actual one (Markman et al., 1993, 1995; Markman & McMullen, 2003; McMullen, Markman, & Gavanski, 1995; Sanna, 1996, 1998). Downward counterfactuals imagine how things might have been worse than they are. Data suggest that upward counterfactuals are more likely than downward ones to motivate action so as to avoid repeating the behavior that is believed to have caused the actual, and unpreferred, event or condition (Epstude & Jonas, 2015; Smallman & Roese, 2009).

The plausibility of counterfactual possibilities can vary over the full range from nearly impossible to imagine at one extreme to very easy to accept at the other. Among the factors that affect plausibility is the extent to which the counterfactual situation differs from the actual one – the "closeness" of the counterfactual to reality. It should perhaps not be surprising that a counterfactual that differs from actuality by only a small amount is considered more plausible than one that differs from actuality by a large amount, but how to measure closeness can be problematic (Kühberger, Großbichler, & Wimmer, 2011; Markman & Tetlock, 2000; McMullen & Markman, 2002).

A common finding is that the negative affect that such imagining has tends to depend in part on how easily one believes the events that produced the undesirable effects could have been avoided; the more easily they could have been avoided (close misses), the stronger the negative affect (Boninger, Gleicher, & Strathman, 1994; Girotto, Legrenzi, & Rizzo, 1991; Kahneman & Miller, 1986; Macrae, Milne, & Griffiths, 1993; Roese, 1997; Wells, Taylor, & Turtle, 1987). Close counterfactuals can also produce positive affect, as when people imagine how things could have turned out worse than they did (Markman et al., 1993; Medvec, Madey, & Gilovich, 1995; Roese, 1994; Taylor, Wood, & Lichtman, 1983).

The tendency to imagine possible differences that are very close to the actual state of affairs – sometimes referred to as the *principle of minimal mutations of reality* (Teigen, Kanten, & Terum, 2011) – has been observed in several studies (Byrne, 1997, 2002; Roese & Olson, 1995). However, when asked to recall events in their own lives that could have turned out differently and to indicate how they could have turned out, people sometimes show a tendency to describe a counterfactual possibility that is a "polar opposite" of what actually occurred. Karl Teigen et al. (2011) obtained this result and found also that the *degree* of positivity (or negativity) of the counterfactual possibility matched that of the reality: "highly positive events had highly negative counterfactuals, whereas moderately positive events had counterfactuals that were moderately negative, and the other way around" (p, 19).

A complication in the interpretation of results of experiments on negative affect of counterfactual thinking about events yielding undesirable consequences is the finding that people's actual reactions to such events do not always correspond to what people predict they will be. Anton Kühberger et al. (2011) found that "closeness effects" that people expected would be found were not always experienced in actuality. A similar disparity between expectations from laboratory experiments and actuality has been found in studies of regret from counterfactual thinking; in laboratory studies, people typically report expecting greater regret from actions taken that they wish had not been taken than from failures to act in ways they wish they had acted (Byrne & McEleney, 2000; Feldman, Miyamoto, & Loftus, 1999; Gilovich et al., 2003; N'gbala & Branscombe, 1997), whereas when asked to reflect about regrets over a lifetime, people often report more regretted failures to act than regretted actions (Erskine, 1973; Kinnier & Metha, 1989; Savitsky, Medvec, & Gilovich, 1997). There is also evidence that what counterfactual thoughts are triggered by events can vary depending on whether one observes the events, reads about them, or experiences them. Stefania Pighin et al. (2011), who obtained such evidence, concluded that observing or experiencing an event engages one's attention more than does reading about it. The finding prompts the question of the applicability of results of laboratory studies of counterfactual reasoning about written scenarios to counterfactual thinking in practical non-laboratory contexts.

Closely associated with the concept of counterfactual is that of *prefactual*, one definition of which is "a conditional (if-then) proposition about an action-outcome linkage that may (or may not) take place in the future, such as 'If I take action X, it will lead to outcome Y'" (Epstude, Scholl, & Roese, 2016, p. 48). Kai Epstude et al. describe "the heart of the definition" as "a causal belief that the action (if taken) will result in the outcome with a high degree of certainty" (p. 48). Other definitions also emphasize the focus on possible future events (Byrne & Egan, 2004; McConnell et al., 2000). Thus defined, a prefactual has the potential of being determined to be true or false – one need only wait and see if the expected result is obtained after the assumed cause occurs. There is no corresponding way to determine the truth or falsity of a counterfactual. Neal Roese (1993), who is credited with coining the term, distinguishes prefactuals not only from counterfactuals, but from expectancies; one may think about a possible future event without necessarily expecting it to occur. As with counterfactuals, upward prefactuals are more likely to motivate action than are downward prefactuals (DeWall et al., 2016; Epstude et al., 2016; Simonson, 1992). It is easy to see that prefactual thinking can play a significant role in planning and decision making for the future.

Perceived Strength of the Relationship between Antecedent and Consequent

Another distinction that may prove useful in understanding conditionals is that between the strength of the coupling between an assertion's antecedent and its consequent and the relative uniqueness of that coupling. A unique coupling, as would be true of an *if-and-only-if* relationship, is necessarily strong, but a strong coupling is not necessarily unique. If *A* is a sufficient cause of *C*, the coupling is strong, but if it is one among several sufficient causes, the coupling is not unique. Presumably most people would consider the claim

> If yesterday was Monday, today is Tuesday

to be highly plausible – indeed certainly true – even though it does not represent a causal relationship. If one happens to know that Kate and Dick make it a point never to be in the same place at the same time, one would find the claim

> If Kate was there, Dick was not

also to be highly plausible; but if one were not aware of this, one would find it hard to judge the plausibility of the claim in the absence of other clues regarding the relationship between Kate and Dick.

Awareness of Alternative Causes or Preventatives

If one is aware that an effect could be a consequence of any of several different causes, one is likely to give less plausibility to a claim that it is the effect of a specified cause than if that were the only possible cause of which one was aware (Byrne, 1989; De Neys, Schaeken, & d'Ydewalle, 2003b). Closely related to the effect of awareness of alternative causes on the plausibility of claims regarding specific causes is the effect of awareness of conditions that could prevent a claimed cause from having its expected effect. Baird (1950) notes this as a consideration in evaluating causal reasoning: "Are other causes operating to prevent the known or alleged causes from producing the known or alleged effects?" (p. 145). Many others more recently have made the same or similar observations (Bonnefon & Hilton, 2002; Cummins et al., 1991; see Nickerson, 2015, chapter 5). The following assertion may be true, generally speaking: "If one graduates from a first-rate college, one will have no trouble finding a good job." But it is unlikely to be deemed plausible of a graduate of a first-rate college who is known to be lazy, narcissistic, arrogant, and expecting of an unrealistically high starting salary.

Unawareness of Counterexamples

Any generalization, or categorical universal claim, can be shown to be false by the production of a counterexample to it. "All As are B" is shown to be false by the identification of a single A that is not B. People may differ with respect to what they will consider to be an example of an A that is not B in specific instances (Weatherson, 2003), but, at least when there is agreement on this point, the identification of a counterexample is generally taken to be compelling evidence that the claim is false. Inability to identify a counterexample is not proof that the claim is true, but when a concerted effort to identify a counterexample has failed, the claim gains credence in proportion to the level of the effort made.

Believed Credibility of Source

We get information from countless sources. Dealing with the variability in the reliability, or veracity, of these sources is a constant challenge. It seems reasonable to assume that one is more likely to accept an assertion as true, or at least plausible, if one considers its source to be trustworthy than if one does not; and evidence bears out that assumption (Dholakia & Sternthal, 1977; Hovland, Janis, & Kelley, 1953; Hovland & Mandell, 1952; Hovland & Weiss, 1951/1952; Kelman & Hovland, 1953; Malka, Krosnick, & Langer, 2009; Miton & Mercier, 2015; Oxley, Vedlitz, & Wood, 2014; Wu & Shaffer, 1987; Yaniv & Kleinberger, 2000). As H. W. B. Joseph (1906) noted over a century ago, one's character bears on one's credibility.

A common experimental procedure for demonstrating the effects of source characteristics on the plausibility of assertions is to have people judge the plausibility of precisely the same assertions attributed to claimants that have been presented as highly credible (trustworthy) or lacking credibility. There is evidence to suggest that the effect of source credibility on the plausibility of claims – greater credibility producing greater plausibility – may decrease over time (Hovland & Weiss, 1951/1952; Kelman & Hovland, 1953), however Hovland et al. (1953) note that the effect may be more lasting if some commitment is made when it is first realized. They speculate that it could be due, at least partially, to memory for content (what was said) being generally better than memory for source (who said it).

Source credibility can have substantial impact on the way evidence is evaluated in courtroom situations (Cleary, 1972; Schum, 1977; Schum & Kelly, 1973). Presumably credibility is a function of many variables, some relevant – like the individual's reputation for honesty or deceit – and some are not – like whether one has an "honest appearance." One obviously relevant factor that often figures in court cases is whether the witness has a personal stake in the proceedings; a witness who has turned state's evidence in exchange for immunity against prosecution, for example, is likely to be less credible because of the deal that has been made.

A source may be credible, or not, for a variety of reasons. One would expect a source that is a recognized expert on the subject of a claim to be more credible than a source that lacks that credential (Harvey & Fischer, 1997; Petty, Cacioppo, & Goldman, 1981). This expectation gets support from evidence that people sometimes judge the credibility of a source on the basis of professional affiliation (Bowden, Caldwell, & West, 1934; Kulp, 1934). However, there is ample evidence that irrelevant factors may also affect judgments of credibility. For example, men may be seen as more credible than women (Whitaker, 1965; Whitaker & Meade, 1967), and more attractive people, whether male or female, may be judged to be more credible than less attractive ones (Andersen & Clevenger, 1963; Mills & Aronson, 1965).

Credibility judgments sometimes appear to reflect certain stereotypical responses to witnesses on the basis of the identifiable groups to which they belong. Witnesses on either end of the age spectrum – the very young and the very old – tend to be viewed as honest but less accurate rememberers than young adult witnesses, for example (Leippe & Romanczyk, 1987; Yarmey, 1984; Yarmey & Jones, 1983).

Perceived trustworthiness can be based, at least in part, on data. If one has frequently received information from a particular source in the past, and has been able to determine, after the fact, the truth or falsity of the assertions that have come from this source, and if those assertions have proved to be accurate, then one may feel justified in having a high degree of confidence in assertions from that source. Presumably something of this sort is behind newscasters' practice of noting, on occasion, that a particular news item was obtained from a "reliable source."

Confidence in the source probably does not have an all-or-none effect on plausibility. It seems more reasonable to assume that it increases plausibility by some amount, making an assertion more plausible than it otherwise would be. How much difference it makes presumably depends on a variety of factors such as how plausible the assertion is independent of its origin, which is to say how plausible it would be if its source were not known. If the assertion is highly plausible for other reasons, the fact that it came from a trusted source would not be able to have much impact. If the assertion is highly improbable a priori, then knowledge that it came from a trustworthy source could increase its plausibility substantially. The way in which an assertion is made may affect the way in which it is received; for example, the intensity or confidence with which a claim is made can affect the credence it is given (Price & Stone, 2004).

Undoubtedly there are instances in which a greater weight is given to the credibility of sources than is justified. The power of demagogues comes largely from the unquestioning credence their followers give to whatever they say. Much advertising seems to be based on the assumption that many people will believe anything a celebrity says. Similar thinking may be behind the use of celebrities to endorse political candidates and support causes. Endorsements by celebrities of commercial products, candidates for political office, and various causes raise the question of what the source(s) of any particular endorsement is.

> Is it the TV star who sells us coffee on TV? Or, is it he and a whole team of production people, script writers, and advertising men? And when he tells us to "buy my Instant Maxwell House" he may sincerely believe it is "better than freeze-dried" but it isn't *his* Instant Maxwell House. Yet we know that the argument he makes is believable to many people. Is it because of his credibility? The credibility of General Foods? The credibility created by the production people? The script writers? The other actors in the commercial? (Rieke & Sillars, 1975, p. 141).

Advertisements provide many examples of claims that are of questionable credibility. Many probiotics, and substances that contain probiotics, that are widely sold in pharmacies and supermarkets, are advertised as beneficial to one's health and well-being in various ways. According to Ferris Jabr (2017), a close look at the relevant science "shows that most of the health claims of probiotics are pure hype. The majority of studies to date have failed to reveal any benefits to individuals who are already healthy" (p. 26). It seems unlikely that the average consumer is in a position to judge the credibility of the claims made in advertisements, but wariness of such claims in general is perhaps not an unreasonable attitude.

Sometimes the settlement of a civil legal dispute includes an apology from the wrongdoer, either spontaneously offered or requested by the plaintiff. Such an apology may be made either by the offender's attorney on the offender's behalf, or by the offender him/herself. Data reported by Jennifer Robbennolt (2013) show an apology to improve perceptions of the offender, whether delivered by an attorney or personally by the offender, but to be more effective in the latter case. Presumably an offender is a more credible source of an apology than is an offender's spokesperson.

Hovland et al. (1953) distinguish between two questions having to do with source credibility: its effect on the perception and evaluation of claims and the degree to which claims effectively modify attitudes and beliefs. The distinction allows the possibility of communication from a source being evaluated as highly plausible, while having little or no effect on one's attitudes or beliefs. Hovland et al. make a related distinction between "(1) the extent to which a communicator is perceived to be a source of valid assertions (his 'expertness') and (2) the degree of confidence in the communicator's intent to communicate the assertions he considers most valid (his 'trustworthiness')" (p. 21). They argue that the weight given to a communicator's assertions will depend on both of these factors, and that it is the value that results from this combination that reflects the credibility of the source. They note that attitudes toward a communicator may be affected by several factors and interactions among them. Such factors include "initial attitudes toward the content, the congruence between what is said and prior knowledge about the source's position on the issue, the complexity of the question raised in the communication, the ambiguity of the proposed answer, and the vividness of the source" (p. 47). Hovland et al. note also "the possible influence of attitudes toward the communicator which are unrelated to credibility, such as affection, admiration, awe, and fear" (p. 47). We will return to the subject of source reliability later in this chapter in a discussion of a theory of plausibility put forth by Nicolas Rescher (1976).

Rieke and Sillars (1975) conclude a discussion of source credibility with the following comment.

> Observation over centuries and experimental research have isolated two primary factors in source credibility: competence and trustworthiness. We tend to believe those persons whom we perceive as competent and trustworthy. There are two other factors that are perhaps present and possibly subcategories of the other two. One is the goodwill that a speaker seems to show for his listener. A second is the dynamism of the speaker. Dynamism . . . can be a negative quality if someone feels it is excessive (p. 155).

Rieke and Sillars were writing forty-five years ago. Whether they would make the same claims today we do not know. Surely perceived competence and trustworthiness would be on any short list of determinants of credibility; nothing has been learned in the intervening years that would diminish their importance.

Believed Intention of Source

People make claims for a variety of purposes. One such purpose is simply to provide information. Weather forecasts fit in this category, as do reports of newsworthy happenings, announcements of upcoming events, and the like. Another purpose is to influence people to behave in certain ways – to buy a specific product, to vote for a particular candidate for political office, to support a cause. Still another is to convince unsuspecting potential victims to fall prey to fraudulent schemes.

Not surprisingly, people tend to give less credence to a claim if they believe the intention of its source is to convince them to do something from which the source will benefit. Citing Paul Lazarsfeld, Bernard Berelson, and Hazel Gaudet (1944), Hovland et al. (1953) describe as a general hypothesis that "when a person is perceived as having a definite *intention* to persuade others, the likelihood is increased that he will be perceived as having something to gain and, hence, as less worthy of trust" (p. 23). Said another way, whether a source has a vested interest in one's acceptance of its claim(s) as true is an important consideration in judging its trustworthiness (Eagly, Wood, & Chaiken, 1978; Hoeken, Šorm, & Shellens, 2014).

Framing Effects

Describing a glass as half full is logically, or mathematically, the same as describing it as half empty; but psychologically the two descriptions can be quite different. Much research has established that the way a claim is framed can have considerable influence on the way it is received (Druckman, 2001a, 2001b; Frisch, 1993; Koehler, 1991; Kühberger, 1995, 1998; Mandel, 2001; Rothman & Salovey, 1997; Teigen & Nikolaisen, 2009). "Framing" in this context refers to aspects of a claim that have nothing to do with its truth or falsity, as illustrated by the half-full half-empty example.

Several types of frames have been distinguished. Here my interest is in frames that make a claim in either positive or negative terms. Such frames may contrast benefits versus costs, gains versus losses, positive (desirable) versus negative (undesirable) outcomes. Framing in such terms is usually done with the intention of influencing someone's beliefs or behavior and are therefore representative of what Irwin Levin, Sandra Schneider, and Gary Gaeth (1998) refer to as goal framing (which is distinguished from risky-choice and attribute framing in their taxonomy).

Researchers have given considerable attention to the question of how the effectiveness of quantitative evidence relates to whether it is presented in statistical or narrative form. Bing Han and Edward Fink (2012) consider the results of research on this question to have been inconclusive. As examples of studies that have shown evidence presented in narrative form to be more persuasive than evidence presented in statistical form, they note Borgida & Nisbett (1977), Kahneman and Tversky (1973), Taylor & Thompson (1982); as an example of a study that showed the reverse, they give Baesler and Burgoon (1994). Hans Hoeken and Lettica Hustinx (2009) present evidence that which type of representation – statistical or anecdotal – is more effective depends on the nature of the argument being represented. The same conclusion is supported by data obtained by Jos Hornikx (2008), who also found that people were quite accurate in judging the relative effectiveness of several kinds of representation (anecdotal, statistical, causal, and expert). Han and Fink (2012) attempted to identify conditions that determine which type of evidence would be the more persuasive. They found that the persuasiveness of statistical evidence was sensitive to the amount of evidence, whereas the persuasiveness of narrative evidence was more sensitive to its vividness.

That the same fact can have different effects when presented in different ways is illustrated by the *ratio bias*, which has been demonstrated in numerous studies (Avnet, Pham, & Stephen, 2012; Dale et al., 2007; Pinto-Prades, Martinez-Perez, & Abellán-Perpiñán, 2006; Yamagishi, 1997). One definition of this bias is "the tendency for people to judge a low probability event as more likely when presented as a large-numbered ratio, such as 20/100, than as a smaller-numbered but equivalent ratio, such as 2/10" (Bonner & Newell, 2008, p. 412), and an explanation of it hypothesizes that some people focus on the numerator of a ratio rather than on the ratio itself (Kirkpatrick & Epstein, 1992). It may perhaps be seen as a special case of the more general finding that in judging contingent relationships people often use less than all of the information that is available and relevant (Arkes & Harkness, 1983; Nisbett & Ross, 1980; Peterson & Beach, 1967), and typically they give too much weight to the frequency of co-occurrences (the numerator of a ratio) and too little to the frequency of the remaining possible combinations (Alonso & Fernandez-Berrocal, 2003; Crocker, 1981; Jenkins & Ward, 1965; Reyna & Brainerd, 2008; Wasserman, Dorner, & Kao, 1990).

Results from research with messages intended to influence people's behavior as it relates to their health have generally shown that messages framed in terms of gains (behaving in such a way will have the following desirable consequences) are more effective in persuading people to behave in the desired way than those framed in terms of losses (failing to behave in such a way will have the following undesirable consequences) (Detweiler et al., 1999; Gerend & Shepherd, 2007; Gray, 2008; McCormick & McElroy, 2009; Rivers et al., 2005; Rothman et al., 1993; Rothman et al., 2006).

Beyond the finding that positively-framed messages are typically more persuasive than negatively-framed ones – or stated more conservatively, negatively-framed messages are almost never more persuasive than positively-framed ones – these studies reveal a number of factors that appear to determine the reliability and magnitude of the effect. These include the level of focused attention that is given to the messages (which can vary with the complexity or number of messages that must be processed) and the processor's affect or mood (which is sometimes induced). In a meta-analysis of ninety-three studies of framing effects, Daniel O'Keefe and Jacob Jensen (2007) found evidence that messages intended to induce preventive behavior related to dental hygiene were more persuasive when they emphasized advantages of compliance with recommendations than when they emphasized disadvantages of noncompliance. However, such a difference was not found for messages aimed at preventive behavior related to other diseases represented in the analysis – sexual diseases, skin cancer, and problems of nutrition and diet.

Environmental scientists have been frustrated by the limited effectiveness of pleas with officials, administrators, and the general public to increase their willingness to put effort into solving, or mitigating, the problem of climate change. Some research has focused on the question of how best to frame messages so as to motivate environmentally friendly behavior. Among the findings of interest is that a given way of framing a message may be reacted to by different people in different ways. For example, for some people, messages regarding energy conservation framed in terms of economic benefits are more effective than are those framed in terms of environmental benefits, while for others the opposite is the case (Xu, Arpan, & Chen, 2015).

That the effectiveness of messages aimed at modifying behavior is much influenced by the way they are framed has been amply demonstrated by the results of numerous experiments, but specification of a set of principles explaining precisely how framing works remains to be done. Discovery of what determines whether an effect will be obtained and, if so, what its magnitude will be remains a challenge for research.

Diversity of Evidentiary Support

A claim is the more plausible the greater the diversity of the evidence that it is true. The principle is apparent in court proceedings. A prosecutor who can present several independent eyewitnesses to a crime will have a stronger case than one who can present only one; a defendant who can find several unrelated people to attest to the truth of his alibi will have a greater chance of acquittal than one who can find only one.

A scientific claim or theory will be considered the stronger, the greater the diversity of the evidence that supports it. Michel Shermer (2015) makes this point with respect to the question of whether human behavior is affecting climate. Noting that there is a strong consensus among tens of thousands of scientists that climate is being affected by humans, he nevertheless contends that it is not the numbers that make the case; rather it is the "convergence of evidence from multiple lines of inquiry – pollen, tree rings, ice cores, corals, glacial and polar ice-cap melt, sea level-rise, ecological shifts, carbon dioxide increases, the unprecedented rate of temperature increase – that all converge to a singular conclusion" (p. 81). Shermer argues that to be credible, naysayers would have to provide equally convergent evidence that the proposition that humans are affecting the climate is wrong.

In sum, diversity of support is widely recognized as an important consideration in judging the plausibility of claims. Adian Feeney and Evan Heit (2011) describe sensitivity to diversity as "a widespread and useful aspect of cognition" (p. 157). Its use in the philosophical literature is reviewed by Heit, Ulrike Hahn, and Feeney (2005).

Tricks of Imagination

Imagining that an event occurred in the past can increase one's confidence that it did in fact occur (Garry et al., 1996; Garry & Polaschek, 2000). Producing reasons why a possible future event might occur can increase one's confidence that it will occur (Anderson, 1983; Anderson, Lepper, & Ross, 1980; Hirt & Sherman, 1985; Hoch, 1984; Koehler, 1991; Ross, Lepper, et al., 1977; Sherman et al., 1983). Even simply calling attention to the possibility of a future event (Fiedler, 2000; Fiedler et al., 1996; Koehler, 1991; Tversky & Koehler, 1994), or imagining its occurrence (Carroll, 1978; Gregory, Cialdini, & Carpenter, 1982; Hirt & Markman, 1995) can have a similar effect. Koehler (1991) characterizes this type of finding thus: "any task that requires a person to treat a hypothesis *as if* it were true can strengthen the confidence with which that hypothesis is held" (p. 499). Asher Koriat, Klaus Fiedler, and Robert Bjork (2006) refer to such findings as indicative of an *overestimation bias.* Closely related to this bias is the *focusing effect* (Legrenzi, Girrotto, & Johnson-Laird, 1993) or *focalism* (Wilson et al., 2000), which refers to a tendency to overstate the consequences of imagined or anticipated events. Antithetically to the focusing effect is the finding that producing reasons why an alternative to a specified event might occur can reduce one's confidence that the specified event will occur (Hirt & Markman, 1995).

There is considerable evidence that in imagining their own futures, people tend to be overly optimistic (Shepperd et al., 2013; Taylor & Brown, 1988; Weinstein, 1980). Other factors aside, overconfidence in one's own beliefs and judgments appears to be a common human trait (Fischhoff, Slovic, & Lichtenstein, 1977; Moore & Healy, 2008).

Emotion

Emotions are generally seen as problematic for reasoning. We know from experience that they can make it difficult for one to be objective and to weigh evidence impartially. On the other hand, a case can be made that they play an important role in facilitating what David Gelernter (1994) calls low-focus thought and mental states that are conducive to the experience of insight and the discovery of analogies. "The cognitive spectrum as I will describe it puts emotion right at the heart of thought" (p. 35). "[E]motions are not a form of thought, not an additional way to think, not a special cognitive bonus, but are *fundamental* to thought. If we subtract emotion, the only part of the cognitive spectrum remaining is the radical high end – and to identify this narrow high-focus band with thought in general is absurd" (p. 47). Affect, Gelernter argues, while not sufficient to make creativity happen, is necessary to it.

Assertions can be made with varying types and degrees of emotion. The effects that assertions expressed with emotion – as distinct from those expressed unemotionally – can have on the plausibility of whatever is being asserted appears to depend on a variety of factors. Marios Eliades et al. (2012) found that reasoning about emotional topics tends to be less logical than reasoning about unemotional topics, and more likely to show a belief bias. Hovland et al. (1953) contend that the effectiveness of what they call "motivating appeals" – emotional appeals aimed at affecting beliefs or behavior – depends on several factors. "Increased incentive to pay attention, to comprehend, or to accept the communication could account for the effectiveness of any given motivating appeal. Accordingly, it is essential to differentiate these effects in order to arrive at systematic knowledge concerning the ways in which motivating appeals bring about opinion change" (p. 59).

Perelman and Olbrechts-Tyteca (1969) contend that to create emotion, it helps to be specific. "General notions and abstract schemes have hardly any effect on the imagination" (p. 147). They illustrate the point by reference to an observation by Richard Whately (from his 1928 *Elements of Rhetoric*). "Whately relates how an audience that had remained unmoved by a general description of the carnage that had occurred at the Battle of Fontenoy was moved to tears by a little detail concerning the death of two young men" (p. 147). Statistics, no matter how dreadful, are seldom, if ever, as effective in stirring emotions as are accounts of suffering by individuals who have names and faces.

Proxy Effect

Sometimes the likelihood that one will accept an assertion, or implied assertion, as true seems to depend, at least in part, on who else appears to believe it to be true. If one is poorly informed about a referendum item that is to appear on a ballot but knows that his/her politically knowledgeable friend thinks it is a bad idea, s/he may be inclined to vote against it on that basis.

Jacoby (2015) describes the results of a poll conducted by the *Huffington Post* that included the question of whether the 1975 Public Affairs Act should be repealed. "When respondents were informed that President Obama favors repeal, Republicans were 13 times more likely than Democrats to insist the law should be preserved. By contrast, when told that the push to scrap the law was coming from GOP leaders in Congress, 28 percent of Democratic respondents – but just 4 percent of Republicans – said they opposed repeal" (p. A11). The law in question, Jacoby notes, does not exist.

Preferences

Philosophers and psychologists alike have observed that there appears to be a universal tendency to give more credence to assertions one would like to be true than to those one would prefer to be false. Probably most of us find this observation to be intuitively compelling, perhaps because we believe we see the principle at work in ourselves and in other people of our acquaintance. There is considerable experimental evidence to support this generalization, which is sometimes discussed under the rubric of *confirmation bias* or *my-side bias* (Baron, 1995; Lefford, 1946; Lund, 1925; Nickerson, 1998; Perkins et al., 1991; Weinstein, 1989).

Matthew Boden, Howard Berenbaum, and James Gross (2016) argue that beliefs, which people may hold with varying degrees of conviction, serve many purposes, one of the more important ones being representational and another hedonic. Representational beliefs, in their view, are beliefs about the way things are; they help us negotiate our way around in the world. Entertaining false representational beliefs is likely to get us into trouble the seriousness of which depends on the aspects of the world to which they pertain. Beliefs also serve a hedonic function; there are some beliefs we hold primarily because we want to do so. We feel better in holding them than we would feel if we discovered them to be false. Sometimes the representational and hedonic functions can reinforce each other; sometimes they can be at odds, as when one wants to believe one is amusing when the evidence is to the contrary.

Multiple Factors

The plausibility, or lack thereof, of any particular assertion may be a function of several factors; indeed, that seems more likely than not to be the case, and to be recognized as such. William Lycan (1988) mentions the following factors as influential in this regard: "ordinary inductive support, explanatory power, coherence with antecedently accepted theories, coherence with our linguistic intuitions, parsimony, fruitfulness, failure to give rise to embarrassing and difficult questions, accessibility to rigorous systematization, and so forth" (p. 118). Lycan also takes the position that inasmuch as these are the sorts of considerations to which the theoretical scientist appeals, the method for acquiring new knowledge in philosophy is essentially the same as that used in science.

> If what I have said here is (more or less) right, then we appear to have vindicated some version of the view that (1) philosophy, except for that relatively trivial part of it that consists in making sure that controversial arguments are formally valid, is just very high-level science and that consequently (2) the proper philosophical method for acquiring interesting new knowledge cannot differ from proper scientific method (p. 118).

That is not to say, of course, that all philosophers, or all scientists, would necessarily agree with this assessment.

Global Fit

How readily one accepts an assertion as true may depend, in part, on how well that assertion fits with one's total system of beliefs about the world. "Fits with" is an imprecise notion, but it will do for present purposes. It means more than logical consistency but does not require logical implication. If an assertion not only tends to support another assertion in a substantive way but is also consistent with one's general system of beliefs about the world, it is more likely to be accepted as true than if it is not. If it tends to be at variance with this system of beliefs, it is likely to be rejected. For example, if I believe that dictatorships are more likely than democracies to indulge in politically motivated imprisonments and executions, I will probably have little trouble in finding media reports of such events in countries ruled by dictators to be plausible.

The idea of global fit is closely related to – if not the same as – that of concept-coherence, which is defined by Connell and Keane (2006) as "how well a particular scenario coheres with prior knowledge" (p. 96). "Although plausibility has not been well explained in the existing literature, there is a rough consensus that it has something to do with the coherence of concepts based on prior knowledge. This view holds that some concept, scenario, event, or discourse is plausible if it is conceptually consistent with what is known to have occurred in the past" (p. 96).

Noting that plausibility has been used in theoretical and computational models across a wide variety of fields despite that there is little consensus regarding its definition, Connell and Keane (2003, 2006) and Connell (2004) propose a model of plausibility, the *Plausibility Analysis Model* (PAM), which they refer to as a *knowledge-fitting* theory. According to this theory, judgments of plausibility are processed in two main stages: a comprehension stage and an assessment stage. Comprehension taps existing knowledge to make a mental representation of – to understand – an assertion, description of an event, etc. In the assessment stage, the mental representation is assessed in terms of the degree to which it is consistent with (fits) prior knowledge. If the fit is good, the plausibility is high; if it is poor, the plausibility is low. "A scenario will be perfectly plausible only if its representation has minimal *complexity* and *conjecture*, and/or maximal *corroboration*" (Connell & Keane, 2006, p. 99).

Plausibility Theory

Clearly, determining the plausibility of an assertion can be a complicated affair. Many variables that can play a role have been identified, and much remains to be learned. Given the importance of the subject, and the attention from researchers it has received, it would be surprising if no attempts had been made to develop a theoretical treatment of it. In fact, several theoretical approaches to assessing or measuring plausibility have been proposed, sometimes as alternatives to the use of probability theory. Nir Friedman and Joseph Halpern (1995) and Halpern (2001) mention Dempster-Shafer belief functions (Shafer, 1976), possibility measures (Dubois & Prade, 1990), lexicographic probability (Blume, Brandenburger, & Dekel, 1991), qualitative probability (Fine, 1973) and propose a plausibility measure of their own.

Especially notable among such attempts, because of its range of influence, is the "theory of plausible reasoning" and a "method of applied logic" proposed by Rescher (1976). The task of plausibility theory, as Rescher conceives it, is "to provide the needed tools for resolving or reducing the perplexity that arises in such cases [of receipt of conflicting information] – for carrying on an orderly process of reasoning in the face of the inconsistency of conflicting information" (p. 2). Neither deductive logic nor probability theory, Rescher contends, is up to the task: "we remain impotent to base any useful substantive inferences upon the claims of less than totally veracious sources .... The declarations of a less than totally veracious source do not authorize one to draw any particularly helpful inference as to the categorical or probable truth of its declarations .... One of the main objectives of plausibility theory is to obviate this sort of limitation" (p. 4).

Rescher describes plausible theses as "*genuine candidates* for potential acceptance-as-true because they have some (reasonable) basis of support" (p. 8). He distinguishes between a plausible thesis and one that is possible but has no support. "A plausible thesis thus articulates a possibility that is not a *mere* possibility but one in whose support there is, under the epistemic circumstances at issue, a body of rational warrant sufficient to establish *some* degree of favorable presumption, at any rate" (p. 9).

A major determinant of the plausibility of a thesis, in Rescher's view, is the reliability of its source(s): "plausibility theory sets out to deal with the 'plausibility' of propositions in a way that reflects the reliability of their sources" (p. 10). Rescher sees reliability as a matter of degree. "The greater the reliability of the source, the greater is the plausibility . . . with which it can endow the theses for which it vouches" (p. 11). This, of course, raises the questions of how to determine the reliability of a source and how to quantify plausibility. Rescher proposes a set of rules for quantifying plausibility that produces quantities between 0 and 1. He contends that plausibility, thus quantified, is not to be confused with probability – that the resemblance between these concepts is "purely adventitious."

Rescher recognizes the possibility that a given thesis may have multiple sources that vary in reliability; and when that is the case, the more reliable sources provide the greater support: "The plausibility status of a thesis is determined through the standing of its most respectable sources ... the reports deriving from sources are evaluated in point of plausibility so as to reflect the reliability of the sources that vouch for them" (p. 12). He provides an algorithm for deriving from the estimates of reliability for each of the sources of a particular thesis a measure of the plausibility of the thesis. The algorithm does not require calculations; the numbers involved are treated as ordinals: "The numbers only play the role of providing us with a sufficiently fine sequence of plausibility-distinctions (highly-plausible, medium-plausible, only-somewhat-plausible, etc.)" (p. 17). Rescher describes the process as "qualitative and comparative" as distinct from "quantitative and mathematical," and of a "cruder and simpler sort than that of probability theory" (p. 17).

In applying the principle of greatest weight to the most reliable sources, Rescher allows for the possibility that in combination, many low-reliability sources could outweigh one high-reliability source. Although he focuses first on the role of sources as determinants of plausibility, he notes that deductive logic and certain "standard inductive desiderata: simplicity, uniformity, specificity, definiteness, determinativeness, 'naturalness,' etc." (p. 25) can serve as validating or warranting principles for establishing plausibility. Also, he concedes that it sometimes may be necessary "to depart from the straightforward course of determining the plausibility of theses on the basis of the reliability of their *testimonial* sources to introduce a more sophisticated conception of 'source' which also embraces such *principles* as, for example, those of majority rule or general agreement" (p. 76).

Acknowledging that his plausibility theory is "strongly reminiscent of the idea of probability," Rescher goes to some length to explain how it differs from probability theory.

> Probability distributes a fixed amount (unity) across the range of various cases (exclusive and exhaustive alternatives). Plausibility just does not behave like this. It does *not* assign weights to propositions in line with their internal content (their accommodation of various alternatives). Rather, it grades these propositions *ab extra*, with a view to the reliability status of the sources that speak on their behalf (p. 31).

The probabilities for a set of exclusive and exhaustive possibilities must add to 1.00; it is not possible for two of them both to have values close to 1.00. Rescher contends that plausibility has no such constraint; that it is possible for a thesis and its negation both to be highly plausible. "[I]t is in principle impossible to have several inconsistent theses all of which are highly probable . . . but there is no anomaly whatever in the prospect of a plurality of inconsistent theses all of which are of relatively high plausibility status" (p. 31). Consistency among the theses in a set under consideration is an objective, however, and Rescher (1976, chapter 6) explains how plausibility makes it possible to realize it.

Rescher describes plausibility analysis as epistemologically more basic and fundamental than probabilistic reasoning, because it requires only classification and comparison, and no calculations. He claims, however, that plausibility theory, as he describes it, is capable of handling all the types of reasoning – inductive inference, hypothetical arguments, reasoning with counterfactuals – that are handled by probabilistic reasoning, and of doing so with fewer constraints. Despite the stress that Rescher puts on the differences between probability and plausibility, as he defines these concepts, he sees them as intended to serve the same purpose: "the same basic root idea underlies both probability and plausibility – that of assessing how solid a claim to truth can be made on behalf of a thesis which is not categorically established" (p. 36).

In an overview of Rescher's theory, Raymie McKerrow (1987) lists the principles that govern the process by which a plausibility rating is assigned to a data set, and describes the process as "a 'decision mechanism' for choosing between incompatible alternatives" (p. 320). Noting that arguments for a particular course of action are likely to be met with equally rational counterarguments, McKerrow sees Rescher's theory as a tool for deciding among the competing claims. What results from the process, he suggests, is "a claim that is an order of magnitude greater than an 'alleged' truth but is not held as 'certainly true.' Instead, the claim is held as 'presumptively true,' as a claim which can be accepted as a contribution toward knowledge that something is the case" (p. 320).

There can be little doubt that Rescher's work has been very influential in stimulating thought and research on how to deal with natural-language arguments, among other topics, notably epistemology. One evidence of this is a book edited by Ernest Sosa (1979) that contains thirteen substantive commentaries on Rescher's work, and a rejoinder to each by Rescher. The commentaries address many of the topics on which Rescher wrote; some of them that pertain most directly to his plausibility theory or his method of applied logic are noted in what follows.

Stephen Barker (1979) gives Rescher's method of applied logic a mixed review, contending that the method poses something of a dilemma.

> If the method is to be presented in an informal, casual manner, the aim of descriptive clarity cannot be met very fully; while if the method is to be presented in a rigorously formal manner, we cannot be confident that the aim of justifying the method will be well served. This is not to say that it is pointless to formulate the method; perhaps some worthwhile combination of moderate clarity with some degree of justificatory plausibility can be attained. But the nature of the dilemma is such as to indicate that there may be fairly narrow limits to what can be usefully achieved through such discussions of philosophico-logical method. Earlier great accounts of philosophical method, such as Descartes's certainly did not make much real headway against the dilemma (p. 15).

Brian Ellis (1979) contends that Rescher's theory of conditionals has stimulated much research to improve it, but to no avail, and speculates that the reason for the failure is that "it is not a truth theory. It does not define truth conditions for conditionals, as Stalnaker's and Lewis' theories purport to do. Hence, it is not a theory of the kind which logicians require as foundations for logical systems" (p. 33). Ellis describes Rescher's theory as an "attempt to state conditions under which belief in the truth or falsity of a conditional may be incorporated into a rational system of beliefs" (p. 42) and, despite shortcomings that he notes, calls it a step in the right direction.

Jonathan Cohen (1979) also notes what he sees as weaknesses in Rescher's theory and contends that it fares unfavorably when compared with the "Pascalian theory of probability."

> One should not underestimate either the attractiveness of probabilistic reasoning or the number and variety of considerations standing in its favor. The Pascalian calculus [probability theory] has afforded an elegant and perspicuous logic for statistical inference, signal-transmission theory, quality-control, gamblers' calculation, and very many other types of intellectual operation. So, the prejudice that all rational judgments in the absence of complete information will turn out in the end to be Pascalian is scarcely an unreasonable one. There is a heavy burden on anyone who wants to challenge that prejudice (p. 59).

Rescher contends that Cohen's critique rests on a misunderstanding of his intent in promoting plausibility theory. He argues that the intent was not to contest probabilism, but to develop

> a different instrument for different purposes. The explicit aim of plausibility theory as I [Rescher] conceive it is to deal with reasoning in the face of *inconsistent premises* – mutually incompatible *data*. This issue lies outside the scope of standard logic. When our premises are inconsistent, logic tells us *that* this inconsistency must be removed, but gives or affords no instructions as to *how* to do it. Nor does probability theory help here (p. 61).

Not surprisingly, other commentaries on Rescher's work, or specific aspects thereof, express a range of reactions, some more complimentary, or more critical, than others. In a review of *Plausible Reasoning*, Paul Humphreys (1978) criticizes it on the grounds that because it was intended to be an introduction to a theory of plausible reasoning, the examples used are overly simple. "It is difficult to assess the merit of principles applied to cases no more sophisticated than arguments in propositional logic and triplets of linear equations" (p. 160).

Humphreys contends too that Rescher makes an erroneous claim about conditional probabilities that is critical to a justification of his distinction between plausibility and probability. The claim is that the conditional probability, $p(A|B)$ is undefined when $p(B) = 0$. Humphreys notes that an axiom system for this case was given by Karl Popper (1965) and elaborated by Robert Stalnaker (1970) and argues that correcting this mistake "removes one of Rescher's principal arguments against probabilistic approaches" (p. 160).

Humphrey's conclusion: "The reviewer's overall impression is that the book contains a novel contribution to a burgeoning field, but that much work needs to be done before it becomes a serious rival to existing probabilistic programs" (p. 160). (Unfortunately, the reading of *Plausible Reasoning* is more difficult than it ought to be, in my view, in part because of a superfluity of minor print errors.)

Rescher (1964a, 1964b, 1976, 2007) is a prolific writer and his work has been influential in many areas of philosophy. Perhaps less well known to cognitive psychologists than to philosophers, he has much to say, not only about argumentation, but about how we come to know what we know (or believe) about the world, about the limitations of knowledge, about modal logic, about reasoning in science, and a host of other topics that are of interest to psychologists. His work on plausibility and argumentation is wide ranging and thought provoking. Whether his plausibility theory does a better job of facilitating our understanding of what makes claims plausible and our ability to distinguish degrees of plausibility than does probability theory is debatable; I personally doubt it, but perhaps a compelling test has yet to be made.

6

Fallacies

> The philosophy of reasoning, to be complete, ought to comprise the theory of bad as well of good reasoning
>
> (J. S. Mill, 1995/1892, p. 85).

> People are people. Therefore fallacies are here to stay
>
> (Rohatyn, 1986, p. 49).

> Only the sluggard never commits a fallacy
>
> (Sidgwick, 1884, p. 318).

What Is a Fallacy?

I use "fallacy" here with some misgivings. The word has a tortured past; philosophers and logicians have argued about what it means – and indeed whether there is such a thing (Boudry, 2017; Boudry, Paglieri, & Pigliucci, 2015; van Eemeren & Grootendorst, 1984, 1992, 2004) – and such arguments will undoubtedly continue. Douglas Walton (1986) considers several traditional definitions and shows them to be inconsistent, if not contradictory. He notes, too, that "in some cases, arguments that seem to be of the same general type as the fallacies are (in some sense) reasonably good arguments, that are, and ought to be, acceptable as legitimate ways of rationally persuading someone to accept a conclusion" (Walton, 1989, p. 7). Moreover, many of the fallacies that have been identified are probably of little practical consequence. Examples of them in the literature often seem contrived, and it is difficult to find, or to manufacture, examples of them that are likely to occur in real life. Nevertheless, I believe the word has enough cachet in common parlance that it can be used without too much fear of gross misunderstanding, and to avoid the term would be a serious omission from any book on argumentation.

A narrow definition of fallacy might limit the domain of the concept to deductive arguments, or more narrowly still, to arguments in syllogistic form: in this case, a fallacious argument would be an argument in which the conclusion does not logically follow from the premises. A broader definition would admit the possibility of inductive and informal arguments being deemed fallacious as well. It can be, and has been, maintained that all inductive arguments are invalid, inasmuch as the conclusions of such arguments state something that is not logically implicit in the premises, and the truth of generalizations usually cannot be verified empirically, because it is not possible to check all instances to which they apply. On the other hand, Hamblin (1970) takes the position: "Until it is clear whether induction is an argument-form in any way comparable with deduction there is nothing to be gained by treating inductive shortcomings as varieties of fallacy" (p. 47).

There is also the view, however, that inductive and informal arguments are not all equally good or equally bad and that it is possible to identify criteria for judging their merits. Whether inductive and informal arguments that fail with respect to the criteria are labeled fallacious is perhaps a matter of terminology; in any case, some of the fallacies that are discussed in what follows pertain to deductive reasoning, some pertain to inductive reasoning, and some to both.

One popular definition of fallacy that has come under fire is an argument that appears to be valid, or conclusive, but is not (Hamblin, 1970, p. 12; Joseph, 1906, p. 525; Pessin & Engel, 2015, p. 105). By their reference to appearance, this definition makes fallaciousness a subjective matter, and it does not provide an example of an argument the invalidity of which is obvious to everyone. It could be amended to the satisfaction of some, perhaps, as "an argument that appears to many or most people to be valid, but that, upon reflection, will be seen not to be." Hamblin (1970) also defines a fallacy simply as "an *invalid argument*" (p. 39) without reference to appearances and contends that "many invalid arguments have no appearance of validity" (p. 194). Hamblin explicitly rules out equating fallacy with false belief: "Someone who merely makes false statements, however absurd, is innocent of fallacy unless the statements constitute or express an argument" (p. 224).

Contrary to the notion that a fallacy is an invalid argument, Richard Whately (1995/1853) makes a distinction between logical and nonlogical fallacies. A logical fallacy is one in which an argument's conclusion does not follow from its premises. A nonlogical fallacy is an argument the conclusion of which does follow from its premises, but the reasoning is unacceptable on other grounds.

Various proposals have been made for broadening, or sharpening (or scuttling) the concept of fallacy, and it is not clear that general agreement on the matter is at hand. Here I can do no more than report a sampling of what various writers have said on the subject and then present a view that seems to me to be sensible, albeit in no sense authoritative.

Some definitions/representations of fallacy:

- "any unsound mode of arguing, which appears to demand our conviction, and to be decisive of the question in hand, when in fairness it is not" (Whately, 1995/1853, p. 67).
- an argument "*that seems to be valid* but *is not so*" (Hamblin, 1970, p. 12).
- an "argument which *should not* persuade a rational person to accept its conclusion" (Kahane, 1971, p. xi).
- "If you add two numbers and get a wrong sum, the mistake is just a mistake. If the wrong answer results from an argument that seems to make it correct, the mistake is a fallacy" (Bunch, 1982, p. 1).
- "[S]omething is only a fallacy within the framework of a properly articulated theory of fallacies" (Grootendorst, 1986, p. 335).
- "an argument that falls short of the appropriate logical standard" (Johnson, 1986, 1995, p. 112). Johnson contends that standards that have traditionally been used are too limiting because they apply only to deductive arguments.
- "an argument is fallacious if and only if the conclusion does not follow from the premises" (Finocchiaro, 1995/1987, p. 125). Finocchiaro describes six ways in which conclusions can fail to follow from premises, only one of which corresponds to the conventional idea of formal invalidity.
- "[A] mistake in reasoning, a mistake which occurs with some frequency in real arguments and which is characteristically deceptive" (Govier, 1986, 1995, p. 172). The notions of repetition and deceptiveness are explicit in Govier's treatment: "A fallacy is a mistake which is of a kind: it is repeatable and repeated in other contexts. A mistake in reasoning which is idiosyncratic and unlikely to be repeated does not qualify as a fallacy" (p. 173). As for deception, Govier contends that there need not be an intent to deceive, but that "What is required is that fallacious arguments will themselves tend to deceive in the sense that people will mistake them for good arguments" (p. 173, Footnote 3).

- "a pattern of argument that violates one of the criteria (relevance, sufficiency, acceptability) which good arguments must satisfy" (Johnson & Blair, 1993, p. 48).
- "a speech act that prejudices or frustrates efforts to resolve a difference of opinion" (van Eemeren & Grootendorst, 1995b, p. 136). Van Eemeren and Grootendorst contend that fallacies should be understood as faux pas of communication and that, according to their "pragmatic-dialectical" perspective, rules for critical discussion, violation of which constitute fallacies, apply only for discourse aimed at resolving differences of opinion. Pragmatic-dialectical rules, of which van Eemeren and Grootendorst propose ten, "are not formulated as production rules for generating rational arguments, but as conditions for resolving differences of opinion" (p. 143).

It is not unusual for writers to identify two or more types of fallacy. T. Edward Damer (1980), for example, identifies three types of fallacious reasoning. One can go wrong, according to this view, by (1) reasoning from an unacceptable premise, (2) reasoning from an irrelevant premise, or (3) reasoning from premises that are acceptable and relevant individually but that collectively do not constitute a warrant for the conclusion drawn.

Howard Kahane (1984) also characterizes fallacious reasoning as reasoning that fails to satisfy one or more of three criteria for cogent or correct reasoning. "To reason cogently, or correctly, we must: (1) reason from justified premises, (2) include all relevant information at our disposal, and (3) reason validly" (p. 47). Correct reasoning, according to this view, requires satisfying all three of these criteria; to reason fallaciously means to fail on at least one of them.

Both of these definitions go beyond the connotation that fallacy is given in the narrow formal-logic sense. From this broader perspective, Damer's and Kahane's definitions are excellent, in my view. The main reservation that I have with them is Kahane's requirement that one considers all relevant information at one's disposal. The problem with this requirement is that more often than not is impossible to meet simply because the amount of information that is relevant to any particular conclusion one may be trying to draw is simply too great.

Trudy Govier (1986, 1995) distinguishes three senses in which the terms *valid* and *invalid* are used by logicians:

(1) An argument is valid if its premises are properly connected to its conclusion and provide adequate reasons for it. It is invalid otherwise. (Umbrella validity).

(2) An argument is valid if its premises deductively entail its conclusion, that is, given the truth of those premises, the falsity of the conclusion is a logical impossibility. It is invalid otherwise. (Semantic validity).
(3) An argument is valid if its conclusion is formally derivable from its premises using the rules of a correct logical system. It is invalid otherwise. (Formal validity) (1995, p. 178).

Rudolf Flesch (1951), in a book titled *The Art of Clear Thinking*, distinguishes four types of fallacies that one should be able to recognize if one wants to know "how not to be bamboozled:" formal fallacies, verbal fallacies (tricky use of words) and two types of material fallacies. The two types of material fallacies, in Flesch's words, are: "You either bring up a point that is irrelevant or leave out a point that is relevant" (p. 96). Leaving out a point that is relevant is an example of a failure of omission, but it is not the only one.

Alfred Sidgwick (1884) contends that the term *fallacy* is used in at least four senses:

> (1) A piece of false reasoning, in the narrower sense; either an invalid "immediate inference," or an invalid syllogism; a supposed equivalent form which is not equivalent, or a syllogism that breaks one of the rules.
> (2) A piece of false reasoning, in the wider sense; whereby, from true facts, a false conclusion is inferred.
> (3) A false belief, whether due to correct reasoning from untrue premises (reasons or sources) or to incorrect reasoning from true ones.
> (4) Any mental confusion whatever (p. 172).

There are many other definitions or characterizations of *fallacy*, but this sample suffices to illustrate the diversity of understandings of the concept. I invite the reader to articulate what, if anything, these representations have in common, or what they collectively purport about the nature of fallacy or about what a fallacy is believed to be. Our concern is with fallaciousness as a property of arguments and I propose to consider a fallacious argument to be an argument that violates a rule of logic or a widely held principle of sound reasoning. The definitions offered by Joseph (1906), Hamblin (1970), Damer (1980), and Kahane (1984) strike me as elegantly simple and adequate for present purposes.

In formal logic, a fallacy is committed when the structure of an argument violates one or more of the rules of deductive inference. The argument, "If p, then q; not p; therefore, not q," is said to be fallacious because the conclusion does not follow from the premises. The validity of an argument, in this sense, has nothing to do with the truth or falsity of any of its premises. Some inferences are easier for people to make than others, or to say the same thing in a different way, some implicative relationships are more intuitively compelling than others. Why this should be so and what determines which inferences will be easy and which difficult, is not well understood. That certain types of fallacies are very commonly made has been recognized, however, for a long time.

Producing a list of common reasoning fallacies is not difficult but producing an exhaustive one is impossible. No matter what terms we use to designate the fallacies, there is likely to be considerable overlap among the types we identify, as well as contention regarding whether they are appropriately considered to be fallacies or not. They do, nevertheless, impair the quality of thinking in various ways.

Types (and Examples) of Fallacies

Specific fallacies that have been considered common have been identified and given names by philosophers and logicians over the centuries. Aristotle (in *On Sophistical Refutations,* circa 359 BC) identified thirteen types of fallacies, six of which he described as fallacies dependent on language and seven of which he called fallacies outside of language. (A translation of *On Sophistical Refutations* by W. A. Pickard is available on the Internet from classics.mit.edu.) The fallacies that Aristotle identified as dependent on language are the following six:

- Equivocation. Any fallacy stemming from the double meaning of a word. For example, when two sentences of a syllogism treat different meanings of the word in two premises as though they had the same meaning. (Recall the example of "cold soup is better than eternal bliss" in Chapter 3.) Lawrence Powers (1995), who notes that the fallacy of equivocation, in its broadest sense, is "the fallacy of trading on an ambiguity" takes the position that there is only one fallacy, and it is this one: "equivocation is not only an important fallacy; it is the only fallacy" (p. 287). Powers contends that many of the "fallacies" that various writers have identified are not really fallacies, because the invalid arguments that are used to illustrate them are obviously invalid – they do not appear to be valid – and the appearance of validity is a requirement of fallaciousness. "Since I believe there is no clear way to make an argument *appear* to have a goodness it really lacks except by playing with ambiguities, every real fallacy will turn out to be a fallacy of equivocation" (p. 290). However, Powers distinguishes several types of ambiguity, so it could be argued that his "One Fallacy Theory" turns out to recognize several types of fallacy – corresponding to his several types of ambiguity – after all.

- Amphiboly. "[T]he same kind of thing as Equivocation except that the double meaning occurs in a construction involving several words unambiguous in themselves" (Hamblin, 1970, p. 16). Said another way, *amphiboly* is to *equivocation* what *sentence* is to *word.* Hamblin confesses that he was unable to find a bona fide example of an amphiboly. Examples of amphiboly are not as easy to construct as are examples of equivocation, but they can be found. Andrew Pessin and Morris Engel (2015, p. 106) offer as an example a Beatles album called *Best of the Beatles,* which refers to Pete Best, a drummer who was once a member of the group, but could lead a purchaser to assume the album contained the best of the Beatles' songs. Amphibolies sometimes show up in (presumably unintentionally) ambiguous headings of newspaper articles.
- Composition (Combinations of words). "What is true of a part is therefore asserted to be true of the whole" (Black, 1952, p. 232). "When an inference is made from properties of the parts of a whole, considered individually, to properties of the whole, considered organically or collectively, it is said that the fallacy of composition has been committed. For what is true of each of the parts may not hold true at all for the whole" (Hamblin, 1970, p. 19). From the fact that a paragraph is well organized, or even all the paragraphs of an essay are well organized, it does not follow that the essay as a whole is necessarily well organized.
- Division (of words). "Illicit replacement of a statement about a whole with a statement about its parts" (Hamblin, 1970, p. 21). This is the reverse of the fallacy of composition.
- Accent. There are many words in English (and presumably other languages as well) the meaning of which depends on which syllable is stressed (*content, object, invalid*). When such a word is used in two different premises that give it different interpretations, but it is treated as though it has the same interpretation in both, a fallacy of accent is said to have been made. (The more general problem is the use of the same word – same spelling, same pronunciation – but with different meanings in different contexts as though the meanings were the same.)
- Figure of speech (Form of expression). The *Encyclopedia Britannica* defines the figure-of-speech fallacy as involving confusion between the ordinary sense of a word and its metaphorical, figurative, or technical

use. Hamblin (1970) does not give it much space, contending that it is not easy to find examples of it. It has been controversial among modern scholars, dismissed as trivial by some, and considered a special case of equivocation by others (Huelsen, 1988).

The fallacies that Aristotle identified as outside of language are the following seven:

- Accident (*Fallacia accendentis*). "The fallacy of accident consists in applying a general rule to a particular case whose 'accidental' circumstances render the rule inapplicable" (Copi, 1961, quoted by Hamblin, 1970, p. 28). Antoine Arnauld and Pierre Nicole (1995/1865) define it as "when we draw a simple, unrestricted, and absolute conclusion, from what is true only by accident" (p. 42). It may also be described as overgeneralizing – applying a rule as though it had no exceptions when, in fact, it has some. Basing an argument on the claim that birds fly, without noting than some birds do not (emus, ostriches, baby birds, etc.), illustrates the fallacy.
- *Secundum quid.* "Fallacies secundum quid [more completely, *a dicto secundum quid ad dictum simpliciter*] are those which involve neglect of necessary qualifications" (Hamblin, 1970, p. 28). This means using propositions that require qualification as though they did not – as though they applied universally without qualification. Hamblin gives an example from John Oesterle (1952): "One thus argues fallaciously that the commandment 'Thou shalt not kill' forbids fighting for one's country. But the meaning and context of the commandment forbids killing an innocent person unjustly, that is, murdering" (p. 30). *Fallacia accendentis* (Accident) and *Secundum quid* are obviously closely related, if not identical. Hamblin notes that they are sometimes considered converses, the former going from general to particular and the latter from particular to general, but he suggests that the distinction is hard to maintain in practice. People use both types of fallacy, he says, "to seek a logical sanction for their personal prejudices," or "to bolster any preconceived notion anyone may happen to have" (p. 30). Hamblin also calls *secundum quid* "an ever-present and unavoidable possibility in practical situations, and any formal system that avoids it can do so only at the expense of features essential to natural language" (p. 213).
- Irrelevant conclusion (*Ignoratio elenchi*). Sometimes referred to as "ignorance of refutation," or "ignoring the issue," the fallacy has been defined also as "the ignorance of that which ought to be proved against an adversary" (Arnauld & Nicole, 1995/1865, p. 39). Hamblin (1970)

says that what Aristotle had in mind was a case in which "an arguer thinks he has proved one thing but has at best proved something else" (p. 31). Whately (1995/1853) points out that it may involve the substitution of various kinds of propositions for the one for which proof is required, and notes that it "may be employed as well for the apparent *refutation* of your opponent's proposition, as for the apparent establishment of your own; for it is substantially the same thing, to *prove* what was not denied, or to *disprove* what was not asserted" (p. 82). Illustrating the elasticity of the boundaries of the fallacies, Sidgwick (1884) says of this one: "in one sense it may be stretched to cover nearly every possible fallacy, while in another sense it is often narrowed to misinterpretation of the meaning of the Thesis" (p. 182).

- Affirming the consequent. Hamblin (1970) notes that Aristotle did not use the phrase "affirming the consequent," but he described the fallacy as supposing "that the relation of consequence is convertible. For whenever, suppose *A* is, *B* necessarily is, they then suppose that if *B* is, *A* necessarily is" (Hamblin, 1970, p. 35). This is the basis of the "conversion error" – inferring "If C then A" from "If A then C" – about which psychologists have made much, and to which we will return presently.
- Begging the question (*petitio principii*, or circular reasoning). Sidgwick (1884) equates this fallacy with tautological reasoning. He goes on to refer to the use of tautology as "chiefly a failing of feeble or timid folk," contrasting it with self-contradiction, which he considers "a danger to which the rash and immature seem especially liable" (p. 129). Arnauld and Nicole (1995/1865) see the fallacy as "assuming as true the thing in dispute" (p. 40). Edith Schipper and Edward Schuh (1960) describe it as "smuggling the conclusion [the answer to the question at issue] into the wording of the premises" (p. 55).

Regarding the last two definitions, one may ask, with respect to deductive reasoning, isn't the conclusion always contained, by implication, in the premises? If so, why should "smuggling the conclusion into the wording of the premises" be considered fallacious? Whately (1995/1853) addresses this question, in effect, in noting that

> it is not possible to mark precisely the distinction between the Fallacy in question and fair argument; since that may be correct and fair reasoning to one person, which would be, to another, "begging the question;" inasmuch as to one, the conclusion might be more evident than the premise, and to the

> other, the reverse. The most plausible form of this Fallacy is arguing in a *circle*; and the *greater* the circle, the harder to detect (p. 74).

Walton (1985, 1986, 1995) also contends that circular reasoning is sometimes fallacious and sometimes not. In his view an economist would not be begging the question by contending that many people are leaving a state because its economy is bad, while at the same time arguing that the economy is bad because many people are leaving the state.

- False cause. Taking for the cause that which is not the cause (*non causa pro causa*). A special case, *post hoc, ergo propter hoc,* involves assuming that because B always follows A, A is necessarily the cause of B. Pinto (1995) argues that the literature reveals at least three different kinds of reasoning that have been labeled post hoc. In the first case, a *particular* event is said to have been caused by another *particular* event simply because the latter preceded the former. In a second case, one *kind* of event is taken as the cause of another *kind* of event because events of the former kind generally have preceded events of the latter kind. To illustrate the third type of post hoc reasoning, Pinto refers to Book V of J. S. Mill's *System of Logic* where he treats it "as a species of faulty generalization and appears to construe it as the attempt to establish a causal law from a single sequence of events" (p. 305). Pinto argues that "*post hoc* reasoning – at least of the sort that proceeds from genuine correlation to cause – need not be fallacious" (p. 306). He questions whether post hoc reasoning, in the sense of concluding that one event caused another *only* on the basis of the temporal sequence, ever really occurs. No one, he contends, would conclude that one event (Madonna's lover cutting himself while shaving) caused another (Gorbachev's fall) simply because the first event preceded the second. For a minimally rational agent to infer causality there must be some reason in addition to temporal succession to infer a causal relationship.

Whately (1995/1853) notes that people may believe, and claim, a cause-effect relationship when they lack compelling evidence that it is so: "[N] othing is more common than to hear a person state confidently, as from his own experience, that such and such a patient *was cured* by this or that medicine: whereas all that he absolutely *knows*, is that he took the medicine, and that he recovered" (p. 79). Lewis Thomas (1983) gives an engaging, but sobering, account of the many treatments of diseases that were in vogue as recently as the early part of the twentieth century – "bleeding cupping, violent purging, the raising of blisters by vesicant ointments, the immersion of the body in either ice water or intolerably hot water, endless lists of botanical extracts cooked up and mixed together under the influence of nothing more than pure whim" (p. 19). Treatments persisted because they were credited with the survival of the survivors, while the possibility that the survivors survived despite the treatments was conveniently ignored.

- Fallacy of many questions. Making of more than one question into one. Aristotle made much of the tendency of people to treat words that have more than one meaning as though they had only one. This tendency, he contends, underlies the fallacy of amphiboly and the general problem of ambiguity.

In addition to identifying these thirteen fallacies, Aristotle mentions, in *Topics,* other kinds of faulty reasoning. Examples include reasoning that appears to be syllogistic but really is not, and reasoning that, although syllogistic, starts from false premises. The second of these examples again illustrates the need to distinguish between validity and truth. From a strictly formal point of view, an argument in which the conclusion is implied by the premises is considered valid, even if one or more of its premises and the implied conclusion are false.

The fallacies and other reasoning problems identified by Aristotle served as the point of departure for many subsequent writers on logic, rhetoric, argumentation and related subjects. Isaac Watts (1995/1796), for example, provides a list that is very similar to that provided by Aristotle. He adds "imperfect enumeration" or "false induction" to connote the leap one takes in generalizing from a few cases to a universal conclusion. Other writers have meddled with Aristotle's taxonomy, adding or subtracting fallacies to or from his list, revising some of his definitions, dividing some of the types into subtypes, arguing that some of the distinctions do not stand scrutiny, and so on. An account of (conflicting) treatments of fallacies by influential writers between Aristotle and relatively recent times (Arnauld, Nicole, Locke, Watts, Whately, Mill) is given by Hamblin (1970) and, in brief, by Hansen and Pinto (1995b).

Hamblin (1970) argues that the distinctions among fallacies that are based on language and those that are not is not very marked in all cases. He notes too that for more than a millennium after Aristotle, very little progress was made in the work on fallacies: "the entire bulk of extant literature on the subject, from the time of Aristotle up to the eleventh century A.D., would hardly fill a small notebook" (p. 89). Eventually, however, numerous lists of fallacies were proposed by logicians and philosophers, the compositions of which reveal a remarkable diversity of thought.

Late in the seventeenth century, John Locke (1995/1690) identified four sorts of arguments, that he believed people commonly use:

- *Argumentum ad verecundiam* (appeal to authority). The defense of a belief or opinion on the basis of its being held by someone who is recognized to be an authority on the subject. Hamblin (1970) notes that the word *verecundia* means "shame," "shyness," or "modesty" and suggests that its use to refer to an argument that rests on authority is not quite appropriate. On the other hand, it is not hard to imagine that people who are shy or modest might be more inclined to defer to authority than are people who have the opposite qualities.
- *Argumentum ad ignorantiam.* Attempting to prove a point by appealing to ignorance. Requiring one's adversary to admit what one proposes as a proof if he or she cannot offer a better one. Fallacious because the fact that I cannot think of an argument that is more compelling than the one you have offered does not mean that yours is necessarily valid. M. Wreen (1986), who describes the fallacy as consisting of arguing that a proposition is true because it has not been shown to be false, or that it is false because it has not been shown to be true, contends that this is not a fallacy, or at least that it is not always a fallacy: "Some *ad ignorantiams* are perfectly in order; sometimes no reason is a good reason" (p. 63). Eric Krabbe (1995) cites an example provided by Walton: "the ignorance premise: *it has not been proven that this gun is unloaded* is, within [certain] contexts, a good reason to accept the proposition that *the gun is loaded*" (p. 260). Ulrike Hahn and Michael Oaksford (2006, 2007) too make a case that *argumentum ad ignorantiam* is not fallacious; and they make similar cases for *petitio principia* and *slippery slope* arguments. They contend that it is not so much the form of an argument that determines whether it is fallacious, but its content.
- *Argumentum ad hominem.* This term has more than one connotation as it is used in the literature. Locke (1995/1690) used it to connote the pressing of an opponent with "consequences drawn from his own principles or concessions" (p. 56). This type of argument is legitimate, Locke contends, when one's purpose is not the truth of a proposition but the self-consistency of its proposer. Maurice Finocchiaro (1986) gives a similar definition: "Ad hominem argument is reasoning where the arguer derives a conclusion not acceptable to an opponent from

premises accepted by the opponent, but not necessarily generally acceptable" (p. 86). A quite different connotation that has been given to argumentum ad hominem is that of disparaging (or commending) an argument on the grounds of the character of the person who advanced it. Although there appears to be general agreement that ad hominem arguments can be, and often are, fallacious, they can also be seen as legitimate as, for example, when one notes that Mr. Smith's explanation of what caused the unusually heavy snowfall last winter is best viewed with some skepticism because Mr. Smith is known to have a ready explanation for everything and is generally proven wrong. Alan Briton (1995) contends that many, if not most, of the ad hominem arguments that occur in real life – as distinct from those found in logic textbooks – are a legitimate form of argument, serving a useful purpose in helping one decide what, or whom, to believe. In contrast, Frans van Eemeren and Robert Grootendorst (1995a), who define an argument as "a critical discussion aimed at resolving a difference of opinion," see ad hominem arguments as invariably fallacious: "In a critical discussion, an *argumentum ad hominem* is, in fact, always highly relevant, but in a negative sense: it hinders, or sometimes even prevents, the resolution of a difference of opinion" (p. 228).

- *Argumentum ad judicium.* "[T]he using of proofs drawn from any of the foundations of knowledge or probability" (Locke, 1995/1690, p. 56). Of the four types of argument he identified, Locke considered only the fourth one to be legitimate in the sense of advancing knowledge; the first three are commonly used, he contended, to get the better of one's opponent in a dispute but are not instructive, or knowledge building.

Late in the eighteenth century, Watts (1995/1796) classified arguments into several types on the basis of a variety of properties or characteristics. Of greatest interest for present purposes is his recognition of several sophisms – arguments that appear to be valid but are not. He identifies the following eight, all of which have already been mentioned, but not always described in precisely the same words:

- *Ignoratio elenchi.* "[W]hen something else is proved which has neither any necessary Connection or Inconsistency with the Thing enquired, and consequently gives no Determination to the Enquiry, tho' it may seem at first Sight to determine the Question" (p. 61).
- *Petitio principii.* "[A] supposition of what is not granted; that is, when any Proposition is proved by the same Proposition in other words, or by something that is equally uncertain and disputed" (p. 61).

- A circle. Very similar to *petitio principii*: "when one of the Premises in a Syllogism is questioned and opposed, and we pretend to prove it by the Conclusion: Or, when in a Train of Syllogisms we prove the last by recurring to what was the Conclusion of the first" (p. 62).
- *Non causa pro causa*. "[T]he assignation of a false cause" (p. 62).
- *Fallacia accidentis*. "[A] sophism wherein we pronounce concerning the Nature and essential Properties of any Subject, according to something which is merely accidental to it" (p. 64).
- *A dicto secundum quid ad dictum simpliciter*. "[W]hen we argue from that which is true in particular Circumstances to prove the same thing true absolutely, simply, and abstracted from all Circumstances" (p. 64). Among several illustrations of this type of argument, Watts gives: "Livy writes Fables and Improbabilities when he describes Prodigies and Omens; therefore, Livy's Roman History is never to be believed in any thing" (p. 64).
- Sophisms of composition and division. The former is "when we infer any thing concerning Ideas in a compounded Sense, which is only true in a divided Sense," and the latter is "when we infer the same Thing concerning Ideas in a Divided Sense, which is only true in a compounded sense" (p. 65).

As time passed, fallacy lists tended to get longer. In 1959, W. Ward Fearnside and William Holther (1959) listed and illustrated fifty-one fallacies, and discussed many of them at considerable length. They gave the term "fallacy" a relatively broad connotation; many of the problems they discussed might better be thought of as examples of faulty reasoning rather than as fallacies in a logical sense. All fifty-one are listed in Appendix A, along with a brief comment on each, representing my effort to convey the gist of the associated fallacy. Certainly, in many cases, others would produce a different synopsis; readers should consult Fearnside and Holther's original list when my synopsis seems inappropriate.

As the number of fallacies continued to increase, efforts were made to organize them in some helpful fashion. Fallacy trees by Alexander, Fraunce, Junge, Whately, and others are described in Hamblin (1970). A. Craig Baird (1950), after contending that "any complete classification of fallacies is probably impossible" (p. 163), offers "for practical purposes," a classification of fifty plus fallacies in eleven categories. The title of the chapter in which the classification appears is "Obstacles to straight thinking," suggesting that "fallacy" here is given a broad connotation. Among the fallacies, aka obstacles, included in the list are vague definitions, loose grammar and syntax, unsupported assertion, ambiguity in statement of facts, ignoring negative instances, and repeated affirmation. Baird's book is essentially a primer on argumentation – full of advice and examples of both how to argue effectively and how to do it wrongly. Baird does not hesitate to base advice on his opinion and is not compulsive about supporting it with pointers to relevant research. The advice that is offered sometimes seems a bit simplistic; a chapter on the use of language for composing arguments contains the following suggestions: "Adapt your language to the audience" (p. 204). "Use accurate language" (p. 205). "Use objective language" (p. 206). "Be concrete" (p. 206). "Be concise" (p. 207). "Use unhackneyed language" (p. 208). "Use illustrative or figurative language" (p. 208). "Use oral language in speech composition" (p. 209). "Use variety in language" (p. 211). Somewhat ironically, Baird writes: "Arguers of all kinds . . . fill their discourse with bold or fairly subdued remarks that ring with confidence but fail to echo facts or sustained arguments. Mere assertion is probably the commonest fallacy in argument and may be technically put down as argument without evidence" (p. 170). These quibbles notwithstanding, the reader will find much in Baird's book that is thought provoking and useful.

For present purposes, the foregoing examples should give a sense of the variety of behaviors the concept of fallacy covers. It should be borne in mind too that, as Hamblin (1970) points out, several writers of note (Cohen & Nagel, 1934; De Morgan, 1926/1847; Joseph, 1916/1906) have argued that fallacies cannot be classified, that there simply are too many ways that reasoning can go wrong. Finocchiaro (1980) contends that "the concept of a fallacy as a type of common but logically incorrect argument is a chimera since the various disputed practices usually referred to as fallacious are either not common or not logically incorrect or not arguments" (p. 337).

The problem of counting fallacies is complicated by the fact that often one may choose whether to consider a given instance of poor reasoning to be an example of one fallacy or several. The longest list of fallacies of which I am aware contains 167 items (Gula, 1979); Hunter Lewis (1990) contends that all 167 boil down to just three: "lack of clarity, irrelevance, or incompleteness" (p. 42). Hans Hansen and Robert Pinto (1995) put the number of the "more or less traditional list of prominent fallacy labels" at around eighteen to twenty. They note, however, that contemporary authors are free to create new labels, and that they often do. An example of a recently created label is the "numbers fallacy," which refers to the commonly held belief that as the number of tosses of a fair coin increases, the numbers of heads and tails become increasingly close to equal; when in fact the *numbers* of heads and tails diverge while the *percentages* of heads and tails converge to 50 percent each (Falk & Lavie Lann, 2015).

It seems safe to say that no list of all the forms of reasoning that have been claimed by one or another authority on the subject to be fallacious would satisfy all the claimants, be it ever so long. Also, in view of the remarkable variety in the number and type of fallacies that have been identified by scholars over the years it is not surprising that there have been efforts to distinguish among them in terms of their relative importance. In the context of a discussion of argumentation and decision-making, Rieke and Sillars (1975) describe the following eleven arguments as especially troublesome:

- Non sequitur argument: "[P]robably the most commonly cited problem in general argumentation" (p. 89). Inferring something that is not supported by the evidence.
- Circular reasoning: Taking A as evidence for B, and B as evidence for A.
- Irrelevant argument: Taking as evidence of the truth of a claim something that is not relevant to the claim.
- Ignoring the opposite: Failure to pay attention to arguments other than one's own, especially arguments that produce conclusions that are inconsistent with one's own.
- Shifting the burden: Claiming that one's protagonist must prove that one's claim is false, rather than taking responsibility for proving that one's claim is true.
- Overstating a claim: Making claims that go beyond what evidence will support.
- Hasty generalization: Going from "some" to "all" before the evidence justifies doing so.
- Insufficient cause: That B invariably follows A does not prove that A causes B. (Tuesday invariably follows Monday, but Monday does not cause Tuesday.)
- Inadequate sign: Signs vary in their reliability. An inadequate sign is a sign that is taken to be adequate (a reliable indication of what it is a sign of) when it is not.
- Inadequate analogies: All analogies have limits. An analogy is inadequate when the analogs fail to correspond with respect to characteristics that are relevant to the point(s) being made. Sidgwick (1884) cautions about the use of analogies; the danger, he says, is "that the resemblance between the cases supposed to be analogous is only a superficial one –

or, more widely still, that the resemblance, even if on the whole real and deep, is not essential for the purpose intended" (p. 253).

- Allness: The tendency to treat claims that pertain to many members of a class as though they pertained to all members of the class.

Rieke and Sillars use the term "problems of argument" in order "to avoid the rigid interpretation of the term fallacy" (p. 94), but many of the problems they list are readily considered examples of fallacious reasoning. We shall see that the term *fallacy*, as it appears in the psychological literature, has been used to refer to a considerable variety of faulty or less-than-perfect reasoning.

Hamblin (1970) himself appears to have despaired of the possibility of producing a classificatory scheme for fallacies that would be an improvement on the many that had been proposed:

> [T]here does not seem to be much point in producing *any* new theory of fallacies in the same vein as the old. There have been too many already. Least of all should one aim at producing a new *classification* of the old material, yet another tree. Classification is sometimes a useful preliminary in dealing with unstudied material, and sometimes – not always – it is the upshot of a successful investigation. Our concern, however, is with the middle part of the study, and so many have failed with this that it should be clear by now that they have been asking the wrong questions. One of the main reproaches that could be brought against the study of fallacies is that it has always remained an appendage, insecurely connected to the main part of Logic. A new classification of fallacies does nothing to remedy this; and if the subject cannot be brought into closer relation with the rest of Logic, a radical reappraisal, either of the study of fallacies, or of the rest of Logic, is called for (p. 190).

Hamblin's book evoked a range of reactions by scholars and students of reasoning and proved to be a major stimulus to further work. As Grootendorst (1986) notes, "His criticism of the so-called Standard Treatment [the typical treatment found in modern textbooks] has to no slight degree influenced almost everyone concerned with fallacies, albeit that the reactions to it were far from unanimous" (p. 331).

> The chief weakness in the Standard Treatment, according to Hamblin, is that quite a high proportion of the sorts of fallacy that are discussed do not answer to the standard definition of a fallacy . . .. But in some of the fallacies described in the Standard Treatment there is no question of an *argument* at all, whereas in some others the argument is not *invalid* (p. 331).

Much recent work on fallacious reasoning has focused on difficulties people have in dealing with statistical relationships (Falk & Konold, 1992): the gambler's fallacy, the conjunction fallacy, the inclusion fallacy, among others. The gambler's fallacy takes many guises, all of which rest on one or another misconception of randomness, of which there are many (Falk, 1991, 2011, 2016; Falk & Konold, 1997, 1998; Zabell, 1992) and manifests itself in choices that reflect the assumption of dependency among independent events. Ruma Falk (2016) provides a comprehensive and insightful treatment.

The conjunction fallacy occurs when one assigns a probability to the joint occurrence of two independent events that is higher than the probability one assigned to either of the two constituent events (Charness, Karni, & Levin, 2009; Kahneman & Tversky, 1982a; Sherman, Judd, & Park, 1989; Tversky & Kahneman, 1983). It has stimulated a great deal of research and much debate about whether it should be considered a fallacy in all the contexts in which it has been found (Bovens & Hartmann, 2003; Crupi, Fitleson, & Tentori, 2008; Hintikka, 2004).

The inclusion fallacy is similar to the conjunction fallacy; in fact, it could be considered a special case of the latter. It occurs when one judges the probability of a statement about all members of a class [e.g., bankers] to be more likely to be true than the same statement about all members of a subset of that class (e.g., young bankers) (Osherson, 1995). It could also be considered an instance of unjustified generalization.

Another example of fallacious reasoning that relates to statistics is the negative effect fallacy. Ryan Enos, Anthony Fowler, and Christopher Havasy (2017) describe this fallacy as a conflation of the philosophical and arithmetic definitions of *negative*. "Although it is often difficult to prove that something does not exist (e.g., can we prove that Santa Claus does not exist?), there is no reason that we cannot show evidence that the effect of a law on an outcome of interest is arithmetically negative" (p. 620). Enos et al. claim that the idea that a negative is hard, or impossible, to prove has been used inappropriately in many court cases, including cases heard by the Supreme Court: "In short, relevant statistical evidence has been repeatedly ignored by federal courts because of an elementary but contagious error of language and logic" (p. 620).

In addition to the fallacies mentioned so far, many others have been given names in the literature. In some cases, the fallacies named are similar, if not identical, to some that have been discussed under other names. In other cases, they stretch the connotation of "fallacy" beyond what many scholars would consider to be appropriate; they may be seen as examples of poor reasoning, but not necessarily as fallacies, unless "fallacy" is defined in such a way as to include all instances of faulty reasoning.

The Relativity of Fallaciousness

> The myriad and intricate schemes for classifying fallacies suggest that there is little theory behind the science of fallacy. This suggestion misleads only by implying that there is any theory at all behind it. The unvarnished truth is this: *there is no theory of fallacy whatsoever*!
>
> (Massey, 1995/1981, p. 160).

We often speak as though "fallacy" were an unambiguous conceptual category and that any bit of reasoning could be identified unequivocally as either valid or fallacious. Things are far from as simple as that. What constitutes an instance of fallacious reasoning can be, and often is, the subject of considerable debate (Cohen, 1981; Finocchiaro, 1981; Henle, 1962; Ulrich, 1985); as the preceding definitions and characterizations show, experts do not always agree as to what is fallacious and what is not.

The lack of a widely endorsed definition or characterization of fallacy is seen by some as an insurmountable hurdle to progress in the study of the subject. This is especially true of informal arguments. Hamblin (1970) describes the problem this way: "Within a *formal language* it is generally clear enough which arguments are formally valid; but an ordinary-language argument cannot be declared 'formally valid' or 'formally fallacious' until the language within which it is expressed is brought into relation with that of some logical system" (p. 193). Karel Lambert and William Ulrich (1980) make a similar point: "Until a general characterization of informal fallacies can be given which enables one to tell with respect to any argument whether or not it exhibits one of the informal fallacies, knowing how to label certain paradigm cases of this or that mistake in reasoning is not really useful for determining whether a given argument is acceptable" (p. 332). Moreover, the situation is complicated by the fact that whether an argument is generally considered fallacious – or how fallacious it is considered to be – can depend on the context in which it is made. More on this point presently.

Hamblin (1970) notes that as of the time of his writing there had not yet been a book-length study of fallacies – or of incorrect reasoning more generally – and that the subject had typically been treated "as an afterthought or adjunct to something else" (p. 10). There did not exist, he claimed, a theory of fallacy in the sense in which there existed theories of correct reasoning.

Later, Gerald Massey (1975a, 1975b, 1995/1981) also argued that there does not exist a theory of fallacy, or a theory of invalidity on which a theory of fallacy might be based. There is a theory of validity, he contended, in the sense that there are forms of argument that are recognized as valid, and if an argument represented in natural language can be translated into a form that is recognized as valid, then that argument is to be considered valid. But there are also forms that are recognized to be invalid, so it would seem natural to claim also that if a translation yields a form that is recognized to be invalid, the original argument should be considered invalid. But Massey contended that to show an argument to be invalid, one must show that there is no way to translate it into a form that would be recognized as valid by any logical system, and this is not possible. Clearly, Massey's criterion for establishing validity is much less demanding than his criterion for establishing invalidity. Massey acknowledged this asymmetry, but did not see it as an impediment to good thinking:

> All of us try to advance good arguments, and validity is one element of the goodness sought. If we devise a seemingly good argument only to find its validity challenged, we can call upon logical theory which will usually establish its validity to everyone's satisfaction.
>
> But suppose none of the arguments we devise for some proposition *p* strikes us as valid? What then? Do we need a theory of invalidity to discredit them? By no means! That these arguments seem upon careful reflection to be invalid is reason enough to abandon them and to look elsewhere for a good argument for *p*. It is much the same with arguments propounded by others. When appropriate, we can invoke logical theory to validate those arguments that appear good to us. Those that upon close scrutiny seem invalid are best set aside unless and until their composers or admirers supply cogent evidence of their validity. In short, the asymmetry inherent in showing validity and invalidity is exactly counterbalanced by a pragmatic asymmetry in burden of proof. Consequently, the asymmetry thesis does not generate any special difficulties for the practical use of logic (p. 167).

Govier (1986, 1995) takes exception to Massey's position in part because of its coupling of fallaciousness with invalidity. She argues that invalidity is neither necessary nor sufficient for fallaciousness. She objects too to Massey's failure to recognize the possibility of having a theoretically adequate method as distinct from a formally adequate method and argues that those who think that respectable informal theories of argument are possible will find this unacceptable.

John Woods (1995b), in contrast, goes even further than Massey in claiming the impossibility of a theory of invalidity that can be applied to natural-language arguments. He contends that it is also impossible to have a theory of validity for what he refers to as "arguments on the hoof." The problem, in his view as I understand it, is that there does not exist an adequate theoretical basis for reliably transforming natural-language arguments into precise logical forms. The conclusion to which he comes is, in his words, not a happy one. "It compromises the ambitions of any formal logician naïve enough to think that a theory of logical forms could be grafted onto natural languages in ways that disclose the logical structures that they 'really' have" (p. 193). As for the informal logician, he or she, Woods contends, "is simply out of business" (p. 193).

Debates about what constitutes fallaciousness, or invalidity, and whether either can be demonstrated conclusively are likely to continue. It is ironic that experts on logic find it so difficult to agree on such fundamental questions about what can and cannot be proved. Perhaps it tells us something about the limitations of human reasoning, or about the extraordinary ability of people to defend positions they advocate and to construct counterarguments to those they oppose. Here it suffices to acknowledge this debate.

A widely recognized problem in the identification of reasoning fallacies is that what constitutes fallacious reasoning often depends on the context. That is to say many of the types or aspects of reasoning that have been classified as fallacious are legitimate in some contexts but not in others. Samuel Fillenbaum (1975, 1976) contends that, unlike the inferential problems that people are often given in psychological experiments, those they encounter in real life are always in a context and their solutions benefit from, or perhaps require, the use of knowledge relating to those contexts. He argues that whether a particular line of reasoning should be considered logically fallacious depends on the frame of reference in which it is viewed, and what appears to be a logical fallacy looked at in one light may be seen as a pragmatically reasonable inference in another; in particular, what is fallacious in the abstract can, in many instances, be pragmatically sound reasoning in real-world situations.

Cohen (1981) makes a similar case in arguing that in order to understand a speaker's intention in normal discourse, one must attend not only to the words that are spoken but to the "total act of communication," which includes the contextual circumstances in which the communication occurs. Comparable arguments have been made by others (Krabbe, 1995; Walton, 1986; Wertz, 1985; Woods, 1995a, 1995b; Wreen, 1986).

From one point of view, we might say that many of the "fallacies" are really fallacious only when misused. Investigators have pointed out, for example, that some norms of reasoning that would be considered fallacious in the sense of violating rules of formal logic are precisely what are needed to make induction and learning possible (Evans, 1993; Stevenson, 1993). Over 160 years ago, Whately (1995/1853) contended that many types of argument that were widely considered fallacious – *argumentum ad hominem, argumentum ad verecundiam, argumentum ad populum* – should be considered fallacious not invariably, but only when used unfairly. Similar points of view have been expressed more recently (Stich & Nisbett, 1984; Toulmin, Rieke, & Janik, 1984/1979; Walton, 1986; Willard, 1995).

Walton (1986), for example, notes that when one begins to study fallacies that are often listed in textbooks on argumentation, one finds that such arguments are not always unreasonable. "So generally speaking, the real problem is that of constructing guidelines to enable a reasonable evaluator to judge in a particular case whether the type of argument can be shown to be reasonable or fallacious" (p. 325). But Walton is not optimistic that such guidelines can be developed; the problem, he suggests, is that the dichotomous distinction between arguments that are fallacious and those that are not is too simple:

> In arguments on controversial subjects in natural language, most often the most useful job of a reasonable critic is not necessarily to show that an argument criticized can be rejected completely. Such strong refutation may be neither possible nor practical. More often the most useful job of the critic is to show that an argument lacks needed support and is therefore open to reasonable questioning. For this weaker kind of criticism is often enough to reserve or withdraw the commitment of the audience to whom the argument is directed. Thus, the broad use of the term "fallacy" has engendered the unfortunate misconception that all kinds of arguments coming under the heading of a recognized type of "fallacy" are essentially worthless, and should be completely refuted by the standards of logic (p. 326).

Walton goes on to contend that examples of fallacies that one is likely to find in textbooks are too simplistic: "Often, particular examples of the so-called 'fallacies' can be defended as not unreasonable arguments in various contexts" (p. 328).

From this perspective, understanding fallacies involves understanding those conditions under which certain types of reasoning are fallacious (i.e., are being used unfairly), and those under which they are not. However, it is not always easy, or perhaps even possible, to make this distinction and to draw the line between fair and unfair behavior. When, for example, does the laudable desire to be self-consistent over time become obstinacy and an objectionable resistance to change? How does one distinguish between an honest effort to understand opposing sides on a controversial issue and moral weakness that manifests itself in an unwillingness to take a position on a matter of controversy? When does a healthy regard for experience, expertise, or tradition cross the line to become unreasonable deference to authority?

Richard Nisbett and Lee Ross (1980) concluded from their review of work on human inference that many of the inferential errors that people commonly make result from the use of inferential strategies that are valid and effective in many, but not all, contexts. This is the nature of heuristic processes, the functional value of which lies in the fact that they typically simplify what might otherwise be overly complex tasks. The cost of this simplification is that the approaches are not guaranteed to work perfectly in all of the instances in which they are applied. Some of the inductive thinking skills that are so useful in many contexts (interpolation, extrapolation, generalization) can also yield erroneous conclusions. Whether the benefit derived from the simplification and the resulting decreased call on one's cognitive resources is worth the cost depends on how effective the approaches are on average.

Nisbett and Ross defend the assumption that the benefits derived from using these strategies – or even overutilizing them, to use their term – is worth the cost of the erroneous results they sometimes produce. "They probably produce vastly more correct or partially correct inferences than erroneous ones, and they do so with great speed and little effort. Indeed, we suspect that the use of such simple tools may be an inevitable feature of the cognitive apparatus of any organism that must make as many judgments, inferences, and decisions as humans have to do" (p. 18). They argue that intuitive strategies, even though normatively inappropriate in a strict sense, can serve us well on balance and that the cost of applying them is typically low relative to the cost of applying more formal or normatively correct strategies.

William Lycan (1988) also suggests that some of the inductive rules that guide our thinking may be overly general in the interest of simplicity, and that we are probably well served by the fact.

> A tendency to jump quickly to conclusions may be more useful on the whole than a respect for textbook adequacy of sample size ... a proneness to false

> beliefs of certain sorts may serve important noncognitive evolutionary needs. We tend to overestimate the attractiveness and other admirable qualities of our own children; we quickly forget the painfulness of certain otherwise useful activities; we habitually deceive ourselves in any number of beneficial ways (p. 345).

It can be, and has been, argued too that reasoning that is technically fallacious, in the sense that it violates the dictates of standard logic, can nevertheless be effective in certain instances. Affirming the consequent and denying the antecedent (see section below) have long been recognized as fallacious forms of deductive argument, but in some contexts committing these fallacies can have practically useful results (Fillenbaum, 1976; Geis & Zwicky, 1971). It has been suggested that a reason why *modus tollens* and contrapositive arguments are (it seems) not part of the repertoire of people's logical intuitions is because they do not have great practical utility (Cheng & Nisbett, 1993).

What follows are brief discussions of examples of reasoning that are generally considered fallacious, at least in certain contexts. A question of interest is whether some of these types of reasoning could be effective in some contexts despite the fact that they would be considered fallacious in those or in others.

Formal and Linguistic Difficulties and Confusions

Some of the reasoning difficulties that have been studied relate directly to logical or syntactical forms. That is not to say that they occur only in the context of using formal logic, but to understand them it is helpful to make the connection to logic explicit.

Premise Conversion

> What seems to be an invalid inference is nothing more than a valid inference from other premises
>
> (Johnson-Laird & Byrne, 1991, p. 18).

As we have already noted, some investigators have defended the position that many, if not most, of what appear to be errors of logic in deductive reasoning are better seen as the consequences of linguistic confusions or misconstruals, the idea being that people often misinterpret the premises of arguments but then draw conclusions that follow logically from the premises as misinterpreted (Chapman & Chapman, 1959; Cohen, 1981; Henle,

1962; Newstead, 1990; Revlis, 1975a, 1975b). People find it easy, for example, to confuse the probability of C, contingent on A, with the probability of A, contingent on C. They often misinterpret the conditional statement "If A then C" with "If C then A" (or equivalently "C if A" with "A if C"). And they sometimes treat "All A are C" as though it were equivalent to "All C are A," or "Some As are not Cs" as though the same in meaning as "Some Cs are not As." These are examples of what has been called the "premise conversion" error.

James Erickson (1974) suggests that the probability that the assertion "All A are C" will be interpreted as expressing the identity or equivalence relationship (all A are C and all C are A) may be as high as 0.75. The probability that "Some A are not C" will be interpreted as expressing an overlap relationship – Some A are not C and some C are not A – may, in his view, be even higher. There is evidence that the probability of a conversion error may depend, in part, on the degree of ambiguity of a premise (Cesaro & Provitera, 1971), and that it can be reduced by instruction (Dickstein, 1975). It has been suggested that the kind of confusion represented by premise conversion explains the behavior of the participants in some of the experiments discussed by Cohen (1981) showing the tendency of people to ignore base rates in decision making (Margalit & Bar-Hillel, 1981).

According to James Roberge (1970), grade school children typically fail to recognize the invalidity of arguments of the form:

All As are Cs
X is a C
Therefore, X is an A

and

All As are Cs
X is not an A
Therefore, X is not a C.

This failure might be considered to be a form of the premise conversion error, because the conclusion in both cases would follow if the major premise were All Cs are As instead of all As are Cs.

When made with conditional assertions, the premise conversion error can be described as failure to distinguish between the conditional (If A then C) and the biconditional (If and only if A then C). This confusion is considered by some investigators to be most likely to occur when the sets represented by A and C are believed to be in a one-to-one relationship (Fillenbaum, 1975; Marcus & Rips, 1979; Rips & Marcus,

1977). When the belief happens to be correct, the confusion would cause no harm because it would square with reality.

Evidence that people often interpret premises of arguments differently from their intended interpretations is compelling (Falk, 1993; Fillenbaum, 1976; Galotti, Baron, & Sabini, 1986; Gebauer & Laming, 1997; Geis & Zwicky, 1971; Osman & Laming, 2001). Whether such changes suffice to account entirely for what otherwise would appear to be errors of logic is not so clear (Evans, 1982). The debate centers not on whether such changes occur but on the tenability of the assumption that they account for all (or most) of the errors that otherwise might be attributed to faulty reasoning. Johnson-Laird and Byrne (1991) point out that the idea that what appear to be errors of reasoning are really errors of interpretation of premises can be carried to the extreme that no conceivable observation can refute it; this would make it uninteresting as a scientific hypothesis.

Affirmation of the Consequent and Denial of the Antecedent

Closely related to problems of linguistic interpretation – one might even see them as examples of them – are the two classical errors associated with the *modus ponens* and *modus tollens* forms of the conditional syllogism. As already noted, the *modus ponens* form of argument is as follows:

If A then C
A
Therefore C,

and the *modus tollens*:

If A then C
Not C
Therefore, not A.

One fallacious form of the conditional, usually referred to as "affirmation of the consequent" (A is called the antecedent and C the consequent) is as follows:

If A then C
C
Therefore, A.

The other fallacious form, known as "denial of the antecedent" is:

If A then C

Not A
Therefore, not C.

The first two forms are sometimes denoted "closed forms" and the latter two as "open forms," because each of the former leads to a conclusion, but neither of the latter does. The *modus tollens* form is referred to as the contrapositive of the *modus ponens* form. The study of conditional reasoning involving these and other forms of argument is reviewed extensively in Nickerson (2015). Here I wish only to note briefly a few particulars that relate relatively directly to the subject of fallacies.

People commonly make both affirmation-of-the-consequent and denial-of-the-antecedent errors when reasoning with conditional statements (Markovits, 1988; Taplin, 1971; Taplin & Staudenmayer, 1973; Wildman & Fletcher, 1977). Galileo famously made the fallacious argument

If the planetary system is heliocentric, Venus will show phases,
Venus shows phases,
Therefore, the planetary system is heliocentric.

He was criticized for doing so by Kepler (Gingerich, 1982).

Affirmation-of-the-consequent and denial-of-the-antecedent forms of argument, slightly modified to acknowledge the tenuousness of their "conclusions," are widely used by scientists today as part of the hypothetico-deductive method. Affirming the consequent becomes

If A then C
C
Therefore, perhaps A.

And denying the antecedent becomes

If A then C
Not A
Therefore, perhaps not C.

In neither case can a firm conclusion be drawn without further investigation of the relationship between A and C. However, in each case a hypothesis regarding the nature of that relationship may be posited: Hypothesis (Affirming the consequent) If it is C it is A (and Denying the antecedent) If it is not A it is not C. To test these hypotheses, one must look hard in the first case for an A that is not a C, and in the second for a not A that is a C.

In general, people find *modus ponens* easier to deal with than *modus tollens* (Marcus & Rips, 1979; Taplin, 1971), and they are more likely to recognize either of these forms as valid than to recognize that the invalid forms do not provide the basis for a conclusion (O'Brien, 1972, 1973). Thomas O'Brien (1972) found, for example, that high-school seniors recognized the invalidity of open syllogisms about one-third of the time. College students in a logic course did equally poorly in this regard (O'Brien, 1973). O'Brien (1973) found that people dealt best with *modus ponens* forms, next best with *modus tollens*, worst with the invalid forms.

Some investigators have taken the position that whether conditional arguments involving denial of the antecedent or affirmation of the consequent should be considered fallacies, pragmatically speaking, depends on the context in which they occur, because under some conditions such forms yield practically useful inferences (Fillenbaum, 1975, 1976; Geis & Zwicky, 1971; Sperber & Wilson, 1986). Michael Geis and Arnold Zwicky suggest that certain linguistic contexts, such as promises and threats, are strongly suggestive of causal relationships between antecedents and consequents and hence invite the affirmation of the consequent or denial of the antecedent in reasoning.

If the assertion "If A then C" can reasonably be interpreted as "Event A causes event C" (e.g., if you touch the stove you will burn your hand) then it may be reasonable to assume that if you do not evoke the cause, you will not get the effect (i.e., If A then C, not A, therefore not C). This involves the assumption that A is the only cause of C; however, in some contexts that is a reasonable assumption to make.

L. Jonathan Cohen (1981) argues that often in discourse, an assertion of the sort "If A then C" makes sense only if it can be assumed to be the case that "If not-A then not-C." Cohen gives the example, "If you interrupt him now, he will be cross," which would not be worth saying unless it could be assumed that if one does not interrupt him now he will not be cross. So, if one's objective is to understand the total message that is being communicated, as distinct from the decontextualized logical implications of the sentence that is uttered, it often is the case that one should assume the converse – "If *C* then *A*" – of a conditional is intended as well as the conditional – "If *A* then *C*" – that is actually spoken. It is important, Cohen argues, to make a clear distinction between the implications of a sentence uttered and the implications of the fact that it is uttered.

Evans (1993) argues that it is not irrational for people to make inferences involving denying the antecedent even with abstract conditionals – it may be illogical, but not irrational, in his view.

> [H]ow is a subject to understand the meaning of an [if-then] utterance in an artificial context ... except by reference to its normal everyday usage? ... Although it may be technically correct to describe certain reasoning patterns as logical errors, the practice imbues logic with an unjustified importance and tempts both author and readers to adopt a judgmental view of the subjects' behaviour (p. 18).

Both mathematicians and scientists use a form of reasoning – abduction – involving affirmation of the consequent in a way. That is to say, both infer from their conjectures consequences that would be expected if the conjectures were true; then, if upon looking, they find these consequences to be true, their confidence in the conjectures from which the consequences were derived is increased. How much it is increased depends on several considerations, which Polya (1954a, 1954b) discusses in some detail (see also Chapter 2). Stove (1986) notes, with a touch of irony, that textbook writers have been able to condemn the affirmation of the consequent in one context while lauding it in another. "The same process of affirming the consequent, which in an early chapter of the textbook had been duly exposed as betraying logical ignorance or unscrupulousness, had a habit of turning up again in the Chapter 5, on scientific method, but this time as nothing less than the logical mainstay of the entire structure of empirical science" (p. 119).

Ambiguity

It is generally agreed that logic, as typically taught, has to do only with the *forms* of arguments and is independent of their semantic content. An argument is said to be valid or invalid depending only on its structure. But real arguments – arguments that matter to most of us – have substance as well as form. And as soon as an argument is expressed in meaningful words, the problem of ambiguity arises. Mill (1995/1892) lumps fallacies that have to do with ambiguity and other linguistic factors under "fallacies of confusion," which are to be distinguished from fallacies of deduction or induction. Although Mill proposes a taxonomy that distinguishes five classes of fallacy, he claims that, in strictness, almost all fallacies can be seen as fallacies of confusion.

Whately (1995/1853) contends that, while there is no hope of the rules of logic ever solving the problem of ambiguous language, they "do point out in *which* term of an argument it is to be sought for: directing our attention to the *middle* term, as the one on the ambiguity of which a fallacy is likely to be built" (p. 70). How ambiguity of the middle term can wreak havoc with a syllogism is illustrated by the following:

No one is bigger than Jack.
Tiny is bigger than no one.
So Tiny is bigger than Jack.

This is the problem of *amphiboly,* which was one of the thirteen fallacies noted by Aristotle and discussed in the foregoing. Here it can be seen as toying with words; taking advantage of the context-dependency of word meanings to produce nonsensical arguments. The following illustration is from *The Dialogues of Plato*, as quoted in Hamblin (1970, p. 57–58). Dionysodorus is speaking to Ctesippus:

You say that you have a dog.
Yes, a villain of one, said Ctesippus.
And he has puppies?
Yes, and they are very like himself.
And the dog is the father of them?
Yes, he said, I certainly saw him and the mother of the puppies come together.
And is he not yours?
To be sure he is.
Then he is a father, and he is yours; ergo, he is your father, and the puppies are your brothers.

Whately (1995/1853) makes a sharp distinction between *logical* fallacies and what he calls *non*logical or *semi*-logical fallacies, or fallacies *in the matter* and fallacies *in the words*, and contends that failure to make this distinction has led to much confusion. Logical fallacies are those in which the conclusion does not follow from the premises and they arise because of faulty reasoning. Nonlogical or semi-logical fallacies generally involve an ambiguous middle term; the fallaciousness of such arguments is revealed when the ambiguity is resolved, and the argument rewritten in an unambiguous way. Whately warns that the problem of ambiguous terms can be subtle, that it is easy for one to use a term – especially a familiar one – as though one fully understands it, when in fact one does not.

Difficulties with Syllogisms

A categorical syllogism is an argument containing three assertions, the third of which, the conclusion, follows from the first two, the premises. The following (invalid) argument is an example.

All dogs are mammals.
All Collies are dogs.
All Collies are mammals.

In this simple form, the argument contains three terms, one of which is called the middle term ("dogs" in our example) and appears in both premises; logicians say that it is "distributed." The middle term serves to link the other two terms, enabling an inference regarding their relationship, which is stated explicitly in the conclusion.

Many forms of the categorical syllogism are possible, representing different combinations of quantifiers (all, some, no) applied to the various terms and the use of both of positive and negative assertions. There is a long tradition of psychological research on the question of how well people can evaluate the validity of these various forms. The least controversial generalization that comes out of this research is that different forms of the syllogism differ greatly in the difficulty they pose, both to people who have had some formal training in logic and to those who have not (Cesaro & Provitera, 1971; Erickson, 1978; Evans, 1982; Johnson-Laird & Bara, 1984; Johnson-Laird & Steedman, 1978; Wilkins, 1928; Woodworth & Sells, 1935). Erickson (1978) claims that the modal response for most syllogisms is incorrect.

Figural Effects in Syllogistic Reasoning

The *figure* of a syllogism is determined by the arrangement of terms, in the premises and conclusion. The syllogisms in the preceding section are in the first figure by virtue of the fact that the predicate of the conclusion is also the predicate of the first (major) premise and the subject of the conclusion is the subject of the second (minor) premise. The second figure has the predicate of the conclusion playing the role of subject in the major premise and the subject of the conclusion playing that of subject also in the minor premise, as follows:

No competent plumbers are available when they are needed.
Plumber White is always available.
Plumber White is not a competent plumber.

Other figures are defined in an analogous way. It suffices for present purposes to note that people find it much easier to deal with some figures than with others and that some figures can be quite difficult indeed

(Dickstein, 1978a; Johnson-Laird, 1975; Johnson-Laird & Bara, 1984; Johnson-Laird & Steedman, 1978; Wetherick & Gilhooly, 1990).

The Atmosphere Effect

The *atmosphere effect,* as first described by Robert Woodworth and S. B. Sells (1935; see also Sells, 1936; Sells & Koob, 1937), refers to the tendency to interpret any syllogism whose statements are all of the same mood as valid. Mood is defined by the types of statements – A, E, I, and O – that comprise the syllogism. A, E, I, and O are, respectively, universal affirmative, universal negative, particular affirmative, and particular negative statements.

A: All logicians are comedians.
E: No carnivores are vegetarians.
I: Some mathematicians are athletes.
O: Some dictators are not benevolent.

Another way to characterize the atmosphere effect noted by Woodworth and Sells is to say that syllogisms that have both premises qualified by "all," "no," "some," or "not" predispose people to draw conclusions qualified by the same terms – positive and negative premises create positive and negative atmospheres, universal and particular premises create atmospheres that promote thinking in universal and particular terms, and so on.

Other structural factors have been identified as important for the interpretation of syllogisms whose premises and conclusions are not all the same type. Ian Begg and J. Peter Denny (1969), for example, have suggested that the conclusion will be expected to be particular if the quantity (universal-particular) of at least one premise is particular and it will be expected to be negative if the quality (affirmative-negative) of at least one premise is negative. An exception to these rules that has been noted involves the quantifier "only." Johnson-Laird and Byrne (1989) found that when both premises were based on "only," only 16 percent of the conclusions that were drawn contained it, and when one premise was based on "only," just 2 percent did so. These investigators interpreted this result to be damaging to the atmosphere hypothesis. Wason and Johnson-Laird (1972) questioned the existence of an atmosphere effect on the strength of their finding that when asked to state the conclusion that followed from given premises, the errors that people made that were incompatible with an atmosphere effect were more numerous than those that would be expected by such an effect. Further Johnson-Laird and Byrne (1993) point out that inasmuch as most of the valid conclusions to syllogisms have the same properties as those associated with an atmosphere effect, a purely logical process could appear to be susceptible to such an effect; conversely deductions that actually stemmed from an atmosphere effect would often prove to be logically sound.

The phenomenon that prompted the idea of an atmosphere effect is the matching of quantifier terms in the conclusion of a syllogism to those in the premises. Sometimes the premises contain two different quantifiers, e.g. "All A are B; Some B are not C." In such cases, a tendency to match the conclusion quantifier with a premise quantifier could take the match from either premise, but still one would expect the conclusion to be more likely to match one of those that occurred than to match one of those that did not – assuming a tendency to match.

Rips (1994) argues that the evidence suggests that when premises have different quantifiers, the pattern of dominance in selecting the conclusion quantifier is No > Some-not > Some > All. He notes that given "All A are B; Some B are C," the modal response is "Some A are C," and that given "Some B are not A; Some C are B," the modal response is "Some C are not A." Rips sees this dominance ordering as reflecting the idea that the best responses are those that posit the least overlap between the terms. He notes also the possibility that conclusions asserting "Some are" or "Some are not" may be perceived as somewhat safer bets than those asserting "All are" or "No are" when guessing is involved.

Citing Pollard (1979), Evans (1982) notes that while people perform well on valid syllogisms this does not demonstrate that they understand validity, inasmuch as most valid syllogisms would be endorsed on the basis of an atmosphere bias. Given that an atmosphere effect would lead to valid conclusions for most syllogisms, there is also the possibility of mistaking the result of such an effect as evidence of valid reasoning (Johnson-Laird & Byrne, 1991).

A criticism that has been made of the atmosphere-effect hypothesis is that it does not predict figural effects of the types that have been found (Dickstein, 1978a; Johnson-Laird & Steedman, 1978). Evans (1982) has argued that this criticism is inappropriate inasmuch as the atmosphere hypothesis was not intended to account for figural effects, but rather for effects of mood. That the atmosphere hypothesis does not account for figural effects limits its applicability to a subset of the errors that people make in syllogistic reasoning, but it does not diminish its ability to help account for that subset.

Johnson-Laird (1983) points out that hypothesized causes of reasoning errors such as the atmosphere effect do not account fully for deduction but must be imposed on some underlying deductive mechanism. Evidence that this is so includes the fact that people are more likely to accept valid conclusions that are consistent with an atmosphere effect than to accept invalid conclusions that are consistent with it, and sometimes, despite conditions that should produce an atmosphere effect, people decide that no valid conclusion can be drawn. Again, the fact that the atmosphere hypothesis does not account for everything proves only that its predictive power is limited but not that the effect does not exist.

After reviewing experimental work on syllogistic reasoning, Evans (1982) concluded that the most obvious result from the studies, as of the time of his writing, was the relatively low level of performance of the subjects and the high frequency of logical errors they made. In his view, the studies established that these errors are systematically related to the structure (mood and figure) of the syllogisms used, but explanations of the effects were not very satisfactory and tended to be paradigm specific. The only investigators who had tried to explain the effects of both mood and figure, he argued, were Johnson-Laird and Steedman (1978) and Dickstein (1978a, 1978b), and he contended that post hoc assumptions were needed in both cases.

The atmosphere effect can be seen as one of several ways in which a matching strategy manifests itself in reasoning situations. The notion of a matching strategy is often seen in accounts of performance of Wason's selection task as well as other reasoning tasks (Evans & Lynch, 1973; Moutier, Angeard, & Houdé, 2002; Ormerod, Manktelow, & Jones, 1993; Prado & Noveck, 2006; Stahl, Klauer, & Erdfelder, 2008). In the case of syllogisms, the idea is that people make conclusions match premises in specific ways. The evidence is strong that matching effects occur, but it is equally strong that they do not constitute a general account of syllogistic reasoning, because effects of other variables are seen when the opportunities for matching are held constant (Johnson-Laird & Byrne, 1993).

Difficulties with Conditional Syllogisms

In the case of conditional syllogisms, *modus ponens* inferences appear to be easier, or more natural, for people to make than *modus tollens* inferences (Evans, Newstead, & Byrne, 1993), as we have already noted. *Modus tollens* arguments are especially difficult when the antecedent in the conditional proposition is negative (If not-A then C; If not-A then not-C) (Evans, 1977a; Pollard & Evans, 1980; Roberge, 1978).

Evans (1993) argues that the failure of people to make *modus tollens* inferences "is not compatible with any sensible interpretation of a conditional statement that one can think of . . . nor is the analogous failure to investigate the not-q [not-C] card when testing the truth value of a conditional statement in the famous and much investigated Wason selection task" (p. 22). Negation, in its various forms, generally complicates arguments as evidenced by an increase in the time required to process negations and in the likelihood of errors (Nickerson, 2015, chapter 5).

Content Effects in Argumentation

The quality of one's reasoning with syllogistic arguments – or at least the likelihood that arguments will be identified as valid or invalid – can be influenced by whether they are expressed in abstract terms or with realistic content. Among the first investigators to report this effect was M. C. Wilkins (1928). In her experiments, subjects did better with syllogisms composed of semantically meaningful statements than with abstract ones.

Much recent work has corroborated the finding that syllogistic reasoning can be influenced by the semantic content of the syllogisms, and that it is not unusual for content to mislead one regarding an argument's validity.

The Difficulty of Judging the Soundness of Reasoning

> [P]resenting a logical problem does not guarantee ratiocination by subjects: They may guess, evaluate the material truth of propositions, apply learned rules, or whatever
>
> (Henle, 1981, p. 339).

It will perhaps be clear from the foregoing that determining whether a specific instance of reasoning is sound can be very difficult, in some cases maybe impossible. This is because it usually is difficult, if not impossible, to know the process by which people choose the responses they make when performing experimental tasks. When one judges a syllogism to be valid, for example, it often is not clear whether the judgment is based on a legitimate analysis of the syllogism's form, a belief that the premises and conclusion are true, a pure guess, or something else.

It is natural to assume, when people's performance on reasoning tasks conforms to the prescriptions of a normative theory, that it does so because people are reasoning as the theory specifies that they should. The theory represents a ready explanation of their behavior (Lopes, 1981), but the fact that people produce the same results that would have been produced by use of the prescriptions of a theory is not compelling evidence that they indeed used those prescriptions. Conversely, as J. S. Mill (1874) pointed out, when people appear to be making invalid deductions, it is hard to be sure they are doing so, because, unless they have made the premises explicit, there is always the possibility they have made valid inferences from false premises.

Non Sequitur Reasoning

Whenever we draw a conclusion that does not follow from the argument advanced in its support, we are engaging in *non sequitur* (it-does-not-follow) reasoning. There are a great many ways of doing this. It would be impossible to identify them all. The following are but a few examples of the guises this type of reasoning can take.

Stereotyping

For good or ill – probably for good *and* ill – we classify people as well as everything else. That is to say we sort people into categories on the basis of such considerations as nationality, race, body type, personality type, religion, vocation, intelligence, economic status, and numerous other properties or characteristics. Sometimes having identified an individual as a member of a certain conceptual category or class, we then impute to the individual all the characteristics of that class, as we believe them to be. This is what is typically referred to as stereotyping, a term coined, I believe, by Walter Lippmann about 100 years ago.

The term has a negative ring to it, suggesting the uncritical treatment of groups as homogeneous and the overlooking of individual differences among their members. Stereotyping – like all classification – simplifies one's conceptual life considerably; by limiting the need to deal with uncertainty and variability, it limits the need to think. There can be no question of the fact that stereotyping does often lead to the unjust treatment of individuals who are credited with, or blamed for, characteristics they do not have. On the other hand, people sometimes wish to be recognized as members of specific groups and to be identified with what those groups stand for, and they advertise their group memberships by wearing rings, pins, uniforms, or other visible emblems and in various other ways.

Whether the imputation to individuals of the characteristics of groups to which they belong should be considered irrational depends perhaps on the attitude with which the imputation is made. On the one hand is the possibility of doing it in an unthinking and inflexible way; on the other is that of recognizing an imputation as a default assumption in the absence of evidence to the contrary, and of leaving open the possibility that it is wrong. Group membership often is informative in a statistical or probabilistic sense – Republicans, on average, presumably really do see things somewhat differently than do Democrats, and knowledge of party affiliation provides some information about probable views on specific issues. Unfortunately, the evidence seems to indicate that we find it easy to carry the kinds of inferences that are associated with stereotyping to excess.

It appears that when one knows the organizational structure of a set of entities, one is likely to overestimate the degree of similarity among entities within the same group and to overestimate the differences among those from different groups. This result has been obtained when the entities in question are physical stimuli (Tajfel & Wilkes, 1963) and when they are people (Tajfel, Sheikh, & Gardner, 1964). One interpretation of such findings is that the categorization process produces perceptual distortions – enhancement of perceived intergroup differences – that can act as a positive feedback mechanism providing the perceiver with "evidence" of the efficacy of the categories being used (Hamilton, 1979, 1981; Hamilton & Gifford, 1976).

Failure to Distinguish between Correlation and Cause-Effect Relationships

Suppose someone discovers that students who have studied a particular subject, say Greek, or Latin, or geometry, score significantly higher in IQ tests, on the average, than do students who have not studied that subject. (I am not claiming that people who study these subjects actually have higher IQs than people who do not, but simply positing a "what if" question.) Should this be taken as evidence that the study of Greek, Latin, or geometry enhances intelligence? The answer, of course, is no. An equally plausible hypothesis, in the absence of any other information, would be that more intelligent students are more likely than less intelligent students to study such subjects.

This illustrates, however, a very common error of reasoning, namely the inference of a cause-effect relationship from the observation of a correlation between two variables. This confusion can be seen as a form of the fallacy of affirming the consequent: If A causes C, then A and C should be highly correlated; A and C are highly correlated; therefore, A must be the cause (or *a* cause) of C. But inasmuch as a causal relationship between A and C is not the only possible basis of a correlation between these variables, the inference is not justified.

The development of statistics as a mathematical discipline was motivated, in part, by an interest in finding regularities in aggregate behavior, and especially regularities that had some significance for public policy. Early in the nineteenth century, two French investigators, Adriano Balbi and Andre-Michel Guerry (1829), found, to their surprise, that when the administrative units of Paris were rank ordered both in terms of educational level and crime rate, those with the higher levels of education also had the greater rates of crime. People who do not understand the difference between correlation and causation might draw a conclusion from this finding that those who do understand the difference would hesitate to draw; the finding caused something of a sensation at the time.

There is nothing wrong, of course, in taking the finding of a correlation between two variables as an indication of the possibility of a causal relationship between them. However, establishment of a causal relationship requires evidence in addition to the correlation.

Reification

A subtle problem relating to classification or categorization is that of reification. We are much inclined to partition the world, or aspects thereof, into specific categories: there are six entities of this sort, four of that, and seven of another. Having imposed a conceptual taxonomy on an area of interest, we then proceed as though the invented classes were something more than a conceptual convenience. The assumption seems to be that the invention of a name guarantees the existence of a real referent. Mill described the problem this way: "The tendency has always been strong to believe that whatever received a name must be an entity or being, having an independent existence of its own. And if no real entity answering to the name could be found, men did not for that reason suppose that none existed, but imagined that it was something peculiarly abstruse and mysterious" (Quoted in Gould, 1981, p. 350).

William Uttal (2001) argues that the tendency within psychology to reify – "to treat as real that which is, at best ad hoc or invented, is pervasive" (p. 91). N. A. Cummings and William O'Donohue (2005) make a similar claim in asserting that psychologists and mental health professionals have made a habit of inventing names – XYZ Disorder – for clusters of symptoms and then acting on the assumption that the named entity is a clinical, and treatable, reality.

John Rosemond and Bose Ravenal (2008) make the case that this habit is seen in the emergence in recent years of a stable of disorders to which children, especially American school children, are highly susceptible: Attention Deficit Disorder (ADD), Attention Deficit Hyperactivity Disorder (ADHD), Oppositional Defiant Disorder (ODD), Childhood-Onset Bipolar Disorder (COBD). Without denying that some dysfunctional behavior may have a physiological or biochemical basis, Rosemond and Ravenal contend that the majority of instances of behavior problems that get diagnosed as a clinical syndrome are the result of approaches to parenting that fail to put an end to the "terrible twos" and allow negative aspects of "toddlerhood" – "tantrums, belligerent defiance, disrespect, destructiveness" – to persist unchecked into school age if not indefinitely.

Psychiatrists have defined a sufficient variety of psychoses and neuroses, it would appear, that all of us can be reasonably assured of finding ourselves in one or more of them (Frances et al., 1994). The questionability of some of the classificatory distinctions that have been made in psychiatry has been captured colorfully by Hervey Cleckley (1988) in his classic discussion of psycho- or sociopathology.

> In more recent decades two tendencies particularly seem to have played a major and persistent role in isolating the psychopath from practical consideration and in concealing him in a strange and gratuitous confusion. One of these tendencies arose from efforts to group these patients with many other types by no means similar. The other seems to have proceeded from ambitious attempts to break down the psychopath's disorder by fine and largely imaginary distinctions, by all sorts of descriptive nuances and diagnostic legerdemain, into theoretical entities to be differentiated and classified under many subheadings.
>
> These attempts at elaborate differentiation have been applied not to a distinguishable group having in common fundamental features that could be brought into conceptual focus but to an essentially heterogeneous referent. A good analogy would arise if someone set out to establish and list scores of inconsequential differences between Buicks, Oldsmobiles, Plymouths, Cadillacs, Lincolns, etc., by studying assiduously a general material in which automobiles, oxcarts, demolished freight cars, jet planes, rural woodsheds, and the village pump were undistinguished, embraced under a single term, and treated through such concepts as can be formed in such an approach. Would it not be

> wiser to put all our automobiles together in a field of reference before attempting to take further steps? (p. 241).

Cleckley's assessment of the invention (reification?) of categories in terms of which problematic forms of behavior are often classified is unquestionably harsh. His book has been extremely influential, and not a little controversial, appearing in six editions between 1941 and 1988.

Proof by Example

A common form of argument begins with a general statement and follows that with one or more specific examples that illustrate the generalization. "Scientists do not make good family men. Einstein was a disaster both as a husband and a parent." "Dobermans are vicious dogs. A neighbor of mine once had one that had to be put down after attacking several people."

Examples do illustrate generalizations, but they do not prove them. When such arguments are made with the intent of demonstrating the truth of general assertions by noting the existence of particular cases, or when one who encounters such arguments takes the existence of particular cases as proof of the general assertions, the reasoning is not sound.

Arnauld and Nicole (1995/1865) contend that overgeneralization constitutes one of the more common sources of false reasoning. "Three or four examples suffice them [people] to make a maxim and a common-place, which they then employ as a principle for deciding all things" (p. 47). Fallacies of generalization (conclusions based on facts but not warranted by them) are one of two main types that Mill (1995/1892) claims are found in inductive reasoning; the other type is inadequate grounding of reasoning on facts. Baird (1950) describes hasty generalization as "perhaps the most common sin of all who argue" (p. 171).

Proof by Analogy

Analogical thinking (discussed in Chapter 2) is useful for many purposes. It becomes problematic when analogies are used as evidence of correspondences that may not exist. From the fact that two entities are alike with respect to certain specific properties, say A, B, and C, it does not follow that they are necessarily also alike with respect to additional specific properties, say D and E.

It is legitimate, of course, to use the fact that two entities are alike with respect to A, B, and C as a basis for raising the question of whether they may also be alike with respect to D and E. If entities are alike in certain known ways, it is not unreasonable to suppose that they might be alike in other ways as well. However, raising a question, which can then be addressed appropriately, is different from simply jumping to the conclusion.

Analogical reasoning plays a very important role in mathematics and science. The more creative mathematicians and scientists have often shown an ability to see analogies that most of us would miss. Analogies serve only, however, as a point of departure for further investigation, or as aids to understanding or exposition. They do not, in themselves, establish new truths.

Premature Closure

Sometimes we draw a conclusion or commit to an opinion before there is adequate evidence to justify doing so. The problem is compounded when, after having accepted a conclusion or formed an opinion, one fails any longer to consider alternative possibilities. One narrows one's focus, as it were, to the conclusion that has been reached or to the opinion that has been formed, and treats it as unquestionably correct, when the evidence for it may be less than compelling.

Undoubtedly most readers will have encountered at one place or another a sign with the message "Do not confuse me with the facts; my mind is made up." It strikes us as humorous not only because we recognize it as an insightful, if somewhat disparaging, comment on human rationality in general, but, if we are honest about it we have to admit, at least to ourselves, that on more than one occasion we probably have, perhaps in a more subtle and less direct way, made exactly the same request.

Jonathan Baron (1985) mentions two reasons why people may stop working on an intellectual problem prematurely: overconfidence in a favored hypothesis or underconfidence in the efficacy of further thinking. With respect to the second possibility, he suggests that one of the reasons we do not think reflectively as much as we should is that we underestimate the value of doing so.

There are other possibilities as well. One may simply be unwilling to make the effort that further thinking requires, or one may be comfortable with a particular conclusion and unwilling to risk the possibility that further thinking would call it to question.

Escalation

Sometimes individuals or groups not only persist in behaving in ways that appear to be contrary to their self-interests, but even intensify, or make more extreme, such behavior in the face of evidence that it is not having, and not likely to have, the desired effect. Such escalation behavior has been of considerable interest to social scientists (Brockner & Rubin, 1985; Staw, 1981; Staw & Ross, 1989; Tegar, 1979). It may sometimes result from simple stubbornness, an unwillingness to admit to being wrong; but it also sometimes may be due to an inability, or failure, to see clearly the ineffectiveness of the escalation.

One thing that appears to happen in escalating situations is that the "stake" that involved parties have in the outcome, in their own eyes, changes as a consequence of the changing situation. What would be an unacceptable outcome, as seen from a given party's vantage point at the beginning of the venture, may become acceptable, or even desirable, from the same party's perspective at a later stage of the venture's unfolding (Brockner & Rubin, 1985). Considerations of face saving, justifying previous decisions, and social approval can loom large and counterbalance or even offset concerns for escalating costs.

Closely related to the phenomenon of escalating costs, perhaps an example of it, is the bidding more for an item at auction than the maximum one had intended to bid. Dan Ariely and Itama Simonson (2003) attribute this behavior to a "pseudo-endowment effect." The "endowment effect" refers to the tendency people have to require more for an article they are selling than they would pay for the item if they did not have it (Kahneman, Knetsch, & Thaler, 1990). It appears that the magnitude of the effect increases with the amount of time one has owned an item (Strahilevitz & Loewenstein, 1998). Overbidding at auction can be seen as a pseudo-endowment effect if one assumes that while the bidding is going on the bidder comes to think of the item as already hers, and she is willing to overbid so as to keep from losing it. (I confess to some ambivalence about auctions; I have occasionally enjoyed participating in one, but after obtaining an item, I am left with the humbling thought that I was the only person in the crowd who believed the item was worth what I paid for it.)

Rationalization

Few of us, I suspect, would admit to being willfully irrational. We wish to be able to justify our actions, at least to the extent of making them consistent with our own value systems. Evidence suggests that we are capable of going to considerable lengths to justify behavior that appears to be inconsistent with our own norms. Thus, when people have broken a pledge they have made (to quit smoking, say), rather than simply admit that they failed in their intentions they may construct a complicated explanation of their behavior that gives it the appearance of rationality.

Rationalization can serve the purpose of justifying beliefs or behavior; people may offer explanations they know to be false in order to protect their image or to avoid censure or criticism. Explanations that one offers of one's beliefs or behavior may be suspect in some instances on the grounds that there may be more plausible explanations that would put the offerer in a less favorable light. But people also undoubtedly sometimes produce explanations that they sincerely believe to be true, even though they are not; the reasons one gives for a particular choice one has made, for example, may not have been operative at the time the choice was made, even though in retrospect one believes, or assumes, that they were (Soelberg, 1967). Similarly, if asked why one believes X, one may in good conscience give "reasons" that, in fact, have little to do with how the belief got established; it is doubtful that we have a clear understanding of why we believe what we do in many instances.

Howard Margolis (1987) makes a distinction between "seeing-that" (something is so) and "reasoning-why" (it is). Seeing-that is an intuitive pattern-recognition process, in Margolis's view, and is fundamental to our functioning in the day-to-day world. It is the process by which we make judgments. Reasoning-why is a more deliberate retrospective process by which we try to figure out why we made the judgment we did. It is more important, for practical purposes, that the seeing-that process be relatively accurate than that the reasoning-why process be so; Margolis sees the latter as quite fallible.

> [S]ometimes there is a reasonable basis for supposing that the reasoning-why a person gives in fact explains the seeing-that he reports. But that is always a question to be explored, never something about which a person can have direct insight. Even under circumstances that might be supposed especially favorable (as in a set-piece puzzle), reasoning-why can never be taken at face value as an adequate account of how a judgment was first reached (p. 78).

However, Margolis contends that although reasoning-why follows seeing-that, the outcome of a reasoning-why occurrence can have an impact on subsequent seeings-that.

Summary Comment

"Fallacy" is a slippery concept. The term has many connotations in the psychological and philosophical literature. The foregoing has noted only a subset of them. Arguments can be fallacious in many ways; and the same argument may be considered fallacious in some contexts and sound in others. Whether one accepts – or should accept – the conclusion of an argument as true depends on much more than whether it is logically valid in form.

One would assume that knowledge of the types of fallacies and other vices, minor and major, that plague human reasoning would facilitate critical thinking; however, as the foregoing demonstrates, knowledge, important as it is, is not enough; motivation plays an important role as well. Regarding the pros and cons of teaching fallacies as a part of teaching critical thinking, see J. Anthony Blair (1995) and David Hitchcock (1995).

7

Biases, Misconceptions, and the Like

A bias is an inclination to see things one way rather than another. Generally, when one encounters the term *bias* in the psychological literature, it has a negative connotation; it represents a problematic aspect of reasoning – an aspect that needs to be fixed. We note at the outset that many biases are commendable and beneficial. Think of a bias to eat fruit instead of candy, to give people the benefit of the doubt when accused of bad behavior, to refrain from drinking when driving, to focus on people's virtues rather than their vices. However, most – nearly all – of the psychological research that has been done on biases has dealt with what are seen as flawed aspects of reasoning and argumentation, and it is that sense in which the term is used in most of what follows.

Much of our reasoning is based on assumptions. These assumptions may or may not be stated; perhaps in most cases they are not. We assume that the floor on which we are standing will not suddenly give way, that the food we buy at the supermarket is edible, that the vast majority of US adults can read and write. Often we are not even aware of having made such assumptions, but if our reasoning requires them, it seems fair that we be held accountable for them. Assumptions, explicit or tacit, may or may not be consistent with known facts or with what are widely accepted as facts. Our interest here is primarily with assumptions the factuality of which is questionable at best.

Questions are often predicated on unstated assumptions, and to such a degree that if the assumptions are faulty, the questions are meaningless. Consider, for example, the question: What are the component skills of critical thinking? The question assumes that critical thinking is decomposable into component skills. It would make little sense to attempt to answer the question if one did not accept this assumption. We shall see that assumptions – especially unstated assumptions – play a significant role in many biases

Peter Medawar (1979) provides an example of how a faulty assumption can have an undesirable effect in medicine. The faulty assumption is that grave diseases have complex causes, while less serious diseases have simpler causes and therefore the latter should be easier to cure. The assumption is often revealed in a quip of the sort "Medicine is not able even to cure the common cold" with emphasis on "even." Such an observation, Medawar notes, is sometimes used to argue against the expenditure of large sums of public money on medical research when medicine "cannot even . . . ."

The idea that causes resemble their effects is a very old one and not unique to medicine, although it has affected medicine in nontrivial ways. Since the discovery of bacteria and viruses and of the roles they play in the transmission of disease, it has been clear, at least to biologists and people trained in medicine, that small causes can have very substantial effects and that the similarity between causes and their effects need not be great.

That small causes can have very large effects in complex systems was recognized by a few mathematicians in the latter part of the nineteenth century, and mathematicians in general have become acutely aware of this fact since the discovery of "deterministic chaos" (Crutchfield et al., 1986; Stewart, 1989). What pertains to mathematics in this regard pertains also to medicine as well as to many other contexts; there is no law that says that causes and effects must be equally complex.

Closely related to faulty assumptions, and similarly related to biases, are misconceptions that are sufficiently pervasive and persistent to warrant being referred to as cognitive illusions. As is true of perceptual illusions, cognitive illusions often are quite compelling and can be "seen through" only with difficulty. Examples include:

Illusions of comprehensibility. Familiarity with subject matter may mislead one into judging difficult text to be clear and easily comprehended (Glenberg & Epstein, 1985, 1987). Being familiar, in other words, may be mistaken for being comprehended, thus making the perception of comprehensibility illusory.

Illusions of competence or proficiency. Short-term effects of training on performance often are not good predictors of what the longer-term effects will be (Jacoby, Bjork, & Kelley, 1994; Schmidt & Bjork, 1992). Aspects of a training regimen that facilitate performance during training do not necessarily produce the most lasting effects; consequently, one may be misled by one's performance during or immediately following training into believing that one has attained a higher level of proficiency than one really has.

Illusion of control. The illusion of control is the belief that one has more control over a situation than one actually has. It is similar to the belief that one is safe and secure when, in fact, one is at considerable risk (Camerer, 1995, 1998).

Illusion of consistency. Is there such a thing as a totally open mind? Possibly not, but some are more open – more willing to consider new ideas and new arguments on their merits – than others. And any given mind may be more or less open, depending on the subject. Suppose that it can be shown that A, which one believes, implies B, which one does not believe. Logic requires that one must either accept B or reject A. This is undoubtedly easier said than done. We appear to be very good at ignoring, or living with, counterindications of strong beliefs; indeed, we may be blissfully unaware of the inconsistencies involved.

Belief can be defined in many ways. A definition that I like links belief to willingness to act: *One believes X to the extent that one acts as though X were true.* Given this definition, it is easy to imagine instances of believing something without realizing that one is doing so and of thinking one believes something that one really does not believe. If I willingly walk across a rustic bridge over a chasm, I give evidence that I believe the bridge will hold me, even if I don't articulate that belief. On the other hand, if I say I believe the bridge would hold me but I refuse to walk on it, one may question whether I really believe what I claim. In general, when one's behavior is inconsistent with a professed belief, we are right to question the genuineness of the professed belief.

People may, for a variety of reasons, knowingly profess beliefs that they do not hold, but here we ignore those cases. Also, for some purposes (e.g., Bayesian decision-making or problem-solving) we recognize degrees of belief, but for many contexts in which the concept is used in everyday parlance, it suffices to treat *belief* as a binary variable; one believes X or one does not. This is reminiscent of Descartes's advice regarding decision-making, which is to act on a decision, once made, as though it were absolutely certain (Watkins, 2002, p. 277).

Biases of Perspective and Preference

As the old saying about the glass that can be seen as either half full or half empty reminds us, it is possible to view the same situation from different perspectives and to get different impressions about what one is seeing. Many of the situations that we encounter in life are ambiguous and open to more than one interpretation. Sometimes people fail to see the ambiguity of a situation, perhaps because their own perspectives are sufficiently fixed as to permit only one interpretation. It can also happen, however, that people recognize that a situation can be interpreted in more than one way but elect to acknowledge only the interpretation they prefer.

We know that expectancy has a lot to do with perception. When we are trying to make sense of indistinct stimuli, we are very likely to see what we are looking for. It would be surprising if there were not similar expectancy effects of a more cognitive sort. We should not be surprised to discover, for example, that when one listens to a political speech expecting the speaker to take certain positions and not others, that ambiguous portions of the speech are interpreted as consistent with the expectations.

Belief Bias

Just as one's knowledge of the truth or falsity of a rule can interfere with one's ability to construct a compelling test of that rule (Pollard, 1979; Pollard & Evans, 1981), one's belief about the truth or falsity of the conclusion of an argument can interfere with one's ability to judge the validity of the argument on which the conclusion is based – generally the argument is more likely to be judged to be valid if its conclusion is believed to be true than if it is believed to be false (Evans, Barston, & Pollard, 1983; Henle & Michael, 1956; Janis & Frick, 1943; Klauer, Musch, & Naumer, 2000; Morgan & Morton, 1944; Morley, Evans, & Handley, 2004; Newstead et al., 1992; Oakhill, Garnham, & Johnson-Laird, 1990). People tend to be more critical of arguments that have conclusions with which they disagree than of arguments that have conclusions they believe to be true (Edwards & Smith, 1996; Nyhan & Reifler, 2010).

The tendency to be less demanding of evidence to support conclusions that one believes, or would like, to be true, than to support conclusions one believes, or would prefer, not to be true is usually referred to as the *belief bias,* and it is well documented. As Thompson and Evans (2012) put it, the "belief bias effect is pervasive and robust, and has been noted on a large variety of reasoning tasks, both formal and informal" (p. 279). Initially it was studied primarily with syllogistic arguments, but more recent experiments have demonstrated that it is also found with informal arguments and other reasoning tasks as well (Klaczynski & Lavallee, 2005; Klaczynski & Robinson, 2000; Neilens, Handley, & Newstead, 2009; Thompson & Evans, 2012). How best to account for the belief-bias effect theoretically has been a matter of debate (Dube, Rotello, & Heit, 2010, 2011; Klauer & Kellen, 2011; Trippas, Verdi, & Handley, 2014).

There is evidence that people are more likely to accept conclusions from premises they believe to be true than from premises they believe to be false, whether or not the argument is valid (Nickerson, Butler, & Barch, in press; Thompson, 1996). It has also been found that people tend to prefer conclusions about which they have no strong belief to those that they believe to be false (Evans & Pollard, 1990; Newstead et al., 1992). Belief bias has been noted as a possible explanation of why many people deny the reality of climate change despite much evidence of its occurrence (Lewandowsky, Oberauer, & Gignac, 2013; Trippas et al., 2015).

The literature on belief bias is not entirely consistent, however, and some investigators have questioned whether there is, in fact, such an effect (Frase, 1966, 1968; Revlin & Leirer, 1978). Russell Revlin et al. (1980), who had expressed reservations regarding the robustness of the belief-bias effect, reported an experiment in which they obtained such an effect but one they considered to be weak compared to the effect of logic. Evans et al. (1983) raised the possibility that Revlin et al. had underestimated the size of the belief-bias effect in their experiment and followed up that experiment with one in which, using all possible combinations of valid and invalid syllogisms with believable and unbelievable conclusions, they found substantial effects of both logic and belief bias: subjects were more likely to accept validly-derived than invalidly-derived conclusions, and also more likely to accept believable conclusions than unbelievable ones.

Johnson-Laird and Byrne (1991) point out that many studies of belief bias have required people to evaluate conclusions that were provided and have not required them to draw conclusions themselves and that, in these cases, the beliefs could have provided a basis for people to reject or "censor" the conclusions without actually reasoning at all. Of course, to the extent that they did this they could be faulted for not distinguishing between the validity of an argument and the believed truth or falsity of its conclusion. Moreover, even when subjects have been required to draw their own conclusions, as they have in some experiments (Oakhill & Johnson-Laird, 1985; Oakhill, Johnson-Laird, & Garnham, 1989), there is no guarantee that they have engaged in reasoning as opposed simply to stating a "conclusion" on the strength of the fact that they believe it to be true. In any case, although the belief-bias effect has been found both in studies in which subjects had to evaluate conclusions provided by the experimenters and in those in which they had to generate them themselves; it appears that the effect is stronger in the latter case (Markovits & Nantel, 1989). The magnitude of the effect has also been found to be greater with more difficult reasoning problems than with less difficult ones (Brisson et al., 2014; Stupple & Ball, 2008) and greater if the focus of reasoning is emotional than if it is not (Eliades et al., 2012).

The extent to which individuals differ with respect to their susceptibility to belief bias has not been studied very much. However, Donna Torrens, Valerie Thompson, and Kenneth Cramer (1999) addressed the question experimentally and obtained results that led them to attribute individual differences in belief bias to individual differences in ability to generate alternatives (e.g., alternative conclusions) rather than to differences in logical ability. Torrens et al. considered their results to be supportive of a mental-models account of belief bias.

The evidence that a belief-bias effect of some magnitude exists is strong; although questions remain as to what determines its strength under various conditions. In general, it appears the effect is more likely to mitigate logical considerations than to override them altogether. One account of the effect – the "selective-scrutiny" account – assumes that people look more critically at arguments leading to conclusions they do not believe than at arguments that lead to conclusions they do believe and are thus more likely to detect logical inconsistencies in the former case (Barston, 1986; Evans, 1989; Evans et al., 1983; Klaczynski & Robinson, 2000).

Johnson-Laird and colleagues (Johnson-Laird & Byrne, 1991; Oakhill & Garnham, 1993; Oakhill & Johnson-Laird, 1985) suggest, from the perspective of the theory of mental models, that people are likely to search more assiduously for models that refute an initial conclusion if they do not believe it than if they do. The assumption that people tend to think harder about arguments that produce conclusions they do not believe than they do about arguments that produce conclusions they believe has promoted the idea of motivated reasoning – the motivation in this case being to search for justification of disbelief (Evans et al., 1983; Oakhill et al., 1989).

This account makes the extent to which one processes an argument contingent on how believable one finds its conclusion to be; if the conclusion is believable, processing of the premises is not extensive. The finding that the verbal protocols of people who show the most belief bias are most likely to mention only an argument's conclusion (Evans et al., 1983), and the relative insensitivity of the bias to the logical complexity of arguments (Evans & Pollard, 1990) are consistent with this aspect of the account. That evidence of a belief bias has been found also in the conclusions that people produce when given only the premises of an argument (Oakhill & Johnson-Laird, 1985; Oakhill et al., 1989) shows that judging the believability of provided conclusions is not all there is to the belief bias. Moreover, apparently the bias can be weakened, if not eliminated, by instructions stressing the importance of analyzing the logic of arguments (Newstead et al., 1992).

The selective-scrutiny account of belief-bias effects is not without critics (Dube, Rotello & Heit, 2010, 2011). Experiments have shown that people sometimes take a relatively long time to evaluate invalid arguments with believable conclusions (Ball et al., 2006; Thompson, Newstead, & Morley, 2011; Thompson et al., 2003). This result appears to be at odds with the selective-scrutiny account.

Evans (1989) has proposed an explanation of the belief-bias effect that applies to syllogisms with conclusions that are false or possibly false, called the *misinterpreted-necessity accoun*t. According to this account, people fail to distinguish between false and possibly-false conclusions and evaluate possibly-false conclusions on the basis of their believability. Newstead and Evans (1993) emphasize that, unlike the selective-scrutiny account, the misinterpreted-necessity account does not provide an expectation for belief-bias effects to occur with valid syllogisms.

Which of the various explanations of the belief-bias effect(s) that have been proposed provides the best account of the findings is a matter of continuing debate (Newstead & Evans, 1993; Newstead et al., 1992; Oakhill & Garnham, 1993). There is little question, however, of the fact that how one produces or evaluates conclusions from premises can be influenced by how those conclusions relate to one's beliefs.

Is it irrational to give preferential treatment to conclusions that one believes to be true over conclusions that one believes to be false? A positive answer can be defended from a strictly formalistic point of view. If one's criterion for rationality includes the ability to make a sharp distinction between empirical truth and logical validity, and to judge accurately the latter independently of the former, then the operation of a belief bias must be taken as evidence of irrationality. From a pragmatic perspective, the answer to the question is less clear.

There is the thought that reasoning more about arguments that go against one's beliefs than about arguments that yield conclusions that are consistent with them may be adaptive, and rational if rationality is defined as behaving in a way that will help one achieve one's goals (as distinct from rationality defined as reasoning in conformity with the principles of logic).

> The maintenance of a large and stable set of beliefs is essential for intelligent behaviour, since this forms the basis for any actions which one may take to

> achieve one's goals. When arguments are encountered which support existing beliefs, the evidence suggests that we do not examine them closely. This is surely rational since (a) it is advantageous to maintain beliefs unless there is good reason to revise them, and (b) the processing effort required constantly to question the evidence of current beliefs would be enormous. The situation when confronted with argument or evidence for a statement which contradicts one's beliefs is quite different. To accept such an argument uncritically would be damaging to the individual since this would introduce a contradiction and disrupt the internal consistency of their belief system. Hence, it is quite rational that such arguments should be subjected to the closest possible scrutiny and rejected if at all possible (Evans, Over, & Manktelow, 1993 p. 174).

As noted several times, it seems reasonable to assume that for most practical purposes, one is likely to be more interested in whether some claim (e.g., the conclusion of an argument) is true or false than whether an argument from which the claim may be derived is valid. In other words, if one finds it important, for practical reasons, to evaluate an argument, one probably is in the position of wanting to know whether to accept the argument's conclusion as true. If one judges a deductive argument to be valid and believes that its premises are true, one can confidently accept its conclusion as true.

But judging the truth or falsity of the premises may be no easier than judging the truth or falsity of the conclusion directly. And, if one believes at least one premise to be false, or indeterminate, then the truth of the argument's conclusion is not assured by the argument's validity and, again, it must be judged directly. Moreover, if one decides that an argument is invalid, then even if the premises are believed to be true, nothing follows from them, so, once more, one is left with the need to judge the truth or falsity of the conclusion directly. In short, if one accepts this view, judging the truth or falsity of claims is, for practical purposes, a more basic process than judging the validity or invalidity of arguments, and therefore it should not be surprising that the former takes precedence over the latter.

It is probably important to make a distinction between the finding of a belief-bias effect in psychological experiments the point of which is to determine whether people can judge validity independently of content when they are asked to do so and the finding of a belief-bias effect in real-life situations in which people are trying to decide whether to accept, as true, conclusions of arguments regarding issues that matter to them. In both cases, there are methodological difficulties. In the laboratory situation, if the point is to determine whether people are able to judge validity independently of content, it must be clear to them that they are being asked to decide whether a conclusion follows from premises and not whether it is true or false. Not all studies have been sufficiently well controlled to leave no doubt as to the subjects' understanding of this point.

Real-life situations in which the individual's intent is to judge an argument's validity, per se, are probably much less common than those in which the intent is to decide whether to accept a conclusion, and whenever the latter is the case, what constitutes a belief bias is not entirely clear. It is hard to rule out the possibility that one judges the plausibility of the conclusion directly; and to say that one is more likely to accept as true a conclusion that one already believes to be true than a conclusion that one believes to be false does not seem like grounds for considering one's behavior to be irrational.

"Truth" Bias

Consider the following two statements: "The population of Chicago is greater than the population of Paris." "The population of Paris is greater than the population of Chicago." Given the task of judging, with respect to each of these statements, whether it is true or false, anyone who judges the first one to be true should judge the second one to be false, and conversely. Imagine a large set of statements constructed so that for every statement there is a contradictory statement somewhere in the set. In other words, the set is composed of pairs of contradictory statements. Assume further that for many of the statements in the set one does not know whether they are true or false, and that the items of any given pair are not adjacent in the set, so that when one is making a judgment with respect to one of the items of a contradictory pair one is not assured to remember what one said when judging the other statement of the same pair.

Thomas Wallsten and Claudia González-Vallejo (1994) did essentially this experiment and found that participants were considerably more inclined to judge both forms of a pair to be true than to judge both of them to be false, which is to say they had a bias for calling statements true. This suggests that if one does not know whether a statement is true or false, one is more likely than not to judge it to be true. Wallsten and González-Vallejo developed a stochastic model of the judgment process that distinguishes between covert confidence in the truth of a statement and overt response selection; according to this model, participants in sentence verification experiments showed a covert bias to believe statements to be true as well as a bias at the level of response selection also in favor of selecting "true" over "false." This is suggestive of what might be called "benefit-of-the-doubt" or "presumption-of-innocence" principle: assume a statement is true unless there is reason to believe otherwise.

They interpreted their results to be generally consistent with those of other investigators who have argued that, in the absence of compelling evidence one way or the other, people are more inclined to assume that a statement is true than to assume that it is false. They saw them as supportive of the idea, put forth by Asher Koriat, Sarah Lichtenstein, and Baruch Fischhoff (1980), that, having made the assumption of truth, people then search memory for information that supports this view. Other investigators who have found evidence of a bias for assuming assertions are true in the absence of compelling evidence that they are false – a *truth bias* – include Charles Bond and Bella DePaulo (2006), Herbert Clark and William Chase (1972), Daniel Gilbert (1991), Timothy Levine (2014) and Tom Trabasso, Howard Rollins, and Edward Shaughnessy (1971).

If people generally do not make false statements either intentionally – lie – (DePaulo et al., 1996) or inadvertently, then the assumption that a random statement is true is perhaps more likely to be correct than the assumption that it is false. Albeit, in deciding whether to accept such a statement as true, one does well to consider the implications of the two possible ways of being wrong.

Evidence of a truth bias has led to the idea that people are generally gullible – too ready to accept claims uncritically. Mercier (2017) notes that belief in human gullibility is widespread among scholars, and that claims to that effect are found in a variety of sources: "in academic journals (Gilbert, Krull, & Malone, 1990), in psychology textbooks (Myers, 2011; Zimbardo, Johnson, & McCann, 2006), in sociology textbooks (Schweingruber & Wohlstein, 2005), in books by psychologists (Gilbert, 2006; Kahneman, 2011), philosophers (Brennan, 2012; Stanley, 2015), economists (Akerlof & Shiller, 2015), and other types of scholars (e.g., Dawkins, 2009; Herman & Chomsky, 2008)" (p. 104). Mercier contends that despite this literature, belief in the pervasiveness of human gullibility is wrong, or at least unduly strong. In his review of the literature, he demonstrates how results of experiments that have been interpreted as evidence of gullibility can often be shown to have equally, or more, plausible interpretations.

The practical implications of a truth bias, to the extent that one exists, are magnified many times by the ease with which claims can be widely distributed, essentially instantaneously, via social media. This illustrates the power of modern communication technology for both good and ill.

Rick Weiss (2017) characterizes this technology as a two-edged sword and argues the importance of nipping misinformation in the bud.

> The internet has vastly expanded the sourcing of news and information, capturing stories that might otherwise go untold and delivering a diversity of perspectives that no single medium outlet could hope to offer. At the same time, this new and open model has given anyone with web access a global platform to propagate information that is mistakenly or intentionally false (p. 427).

Fact-checking services have been established to expose misinformation for what it is, but research has shown that false claims, once accepted as true, can be retained even after having been shown to be false.

Survivorship Bias

We read about the winners of lotteries, and seldom about losers, although the latter outnumber the former by many orders of magnitude. Similarly, new companies that have survived long enough to become traded on a stock exchange are much more likely to be visible to the general public than the many times as many start-ups that failed to get to that point. People who survive a typically fatal disease or accident are often subjects of human-interest stories in the media, while most of those who succumb – in keeping with the normal expectation – are mentioned only in a death notice in the local newspaper.

The attention that is given to winners of lotteries and other long-odds gambles may skew people's appreciation of the probabilities involved, giving them the impression that the probability of winning is much greater than it really is. As Nassim Taleb (2004) puts it, "one sees only the winners – it is natural for those who failed to vanish completely. Accordingly, one sees the survivors, and only the survivors, which imparts such a mistaken perception of the odds" (p. 127). "[T]he survivorship bias implies that *the highest performing realization will be the most visible*. Why? Because the losers do not show up" (p. 136).

Underestimation Bias with Fault Trees

A specific example of uncritical assumption of completeness or adequacy, which is worthy of special notice, involves the use of *fault trees*. Laurette Dube-Rioux and J. Edward Russo (1988) describe what they refer to as an *underestimation bias*, which they define as what occurs "when those events not brought to mind are overlooked and the probabilities of retrieved events are distorted upward" (p. 223). Such a bias could equally well be described as an "overestimation bias," inasmuch as it involves overestimation of the completeness of the items explicitly identified. The bias has been demonstrated with the use of diagnostic fault trees, which are hierarchical delineations of possible causes of specified events.

A fault tree shows explicitly various conditions that could have given rise to a problem that is being diagnosed. Sometimes it identifies each of several major system components (subsystems) that could be responsible for a problem. For each of these components, the tree might identify (at a second level) a specific type of malfunction. Even more detailed information may be provided in some trees (at a third level) in the form of lists of specific causes of these malfunctions.

Fault trees usually are constructed by people who know enough about a system to be able to itemize many of the various things that could go wrong with it. However, two experts designing a tree for the same system will not necessarily come up with the same representation. Even given the same level of understanding of a system, representations produced by different experts can differ with respect to the amount of detail they contain and the way in which the tree is organized. More specifically, they can differ in terms of the number of major subsystems identified and/or the amount of diagnostic detail provided for identifying a problem within a given subsystem.

Because it usually is not feasible to list all possible causes of a problem, a catchall category labeled "other" may be included at any level of a tree. The designer of a tree must decide which of the potential faults to list explicitly and which to include in the "other" category. Such a decision might be based on the designer's own estimates of the relative likelihoods of the possible causes of a problem. However, other factors could also influence one's behavior: a desire to create the impression that certain problems are more likely than others, an unwillingness to admit the possibility of some types or causes of failure, or simply a lapse of memory regarding what some of the possibilities are.

Fischhoff, Slovic, and Lichtenstein (1978) have shown that people's estimates of the probable causes of problems can be strongly influenced by the information contained in a fault tree, and this is true of both expert and novice diagnosticians. In particular, people appear to be likely to overestimate the probability of a fault that is listed in the tree, and to be relatively insensitive to possibilities that are not shown explicitly. Participants in an experiment who worked with trees from which some potential faults had been pruned "clearly did not appreciate how much had been left out, and, as a consequence, they overestimated the exhaustiveness of the branches they saw" (Fischhoff et al., 1978, p. 355). Calling attention to the "other" category increased the use of it somewhat but not enough to compensate for the deleted items. That is to say, deletion of items had the effect of increasing the proportion of problems attributed to the remaining explicitly specified possibilities even when subjects were warned that not all possibilities were listed and were encouraged to consider the "other" category.

The effect of top-level organization of a tree was also seen in the results of Fischhoff and his colleagues in another way. When a given branch was split into two, the proportion of problems assigned to the two branches was invariably greater than the proportion assigned to the single branch before it was split. In contrast to the large effect of the top-level organization of the tree, how much detail was supplied on individual branches had relatively little impact on subjects' judgments, except that the more detail supplied, the smaller the proportion of problems attributed to the "other" category. These results demonstrate the ease with which people overlook or discount possibilities that are not explicitly identified in a problem representation. Moreover, as the investigators point out, they lead one to the socially significant conclusion that "one can get the public to focus on those issues one thinks are important by never mentioning other issues" (p. 343).

Fischhoff et al.'s results support the idea that people overestimate the completeness of a list of possible faults that is provided to them in diagnostic situations. Again, the question arises as to whether people would overestimate the completeness of a list of possibilities that they themselves had generated. I suspect they would. If this suspicion proved to be true, it would illustrate another way in which memory limitations can constrain problem-solving. Failure to think of possible solutions to a problem is compounded by the failure to be sufficiently sensitive to the incompleteness of the possibilities one does generate and the result is overestimation of the probability that the correct answer is on the list one has produced.

The results obtained by Fischhoff and his colleagues were replicated in most respects by Dube-Rioux and Russo (1988). Failure of subjects to increase the probability of the catchall branch by an amount equal to the probability associated with pruned branches is what Dube-Rioux and Russo referred to as the underestimation bias. What is underestimated is the probability of the catchall category in the pruned tree relative to the sum of the probabilities associated with the pruned possibilities, but, as noted above, one might equally well think of the problem as that of estimating the completeness of the pruned tree. Whichever way one looks at it, the problem is a result, at least in part, of our limited ability to retrieve on demand from memory all that is there that is relevant to a topic of interest.

The "at least in part" qualification in the last sentence is necessary because the fact that one can "recognize" something as relevant to a decision does not require the assumption that what is recognized was once explicitly in memory. We use such expressions as "I forgot to consider . . ." which sounds as though we are pinning the blame for the problem on a faulty memory, but forgetting in this sense does not necessarily entail that what was "forgotten" was in memory at one time. A similar observation can be made with respect to the notion of insufficient search. Usually when psychologists talk about search they are talking about search of memory; however, one can make an argument that searching for solutions, searching for ideas, searching for X is not necessarily limited to searching memory, unless memory is more or less equated with mind.

Desirability Bias/Wishful Thinking

There is evidence of a positive correlation between the probability that one will believe a proposition to be true and the probability that one will consider it to be desirable (Lefford, 1946; McGuire, 1960; Price, 2000; Russo et al., 2008; Russo & Corbin, 2016; Slovic, 1966). Russell Russo and Joseph Corbin define *desirability bias* this way: "The desirability bias (DB) is the upward distortion of the estimated likelihood of a desired event and, less frequently, the downward distortion of an undesired event" (p. 449). This could reflect a relationship between desirability and truth in the real world, whereby what is likely to be desirable is likely also to be true. On the other hand, the correlation could also be the result, at least in part, of beliefs being influenced by preferences. This seems likely to be the explanation, for example, of why smokers find the Surgeon General's warning of the risks of smoking to be less persuasive than do nonsmokers (Kassarjian & Cohen, 1965).

We have already noted several times that people find it easier to believe propositions they would like to be true than propositions they would prefer to be false. This has been seen as one manifestation of the Pollyanna principle, according to which we are likely to give preferential treatment to pleasant thoughts and memories over unpleasant ones. Daryl Bem (1970) notes that rationalization can also work in the other direction.

Having come to believe that something is true, we may persuade ourselves that it is desirable as well.

Suppose I believe that if A is true, then B is necessarily also true, which is to say that A is a sufficient cause of B. Suppose further that I do not know whether A is true. Is the likelihood that I attach to A influenced by how desirable I find B to be? The results of a study by William McGuire (1960) suggest that I will find A more believable if B is desirable to me than I will if it is not.

Several investigators have documented the fact that we tend to judge ourselves to be more likely than our peers to experience pleasant or positive events in the future and less likely to experience unpleasant or negative ones (accidents, health problems). Pointers to some of the relevant studies are given below in a discussion of "I'm special" biases. It appears that we also may be inclined to have rosier expectations for people we like or support (as, for example, political candidates) than for those for whom we have negative or neutral feelings (Babad & Katz, 1992; Granberg & Brent, 1983).

Evidence of what seems to be appropriately interpreted as wishful thinking comes from studies in which participants have been given information about individuals they have never met. In general, they expressed a greater liking for individuals if they expected to interact with them than if they did not (Berscheid et al., 1976; Darley & Berscheid, 1967). Wishful thinking in this context might be seen as having some social benefit; one might argue that it is good for people to find reasons to like those with whom they expect to interact. It appears to be the case also, however, that people are likely to assess another's ability to be lower if they believe the individual is to be an opponent than if they expect him or her to be a partner (Klein & Kunda, 1989); this seems a little less easy to see as a beneficial misperception.

Evidence of wishful thinking has also been found with laboratory tasks for which it is not so easy to imagine a social benefit. For example, when asked to predict cards that are to be drawn at random from packs containing cards representing different payoffs, people often tend to overestimate the likelihood of drawing the more desirable cards (Irwin, 1953; Irwin & Grace, 1968; Irwin & Metzger, 1966; Irwin & Snodgrass, 1966). Many people appear to have a generally optimistic outlook on life as evidenced by an inclination to overestimate the probability of occurrence of positive events and underestimate the probability of negative events (Sharot, Korn, & Dolan, 2010; Taylor & Brown, 1988). What has sometimes been referred to as a planning fallacy or planning bias is the tendency to underestimate the time it will take to finish a task (Buehler, Griffin, & McDonald, 1997; Buehler, Griffin, & Ross, 1994; Griffin & Buehler, 1999; Kahneman & Tversky, 1979); a tendency that appears to be ubiquitous at all levels of activity, from mundane projects of individuals to major undertakings of corporations and governments, which characteristically require much more time and money than initially anticipated.

Maya Bar-Hillel and David Budescu (1995) did a series of experiments in which participants were asked to estimate the probabilities of occurrence of various events of different degrees of desirability. They found little evidence of a desirability effect when participants were given an incentive to be accurate. These investigators do not question the claim that people often display a desirability bias, but they argue that the locus of the bias, at least as it is manifested in probability judgments, may not be the probability judgments, per se. "Rather, it may lie at a prior stage, when the considerations deemed relevant to that judgment are recalled or generated. Our claim is that previous reports of wishful thinking can be interpreted as an unbiased evaluation of a biased body of evidence" (p. 100).

The idea that people find it easier to believe what they would like to believe is closely related to a variety of manifestations of what has become known as the *confirmation bias*. I have discussed this bias elsewhere (Nickerson, 1998). For the present, it suffices to quote Thomas Gilovich's (1991) conclusion regarding our propensity to be less than evenhanded in our evaluation of favored and unfavored claims on our credulity.

> [I]t is clear that we tend to use different criteria to evaluate propositions or conclusions we desire, and those we abhor. For propositions we want to believe, we ask only that the evidence not force us to believe otherwise – a rather easy standard to meet, given the equivocal nature of much information. For propositions we want to resist, however, we ask whether the evidence *compels* such a distasteful conclusion – a much more difficult standard to achieve. For desired conclusions, in other words, it is as if we ask ourselves, *"Can* I believe this?," but for unpalatable conclusions we ask, *"Must* I believe this?" (p. 83).

The evidence that beliefs can be influenced by preferences is very strong. It is important not to lose sight of the fact, however, that there is a limit to how much influence on our beliefs our preferences can have. It is not the case, for most of us at least, that we are free to believe anything we want; what we believe must appear to us to be believable. We can be selective with respect to the evidence we seek and we can tilt the scales somewhat when we weigh what we find, but we cannot completely ignore counterindicative evidence of which we are aware. Ziva Kunda (1990) makes this argument persuasively. The very fact that we *seek* to ignore or discount evidence that counts against what we would like to believe bears witness to the importance we attach to holding beliefs that are justified, or at least that appear to be justified, by sound reasons.

Although not as aggressively researched as the effect of personal preferences on one's own beliefs and behavior, there is evidence that people are sensitive also to the preferences of others and this sensitivity may affect their behavior. If, for example, a speaker knows that his audience prefers A to B, he may slant his remarks to be partial to A, even if he would not strongly support A in a different context (Brown, 1999).

A caveat regarding the interpretation of predictions. Because predictions are typically made for the purpose of guiding action, they can become causal agents in helping determine the future course of events (Einhorn & Hogarth, 1978). A prediction of an impending economic problem, for example, may move economic policymakers to take steps to avoid the problem. If the steps are effective, then the problem will not materialize and the prediction will prove to have been wrong, which obviously is not to say that it was a poor prediction.

There are also such things as self-fulfilling predictions (Merton, 1948). The prediction that the price of some commodity is about to fall, even if baseless, could, if believed, precipitate a wave of selling that would cause the prediction to become true. One would be reluctant to judge such a prediction to have been a good one, however, unless it was the predictor's intention to cause a selling stampede.

Citation Bias

Some especially thought-provoking data have been reported by Jay Christensen-Szalanski and Lee Beach (1984) that suggest that the appearance of the prevalence of reasoning biases may be, to some degree, a consequence of selective attending by the research community to studies that have yielded evidence of such biases as distinct from those that have not. In examining the *Social Science Citation Index* for a ten-year period, these investigators found that articles that reported poor performance on reasoning tasks were cited about six times as frequently as were comparable articles that reported good performance on such tasks, and that the discrepancy increased as a function of the number of years that the articles had been in print. They found too that members of the *Judgment and Decision-Making Society* who responded to a questionnaire were better able to recall documented examples of poor performance of which they were aware than documented examples of good performance.

These findings suggest that reports of poor performance are more likely to be noted and cited by other researchers than are reports of good performance, and the consequence is that the attention that is given to poor performance in the literature is out of proportion to the number of times it has been found in experiments relative to the number times performance has proved to be sound. As to why researchers would demonstrate a bias for citing examples of poor performance, Christensen-Szalanski and Beach consider several possible reasons. Among them is the possibility that poor performance simply seems more newsworthy.

> When people behave the way they are "supposed to," it often does not seem particularly remarkable. But when people behave in what appears to be an irrational manner, it is not only remarkable, but we can give it a name. Names like *representativeness, availability bias,* and *overconfidence bias* make the unfelicitous performance seem like a concrete phenomenon and create the illusion that we have actually explained something merely by naming it (p. 77).

Although their study does not speak to the possibility, it could be too that investigators are more likely to submit for publication results that demonstrate biases than results that do not.

Attribution Bias

Effects have causes, and people like to know what they are. How people attribute specific effects to specific causes has been a focus of research for a long time (Heider, 1944; Jones & Davis, 1965; Kelley, 1967; Nisbett & Borgida, 1975). Effects that can be attributed to human behavior have been of special interest. Many such effects might be attributed either to personality traits or to situational circumstances, and much research has addressed the question of what determines whether people will make the one attribution or the other. This work has revealed what is generally called the *fundamental attribution error* – a tendency to attribute a person's behavior to his or her disposition or personality traits and to overlook possible situational determinants of that behavior (Jones, 1976, 1979; Jones & Davis, 1965; Jones & Harris, 1967; Mischel, 1968; Ross, 1978; Ross & Anderson, 1982). I have discussed much of the relevant research elsewhere (Nickerson, 2008, chapter 6). (See also Borgida & Brekke, 1981; Kelley, 1967, 1971; Gilbert & Malone, 1995; Pal, 2007; Ross & Fletcher, 1985.)

Much of the research and theorizing on the fundamental attribution error is also reviewed by Abigail Gertner et al. (2016). For challenges of the concept, see John Sabini, Michael Siepmann, and Julia Stein (2001) and David Funder (2001).

Retrospective Biases

The idea that memories are not simply "retrieved" from a repository where they lie in a pristine state between activations, but that they are, to some degree, "constructed" has considerable currency among psychologists today. When people attempt to recall attitudes or things they have said or done in the past, they sometimes display what Robyn Dawes (1988) refers to as "biases of retrospection."

Presumably there are many reasons why we remember, or reconstruct, some events or incidents better than others. One such reason may be that we prefer to remember some things more than others. Pleasant memories are more likely to be rehearsed, perhaps, than unpleasant ones, although some people appear too to have a tendency to dwell on unpleasant events in their lives.

Selective remembering can also be ego-building or ego-protecting. People who have been led to believe that a particular type of activity is good for one's health are likely to report having engaged in that activity more frequently than are people who have been led to believe that that activity is bad for one's health (Ross, McFarland, & Fletcher, 1981). This result seems consistent with the idea that what is affected by the belief about the desirability of the activities is not the encoding in memory of representations of having engaged in the activities, but the way in which memory is searched for instances of those representations (Kunda, 1990).

In a longitudinal study, Gregory Marcus (1986) surveyed the attitudes of the same group of people in 1965, 1973, and 1982 with respect to several politically controversial issues. In 1982, he asked the participants not only to indicate their current attitudes on these issues, but to indicate retrospectively what their attitudes had been in 1973. For the most part, the recalled attitudes were more similar to the 1982 attitudes than to those that were actually expressed in 1973. Evidence of a similar shift of retrospective reports of earlier behavior in the direction of behavior that is more similar to that that prevails at the time of the report has been obtained also by L. N. Collins et al. (1985).

There is, of course the possibility that subjects' memories in such studies are more accurate than their reports, which is to say that they may deliberately report past attitudes or behavior that are more consistent with their present attitudes or behavior than they know them to have been. Alternatively, their memories may really have been affected by an unwarranted assumption of consistency on their part.

Dawes (1988) points out that retrospective biases can also work in the direction of making the past appear less, rather than more, consistent with the future. If, for example, one *believes* that things have changed, one may exaggerate (perhaps intentionally, perhaps not) how different things used to be. He cites a study by Michael Conway and Michael Ross (1984) in which students who had completed a program to improve study skills assessed their pre-participation study skills to have been worse than they had originally assessed them to be, and this despite the fact that participation in the program had failed to improve their skills.

Explanation Bias

Much conditional reasoning is prefactual (the antithesis of counterfactual) in that it has to do with the future – what is likely to be a consequence of doing X? (Byrne & Egan, 2004; McConnell et al., 2000; Sanna, 1996, 1998). Numerous studies have demonstrated what has been referred to as an *explanation bias*, which is related to retrospective biases, but prospective in orientation: explaining why or how a possible future event might occur – or simply imagining its occurrence – can increase one's estimate of the probability that the event will, in fact, occur (Campbell & Fairey, 1985; Carroll, 1978; Hirt & Sherman, 1985; Johnson & Sherman, 1990; Koehler, 1991; Ross, Lepper et al., 1977; Sherman et al., 1981). The effect is more pronounced under some conditions than under others, and there are various theories of why it occurs at all (Hirt & Markman, 1995), but the fact that it occurs is not disputed.

Context Bias

In medicine, *context bias* refers to the tendency of diagnoses to be unduly influenced by the diagnostic context in which they are made – e.g., a radiologist's interpretation of an x-ray being influenced by his/her knowledge of the interpretation by other radiologists (Egglin & Feinstein, 1996). Robert Warren et al. (2017) present evidence that the interpretation of results of studies of the effects of invasive biological species have sometimes been overly negative because of the prevailing tendency to frame studies of biological invasion in negative terms. Context bias is also given other connotations; my sense is that they are not widely recognized.

Egocentric Biases

> [T]he evidence is clear that we often hold false beliefs about our own cognitive processes. In most cases, these false beliefs are self-flattering. We are convinced of the rationality of our reasoning, highly adept at constructing plausible explanations for our decision behavior, too confident that our judgments are correct, convinced that we could have predicted uncertain matters after the event, and so on
>
> (Evans, 1989, p. 109).

Some biases can be seen as *egocentric* in the sense that they either take one's own experience as being more representative of that of others than it probably is, or they rest on the assumption, probably tacit, that one is special in some way. This is not to suggest that all such biases have the effect of flattering one's ego, although some of them undoubtedly do. The tendency of experts to overestimate the complexity of their own decision-making and to believe that they make use of more information than they actually do (Slovic & Lichtenstein, 1971) might be considered a case in point. Another is our inclination to take credit for our successes while finding ways to attribute our failures to external causes (Miller & Ross, 1975; Ross, 1977; Snyder, Stephan, & Rosenfield, 1976).

"False Consensus," Effects, and Projection

It was July 16, 1985. On my way to the airport I had tuned into a radio talk station. President Ronald Reagan was still in the hospital recuperating from the removal of a section of his large intestine that contained a malignant polyp. The topic of conversation on the radio station was colonoscopy, a procedure used to inspect the large intestine visually. One caller who had experienced the procedure described the instrument that is used as "an 8-foot garden hose" and warned the radio audience that anyone who has to be inspected with this device will find the experience excruciatingly painful. A subsequent caller, who some years ago had had a section of his intestine removed because of cancer, reported that he has the procedure performed periodically and assured the audience that while it is mildly uncomfortable, it is not painful and should not be feared. Both of these men were speaking from experience. Assuming that neither of them was intentionally lying, how do we reconcile their conflicting claims?

They were on safe ground as long as they were only reporting their own experiences; each was on thin ice, however, when he assumed that everyone else would react as did he. And this appears to be what each was doing: projecting his experience onto everyone else. Projecting in this way overlooks that the amount of discomfort or pain associated with a medical procedure may depend on the skill of the physician, the physical and mental state of the patient, the patient's tolerance for pain generally, among a variety of other factors, and that, consequently, it is likely to vary considerably from case to case.

Many biases appear to stem from the tendency to view oneself as more representative of other people in specific respects than one really is. Such biases are manifest in the imputation, or projection, of one's own behavior, opinions and knowledge to other people. An example is what has become known as the *false-consensus effect,* which refers to the fact that people who engage in a particular behavior tend to estimate that behavior to be more prevalent than do people who do not engage in that behavior (Baumeister, Dale, & Sommer, 1998; Dunning & Hayes, 1996; Mullen et al., 1985; Ross, Greene, & House, 1977). A relatively early report of this phenomenon was Daniel Katz and Floyd Allport's (1931) finding that students' estimates of the prevalence of cheating was positively related to their own admitted level of cheating. Discussions of the false-consensus effect, or *social projection* more generally, include those of David Holmes (1968), Brian Mullen et al. (1985), Gary Marks and Norman Miller (1987), Joachim Krueger (1998) and Jordan Robbins and Krueger (2005).

The phenomenon appears to pertain not only to behavior, but to feelings, attitudes, opinions, beliefs, preferences, and experiences as well. How happy one perceives others to be appears to depend to some degree on how happy one considers oneself to be (Goldings, 1954). Competitors are likely to consider most other people also to be competitive, and cooperators tend to see most others as cooperative (Dawes, McTavish, & Shacklee, 1977). People with hostile attitudes are likely to perceive hostility in others (Nasby, Hayuden, & DePaulo, 1980). People tend to consider their own opinions to be representative of – though less prejudiced than – the opinions of the general public (Fields & Schuman, 1976). Victims of crime estimate the incidence of crime to be higher than do people who have not been victims (Bennet & Hibberd, 1986). People's judgments of how difficult anagram or other problems are likely to be for others have been found to correlate highly with difficulty of the problems for themselves (Kelley & Jacoby, 1996; Nickerson, Butler, & Carlin, 2009). People are more likely to believe that others know the answer to a question if they themselves know it, or erroneously believe they know it, than if they do not know it and realize they do not know it (Nickerson, Baddeley, & Freeman, 1987; Nickerson et al., 2009). When children were asked to estimate the age of Peter Pan, their estimates correlated with their own ages (Mintz, 1956). Sometimes people impute knowledge to others that they should realize that only they themselves have (Keysar et al., 2000). Several other illustrations of a tendency to see oneself as more representative of others in various ways than one really is are given in Nickerson (1999).

One can make an argument – the argument has been made (Dawes, 1989; Hoch, 1987; Krueger & Zeiger, 1993; Nickerson, 2001) – that one's knowledge or belief about how one would behave in specific situations can be a useful basis, possibly the best basis one has, for anticipating how random other people would behave in those situations. If this were not the case, how would we be able to understand other people's reactions, to be happy with them when they have cause to celebrate or to empathize when they are in pain? This idea is captured in the *principle of humanity* according to which when trying to understand what someone has said, especially something ambiguous, one should impute to the speaker beliefs and desires similar to one's own (Gordon, 1986; Grandy, 1973). And there is evidence that, under certain conditions, people who project their own opinions on others may indeed predict other people's opinions better than those who do not (Stanovich & West, 1998b).

There is a need for caution here, however; although one's own reaction to a situation may be the best model one has of how random other people will react, it is important to recognize the limitations of this model, and to understand that not all people are likely to react to any situation in precisely the same way. The risk in using one's own experience, knowledge, or reactions to specific situations as a basis for predicting what other people have experienced or know or will react is that of overgeneralizing.

Much of the research relating to the false-consensus effect has shown only that people tend to impute their own knowledge, attitudes, beliefs, behavior, and so forth, to others; it has not dealt much with the question of the accuracy of those imputations (Campbell, 1986; Hoch, 1987). It could be that people perceive other people's behavior and states of mind more accurately when they assume them to be similar to their own than when they do not, but evidence on the question is sparse. There is the possibility, too, that in imputing one's own knowledge to others, one complicates communication by assuming people have knowledge they do not have (Gilovich, Savitsky, & Medvec, 1998; Keysar & Henbly, 2002; Nickerson, 1999; Thomas & Jacoby, 2013).

A particularly thought-provoking result from research that has focused on the question of accuracy is the finding that people who are depressed have sometimes been shown to perceive themselves and/or others more accurately than those who are not depressed; such results make it appear that the social perceptions of depressed people are more realistic than those of nondepressed people, the latter being more subject to certain distorting biases, at least insofar as the perception of oneself and how one compares with others is concerned (Alloy & Abramson, 1979; Golin, Sweeney, & Shaeffer, 1981; Lewinsohn et al., 1980; Mischel, 1979; Tabachnik, Crocker, & Alloy, 1981).

Although one might expect, on common-sense grounds, that depressed people would see themselves more negatively, at least with respect to depression-relevant attributes, than they see other people, it seems to be more the case that the greater accuracy of the imputations of depressed people stems from the fact that nondepressed people tend to see themselves more positively with respect to such attributes than they see others (Tabachnik et al., 1981). This suggests the interesting possibility that some self-serving biases in self-perception may contribute to mental health, to a degree, and that the absence of such biases may be conducive to depression. Of course, we cannot conclude causation from correlation, but the possibility is an interesting one to consider. Naomi Tabachnik et al. relate this association with the idea that nondepressed people, but not depressed people, tend to overestimate the degree to which they control the positive events in their lives and underestimate the degree to which they control negative events, whereas depressed people tend to make relatively accurate judgments of degree of control.

We all must have a great deal of knowledge in common; if that were not the case, we could not communicate effectively. That the assumption of common knowledge is essential to most of our everyday conversations, and that we all make this assumption more or less constantly, are facts that have been made very clear by the enormous difficulties that have been encountered by researchers in their efforts to give computers the capability to converse with people in natural language. So far such efforts have been successful only when the domain of discourse has been greatly restricted so that the amount of knowledge needed to support a conversation is manageably small. No natural-language system that has yet been built has enough "common-sense" knowledge about the world to support a random conversation such as one might overhear by eavesdropping on two five-year -olds. (But speech – natural language – understanding by computer is progressing rapidly and it may soon be the case that this observation will no longer hold.)

Although the assumption of common knowledge is a necessary one and one that serves us well, it also can be the basis for misunderstandings and failures of communication. The problem is that we make it not only when it is justified, but also sometimes when it is not. Mark Steedman and Philip Johnson-Laird (1980) suggest that, in a conversation, "the speaker assumes that the hearer knows everything that the speaker knows about the world and about the conversation, unless there is some evidence to the contrary" (p. 129).

Evidence that people overestimate the degree to which what they happen to know (or think they know) is representative of what people in general know comes from a study in which college students attempted to answer general-knowledge questions and to estimate, for each question, the percentage of other college students who would be able to answer that question correctly. Subjects gave higher estimates for questions the answers to which they knew (or thought they knew, as indicated by confidence ratings) even when their own answers were wrong than for those the answers to which they did not know (and knew they did not know) (Nickerson et al., 1987).

Although I am not aware of experimental evidence on the question, we might surmise that, in keeping with other manifestations of egocentric biases, people tend to overestimate the level of other people's interest in things in which they themselves are very interested. I suspect that researchers tend to overestimate the importance attached to their own problem areas by others. This might help explain why public speakers often find it difficult to stay within their allotted time. I am not suggesting that this is the only reason that speakers become oblivious to the clock, but it must be among the more important ones; a speaker would hardly drone on interminably if he really believed he was boring the audience to tears. It might also help account for the sometimes unwelcome insistence of people to tell more than others may want to hear about their personal lives, families, travels, and so on.

G. H. Hardy (1989/1940) made an interesting defense of an egocentric bias of a sort among people engaged in creative work as, say, in mathematics or science.

> Good work is not done by "humble" men. It is one of the first duties of a professor, for example, in any subject, to exaggerate a little both the importance of his subject and his own importance in it. A man who is always asking "is what I do worthwhile?" and "am I the right person to do it?" will always be ineffective himself and a discouragement to others. He must shut his eyes a little and think a little more of his subject and himself than they deserve (p. 66).

Hardy seems to be suggesting that people who wish to do good work should intentionally exaggerate the importance of themselves and their research focus. My conjecture is that most of us have a natural tendency to do this without realizing it; that is, we exaggerate our own importance but do not recognize the exaggeration as such. Perhaps Hardy also suspected this tendency to a degree, inasmuch as he noted that one would not find it difficult to take his advice to shut one's eyes a little, but would find it harder "not to make his subject and himself ridiculous by shutting his eyes too tightly" (p. 66).

An example of what might be considered an egocentric bias has been observed in the peer review process that editors of most scientific journals use to determine what will and what will not be published in them. Michael Mahoney (1977) found that the accept-reject recommendations made by manuscript reviewers were strongly influenced by whether or not the author's findings were consistent with their own theoretical positions. Undoubtedly there are other ways in which a tendency to project one's own knowledge, opinions, or interests to others manifests itself.

The false-consensus effect may rest on several factors, but one that seems likely to play a more-than-incidental role is the tendency that people appear to have to associate with others who share their attitudes, opinions, interests, and values. The old saying that "opposites attract" may be true in physics, but it cannot be considered a general principle in psychology. The evidence is strong that people tend to be attracted to others who are like themselves in various ways (Byrne et al., 1975; Rosenbaum, 1986). To the extent that people choose friends and associates on the basis of shared characteristics, they are bound to get first-hand evidence that others think as they do themselves (Berscheid & Walster, 1978), and may find it easy to make unwarranted generalizations from their peer group to the general population (Perloff & Fetzer, 1986). Krueger (1998) makes a strong argument that, although selective exposure may be a causal factor in false consensus, it cannot be the whole story.

There is also the possibility of a statistical artifact. Imagine a group of people 75 percent of whom believe chocolate is good for you and the other 25 percent believe it is not. Assume they all project their own beliefs to others: those who believe chocolate is good for you believe that everyone believes this and those who believe chocolate is not good for you believe that everyone believes that. The people who believe chocolate is good for you will be correct in their belief about the beliefs of others regarding chocolate more often than will the people who believe chocolate is not good for you, not because they are wiser or psychic, but simply because they are in the majority with respect to their belief about the virtues of chocolate. More generally, simply as a matter of statistics, when a majority shares some bit of knowledge, belief, or behavior and projects it onto others, they are bound to be correct more often than will others – who are not in the majority – when they project their knowledge, beliefs, or behavior.

Dawes (1989) makes this point in general terms and contends that if everyone in a group takes his or her own opinion as representative of that of other members of the group, on average they will be right more often than they will be wrong. Richard Wallen (1943) reports experimental data showing a tendency of subjects "to estimate the attitudes of others so that their own opinion coincides with that of the estimated majority" (p. 272) and notes the possibility that "subjects thought of themselves as typical and ascribed their own views to the majority of the group" (p. 273).

Another factor that has been suggested as possibly being at least partially responsible for the false-consensus effect is the *availability* heuristic (Tversky & Kahneman, 1973). One's own behaviors, opinions, preferences, and so on are likely to be projected simply because they are more available for projection than are behaviors, opinions, or preferences that are not one's own.

The false-consensus effect and related egocentric biases may be viewed as self-serving types of estimation bias. To the extent that we like to think of ourselves as typical, normal, mainstream, middle-class, individuals, seeing our own behavior, knowledge, opinions, and interests as more common than they actually are may serve to support that view. The tendency to take oneself as the norm may result in perceiving views that differ from one's own as being extreme. In an analysis of survey data from 1,468 respondents, Donald Granberg and Carol Robertson (1982) found a strong contrast between respondents' attitudes and their estimations of government policies on three national issues: as one might guess, the more conservative the respondent, the more liberal the policies of the government were seen to be.

Egocentric biases of the false-consensus type help one maintain an image of oneself as a typical individual whose behavior, knowledge, and opinions are representative of those of people in general. Why we should want to see ourselves as typical – indeed whether we do – are questions for research. One possibility that seems worth considering as a hypothesis is that to the extent that one considers one's own behavior and opinions to be representative of those of people in general, one feels no further need to justify them. Also, the assumption that one is representative of people in general with respect to how one behaves, what one knows, what one believes, and so on, provides one with a basis for understanding other people. One's default model of how other people act, and of what they know or believe, is what one knows about oneself, and for many purposes this model is quite adequate.

I have focused here on what has been called the *false*-consensus effect, according to which we may see our own knowledge, beliefs, attitudes, and actions as *more* representative of those of others than they really are. Before leaving this topic, it must be noted that the assumption that one is very much like everyone else in most ways is not only a functional one, but essential to communication and understanding. We must assume that other people mean by words more or less what we do when we use the same words. We must assume that when they say they are happy or sad, energized or tired, comfortable or in pain, what they are experiencing is similar to what we experience when we describe our feelings the same way.

It must be noted too that what people know or believe about other's characteristics can influence how they perceive their own (Valins & Nisbett, 1972; Weiner et al., 1972). This is not surprising. Whether one views one's own behavior as "normal," for example, must depend, to some degree, on what one believes the prevailing behavioral norms to be; judgments of knowledgeability, intelligence, optimism, enthusiasm (or their opposites) are comparative in essence and presumably are made relative to some model of how people differ in these regards.

"I'm Special" Biases

The false-consensus and common-knowledge biases are representative of those in which one sees oneself as more typical of people in general than one really is. There are other biases that can be considered egocentric, but that involve seeing oneself as atypical in certain ways. Some of these biases have been taken as evidence of cognitive conceit, because they appear to be based on an inflated appraisal of one's own cognitive abilities. The term "cognitive conceit" was used first, I believe, by Dawes (1976, 1977) who attributed the reluctance of people in decision-making situations to rely on mechanized decision processes to a tendency to overestimate their own cognitive abilities.

This unrealistic assessment of our own competencies, Dawes suggests, explains how some educators or employers can believe they can do a better job of selection on the basis of briefly reviewing applicants' transcripts, or interviewing applicants, than could be done simply by relying on such standardized indicators as undergraduate grade-point average, Graduate Record Exam score, and letters of recommendation. The general tendency to be overconfident of the accuracy of one's own judgments may be seen as a, perhaps mild, type of cognitive conceit.

Numerous other findings that are suggestive of self-serving biases have also been reported (Dunning, Heath, & Suls, 2004; Dunning, Perie, & Story, 1991). It appears that, even outside the boundaries of Lake Wobegon, well more than half of us consider ourselves to have above-average intelligence (Wylie, 1979), to have more positive and fewer negative character traits than our peers (Alicke, 1985), to be better students (Falchikov & Boud, 1989), to anticipate better interpersonal relationships (Baker & Emery, 1993; Lemay & Venaglia, 2016; Murray & Holmes, 1997), lesser risks of health problems (Sparks & Shepherd, 1994), longer lives (Puri & Robinson, 2007), and better futures generally (Taylor & Brown, 1988; Weinstein, 1980).

We believe ourselves to be more fair-minded (Liebrand, Messick, & Wolters, 1986; Messick et al., 1985), more objective (Armor, 1998), less prejudiced (Fields & Schuman, 1976; O'Gorman & Garry, 1976), less susceptible to various biases (Pronin, Lin, & Ross, 2002), and better equipped for academic success or marital happiness (Kunda, 1987; Lavner, Karney, & Bradley, 2013) than the typical person. Drivers are likely to consider themselves more expert and safer than average (Svenson, 1981; Svenson, Fischhoff, & MacGregor, 1985); people appear to consider their chances of being involved in an automobile accident to be higher when they are a passenger than when they are the driver (Greening & Chandler, 1997; McKenna, 1993; McKenna, Stanier, & Lewis, 1991). In the face of well documented evidence that the majority of small businesses fail within a few years of establishment, fledgling entrepreneurs typically estimate their chances of success to be high (Cooper, Dunkelberg, & Woo, 1988; Lovallo & Kahneman, 2003); of course, presumably few people would be motivated to start a business if they really believed their probability of success to be low.

All the respondents in one large survey of high-school seniors believed themselves to be better able than the average student to get along with others; most thought themselves above average in leadership ability (College Board, 1976–1977). The tendency of some parents to overestimate the sizes of their children's vocabularies might be seen as a self-serving bias, inasmuch as a child with a larger-than-average vocabulary reflects well on parental performance.

As to whether unduly optimistic or self-aggrandizing beliefs are more or less beneficial to the individual than realism, the answer is perhaps more complicated than it might at first seem. Roy Baumeister, Kathleen Vohs, and Gabriele Oettingen (2016) argue that it can work both ways.

> First, when optimism comes in the form of expectancy judgments built on past performance (Bandura, 1997; Taylor, 1989), it can be helpful for effort and success; however, when it comes in the form of sheer positive fantasies and daydreams, it saps energy (Kappes & Oettingen, 2011; Kappes, Oettingen, & Mayer, 2012; Kappes, Schwörer, & Oettingen, 2012; Oettingen & Mayer, 2002). Though such indulging in positive fantasies and daydreams is highly problematic, when these fantasies are complemented with a realistic view of the obstacles in the way, these fantasies stir beneficial behavior change (p. 6).

Self-serving biases may extend to the interpretation of data in ways that are ego-building or ego-protecting. In one study, people who had just been told that they did well on an intelligence test judged such tests to be more valid than did people who had been told that they did poorly (Wyer & Frey, 1983). It appears that people may even discount the seriousness of a medical risk if they have reason to believe themselves to be especially susceptible to it (Block & Keller, 1995; Ditto, Jemmott, & Darley, 1988; Ditto & Lopez, 1992; Jemmott, Ditto, & Croyle, 1986; Kunda, 1987).

When people have been involved in a group effort, they often overestimate the size or importance of their own contribution, relative to the sizes or importance of the contributions of other members of the group (Brenner, 1973, 1976; Dawes et al., 1986; Johnston, 1967; Ross & Sicoly, 1979). It is to be expected, of course, that people are likely to have a fuller and clearer memory of their own contributions to a group activity than of the contributions of individual others, but the evidence seems to suggest that, in assessing our own contributions, we tend not to take this into account, and consequently are likely to believe that our contributions, relative to those of others, have been greater than they actually have been.

There is some suggestive evidence, not hard to believe, that we may see our behavior as more socially responsible than it actually is. It appears, for example, that people's behavior with respect to certain activities expected of good citizens, such as trash recycling, is more accurately predicted by their descriptions of the behavior of neighbors than by their descriptions of their own behavior; in particular it seems that people recycle not as much as they say they do, but about as much as they say their neighbors do (Rathje, 1989).

Even the false-consensus effect, discussed in the foregoing, has a variant that might be considered an example of an *I'm special bias.* Apparently we are prone not only to overestimate the probability that other people's beliefs are similar to our own, but we are especially likely to expect this to be true of the beliefs of people who are admirable for one or another reason (Grandberg & King, 1980; Marks & Miller, 1982).

It appears also that we are good at finding evidence introspectively that we have character traits that we have been told are necessary for success or otherwise desirable. Ziva Kunda and her colleagues have shown that people's self-assessment with respect to personality traits can be influenced by the way they have been predisposed to view the traits. People induced to see a given trait (extraversion or introversion) as beneficial (e.g., conducive to academic success) rated themselves as more characterized by that trait than did people not so induced (Kunda & Sanitioso, 1989; Sanitioso, Kunda, & Fong, 1990).

Kunda (1990) attributes such effects to motivation biasing the search of autobiographical memory for evidence that supports desirable beliefs. She argues that such effects tend to be constrained by prior knowledge; the fact that people induced to see extraversion as beneficial judged themselves as more extraverted than did people not so induced was true of extraverts and introverts alike, but extraverts saw themselves as more extraverted than introverts saw themselves as extraverted, independently of the inducement.

Although many of these biases that appear to be motivationally based are self-serving in effect, the assumption that they are held *because* they are self-serving is not beyond debate. The possibility that a *positivity bias* plays some role in them gains credence from findings like that of Sanitioso (1989, reported in Kunda, 1990), who showed that people who were asked whether they were extraverted were likely to recall more about themselves that suggests that they are extraverted and were more likely to judge themselves to be so than people who were asked whether they were introverted. In this case, what appears to be a biased search of memory may be motivated by nothing deeper than the desire to give a positive answer to the question asked.

Not all "I'm special" biases relate to personal capabilities or social virtues. When college students were asked to estimate how much their own chances of experiencing each of forty-two events differed from the chances of their classmates, they estimated their own chances to be above average for positive events and below average for negative events; most of them expected to live longer than average (Weinstein, 1980).

Other investigators have also found that people tend to consider specified positive events to be more likely to happen to themselves than to another person, and to consider specified negative events to be more likely to happen to someone else than to themselves (Bauman & Siegel, 1987; DeJoy, 1989; Dunning, 1993; Harris & Guten, 1979; Linville, Fischer, & Fischhoff, 1993; Perloff & Fetzer, 1986; Robertson, 1977; Svenson, 1981; Zakay, 1983, 1984). Expectations about the future are susceptible also to present mood, however, so that people are likely to see a rosier future for themselves when in a happy frame of mind than when in a sad one (Wright & Bower, 1992). And they are somewhat conditional on the extent to which the future events in question are perceived to be under one's control; one is likely to be more optimistic about events that are so perceived (whether correctly or incorrectly) than about those that are not (Budescu & Bruderman, 1995; DeJoy, 1989; Harris, 1996; Hoorens & Buunk, 1993; Zakay, 1984).

Self-serving biases obviously can have the effect of protecting or pumping up one's ego. Biases that contribute to a generally optimistic outlook can reduce the probability of depression (Alloy & Ahrens, 1987) and have a positive effect on health (physical and mental) more generally (Scheier & Carver, 1987; Taylor, 1989). Perhaps such biases have a motivational basis (Zuckerman, 1979); however, the fact that a bias is self-serving does not force the conclusion that it is intentionally indulged for that purpose and alternative explanations that trace them to cognitive limitations have also been proposed (Miller & Ross, 1975). A not unlikely possibility is that the question does not have an either-or answer and that both motivational and cognitive factors are involved in these biases to some degree (Anderson & Slusher, 1986; Gilovich, 1991; Kruglanski, 1989; Pyszczynski & Greenberg, 1987; Tetlock & Levi, 1982).

Presumably we all like to think well of ourselves – we like to see ourselves as others see us only to the extent that others see us in a reasonably favorable light. Is it the case that, as a rule, we see ourselves as better than we are? Or at least as better than others see us to be? This appears to be an unsettled question, but the agreement between self-judgments of personality traits and judgments made by others has been found by several investigators to be higher the better the individual in question is known to those doing the judging (Funder, 1980; Kusyszn, 1968; Norman, 1969; Norman & Goldberg, 1966). On the basis of these and other results, Funder (1987) concluded that "if proper care is taken to use valid rating scales and peer judges who know us well, then by and large we do tend to 'see ourselves as others see us'" (p. 84).

It may occur to the reader that the biases of the false-consensus type that overestimate the degree to which one's own knowledge, beliefs and behavior are representative of those of people in general and biases of the "I'm special" variety that overestimate the extent to which one differs from others are mutually contradictory. Although superficially this may appear to be the case, I think it is not. Both of these biases, as described here, can be self-serving; both can support the desire, which appears to be relatively universal, to present oneself in socially-commendable ways (Crowne & Marlowe, 1964; Edwards, 1957). The false-consensus bias can help one justify one's beliefs and behavior on the grounds that they represent the norm; "I'm special" biases can help one see oneself as better than average, at least in certain respects. (Even a negative "I'm special" bias, which makes one see oneself as unrepresentative in undesirable ways – chronically unlucky, say – can be self-serving and used to absolve oneself from personal responsibility, though I do not want to argue that it always is.) It is not difficult to imagine the same individual exercising both types of bias simultaneously; there is nothing to prevent one from overestimating the amount of interest that other people have in one's own area of work and, at the same time, believing that almost no one else is likely to appreciate its true significance to the degree that one does oneself.

Hindsight Bias and "I-knew-it-all-along" Phenomenon

There is considerable evidence to support the view that following the occurrence of an event, people are likely to overestimate the degree to which they had expected the event to occur (Bernstein et al., 2015; Christensen-Szalanski & Fobian Willham, 1991; Hawkins & Hastie, 1990; Hoffrage & Hertwig, 1999). This finding is sometimes referred to as the *hindsight bias*, and sometimes as the *I-knew-it-all-along phenomenon*. The distinction between hindsight and knew-it-all-along studies has not been maintained in the literature and the two terms have often been used interchangeably. However, Ralph Hertwig, Gerd Gigerenzer, and Ulrich

Hoffrage (1997) have distinguished between them on the basis of whether the experimental design required participants to make judgments of their memories.

The hindsight design, according to this distinction, involves having people express their confidence in the outcome of some future event (or past event the outcome of which they do not yet know) and then, after the event has occurred and they know the outcome, having them report the degree of confidence they had previously expressed. One is said to display a hindsight bias when one's recalled confidence differs from the confidence actually expressed in a direction that would indicate greater foresight than one actually had. If, for example, one expressed a confidence (probability) of, say, .6 that JP would win an upcoming election, and then after JP did in fact win, one recalled expressing a confidence of .8 that she would do so, this would be evidence of a hindsight bias; similarly if one expressed a confidence of .6 before the fact and then, after learning that JP had lost, remembered the original confidence as .4.

The knew-it-all-along design does not require people to express their confidence in the outcome of a future event, but has them judge, regarding an event the outcome of which they already know, what they think their confidence in that outcome would have been, if they had been asked to give it before the outcome was known to them. In this case, responses are compared with confidence expressed by people who do not know the outcome, and a bias is revealed when the hypothesized confidence is greater than the confidence expressed by people to whom the outcome is not known. The distinction between hindsight bias and knew-it-all-along bias will not be stressed in what follows; for present purposes, it suffices to consider them sufficiently similar to be treated as the same. The bias has been found experimentally with people from various cultures, although not necessarily with the same strength in all cases (Choi & Nisbett, 2000; Yama et al., 2010).

Fischhoff (1975) had people judge the likelihoods of specified alternative outcomes of various historical events on the basis of written descriptions of those events. Those who had been informed of the actual outcomes assigned higher "before-the-fact" likelihoods to these outcomes than did those who had not been so informed; the former participants also judged information that pointed in the direction of the actual outcomes to be more relevant than information that pointed to other possibilities. Slovic and Fischhoff (1977) got a similar hindsight effect when people were asked to estimate retrospectively the probabilities of various scientific results.

Several other investigators have obtained data that demonstrate the hindsight bias in one or another form. When members of the Conservative and Labour parties made forecasts and hindsight estimates of the outcome of the British General Election of May 1979, the results gave only weak support to the idea of a hindsight bias, while they showed a strong effect of party affiliation on both foresight and hindsight judgments; in both cases outcomes favorable to the individual's party were estimated to be more likely than those favorable to the opposing party (Pennington, 1981). However, in a second study in which subjects made hindsight and foresight estimates of the percentages of females in various roles in society, evidence of a strong hindsight bias was obtained.

Mark Leary (1982) had college students predict the outcome of the 1980 US presidential election before it occurred and compared their predictions with the responses of another group that was asked, following the election, what they would have predicted had they been asked to do so before the election occurred. The retrospective "predictions" of the latter group were closer to the actual election results than were the predictions of the former group.

Women who knew the results of a pregnancy test to be positive gave hindsight estimates of a positive outcome that were higher than the estimates produced by women about to have a test that later proved to be positive (Pennington et al., 1980). Interpretation of this result as a straightforward hindsight effect is complicated, however, by the fact that the same difference between hindsight and foresight estimates was not obtained for women who tested negative.

Hal Arkes et al. (1981) had one group of physicians read a case history and estimate for each of four possible diseases the probability that the patient had that disease. Another group of physicians was divided into four subgroups. Each subgroup read the same case history and was told that it was a case history of a patient with a particular disease. The particular disease identified (one of the four) was different for each subgroup. Physicians in these subgroups were asked to specify for each of the four diseases the probability they would have assigned to that disease had they done the diagnosis. A strong hindsight effect was obtained for each of the four hindsight subgroups; the highest probabilities being associated with the diseases the patient had been identified as having.

These results were seen by the investigators to be particularly important, inasmuch as, unlike some other studies of hindsight bias, in this case the subjects were professionals qualified to make informed decisions. The investigators note also the possible implication of the study for the practice of seeking second opinions regarding medical diagnoses. In particular, the results suggest that when physicians know what a previous diagnosis was, they may be inclined to attempt to make sense of that diagnosis rather than to analyze the data independently of it. If this is true, then if one wants a truly independent second opinion, the physician who is asked to give it should not be informed of the original diagnosis.

When people are induced, say by role-playing, to modify their opinion on a controversial issue, they may remember their previous opinions as being more consistent with their opinions as modified than they actually are (Bem & McConnell, 1970; Wixon & Laird, 1976). Michael Conway (1990) had students predict their performance on an upcoming exam and then asked them, after learning of their results, to recall what they had predicted. Students who did better than they had anticipated recalled a higher-than-actual predicted score, whereas those who did more poorly than they expected recalled a lower-than-actual prediction.

In early demonstrations of hindsight bias, Fischhoff and Beyth-Marom (1975) and Fischhoff (1977) found the bias to be larger for true assertions than for false ones. That is to say retrospective estimates of foresight were influenced to a greater degree when the participants were informed that statements were true than when they were informed that statements were false. Other investigators have reported a similar result (Hasher, Attig, & Alba, 1981; Wood, 1978).

Hertwig et al. (1997) offered an explanation of this asymmetry that attributes it to the combined effects of hindsight and reiteration. The hindsight effect is considered to be directional in the sense that learning that an assertion is true increases one's retrospective confidence in that assertion, whereas learning that it is false decreases one's retrospective confidence in it. The reiteration effect is seen as always positive in the sense that hearing an assertion repeated increases one's confidence in it, whether it is true or false. If the effect of the hindsight bias is generally larger than the effect of reiteration, the result would be that, other things equal, their combined effects would increase one's retrospective confidence in a true assertion more than they would decrease one's retrospective confidence in a false one.

Many other studies have yielded evidence of a hindsight bias, or something like it (Arkes et al., 1988; Campbell & Tesser, 1983; Hoch & Lowenstein, 1989; Mitchell & Kalb, 1981; Snyder & Uranowitz, 1978; Synodinos, 1986). The complexity of the bias is seen in the fact that it is possible under some conditions to get the reverse effect, in which after-the-fact probability estimates are lower than estimates made before the fact (Verplanken & Pieters, 1988), but this outcome is exceptional.

The tendency that people have to be overconfident of the accuracy of their opinions can sometimes be reduced if they are required to give reasons for and against those opinions. A similar effect has been found with respect to the hindsight bias. When neuropsychologists were asked to give for each of three possible diagnoses of a clinical presentation a reason why it might be correct, their susceptibility to the hindsight bias was reduced (Arkes et al., 1988). Simply explaining to people what the bias is and asking them to avoid it appears not to be an effective antidote (Fischhoff, 1977, 1980; Wood, 1978).

Something similar to a hindsight bias has been observed in young (three-year-old) children. If a candy box is opened to reveal that it contains pencils, and they are asked what they thought was in the box before it was opened, they may say pencils (Gopnik & Astington, 1988). This seems likely to be different from the hindsight bias that has been observed in adults; one interpretation of it is that young children do not distinguish between beliefs and reality and thus do not recognize the possibility of entertaining beliefs that are at odds with what is objectively true. This idea gets some support from the fact that when asked what someone else will think is in the candy box when they first see it, they are likely also to say pencils if they themselves know that that is what the box contains (Perner, Leekam, & Wimmer, 1987).

Various explanations of the hindsight bias have been proposed. Some emphasize information-processing limitations of human beings, such as the possibility that one's memory for one's prior expectancy of an event may be modified as a consequence of one's knowledge of the event's occurrence (Fischhoff, 1975). Some researchers stress the role of motivational factors, such as the desire to present oneself as more knowledgeable than one really is. Both of these lines of reasoning could apply to other manifestations of tendencies to reconstruct history as well as to the hindsight bias. Imre Lakatos (1970) surmises that scientific experiments that are viewed as crucial, in the sense of being decisive in favor of one competing theory over another, usually are seen as crucial only with the benefit of hindsight.

Peter Mitchell et al. (1996) suggest that the hindsight bias may be a special case of what they call a "realist bias," according to which people's judgments of beliefs (their own and others') are influenced by their current perceptions of reality. In particular, according to this view, the beliefs that others hold or held, or that one once held oneself, are judged to correspond more closely to what one now believes to be true than they actually do, or did. These investigators liken this distortion to the type of perceptual illusion in which what one "sees" is a compromise between the physical stimulus and what one believes one is looking at, the prototypical case being the demonstration by Thouless (1931) that people typically judge the apparent shape of what they know to be a circle seen from an oblique perspective to be more nearly circular than the physical image really is.

Hertwig et al. (1997) have linked the hindsight bias with the reiteration effect, whereby the plausibility of a claim is increased by repeating it. They suggest that what has usually been considered the effect of hindsight bias is, in fact, the combination of the hindsight bias and the reiteration effect. This view explains, they argue, an asymmetry that has been found in hindsight studies, whereby the hindsight effect tends to be larger for true assertions than for false ones (Fischhoff & Beyth-Marom, 1975; Fischhoff, 1977). The hindsight and iteration effects are assumed to be additive. The hindsight effect is directional in the sense that learning that an assertion is true increases one's retrospective confidence in that assertion, whereas learning that it is false decreases one's retrospective confidence in it. The reiteration effect is always positive in the sense that hearing an assertion repeated increases one's confidence in it, whether it is true or false. If the effect of the hindsight bias is generally larger than the effect of reiteration, the result would be that, other things equal, their combined effects would increase one's retrospective confidence in a true assertion more than they would decrease one's retrospective confidence in a false one. Hertwig et al. note that the asymmetry that has characterized hindsight studies has not been found consistently with knew-it-all-along experiments, and argue that this is because, unlike the hindsight design, the knew-it-all-along design does not involve repetition of the assertions in questions and therefore does not elicit a reiteration effect.

The hindsight bias might be viewed as a type of retrospective bias. In this case, recalled beliefs, as reported, are more consistent with what the truth turned out to be than the original beliefs were. Again, how much of this migration to the truth reflects actual memory changes and how much is due to misrepresenting what one recalls in such a way as to make oneself appear to be smarter than one is, is difficult to say.

Confirmation Bias

Confirmation bias usually connotes a tendency, not necessarily conscious, to overweight evidence that supports a favored view while underweighting or discounting evidence that favors alternative views (Beattie & Baron, 1988; Kuhn, Amsel, & O'Loughlin, 1988; Mynatt, Doherty, & Tweney, 1977; Nickerson, 1998). Francis Bacon recognized this bias and wrote about it in 1620:

> The human understanding when it has once adopted an opinion (either as being the received opinion or as being agreeable to itself) draws all things else to support and agree with it. And though there be a greater number and weight of instances to be found on the other side, yet these it either neglects and despises, or else by some distinction sets aside and rejects; in order that by this great and pernicious predetermination the authority of its former conclusions may remain inviolate .... And such is the way of all superstitions, whether in astrology, dreams, omens, divine judgments, or the like; wherein men, having a delight in such vanities, mark the events where they are fulfilled, but where they fail, although this happened much oftener, neglect and pass them by (p. 36).

Somewhat more recently, but still over 130 years ago, Sidgwick (1884) had this to say about it, calling it the "empirical fallacy:"

> the empirical fallacy consists in resting our proof of a law or theory on confirmatory (i.e., congruent) facts *alone*. If the facts around us do not fit our theories we have of course unanswerable disproof: but if the facts do fit them, the theories are not yet necessarily secure. We need besides such facts, in every case the further assurance that any contradictory facts, if existing would have come to light. And so far as this assurance is wanting, so far the proof is weak (p. 279).

Mercier and Sperber (2011) see evaluations of arguments as biased in the sense that supportive reasons are sought for beliefs and actions people like and unsupportive ones are sought for those they dislike. In promoting the idea that most, if not all, beliefs are formed, and actions decided, via intuitive inference, they appear to rule out the possibility that people sometimes seek reasons for or against some belief or action in order to make a rational decision regarding whether or not to accept the belief or to take the action.

Emphasis on the role of bias in argument evaluation is justified by much research, but ruling out the role of reason in belief formation seems to me to be a mistake; recognition that people may often look selectively for reasons to justify an opinion they want to hold or an action they want to take does not preclude the possibility that they also sometimes attempt to weigh impartially the reasons for and against adopting some belief or acting in a specific way, and sometimes – though perhaps not as often as one would like – try to take a fresh look at existing opinions or habitual actions to determine whether their retention is justified.

A confirmation bias can also refer to a tendency to seek evidence that supports a hypothesis rather than to seek evidence that tells against the hypothesis, even if one has no preference for the hypothesis over its antithesis. Intelligence analysts, for example, may put more effort into seeking evidence that supports a hypothesis under consideration than into seeking evidence that would show the hypothesis to be false (Cook & Smallman, 2008). The same phenomenon has been documented in a variety of contexts (Baron, 2000; Nickerson, 1998). Most treatments of confirmation bias have presented it as an example of how reasoning can, and does, go wrong; however, there is an argument that, under the right conditions, seeking confirmatory evidence may be the optimal way to proceed (Klayman & Ha, 1987; McKenzie & Mikkelsen, 2000). An extensive review of confirmation bias and other cognitive biases as they have been documented in numerous contexts has been provided by Abigail Gertner, Franklin Zaromb, Robert Schneider, and others (2013, 2016).

My-side Bias

The tendency to give preferential treatment to data that support one's own views is often referred to as *my-side bias* (Baron, 1995, 2008; Perkins, 1985; Perkins, Farady, & Bushey, 1991; Sá et al., 2005; Stanovich & West, 2007; Toplak & Stanovich, 2003). It is similar in many respects to what is referred to as the *confirmation bias*, as just described. My-side bias appears to be very common, people with high cognitive ability and/or many years of education being as susceptible to it as people with less cognitive ability or fewer years of education (Perkins, 1985; Stanovich & West, 2007, 2008); and it is relatively difficult to counteract (Drummond & Fischhoff, 2019).

Christopher Wolfe and Anne Britt (2008) make the important and intuitively compelling point that the fact that people tend to make stronger arguments for propositions they believe than for those they disbelieve is neither surprising nor evidence of faulty reasoning. Presumably they have stronger evidence (in their view) for what they believe than for what they do not believe; if that were not true, their beliefs would be different from what they are. "[W]ith respect to written argumentation, it is not at all clear that the tendency to generate more evidence on myside is an adequate definition of the myside bias, or if it even constitutes a bias of any kind. Indeed, it would be surprising and generally counterproductive for authors to write more other side arguments than myside arguments" (p. 3). This line of reasoning led Wolfe and Britt to define my-side bias in written argumentation as "the failure to include *any* reference to other side arguments or positions" (p. 3, emphasis added).

This makes the question of whether a my-side argument should be considered a biased argument to some degree. Wolfe and Britt take the position that to be considered biased an argument should not acknowledge the possibility of any meritorious counterarguments. A less extreme position might consider an argument to be (my-side) biased despite acknowledging the possibility of counterarguments, but without giving them the credence they deserve. Where to draw the line is a judgment call and one that is not likely to be easy to make – which presumably is why Wolfe and Britt opted for the definition they proposed.

Rieke and Sillars (1975) contend that one thing about my-side bias seems clear: "the arguer who only looks to his own arguments, who does not consider carefully what the possible opposition arguments are is doing no one a disfavor but himself" (p. 58).

It will be clear to the reader that the hindsight, I-knew-it-all-along, confirmation and my-side biases have much in common. Some might contend that they all amount to the same thing; although it is not entirely clear how best to capture their common focus. For purposes of this book it suffices to acknowledge their similarity while maintaining the terminology used by their investigators.

Transient Biasing Effects

For the most part, the biases that have been discussed in the foregoing may be considered to be relatively long-lived. In many cases, they can be viewed as tendencies or propensities that persist more or less indefinitely. We should not overlook the possibility, however, of biases that can come and go as consequences of temporary changes in physiological state or mood, recent activation of specific thoughts or memories, or other transient events.

Apparently our judgments and decisions can be biased by short-term events and temporary conditions of various sorts. How generally satisfied with life we will claim to be may depend to some degree, for example, on what the weather is when we are asked (Schwartz & Clore, 1983). Our assessment of the quality of the performance of an individual may be influenced by our reaction to the individual per se; our judgment of a film may be affected by the presence of distracting noise; and we may fail to recognize the effects of the extraneous influences on us (Nisbett &

Wilson, 1977b). Our interpretation of ambiguous behavioral cues to personality characteristics may be influenced by the immediate relative accessibility (recency of activation) of relevant classificatory concepts (Schwarz, 1995; Wyer & Srull, 1989). Our assessments of our satisfaction with our own lives can be affected by recently induced pleasant or unpleasant events (Strack, Schwarz, & Gschneidinger, 1985).

The Big Picture: How Biased Is Human Reasoning?

In the aggregate, the studies reviewed in this chapter present a somewhat discouraging view of human reasoning. The general impression one gets from the literature on the whole is that of reasoning processes that go wrong in an astonishing variety of ways. One is led to wonder how, if our thinking is so faulty, we manage to survive as a species.

This line of reflection prompts two questions: (1) Is the general impression one gets from the literature as a whole correct? Are people as biased in their thinking as the literature seems to indicate? (2) To the extent that specific biases really are prevalent, what causes them and might they serve some useful ends?

On Biased Reasoning in the Laboratory

Most of the empirical research that has been done on reasoning has made use of situations that lend themselves to laboratory control. In many of these cases the problems have been somewhat artificial and the question has been raised as to their representativeness of the kinds of problems that people typically face outside the laboratory. How much can we hope to learn about human reasoning, as it occurs in meaningful contexts, through laboratory studies of performance on contrived tasks?

In defense of the use of artificial situations for research on reasoning, the argument can be made that if one wants to assess an individual's ability to reason, as distinct from one's ability to apply factual knowledge about the world that has been gained from experience, reasoning problems must be used that cannot be solved simply by pattern matching or some other memory-based technique.

On the other hand, the question of the generalizability of the results obtained in artificial situations to real-world contexts is a legitimate one that deserves to be addressed. Several investigators have taken the position that some of the principles and strategies that have been observed in the performance of laboratory tasks are appropriately seen as biases in the laboratory context but not in the real-world contexts in which they are normally applied (Bar-Hillel, 1979; Campbell, 1959; Evans, 1989; Hogarth, 1981; Macdonald, 1986; Oaksford & Chater, 1995). Biases of various types can be viewed as adaptive for an overburdened information-processing system; many of the errors that people make in laboratory contexts may be seen as adaptively useful when viewed from a broader perspective.

Mike Oaksford and Nick Chater (1995) contend that, "if psychologists of reasoning intend their accounts of laboratory reasoning tasks to generalize to everyday reasoning, they face a paradox: although they can account for people's poor performance on explicit reasoning tasks, it appears that [because of the problem of computational complexity] they cannot account for how everyday reasoning is possible at all" (p. 128). Several investigators have either expressed similar doubts about the applicability of results obtained in laboratory investigations of reasoning to real-world situations, or have urged caution in making the leap from the one context to the other (Ebbesen & Konecni, 1980; Funder, 1987; Harkness, DeBono, & Borgida, 1985; Hogarth, 1981).

Funder (1987), among others, argues that many of the errors of reasoning that have been demonstrated in the laboratory may represent adaptive processes in real-world contexts. The argument applies, in his view, to such phenomena as illusory correlation, the tendency to be insensitive to regression effects, the illusion of control, and the fundamental attribution error. Funder contends that each of these phenomena may serve useful purposes under circumstances not uncommon outside the laboratory. The claim is not that people are always consistent in their behavior or that these phenomena are always functional, but only that the demonstration that errors of these sorts occur in situations structured for experimental purposes is not compelling evidence that reasoning is necessarily dysfunctional when it involves similar processes in life outside the laboratory. The other side of the argument is that failure to make errors in experimental situations does not mean that one will necessarily do as well in related real-life situations. In short the quality of reasoning in social situations cannot be inferred very well from performance on laboratory tasks; the best criteria for judging that quality are agreement between the judgments of different people and the ability of judgments to predict behavior, on both of which criteria people tend to do quite well.

Observing that much of the research on social judgment in recent years has focused on "error" and has led to the general conclusion that many if not most of the social judgments people make are wrong, Funder (1987) makes a distinction between *errors* and *mistakes.* "An 'error' is a judgment of a laboratory stimulus that deviates from a model of how that judgment should be made . . .. A 'mistake,' by contrast, is an incorrect judgment in the real world, such as a misjudgment of a real person, and so must be determined by different criteria" (p. 76). Errors made in laboratory tasks do not necessarily translate to mistakes in social settings, because a judgment that is wrong in a laboratory context may be correct in an ordinary social situation.

Ranald Macdonald (1986) argues that many of the reasoning inadequacies that have been identified in laboratory research have been demonstrated in contrived situations involving unfamiliar games of chance and that the answers subjects often give in these tasks can be defended as they apply to more general cases. He suggests that subjects may view the problems they are given to solve differently than do the experimenters. And when this is the case, what constitutes faulty reasoning from one perspective may be appropriate from another.

Macdonald lists three sources of confusion:

> (1) The definition of probability is controversial, even in the technical sense, and it has several meanings in ordinary language. A failure to distinguish between these uses is bound to lead to confusion especially if the possibility of different meanings is not appreciated. (2) The sample space on which the probabilities are to be defined is not made explicit in many of Tversky and Kahneman's problems. Hence the subjects' conceptualization may well be different from the experimenters', and different probabilities assigned, even if one of the usual definitions of probability is mutually accepted. (3) In ordinary life communications are normally sent for some reason, reporting is rarely impartial and pieces of information vary in the extent to which they are reliable. Subjects may well take such factors into account when assessing the information given in these problems. Natural-language rules for assigning non-surface meanings are relevant here (p. 15).

After Ian Hacking (1975), among others, Macdonald distinguishes between aleatory probability, which has to do with idealized games of chance and long-term stable frequencies, and epistemic probability, which refers to a state of belief. Citing what Tversky and Kahneman have referred to as violations of the conjunction rule (mentioned in Chapter 6), whereby subjects have considered the probability of the conjunction of two events to be greater than the probability of the less probable of the component events, Macdonald argues that if subjects in this situation are interpreting probability as epistemic probability, reporting the probability of the conjunction to be greater than that of one of its components is not wrong. "A story can become more believable as it develops, despite the fact that there is necessarily more to believe" (p. 19). If this were not the case, he contends, we would have the curious state of affairs that unexplained events would be more likely than those for which we have an explanation. He contends too that in natural language, questions are always motivated and are only asked when there is some reason to expect a positive answer. It should not be surprising therefore to discover that subjects in these experiments are treating the questions as though they carried useful information.

Another point emphasized by Macdonald and others is that probabilities are mathematically meaningful only if the sample space to which they relate is clear. A given event typically can be described in more than one way and can be treated as a member of any of several categories. To speak unambiguously about the probability of an event, one must be clear as to the reference category intended; comparisons across categories, especially when one category is a subset of the other (as the category feminist bank tellers is a subset of the category bank tellers, and of the category feminists), can yield results that are inconsistent with respect to a fixed frame of reference. As Macdonald puts it: "when subjects are asked to assess the likelihood of a result, they are biased, not surprisingly, by their preferred level of description and may not give the required weight to the level of description given in the problem. Difficulties arise only when the level of description is abnormal or when levels of description are mixed" (p. 22).

Howard Margolis (1987) too argues that "what has usually been taken to be incorrect reasoning leading to cognitive illusions in fact is better characterized as normatively plausible responses to a question different from what the experimenters intended" (p. 141). He emphasizes the roles of both semantic ambiguities and scenario ambiguities (the latter arising from the impoverished context of typical laboratory problems), and the interaction between them in enabling participants in reasoning experiments to interpret problems in ways unintended by experimenters.

Jay Christensen-Szalanski and L. R. Beach (1984) found that when people who were familiar with work in judgment and decision-making attempted to recall reports of poor or good performance on reasoning tasks, the most common examples of poor performance were from laboratory studies with college students as subjects, whereas a majority of the most common examples of good performance were from studies done in applied settings and/or used experts as subjects.

W. Todd DeKay, Martie Haselton, and Lee Kirkpatrick (2000) argue that the psychological architecture that humans evolved was suited to produce inferences that were adaptive, not necessarily normatively logical. They give three reasons why people make errors in solving reasoning problems of the type they typically encounter in the psychological laboratory.

> First, people bring into the lab a toolbox packed with specialized implements, none (usually) designed expressly for the task at hand .... Second, logic problems typically require one to ignore vast amounts of real-world knowledge to focus entirely on abstractions .... Third ... our evolved psychological mechanisms succeeded or failed historically not as a function of their adherence to symbolic logic, but rather as a function of their effects on survival and reproduction (p. 670).

DeKay et al. argue that in view of the favoring of natural selection of designs that out reproduce others rather than designs that are normatively rational, it is astonishing that we are able to deal with the kinds of reasoning problems typically encountered in the laboratory at all.

It would be easy to add to these examples of expressed reservations about the applicability of many laboratory results on reasoning tasks to the ways in which people do, or should, function in real-world situations. The general point, however, is not that laboratory research on reasoning is futile, but rather that the results of such research should not be applied – as they sometimes are – to real-world contexts in an unthinking way. A view to which many researchers would subscribe is that laboratory studies can provide useful clues to how we are likely to reason, or fail to reason, in practical situations, but that these clues need to be checked in real-world contexts before they can be considered accurate representations of what actually happens, or should happen, there.

Bases of Biases

Some of the biases and other ostensibly problematic aspects of reasoning that have been discussed in this chapter appear to be not only quite pervasive, but persistent and unlikely to be self-correcting. Their pervasiveness and persistence prompt two questions: What causes them and why do they persist?

Many reasons have been proposed as to why we have biases of the types on which we have been focusing. Broadly speaking, the explanations usually emphasize either motivational factors or cognitive limitations. Tom Pyszczynski and Jeff Greenberg (1987) summarize the situation this way.

> Although virtually all psychologists agree that cognitions are often subject to bias, there is very little agreement concerning the mechanisms responsible for such bias. One group of theorists, those espousing a motivational position, argue that cognitions are biased to meet the needs or desires of the individual. Influenced by the psychodynamic theories of Freud and others, these theorists maintain that cognitive biases result from powerful drives, internal conflicts, and affective states. They posit a variety of motives, such as needs for self-esteem, cognitive consistency, and a belief in a just world, that lead to inferences other than those which would result from a purely logical consideration of evidence.
>
> The other group of theorists, those espousing a purely cognitive perspective, view cognitive biases as the result of rational, albeit imperfect, inferential processes. Influenced by recent developments in cognitive psychology and information processing, these theorists focus on the way people encode, organize, and retrieve information and on the knowledge structures, transformation rules, and heuristics that are used to make inferences of various kinds. Rather than viewing cognitive bias as a result of the affective consequences of various cognitive configurations, they view it as a consequence of the dispassionate workings of the cognitive system (p. 297).

Sometimes the two types of explanation are said to invoke notions of hot and cold cognition respectively.

The motivational accounts of biases predominated until relatively recently; explanations emphasizing the role of cognitive factors began to emerge and gain some prominence as part of what is sometimes called the "cognitive revolution" in psychology. Today some theorists continue to emphasize motivation while others stress cognitive factors; many consider both types of factors to be important. Pyszczynski and Greenberg (1987), for example, suggest that self-serving attributions have both motivational and cognitive roots: "self-serving attributions are usually the result of a self-esteem motive's influence on the same processes that produce attributions when such a motive is not exerting an influence" (p. 302).

Hoffrage and Hertwig (1999) consider hindsight bias to be the "by-product of two generally adaptive processes: first, updating knowledge after receiving new information; and second, drawing fast and frugal inferences from this updated knowledge" (p. 191). The argument, in short, is that memory is largely a reconstructive process; much of what we appear to remember we actually reconstruct by making inferences based on other things we know. One may not remember what one expected the outcome of an upcoming election to be, but if asked, after the event, it is natural to infer what it was on the basis of what one now knows.

The belief that some biases are reflective of cognitive limitations gets support from the work of Keith Stanovich (1999) and Stanovich and Richard West (1998a, 1998b, 1998c, 2000b) showing differences among individuals with respect to their proneness to certain biases and correlations between that proneness and measures of cognitive ability, such as SAT scores and performance on various tests of intelligence. Generally speaking, people who do better on the various tests of cognitive ability tend to be less likely to display the more common biases. And people who perform normatively, or nearly so, with one task, are likely to perform normatively, or nearly so, on other tasks as well.

Evans (1989) argues that all the kinds of biases that have been found in reasoning tasks stem primarily from selective processing of problem information: "the major cause of bias in human reasoning and judgment lies in factors which induce people to process the problem information in a selective manner. Such selection may arise either in the process of forming mental representations of the information presented in the problem or else in the actual manner in which it is subsequently processed" (p. 19). The impossibility of processing all the sensory data with which we are continually bombarded makes selection essential; the challenge to the student of cognition, Evans argues, is to discover why the selection process sometimes yields systematic mistakes in reasoning.

The Functionality or Dysfunctionality of Biases

A tacit assumption underlying much of the relevant psychological literature is that biases of the sort described are bad – irrational aspects of human cognition. They cause people to reason illogically, to draw unwarranted conclusions, and to form and retain unfounded beliefs. Jonathan Baron (1985) summarizes his view of the situation the following way. "People will in general think too little, search for evidence to confirm what they already favor, and use evidence the same way – unless corrective action has been provided. We may thus expect people (without corrective education) to exhibit biases predominantly in one direction, and therefore to be generally irrational. This is the main empirical prediction of the present theory" (p. 129). This is a fairly negative general assessment of the role of biases in thinking and of the prospects for changing things much for the better. Strong arguments can be made in defense of this view.

On the other hand, one is led to wonder why, if these biases are so bad, do they persist. At least if they are bad in the sense of promoting dysfunctional behavior, they should contribute to their own extinction over time because of the negative consequences they incur. The entertaining of false beliefs about the world should, as a general rule, put one at some disadvantage in a competition for survival. If I believe that I can defy the law of gravity, or that I can drink contaminated water with impunity, or that I can mistreat people with no serious consequences, such beliefs are not likely to make me a better insurance risk.

Gigerenzer and Brighton (2009) make a case for the idea that many of the biases and alogical heuristics that have been shown to be pervasive in human reasoning may, in fact, be effective strategies in the contexts in which they occur. They review numerous studies that support the conclusion that what are generally seen as instances of biased heuristics are often more efficient and/or more accurate in decision-making or problem-solving than are more logically copacetic approaches. "A biased mind that operates with simple heuristics can thus be not only more efficient in the sense of less effort but also more accurate than a mind that bets only on avoiding bias" (p. 125). Gigerenzer and Brighton are not arguing, as I understand them, that people invariably do better by relying on biased heuristics rather than on more conventionally analytic approaches, but that they often do so.

There is the view that some of the biases that have been observed were functional at an earlier time in the history of the species, but no longer are. Here the question of interest is whether some biases can serve useful purposes at the present time. One can certainly argue that some egocentric biases have the effect of bolstering personal egos. The idea of "defensive projection," according to which people often project onto desirable other people undesirable traits that they see in themselves, illustrates this possibility (Bramel, 1962; Edlow & Kiesler, 1966; Holmes, 1968).

Suppose I believe myself to be more intelligent than I really am, or more attractive, or more tolerant of others' quirks, or better adjusted psychologically. Are such delusions necessarily bad for me? Some psychologists have argued that a certain amount of self-deception of this type may make me happier than I would otherwise be (Greenwald, 1980; Taylor & Brown, 1988, 1994). At risk, of course, is the possibility of discovering the belief to be false.

Certainly, biases can serve the purpose of protecting existing beliefs. On the assumption that people everywhere and always are truth seekers, biases that protect existing beliefs against counterindicative evidence are clearly dysfunctional. On the other hand, it must be the case that a large proportion of the average person's beliefs about the world are true in a practical sense – water is wet; fire is hot; if I jump out of a three-story window I am likely to get hurt; a toothache requires a trip to the dentist, while a burst water pipe requires a call to the plumber – anyone who holds mostly false beliefs about the world is likely to be in serious trouble, or dead. This being so, the perseverance of existing beliefs can serve to facilitate the correct interpretation of new data, as Hilary Kornblith (1993) points out, as well as sometimes to distort it.

But the assumption that people everywhere and always are truth seekers is not tenable; for many people the desire to preserve existing beliefs trumps the desire to know the truth, whatever it may be. Alfred North Whitehead (1994/1967) puts it this way.

> Every age produces people with clear logical intellects, and with the most praiseworthy grasp of the importance of some sphere of human experience, who have elaborated, or inherited, a scheme of thought which exactly fits those experiences which claim their interest. Such people are apt resolutely to ignore, or to explain away, all evidence which confuses their scheme with contradictory instances; what they cannot fit in is for them nonsense. An unflinching determination to take the whole evidence into account is the only method of preservation against the fluctuating extremes of fashionable opinion. This advice seems so easy, and is in fact so difficult to follow (p. 222).

This observation – of the confirmation bias at work – was made in the context of a discussion of the relationship between science and religion, but it pertains more broadly, and it is doubtful that any group is devoid of people who fit the description.

In many real-life situations the various types of errors one might make are not equally undesirable. It is almost tautological to say that when choices really matter to the people who are making them, some ways of being wrong are likely to be more regrettable than others. This is illustrated by the rules of jurisprudence used by the legal systems of most of the civilized world, which are set up to make it much more difficult to convict an innocent person than to acquit a guilty one. It is illustrated too by the application of a similar principle in the making of judgments about people in everyday life; who can doubt the wisdom of Isaac Watts's (1995/1796) advice: "'Tis hard for us to determine with Assurance what are the inward Springs and secret Causes of every Man's Conduct; and therefore we should be cautious and slow in passing a Judgment, where the Case is not exceeding evident: And if we should mistake, let it rather be on the charitable than the censorious Side" (p. 63).

Several investigators have argued that this type of consideration makes certain types of "biases" functional in specific situations (Cosmides, 1989;

Friedrich, 1993; Hogarth, 1981; Klayman & Ha, 1987, 1989). Consider the problem of hypothesis testing. When the undesirable consequences of judging a true hypothesis to be false are greater than those of judging a false hypothesis to be true, a bias toward confirmation is not only understandable, but dictated both by some normative models of reasoning and by common sense.

James Friedrich (1993), for example, argues that

> our inference processes are first and foremost pragmatic, survival mechanisms and only secondarily truth detection strategies. As such, these inferential strategies are well suited to identifying potential rewards and minimizing costly errors; they are not, and in fact *need not* be, well suited to "rational" hypothesis testing as prescribed by the logic of science. Thus, strategies often viewed as seriously flawed may not only produce adaptively accurate judgments in the real world (Arkes, 1991; Funder, 1987), they may also cease to appear error prone (deviating from some standard) when a more appropriate normative model is considered (p. 298).

To illustrate the point, Friedrich uses the example of an employer who wants to test the hunch that extraverts make the best sales people. If the employer checked the sales performance only of extraverts, found it to be very good and, on this basis, decided to hire only extraverts for sales positions, we would say that she had not made an adequate test of her hunch, because she did not rule out the possibility that introverts might do well at sales also. But if her main objective is to *not* hire people who will turn out to be *poor* at sales, satisfying herself that extraverts make good sales people suffices; the fact that she has not discovered that introverts can be good at sales too could mean that she will miss some opportunities by not hiring them, but it does not invalidate her decision to hire extraverts if her objective is to avoid hiring poor performers.

An obvious implication of the hypothesis that people are generally more motivated to avoid certain types of errors than to determine the truth or falsity of generalizations is that the strategies people use to test hypotheses or make choices should be sensitive to changes in what constitutes the primary error(s) they seek to avoid. Friedrich argues that for many of the decisions we make we are more concerned to avoid false-positive errors than to avoid false-negatives. When we are deciding what make of car to buy, for example, it is probably more important to us to avoid getting a lemon than to ensure making the best selection possible. In Friedrich's terms, buying a car that turns out to be a lemon is making a *primary* error, and it is this sort of error that the strategies people often use in making decisions or testing hypotheses are intended to avoid.

> If one accepts *p*rimary *e*rror *d*etection and *min*imization (PEDMIN) goals as reasonable and appropriate for the pragmatic social thinker, then the tendency to focus most heavily on cases or data possessing the hypothesized quality is, in a sense, a normatively appropriate strategy. It is not an optimal way of testing the truth value of hypotheses, but it *is* an appropriate means of answering the decision maker's likely questions, questions fundamentally different from those the scientist might ask in the same situation (p. 299).

Friedrich (1993) contends that, as a general rule, false-positive and false-negative errors are of unequal importance and that which of them is of greater concern will shape one's hypothesis-testing behavior in any given case. He presents evidence that people will modify their hypothesis-testing strategy in such a way as to decrease the probability of false-negative errors if such errors are given primary status by being made more salient or costly. Such a shift, he argues, can be accounted for completely in terms of error avoidance, so it is not necessary to assume increased awareness of the importance of diagnosticity or a shift to the logic of falsification.

Sometimes use of a truth-seeking strategy would require exposing oneself to a perceived risk. In such cases, survival presumably takes precedence over truth-finding, and it is hard to argue that rationality would dictate otherwise. It would seem odd to consider irrational the refusal, say, to eat mushrooms that one suspected of being poisonous, because the decision is calculated to preserve one's well-being (to avoid the dire consequences that would result if the suspicion turned out to be justified) rather than to shed light on the question of whether the suspicion is indeed true. Friedrich argues that, in general, the objective of avoiding disastrous errors is more conducive to survival than is that of truth determination: "Evolution should favor the survival and reproductive success of individuals who do not make costly errors, not of those who expend unnecessary energy or expose themselves to likely true negatives in the course of truth detection" (p. 313).

We should note, as does Friedrich, that the desire to avoid a specific type of error may coincidentally dictate the same behavior as would the intention to determine the truth or falsity of a hypothesis. When this is so, the behavior itself does not reveal whether the individual's intention is to avoid the error or to test the hypothesis. Friedrich suggests that some behavior that has been taken as evidence of people's preference for normative diagnostic tests of hypotheses, and of their interest in accuracy, could have been motivated instead by the desire to avoid specific types of errors. In general, he sees people as "pragmatic reasoners more concerned with minimizing crucial errors or mistakes than with testing for truth," and contends that this is appropriate and adaptive "given the time constraints and imperfect data bases that characterize the real world" (p. 304). Thus, error detection and minimization are presented not only as a descriptive model of hypothesis-testing behavior, but as a normative one, in the context of the natural environment. Even when behavior is consistent with the assumption of truth-seeking, or confirmation, it is likely to be easily interpreted, Friedrich argues, in terms of error-minimizing strategies.

The Ubiquity of Bias

The term "bias" covers a lot of ground, as used in the press and other media. It is not possible to list all the behavioral connotations it has been given. Here we have only noted some of the more well-researched uses. Among others we have not addressed: outcome bias (Baron & Hershey, 1988), positive bias (Kareev, 1995), sampling bias (Lann & Falk, 2006), contraction bias (Poulton, 1982; Stevens & Greenbaum, 1966), hot-hand bias (Falk, 2016), publication bias (Easterbrook et al., 1991; Rothstein, Sutton, & Borenstein, 2005), reporting bias (McGauran et al., 2010; Sterne, Egger, & Moher, 2008), self-serving biases (Campbell et al., 2000; Ross & Sicoly, 1979), group-serving biases (Taylor & Doria, 1981), status quo bias (Cinner, 2018). The list could easily be extended. It is to be expected that not everyone will agree that all the phenomena that have been described as biases are truly biases, as opposed to other types of phenomena, but in the aggregate, the innumerable discussions that pertain to "biases," however defined, attest to the complexity of cognition and the many forms and interpretations that arguments can have.

Three Points

Three points need to be made, I think, with respect to the costs and benefits that may attach to biases that may lead to false beliefs of various types. First, some of them may indeed be beneficial to the individuals or groups who have them. The belief that one is luckier than most people has undoubtedly led some individuals to succeed at very risky undertakings (which is not to deny that others have paid a dear price for acting on the same belief); people who have an unjustifiably high regard for the prestige of groups to which they belong may derive great satisfaction from their membership in these groups; the same view if widely shared within a group may contribute to the strength and longevity of the group itself.

But even beneficial self-serving biases are likely to be beneficial only if they do not support beliefs that are grossly inaccurate. Believing that one is somewhat more intelligent than one really is, is not the same as believing that one is a genius or incapable of being wrong; to overrate the elitist significance of membership in a group it is not necessary to believe that the group's survival and well-being are worth ensuring at any cost. Self-serving beliefs that become too extreme are likely not to serve well those who hold them.

Second, what is beneficial to one individual is not always beneficial to others or to society in general. I may exercise certain biases that benefit me at the expense of others. And all of us may exercise biases that would benefit us individually if only a small minority of people exercised them but will hurt us all if everyone does so. This is the well-known phenomenon of the "tragedy of the commons" (Hardin, 1968; Swap, 1991), often used as an example of a "social trap" (Platt, 1973) or "social dilemma" (Glance & Huberman, 1994; Komorita & Parks, 1996).

Third, there can be little doubt that biased thinking can lead to and reinforce extreme views of many types that would be untenable if judged objectively in light of all the relevant evidence. Extreme views, especially when opposing extreme views are held by members of different groups, can evoke extreme behavior, often with disastrous consequences for all involved. Increasing people's awareness of the more common types of reasoning biases, their ability to countermand them in their own thinking, and their motivation for doing so surely should be major goals of education.

Most of us find it much easier, I assume, to act in ways that are personally beneficial than in ways that are in the best interest of society as a whole, when the two are not identical. This does not necessarily mean that we are irrational, because rationality is sometimes defined, especially within economic theories, as behaving in one's best self-interest. But it does mean that to the extent that survival and well-being of the species are considered goals to which individuals should attach a high priority, the tendency of all of us to put individual interests ahead of societal interests represents a continuing challenge to find effective ways to ensure that in the pursuit of our own interests we naturally further, and not work against, the interests of society as a whole.

The question of what the demonstrable existence of certain persistent biases means vis-à-vis human rationality is not as simple as it might appear. One position that can be taken is that any bias is evidence of irrationality, but I do not think that is a tenable view. It seems to me that many biases can be functional in some situations and dysfunctional in others, and that whether, on balance, we see the mix as indicative of a lack of rationality depends to some extent on what we assume about what people *should* be striving for and about the limitations of the cognitive resources at their disposal. Some biases may represent reasonable trade-offs that have the effect of permitting us to deal about as well as can be expected, given our limitations, with a wide range of complex situations. In effect, we learn to deal with classes of situations in the interest of keeping things manageably simple, and this makes our behavior suboptimal with respect to very specific situations, relative to that of an organism that did not have the same limitations.

There is also the possibility, however, and I think it is a good one, that many biases persist simply because we do not take the trouble to understand and attempt to deal with them. They do not cause us enough trouble as individuals, or at least it is not sufficiently clear to us that they are causing us trouble, to motivate us to make the effort that would be necessary to correct them. There is some chance, however, that biases and other reasoning problems that fail to cause us grief as individuals can, in the aggregate, be problematic for the well-being of humankind as a species.

Many biases in addition to those mentioned here have been identified and named; it should be clear that if one's definition of bias is broad enough, one can produce a very long list indeed. Those mentioned here give a sense of the numerous ways in which reasoning can be influenced, for good or ill.

8

Other Flaws and Foibles

In Chapters 6 and 7 we have considered examples of fallacious thinking, or what are considered by some to be examples of fallacious thinking, and biases, or what are often considered to be biases, at least in certain contexts. These are topics of special interest to cognitive psychologists among other researchers and scholars. The lists of fallacies and biases considered here are by no means exhaustive in either case. Moreover, there are many reasoning problems that would probably not best be classified as either fallacies or biases, but have nevertheless been objects of study. We turn in this chapter to a consideration of some of these, which I will refer to collectively, for want of better terms, as flaws and foibles. For expository convenience, I have classified the flaws and foibles that are discussed into four categories: Oversimplification; Saying the same thing in different ways; Failures of omission; and, The myth of objectivity.

Oversimplification

The world is complex. We are obliged to simplify it in our thinking or it would be incomprehensible to us. This was noted, at least implicitly, in the comments on classification and stereotyping in Chapter 6. An argument can be, and has been, made, however, that we often go too far in this direction and oversimplify beyond reason. Robert Thouless (1950/1940) refers to the tendency to think in terms of broad unqualified generalizations – "High tariffs make high wages," "Everything is relative" – as "tabloid thinking." Thouless's assessment of the quality of human thinking in general is not high. Appendix C is a list of thirty-eight "dishonest tricks" that he contends are "commonly used in argument." With each of the items on his list, Thouless offers a method for overcoming it. Data are not presented regarding whether, or how well, the methods work. [The list in Appendix C is from the edition of *How to Think Straight* that was published in 1950. Several editions of *How to Think Straight* were published between

1940 and 2004, each also containing a list of 'dishonest tricks' that differs slightly from the list given in Appendix C.

Ernst Schumacher (1973) argues that the great appeal of private enterprise lies, at least in part, in its "terrifying simplicity." "Everything becomes crystal clear after you have reduced reality to one – one only – of its thousand aspects. You know what to do – whatever produces profits; you know what to avoid – whatever reduces them or makes a loss. And there is at the same time a perfect measuring rod for the degree of success or failure" (p. 272).

The tendency to oversimplify can be seen in many examples of what might be called "one-dimensional thinking" or "single-issue focusing." Often when faced with complex issues or the need to make choices among alternatives that differ in complex ways, we simplify things for ourselves by focusing on only one, or a small subset, of the relevant considerations. Perhaps this is especially likely to be the case when one aspect of the issue or one of the ways in which choice options differ is particularly salient or has received an unusual amount of attention from the media.

The point may be illustrated by reference to an example I have noted before (Nickerson, 2003, p. 149): the use of polystyrene for disposable cups and other food containers. This practice received enough criticism from environmentalists to convince some major fast-food companies to discontinue it – largely because of the nonbiodegradable nature of the material. My purpose in mentioning this is not to second guess this decision or to question the legitimacy of the concern about problems arising from nonbiodegradable disposables, but to point out that a comparison that appears to be one-dimensional at first glance can prove to be considerably more complicated when looked at more closely.

A fair environmentally-sensitive comparison of paper and polystyrene as materials for disposable food containers would take not only ultimate disposability into account, but many other factors as well. A comparison involving the environmental implications of their production (raw materials consumed, energy used, waste effluents, and atmospheric emissions produced) and recyclability showed polystyrene to be superior to paper with respect to several of these factors (Hocking, 1991a, 1991b). How one would judge the relative merits of the two options overall would depend on how one weighted the several individual factors, but it is difficult to imagine any reasonable weighting that would make paper the undisputed winner that it appears to be when only biodegradability is taken into account. Recognizing the multidimensional nature of such issues complicates the problem of choice and it can take the thunder out of much debate.

That care in the use of language is important to good thinking can hardly be doubted. As Friedrich Müller (1887) put it, "Right language is right thought, and right thought is right language; and if we want to understand, not only the disease, but the health also of our thought, we can study it nowhere more efficiently than in the pathology of language" (p. 7). Thouless (1950/1940) makes the interesting observation, however, that the time-honored principle of insisting on defining terms when engaged in a verbal dispute holds a risk that is easy to overlook. A good definition gives an idea precision and distinction from other ideas, and the risk is that it makes whatever is defined more precise and distinct in our thinking than it is in actuality. "The worst danger of all in too great reliance on definitions is that one may be creating conceptions by definition which correspond to nothing whatever in fact" (p. 131). Because something has a definition (tooth fairy: a fairy that replaces a tooth with money) does not guarantee that what is defined exists. (See the problem of reification, noted in Chapter 6.)

Although Thouless's point is well taken, in my view, it does not demonstrate that definitions are useless as aids to the resolution of disputes. When two parties to a dispute agree on the definitions of critical terms, what they have done, presumably, is establish a common usage of language for purposes of the dispute. The common usage may be wrong, if their agreed-upon definitions do not reflect reality, but at least there is agreement between the disputants as to what they *think* they are talking about, and this seems like a minimal requirement for a meaningful exchange between two minds.

False Dichotomies

> In all periods of life there is an equally powerful urge to dichotomize, to classify other human beings into two artificially sharpened categories. We seem able to be fully comfortable only when the remainder of humanity can be labeled as members versus nonmembers, kin versus nonkin, friend versus foe
>
> (Wilson, 1978, p. 70).

Unjustified dichotomization involves proceeding as though there were only two possibilities – black or white, either-or – when, in fact, there are more, perhaps many more. Fearnside and Holther (1959) refer to this as the "all-or-nothing mistake" which "assumes a naked dichotomy where no such simplification is warranted" (p. 30). "The assumption that there is no middle ground is a favorite weapon of persons desiring to force others to take sides in black-white terms even though the problem is not simple and though its fair solution requires an evaluation of several possibilities" (p. 30). Who has not experienced pressure from opponents on some contentious issue to take one side or the other, without acknowledgment that there might be viable points of view other than those represented by the extremes?

The tendency to see dichotomies where gradations actually exist, and to engage in "either-or" thinking as a consequence, is a form of oversimplification, but a sufficiently prevalent and important one to warrant special emphasis. Many characteristics of the world vary continuously over some range from one extreme to the other. Often we give labels to the extremes of these characteristics and treat them as though only the extremes exist. Examples of such false dichotomies include right- and left-wing politics, totalitarianism and democracy, sadness and happiness, stinginess and generosity, bravery and cowardice, wealth and poverty, sickness and health, ...

Psychologists seem to have a penchant for dichotomizing people. Individuals are categorized as either introverts or extroverts (Jung, 1971/1921), field-dependent or field-independent perceivers (Witkin et al., 1954), levelers or sharpeners (Holzman & Klein, 1954), activists or pacifists (Rotter, 1966), instance learners or rule learners (Snow & Hoefnagel-Hohle, 1979), structural or analytical processors (Hock, 1973), ... Binary distinctions are made between primary- and secondary-process thinking (Freud, 1957/1923), narrative and paradigmatic modes of knowing (Bruner, 1986), crystalized and fluid intelligence (Cattell, 1971), ... It is almost as though in learning to count we got stuck at two.

Such distinctions may serve useful purposes. At the least, they identify properties, characteristics, and traits with respect to which people differ. There is a danger in such dichotomous distinctions, however. Treating continua as binary variables tends to obscure the fact that human differences extend over a considerable range and do not simply fall at one or the other of two extremes. Dichotomizing is a form of oversimplification, one consequence of which can be stereotyping in objectionable ways.

Failure to recognize the existence of continua leads us to see things in black and white terms, to become easily polarized on controversial issues, and to be vulnerable to demagoguery. It simplifies one's outlook on life. It minimizes the need to confront complicated issues and to struggle with them, and it reduces the burden of uncertainty that comes with recognition of the complexity of life. But this simplification is gained at a considerable price that appears often not to be recognized.

Mistaking Form for Substance

Appearances matter. Elain Hatfield and Susan Sprecher (1986) document the truth of this observation. (See also Hatfield & Rapson, 2000.) People react to "attractive" people differently than they react to "unattractive" people, despite that what constitutes attractiveness differs across cultures and changes over time (Banner, 1983; Bull & Rumsey, 1988).

When George Washington was president of the United States, the average height of US males was 5'8". Washington himself was 6'2". Today the average height of US males is approximately 5'9". The average height of the thirty-nine US presidents who were elected to the office (excluding the five who came to the presidency without being elected to it) is approximately 5'11". Might it be that being relatively tall is a plus for anyone who aspires to be a leader? I suspect that few people would argue that it is essential, but it does not follow that height, among other irrelevancies, plays no role in the selection of leaders.

Anyone who has had much involvement with the processing of written material is aware that an argument neatly arranged on a printed page appears more compelling than the same argument scribbled in longhand on a piece of paper, showing cross outs and inserts made during the process of its construction.

Misjudging Knowledge

In an experiment that produced thought-provoking results, Lee Ross, Teresa Amabile, and Julia Steinmetz (1977) had pairs of subjects play the roles of questioner and contestant in a general-knowledge quiz game. "Questioners" made up questions and posed them to the "contestants" who tried to answer them. The questioners indicated in each case whether contestants had given the right answer, and if they had not, the questioners supplied it. Following the playing of the game, questioners, contestants, and observers rated the general knowledge of both questioners and contestants. Questioners had to know at least as many answers as the contestants inasmuch as they themselves made up the questions, so the fact that questioners knew more of the answers to the specific questions asked than did observers is not good evidence that they were more knowledgeable in general. Nevertheless, both contestants and observers judged the questioners to be more knowledgeable *generally* than the contestants. (The questioners judged the knowledge ability of the two groups to be about equal.)

Funder (1987) points out the possibility of a misinterpretation of performance in this paradigm. People who judge the questioners to be more knowledgeable than the contestants in this situation are said to be insensitive to the role of the questioners in making up the questions. People who judge the questioners and contestants to be about equally knowledgeable, or who say that they do not know who is the more knowledgeable, would be considered to be more sensitive to the realities of the situation. But Funder notes that it is also possible that these people have simply failed to perceive the (admittedly misleading) difference in performance. In support of this possibility, he cites the finding of Block and Funder (1986) that participants in one study who were least susceptible to the role effect were also the least socially competent and well adjusted, according to an independent characterization.

Misleading Truths

Certain diseases, such as cancer and heart disease, are sometimes referred to as diseases of civilization. The ascription is true in that a greater proportion of people die of these diseases in developed countries than in undeveloped ones. It does not follow, as is sometimes suggested, that industrialization is the cause of these diseases. An alternative possibility is that people are more likely to contract these diseases in developed countries simply as a consequence of being more likely to live long enough to do so, because many other causes of death have been reduced.

I am not fond of maxims; they can stifle thought in an insidious way. Often they seem not only obviously true but to encapsulate some profound bit of wisdom, and because of their pithiness they engrave themselves on one's mind and are always available for use at opportune times. The problem is that they can be used to justify just about anything. Given a maxim expressing a particular thought, one can usually find another equally clever maxim expressing precisely the opposite thought. You wish to do something quickly? Justify it with "a stitch in time saves nine." You prefer to put it off, use "haste makes waste." You would like a large committee? "Many hands make light work." You prefer to keep it small? "Too many cooks spoil the broth." And so on.

One- or Two-Sided Argument Preference

By definition, there are at least two sides to any controversial issue. When supporters of one side of such an issue wish to persuade others to their position, they may try to do so by presenting arguments for both sides of the issue (from their perspective) and explaining why they believe their side to be the correct one, or they may present only an argument supporting their position and perhaps not even acknowledge that an argument can be made for an opposing view. There is evidence that professional writers typically use two-sided arguments in their published works whereas college students tend to use one-sided arguments when writing essays as participants in psychological experiments (Wolfe & Britt, 2005, 2008). However, Stanovich and West (2008) found the tendency to avoid one-sided thinking to be relatively independent of cognitive ability as assessed by conventional psychometric indicators.

One might expect that two-sided arguments would be the more effective for a variety of reasons – they suggest reflectiveness and open-mindedness on the part of the arguer; they may "inoculate" one against counterarguments that may be raised against one's position by demonstrating that one is well aware of them. However, as to the question of whether one- or two-sided arguments are the more effective, the answer seems to be "it depends." Several studies have found that people often judge one-sided arguments to be more persuasive than two-sided arguments (Baron, 1991, 1995; Buehl et al., 2001; Kuhn, 1991). The results of one meta-analysis suggest that two-sided arguments are likely to be more persuasive than one-sided arguments, but only if they include refutations of possible counterarguments, and that one-sided arguments tend to be more persuasive than two-sided arguments that do not include such refutations (Allen, 1991). In the same study, Allen notes that the persuasiveness of an argument depends also on other factors, such as the receptiveness of an audience to the conclusion it is asked to draw:

> The one-sided message is superior for a favorable audience because the message focuses on the agreeable arguments. Failure to mention possible counterarguments assures that the attention of the audience (and the cognitive processing of the audience) remains focused on the opinion advocated by the message sender. The two-sided or one-sided message under different conditions of audience favorableness will be more or less persuasive (p. 391).

Allen hypothesizes that, in general, one- and two-sided messages will be more persuasive for favorable and unfavorable audiences respectively. He knows too however that there are other variables at work determining the persuasiveness of arguments and that, in any case, the difference in the persuasiveness of one- and two-sided arguments tends to be small.

Saying the Same Thing in Different Ways

Any fact, or claim, can be presented in more than one way and the effect on a listener or reader can depend as much as, or more than, on the form of presentation as on the content. Consider, for example, the fact (reported in *Power On! New Tools for Teaching and Learning*, Congress of the US OTA, 1988) that $2 billion was spent on computer hardware for instructional purposes in American schools over a ten-year period from about 1977 to about 1987. If one wished to create the impression that this was a large expenditure, one might note that $2 billion is – or was at the time – enough to pay for ten year's tuition, room and board for 20,000 college students, or to cover the home electric and heating bills of 165,000 households or medical expenses for 130,000 elderly Americans. If, on the other hand, one wished to convey the idea that this was a small expenditure, one might note that it amounts to about $5.00 per student per year and represents two-tenths of 1 percent of the total elementary and secondary school expenditures and about 3 percent of what is spent on pet food.

Choice of Words for Comparisons

Choices that people make when gambling can depend on how particular gambles are expressed. Probabilistically identical outcomes can be expressed in terms either of possible gains or of possible losses, and which way it is done appears to matter (Levin, Chapman, & Johnson, 1988; Levin et al., 1986; Levin et al., 1985). Framing in terms of possible gains often induces risk-seeking choices, whereas framing in terms of possible losses seems to encourage risk-avoidance behavior (Tversky & Kahneman, 1981).

In the medical context patients' preferences among possible treatments may depend on precisely how the expected outcomes are compared. In particular, preferences that hold when treatments are compared with respect to their beneficial effects may differ from those that hold when they are compared with respect to their potential adverse effects (Eraker & Sox, 1981). In one study, for example, it was found that the relative attractiveness of different hypothetical therapies for lung cancer differed for both physicians and patients depending on whether the probable outcomes were described in terms of mortality or survival rates (McNeil et al., 1982).

The preceding examples involve alternative ways of making comparisons, one of which uses positive terms and the other of which uses negative ones. Wording effects have also been obtained even when both alternatives are expressed in negative terms. For example, the report of a tiny reduction in the average life expectancy of people living near a nuclear reactor is less likely to cause concern among the recipients of the information than is the same information expressed in terms of an increase in the expected number of radiation-caused deaths (Slovic, Fischoff, & Lichtenstein, 1976).

The Principle of Invariance

According to the principle of invariance, as defined by Kahneman and Tversky (1984), when a problem is presented in two ways such that it is not fundamentally altered, people should respond to the two presentations in the same way. Consider, for example, the contrast between losing a $10.00 admissions ticket to a play and losing $10.00 in cash. Some people claim they would purchase a ticket after losing $10.00 in cash but would not purchase a second ticket after losing one. Such behavior, Kahneman and Tversky contend, violates the principle of invariance.

This characterization of the behavior has been challenged on the grounds that the two problem presentations may not be identical from all points of view. Macdonald (1986) notes, for example, that people may see an attempt to get in the theater without a ticket as morally justifiable if they had purchased a ticket and lost it but not if they had lost $10.00 in cash. Whether this difference justifies the differential willingness to purchase a ticket in the two situations is debatable. We should note, however, that it does not necessarily invalidate the principle of invariance; it simply calls into question its applicability in this instance.

Vividness

Information that is represented in an especially vivid way is likely to have more effect on human attitudes and behavior than similar information presented in a less vivid or interesting form. Pallid statistical summaries are likely to count for less than information that is presented in more interesting case-history style (Nisbett et al., 1976).

In an unpublished study by Hamill, Wilson, and Nisbett (described in Nisbett and Ross [1980]) a vivid (and uncomplimentary) description of a single family living on welfare changed subjects' attitudes toward welfare, whereas the presentation of dry statistics regarding how long people stay on welfare on the average had no effect on attitudes. Nisbett et al. (1976) also illustrated the effectiveness of vividness by pointing out that the publicity regarding the mastectomies performed on Mrs. Ford and Mrs. Rockerfeller in 1974 prompted many more women to get checked for breast cancer than had widely disseminated statistical information regarding breast cancer risk.

Alvin Goldman (1986) cautions against taking such findings as evidence that people necessarily attach greater weight to vivid information than they do to the same information presented in more pallid form. An alternative hypothesis is that the vivid information and the pallid information are not equally accessible to people, either because the vivid information gets disseminated more effectively or because it is more memorable and hence more accessible for use at a later time. The alternative hypothesis does not contest the idea that vividness is an important determinant of how influential information is likely to be on people's attitudes and behavior, it simply provides an account of that effect that does not require the assumption that people judge vividly presented information to be more compelling than equally accessible information that is represented in a less vivid form.

Failures of Omission

Many of the problematic aspects of human reasoning result from the misunderstanding of concepts, the misuse of logical forms, the acceptance of faulty assumptions, the application of misinformation, and other errors of commission. It is important to understand these various overt ways in which reasoning can go astray. Also important, though perhaps less obvious, are the many ways in which we reason less effectively than we should because of what might be called failures of omission.

There are two ways to go wrong in brainstorming activities. One is to accept poor ideas; the other is to fail to produce ideas that would have been recognized as good ones, had they been expressed. Given the participation of knowledgeable people who are willing to be critical, the second possibility seems likely to be a more serious problem than the first; truly poor ideas are unlikely to survive critical evaluation, but good ideas may easily be overlooked. One consequence of the failure to produce certain good ideas may be that evoked ideas that survive the filtering process look to be better than they really are, because they are judged relative to the other ideas on the table and not relative to possibly better ones that were not forthcoming.

A similar observation applies to the selection of people for awards and other types of special recognition. Selection of an undeserving recipient seems like a lower-probability outcome than failure to identify for consideration some of the worthy candidates. Imagine a group of n people m of whom would qualify for a particular award. Assume that n is much larger than m, but that both are large. In order to be considered for the award, one must be proposed. It is easy to imagine that most of those who are proposed are qualified and that any unqualified people who are proposed are eliminated by the selection process (committee narrowing of slate, voting, etc.) and that, consequently, few, if any, unqualified people are selected. It is also easy to imagine, however, that many of the m qualified people are never proposed. In short, the suggestion is that it is easier to imagine qualified people being overlooked than to imagine unqualified people making it through the process.

In assessing risks, it is necessary not only to assign probabilities to the various things that could go wrong but to identify the possibilities in the first place. The latter of these tasks, which logically precedes the former, may be the more problematic of the two. A similar observation can be made with respect to the application of a Bayesian analysis in decision-making. An essential aspect of this approach is the identification of the possible states of the world (a priori hypotheses). An obvious way in which one can fail with a Bayesian analysis is by working with a set of hypotheses that does not include the correct one.

Such examples of failures of omission might be considered instances of premature closure. One might argue that the brainstorming session should not be terminated until all the good ideas are on the table, or that the search for an award recipient should not be ended until all worthy candidates have been considered, or that the Bayesian analysis should not be done until all possible a priori hypotheses have been specified. But this would be an impractical position; one can never be sure that all the good ideas, every last worthy candidate, or all possible a priori hypotheses have been identified. On the other hand, it seems safe to assume that attempts to generate ideas, candidates, or hypotheses often are terminated before they should be, and among several reasons why that might be so is a failure to appreciate the incompleteness or inadequacy of the information in hand.

Uncritical Assumption of Completeness or Adequacy

The problem of uncritically assuming completeness or adequacy is easily seen in the context of advertising. An advertisement identifies four factors in terms of which the product being advertised should be compared with competing products, and it goes on to make the comparison on a factor-by-factor basis, showing, of course, that the product being advertised is superior in each case. Dubious prospective purchasers may give some thought to the individual factors and consider whether they believe the claim of superiority is justified. They may be less likely to question whether the four factors identified by the advertiser are indeed the ones in terms of which the products should be compared. They may simply accept the list as complete without thinking much about it.

We often encounter lists that are presented as exhaustive or complete. We read a claim that there are seven things to consider in choosing a vocation or career and see the considerations laid out in a list. We hear a news commentator run down the three possible reasons for the recent surprising behavior of a particular world leader. We see an economist's enumeration of the four world-event scenarios that could significantly alter the flow of goods and money among the world's major trading partners.

When such lists pertain to matters about which we do not have extensive knowledge, we are unlikely to be keenly aware of items that could be added to them. And when we can assume that a list has been generated by an expert, we may be inclined to assume its completeness uncritically. Even if a list pertains to a subject about which we have substantial knowledge, it does not follow that its incompleteness will be recognized. We cannot recall all we know about any subject on demand, and, again, when we can assume that a list has been generated by an expert, we may make little or no effort to extend it.

In the context of Bayesian decision-making it has been found that people often overestimate the completeness of the sets of hypotheses provided about the possible states of the world (Fischhoff, Slovic, & Lichtenstein, 1978; Gettys, Fisher, & Mehle, 1978; Mehle et al., 1981). Given this tendency, the use of previously prepared checklists in decision-making situations would appear to have some merit, and there is evidence that decision-making can be improved in this way (de Dombal et al., 1974). There is also evidence that users of electronic document searches tend to overestimate, sometimes by large amounts, the percentage of the relevant documents that a search has returned (Blair & Maron, 1985; MacGregor, Fischhoff, & Blackshaw, 1987).

In all of the examples of lists given above, a tendency to overestimate completeness might be attributed to assumptions about the competence and thoroughness of whoever or whatever has generated the list. One might simply assume, for example, that an economist's enumeration of possible economic scenarios would include all of them, or that the returns from an electronic document retrieval system would be relatively exhaustive. Are people likely to overestimate the completeness of lists that they themselves generate (excluding sets that are sufficiently small and familiar that they know the entire set and those, e.g., the states of the union, for which they are likely to know the number)? When asked to generate as complete a list as possible of, say, countries, birds, or major classical composers, and then to estimate what percentage of the total set of members of that category they have generated, will their estimates tend to be inappropriately high? It is an interesting question the answer to which, to my knowledge, is not known.

If it is the case that we tend generally to accept lists or sets as more complete than they really are, this fact has important implications for reasoning and in particular for argument evaluation. Our limitations of knowledge and memory can make arguments appear to be stronger than they are. In general, an essential aspect of sound reasoning is a continuing awareness that the fact that one cannot construct a compelling counter to an argument on a moment's notice does not mean that the possibility of constructing one does not exist.

A failure of omission that is closely related to that of assuming the completeness or adequacy of sets or lists is the tendency to accept uncritically a problem as structured by someone else. What one is omitting in this case is consideration of alternative ways in which the problem might be structured. The point is illustrated by the finding that people are likely to accept without complaint the set of options provided on multiple-choice questions, even when the best option is not among them (Schuman & Scott, 1987).

Sometimes one finds oneself presented with a dilemma. A and B are represented as exhaustive, mutually exclusive, and contrary possibilities of belief or action. One is told that one must believe (or do) either A or B. If neither A nor B is something one is comfortable believing or doing, one is an awkward position.

What one should do in such cases, before selecting between the alternatives, is question whether in fact the problem has been posed in the only feasible way. Is it really true that there are only two possible beliefs or two possible courses of action, and in particular two that are mutually exclusive as represented? Maybe A holds under some conditions and B under others, or perhaps there are more than two alternatives. The point is, one should not be quick to accept the problem as posed, especially if by doing so one finds oneself in a box from which there is no apparent exit.

Overweighting the Here-and-Now

Many failures of omission may be instances of a general tendency to overestimate the importance, representativeness, or comprehensiveness of the "here-and-now." It would be hardly surprising to discover that whatever occupies our immediate attention is considered more important and given more weight in our thinking than other, possibly equally, or more, important factors that, for whatever reason, are not in our consciousness at the time. A greater sensitivity not only to our limitations as information processors but also to our tendency to discount the importance of whatever happens to be out of sight and out of mind might give us a more modest, and more realistic, view of the quality of our own judgments.

If people do characteristically overestimate the importance or completeness of whatever they happen to be attending to, we would expect such a tendency to lead to the overestimation of the completeness of lists, the insufficiently critical appraisal of proposed problem structures, and the perceived comprehensiveness of incomplete fault trees – even by experts. Such a tendency could help account also for a variety of other phenomena, including the confirmation bias, the availability heuristic, and the difficulty we sometimes have in constructing counterarguments.

Failure to Write off Sunk Costs

According to most prescriptive models of rationality, one's present behavior should be guided by expected present or future effects of that behavior. In economic terms, new investments are said to be justified only when marginal revenues (revenues resulting from the amount to be invested, not counting those resulting from investments already made) are expected to exceed marginal costs (Samuelson, 1988).

When I am deliberating about what to do now, I should not take into account costs that I have incurred in the past; such costs, assuming they have been spent irretrievably, are irrelevant to current decisions. To illustrate the inappropriateness of taking into account sunk costs, Richard Thaler (1980) uses the example of a person who continues to play tennis in agony, after developing tennis elbow, simply because of not wishing to have wasted the cost of membership in a tennis club. This person is failing to discount sunk costs and is suffering needless pain as a consequence. Or, to take another example from Thaler (1980), consider the individual who has paid $40 for tickets to a basketball game that is to be played sixty miles from home. On the day of the game there is a snowstorm, but the ticket holder decides to go to the game anyway, although he admits that had he been given the tickets, instead of having bought them, he probably would stay home. Again, it appears that one is doing something that one really prefers not to do, simply because of a cost incurred in the past.

Both of these actions appear to be irrational inasmuch as present behavior is being determined by costs incurred in the past, the behavior is not what the individuals would elect if it were not for those costs, and the costs are gone – sunk – irrespective of what they do. The behavior seems to violate the principle that a rational person always tries to maximize expected utility; these folks are following the expenditure of some capital with unpleasant actions that they are not obliged to take.

The "sunk-cost fallacy," as it has been called, has been investigated in a variety of personal and corporate contexts (Arkes & Blumer, 1985; Dawes, 1988; Dawkins & Carlisle, 1976; Staw, 1976; Staw & Huang, 1995). Hal Arkes and Catherine Blumer found that, at least in simulated business situations, people were more likely to express a willingness to commit a significant amount of money to a project with a small estimated likelihood of success if they had already spent money on the project than if they had not. Sometimes the sunk-cost fallacy is discussed in connection with the concepts of entrapment (Rubin & Brockner, 1975), escalation (Staw, 1976, 1981), or unjustified commitment or persistence (Garland & Newport, 1991). Who has not heard the argument that some controversial policy of a government, such as the continued waging of a war, must be continued because to discontinue it would be to mean that the costs incurred in the past in the execution of this policy would have been incurred in vain.

Hermann Bondi (2003) notes how the sunk-cost fallacy can affect the pursuit of science.

> The "softest" part of science is the choice of topics to be researched. Fashion plays an important role here; once a costly instrument has been built, it is going to be used, whether the scientific justification that led to the decision to construct it has strengthened during the building period or weakened. When an institute or grouping has been established to research a particular, originally very important, topic, its existence may well outlast the validity of that line of investigation (p. 146).

Arkes and Blumer (1985) suggest that one reason why people fail to discount sunk costs is that they apply the principle "waste not, want not" inappropriately. The principle is appropriately applied to costs that one has yet to incur (one should not spend money on something that one expects to be a waste) but not to costs that have already been incurred. Deciding on a future course of action for no other reason than to not perceive an already incurred cost as wasted is, in this view, not rational.

Although the failure to discount sunk costs may be irrational in specific instances, it is not necessary to consider it to be so in all cases. Whether it is seen as irrational in any particular instance depends, at least in part, on what one's objectives or values are assumed to be; as Larrick, Morgan, and Nisbett (1990) note, any complete set of prescriptive principles of choice should include not only economic principles but moral ones as well, and rules for adjudicating when the two are in conflict. In terms of narrowly conceived economics, the tendency to take account of sunk costs must usually be seen as irrational, inasmuch as it generally results in avoidable additional costs for which there are not commensurate gains. If, however, one factors into the equation the value that one attaches to being consistent, following through on commitments – even those that were better never made – justifying one's past behavior, avoiding embarrassment, and so on, the costs of perseveration may be less than those of discontinuing the behavior (Bazerman, Beekum, & Schoorman, 1982; Brockner, Rubin, & Lang, 1981; Staw, 1976). Of course, one may take the position that attaching values to psychological variables in such a way as to justify perseverative behavior in situations like those described is itself irrational; one cannot get away from opinion in these matters.

People may decide not to ignore sunk costs for reasons that, judged by their own values, legitimize their behavior. The person who elects to play tennis with a sore elbow, for example, may attach a greater utility to being able to play despite pain than to having an elbow that does not hurt. Who is to say that a person who choses peace of mind over an unsore elbow is irrational? And the one who decides to drive through a snowstorm to use tickets for which he has paid (but who would not do so to use tickets that he had received as a gift) could be motivated to teach himself a memorable lesson to be careful in the future about buying tickets to games sixty miles from home in the winter unless it is a game he very much wants to see. The argument here is not that the behaviors in question are rational, but that they could be, and that without knowing what the people involved are thinking, one is on shaky ground in saying that they are not.

Ken Manktelow and David Over (1993) note that some of the situations that have been used to investigate how people deal with sunk costs may involve, in participants' minds, issues of fairness or justice that could influence their decisions. The scenario in which one is faced with the decision of whether to buy another $40 pair of theater tickets after losing a pair, or with the decision of whether to buy an initial pair after losing $40 (Kahneman & Tversky, 1982b) is a case in point. The conventional argument is that if one decides to buy the tickets in the latter case, one should do so also in the former; the lost tickets and the lost money both represent the same sunk cost of $40. Manktelow and Over point out, however, that from the theater goer's point of view, the theater is getting paid twice for the same event in the former case but only once in the latter, and that the decision as to whether or not to purchase may be influenced by this consideration.

Failure to Consider Opportunity Costs

Almost invariably when one chooses one from among a set of alternatives, one, in effect, closes off the opportunities represented by the alternatives not chosen. If one has a certain amount of money to invest and one chooses to invest it in a particular business venture, one thereby closes the door to the possibility of investing it in other ventures that were options before the decision was made. When one decides to prepare for a specific profession, one forecloses the opportunity to prepare for a different profession. And so on.

Not considering opportunity costs as part of the equation in selecting among alternatives in decision situations appears to be a common failing (Neumann & Friedman, 1980). This might be attributed, in many cases, to unawareness that such costs exist, or simply a failure to call the fact to mind. However, there is evidence that people may underestimate their magnitude even when their existence is understood (Hoskin, 1983).

The Role of Salience

"It is one of the humiliating features of human nature that we resent a few little things which happen to irritate us more than we appreciate a great deal for which we ought to be grateful" (Dimnet, 1928, p. 17). If this is true, and I am not inclined to argue that it is not, perhaps the reason is that the irritating things are more salient, more attention-getting, than those for which we should be grateful. We do not, in general, appreciate how good it is to feel good, but when we are sick we are very conscious of how unpleasant it is to feel bad.

As a rule, we are aware of calamities that befall us but not of those we could have experienced but did not. If I break my leg, I am likely to say to myself, "I would be so happy if only I had not broken my leg." But in fact, if I had not broken my leg, the possibility of doing so at that particular time would probably not have entered my mind and the chance that I would have felt particularly fortunate for having escaped this unhappy experience is small.

Many of the things for which many of us should be grateful, but probably are not, are in the same category as the broken leg that did not happen. If it were not for the advances that were made over the last couple of hundred years in sanitation and preventive medicine, many of us who are alive today would have been dead years ago of tuberculosis, dysentery, small pox, poliomyelitis, or any of a number of other diseases that were once beyond control. But, for the most part, we do not know who we are and consequently are not aware of our good fortune.

Causes of Failures of Omission

It was suggested in the preceding comments that failures of omission such as those mentioned may be attributable, to some degree, to knowledge limitations and memory constraints. It seems also likely that people sometimes overlook the possibility of events that have never occurred in the past, precisely because they have never occurred and therefore are not part of one's memory store. Robert Kates (1962) argues, for example, that people have difficulty in conceiving of floods that have never occurred and consequently when they make decisions about flood control, they tend to be limited in their thinking by their immediate past experience.

Undoubtedly knowledge limitations and constraints of memory or imagination are all contributory causes of failures of omission, but from the fact that performance improves when people are forced to try to extend lists or fill in fault trees, we can conclude that they do not tell the whole story. Another possible contributing factor is motivation. It may be that under normal circumstances, people are not willing to make the effort required to access from their memories the information needed to round out what they have been given.

There is also the possibility that subjects in psychological experiments simply assume, unless told differently, that the lists (or fault trees) they have been given are relatively complete, or are intended to be treated as though they were. Laurette Dube-Rioux and J. Edward Russo (1988) note the possibility that subjects expect the catchall probability to be low in any good fault tree. This explanation is similar to one that will be encountered in other contexts to account for what appears to be irrational behavior of subjects in certain experimental situations. The behavior appears irrational if judged only in the experimental situation in which it is observed, but may make sense if one takes into account expectations that are likely to be appropriate to similar situations outside the laboratory.

Whether it is appropriate to assume that lists that are given to us for various purposes outside the laboratory tend to be relatively complete is an open question. My sense is that this is not a safe assumption. I suspect that we tend to accept whatever is given as sufficient to a problem-solving or decision-making process whether or not it really is. Where the tendency itself, assuming there is one, comes from is an interesting question. One possibility is the considerable experience that most of us have had with ostensibly complete lists in textbooks, the completeness of which we have not been encouraged to question.

Counteracting Failures of Omission

Forcing people to give more thought to the possibilities that are not explicitly identified in a fault tree can mitigate the tendency to overestimate the completeness of the tree. Among the tactics that Dube-Rioux and Russo (1988) note as having succeeded in improving estimation of probabilities are "imagining events (Caroll, 1978), explaining events (Sherman et al., 1981), developing scenarios for an event (Gregory, Cialdini, & Carpenter, 1982), listing pro and con reasons (Koriat, Lichtenstein, & Fischhoff, 1980; Hoch, 1984) and considering opposite possibilities (Lord, Lepper, & Preston, 1984)" (p. 225).

In their own study, in which people, all of whom were employed in restaurants or restaurant-related jobs, estimated the likelihood of various possible causes of failure of a restaurant, Dube-Rioux and Russo (1988) showed that having people attempt to extend pruned fault trees by adding possibilities that they themselves thought of was effective in increasing their sensitivity to the importance of possibilities not originally represented explicitly in the tree. This result corroborated one reported by Thomas Mehle et al. (1981). In this case people estimated the probability that a student was majoring in one of three specified subjects or a fourth catchall category, and their utilization of the catchall category was increased by having them specify some of the majors that could be included in this category.

The Myth of Objectivity

> We must have somewhere to stand when we survey the world, but we must bear in mind the possibility that our vantage point obscures from us important features of the scene which others will more readily discern
>
> (Polkinghorne, 1989, p. 84).

"What indulgence ought we not then to have," Pierre-Simon Laplace (1951/1814) admonished, "for opinions different from ours, when this difference often depends only upon the various points of view where circumstances have placed us! Let us enlighten those whom we judge insufficiently instructed; but first let us examine critically our own opinions and weigh with impartiality their respective probabilities" (p. 9). Excellent advice, without doubt. But can we follow it? Can we really weigh our own opinions impartially? Is it the case, as Henry Bauer (1994) claims, that "[d]ispassionate, objective, systematic pursuit of knowledge is profoundly unnatural" (p. 147).

People perceive the world from different perspectives. The physicist is likely to be attuned to different aspects of the everyday world than is the economist. This applies not only to the "intellectual spaces" where they do their work, but to those aspects of everyday life that they have in common. The carpenter, the electrician, and the plumber are likely to notice quite different things when visiting the same housing development. Trees looked very different to me after spending a couple of years during student days as a climber with a tree company than they did before. Are we as sensitive to differences in perspective as we should be? Do we naturally assume that other people see events and situations pretty much as we ourselves do, when in fact the differences could be substantial?

Francis Bacon (1939/1620) stressed the subjectivity of perception and of the understanding of the world that has its roots in perception:"... the human understanding is like a false mirror, which, receiving rays irregularly distorts and discolors the nature of things by mingling its own nature with it" (p. 32). He also saw in the understandings that we develop a tendency to simplify the complexity of nature by imposing on it more order and regularity than it has. He warned against certain failings of reasoning that he considered common to humankind and that he called the "idols of the mind." E. O. Wilson (1999) characterizes four idols that Bacon discussed this way: "idols of the *tribe* assume more order than exists in chaotic nature; those of the imprisoning *cave*, the idiosyncrasies of individual belief and passion; of the *marketplace*, the power of mere words to induce belief in nonexistent things; and of the *theater*, unquestioning acceptance of philosophical beliefs and misleading demonstrations" (p. 29).

Given the constructive nature of memory, we should not be surprised to discover that one's memory for an event or for an argument, especially an argument the conclusion of which one does not believe, may differ sometimes from the event or argument as it actually occurred. It is not necessary to attribute such changes to devious intentions. The fact that memory is constructive is supported by a wealth of evidence and it seems only reasonable to assume that whatever construction that occurs would be consistent with one's underlying relevant beliefs and attitudes. We know too from research that people are largely unaware of the constructive nature of memory so they do not view what they remember as the result of a construction or even a reconstruction, but rather as a record of events as they occurred.

That witnesses of the same event may describe it very differently was demonstrated in a study by Albert Hastorf and Hadley Cantril (1954) that showed that descriptions of a Princeton/Dartmouth football game differed considerably depending on whether they were produced by Princeton or Dartmouth supporters. Subjectivity could have entered the picture here at several points and in various ways. Spectators' predispositions could have affected the way they perceived the event, the way they remembered it, or the way they chose to report it.

What an observer sees in an event depends in large part on the observer's background knowledge about events of the type being observed. An individual watching a football game for the first time and without knowledge of the rules of the game sees little of what the seasoned football fan sees and his description of a game would be quite different. In pointing this out, Schmidt (1976) argues that the description of human action "is *inherently* interpretive because what is seen and reported depends on a property of the observer" (p. 50). Hastorf and Cantril's observation assumes that perception is influenced by vested interests, and Schmidt's assumes it is affected by one's level of knowledge about the perceived event. These are but two of the subjective factors that can have an impact on what one perceives, or believes one perceives.

It is difficult, perhaps impossible, for any of us to represent a view that we do not hold in a way that would be considered fair by someone who does hold that view. So, when one who has a strong opinion on a controversial issue sets out to present all sides of the issue fairly to an uncommitted listener, there is reason to question whether that really can be done. Of course, people sometimes present the various positions on an issue without any intention of doing so fairly, the goal being to show one's favored view to advantage. What are offered as accurate representations of opposing views may, in fact, be deliberate caricatures or distortions of them. But the point I wish to make here is that there is some question as to whether it is possible for one to represent fairly a view one does not hold even when one tries hard to do so. It is not entirely clear that one who does not hold a particular view can even understand that view in the same way that one who holds it does.

Consider the philosopher who wishes to present an accurate representation of some thesis that he considers worthy of belief. Robert Nozick (1993) describes the typical philosophy journal article that is structured to induce rational belief in readers this way.

> Usually, a philosophical proposition or thesis is propounded as worthy of belief, and reasons for and against it are considered. Among the reasons in favor of the thesis are: general and acceptable statements from which it follows; other acceptable things it fits in with or alongside of; its consequences, which are acceptable and so support it; instances of it or examples that fit it and so provide some evidence for it. Among the reasons against the thesis that are considered are: possible objections to it (these are replied to, weakened, undercut, or somehow avoided); possible counterexamples (these are neutralized *or* used to modify the thesis into another proposition that is not subject to that counterexample, so that now it is the modified statement that is propounded as worthy of rational belief) (p. 72).

The question one must raise is whether one can reasonably expect a philosopher who believes the thesis that is being put forward to be able, even assuming a best effort, to do as good a job at presenting the arguments that can be made against it as can one who strongly disbelieves it.

Subjectivity in Journalism

> [O]ne cannot judge the importance of a story by the prominence of its treatment without considering the incentives of those treating the story
>
> (Nozick, 1993, p. 103).

> Like the lawyer ... who does not care about the truth, but about arguments that can sway a jury whose intellectual defects he knows intimately, journalism goes to what can capture our attention, with adequate sound-bites
>
> (Taleb, 2004, p. 63).

Journalists make a distinction between editorializing and objective reporting of news. The writer of an editorial is expected to inject a good bit of opinion. Even when news events are discussed, the reader expects to find interpretations from the writers' perspectives on the editorial pages. In the case of objective reporting of news, however, what one hopes to get is an unbiased presentation of facts.

While this distinction seems a useful one, it can be overly sharply drawn. What exactly might objective reporting mean? It cannot be the case that objective reporting involves no human judgment or interpretation. Reporting invariably represents a condensation, and even the most straightforward reporting of facts involves deciding what facts to report; and, as A. K. Dewdney (1993) reminds us, "Selective sampling can be made to produce almost any result you want" (p. 37). The *New York Times's* claim to the contrary notwithstanding, no newspaper prints even all the news that is fit to print, unless of course one defines news as that and only that that makes its way into the newspaper or other news media.

Reporting what someone has said in a public speech involves selection from possibly thousands of words, a few that the reporter considers, for whatever reason, to be worth quoting. Coverage of any extended event requires focusing on highlights; exhaustive coverage is simply impossible. The description of highlights can easily produce an oversimplified understanding of what actually transpired and, of course, what constitutes the highlights is a matter of judgment.

From whom a journalist seeks input when preparing a story is a matter of choice and it is hard to believe that personal views and opinions – and personal preferences with respect to the various messages the story could convey – have no effect on such decisions. That journalists, whether wittingly or not, are more likely to select inputs from people who share their views than from those who do not is not beyond the realm of possibility (Goodfield, 1996; Lichter, Rothman, & Lichter, 1986).

I recently heard on the radio of an individual suing a newspaper reporter for libel, not because of what the reporter had said about him, but because of what he had failed to say. The allegation was that the reporter had so selectively presented facts about the individual (who, I believe, was a candidate for political office) that he had falsely represented the individual's character and beliefs and had done so deliberately. The factualness of what the reporter had written was not contested; the claim was that he had selected information to include in his report that would give an uncomplimentary picture of the individual and had deliberately failed to include information that would have shown that picture to be false.

Whether this ever came to trial, I do not know. The radio announcer noted in his commentary that the newspaper involved saw the possibility of a conviction as a serious threat against freedom of the press and held that, while reporters have an obligation to report only the truth, they are not obliged to report all the truth as they know it, and that successful prosecution of a libel suit based solely on failing to include certain information in a news report would greatly dampen the enthusiasm of reporters for investigative reporting and would decrease the effectiveness of the news media as guardians of democracy.

I find the case interesting because it poses a real dilemma. On the one hand, freedom of the press is not only cherished by all free societies, but a compelling argument can be, and has been, made that it is essential to any society that would remain free. On the other hand, one does not normally think of legal prohibitions against libel as an undo restriction of freedom of the press and there seems little doubt that one can unjustly damage an individual's reputation by telling selective parts of the truth just as one can do so by telling explicit lies.

I do not wish to suggest that reporters do not make an effort to report the facts objectively. I am willing to assume that in most cases that is the intent. Reporting selectively and from a perspective is not necessarily the same as intentional biasing. The point is, however, that any description of an event, a person, a viewpoint is an abstraction, and even given the best of intentions on the part of the reporter, one cannot escape the fact that subjectivity is involved in deciding what should, or should not, be reported. As I. J. Good (1983) reminds us, "All judgments are subjective, but some are more subjective than others" (p. 127).

Gilovich (1991) has discussed a variety of ways in which news reports can be distorted, sometimes for the sake of increasing the interest that a story will hold for the intended audience, sometimes as a result of the need to compress the report of a complicated event into a small space or time slot, sometimes in the interest of helping to make a case or support a cause. Distortions may sometimes be intentional, but they need not be so in order to be distortions.

Much of the knowledge of the world that we have, especially of current events, is obtained through the media. Especially in view of the considerable pressures on media organizations to present news that will capture and hold the attention of the public more effectively than does that of competitors, one may hesitate to assume that the events that are reported in the news are a representative sample of all the events that are occurring. Consequently, to the extent that one's knowledge of what is happening in the world or in one's locale depends exclusively on what one learns through the media, one's view is likely to be incomplete and to some extent distorted. Frequently-reported events may be taken to be more common than they really are.

Even discounting any biases that may have their roots in our own cognitive and inferential limitations, there are biases inherent in the data upon which we base our beliefs; as Gilovich (1991) puts it, "the world does not play fair. Instead of providing us with clear information that would enable us to 'know' better, it presents us with messy data that are random, incomplete, unrepresentative, ambiguous, inconsistent, unpalatable, or secondhand" (p. 3). Sorting it all out and drawing inferences in an unbiased way is a tall order.

Subjectivity in Historical Reporting

> One of the greatest Greek inventions was the idea of history
> (Boorstin, 1985, p. 562).

What has been said of journalism is true of historical reporting as well. Any presentation of history is necessarily an oversimplification of the facts. In putting on paper an account of a historical event, person, or era, historians have no choice but to be selective. They cannot describe all that is describable. The recording of history necessarily requires condensation and abstraction. Even with the purest of intentions for accuracy, historians are limited both by their sources of information and their own inability to know all there is to know about any given period, any given country, any given individual, or even any given event.

In deciding what to describe, historians must exercise judgment. Their choice of details for inclusion may be determined by how they relate to a question they wish to answer, a theme they wish to develop, or a theoretical perspective that is influencing their research. They may select on the basis of the importance they attach to events as causal agents in shaping subsequent history, or on the basis of what they believe will be of greatest interest to their readers, but select they must. It is not possible to describe everything as it happened.

Add to these considerations the fact that all history is history from a point of view. The same events can appear quite different to people observing them from different perspectives. Even unembellished "bare facts" may differ in subtle and not-so-subtle ways in different "objective" accounts. The evidence of this is in the differences in the accounts of the same events by different historians. The War of the American Revolution, for example, does not look the same when viewed through the eyes of a British historian as when viewed through those of an American one. In some cases, differences between accounts are not subtle but amount to flat contradictions.

When even historians have great difficulty establishing the accuracy of many particulars, what is the average person to do? How is one to decide what to believe? What criteria might one use to determine how much credence to give to any particular claim?

The answer, in my view, is that one should use the same criteria that are appropriate for any situation in which it is impossible to check directly the accuracy of any particular claim. These include self-consistency (an account that contradicts itself is or should be suspect), consistency with other known or believed facts, credibility of source (reputation for accuracy), although this criterion may beg the question, because one now has the problem of deciding how to determine one's credibility.

One might argue that these points are obvious, and that when we speak of complete and accurate reports of historical events, of printing all the news, or – in the case of the witness in a trial – of telling the whole truth, we do not mean to imply the impossible. We use these absolute terms in relativistic ways, and mean only to claim that the historian or reporter is careful and unbiased, as historians and reporters go, that the newspaper is thorough relative to other newspapers, and that the witness is not to withhold critical evidence intentionally. I believe, however, that there is a problem, and that we are not as sensitive as we should be to the incompleteness and selectivity of *all* reporting.

One of the consequences of our lack of sensitivity to this fact is a willingness to accept overly simple accounts and cause-effect explanations of complex events. We tend, for example to credit individuals with discoveries and inventions in which many people may have had a hand. Despite the fact that it is very difficult, if not impossible, to pinpoint the origin of atomism – the idea that all matter is made of indivisible particles – or to say with any surety who first conceived of energy conservation, we insist on having answers to such questions and to view science as a cumulative process involving the compounding of individual discoveries and inventions (Kuhn, 1970).

We tend to think of history in terms of cause-effect relationships, but such relationships are extremely difficult to establish when we look beyond superficial accounts. Aron, Keller, & Davidson (1958) illustrate the problem by reference to the question of what caused the world war that started in 1914. Some historians focus on the events immediately preceding the war, others consider those events to be incidental on the assumption that the long-term situation insured the inevitability of the war with or without the immediately preceding incidents. Of interest in the present context is Aron et al.'s contention that such propositions are, in principle, untestable. "How can such propositions be proved? And again, the answer is that irrefutable proof is impossible. We cannot repeat the experiment, eliminate the incident of July 1914, so that history may take another course – which might confirm or refute the hypothesis of 'inevitability'. All we can do is to perform mental experiments" (p. 31).

Aron et al. conclude that "when we assert a causal relation between a situation and a past event, our assertion is no more indisputable than is the forecast of such an event. (The judgment that an event occurred is indisputable. The judgment that it was the effect solely of a given situation is not indisputable.)" (p. 32). An even stronger reservation about cause-effect analyses of historical events comes from Garrett Hardin (1985): "Cause-effect assertions about history are forever dubious because of the logical flaw of *post hoc ergo propter hoc* reasoning. Out of a multitude of contributing factors how can we be sure that a particular one is, or is not, determinative?" (p. 61).

My purpose is not to cast aspersions on historical scholarship, but simply to call attention to the fact – I believe it is a fact – that history is bound to be more complex than any account of it can reveal it to be. Historical accounts *must* be simplifications. That fact, in itself, is not a problem, provided we recognize the situation for what it is. Failure to recognize the necessity for simplification, however, can reinforce the assumption that every event has a readily identifiable cause, and this can lead to a variety of reasoning difficulties that go along with an overly simplistic view of the world.

More generally, the need is to see that in all contexts each of us necessarily sees things from a particular perspective; there is no such thing as a completely objective observer. Evidence is always evaluated from some point of view. As Richard Messer (1997) puts it: "The influence of one's personality, background, social culture, religious and philosophical beliefs, and so on, casts doubt upon the possibility of providing a non-relative set of criteria for making philosophical judgments" (p. 92). Or, we might add, any other kinds of judgments as well.

Subjectivity in Science

> Science can, and does, strive to grasp nature's factuality, but all science is socially embedded, and all scientists record prevailing "certainties," however hard they may be aiming for pure objectivity (Gould, 1994, p. 86).

Surely if we are to find objectivity anywhere, we should find it in science. But even here, despite intentions to be objective, and institutional conventions designed to discredit views that are not backed by empirical evidence, subjectivity is not to be denied a substantive role. Scientists' thoughts, like everyone else's, are conditioned by knowledge and theories of the day in which they live; it is impossible to view the world from the vantage point of a theory that might have been developed, but was not.

Kitty Ferguson (1994) describes the lack of complete objectivity in science this way:

> How are we to find a way of looking at the universe free from any bias whatsoever? How are we to recognize ultimate truth when and if we find it? How are we to prove we've found it? The naïve view is that these are precisely the problems science solves: it enables us to study reality without a bias, with pure objectivity, and prove conclusively what is true and what isn't. That is a *very* naïve view of science (p. 37).

In Sum

So, we see that human reasoning is plagued not only with many fallacies and biases but with sundry other flaws and foibles, only a sampling of which has been noted here. All of these difficulties show up in arguments that we construct for the purpose of influencing the beliefs and behaviors of others and ourselves. So, the question is forced: given the myriad of ways in which human reasoning goes awry, how is it that we, as a species, have lasted as long as we have? Apparently the problems have not (yet?) been collectively bad enough to do us in, but can anyone doubt that their effects have made things worse than they need to be?

9

Stratagems

> There are brilliant tricks for getting people to accept all sorts of false premises as true . . . and these tricks of argument are so prevalent that even when people realize that something is being pulled on them, they tend to let it pass
>
> (Fearnside & Holther, 1959, p. 2).

There is the view that "the point of argument is not to produce involuntary acquiescence, but to seek voluntary agreement" (Soeteman, 1986, p. 102). Undoubtedly this is true in many cases, and one could wish it were invariably true, but it seems clear that the objective of the participants in many arguments is less to seek voluntary agreement than to "win" the argument or to modify an opponent's behavior in some way. People use many techniques – or stratagems – to accomplish such goals in argumentation. The term *stratagem* is borrowed from Arthur Schopenhauer (undated/1896) to whom it connoted an alogical ploy that is used for the purpose of winning debates or disputes. I would extend the connotation to include any effort to shape or mold beliefs or behavior by a method other than appeal to relevant information and cogent reasoning.

Stratagems differ from fallacies, at least as I am using the terms. As is true of most distinctions of this sort, the line between the two concepts is a fuzzy one. The distinction is helpful, nonetheless. The distinguishing feature is intentionality. Fallacies are unintentional violations of principles of sound reasoning; one intends to reason soundly and generally is unaware that one is not doing so. Stratagems are rhetorical tricks used for the purpose of persuasion or winning debates without regard for being logical, or perhaps even fair, about it. When one intentionally constructs a knowingly fallacious argument for the purpose of getting the better of an opponent in a dispute, I would say that one is using a stratagem; when one constructs the same argument, believing it to be logically sound, I would say one is committing a fallacy. I do not mean to suggest that whenever one uses a stratagem, one is fully aware of what one is doing; I mean only that one's primary goal is that of persuading, or winning a dispute, and not that of converging on whatever conclusion sound reasoning dictates. Stratagems often, perhaps typically, though not always, involve some degree of deception of one form or another.

There are numerous identifiable stratagems for getting the better of one's opponent in a verbal dispute. Many have been recognized and discussed by philosophers for hundreds, if not thousands, of years. Aristotle mentions some in his *Rhetoric*. Schopenhauer describes and illustrates thirty-eight of them in *The Art of Controversy* (summarized in Appendix B). Thouless (1947) lists thirty-eight "dishonest tricks which are commonly used in argument" (see Appendix C) and suggests methods for overcoming them.

The connotation that is given to stratagems in these references is decidedly negative. If one believes that disputes should be won or lost on the basis of the relative strengths of rational arguments, then the use of stratagems might be considered cheating, inasmuch as they represent ways of attempting to win disputes without relying on the rationality of the disputants. On the other hand, this might be considered an unduly harsh generalization, inasmuch as some ways of making an audience receptive to one's argument seem relatively innocuous. Noting the importance of the manner in which an argument is made, as well as that of its substance, Arnauld and Nicole (1995) recommend to "those who wish to persuade others of any truth which they have discovered" "to clothe it in the garb most suitable for making it acceptable, and to avoid those revolting ways of stating it which only lead to its rejection" (p. 53). Who can object to such advice? However, the intention of clothing a discovery in the "garb most suitable for making it acceptable" can easily morph into the stratagem of withholding evidence that is inconsistent with the discovery one wishes to share.

Here I want to give *stratagem* a sufficiently broad connotation to include things that people do to influence others' beliefs or behavior other than by engaging in rational discussion and argumentation – presenting and evaluating evidence impartially and going where the evidence leads. To be a stratagem, according to this connotation, it is not essential that the motivation for its use be nefarious or that its user intends to cheat; it is essential only that the purpose for its use is that of influencing beliefs or behavior.

The careful observer will have no trouble finding examples of the use of the stratagems that are discussed here, especially in situations in which people are heatedly debating controversial issues. It is an interesting commentary on the way our minds work to note how intuitive and natural many of them seem to be. We use some of them more or less effectively without any special training on how to do so, and often without being sufficiently aware of the stratagems we are using to be able to describe them in precise terms.

A Sample of Stratagems

The stratagems discussed in what follows constitute only a sample of those that could be noted. My intention is to provide a sense of the diversity of those that are widely used; I doubt if it would be possible to generate a complete list. Those mentioned here include some that have been the focus of considerable research, as well as some that are conjectural on my part. My failure to cite references in some cases should not be taken as evidence that relevant references do not exist, but only of my unawareness of any. Some of the stratagems mentioned have been noted in the context of the discussion of fallacies and biases in Chapters 6 and 7. Sometimes it is difficult to tell whether something is better considered a fallacy, a bias, or a stratagem; it is more frequently the case, I suspect, that it may be considered one under some circumstances and another under others.

Appeal to Authority

A person who has made a study of a particular subject surely speaks with greater authority on that subject, other things being equal, than does one who has not made such a study. It seems right that we respect that authority. If I have reason to suspect that there may be something seriously wrong with my liver, I would do better to consult with a medical specialist who is expected to know something about livers than with my dentist. We seek advice from people we believe to be qualified to give it and this seems as it should be.

Similarly, we are likely to give more credence to a claim, especially a surprising one, if it is made by someone whom we believe is knowledgeable about the subject than if made by someone whom we believe is not. If you, a person of some means, were presented with the opportunity of purchasing a painting that is reputed to be an early work of Rembrandt, but you had some misgivings about its authenticity, you surely would consider the opinion of an authority on Rembrandt to be considerably more helpful to you than that of a random cousin as you attempted to decide whether to make this purchase. Taking into account the qualifications of the sources of claims and opinions in determining how much credence one should give to them is an eminently reasonable thing to do.

A very significant percentage of our learning is based on a trust of authorities in various fields and acceptance of what they say. And we are fortunate that there are authorities who can serve this educational function. If what each of us could know about the world were limited to what we can discover directly through our own observation, exploration, and experimentation, our knowledge would be limited indeed.

The idea that appealing to authority can be legitimate and useful, under some circumstances, is widely acknowledged. Kitty Ferguson (1994) argues that even in science, where objective evidence is considered the ultimate arbiter of what to believe, appeal to authority is common: "The opinions and prejudices of the acknowledged experts of our generation strongly influence which theories other scientists take seriously, which they scoff at, and what avenues of inquiry they follow" (p. 66). More generally, Richard Swinburne (1981) notes, what is obvious on reflection, that "Most of what we believe, we believe on authority" (p. 42). Even our questioning of authority is generally based on what we learn from other authorities. James Bachman (1995), speaking from the vantage point of an interrogative model of reasoning (Hintikka & Bachman, 1991), also defends appeal to authority as a strategy that can be effective in obtaining answers to questions, if not necessarily consistent with rules of logical inference.

Appeal to authority becomes a stratagem, as the term is used here, when it is used in extreme, biased, or uncritical ways. It is abused when one uses it in lieu of appealing to more direct relevant evidence that is available, or when one appeals to an authority on X who is not an authority on Y when the question at issue is on the subject of Y. Isaac Watts (1995/1796) referred to this type of argument as one addressed to our modesty: "When the Argument is fetch'd from the Sentiments of some wise, great, or good Man, whose Authority we reverence, and hardly dare oppose" (p. 59). Attempting to get someone to accept a claim as true by attributing it to someone who has much cachet with the person one is trying to convince can be a stratagem: "I am not making the claim, Prof Smith, a Nobel laureate is."

One is giving authority more than its due when one fails to recognize the possibility that authorities can be wrong even in their areas of expertise, or when one discounts or disregards all factors other than the authoritativeness of a source in judging the credibility of some claim. Or when the authority is used selectively and in a biased way, as when I appeal to authorities who agree with my position but choose to ignore equally authoritative persons whose views are at variance with mine. Or when the reason for appealing to authority is to avoid thinking about an issue and doing the digging necessary to develop a well-informed opinion of my own.

On average, people who are knowledgeable with respect to a specific subject are going to be more reliable sources of information on that subject than people who are less knowledgeable with respect to it, but knowledgeable people can be wrong, they can make mistakes, and they do on occasion deliberately mislead. So, while authoritativeness is a legitimate factor to weigh in judging credibility, it is by no means the only one and seldom is it sufficiently strong to overwhelm all the rest.

It is customary in our society for individuals who are well-known and admired by the general public (movie stars, outstanding athletes, television personalities) to be engaged by companies, political parties, or special-interest groups to endorse commercial products, promote political candidates, support specific causes, or influence people's opinions and actions for a variety of other purposes. Seldom is it a requirement that such individuals be experts with respect to the topics about which influence is sought. It is necessary only that they be well-known and highly-regarded by the intended audience. Popularity is a stand-in for authority in this case, and judging from the willingness of influence brokers to pay highly visible and popular people large sums of money for public endorsement services, the approach works rather well.

In the context of the report of a study of consumer behavior, Grant McCracken (1989) defines "the celebrity endorser," for his purposes, as "any individual who enjoys public recognition and who uses this recognition on behalf of a consumer good by appearing with it in an advertisement" (p. 310). He distinguishes four forms of endorsement: "explicit mode ('I endorse this product'), the implicit mode ('I use this product'), the imperative mode ('You should use this product'), and the copresent mode (i.e., in which the celebrity merely appears with the product)" (p. 310). As to why celebrity endorsements work, when they do, there are several explanations. McCracken notes two prominent possibilities, one of which invokes the idea of source credibility and the other of source attractiveness; and he proposes a third one, which assumes a meaning transfer process – a process in which certain properties are transferred from celebrity to a consumer good and then from the consumer good to the consumer. The "when they do" hedge is worth a comment. As McCracken notes, not only do celebrity endorsements sometimes fail, it is not uncommon for endorsements by the same celebrity to be successful for some companies/products while failing for others.

Appeal to Tradition

The argument that it *should* be thus because it always *has been* thus, or because it has been thus for a long time, is not compelling from a logical point of view. Nevertheless, although this argument may not often be expressed explicitly, tradition clearly is a major determinant of much of what we believe and do.

Tradition can be a stabilizing influence and we should be careful about throwing it off too lightly; cavalier dismissal of a tradition that one finds personally onerous or unappealing is a temptation that should be resisted (Blackstone, 1962/1769; Leftow, 1994). As in the case of long-standing personal beliefs, the fact that one may not be able to bring to mind immediately a completely satisfactory rationale for a traditional practice or point of view does not necessarily mean that one does not exist. Traditions become traditions over many years and sometimes the reasons for them become obscured.

Appealing to tradition becomes a stratagem when it is done in a dogmatic and unthinking way – "we have always done it thus and so, so we should continue to do it thus and so." Refusal to consider the possibility that the traditional way of doing something might be improved upon can make the appeal to tradition an impediment to progress.

It is possible for traditions to become established on the basis of unworthy or invalid reasons, or on reasons that were once valid but are no longer so, as the consequence of changing circumstances over time. So, it is right to challenge traditions, to reassess them from time to time, and to attempt to understand the arguments that can be made for modifying them or for keeping them as they are. Reassessing a tradition thoroughly and fairly may require more of an effort than many of us are typically willing to make.

Appeal to Common Knowledge or Numbers

Argumentum ad populum. The fact that many people believe something does not make it true. That many people engage in a specific type of behavior does not make it a good idea to engage in it oneself. Even when most people agree, it does not follow that what they agree on is right; there is no law of nature that says the majority cannot be wrong.

On the other hand, although history makes it clear that majorities can be wrong, it can be argued, as Nozick (1993) has done, that "[s]ometimes it will be rational to accept something because others in your society do .... We are all fallible, so the consensus of many other fallible people is likely to be more accurate than my own particular view when it concerns a matter to which we all have equal access" (p. 129). A similar point is made by James Surowiecki (2005) in *The Wisdom of Crowds.* Citing Reid Hastie and Tatsuya Kameda (2005) and Krishna Ladha (1992), Hugo Mercier (2017) puts the matter this way: "in the absence of sounder cues, majority is a robust cue to accuracy, so that it is far from unreasonable to follow it" (p. 107).

Appealing to numbers becomes a stratagem when it is used in lieu of, or to the neglect of, other evidence that is relevant to the claim in question. James Freeman (1995) distinguishes between appeal to popularity and appeal to common knowledge and considers the former to be problematic but not the latter. The appeal to popularity he refers to as the *bandwagon appeal*, "an argument which claims that because many, most, or all people accept a certain belief or approve a certain course of action, that belief must be true or that course of action must be right" (p. 265). Freeman argues, however, that, interpreted correctly, common knowledge – e.g., that human beings have hearts, that there are many trees in Canada – can be a legitimate though fallible basis of a presumption of truth.

The idea of common knowledge is closely related to the assumption, borne out by many experiments, that people use their own knowledge, behavior, and states of mind as a basis for judging what others know or will do or think in specific contexts (Katz & Alport, 1931; Marks & Miller, 1987; Mullen et al., 1985; Nickerson, 1999; Nickerson, Baddeley, & Freeman, 1987; Ross, Greene, & House, 1977). The phenomenon is sometimes referred to as the *principle of humanity* (Gordon, 1986; Grandy, 1973). Use of the principle can facilitate communication, but applied uncritically, it can also make communication more difficult than it need be (Nickerson, 1999, 2001).

Appeal to Emotion

In theory, the persuasiveness of an argument should be independent of the emotion with which it is expressed, but surely no one can believe that it is so. Emotions of various types and intensities are much in evidence in arguments. Playing to feelings of compassion, guilt, despondency, or other emotional states has long been recognized as an effective means of influencing beliefs and behavior. Watts (1995/1796) described the intended use of such arguments as to "engage the Inclinations and Passions of the Hearers on the Side of the Speaker" (p. 59). Frans van Eemeren and Rob Grootendorst (1992) speak of "putting pressure on the other party by playing on his feelings of compassion" (p. 213).

Although recognizing *argumentum ad misericordiam* as a fallacious argument, Charles Hamblin (1970) qualifies that assessment: "more depends on a lawsuit, or a political speech, than assent to a proposition. A proposition is presented primarily as a guide to action and, where action is concerned, it is not so clear that pity and other emotions are irrelevant" (p. 43). A book-length treatment of appeal to pity has been produced by Douglas Walton (1997).

Thouless (1947) notes that words implying moral judgments may be injected into arguments for the express purpose of attempting "to distort the hearer's view of the truth by arousing emotions" (p. 16). The assumption on which this contention rests is that emotional reasoning is more likely to be faulty than is unemotional reasoning; an assumption that many people may find it easy to accept. Thouless offers this advice.

> When we catch ourselves thinking in emotional phraseology, let us form a habit of translating our thoughts into emotionally neutral words. So, we can guard ourselves from ever being so enslaved by emotional words and phrases that they prevent us from thinking objectively when we need to do so – that is whenever we have to come to a decision on any debatable matter (p. 19).

Appeal to Ignorance

The stratagem of appealing to ignorance involves invoking concepts with which one is familiar but that one believes one's opponent in a dispute is unlikely to be. This is a stratagem that is easy for an expert in a field to use when arguing with someone who knows little about that field. One might take the position that one should not argue about a field that one does not understand and that having to confront unfamiliar terms is only one of the risks that one takes in doing so.

My point here, however, is that concepts that are unlikely to be familiar to one's opponent can be introduced into an argument for no better reason than to confuse the opponent and perhaps impress upon him his lack of qualifications to debate an issue. But a superior or more technical vocabulary is not the equivalent of more compelling reasons in a debate. The appropriate counter to this stratagem is to insist on definitions of terms or explanations of how they are being used. Pretending one understands terms that one does not understand – perhaps from a reluctance to admit to a lack of specific knowledge – only digs deeper the hole into which one is likely eventually to fall.

Appeal to Vanity

"As a recognized leader (major contributor, concerned citizen, ...) ...." One way or another, the enclosed letter is calculated to make me feel important – and generous. It invariably contains an envelope, usually with a suggested amount of a contribution, which, if I have contributed to this organization before, is somewhat larger than my latest contribution. Sometimes the ploy is to make me feel important: "You have been selected to represent (your town, state, party) in an important survey." Again, in addition to the survey, the packet contains a return envelope so I can demonstrate my concern for the subject of the survey with a donation.

Appealing to vanity – ego-stroking, flattery – is much in evidence in many requests for financial support of various causes or in efforts to persuade one to purchase some product – any of a variety of *Who's Who*, alumni or organization member directories. I receive a postcard from a scientific organization to which I belong, requesting that I call a specified toll-free number in order to verify the completeness and accuracy of the biographical information about me that is included in a directory the organization is about to publish. I call. The information is verified. Before the conversation is ended, the interviewer describes the various editions of the directory that will be available and the special prices that are being offered to members who order in advance. The final question: "*Which* of them would you like me to reserve for you?"

The message on the postcard gave no warning that the conversation would include an attempt to sell me something. The solicitation, when it came, explicitly offered me a choice among several purchases, but not a choice between purchasing or not purchasing. The question was not "Would you like me to reserve a copy?" but "Which edition would you like me to reserve?"

This approach set me, the potential buyer, up in several ways. It projected the idea that the organization was sufficiently interested in me, as a member, to want to get my listing in its directory correct, and I have no reason to believe that this was not the case. By not mentioning that it hoped to sell me something, it projected the idea that its *only*, or at least its *main*, reason for wanting to talk with me was to get my biographical information straight; this idea was considerably less credible after the phone conversation than before. Deferring any mention of the possibility of a purchase until after some conversation focused on my listing for the directory – all reminding me what an impressive person I am – more or less guaranteed that my resistance to a subtle sales pitch would be at its nadir, especially in view of the fact that the preferred item for sale was a gold-embossed leather-bound volume the purpose of which was to inform the world of my existence and accomplishments along, of course, with those of other members of the organization. Presenting me with a choice among different editions of the directory meant that in order to select *no* edition, I had to introduce that option myself, which I ungraciously did.

The following is an account of the experience of one person, call him Sam, with Marquis *Who's Who in the World* (hereafter *WW*). One day Sam received a phone call congratulating him on being accepted into this organization. Follow-up emails informed him that *WW* is composed of the top 3 percent of professionals in the world, and provided some information regarding what *WW* is and does:

> Reservation in our network is honored to individuals who have demonstrated leadership, excellence, and longevity within their respective industries and professions. Lifetime affiliation with Marquis *Who's Who* entitles biographees to an expanded biographical profile online, as well as a professional news release detailing induction into Marquis *Who's Who in the World.*
>
> Award recipients are entitled to a professionally written personal narrative announcing this honor as well as your accomplishments. The narrative comes with online distribution to all the major search engines for higher visibility and each winner is given an expanded biography and exclusive access to Marquis Biographies Online (MBO), our database of more than 1.5 million of the most distinguished professionals from around the globe. Lastly, all narratives are also offered in a lovely custom framed display piece [trophy] for the home or office.

Sam is vain enough to have been pleased by his selection by *WW*, but he is something of a penny-pincher, and was put off by the fact that the benefits came at some not-incidental cost for the awardee (approximately $800, as he recalls). He informed *WW*, by email, that he was pleased with the honor, but he did not wish to spend money on a personalized news release or a trophy. He received no reply to this email, but the notices kept coming. After several of them, he responded as follows:

> A month or so ago I replied to this notice with the following message: I am very pleased to have been selected to be listed in *Who's Who in the World.*

> However, if that selection is contingent on my purchasing something, which this and previous emails appear to indicate, then I must decline, inasmuch as I consider any honor for which one must pay to be no honor at all.
>
> If I have misunderstood, please advise.
>
> I now reiterate. I am very pleased to have been selected to be listed in Who's Who in the World, and am happy to accept the honor; but I do not wish to purchase anything. I would much appreciate a reply informing me whether I am wrong in assuming that the listing is contingent on my purchasing something.
>
> Thank you.
>
> Sincerely,
> Sam . . .

This message, like the preceding one, received no reply. Over a period of ten-and-a-half months, Sam received essentially the same email regarding his selection by *WW* twenty-three times, the major difference being that they were identified as "final offer," "last chance," or "last reminder," and sometimes referred to the award as a "lifetime award," or the "Albert Nelson Marquis Lifetime Achievement Award." Each email urged Sam to participate in helping prepare an announcement to the press of his selection to *WW* and to purchase the impressive looking trophy proclaiming it.

I tell this (true) story not to disparage people listed by *WW*; I suspect that a large majority of them are fully deserving of the recognition listing provides. I tell it to illustrate how the appeal to vanity can be used to affect behavior in this context. (On the question of what listing in *WW* is worth, Googling *Is "Marquis Who's Who" still reputable? – ResearchGate* will turn up a variety of stories not unlike Sam's and opinions re the question of worth.)

Proof by Selected Instances

> [T]o tell the truth but not the whole truth is the basic trick of any propaganda service that has risen above outright lying
>
> (Beckman, 1971, p. 59).

Whenever one attempts to support the claim that "All As are Bs" by pointing out specific As that are Bs and ignoring the possibility that there are As that are not Bs, one is engaging in a type of argument that Thouless (1947) refers to as "proof by selected instances." That some As are

Bs is not compelling evidence that all of them are, or even that most of them are. Presumably this is obvious to anyone who thinks about it, but we find it easy to ignore the fact when it is convenient to do so and especially when we are evaluating evidence for claims that we believe, or want to believe, to be true.

A related form of selectivity involves attacking a minor point in a complicated argument and taking the position that the entire argument is brought down by virtue of the untenability of that point. To be sure, the undercutting of any component of an argument weakens the argument as a whole, but the conclusion of a complicated argument that has many supporting claims is not shown to be false by a successful refutation of one, or a subset, of them, especially if the refuted claim(s) is (are) supplemental to other more critical ones.

A clever variant of proof by selective instances has been used to win the confidence of unsuspecting investors in the ability of an individual to forecast, say, changes in prices of commodity futures. The forecaster calls a large number of people to introduce himself, telling them that he has nothing to sell them, but to let them know that he deals in commodity futures and that he is available to accommodate them if they ever decide to invest in this market. Before hanging up, he mentions in passing that they should keep an eye on a specific commodity over the next few days. To half of the people he calls, he predicts that the price is going to rise, and to the other half, he predicts that it is going to fall. Sometime later he again calls the half for which his prediction proved to be correct, just to remind them of his existence; to half of this group he predicts that the price of the same commodity will rise again, and to the other half, he predicts that it will now fall. By the time he makes his third call, which he places of course only to those people for whom both the first and second prediction proved to be true, he is likely to find a few people who are sufficiently impressed with his prescience to be willing, if not eager, to talk business with him.

Proof by Blatant Assertion

A stratagem commonly used in disputation is that of simply asserting, in forceful and unequivocal terms, whatever one wishes to claim to be true. One finds the stratagem used by learned and unlearned people alike. Consider the following pronouncement by Bertrand Russell (1961/1923):

> That Man is the product of causes which had no prevision of the end they were achieving; that his origin, his growth, his hopes and fears, his loves and

> his beliefs, are but the outcome of accidental collocations of atoms; that no fire, no heroism, no intensity of thought and feeling, can preserve an individual life beyond the grave; that all the labors of the ages, all the devotion, all the inspiration, all the noonday brightness of human genius, are destined to extinction in the vast death of the solar system, and that the whole temple of Man's achievement must inevitably be buried beneath the debris of a universe in ruins – all these things, if not quite beyond dispute, are yet so nearly certain, that no philosophy which rejects them can hope to stand (p. 67).

Russell was stating a point of view that he and others have held, and of course he had every right to do so. But he stated it not as a personal belief but as a set of facts "so nearly certain that no philosophy which rejects them can hope to stand." In doing this he went considerably beyond what the evidence warrants and pronounced assertions to be factual that are by no means settled in the minds of many others as well-informed on the issues as he.

Frederic Bartlett (1958) notes the commonness of the habit of asserting opinions as facts in everyday discourse, and points out that it is often done with not a little emotion.

> It is not in the nature of the assertion, but in the manner of assertiveness that everyday thinking seeks to attain necessity. Its commonest introductory phrases, when it is expressed in words, are "of course," "beyond a doubt," and – especially perhaps in political circles – "I am (or "we are") confident that." The source of the compulsion being now within the thinker, and particularly in his social group, it is possible, and indeed common, for completely contradictory issues to claim the same necessity. Then the only way either side has of enforcing its claim is yet more violent assertiveness. It is partly on account of this that many people have said that everyday thinking is largely emotional thinking (p. 182).

Proof by Frequent Repetition

Closely related to the idea of proof by blatant assertion is that of proof by frequent repetition. Baird (1950) refers to frequent repetition as a fallacy, which occurs "when, in lieu of an argument methodically unfolded, the speaker or writer merely repeats, again and again, his own proposition" (p. 182). It appears that, other things equal, if a claim is made frequently enough it is likely to be believed by many people, irrespective of whether there is any objective evidence of its truth (Hasher, Goldstein, & Toppino,

1977; Schwartz, 1982). One presumes that this principle is well understood by the advertising industry.

Thouless (1947) discusses the use of repetition as a "trick of suggestion" and notes that orators who use the method of suggestion rely on three things: "(1) repeated affirmation, (2) a confident, insistent method of speaking, and (3) prestige" (p. 58). Frequent repetition is a well-known method of brainwashing and propaganda; Karl Jaspers (1952) points out its importance as a stratagem used by repressive governments for controlling their citizens: "Totalitarian states show that whole populations can be reduced to ignorance by the withholding of news, the prohibition of free public discussion, and by becoming accustomed to constantly repeated falsehoods" (p. 51).

Experimental findings indicate that repetition does not have to be frequent or made by authoritative figures to have an impact; a single repetition of an assertion under unremarkable circumstances can increase the hearer's confidence in the assertion's truth whether or not it is true (Arkes, Boehm, & Xu, 1991; Bacon, 1979; Begg & Armour, 1991; Begg, Armour, & Kerr, 1985; Gigerenzer, 1984; Hasher, Goldstein, & Toppino, 1977; Schwartz, 1982). This has been called by Hertwig, Gigerenzer, and Hoffrage (1997) the *reiteration* effect. It has been referred to also as *the conference of referential validity* (Hasher et al., 1977), the *frequency-validity relationship* (Gigerenzer, 1984), *the familiarity-validity relationship* (Arkes, Hackett, & Boehm, 1989), and *the illusion of truth* (Begg, Anas, & Farinacci, 1992). Theoretical accounts of the effect have treated it as a memory phenomenon: one is more likely to consider assertions to be true that one realizes one has heard before or that one recognizes as familiar (Arkes et al., 1989; Begg et al., 1992).

Proof by Obfuscation

> Not all that is obscure is necessarily profound. There is a huge difference between discourses that are difficult because of the inherent nature of their subject and those whose vacuity or banality is carefully hidden behind deliberately obscure prose
>
> (Sokal & Bricmont, 1998, p. 186).

Every community of people with common interests evolves its own jargon. Physicians have theirs, physicists theirs, and lawyers theirs. So do truck drivers, baseball fans, and computer hackers. Discipline-specific, or domain-specific, language has two important effects. It facilitates communication among people who understand it, making the exchange of ideas more efficient than it otherwise would be, and it increases the difficulty of communication between people who understand the language and those who do not. Physicians, for example, who have learned not only to communicate with, but to think in the language of, medical terminology may find it difficult, on occasion, to communicate as effectively as they would like with people outside the profession.

This is neither surprising nor objectionable, which is not to deny that it can sometimes be frustrating; it is the price of specialization. What is objectionable is the use of jargon for no other purpose than to give oneself an advantage in a dispute with someone who does not understand it. As Thouless (1947) notes, "It is unfortunately true that many people are more easily persuaded by what they cannot understand" (p. 64). Use of this stratagem is tantamount to using a weapon against an unarmed opponent in a hand-to-hand tussle. The defense is to insist on the use of terms that both parties to the dispute understand, or to require that specialist terms be defined when that is not possible.

Arguing Cause from Correlation

When events are observed to be highly correlated, the assumption is often made that they are related in a cause-effect way, as indeed they may be. Causes and their effects are highly correlated, so if there is a cause-effect relationship, a high correlation is very likely to be observed. Events that are not related as cause and effect can also be highly correlated, however, so an inference from correlation to cause-effect is not a safe one to make. (Arguing from correlation to cause-effect can be seen as a case of affirming the consequent: If A, then C; C, therefore A. If there is a cause-effect relationship, then a high correlation will be observed; a high correlation is observed; therefore, there is a cause-effect relationship.)

The question of how useful, or how problematic, inferences from correlation to cause-effect are, from a practical point of view, has never been answered, to my knowledge. Sometimes the inference, though logically unwarranted, yields a true belief; sometimes it does not. We do not know what percentage of beliefs produced by this type of inference are true. It might be high – and would be so if a large percentage of the correlations that are observed in the natural course of events are, in fact, based on cause-effect relationships. If that percentage is high, and if it is more important for one to identify cause-effect relationships that occur than to be fastidiously logical, and if an occasional misidentification of a noncausal relationship as a causal one is of no great consequence, then inferring cause-effect relationships from high correlations may be a generally reasonable thing to do. However, claiming a cause-effect relationship solely on the basis of a high correlation is risky, and one should not do it without acknowledging the possibility that the claim could be wrong.

Straw Man

When one wishes to show the weakness of a belief or opinion and, in doing so, one describes that belief or opinion inaccurately and in a way that makes it especially vulnerable to criticism, we say that one has attacked a *straw man*. Sometimes the term is used to refer to an argument that one refutes when, in fact, the refuted argument is one that no one has made, or is likely to make. Use of the straw-man tactic is very common in debates. Although it undoubtedly often is done wittingly, we need not assume that intentional distortion is always the case.

Philosophers, among others, sometimes lay out the two sides of an argument in dialog fashion. Often the arguments are notably one-sided – designed to demonstrate the superiority of the position one supports. It is very hard (impossible?) for one to do justice to a position he/she does not hold.

Perhaps it is only natural for one to present a position with which one does not agree in the poorest possible light. At least it seems reasonable to assume that people who disagree with a position or belief are likely honestly to see it as more vulnerable to criticism than are those who hold it. Peter McKellar (1957) argues that "opposing theories tend to develop over-simplified notions about the mental models of their opponents" (p. 180).

A straw-man version of a position may distort the position in subtle ways through selective emphasis; or it can be factually wrong. At least in the latter case, there is an obvious fix. One simply informs the holder of the straw-man view of the way or ways in which it is factually incorrect. Whether this suffices will depend on how open the proposer of the straw-man view is to having the erroneous conception corrected.

A more subtle form of the straw-man stratagem involves pretending that some refutable claim is essential to the truth of some other claim when it really is irrelevant. You say "I believe X." I say, "If you believe X, you must believe Y, because X cannot be true unless Y is also." I am motivated to make this connection because I am quite sure you do not believe Y, and

I want to convince you of the untenability of X. If the truth of X is not dependent on the truth of Y, I have used a straw-man stratagem. Your defense is to deny the truth of my assertion that X cannot be true unless Y is also. If you do not know enough about the relationship between X and Y to be able to do this, my stratagem may work.

It should be clear from this example that when one of two parties to a dispute knows much more about the subject than does the other, the more knowledgeable person has a considerable advantage in more than one way. Not only can s/he bring more knowledge to bear legitimately, but, if s/he is unscrupulous, s/he can also invent nonexistent dependencies that his/her opponent will be unable to challenge effectively.

A common variant of the straw-man stratagem involves the intentional misrepresentation of a belief or opinion that differs from one's own by stating it in an extreme or exaggerated form. This is an irksome trick but a common one. It is used with abandon by some opinionated radio talk-show hosts to discredit statements of callers with whom they disagree. It is most offensive when it is done after a caller has hung up and therefore has no chance for rebuttal. In stating the opinion in an extreme form, one caricaturizes it and thereby sets it up it for easy refutation.

Diversion

A stratagem that is often used when one of the parties in a verbal dispute is unable to answer directly some point that an opponent has made is diverting the focus of the discussion. The diversion can be accomplished in many ways, but it seems likely to be most effective when the shift of focus is sufficiently subtle that it is not obvious the stratagem is being used. One may, for example, address a claim that is slightly different from the one that is being made, or answer a question that is not quite the one that was asked. In the extreme, one may introduce a "red herring," something that is completely irrelevant to an argument as though it were relevant.

This stratagem is much in evidence in political debates. Often a participant will give a nod to a question that has been asked, without really answering it, and quickly use it as a springboard to a different point. A finely tuned ability to evade questions while appearing to answer them is arguably almost a requirement for success in politics, which is not to suggest that this is the only context in which such an ability can be used to advantage.

Diversionary tactics in disputes may move the focus from the original point of contention to irrelevancies involving personal traits of the disputants. When this happens, what started as an intellectual disagreement can evolve into an exchange of personal insults. Even when it does not have such an unhappy outcome, diversion can cause a dispute to wander far from its original focus.

Charles Willard (1995) points out that distraction can be effected by the use of emotional appeals or esthetic images. "Music and visual imagery in television commercials divert attention from argumentatively weak messages yet leave enduring general impressions. And there is evidence that when persuadees find the topic personally irrelevant, they are vulnerable to *peripheral route persuasion*" (p. 149). Petty and Cacioppo (1986) make the argument: "It is *easier* to accept influence from ethos, slogans, or other oversimple decision heuristics than to engage in issue-relevant thinking" (p. 149).

Incredulity and Ridicule

> Where two principles really do meet which cannot be reconciled with one another, then each man declares the other a fool and a heretic
> (Wittgenstein, 1972/1950, p. 81).

Persuasive arguers often use humor to good effect. As Perelman and Olbrechts-Tyteca (1969) put it, "humor is a very important factor in winning over the audience or, more generally, in establishing a communion between a speaker and his hearers" (p. 188). But as these authors also point out, it can be used to make fun of the views of one's opponent. "To say of a writer that his views are inadmissible because their consequences are ridiculous is one of the strongest objections that can be made in argumentation" (p. 207).

Sometimes people dismiss claims or ideas with which they do not agree with an authoritative pronouncement: "That's ridiculous;" "No one could believe such a thing;" or "You can't be serious!" The right intonation and body language can help give the assertion force, creating the impression of being dumbfounded or horrified to discover that one could hold such a view. An expression of incredulity may be prelude to a reasoned rebuttal of the claim or criticism of the idea, in which case it can be viewed as a harmless clearing of the throat, and attention should be given to the substance of the rebuttal or criticism that follows it. Sometimes, however, such comments are given without any elaboration; their justification is left as an exercise for the listener, as it were. They may, in these instances, represent all one can think of to say about a claim or idea one does not wish to accept. Obviously they do not constitute legitimate counters to the claims or ideas that prompted them, but, given the right social dynamics, they can be intimidating.

David Lewis (1990) quotes some remarks of Maynard Keynes at length in which he reminisces about the formation of some of his (Keynes's) early beliefs while a student at Cambridge University. Keynes described G. E. Moore, then a Cambridge professor, as a master of the technique of speaking with "the greatest appearance of clear, undoubting conviction" and use of "the greatest accents of infallibility." Moore would greet another's remarks, Keynes recalled, "with a gasp of incredulity – *Do* you *really* think *that*, an expression of face as if to hear such a thing said reduced him to wagging his head in the negative so violently that his hair shook. *Oh*! he would say, goggling at you as if either you or he must be mad; and no reply was possible . . . " (p. 231).

Incredulity may be real or feigned, of course. Keynes's description gives Moore's reaction, to this reader at least, the appearance of incredulity expressed for the sake of the expected effect. It may be difficult to tell sometimes whether a claim of incredulity is sincere or shammed. How we should feel about such a claim should depend, it seems to me, on what we consider to be the knowledgeability of the person who makes it. If I claim to be incredulous about a matter that I know little about, my inability to believe something about that matter should not count for much, but if I claim to be incredulous with respect to a matter pertaining to a subject about which I am an expert, my reaction should carry some weight. In the latter case, but not in the former, one might reasonably expect me to do more than simply express my incredulity; I should be able to give a reason for it. I have been more than a little surprised, however, at how often an author who is an expert in a field will dismiss some view of another recognized expert in the same field by simply classifying it, without elaboration, as preposterous, ridiculous, or absurd.

If one can find no rational argument against a position one wishes to oppose, one can always resort to ridicule, which is only a short step from expressions of incredulity. The technique is easy to apply; just laugh. Make it clear that you consider the position to be ridiculous to the point of being hilarious. This is a form of intimidation, and is most likely to be effective against timid opponents.

A somewhat milder form of intimidation is the use of "as everyone knows," as the lead-in to some claim that one does not wish to have to justify. Sokal and Bricmont (1998, p. 45, footnote 42) refer to this usage as a form of intellectual terrorism. This seems a bit overly dramatic, but there can be little question that the intent of this comment often is to establish acceptance of a claim without having to justify it explicitly.

Exploitation of Linguistic Ambiguity

> "[T]he greatest part of controversies in the sacred or civil life arise from the different senses that are put upon words, and the different ideas which are included in them"
>
> (Watts, 1995/1796, p. 287).

In Chapter 6 sophisms arising from abuse of the ambiguity of words were described as a type of fallacy. Watts (1995/1796, p. 286) called this "the largest and most extensive kind of fallacy." Here the point to be made is that the ambiguity of language can be exploited in argumentation effectively. The assertion "Norts are glame" is ambiguous, for example, because it is not clear whether I am claiming that *all* norts are glame, *some* norts are glame, *as a general rule* – to which there may be exceptions – norts are glame. This ambiguity is exploited when one makes an assertion of this type and treats it, for purposes of argument, as a universal (all) claim when in fact a nonuniversal (most, many, some) interpretation is correct.

Sokal and Bricmont (1998) note that ambiguity can be, and sometimes is, used as subterfuge. They give examples of expository text that can be given two interpretations, one of which is true but relatively banal and the other of which is radical but manifestly false. They speculate that many of the ambiguities they consider are deliberate. "Indeed, they offer a great advantage in intellectual battles: the radical interpretation can serve to attract relatively inexperienced listeners or readers; and if the absurdity of this version is exposed, the author can always defend himself by claiming to have been misunderstood, and retreat to the innocuous interpretation" (p. 189).

The vagueness of language and the fuzziness of category boundaries provide countless opportunities for exploitation in argumentation. How many years must a person have lived be to be considered elderly? How little hair must a man have to be considered bald? How giving must a person be to be considered a philanthropist? How one answers such questions may well depend on one's reasons for referring to the categories in argumentation.

Linguistic Preemption

Thomas Sowell (1995) gives examples of how people can gain apparent advantage in disputes by preemptive appropriation of words. One might, for example, describe one's own approach to a problem as a "rational" one, thereby subtly implying that one's adversary's approach is irrational. One of the examples Sowell uses is that of the appropriation of a phrase like "the peace movement" to refer to advocates of disarmament, thereby preempting the question of whether peace is more likely to be realized through disarmament or through military deterrence. "With untold millions of lives depending on the answer to that question, something more substantive than a presumption that some people like peace more than others might be expected. But here, as elsewhere, all sorts of factual and analytical issues are reduced to psychological propensities" (p. 164).

When innocent people suffer from natural disasters (hurricanes, tornados, earthquakes), epidemics, wars, unavoidable accidents, or unprovoked assaults by other people, they are appropriately referred to as victims. But the undisciplined use of "victim" to refer to anyone who has experienced some problem that can, by the greatest stretch, be attributed to someone else's doing is another example of the preemptive use of language. Rogers Wright and Nicholas Cummings (2005) point out how the wholesale application of the concept of victimhood "which allows escape from personal responsibility and elicits redress by others" can, with the help of some trial lawyers and mental health providers, sometimes lead to absurd situations.

> Thus, spilling hot coffee is not due to personal carelessness but reflects its being served at an incorrect temperature. A weight problem is no longer overeating but the result of food addiction exploited by fast-food interests. Lung cancer following a lifelong consumption of cigarettes is the fault of a conspiracy among the tobacco companies to addict large numbers of the public, the warning label on the cigarette package notwithstanding (p. xxv).

The pervasiveness of victimhood is characterized by Ofer Zur (2005) this way: "We have become a nation of victims, leapfrogging over one another to compete publicly for the status of victim and defining everyone as some sort of survivor" (p. 49). What one gains in claiming victim status, Zur contends, is the ability to assign blame to others thereby achieving moral superiority and lack of responsibility for one's own behavior and its consequences. Among the unintended negative consequences of the politics of victimization, according to Jason Lillis et al. (2005) are: "infantalizing minorities, giving incentive for people to claim victim status, creating group polarization, and encouraging reverse discrimination" (p. 289). I do not mean, by these observations, to deny that people can be victims in the sense of suffering harm as a consequence of other people's behavior, but only to concur with the idea that the use of "victim" can be a form of verbal preemption and that there also is such a thing as victimhood being carried to an absurd extreme.

The use of euphemisms can also be a form of linguistic preemption: "previously-owned" for "used," "wetland" for "swamp," "physically (or mentally) challenged" for "handicapped," "participant" for "subject," . . . . The acceptability of specific words in polite discourse changes over time, which makes it sometimes difficult, if not impossible, to know how to be politically correct. Cummings and O'Donohue (2005) point out that the use of politically correct terminology can have the effect of making people feel good in the absence of solutions to the problems to which the changes in terminology relate. They contend that in psychology and psychiatry today concern for politically correct verbiage appears to have precedence over sound professional experience and scientific validation.

Preemption of Criticism

If one anticipates that one is likely to be criticized, justly, for things one has done or failed to do, one may avoid, or at least blunt, the criticism by acknowledging the transgressions before the criticism is made. Studies have shown that voluntarily acknowledging characteristics, features, or facts that would be expected to evoke negative reactions when they came to light softens or mitigates the expected negative effects (Pfeiffer et al., 2014; Ward & Brenner, 2006).

A related stratagem that may be used to blunt the emotional effect of poor performance in some future undertaking is "self-handicapping" (McCrea & Flamm, 2012), or practicing "defensive pessimism" (Sanna, 1996, 1998). "I probably won't do well on the test, because I have very little time to study for it." By noting factors that could impair performance, one presumably lessens the disappointment if the performance in fact is poor and increases the pleasure if it is better than expected.

Selective Use of Statistics

The same statistical information can be packaged in different ways to create different impressions or get different effects. More than sixty years ago, Darrell Huff (1954) made the point in a captivatingly humorous way. If, in describing the prevalence of a problem (disease, crime, automobile fatalities), one wishes to stress its severity, one does well to use natural frequencies (between 30,000 and 40,000 people lose their lives on U.S highways every year). If one wishes to play down the problem's severity, one should report rates or probabilities (the average person's probability of being killed in a traffic accident in any given year is about .0001). More generally, one who understands something of how people interpret quantitative claims can evoke opposing reactions by presenting the same facts in different ways. As John Paulos (1995) illustrates with numerous cases, "almost any mathematically expressed scientific fact can be transformed into a consumer caveat (or lure) that will terrify (or attract) people" (p. 142).

Many examples could be given of how different impressions can be created by clothing the same information in different words. I recently took some area rugs to be cleaned. I mentioned to the rug cleaner that I also had a rug too large to transport easily by car that we would like to have cleaned and asked what the charge would be for pickup and delivery. He said there was no charge for that. When he gave me the bill for the rugs that I had brought to be cleaned, I noted a 20 percent discount. I asked if the company was having a special. He said they standardly give a 20 percent discount for the cleaning of any rugs that one delivers and picks up oneself.

If one wanted to create the impression that the standard of living did not improve much during the latter part of the twentieth century, one might point out that from 1969 to 1996 the annual income of the average American household rose only about 6 percent in constant dollars. One would not mention that during this period, the number of people in the average household declined and the per-capita increase in income was 51 percent. (Figures from Sowell, 2004, p. 147.)

Eric Larson, Marc Ross, and Robert Williams (1986) begin a discussion of how the use of raw materials has been changing over time with acknowledgment that in their view "the primary factors that are affecting the changing role of materials involve consumption rather than production," and consequently they focus on demand.

> We measure the consumption of materials in physical quantities (kilograms) rather than economic ones (dollars) to give a sharper picture of the changing role of materials. We represent the physical quantities in two main ways. If the physical quantity is divided by the population, the result is the consumption of a material per capita at a particular time. If the quantity is divided by the Gross National Product (GNP) in constant dollars, the result is an index of the significance of a material in the economy as a whole (p. 34).

Graphs of these two measures for the 100-year span from 1880 to 1980 show consumption per unit of GDP peaking in about 1920 and falling off

Table 9.1 *Performance of umpires in the aggregate*

	"ball"	"strike"	Total
ball	219,943	20,856	240,799
strike	19,511	99,933	119,444
Total	239,454	120,789	360,243

steadily thereafter, and consumption per capita increasing until 1970. The point is that both of these measures provide pictures of how the consumption of materials has been changing over time, but the pictures they provide are quite different.

Another example of how the same data can be presented in ways that give different perspectives involves Major League Baseball (MLB). In the 2016 season 715,761 pitches were thrown during regulation MLB games. Almost precisely half of the pitches (360,243; 50.33 percent) were *called* (balls or strikes) by the umpires; the other half included hits, foul balls, balls swung on and missed, hit batters, etc. and did not have to be called. Table 9.1 summarizes the performance of the umpires. "Ball" and "strike" refer to umpires' calls; ball and strike (without quotation marks) refer to what pitches actually were (as determined by the electronic strike-zone indicator).

Each of the following statements is true:

- Considering only the balls, 20,856/240,799 = 8.7 percent were incorrectly called "strikes;" considering only the strikes, 19,511/119,444 = 16.3 percent were erroneously called "balls."
- When umpires called "ball," they were wrong 19,511/239,454 = 8.1 percent of the time, and when they called "strike," they were wrong 20,856/120,789 = 17.3 percent of the time.

The first of these facts looks like a bias favoring batters; the second looks like a bias favoring pitchers. Take your pick.

The moral of this story is that the same set of data often can be presented in more than one way and before unquestionably accepting one presentation, one does well to consider if there might be other reasonable ways of interpreting it as well. How to help people to do that effectively is a challenge to the teaching of critical thinking.

Ploys and Entrapments

Explicit verbal argumentation is only one of many means that are used to influence beliefs and behavior. It is not necessarily either the most pervasive or the most effective means, but because it is explicit it lends itself to analysis and criticism. From the perspective of one who wants to influence other people's beliefs and behavior, these may be good reasons for looking to other methods.

Robert Cialdini (2001a, 2001b) has proposed a classification of human tendencies that are widely exploited, wittingly or otherwise, in getting people to comply with requests. The scheme distinguishes six tendencies: reciprocation, consistency, social validation, liking, authority, and scarcity. *Reciprocation* refers to the feeling of obligation to repay in kind for what one receives (exploited, for example, by organizations that include a free gift in a solicitation for funds). The desire to be *consistent* (or at least to appear to be consistent) in one's behavior can be used to increase the chances that one will follow through on a commitment by getting one to make the commitment public in some fashion. *Social validation* of requested behavior is accomplished by showing (or claiming) that others, like the requestee, have complied with the same request. *Liking* refers to the fact that people find it easier to say yes (and more difficult to say no) to requests that come from friends than to those that come from strangers. *Authority* is exploited when requests are backed by endorsements by knowledgeable people (four out of five doctors recommend) or that are channeled through what appear to be authority figures (celebrities, actors in medical attire). The persuasiveness of *scarcity* (or claims of same – "the supply is limited") reflects the tendency of people to find things to be the more desirable the less abundant they appear to be (if oak trees shed diamonds instead of acorns, who would buy them?).

Even very simple ploys to give arguments, or other types of interaction, a personal touch can have notable effects on behavior. Randy Garner (2005) found, for example, that sticking a Post-it note on a survey packet increased the percentage of recipients who completed and returned the survey. Personalizing the note increased the percentage more than simply attaching the Post-it when the survey was long and time consuming but not when it was short and simple.

Here are a few other ploys that are commonly used to influence people's beliefs or behavior in ways other than explicit argumentation.

- Misleading claims. From *Consumers Digest* in 1998. In bold print below a color picture of an impressive chalet with wrap-around deck in a wooded area: "DORIS NICKERSON, YOU'VE WON THIS FABULOUS VACATION HOME!" Small print elsewhere makes it clear that my wife has not quite yet actually won this fabulous prize, but that if she returns "the winning entry" by a specified date, she will receive a certified letter indicating that she is in the running for this prize. She will also receive a free issue of *Consumers Digest* and the opportunity to subscribe for two years at the price of one.

- Misrepresentation via paraphrase. Restating something that someone has said, but tweaking the wording enough to make it sound outlandish, or at least more extreme than the original statement.
- Playing with words. Sometimes politicians talk about budget cuts as though they were reductions in spending when they are not. A budget is a proposal for spending, but if I prepare a budget for next year that is twice as great as my spending last year, and then reduce the budget by 10 percent, I have reduced the proposed rate of growth, but I have not reduced spending, nor have I proposed to reduce spending.
- Quoting out of context. Quoting, but failing to provide the context in which what is quoted was originally said and that is necessary to reflect the original source's intent. Partially quoting can also convey something other than the source's intent. Sound bites in newscasts provide many examples of the use of this stratagem.

Arguments without Arguments

Sowell (1995) gives several illustrations of what he calls "arguments without arguments" – ways of getting the better of one's opponent in a dispute other than by force of relevant reasons.

- *The "complex" complex:* the stratagem of claiming that the issue in dispute is complex, by which one really means "it is just complex enough that intelligent and compassionate individuals should clearly be on one side, while those on the other side are considered deficient in at least one of these qualities" (p. 90).
- *All or nothing* (already noted): differences in degree are ignored in order to provide the appearance of a forced choice between two alternatives. Sometimes referred to as "false dilemma" or "either-or fallacy," among other things: presentation of a binary choice as though it were forced when it really is not. "Would you rather live in a police state or in anarchy?"

- *Innocuous generalities:* the technique of burying "the specifics of one's policy preferences in a vast generality, so diffuse that no one can effectively oppose it" (p. 93). The claim to be "in favor of change," for example, may be invoked in order to create the impression that anyone who opposes a specific change that is advocated is opposed to change generally.
- *The shifting viewpoint:* attributing some point of view that one wants to promote, not to oneself but to others, e.g., "students everywhere," "advocates," "critics."
- *"Rights" rites:* endowing a group with a "right" that one would like the group to have, without justifying the claim that it should be considered a right, as distinct from a privilege.
- *General proclamations:* pronouncing something inevitable, an inherently untestable assertion.

Camouflage/Obscure Intent

There are very few days that go by on which I do not receive (by mail, email, or phone) offers of special deals on goods or services, invitations to special events (open only to a "select few"), and so on. In that respect, I strongly suspect that I am in the same boat as a large majority of my compatriots. Of course, hawking goods and services is hardly a new phenomenon, nor is the shilling of bogus prizes or promises aimed at relieving unsuspecting targets of some of their legal tender. What is new is the unprecedented access to potential targets that modern communication technology provides. What is of special interest here is the fact that such appeals and offers often obscure or camouflage their intended purpose.

Sometimes when people ask you what you think about X, it is because they are interested in knowing what you think about X; however the question can also be a way of broaching a topic when the real desire is to tell you what you *should* think about X.

Fundraising is sometimes camouflaged as requests for information. Senator Joe Smith urgently requests your input on a number of issues that will provide him the guidance he needs to accurately represent your interest in the congress, and, by the way, along with your answers to his questions, please send a donation to help underwrite his reelection.

Evert Vedung (1986) notes how intentional obscuration can be used to advantage in politics, and gives examples of its use sometimes in the careful wording of resolutions. He contends that a "common political stratagem is balancing options in a misleading way. Political leaders put emphasis on things that actually carry less weight to conceal motives and facts that are of greater importance to them" (p. 361).

Certification: What Does It Signify?

I receive in the mail an invitation to apply for membership in the American College of Forensic Examiners (ACFE), "the world's leading forensic association with over 10,000 members. Association with our eminent society not only brings prestige as a member of a distinguished assembly, but also networking with noted colleagues in various fields of expertise, ..." An enclosed brochure informs me that after acceptance by the ACFE, I can make application for Diplomate Status in any of several specialty boards. Among the noted benefits of such status: formal recognition of excellence and achievement, identification of competence at the highest level, possible career advancement, greater credibility with prospective patients and clients, and so on. The letter and brochure also inform me that if I can reach 100 points on a "petition for waiver of examination," I can receive a diploma without taking an exam. Fifty points are given for having a PhD, fifteen for being an author, coauthor or editor of a book, ten for being an author or coauthor of an article (ten for each such article), and so on. So, it is possible to be an honored diplomate even if one has had no forensic experience whatsoever. As of 1997, the date on my invitation letter, the cost of membership was $100 (one year's annual dues), but for Diplomate Status it was $450 (one-time certification fee of $350 plus one year's dues of $100). Never having been engaged in any forensic examining activities, I did not jump at the chance of joining the ACFE, despite the chance of becoming an honored diplomate on the strength of professional activities having nothing to do with forensics.

This experience raises questions of the pros and cons of certification (and accreditation), and of how to certify the legitimacy of certification processes and organizations. There are many certifying organizations serving a variety of professions. Undoubtedly many of the certified, or accredited, members of those professions are highly qualified to be so, but if the bar for becoming a diplomate is very low, one must wonder what the recognition is worth. (The founding and subsequent history of the ACFE and several related organizations has been told by Radley Balko in the August 31, 2017, edition of the *Washington Post*.)

Misleading (Not Necessarily False) Claims

From Publishers Clearing House Prize Patrol, To Raymond S. Nickerson, in an envelope marked in bold print: "FINAL PRIZE DOCUMENTS." "CONGRATULATIONS! YOU ARE NOW SCHEDULED TO WIN $10,000,000.00 in the Publishers Clearing House Sweepstakes provided you have and return the winning number by the JANUARY 21 contest ending date." In the accompanying personalized letter:

> This is your personal file folder we told you to watch for. After careful consideration of your candidacy, our Contest Administration has approved your name for endorsement as a potential winner of our $10 Million SuperPrize which ends just a few short weeks from now .... We carefully scrutinized names on our list before we finalized who would get this invitation .... Endorsement was given only to those who met our selection criteria. Believe me not everyone on our list was chosen ... be sure to get your Winners Documents back to us by January 21.

Among the material enclosed: a form for signature granting permission to have a live TV announcement of my winning the $10,000,000 prize, should I do so, at my home. "We'd like your permission in advance to broadcast live from your door at [my home]" Also a request to call a specified number to let the Clearing House staff know if I planned not to be home (to receive a phone call) on the day the winner is to be announced.

Enclosed also were three official-looking forms each to be signed and returned: (1) a "Prize Payment Method Selection" on which I am to designate whether I prefer to receive my $10,000,000, should I win it, in certified checks or by electronic transfer, (2) an "Eligibility Confirmation" on which I am to affirm that I am not related to any employee of Publishers Clearing House and that I am willing to have my winning moment broadcast live on TV at the conclusion of the Super Bowl football game, and (3) a "Prize Acceptance Affidavit" on which I am to affirm that I will accept the ten million dollars in prize money if my number is chosen as the winning one. On the third form there are also four places for "order stamps." The packet includes 100 plus labels, each of which identifies a magazine or some other product that can be ordered by affixing it to one of these spots.

The documentation makes it clear that it is not necessary to order anything to enter the contest, but in a letter addressed to "Dear Winner Candidate," a favor is asked.

> If indeed you are our Ten Million Dollar winner, we'll soon be at your door, along with the news crew from your local TV station, to record the winning moment for the entire country to see. The TV folks will ask you "What are you going to do with all that money?" And they'll ask me questions like, "How can you afford to give away all that money?" and "Do most people order when they enter?" While we have had winners who admitted on TV that they hadn't ordered anything when they entered, I'd love to say you don't just enter for the prizes. I'd like to answer, "This winner is a smart customer who takes advantage of our unbeatable deals as well as our Sweepstakes!" As a friend [I am?] and potential multimillionaire [Oh joy!] you understand that the only way we can afford to give away so much money is to sell magazines [Of course] . . . . Won't you please take advantage of your "On the house" or Free Inspection privilege and order something at this time?

[How can I refuse?] The packet contains also registration forms for winning a Range Rover or Jaguar. Submission of either of these forms must be accompanied with an order.

I did not return this document by the January 21 deadline. But not to worry; I received a similar package a few months later with a return deadline of July 31 (although the prize I was scheduled to win this time was only $1,000,000.00).

Since 2007, the United States Mint has issued thirty-nine one-dollar coins each bearing the likeness of a US president, starting in the first year of the program with presidents Washington, Adams, Jefferson, and Madison. The plan was to issue four such coins per year for the succeeding ten years, honoring the now-dead presidents in the order in which they served. The last president to be honored with a one-dollar coin was Ronald Reagan; this was minted, along with coins for presidents Richard Nixon and Gerald Ford, in 2016.

The following advertisement appeared in *Parade Magazine* on January 27, 2008 with the headline: "Handout of new U.S. Gov't Presidential Dollar coins surge as public snaps them up for free." In smaller, but still bold, print below the headline: "Valuable Presidential Golden Dollar coins being given away free with orders for Framed Money Gallery, but frame shop workers under strain of Public rush, impose household limit of 2. Free money: national handout clogging phone lines as people everywhere scramble to beat 72-hour deadline."

The two-page ad features a fuzzy picture of persons, standing in front of a US flag, who could easily be mistaken for Presidents Bill Clinton and George W. Bush. (The small print under the photo mentions "presidential performers" Tim Watters and Brent Mendenhall.) In the foreground there is a pile of what appear to be blocks of gold bullion. The pictured coins also are gold in color, but their composition is not mentioned. The ad promises to deliver four of the presidential coins free of charge when one purchases a "Framed Money Gallery" at the "discounted" price of $28. The offer purported to be good for only seventy-two hours and could be accepted only by calling a "Direct Claim Hotline," phone numbers provided. I did not verify this, but feel confident in assuming that a phone call would have revealed also a handling and shipping fee as well as opportunities to make other stunningly valuable purchases at bargain prices. (I was tempted to call and ask if I could just have the free money, please, and not buy the gallery frame, preferring to keep the money in a strong box. The reader may guess what the answer would have been.) At the time of the offer, one could buy a bag of 100 of the latest presidential coins from the mint for $111.95, i.e., $1.12 per coin.

Indirect Arguments and Devious Claims

Arguments are often stated indirectly and sometimes deviously. An assertion can be both true and misleading. This being so, arguments can be stated in such a way as to lead the reader or listener to draw a conclusion that is not true even though the premises are true. Consider the following advertisements for toothpaste, which are not unlike some often seen on TV.

> In a nationwide survey, dentists were asked which of several leading brands of toothpaste they preferred. More dentists selected Brand X than any of the other brands tested.
>
> In test after test, Brand Y toothpaste has been shown to be effective in preventing tooth decay, when used in a conscientious program of oral hygiene.
>
> In a year-long laboratory test, children who brushed their teeth regularly with Brand Z toothpaste developed fewer cavities than children who brushed with either of the other two leading brands.

Let us assume that all of the ads are factual, that none of them is claiming something that is not true. What could one conclude about the relative merits of the different brands? Not much. The first ad does not tell us which other brands were tested. In fact, as stated, it does not rule out the possibility that several nationwide surveys were conducted (a survey need not be a major undertaking to be "nationwide"), each involving a different subset of "leading brands," and that the one that produced results most favorable to Brand X was the basis for the ad.

The second ad tells us nothing about the relative effectiveness of Brand Y; probably any toothpaste, or simply a wet toothbrush, would be effective "when used in a conscientious program of oral hygiene."

The third ad is also unconvincing. Again, we do not know how many year-long tests were conducted and whether the one reported was selected because of its favorable results (we can be quite sure that no manufacturer is going to report the results from an unfavorable test). We are not assured that the children in all three groups brushed equally often and effectively. And, if one wants to be really cynical, the ad, as stated, leaves open the possibility that the fewer cavities among the children who brushed with Brand Z resulted from there being fewer children in that group!

I do not mean to suggest that all advertising is misleading or even that these particular three ads are. The point is that in these cases, one cannot tell, and in that respect they are not unlike many ads that one sees all the time. What ads do not say is at least as important as what they do say. We tend not to be very good at making effective use of missing information, which, perhaps, is one of the reasons that noninformative advertising can be effective.

The importance of awareness of the stratagems that can be, and are, used in advertising is difficult to overstate. Especially is this true in view of the frequency with which people encounter advertisements in the normal course of events. Susan Koger and Deborah Winter (2010) describe the situation this way. "Today, the most frequent and explicit messages are sales pitches, which use social norms, reference groups, and appeals to egocentric values to sell products and services to consumers. Commercials have increasingly become a ubiquitous part of daily life" (p. 123).

The Slippery Slope

One is said to be on a slippery slope when one is engaging in undesirable behavior that is relatively inconsequential but that can easily lead to undesirable behavior that has significant consequences. The slippery slope argument can be, and has been, used as a bogeyman. That is not to suggest that the argument never carries any weight and that slippery slopes should be of no concern. The point I wish to make is that almost anything can be carried to an unreasonable extreme, but from the fact that too much of X is not good it does not follow that a small or modest amount of X is not good either. Nor is it the case that a little bit of X must invariably lead to an excessive amount of X.

When the slippery slope argument is raised as an objection to going down a certain path a little way, it should be heeded. In some cases, one may decide, on the evidence, that going down the path even a little way does indeed risk the possibility of going farther than one should. One may decide too, however, that going down a little way is precisely the correct thing to do, and that the slope is not as slippery as it has been made out to be.

Fundraising

There are many situations in which stratagems like those described in the foregoing are employed in efforts to influence people's beliefs or behavior. One activity in which the use of such stratagems is highly visible is fundraising. In what follows, I will give examples from two major fundraising contexts: political solicitations and solicitations by charitable organizations.

Political Solicitations

My wife and I have occasionally made a modest contribution to a political party during a congressional or presidential campaign. The stratagems that have been used in the subsequent deluge of mailings (the examples are from several years ago) include: making us members – without our consent – of the Presidential Task Force or Party National Committee (and sending periodic reminders that we have not paid our "Sustaining Membership Dues"); sending a national-committee member card (similar in look to a credit card) and later (this is one of my favorites), when this did not effect a reply, sending a gold "charter member" card with a sugary letter with profuse apologies for any inconvenience receiving the wrong card might have caused and a request to return the enclosed "verification receipt" with whatever contribution we are able to make; sending a survey questionnaire with a request to return it – preferably with a check – to let the party know where the country's "Opinion Leaders" stand on critical issues; sending a personalized and duly signed "Certificate of Appreciation" "for the unique commitment and sacrifice . . .;" . . ..

Flattery and ego-stroking are much in evidence. Making one an "Honoree" – one of only 250 in one's state (at a cost of a $120 contribution, payable in full, with return envelope or in pledged installments). Recognition that places one in an "elite group" of supporters from across the nation. Enclosing a "distinctive Honoree Commission . . . that one will want to display prominently." An Honoree Lapel Pin. Addition of one's name to a "distinguished Founders Wall list" at party headquarters. "As you can expect, with only 250 spots available for [this year's] Honorees, demand for this recognition is immense .... If you cannot participate, please let me know so I may extend this honor to those who are currently on the reserve list."

A letter containing a one-dollar bill, with an explanation for its inclusion: "we have a VERY URGENT situation on our hands and I had to do something to get your attention – FAST." The letter went on for four pages to explain the direness of the situation and was followed with an EMERGENCY DONATON form (with a Member ID number as well as a Reply number) requesting return of the enclosed one-dollar bill along with a substantive donation – or at least return of the one-dollar bill if a donation is not possible.

Pleas from individual senators and congressmen for money to help fund reelection campaigns (one with a "confidential briefing report" enclosed – inasmuch as this report was confidential, I am not at liberty to divulge what was in it).

In the interest of full disclosure, I am a registered Republican and my wife was an Independent. This being the case, most of the preceding, and following, examples of mailings are from Republicans or Republican organizations. I have little doubt, however, that registered Democrats receive comparable solicitations from Democratic sources. Appeals are made without respect to potential contributors' financial situation or cognitive ability to assess claims – often unsubstantiated and sometimes ludicrous – of the consequences of not giving. And the rule seems to be that the more often one gives, the more requests for additional contributions one will receive.

Often solicitations for money are embedded in policy questionnaires or surveys. "What we really want is your opinion on these important issues. But we are desperately in need of any financial help you can give us." And much attention may be given to projecting a sense of urgency and an obligation to respond. An example is a letter with all of the following showing through the transparent envelope face: "Registration #: xx.xx. xxxx. **NOTICE**: This **SURVEY DOCUMENT IS REGISTERED IN YOUR NAME** and *must be accounted for upon completion of this project.* If you choose not to participate in this crucial Republican Senate Leadership Survey, return this Survey Document at once using the postage-paid envelope provided. **OFFICIAL REPUBLICAN PARTY DOCUMENT – DO NOT DESTROY.**" Inside was a four-page questionnaire form, with thirty-six mostly "yes-no" option questions, and – surprise – an opportunity to make a financial contribution to the National Republican Senatorial Committee. With respect to the latter, three options were provided: "**YES!** I want to help . . . I am enclosing my most generous contribution of : ___; **NO.** I do not wish to participate in this vital Republican Senate Leadership Survey. However, I am returning my Survey Document along with a generous contribution . . . ; **NO.** I do not wish to participate in this Survey, but am returning my Survey Document along with a contribution of $11 to help cover the cost of tabulating and redistributing my Survey." The cover letter that came with this survey opens with "Your immediate attention is *required* on a confidential and time-sensitive matter." It references my "vital role in the resurgence of the Republican Party" and tells me that I "have been selected to represent your [my] voting district in the Republican Senate Leadership Survey." It goes on to say that the survey document has been registered in my name only and assigned to me "as a REPRESENTATIVE of ALL REPUBLICANS living in your [my] voting district." (I have never volunteered to be a political representative of anyone.)

A letter from the chairman of the Republican National Committee (RNC) (undated, but sometime during the first term of President Obama) referring to me as a member of "a select group of Republicans who have been chosen to take part in a new CENSUS OF THE REPUBLICAN PARTY" and enclosing an "official GOP CENSUS DOCUMENT . . . assigned and prepared especially for you [me] as a representative of all Republications living in your voting district" [I wonder if there are any registered Republicans in my voting district who did not receive the same letter notifying them that they are "a representative of all Republicans" in the district.] On the third page of the letter:

> Based on your response, the RNC plans to print and mail a REPUBLICAN PARTY CENSUS to 6.2 million of your fellow Republicans so that we can get a statistically reliable sampling of our party. (Professional pollsters generally consider a random sample of a few thousand to produce reliable results.) But at the cost of $0.42 each, our CENSUS OF THE REPUBLICAN PARTY will cost the RNC more than $2.6 million. So along with your completed GOP CENSUS DOCUMENT, won't you please enclose a contribution of $500, $250, $100, $50, $35, or even $25 to the RNC?

The enclosed questionnaire contains twenty-six questions each of which can be answered "Yes," "No," or "Undecided." It contains also a set of

"Special questions for RNC members only," with notification that a "gift today makes you a member in good standing of the RNC."

Although my leanings are Republican (somewhat right of center, I would say), I do not vote straight party line, so I sometimes feel neglected by the fundraisers for the Democrats. Not to worry, I found myself receiving regular appeals, via email, from MoveOn.org, referring to me as a member. To my email noting that I was not aware of ever joining this organization, I received no reply, but the solicitations kept coming.

Solicitations from Charitable Organizations

I want to make it clear here that in noting certain stratagems (a small subset of those that could be noted) that are used in fundraising by charitable organizations, it is not my wish to disparage charities that do good and important work, or to imply that in appealing for donations they invariably use deceptive methods. My intention is merely to note various techniques that are sometimes used in attempts to get people to behave in certain ways in this context. It would be disingenuous to fail to acknowledge that techniques that many charitable organizations use in fundraising are not much different from those used by other organizations for other purposes.

I get a notice that I have been selected as someone who might agree to serve as a volunteer for an upcoming fund drive by a specific charitable organization. My help is "desperately needed." The requested help involves sending a letter to neighbors to "ask their contributions to fight heart disease to help us with our patient assistance and public health education programs." Presumably, the idea behind having people mail requests for donations to one's neighbors is that it is much more difficult for one to say no to a friend or acquaintance than to an unknown solicitor.

The FACTS disclosure on the back of the request reveals that in the preceding fiscal year the organization distributed the funds it raised as follows: 54 percent to fundraising, 10 percent to administration, 6 percent to program services, and 30 percent to public education in conjunction with fundraising appeals. Classifying 30 percent of expenditures as public education in conjunction with fundraising appeals permits reporting that which is classified as fundraising at 54 percent instead of 84 percent (not to mention that a portion of administration may be administration of fundraising activities). What justifies classifying expenditures as public education is inclusion on the back of letters like the one I received such educational admonitions as "Learn emergency heart attack first aid," "Have your emergency phone numbers close to your phone," and so on.

The disclosure statement notes that the cost of this particular solicitation "is charged partly to fundraising and partly to public education." I do not know whether any "public education" is disseminated independently of solicitations for help in fundraising; from the wording of the disclosure statement, I doubt it.

Of course, the letter reminds me of what a serious problem heart disease is: "As you know, heart disease is one of America's leading killers. In fact, as I write to you today, one out of two Americans will eventually be stricken with this dread disease." Presumably, the inference I am supposed to draw is that helping this organization raise money is an effective way to contribute to the solution of this problem.

Additional little touches: A "personal" note on a yellow Post-it: My first name: "I hope we can count on you ...." Signed with association president's first name. On the volunteer reply form: "Please indicate your choice of how you will be participating in this year's Heart Drive and return this form in the enclosed envelope."

My wife receives an oversized envelope with CHECK ENCLOSED in large letters on the front. Inside is a check for $2.25, a letter explaining the mission of the organization and a request for a contribution. Within the letter: "Even though you can certainly cash the $2.25 check I've enclosed, I hope you will return it along with a generous donation ...." In the fine print: "Please be advised that some of the cost of this appeal is regarded by ... as a public education program rather than as a fundraising expense. Most of ...'s public education program efforts are carried out in its direct mail material, such as the one you are now reading."

Some organizations that solicit financial support make a first-time donor a "member" of the organization. Future requests can then appeal to a sense of belonging and loyalty to the group of which one is now a valued member. And requested contributions may be treated as obligations – responsibilities of membership. Sometimes the request is even expressed as a bill for "dues," or a condition for maintaining membership. Often the membership that is bestowed is a "life membership," signifying subtly that the expectation is for support continuing for the rest of one's life. Membership may be hierarchically tiered so one finds oneself a supporting member at the bronze, silver, gold, or platinum level, and in receipt of congratulatory comments appropriate for the level attained. There may be some urging of moving up with a larger contribution; the possibility of moving down is not likely to be noted.

Requests for donations often are accompanied with some tangible "gift" (return address labels, note paper, greeting cards, ...). Presumably the rationale for this is the assumption that acceptance of the gift (typically there is no way to decline or return it) will induce a feeling of obligation to make a contribution. And the ploy appears to work; Cialdini (2001b) notes that "When the Disabled American Veterans organization mails out requests for contributions, the appeal succeeds only about 18 percent of the time. But when the mailing includes a set of free personalized address labels, the success rate almost doubles, to 35 percent" (p. 76).

I receive a letter with "YOUR 2017 STATEMENT IS ENCLOSED" printed prominently on the envelope. I open the envelope to find in it a "Statement of Activity" reporting my "Giving Activity Summary" for the years 2015, 2016, and 2017. I find another envelope on the same day, this one with a note written in faux script on the envelope just above a cellophane window. The note says "I'm worried that this is wrong. Take a look and let me know." The note refers to a "Data File Card" which contains information about the recipient's giving history and is stamped in red with "FILE COPY must be returned." When I open the envelope, I find a letter urging me to make a contribution to the cause. I also note that I have a "member number" though I have no recollection of joining the organization.

I receive a letter with URGENT NOTICE in bold print on the envelope, "DEADLINE" and a date showing through the plastic window and "IMMEDIATE ACTION REQUIRED" on the back of the envelope. The enclosed letter informs me that if I make a gift now, it will be matched by a gift four times as large as mine, but the opportunity to take advantage of this offer will expire soon. The letter is carefully worded and it is not clear whether the money that is intended to multiply my gift will disappear if I do not make one – or whether the entire pledged matching grant will be lost if the quota is not reached.

Another letter, from a different organization, with bold print URGENT NOTICE and, in slightly smaller font, DEADLINE with a date on the front and IMMEDIATE ACTION REQUIRED on the back.

It would be easy – much too easy – to extend this list of examples of stratagems organizations sometimes use to motivate people to contribute to various causes. So far as I know, there is nothing illegal about these and other stratagems that are widely used in fundraising, but there can be little doubt that many of them are misleading and calculated to convince people to do something they otherwise might not be inclined to do.

Obviously, stratagems of the sort noted here work; if they did not, they would not continue to be used. Presumably, some work better than others, but the search for evermore effective techniques is intense. Fundraising is big business. According to Giving USA 2018, Americans gave an estimated $410 billion dollars to charities in 2017.

Again, I want to make it clear that it is not my intention to disparage all efforts by charitable organizations to raise funds by appeals for donations, or to imply that all such organizations use deceptive means to do so. Decisions regarding whether, and/or how much, to contribute in response to specific appeals should be determined not only by one's interest in, and desire to support, the organization's stated purpose(s) and its record of accomplishments – which usually can be discovered by a modest amount of research. Awareness of stratagems that are often used in fundraising should make one more selective, and perhaps more effective, in one's support of charitable organizations.

***

There are many stratagems in addition to those noted here that are commonly used in efforts to influence people's beliefs and behavior, far too many to justify an attempt to list them all. I suspect that production of an exhaustive list would be impossible, not just because it would be so long, but because it is always possible to invent new stratagems.

As noted at the beginning of this chapter, the connotation that is given to stratagems in many references is decidedly negative. And I think it fair to say that the examples of stratagems that have been used as illustrations in the foregoing are predominantly negative. However, the thoughtful reader will realize that real arguments tend to be complex and may be a mix of stratagems in the negative sense, on the one hand and rational strategies on the other.

Why should one want to know about stratagems? There are at least three possible answers to this question: (1) so that one will be able, with this bag of tricks in hand, to get the better of one's opponents in disputes; (2) so that one will recognize stratagems for what they are when they are used by someone else and will be able to defend against them effectively; and (3) so that one will recognize stratagems when one uses them oneself, or is tempted to do so, and will be able to modify one's approach in the interest of making it more logically sound. Hopefully, readers of this book will be motivated most by the third of these reasons, somewhat by the second and rarely by the first.

10
Improving Argumentation

The point was made in Chapter 1 that argumentation and reasoning are closely related concepts and that some writers contend that they are the same thing, or nearly so (Kuhn, 1991; Mercier, 2017; Mercier et al., 2016; Perelman & Olbrechts-Tyteca, 1969). Much of the reasoning we do, it is held, is best described as arguing – debating – with oneself about what to believe, or what to do in specific situations. I find that equivalence easy to accept. Among other implications of it is the idea that teaching argumentation means teaching reasoning, and conversely.

The ability to reason effectively about arguments is an immensely important one in daily life, simply because arguments confront us all more or less continuously. Without the ability to construct and evaluate arguments effectively we would be at a loss to know which of the numerous claims that we encounter daily to accept and which to reject.

Cultivation of the ability to argue persuasively has been recognized as a major goal of education at least since the days of the classical Greeks who made rhetoric – the art of persuasion – an essential aspect of what it means to be educated. Today the term *rhetoric* is sometimes used in a disparaging way to connote arguments without substance, but the art of persuasion is as important as it has ever been.

The Teaching of Higher-Order Cognitive Skills

Interest in the teaching of "higher-order cognitive skills" was, and is, motivated by realization that high school students, even those who plan to go to college often prove to be deficient in the kinds of cognitive skills that effective learning in college courses requires. Much research has focused on the question of the extent to which higher-order thinking skills can be taught. Specific abilities that have been targets of this research include the ability to analyze and evaluate arguments, the ability to exercise good judgment, the ability to estimate, sensitivity to missing information, the ability to deal effectively with uncertainty, to take alternative perspectives, and to engage in counterfactual thinking. Much of this work is reviewed in Nickerson (1986c, 1990, 1991, 1994, 2004). Efforts to teach such skills have had mixed results, but enough successes to warrant continued attempts to develop more effective teaching techniques.

Creative versus Critical Reasoning

A distinction that one frequently encounters in the literature on reasoning is the distinction between creative and critical thinking. As this distinction relates to argumentation, one might say that creative thinking is required for building persuasive arguments that can withstand efforts to show them to be faulty, while critical thinking has to do with argument evaluation – determining how compelling an argument is, what is right or wrong with it, how it might be improved. It seems clear that skill in argumentation must include competence with both types of reasoning, to the extent that they can be separated.

The ability to build and evaluate arguments effectively is immensely important, not only in the study of science and math, but in dealing with the problems encountered in everyday life as well. Moreover, it seems reasonable to assume, or at least hypothesize, that skills that prove to be useful in argument construction and evaluation will be broadly representative of those required by many other cognitively demanding tasks. In other words, ability in argumentation is sufficiently important in its own right to warrant making its development a primary educational objective whether or not what is learned can be expected to generalize; and it is not unreasonable to expect some generalization to occur.

It would be helpful to have a theory of reasoning as it pertains to argumentation. Such a theory would provide not only a general conceptualization of argument, but also a framework for classifying the various types of argument that exist. It would provide conceptual tools to facilitate analyses and a basis for characterizing arguments with respect to such properties as structural complexity and difficulty of evaluation. It would indicate how competency in argumentation might be expected to increase with age and education. And so on.

Although, much of a theoretical nature has been written about reasoning and argumentation, separately or in combination (Blair, 1986; Cohen, 1979; Collins & Michalski, 1989; Dillard & Shen, 2012; Green, 2007; Hahn & Hornikx, 2016; Hoeken, Timmers, & Schellens 2012; O'Keefe, 2017;

Rescher, 1976, 1979; van Eemeren & Grootendorst, 2004), to my knowledge there is no widely accepted theory of how best to teach these subjects.

To be sure, there are taxonomies of thinking skills or intelligence components that should be helpful (Ekstrom et al., 1976; Ennis, 1985; Erstad, 2018; Govier, 1999; Kelly, 2015; Scheffer & Rubenfeld, 2000, 2001; Skyrms, 1975; Sternberg, 1981; Wagemans, 2016, 2019). One or more of these taxonomies – perhaps an amalgam of them – might provide the basis for a conceptual framework on which a theory of reasoning and argumentation could be built, but no theory that is sufficiently widely accepted to guide the development of teaching/learning of reasoning/argumentation yet exists.

Teaching Fallacies

It seems clear from much research that human reasoning can go wrong in a multitude of ways. How best to address the failings that have been identified? One possibility is to teach fallacies explicitly as a means of improving students' reasoning either by decreasing their use of them or by improving their ability to recognize them when they are used by others. As recent examples of the teaching of fallacies, Mercier et al. (2016) cite John Carroll (2012), Irving Copi, Carl Cohen, and Kenneth McMahon (2010) and Christopher DiCarlo (2011).

Mercier et al. (2016) recommend, with some caveats, eschewing the teaching of fallacies. They contend that the approach does not work because the concept of a fallacious argument is too vague and too comprehensive: the line between fallacious and non-fallacious arguments is impossible to draw and many "fallacious" arguments are perfectly acceptable in certain contexts. Moreover, Mercier et al. contend, even if a method could be described for telling the difference between fallacious and non-fallacious arguments, "it is far from clear that people would be able to consistently apply this method to scrutinize their own reasons" (p. 10).

They summarize their position regarding the teaching of fallacies as a means of improving reasoning thus: "the main features of reasoning that one should aim at are those of argument production, not argument evaluation: how to overcome the my-side bias and think of arguments for the other side, and of potential counterarguments to our own arguments" (p. 10). The question of whether teaching fallacies is an effective way to improve argumentation, or critical reasoning more generally, continues to be a subject of debate (Blair, 1995; Finocchiaro, 1981; Govier, 1995;

Hitchcock, 1995; Massey, 1991). The safest, conclusion one can draw from the research that has been done is the unhelpful one that sometimes it works and sometimes it does not.

Reducing Biases

Given the commonness of biases and related problems of reasoning, it is not surprising that considerable attention has been given to whether anything can be done to eliminate them or to reduce their negative effects on reasoning (Camerer & Hogarth, 1999; Evans et al., 1994; Larrick, 2004; Nisbett et al., 1983; Tetlock, 1985). In theory, any technique that is effective in modifying behavior, should be a candidate for modifying biased behavior. Presumably if a bias is a consequence of a cognitive illusion, one way to eliminate or reduce the bias is to convince one that the illusion really is an illusion. This is more easily said than done; many illusions are persistent even when exposed as such by compelling evidence. However, some techniques for modifying behavior do not require that illusions be recognized as such; they simply aim at modifying the behavior.

Attempts to eliminate the effects of biases on reasoning in various contexts – economics (Larrick, Morgan, & Nisbett, 1990), forensics (Williams, 1992), medicine (Croskerry, 2003), intelligence analysis (Fischhoff & Chauvin, 2011), politics (Lockwood, 2016), among others – have had mixed results. Evidence shows that many biases are remarkably robust. It is difficult to eliminate them or to mitigate their negative effects. Evidential discrediting, or even notice of retraction, of a scientific article has proved to be insufficient to destroy confidence in the article's claims (Davies, 1997). Misinformation in memory can continue to be utilized long after it has been recognized as false (Seifert, 2002). The same may be said of disinformation, which differs from misinformation by its perpetrator intentionally being deceptive (Lewandowsky et al., 2012).

The tendency for beliefs to linger even after having been discredited is widely known and is sometimes referred to as *belief perseverance* or *persistence* (Anderson, 1995; Nestler, 2010; Thorson, 2016). Brian Southwell, Emile Thorson, and Lara Sheble (2017) argue that misinformation (and presumably disinformation as well) is problematic in three ways: "people who encounter misinformation tend to believe it, at least initially. Secondly, media systems often do not block or censor many types of misinformation before it appears in content available to large audiences. Thirdly, countering misinformation once it has enjoyed wide exposure can be a resource-intensive effort" (p. 373).

On the other hand, the literature contains enough success – or partial-success – stories to demonstrate that debiasing is possible and that the search for more effective techniques is not doomed to failure. Training with respect to certain aspects of logic (e.g., the difference between logical necessity and possibility) has sometimes increased people's accuracy (calibration) in evaluating their own performance on judgment tasks (Turner & Thompson, 2009). Training with interactive computer games and videos aimed at making people aware of their biases has also sometimes proved to be effective in reducing them in decision-making contexts (Fischhoff, 1982; Morewedge, 2015; Morewedge et al., 2015; Sellier, Scopelliti, & Morewedge, 2019). Training in statistics has improved people's ability to deal with probabilities generally (Fong, Krantz, & Nisbett, 1986). Large-scale efforts to improve reasoning have sometimes produced positive, if modest, results (Campbell & Burchinal, 2008; Campbell & Ramey, 1994, 1995; Campbell et al., 2002; Clarke & Campbell, 1998; Herrnstein et al., 1986; Nickerson, 2020).

Instructions stressing the importance of analyzing the logic of arguments can weaken the effects of belief bias (Newstead et al., 1992). Having people attempt to explain in writing the strength of an argument has also proved to be effective in decreasing or eliminating belief bias in some cases, when, under the same conditions, rating arguments did not have the same effect (Neilens, Handley, & Newstead, 2009). Getting people to consider alternatives to expected outcomes of decisions (Anderson, 1982; Anderson & Sechler, 1986; Hirt & Markman, 1995; Lord, Lepper, & Preston, 1984) or to look at things from perspectives other than, perhaps opposite to, their own (Galinsky & Ku, 2004; Galinsky & Moskowitz, 2000; Mussweiler, Strack, & Pfeiffer, 2000) has been effective in some cases. The tendency of people to be overconfident of the accuracy of their opinions has sometimes been reduced by having them give reasons for and against those opinions (Arkes et al., 1988).

Explicitly holding people accountable for decisions they make has improved the quality of decisions in some instances (Lerner & Tetlock, 1999). Listing reasons why an anchor is inappropriate can eliminate or reduce the typical anchor effect (Mussweiler et al., 2000). Use of statistical, or other decision-making, models can sometimes improve decisions made by unassisted humans (Dawes & Corrigan, 1974; Dawes, Faust, & Meehl, 1989; Fong et al., 1986). Giving people an incentive to be accurate may increase the accuracy with which they estimate the probabilities of events of different degrees of desirability (Bar-Hillel & Budescu, 1995). Other techniques have been tried and have sometimes worked, at least to decrease the negative effects of biases, if not to eliminate them altogether (Dube-Rioux and Russo, 1988).

Sometimes training in debiasing techniques has proved to be effective in laboratory settings but the effectiveness has failed to transfer to real-life situations, or it has not been checked there (Fischoff, 1982; Kahneman & Egan, 2011; Milkman, Chugh, & Bazerman, 2009). Anne-Laure Sellier et al. (2019) addressed this question and demonstrated the possibility of obtaining transfer of effectiveness of one-shot training aimed to reduce the effects of confirmation bias in their decision-making. They gave a single training session to over 300 participants on lab-type problems (e.g., the Wason selection task) designed to illustrate the importance of looking for evidence against a hypothesis when attempting to determine if the hypothesis is correct. Several days later, without warning or reference to their training, they had the same participants attempt to solve real-world business cases. They found that the participants who had had the training session showed less confirmation bias on the business cases than did those who did not have the training; the former used more disconfirming arguments and fewer confirming arguments than the latter. Sellier et al. saw the absence of any explicit connection between the training session and business cases as a noteworthy aspect of the study. Their conclusion: "The results provide promising evidence that debiasing training effects transfer to field settings and can improve consequential decisions in professional and private life" (p. 2). Sellier et al. noted too the possibility that "games may be uniquely engaging training interventions" (p. 18).

Among the approaches that have been used in efforts to decrease the effect of the confirmation bias on decision-making is one known as the Analysis of Competing Hypotheses (ACH) approach (Hallihan, Cheong, & Shu, 2012). The method requires users to rate data with respect to their relevance to a decision that is to be made and their diagnostic value. Hallihan et al. found that the procedure can be effective in decreasing the effect of confirmation bias, at least in some cases. The ACH approach was used by Thomas Nelius et al. (2019) with mixed results. Reflecting on their performance on an initial task designed to teach them something about how biases work increased participants' motivation to learn more about biases, but it did not eliminate the effects of the confirmation bias on a subsequent task.

Evaluating debiasing techniques is complicated by the fact that people often resist adopting them even if they have been shown to be effective. Richard Larrick (2004) reminds us of this and, citing Arkes (2003) and Kleinmuntz (1990), he suggests some reasons for the resistance:

> They do not want to be told that they have been "doing it wrong" all these years. They do not want to relinquish control over a decision process. And, perhaps most importantly, they fail to understand the benefits of many debiasing techniques relative to their own abilities, not just because they are overconfident, but because the techniques themselves are alien and complex, and the benefits are noisy, delayed, or small (p. 331).

Larrick notes, too, the relative paucity of attempts to determine what makes debiasing techniques acceptable to people who could benefit from using them, and on how such techniques are adopted and diffused.

In sum, many, if not most, biases and closely related problems tend to be remarkably persistent, even when concerted efforts are made to eliminate them, but the successes, or partial successes, that have been realized should incentivize the search for more effective and palatable debiasing techniques and justify the hope that such can be found. However, the search for such techniques should be done bearing in mind the claim by Gigerenzer and Brighton (2009), among others, that many of the biases and other reasoning foibles that have been identified may actually be effective strategies for navigating the challenges of everyday life in certain contexts.

Collaborative Learning

As a means of improving peoples' reasoning skills, Mercier et al. (2016) recommend motivating them to engage more in argumentation and creating conditions in which they feel free (encouraged) to do so. Discussion and debate in small groups with initially diverse opinions on issues of interest are promoted as an effective approach to teaching/learning better reasoning. What is learned in small-group discussions and debates – e.g., how to find/construct counterexamples – presumably can be applied to one's solitary thinking.

Collaborative airing of arguments and counterarguments should, Mercier et al. (2016) contend, produce better arguments.

> When people solve problems together, cogent argument evaluation – paired with the ability to produce arguments to defend one's side – should lead to good outcomes: The best arguments should carry the day and discussion should allow an improvement in the members' answers. The exchange of arguments and counterarguments should help people realize the strength of arguments, even when these arguments challenge their views (p. 7).

As evidence that this expectation is plausible, Mercier et al. cite Nicolas Claidiére, Emmanuel Trouche, and Mercier (submitted), Patrick Laughlin

(2011), David Moshman and Molly Geil (1998), and Trouche, Emmanuel Sander, and Mercier (2014). They contend too that groups can sometimes converge on solutions to problems that are better than those produced by any of the group's members (Mellers, et al., 2014). Studies showing that discussion about a topic can lead to improvement in arguments produced by the discussants include those of Deanna Kuhn and Amanda Crowell (2011), Kuhn, Victoria Shaw, and Mark Felton (1997), E. Michael Nussbaum and Carol Anne Kardash (2005), Lauren Resnick, Christa Asterhan, and Sherice Clarke (2013), and Amaras Vinokur and Eugene Burstein (1974). Other recent studies providing evidence of the effectiveness of collaborative reasoning and problem solving include Julia Minson, Varda Liberman, and Lee Ross (2011), Tamar Kugler, Edgar Kausel, and Martin Kocher (2012), and Christin Schulze and Ben Newell (2016).

Mercier et al. (2016) contend that for argumentative groups to be effective they must satisfy certain criteria. They should be neither too small nor too large (they suggest five as a good number of members), members should represent a diversity of opinions re the issue(s) of concern, members must feel free to express their opinions, and they must respect the opinions of others. Mercier et al. stress the importance of diversity of opinions among participants in an argument group. "The dependency of performance improvements on genuine debate, which requires a measure of disagreement, is expected by the argumentative theory of reasoning. When people agree with one another, they are not very critical of one another's arguments, and they do not offer arguments that challenge the consensus" (p. 8).

Although the emphasis is on argumentation within diverse groups as a means of attempting to arrive at a consensus, one can imagine that even if the members of a group all share the same opinion to begin with, there could be something to be gained from argumentation – say a better understanding of the issue of interest and of reasons for the shared opinion about it. However, one can be reasonably sure that groups lacking people who sincerely disagree with prevailing opinions are unlikely to give possible counterarguments the attention they deserve.

Mercier et al. (2015) claim that people – experts and nonexperts alike – underestimate the benefits of argumentation for reasoning. They review data from several studies that show that groups of three to five people working collaboratively on the well-known Wason (1966) selection task yield success rates of better than 65 percent as compared with success rates of about 15 percent by people attempting to solve the problem on their own. In a series of experiments in which participants estimated the percentage of people working alone or in small groups would solve the selection task, Mercier et al. (2015) found that participants, including psychologists who were familiar with the problem, underestimated the benefits of interacting (arguing) with others in performing the task.

I have devoted considerable space to the work of Mercier and colleagues on the possibility of improving people's argumentative skills via interaction among people with differences of opinion on issues of interest in small-group settings, because it is a well-documented set of studies that provide much food for thought regarding one way in which argumentation may be improved. Moreover, whether one finds the case for the approach persuasive, or not, its existence invites comparison with alternative approaches that might be used in place of, or in conjunction with, this one.

The Basics of Formal Logic

The teaching of formal logic as a normative or prescriptive model of deductive thought is a tradition that goes back as far as institutionalized education and there are numerous books on the subject, aimed primarily at college and, to a lesser degree, high school students. However, the teaching of formal logic does not receive the emphasis today that it once did. Some argue that it has little to do with the way people actually think (Cheng & Holyoak, 1985; Evans, 1989). Despite this, I lean toward believing that neglecting formal logic in secondary and post-secondary education is a bad idea; and there is some empirical evidence to support this view (Dickstein, 1975; Rips & Conrad, 1983).

The assumption is made here that some knowledge of logic, while perhaps not a necessary, and certainly not a sufficient, cause of competence in everyday argumentation, is probably some – and possibly considerable – help; few, if any, researchers would claim that it hurts. The insufficiency of knowledge of logic to guarantee competence in argument evaluation is not a controversial issue, however, because most of the arguments one encounters in everyday life are neither exclusively deductive nor expressed in a canonical logical form. Evaluation of these arguments requires much more than the ability to distinguish between valid and invalid syllogisms.

Principles of Informal Reasoning

The explicit teaching of informal reasoning and, more precisely, reasoning with informal argumentation, is not an old established tradition. There are, however, a number of books that deal with this subject (Cavender &

Kahane, 2013; Crews-Anderson, 2007; Damer, 1980; Fisher, 1988; Larson, Hodge, & Perrin, 2003; Nickerson, 2004; Ruggiero, 1981; Scriven, 1976; Walton, Reed, & Macagno, 2008). These typically focus on various ways in which informal reasoning is, or appears to be, ineffective or wrong. Lauren Resnick (1986) points out that the work of philosophers in this area, while featuring a new emphasis on informal logic, still reflects a normative or prescriptive stance, whereas psychologists have tended to be more inclined to study how people who are judged to be good thinkers think and then to try to teach these techniques to others. There is, however, no well-developed and clearly articulated theory, either descriptive or prescriptive, of informal reasoning that is espoused by any major subset of either the philosophers or psychologists whose research focuses on human thought.

One motivation for the recent focus on informal reasoning is the assumption that formal deductive reasoning plays a relatively small role in everyday life; some (e.g., Toulmin, 1958) hold that even when it is relevant, it is too difficult to apply to the kinds of arguments one tends to encounter in daily life to be of much practical use.

Informal or *inductive* arguments are considerably more difficult to evaluate than formal deductive ones inasmuch as they can take any of countless forms and there are no well-known rules for judging them. Indeed, it is not clear that the concept of validity is appropriately applied to them. In general terms, an informal argument may be described as a collection of assertions intended to support another assertion (conclusion). Seldom does such an argument demonstrate the truth of its conclusion beyond any doubt. Typically, the most one can reasonably hope for from such an argument is to make its conclusion more believable than it otherwise might be.

As noted in Chapter 3, to evaluate informal arguments, one must, at least, recognize the claims that are made, decide how much support each of these claims, if true, gives to the conclusion the argument is intended to support, decide whether to accept the claims as true, and somehow aggregate the results of these considerations into an overall assessment of the persuasiveness of the argument as a whole. In other words, evaluation of informal arguments of any substance and complexity involves, at least implicitly, the following components: analysis, judgments of relevance and weight, judgments of truth or falsity, and aggregation or synthesis.

A Perspective

In view of what has been said about argumentation in this book, what should the goals of the teaching of argumentation, or reasoning, more generally be? The following, in no particular order, are among the items (concepts, principles, facts) that, in my view, an individual who is competent in argumentation should know or understand (adapted from Nickerson, 1986a).

- the importance, but limitations, of definitions.
- the difference between logical validity and empirical truth.
- that an argument need not be logically valid to be persuasive.
- what constitutes a contradiction.
- what is required to disprove a universal statement.
- how to explicate tacit assumptions underlying an argument.
- how to design tests of hypotheses.
- the difference between a correlational relationship and a cause-effect relationship.
- the difference between corroborating evidence and proof.
- the difference between necessary and sufficient conditions.
- the difference between explanation and rationalization.
- the limitations of argument by analogy.
- the difference between A conditional on B and B conditional on A.
- that we all have biases.
- what some of the more troublesome biases and other common reasoning problems are.
- how to apply various debiasing techniques.
- the importance of motivation to sound reasoning.
- the difference between exploratory search and confirmatory search.
- the difference between truth-seeking and case making.
- what counterarguments are and the role they can play in argument evaluation.
- how to judge the persuasiveness of an argument and counterarguments that could be made.
- the importance of the ability to take perspectives that differ from one's own.
- that changing one's mind in response to evidence that one should is no great sin.

The list could easily be extended.

In Chapter 1, a distinction was made between two purposes of argumentation – seeking consensus and winning disputes. Richard Paul (1986) makes essentially the same distinction, the nub of which, he says, is

> that it is possible to develop extensive skills in argument analysis and construction without ever seriously applying those skills in a self-critical way to one's own deepest beliefs, values, and convictions. In fact, it is possible to use the traditional argumentative skills as tools for rationalization and self-deception. It is possible to use them in a selective way to attack unsympathetically the views of those with whom we disagree and to defend un-self-critically our own views. A person who can think critically only in this restricted sense has little hope of becoming a genuinely open- or fair-minded person, little hope, in other words, of becoming a rational person (p. 379).

A similar distinction, noted in Chapter 2, that I find especially useful differentiates reasoning as a process of coming to conclusions (exploratory or investigative reasoning) from reasoning as justification of conclusions already drawn (justificatory or confirmative reasoning). Making people aware of this distinction and able to apply it effectively must be among the more important goals of the teaching of argumentation.

There can be little doubt that it is easier to teach people to win disputes than to teach them to be self-critical. People generally appear to be naturally highly motivated to try to win disputes, so are likely to have a keen interest in learning strategies or stratagems for doing that. In contrast, there is little reason to assume that people are naturally inclined to be self-critical. The evidence supports a contrary conclusion.

Not surprisingly, the proliferation of interactive games and challenges available on the Internet has included a rash of "brain-training" programs intended – and claimed – to improve one's thinking in a variety of ways. On the basis of examination of many of these programs and the claims that have been made in their favor, Walter Boot (2019) concluded "my optimistic answer to the question of whether brain training is worth it would be 'we just don't know.' But the actual answer may very well be 'no'." The most important lesson from the literature, he contends, is this: "If you want to improve your performance on a task that's important to you, practice that task. Playing brain games may only make you better at playing brain games."

In my opinion, the larger truth that Boot's conclusion – as well as those of many other researchers – supports is that there is no quick fix to the fallacies, biases, and other foibles that characterize much of human reasoning and argumentation. There are many books that are intended to help one to become a more effective thinker (Bartlett, 1958; Beardsley, 1975; Carroll, 2012; Dimnet, 1928; Flesch, 1951; Moore & Parker, 1993; Nickerson, 1986b; Ruggiero, 1984; Templin & McCracken, 1927;

Thouless, 1950). They can be helpful, but a quick reading of one or two of them is unlikely to make one an effective reasoner. The ability to reason well and effectively requires years of study and practice. To do it habitually also requires a long-term commitment and determination.

Some Grandfatherly Advice

Arguments (disputes) seldom change minds, but they can sour friendships and cordial relationships. The desire to know the truth is too often trumped by the desire to be proved right.

Thomas Jefferson understood this well. In a far-ranging letter, written to his grandson Thomas Jefferson Randolf (Jefferson, 2018), he shared some reflections regarding what he had learned from an active life, which had included stints as Secretary of State, vice president and president of the United States. With respect to "prudential rules for our government in society," he had this to say: "I must not omit the important one of never entering into dispute or argument with another. I never saw an instance of one of two disputants convincing the other by argument. I have seen many, on their getting warm, becoming rude, and shooting one another" (Jefferson, 2018, p. 170). Jefferson described Benjamin Franklin as "the most amiable of men in society," and justified this description with the observation that Franklin lived by the rule of never contradicting anybody.

In the same letter, Jefferson distinguished two major classes of disputants:

> The first is of young students, just entered the threshold of science, with a first view of its outlines, not yet filled up with the details and modifications which a further progress would bring to their knowledge. The other consists of the ill-tempered & rude men in society, who have taken up a passion for politics. (Good humor and politeness never introduce into mixed society, a question on which they foresee there will be a difference of opinion.) From both of those classes of disputants, my dear Jefferson, keep aloof, as you would from the infected subjects of yellow fever or pestilence. Consider yourself, when with them, as among the patients of Bedlam, needing medical more than moral counsel. Be a listener only, keep within yourself, and endeavor to establish with yourself the habit of silence, especially on politics. In the fevered state of our country, no good can ever result from any attempt to set one of these fiery zealots to rights, either in fact or principle. They are determined as to the facts they will believe, and the opinions on which they will act. Get by them, therefore, as you would by an angry bull; it is not for a man of sense to dispute the road with such an animal (p. 170).

Jefferson warned his grandson that he would be more exposed to the "animals" of which he had been speaking "shaking their horns" at him simply because of the familial connection. The acrimonious language in which the warning was delivered is a cogent reminder that political beliefs and attitudes were every bit as partisan and charged with emotion in the early days of the republic as they are today.

A Metaphor

Trial by jury relates to the subject of this book in several ways, one of which I wish to highlight, namely that it can serve as a metaphor for reasoning as arguing with oneself – assuming the roles of fact producer (witness), lawyer (both sides), judge, and jury. As fact producer or witness, one's task is to attempt to bring to light – in an unbiased way – facts that are germane to the conclusion one is considering drawing. In playing attorney – both for the prosecution and for the defense – one imagines the case that can be made from each perspective. As judge and/or jury, one attempts to weigh the evidence that has been presented and the inferences that have been made and to arrive at a warranted conclusion.

The judicial system, as a whole, is fallible. There is no guarantee justice will prevail in any particular trial. In this respect too, the system serves as a metaphor for argumentation with oneself, inasmuch as there is no process that one may follow that will ensure that all the conclusions one draws will be correct. So just as the judicial system is designed to make it more difficult to convict an innocent person than to exonerate a guilty one, it is well to bear in mind that some wrong conclusions are more acceptable – less detrimental – than others.

Final Thought

The December 2018, issue of *Scientific American* contained a special section featuring the "Top 10 emerging technologies of 2018," edited by Mariette DiChristina and Bernard S. Meyerson (2018). Number four on the list, written by Meyerson, was "Bots that argue and instruct" (p. 34). Meyerson notes:

> technologies are now being developed to allow the next generation of such systems [systems that can learn and converse to a limited extent] to absorb and organize unstructured data (raw text, video, pictures, audio, e-mails,

> and so on) from myriad sources and then autonomously compose cogent advice – or debate an opponent on a subject they have never been trained to handle (p. 34).

It will be interesting to see how people's ability to argue is affected by the appearance, and progression, of such systems. The attention that argumentation has been, and is, receiving from artificial intelligence researchers makes it unlikely that we will have to wait very long to find out (Bench-Capon & Dunne, 2007; Rahwan & Simari, 2009).

APPENDIX A

Fallacies Listed by Fearnside and Holther (1959)

1. **Faulty generalizations.** Treating general statements as though they pertain to all members of a category when, in fact, they do not: "Engineering students study hard" interpreted as "All engineering students study hard."
2. **Faulty causal generalizations.** Special case of 1. If X is known to often be the cause of Y, the problem comes when it is assumed always to be the cause of Y.
3. **Assuming the cause: "Post hoc reasoning."** Assuming that because Y always follows X, X is the cause of Y.
4. **Faulty analogy.** Assuming that because X and Y are alike with respect to properties a, b, and c, they must be alike with respect to d, as well.
5. **Composition and division.** Composition: Assuming that what holds for every member of a class holds for the class as a whole. Division: Assuming that what holds for a class holds for every member of that class.
6. **The all-or-nothing mistake.** In an either-or discussion, failure to recognize that it might be neither-nor – that there may be a middle ground.
7. **The false dilemma.** Similar to the all-or-nothing mistake, but when both of the presumed alternatives are undesirable.
8. **Faulty classification.** Taking a classification scheme to be exhaustive or exclusive when it is not.
9. **Misconceptions about classification.** Reification: Assuming that because there is a name, what is named must exist – "thing-ization." Relativism: Everything is relative; everyone is entitled to his/her opinion, independently of evidence. "If the present book can be said to have a general thesis, it is that nobody is entitled to an irresponsible opinion on anything" (p. 53).

10. **Unnecessary vagueness.** In classificatory schemes divisions between classes often are insufficiently precise to preclude problems with marginal cases.
11. **Overprecision.** The opposite of unnecessary vagueness; rejecting serviceable concepts (baldness) "for the sole reason that there are cases that are marginal or doubtful" (p. 66). "Bald" is a useful concept even though in marginal cases whether it is descriptive of specific heads might be debatable.
12. **Word magic.** Similar to reification: "the existence of a name does not guarantee the existence of any corresponding entity in the situation .... The name, like a spell, conjures an entity into being" (p. 68).
13. **Emotive language.** Often the same fact can be expressed in either bland or emotive (approving or disparaging) terms.
14. **Ceremony or setting.** "The physical circumstances forming the background of an argument often affect the notice the argument gains" (p. 82).
15. **Appeal to authority.** Appealing to authority is reasonable and often very helpful, but an authority has to satisfy certain rules to be reliable.
16. **Appeal to tradition or faith.** Can be appropriate, but not always is. A principle that was appropriate at one time may not be at a later time.
17. **Impressing by large numbers.** Because many people believe it does not make it true; because many people do it does not make it right.
18. **Popular passions.** Playing to popular likes and dislikes.
19. **Damning the origin.** Rejecting an argument on account of its undesirable source.
20. **Personal attacks.** Casting doubt on a claim or argument by attacking the character of its originator.
21. **Forestalling disagreement.** "Forestalling disagreement ranges from mild devices calculated to make agreement easy ('Of course we all believe . . . ') to highly prejudicial assertions to intimidate opposition ('Only a muddled headed person would suggest . . .'). They are characteristically question begging" (p. 101).
22. **Creating misgivings.** Allegations of objectionable (illegal, immoral) behavior, whether true or false, can produce misgivings that last long after the specific allegations have been forgotten.
23. **Self-righteousness.** "[T]he error of confusing self-interest or good intentions with justice and truth" (p. 105).

24. **Finding the "good" reason.** "[T]he process of selecting a fact which is creditable, or, at least, not discreditable, and proposing it as the explanation for one's actions" (p. 106).
25. **Wishful thinking.** Building unreasonable expectations, risking disappointment.
26. **Special pleading.** "One-sided pleading becomes special pleading when you 'have it both ways'" (p. 108); ignoring or twisting facts to one's own advantage.
27. **Lip service.** Publicly endorsing a principle in which one privately does not believe.
28. **Apriorism.** "Closing one's eyes to evidence alleged against something one believes in . . . frequently described as an attempt to deduce facts from principles, instead of inducing principles from facts" (p. 111).
29. **Personification.** Attribution of human traits (motivation, purpose) to nature.
30. **Cultural bias.** Seeing the world through the lens of one's own culture; assuming that what one sees is the way things are.
31. **The gambler's mistake.** Expectations based on a faulty understanding of probability theory, for example, belief that the probability the next toss of a coin will come up tails is greater following a run of ten heads than it is following a run of ten tails.
32. **Humor and ridicule.** Inserting irrelevant humor into an argument to influence the argument's outcome.
33. **Demand for special consideration.** Playing to an audience's good will, empathy, pity to make it more receptive of one's argument.
34. **Clamorous insistence on irrelevancies.** Hiding the weakness of an argument by insistently changing the focus to an irrelevant side issue.
35. **Pointing to another wrong.** Countering an accusation of wrongdoing by accusing the accuser of wrongdoing of equal or greater magnitude.
36. **The wicked alternative.** Defending a position, *A*, by denouncing its opposite, *not-A*; legitimate only if *not-A* really is the opposite of *A*.
37. **Nothing but objections.** When one has objections to all the possible courses of action, one may fail to act without taking into account the consequences that the failure to act may have.
38. **Impossible conditions.** Making action contingent on conditions that, for practical reasons, cannot be realized; for example, objection to a proposal to decrease poverty: It won't work until people become much more magnanimous than they now are.

39. **Abandonment of discussion.** Refusal to participate in a substantive argument, as opposed to "claiming that discussion is unnecessary, irrelevant, indecent, immoral, unpatriotic, and the like" (p. 132).
40. **The undistributed middle term.** Violation of a basic rule of propositional logic.
41. **Suppressed quantification.** Interpreting "*Xs are Ys*" as "*All Xs are Ys*" when "*Some Xs are Ys*" is true. The ambiguous "*Xs are Ys*" may be used in the hope that it will be interpreted as "*All Xs are Ys,*" preserving the claimant's ability to truthfully deny having said "*All Xs are Ys.*"
42. **False conversion of propositions.** People often convert propositions by interchanging antecedents and consequents, and in other ways, that do not preserve truth value.
43. **Non sequitur.** Treating an assertion as though it follows logically from what precedes it when it does not.
44. **Trouble with conditionals and alternatives.** Treating conditional (*If A then C*) assertions as equivalent to biconditional (*If, and only if, A, then C*) assertions.
45. **Ambiguous terms.** Treating a word that has different meanings in different contexts as though it had the same meaning in both contexts. *If* A_1 *then C;* A_2*; therefore, C* is a valid argument if, and only if, A_1 and A_2 have precisely the same meaning.
46. **Amphibole.** Taking advantage of ambiguity in sentence structure; structuring assertions so that it is not clear whether a particular word is to be treated as an assertion's subject or its predicate.
47. **Ambiguous accent.** The same assertion can take on different meanings depending on the use of accent, stress, inflection. "A malicious person finds endless opportunities for giving false impressions, while staying within the literal truth, by subtle shifts of accent in reporting the words of others" (p. 163).
48. **Ambiguous punctuation and word order.** "The order of modifiers and the placing of punctuation marks can considerably affect the sense of what is said" (p. 164).
49. **Circular definitions and question begging.** "By 'circular definition' is meant a definition which attempts to resolve a point at issue by defining a term so as to preempt the point" (p. 165), and circular definitions are cases of question begging.

50. **Misuse of etymology.** Making unjustified inferences from the etymology of words, so as to change the meaning of an assertion from its intended one.
51. **Idiosyncratic language.** "[T]he sort of paradoxical talk that attempts to sound profound . . . a sort of personal or private charging of words with meanings different from, and sometimes opposite to, the usual range of the words in their conventional contexts" (p. 170).

APPENDIX B

Schopenhauer's Art of Controversy

Schopenhauer's *Art of Controversy* was translated and published posthumously in 1896 by T. Bailey Saunders. It is, among other things, a listing of thirty-eight stratagems that people use in efforts to win arguments. Possibly the list, or at least a subset of the items on it, was offered somewhat tongue in cheek. However, the fact that something is said in jest does not make it false; and whatever Schopenhauer's intentions in offering his list, I venture the guess that readers will recognize more than a few of the tricks that are listed, having encountered them, or used them, in disputes.

Before getting to his list, Schopenhauer makes some observations about human nature – of which he did not have a high regard – as it influences the way people think and interact:

- [H]uman nature is such that if A and B are engaged in thinking in common, and are communicating their opinions to one another on any subject, so long as it is not a mere fact of history, and A perceives that B's thoughts on one and the same subject are not the same as his own, he does not begin by revising his process of thinking, so as to discover any mistake which he may have made, but he assumes that the mistake has occurred in B's (p. 3).
- If human nature were not base, but thoroughly honorable, we should in every debate have no other aim than the discovery of truth; we should not in the least care whether the truth proved to be in favor of the opinion which we had begun by expressing, or of the opinion of our adversary. That we should regard as a matter of no moment, or at any rate, of very secondary consequence; but as things are, it is the main concern. Our innate vanity, which is particularly sensitive in reference to our intellectual powers, will not suffer us to allow that our first position was wrong and our adversary's right (p. 4).

Schopenhauer contends that much of the problem stems from our tendency to speak before thinking. When we do that, and later discover that what we said was wrong, we are not inclined to acknowledge our mistake but rather to defend what we said, despite realizing that it was wrong. Vanity, he argues, trumps interest in the truth; "a disputant fights not for truth, but for his proposition" (p. 5).

Schopenhauer makes a distinction between logic and dialectic; the former, in his view, has to do with truth, whereas the latter has to do with winning arguments. "It [dialectic] is the art of intellectual fencing used for the purpose of getting the best of it in a dispute" (p. 10).

Stratagems noted by Schopenhauer follow (paraphrased and in abbreviated form). Some of them Schopenhauer credits to Aristotle. I may have taken undue liberties in paraphrasing in some cases when Schopenhauer's intent was less than crystal clear to me; the reader is encouraged to consult Schopenhauer's original list. Not surprisingly, some of the stratagems on Schopenhauer's list, or something close to them have been noted in the foregoing; they bare repeating here.

1. The *extension*. Interpreting an opponent's proposition as broadly as possible, while interpreting one's own as narrowly as possible. The rationale is that more sweeping statements are more vulnerable to objections.
2. The *homonymy*. Refuting an opponent's proposition by giving its words meanings other than those intended by the utterer (e.g., refuting argument by using homonyms of intended words in lieu of the intended words).
3. Take a proposition that pertains to a particular matter and generalize it to make it pertain to more than the utterer intended. Schopenhauer notes that these three tricks are "of a kindred character" in that in each case "something different is attacked from what was asserted" (p. 18).
4. Get your opponent to agree to the premises of a conclusion you want to make, but do so in a way (e.g., by presenting them in random order and mixed in with other matter) that does not reveal the conclusion you want to make until he/she has agreed to them.
5. To prove a proposition to be true (to your opponent's satisfaction), use supporting propositions that are false but your opponent believes are true.
6. Beg the question by postulating what has to be proved (e.g., by making a general claim that encompasses the particular proposition to be proved – supporting the claim that medicine is uncertain by asserting that all knowledge is uncertain).

7. Ask many wide-ranging questions rapidly, "so as to hide what you want to get admitted, and ... quickly propound the argument resulting from the admissions" (p. 20). Schopenhauer surmises that this stratagem will work well with those who are "slow of understanding" because they will not follow the argument well enough to notice any mistakes in it.
8. Make your opponent angry, because anger impairs one's judgment.
9. Put questions in an order different from that which the conclusion you want to draw requires.
10. If your opponent always answers negatively to your questions, transpose them so as to mask your intentions.
11. If your opponent grants you the particulars that support your intended conclusion, refrain from asking him directly whether he accepts that conclusion; rather simply present it as an admitted fact.
12. When the same entity is called by different names reflecting different attitudes about it (e.g., "zeal" – "fanaticism"), use the name that best supports your perspective (substituting your preferred word for the one used by your opponent).
13. Give an opponent the choice between your proposition and a counterproposition (as if these were the only two possibilities), making the difference sharp and the desired conclusion reasonable by contrast.
14. When your opponent answers questions in a way that does not support the conclusion you want, simply pretend that they do and declare the conclusion to be true "in a tone of triumph. If your opponent is shy or stupid, and you yourself possess a great deal of impudence and a good voice, the trick may easily succeed" (p.23).
15. If you have trouble proving a proposition, submit another (true, but not palpably so) proposition as though you intended to use it to establish the proof of your original proposition. If your opponent accepts it, declare your original proposition proved; if he rejects it, demonstrate its proof and show how absurd your opponent is for not seeing it.
16. Note inconsistencies between your opponent's proposition and other propositions he has (actually or allegedly) made or admitted; or inconsistencies between his proposition and his behavior: "should he defend suicide, you may at once exclaim, 'Why don't you hang yourself?' .... Some such claptrap is always possible" (p. 24).
17. Challenge your opponent's proposition by making some subtle distinction, taking advantage of any ambiguity that can be found in it.

18. If your opponent is on a course that will end in your defeat, change the subject or terminate the argument.
19. If unable to produce an objection to a definite point in your opponent's argument when challenged to do so, "give the matter a general turn and then talk against that" (p. 25).
20. When your opponent has agreed to the premises that support your conclusion, do not ask him to draw the conclusion, but draw it yourself – and do so even if some of the necessary premises are lacking. (Similar to 11)
21. If your opponent uses a superficial or sophistical argument, rebut it with a similarly superficial or sophistical argument.
22. If your opponent requires you to admit something from which the proposition in question will immediately follow, refuse to do so on the grounds that would involve *petitio principii,* making the argument circular or begging the question.
23. Contradicting your opponent may cause him to extend the limits of his proposition (which was true within the limits originally intended) thereby making it easier to refute. (Similar to 3, 6, and 19)
24. Distort your opponent's proposition making it appear that it entails others (false and absurd) that he would not accept, thereby showing it to be false.
25. To refute a general proposition, note a single instance to the contrary. Whether the instance to the contrary really is an instance may be a matter of opinion or definition.
26. Turn an opponent's argument against himself; meet a cliché or adage with a cliché or adage that makes an opposing point.
27. If your opponent becomes angry, it may be because you have hit upon a weakness in his position; press your argument so as to make him more angry and hence less rational. (Similar to 8)
28. "[P]racticable in a dispute between scholars in the presence of the unlearned" (to convince the latter of one's position). If you can think of no valid objection to your opponent's proposition, make an abstruse invalid one – preferably one that will make your opponent appear ridiculous – which he will recognize as wrong, but the unlearned audience will not, and claim victory. It would take too long for your opponent to explain to the audience what is wrong with your argument in terms it can understand, so, in the minds of the audience, you will have won.

29. If you are being worsted, change the subject. The diversion may or may not have something to do with the case; what matters is that it appears to be germane.
30. Make an appeal to authority (rather than reason), choosing an authority, if possible, that your opponent respects. (Schopenhauer contends that the more limited an opponent's knowledge, the greater the number of authorities that will count with him.) Among authorities to which one might appeal is the number of people holding a view.
31. If you have no reply to an opponent's argument, feign humility, claiming the argument to be beyond your comprehension, hoping the audience will take that as an indication that what your opponent is promoting is nonsensical. "This is a trick which may be used only when you are quite sure that the audience thinks much better of you than of your opponent. A professor, for instance, may try it on a student" (p. 35).
32. Throw suspicion on a proposition by classifying it as a proposition that is (or would be) taken by some nefarious or unpopular group. (That is what anarchists say.)
33. Challenge a proposition on the grounds that, while good in theory, it won't work in practice.
34. When you state a question or an argument and your opponent tries to change the subject, you have probably touched a weak spot in his position, so you should disallow the evasion and urge the point all the more.
35. "Instead of working on your opponent's intellect by argument, work on his will by motive; and he, and also the audience if they have similar interests, will at once be won over to your opinion, even though you got it out of a lunatic asylum; for, as a general rule, half an ounce of will is more effective than a hundredweight of insight and intelligence" (p. 37).
36. Be bombastic. Works best if one's opponent is accustomed to hearing much that he does not understand, but pretends that he does.
37. If your opponent's proposition is true, but his proof of it is faulty, refute the proof and claim that the proposition is thereby shown to be false.
38. If your opponent gains the upper hand, become "personal, insulting, rude" (p. 40).

APPENDIX C

Thouless's Thirty-Eight "Dishonest Tricks" [from Thouless 1950]

1. The use of emotionally toned words.
2. Making a statement in which "all" is implied but "some" is true.
3. Proof by selected instances.
4. Extension of an opponent's proposition by contradiction or by misrepresentation of it.
5. Evasion of a sound refutation of an argument by the use of a sophistical formula.
6. Diversion to another question, to a side issue, or by irrelevant objection.
7. Proof by inconsequent argument.
8. The argument that we should not make efforts against X, which is admittedly evil because there is a worse evil Y against which our efforts should be directed.
9. The recommendation of a position because it is a mean between two extremes.
10. Pointing out the logical correctness of the form of an argument whose premises contain doubtful or untrue statements of fact.
11. The use of an argument of logically unsound form.
12. Argument in a circle.
13. Begging the question.
14. Discussing a verbal proposition as if it were a factual one, or failing to disentangle the verbal and factual elements in a proposition that is partly both.
15. Putting forward a tautology (such as that too much of the thing attacked is bad) as if it were a factual judgment.
16. The use of a speculative argument.
17. Change in the meaning of a term during the course of an argument.

18. The use of a dilemma which ignores a continuous series of possibilities between the two extremes presented.
19. The use of the fact of continuity between them to throw doubt on a real difference between two things (the "argument of the beard").
20. Illegitimate use of or demand for definition.
21. Suggestion by repeated affirmation.
22. Suggestion by use of a confident manner.
23. Suggestion by prestige.
24. Prestige by false credentials.
25. Prestige by the use of pseudo-technical jargon.
26. Affectation of failure to understand backed by prestige.
27. The use of questions drawing out damaging admissions.
28. The appeal to mere authority.
29. Overcoming resistance to a doubtful proposition by a preliminary statement of a few easily accepted ones.
30. Statement of a doubtful proposition in such a way that it fits in with the thought–habits or the prejudices of the hearer.
31. The use of generally accepted formulae of predigested though (sic) [thought] as premises in argument.
32. "There is much to be said on both sides, so no decision can be made either way," or any other formula leading to the attitude of academic detachment.
33. Argument by mere analogy.
34. Argument by forced analogy.
35. Angering an opponent in order that he may argue badly.
36. Special pleading.
37. Commending or condemning a proposition because of its practical consequences to the bearer [hearer?].
38. Argument by attributing prejudices or motives to one's opponent.

References

Ackerknecht, E. H. (1981). *Rudolf Virchow: The development of science*. New York: Arno Press.

Adaval, R. (2001). Sometimes it just feels right: The differential weighting of affect-consistent and affect-inconsistent product information. *Journal of Consumer Research, 28*, 1–17.

Adelswärd, V. (1986). The argumentation of self in job-interviews. In F. H. van Eemeren, R. Grootendorst, J. A. Blair, & C. A. Willard (Eds.), *Argumentation: Analysis and practices* (pp. 327–336). Dordrecht, Holland: Foris Publications.

Adler, J. (2013). Are conductive arguments possible. *Argumentation, 27*, 245–257.

Akerlof, G. A., & Shiller, R. J. (2015). *Phishing for phools: The economics of manipulation and deception*. Princeton, NJ: Princeton University Press.

Albarracin, D., & Kumkale, G. T. (2003). Affect as information in persuasion: A model of affect identification and discounting. *Journal of Personality and Social Psychology, 84*, 453–469.

Albarracin, D., & Wyer, R. S. (2001). Elaborative and nonelaborative processing of a behavior-related communication. *Personality and Social Psychology Bulletin, 27*, 691–705.

Alicke, M. D. (1985). Global self-evaluation as determined by the desirability and controllability of trait adjectives. *Journal of Personality and Social Psychology, 49*, 1621–1630.

Allen, M. (1991). Meta-analysis comparing the persuasiveness of one-sided and two-sided messages. *Western Journal of Speech Communication, 55*, 390–404.

Allen, M. (1994). The persuasive effects of one- and two-sided messages. In M. Allen & R. W. Preiss (Eds.), *Prospects and precautions in the use of meta-analysis* (pp. 101–125). Dubuque, IA: Brown & Benchmark.

Alloy, L. B., & Abramson, L. Y. (1979). Judgment of contingency in depressed and nondepressed students: Sadder but wiser? *Journal of Experimental Psychology: General, 108*, 441–485.

Alloy, L. B., & Ahrens, A. H. (1987). Depression and pessimism for the future: Biased use of statistically relevant information in predictions for self versus others. *Journal of Personality and Social Psychology, 52*, 366–378.

Alonso, A., & Fernandez-Berrocal, P. (2003). Irrational decisions: Attending to numbers rather than ratios. *Personality and Individual Differences, 35*, 1537–1547.

Amgoud, L., & Cayrol, C. (2002). A reasoning model based on the production of acceptable arguments. *Annals of Mathematics and Artificial Intelligence*, *34*, 197–215.

Andersen, K., & Clevenger, T. Jr. (1963). A summary of experimental research in ethos. *Speech Monographs*, *30*, 50–78.

Anderson, C. A. (1982). Inoculation and counterexplanation: Debiasing techniques in the perseverance of social theories. *Social Cognition*, *1*, 126–139.

Anderson, C. A. (1983). Imagination and expectation: The effect of imagining behavioral scripts on personal intentions. *Journal of Personality and Social Psychology*, *45*, 293–305.

Anderson, C. A. (1995). Implicit personality theories and empirical data: Biased assimilation, belief perseverance and change, and covariation detection sensitivity. *Social Cognition*, *13*, 25–48.

Anderson, C. A., & Sechler, E. S. (1986). Effects of explanation and counterexplanation on the development and use of social theories. *Journal of Personality and Social Psychology*, *50*, 24–34.

Anderson, C. A., & Slusher, M. P. (1986). Relocating motivational effects: A synthesis of cognitive and motivational effects on attributions for success and failure. *Social Cognition*, *4*, 270–292.

Anderson, C. A., Lepper, M. R., & Ross, L. (1980). Perseverance of social theories: The role of explanation in the persistence of discredited information. *Journal of Personality and Social Psychology*, *39*, 1037–1049.

Ariely, D., & Simonson, I. (2003). Buying, bidding, playing or competing? Value assessment and decision dynamics in online auctions. *Journal of Consumer Psychology*, *13*, 113–123.

Arkes, H. R. (1991). Costs and benefits of judgment errors: Implications for debiasing. *Psychological Bulletin*, *110*, 486–498.

Arkes, H. R. (2003). The non-use of psychological research at two federal agencies. *Psychological Science*, *14*, 1–6.

Arkes, H. R., & Blumer, C. (1985). The psychology of sunk cost. *Organizational Behavior and Human Decision Processes*, *35*, 124–140.

Arkes, H. R., & Harkness, A. R. (1983). Estimates of contingency between two dichotomous variables. *Journal of Experimental Psychology: General*, *11*, 117–135.

Arkes, H. R., Boehm, L. E., & Xu, G. (1991). Determinants of judged validity. *Journal of Experimental Social Psychology*, *27*, 576–605.

Arkes, H. R., Hackett, C., & Boehm, L. E. (1989). The generality of the relation between familiarity and judged validity. *Journal of Behavioral Decision Making*, *2*, 81–94.

Arkes, H. R., Faust, D., Guilmette, T. J., & Hart, K. (1988). Elimination of the hindsight bias. *Journal of Applied Psychology*, *73*, 305–307.

Arkes, H. R., Wortmann, R. L., Saville, P. D., & Harkness, A. R. (1981). Hindsight bias among physicians weighing the likelihood of diagnosis. *Journal of Applied Psychology*, *66*, 252–254.

Armor, D. A. (1998). *The illusion of objectivity: Bias in the belief in freedom from bias*. Los Angeles, CA: University of California, Los Angeles.

Arnauld, A., & Nicole, P. (1995). Concerning sophisms and bad reasonings which are common in ordinary discourse. In H. V. Hansen & R. C. Pinto (Eds.), *Fallacies: Classical and contemporary readings* (pp. 39–54). University Park, PA: The Pennsylvania State University Press. (Originally published in 1865.)

Aron, R., Keller, S., & Davidson, J. K. (1958). Evidence and inference in history. *Daedalus*, *87*, 11–39.

Attridge, N., & Inglis, M. (2014). Intelligence and negation biases on the conditional inference task: A dual process analysis. *Thinking and Reasoning*, *20*, 454–471.

Avnet, T., Pham, M.T., & Stephen, A. T. (2012). Consumers' trust in feelings as information. *Journal of Consumer Research*, *39*, 720–735.

Babad, E., & Katz, Y. (1992). Wishful thinking – against all odds. *Journal of Applied Social Psychology*, *21*, 1921–1938.

Bachman, J. (1995). Appeal to authority. In H. V. Hansen & R. C. Pinto (Eds.), *Fallacies: Classical and contemporary readings* (pp. 274–286). University Park, PA: The Pennsylvania State University Press.

Back, K. W. (1951). Influence through social communication. *Journal of Abnormal Social Psychology*, *46*, 9–23.

Bacon, F. (1939). Novum organum. In E. A. Burtt (Ed.), *The English philosophers from Bacon to Mill* (pp. 24–123). New York: Random House. (Original work published in 1620.)

Bacon, F. T. (1979). Credibility of repeated statements: Memory for trivia. *Journal of Experimental Psychology: Human Learning and Memory*, *5*, 241–252.

Baesler, F. J., & Burgoon, J. K. (1994). The temporal effects of story and statistical evidence on belief change. *Communication Research*, *21*, 582–602.

Baird, A. C. (1950). *Argumentation, discussion, and debate*. New York: McGraw-Hill.

Baker, L. A., & Emery, R. E., (1993). When every relationship is above average. Perceptions and expectations of divorce at the time of marriage. *Law and Human Behavior*, *17*, 439–450.

Balbi, A., & Guerry, A.-M. (1829). *Statistique comparée de l'état de l'instruction et du nombre des crimes dans les divers arrondissements des Académies et Cours Royales de France*. Paris: Everat.

Balko, R. (2017). The emperor of junk science forensics has died. *Washington Post*, August 31.

Ball, L. J., Phillips, P., Wade, C. N., & Quayle, J. D. (2006). Effects of belief and logic on syllogistic reasoning: Eye-movement evidence for selective processing models. *Experimental Psychology*, *53*, 77–86.

Bandura, A. (1997). *Self-efficacy: The exercise of control*. New York: Freeman.

Banner, L. W. (1983). *American beauty*. Chicago, IL: Chicago University Press.

Bar-Hillel, M. A. (1979). The role of sample size in sample evaluation. *Organizational Behavior and Human Performance*, *24*, 245–257.

Bar-Hillel, M. A., & Budescu, D. (1995). The elusive wishful-thinking effect. *Thinking and Reasoning*, *1*, 71–103.

Barker, S. F. (1974). Is there a problem of induction? In R. Swinburne (Ed.), *The justification of induction* (pp. 57–61). London: Oxford University Press.

Barker, S. F. (1979). The method of applied logic: Some philosophical considerations. In E. Sosa (Ed.), *The philosophy of Nicholas Rescher* (pp. 1–16). Dordrecht, Holland: Reidel.

Baron, J. (1985). *Rationality and intelligence.* New York: Cambridge University Press.

Baron, J. (1991). Beliefs about thinking. In J. Foss, D. Perkins, & J. Segal (Eds.), *Informal reasoning and education* (pp. 169–186). Hillsdale, NJ: Erlbaum.

Baron, J. (1995). Myside bias in thinking about abortion. *Thinking and Reasoning, 1*, 221–235.

Baron, J. (2000). *Thinking and deciding* (3rd ed.). New York: Cambridge University Press.

Baron, J., & Hershey, J. (1988). Outcome bias in decision evaluation. *Journal of Personality and Social Psychology, 54*, 569–679.

Barrow, J. D. (1990). *The world within the world.* New York: Oxford University Press.

Barry, H., Jr. (1931). A test for negativism and compliance. *Journal of Abnormal Social Psychology, 25*, 373–381.

Barston, J. I. (1986). *An investigation into belief biases in reasoning.* Unpublished PhD thesis, Plymouth Polytechnic.

Bartecchi, C. E., MacKenzie, T. D., & Schrier, R. W. (1995). The global tobacco epidemic. *Scientific American, 272*, 44–51.

Barth, E. M. (1986). Logic to some purpose. In F. H. van Eemeren, R. Grootendorst, J. A. Blair, & C. A. Willard (Eds.), *Argumentation: Across the lines of discipline* (pp. 33–45). Dordrecht, Holland: Foris Publications.

Bartlett, F. E. (1958). *Thinking: An experimental and social study.* London: Allen and Unwin.

Bartley, W. W., III (1977). Appendix C: Editor's note on Carroll's "What the tortoise said to Achilles." In W. W. Bartley, III (Ed.), *Lewis Carroll's symbolic logic.* New York: Clarkson N. Potter.

Barton, K., Fugelsang, J., & Smilek, D. (2009). Inhibiting beliefs demands attention. *Thinking and Reasoning, 15*, 250–267.

Bauer, H. H. (1994). *Scientific literacy and the myth of the scientific method.* Chicago, IL: University of Illinois Press.

Bauman, L. J., & Siegel, J. (1987). Misperception among gay men of the risk of the risk for AIDS associated with their sexual behavior. *Journal of Applied Social Psychology, 17*, 329–350.

Baumeister, R. F., & Vohs, K. D. (2016). Introduction to the special issue: The science of prospection, *Review of General Psychology, 20*, 1–2.

Baumeister, R. F., Dale, K., & Sommer, K. L. (1998). Freudian defense mechanisms and empirical findings in modern social psychology: Reaction formation, projection, displacement, undoing, isolation, sublimation, and denial. *Journal of Personality, 66*, 1081–1124.

Baumeister, R. F., Vohs, K. D., & Oettingen, G. (2016). Pragmatic prospection: How and why people think about the future. *Review of General Psychology, 20*, 3–16.

Bazerman, M. H., Beekum, R. I., & Schoorman, F. D. (1982). Performance evaluation in a dynamic context: A laboratory study of the impact of a prior commitment to the rate. *Journal of Applied Psychology, 67*, 873–876.

Beardsley, M. (1975). *Thinking straight.* Englewood Cliffs, NJ: Prentice-Hall.

Beattie, J., & Baron, J. (1988). Confirmation and matching biases in hypothesis testing. *Quarterly Journal of Experimental Psychology, 40*A, 269–298.

Beck, S. R., Riggs, K. J., & Gorniak, S. L. (2009). Relating developments in children's counterfactual thinking and executive functions. *Thinking and Reasoning, 15*, 437–454.

Beckman, P. (1971). *A history of pi.* New York: St. Martin's Press.

Begg, I., & Armour, T. (1991). Repetition and the ring of truth: Biasing comments. *Canadian Journal of Behavioral Science, 23*, 195–213.

Begg, I., & Denny, J. P. (1969). Empirical reconciliation of atmosphere and conversion interpretations of syllogistic reasoning. *Journal of Experimental Psychology, 81*, 351–354.

Begg, I., & Harris, G. (1982). On the interpretation of syllogisms. *Journal of Verbal Learning and Verbal Behavior, 21*, 595–620.

Begg, I., Anas, A., & Farinacci, S. (1992). Dissociation of processes in belief: Source of recollection, statement familiarity, and the illusion of truth. *Journal of Experimental Psychology: General, 121*, 446–458.

Begg, I, Armour, T., & Kerr, T. (1985). On believing what we remember. *Canadian Journal of Behavioral Science, 17*, 199–214.

Bell, E. T. (1991). *The magic of numbers.* New York: Dover. (Originally published in 1946.

Beller, S., & Kuhnmünch, G. (2007). What causal conditional reasoning tells us about people's understanding of causality. *Thinking and Reasoning, 13*, 426–460.

Bem, D. J. (1970). *Beliefs, attitudes, and human affairs.* Belmont, CA: Brooks/Cole Publishing Company.

Bem, D. J., & McConnell, H. K. (1970). Testing the self-perception explanation of dissonance phenomena: On the salience of premanipulation attitudes. *Journal of Personality and Social Psychology, 14*, 23–31.

Bench-Capon, T. J. M., & Dunne, P. E. (2007). Argumentation in artificial intelligence. *Artificial Intelligence, 171*, 619–641.

Bennett, M., & Hibberd, M. (1986). Availability and the false consensus effect. *Journal of Social Psychology, 126*, 403–405.

Benoit, W. J. (1986). Argumentation evaluation. In F. H. van Eemeren, R. Grootendorst, J. A. Blair, & C. A. Willard (Eds.), *Argumentation: Across the lines of discipline* (pp. 299–305). Dordrecht, Holland: Foris Publications.

Bernstein, D. M., Aßfalg, A., Kumar, R., & Ackerman, R. (2015). Looking backward and forward on hindsight bias. In J. Dunlosky & U. Tauber (Eds.), *Handbook of metamemory* (pp. 289–304). New York: Oxford University Press.

Berscheid, E., & Walster, E. H. (1978). *Interpersonal attraction.* Reading, MA: Addison-Wesley.

Berscheid, E., Graziano, W., Monson, T., & Dermer, M. (1976). Outcome dependency: Attention, attribution, and attraction. *Journal of Personality and Social Psychology, 34*, 978–989.

Billig, M. (1991). *Arguing and thinking: A rhetorical approach to social psychology* (2nd ed.). New York: Cambridge University Press. (Originally published in 1987.)

Black, M. (1952). *Critical thinking: An introduction to logic and scientific method.* New York: Prentice-Hall.

Black, M. (1974). Self-supporting inductive arguments. In R. Swinburne (Ed.), *The justification of induction* (pp. 127–134). London: Oxford University Press. (Originally published in 1958.)

Blackstone, W. (1962). *Commentaries on the laws of England of public wrongs.* Boston, MA: Beacon. (Original work published in 1769.)

Blair, D. C., & Maron, M. E. (1985). An evaluation of retrieval effectiveness for a full-text document retrieval system. *Communications of the ACM, 28*, 289–299.

Blair, J. A. (1986). Argumentation, inquiry and speech act theory. In F. H. van Eemeren, R. Grootendorst, J. A. Blair, & C. A. Willard (Eds.), *Argumentation: Across the lines of discipline* (pp. 189–200). Dordrecht, Holland: Foris Publications.

Blair, J. A. (1995). The place of teaching informal fallacies in teaching reasoning skills or critical thinking. In H. V. Hansen & R. C. Pinto (Eds.), *Fallacies: Classical and contemporary readings* (pp. 328–338). University Park, PA: The Pennsylvania State University Press.

Blair, J. A. (2013). Are conductive arguments really not possible? OSSA Conference Archive. 24. https://scholar.uwindsor.ca/ossaarchive/OSSA10/papersandcommentaries/24

Blair, J. A., & Johnson, R. H. (Eds.) (2013). *Conductive argument: An overlooked type of defeasible reasoning.* London: College Publications.

Block, J., & Funder, D. C. (1986). Social roles and social perception: Individual differences in attribution and "error." *Journal of Personality and Social Psychology, 51*, 1200–1207.

Block, L. J., & Keller, P. A. (1995). When to accentuate the negative: The effects of perceived efficacy and message framing on intentions to perform a health-related behavior. *Journal of Marketing Research, 32*, 192–203.

Blume, L., Brandenburger, A., & Dekel, E. (1991). Lexicographic probabilities and choice under uncertainty. *Econometrica, 59*, 61–79.

Boden, M. T., Berenbaum, H., & Gross, J. J. (2016). Why do people believe what they do? A functional perspective. *Review of General Psychology, 20*, 399–411.

Boltzmann, L. (1974). The second law of thermodynamics. In B. McGuinness (Ed. and trans.), *Theoretical physics and philosophical problems: Selected writings* (pp. 13–32). Dordrecht: Reidel. (Originally published in 1886.)

Bond, C. F., Jr., & DePaulo, B. M. (2006). Accuracy of deception judgments. *Personality and Social Psychology Review, 10*, 214–234.

Bondi, H. (2003). Uniting the world—or dividing it: Which outlook is truly universal, which parochial in the extreme? In P. Kurtz (Ed.), *Science and religion: Are they compatible?* (pp. 145–148). Amherst, NY: Prometheus Books.

Boninger, D. S., Gleicher, F., & Strathman, A. (1994). Counterfactual thinking: From what might have been to what may be. *Journal of Personality and Social Psychology, 67*, 297–307.

Bonnefon, J. F. (2010). Deduction from if-then personality signatures. *Thinking and Reasoning, 16*, 157–171.

Bonnefon, J. F., & Hilton, D. J. (2002). The suppression of Modus Ponens as a case of pragmatic preconditional reasoning. *Thinking and Reasoning, 8*, 21–40.

Bonnefon, J. F., & Hilton, D. J. (2004). Consequential conditionals: Invited and suppressed inferences from valid outcomes. *Journal of Experimental Psychology: Learning, Memory, and Cognition, 30*, 28–37.

Bonner, C., & Newell, B. R. (2008). How to make a risk seem riskier: The ratio bias versus construal level theory. *Judgment and Decision Making, 3*, 411–416.

Boorstin, D. J. (1985). *The discoverers: A history of man's search to know his world and himself.* New York: Vintage Books.

Boot, W. (2019). Are brain games mostly BS? *The conversation.* theconversation .com

Borgida, E., & Brekke, N. (1981). *New directions in attribution research,* Vol. 5, Hillsdale, NJ: Erlbaum.

Borgida, E., & Nisbett, R. E. (1977). The differential impact of abstract vs. concrete information on decisions. *Journal of Applied Social Psychology, 7*, 258–271.

Bostrom, N. (2003). Are you living in a computer simulation? *Philosophical Quarterly, 53*, 243–255.

Boudry, M. (2017). The fallacy fork: Why it's time to get rid of fallacy theory. *Skeptical Inquirer, 41*, 46–51.

Boudry, M., Paglieri, F., & Pigliucci, M. (2015). The fake, the flimsy and the fallacious: Demarcating arguments in real life. *Argumentation, 29*, 431–456.

Bovens, L., & Hartmann, S. (2003). *Bayesian epistemology.* Oxford: Oxford University Press.

Bowden, A. O., Caldwell, F. F., & West, G. A. (1934). A study in prestige. *American Journal of Sociology, 40*, 193–204.

Bower, G. H., (1981). Mood and memory. *American Psychologist, 36*, 129–148.

Boyer, C. B., & Merzbach, U. C. (1991). *A history or mathematics* (2nd ed.). New York: Wiley.

Braine, M. D. S., Reiser, B. J., & Rumain, B. (1984). Some empirical justification for a theory of natural propositional logic. In G. H. Bower (Ed.), *The psychology of learning and motivation*, Vol. 18 (pp. 313–371). New York: Academic Press.

Braithwaite, R. B. (1974). The predictionist justification of induction. In R. Swinburne (Ed.), *The justification of induction* (pp. 102–126). London: Oxford University Press. (Originally published in 1953.)

Bramel, D. (1962). A dissonance theory approach to defensive projection. *Journal of Abnormal and Social Psychology, 64*, 121–129.

Brennan, J. (2012). *The ethics of voting*. New York: Princeton University Press.

Brenner, M. W. (1973). The next-in-line effect. *Journal of Verbal Learning and Verbal Behavior, 12*, 320–323.

Brenner, M. W. (1976). *Memory and interpersonal relations*. Unpublished doctoral dissertation, University of Michigan.

Briñol, P., & Petty, R. E. (2012). The history of attitudes and persuasiveness research. In A. Kruglanski & W. Stroebe (Eds.), *Handbook of the history of social psychology* (pp. 285–320). New York: Psychology Press.

Briñol, P., Petty, R. E., Durso, G. R. O., & Rucker, D. D. (2018). Power and persuasion: Processes by which perceived power can influence evaluative judgments. *Review of General Psychology, 21*, 223–241.

Briñol, P., Petty, R. E., Valle, C., Rucker, D. D., & Becerra, A. (2007). The effects of message recipients' power before and after persuasion: A self-validation analysis. *Journal of Personality and Social Psychology, 93*, 1040–1053.

Brisson, J., de Chantal, P-L., Forgues, H. L., & Markovits, H. (2014). Belief bias is stronger when reasoning is more difficult. *Thinking and Reasoning, 20*, 385–403.

Briton, A. (1995). The *ad hominem*. In H. V. Hansen & R. C. Pinto (Eds.), *Fallacies: Classical and contemporary readings* (pp. 213–228). University Park, PA: The Pennsylvania State University Press.

Brock, T. C. (1965). Communicator-recipient similarity and decision change. *Journal of Personality and Social Psychology, 1*, 650–654.

Brockner, J., & Rubin, J. Z. (1985). *Entrapment in escalating conflicts*. New York: Springer-Verlag.

Brockner, J., Rubin, J. Z., & Lang (1981). Face-saving and entrapment. *Journal of Experimental Social Psychology, 17*, 68–79.

Bronowski, J. (1965). The abacus and the rose. In J. Bronowski (Ed.), *Science and Human Values* (pp. 77–119). New York: Harper and Row.

Broockman, D., & Kalla, J. (2016). Durably reducing transphobia: A field experiment on door-to-door canvassing. *Science, 352*, 220–224.

Brown, B. R. (1968). The effects of need to maintain face on interpersonal bargaining. *Journal of Experimental Social Psychology, 4*, 107–122.

Brown, B. R. (1970). Face-saving following experimentally induced embarrassment. *Journal of Experimental Social Psychology, 6*, 255–271.

Brown, C. L. (1999). "Do the right thing:" Diverging effects of accountability in a managerial context. *Marketing Science, 18*, 230–246.

Brown, P., & Levinson, S. (1978). Universals in language usage: Politeness phenomena. In E. N. Goody (Ed.), *Questions and politeness: Strategies in social interaction*. Cambridge: Cambridge University Press.

Bruner, J. (1962). *On knowing: Essays for the left hand*. Cambridge, MA: Harvard/Belknap Press.

Bruner, J. (1986). *Actual minds, possible worlds*. Cambridge, MA: Harvard University Press.

Buchanan, R. W. (1986). The American jury trial: The art of argument in voir dire and opening statements. In F. H. van Eemeren, R. Grootendorst, J. A. Blair, &

C. A. Willard (Eds.), *Argumentation: Analysis and practices* (pp. 131–140). Dordrecht, Holland: Foris Publications.

Budescu, D. V., & Bruderman, M. (1995). The relationship between the illusion of control and the desirability bias. *Journal of Behavioral Decision Making, 8*, 109–125.

Buehl, M. M., Alexander, P. A., Murphy, P. K., & Sperl, C. T. (2001). Profiling persuasion: The role of beliefs, knowledge and interest in the processing of persuasive texts that vary by argument structure. *Journal of Literary Research, 33*, 269–301.

Buehler, R., Griffin, D., & McDonald, H. (1997). The role of motivated reasoning in optimistic time predictions. *Personality and Social Psychology Bulletin, 23*, 238–247.

Buehler, R., Griffin, D., & Ross, M. (1994). Exploring he "planning fallacy": Why peoples underestimate their task completion times. *Journal of Personality and Social Psychology, 67*, 366–381.

Bull, R. (1989). Can training enhance the detection of deception?. In J C. Yuille (Ed.), *Credibility assessment* (pp. 83–99). London: Kluwer Academic Publishers.

Bull, R., & Rumsey, N. (1988). *The social psychology of facial appearance.* New York: Springer-Verlag.

Bunch, B. (1982). *Mathematical fallacies and paradoxes.* Mineola, NY: Dover Publications.

Butler, C. (1970). *Number symbolism.* London: Routledge and Kegan Paul.

Byrne, D., Gouaux, C., Griffitt, W. et al. (1975). The ubiquitous relationship: Attitude similarity and attraction. *Human Relations, 24*, 201–207.

Byrne, R. M. J. (1989). Suppressing valid inferences with conditionals. *Cognition, 31*, 61–83.

Byrne, R. M. J. (1997). Cognitive processes in counterfactual thinking about what might have been. In D. Medin (Ed.), *The psychology of learning and motivation: Advances in research and theory* (Vol. 37, pp. 105–154). New York: Academic Press.

Byrne, R. M. J. (2002). Mental models and counterfactual thoughts about what might have been. *Trends in Cognitive Sciences, 6*, 426–431.

Byrne, R. M. J. (2016). Counterfactual thought. *Annual Review of Psychology, 67*, 135–157.

Byrne, R. M. J., & Egan, S. M. (2004). Counterfactual and prefactual conditionals. *Canadian Journal of Experimental Psychology, 58*, 113–120.

Byrne, R. M. J., & McEleney, A. (2000). Counterfactual thinking about actions and failures to act. *Journal of Experimental Psychology: Learning, Memory, and Cognition, 26*, 1318–1331.

Camerer, C. F. (1995). Individual decision making. In J. H. Kagel & A. E. Roth (Eds.), *Handbook of experimental economics* (pp. 587–703). Princeton, NJ: Princeton University Press.

Camerer, C. F. (1998). Bounded rationality in individual decision making. *Experimental Economics, 1*, 163–183.

Camerer, C. F., & Hogarth, R. M. (1999). The effects of financial incentives in experiments: A review and capital-labor-production framework. *Journal of Risk and Uncertainty, 19*, 7–42.

Campbell, D. T. (1959). Systematic error on the part of human links in communication systems. *Information and Control, 1*, 334–369.

Campbell, F. A., & Burchinal, M. R. (2008). Early childhood interventions: The Abecedarian Project. In P. C. Kyllonen, R. D. Roberts, & L. Stankov (Eds.), *Extending intelligence: Enhancement and new constructs* (pp. 61–84). New York: Erlbaum.

Campbell, F. A., & Ramey, C. T. (1994). Effects of early intervention on intellectual and academic achievement: A follow-up study of children from low-income families. *Child Development, 65*, 684–698.

Campbell, F. A., & Ramey, C. T. (1995). Cognitive and school outcomes for high-risk African-American students at middle adolescence: Positive effects of early intervention. *American Educational Research Journal, 32*, 743–772.

Campbell, F. A., Ramey, C. T., Pungello, E., Sparling, J. & Miller-Johnson, S. (2002). Early childhood education: Young adult outcomes from the Abecedarian Project. *Applied Developmental Science, 6*, 42–57.

Campbell, J. D. (1986). Similarity and uniqueness: The effects of attribute type, relevance, and individual differences in self-esteem and depression. *Journal of Personality and Social Psychology, 50*, 281–294.

Campbell, J. D., & Fairey, P. J. (1985). The effects of self-esteem, hypothetical explanations, and verbalization of expectancies on future performance. *Journal of Personality and Social Psychology, 48*, 1097–1111.

Campbell, J. D., & Tesser, A. (1983). Motivational interpretations of hindsight bias: An individual difference analysis. *Journal of Personality, 51*, 605–620.

Campbell, K. (1974). One form of scepticism about induction. In R. Swinburne (Ed.), *The justification of induction* (pp. 145–148). London: Oxford University Press. (Originally published in 1963.

Campbell, W. K., Sedikides, C., Reeder, G. D., & Elliot, A. J. (2000). Among friends? An examination of friendship and the self-serving bias. *British Journal of Social Psychology, 39*, 229–239.

Carpenter, E. T. (1982). Piagetian interviews of college students. In R. G. Fuller (Ed.), *Piagetian programs in higher education* (pp. 15–21). Lincoln, NB: University of Nebraska-Lincoln.

Carroll, J. S. (1978). The effect of imagining an event on expectations for the event: An interpretation in terms of the availability heuristic. *Journal of Experimental Social Psychology, 14*, 88–96.

Carroll, R. T. (2012). *Becoming a critical thinker: A guide for the new millennium* (2nd ed.). Boston, MA: Pearson Learning Solutions.

Cattell, R. B. (1971). *Abilities: Their structure, growth, and action.* Boston: Houghton Mifflin.

Cavender, N. M., & Kahane, H. (2013). *Logic and contemporary rhetoric: The use of reason in everyday life* (12th ed.). Boston, MA: Cengage Learning.

Cesario, J. F. (2006). Regulatory fit from nonverbal behaviors: How source delivery style influences message effectiveness (Doctoral dissertation, Columbia University, 2006). *Dissertation Abstracts International, 67*, 2276.

Cesario, J. F., & Higgins, E. T. (2008). Making message recipients "feel right:" How nonverbal cues can increase persuasion. *Psychological Science, 19*, 415–420.

Cesaro, J. F. & Provitera, A. (1971). Sources of error in syllogistic reasoning. *Cognitive Psychology, 2*, 400–410.

Cesario, J. F., Grant, H., & Higgins, E. T. (2004). Regulatory fit and persuasion: Transfer from "feeling right." *Journal of Personality and Social Psychology, 86*, 388–404.

Cesario, J. F., Higgins, E. T., & Scholer, A. A. (2008). Regulatory fit and persuasion: Basic principles and remaining questions. *Social and Personality Psychology Compass, 2*, 444–463.

Chaiken, S. (1980). Heuristic versus systematic information processing and the use of source versus message cues in persuasion. *Journal of Personality and Social Psychology, 39*, 752–766.

Chaiken, S. (1987). The heuristic model of persuasion. In M. P. Zanna et al. (Eds.), *Social influence: The Ontario symposium* (Vol. 5, pp. 3–39). Hillsdale, NJ: Erlbaum.

Chapman, L. J., & Chapman, J. P. (1959). Atmosphere effect revisited. *Journal of Experimental Psychology, 58*, 220–226.

Charness, G., Karni, E., & Levin, D. (2009). On the conjunction fallacy in probability judgment: New experimental evidence regarding Linda. *Games and Economic Behavior, 68*, 551–556.

Chater, N., & Oaksford, M. (2009). Local and global inferential relations: Response to Over (2009). *Thinking and Reasoning, 15*, 439–446.

Cheng, P. W., & Holyoak, K. J. (1985). Pragmatic reasoning schemas. *Cognitive Psychology, 17*, 391–416.

Cheng, P. W., & Nisbett, R. E. (1993). Pragmatic constraints on causal deduction. In R. E. Nisbett (Ed.), *Rules for reasoning* (pp. 207–227). Hillsdale, NJ: Lawrence Erlbaum Associates.

Chesterton, G. (1959). *Orthodoxy*. Garden City, NY: Image Books.

Choi, I., & Nisbett, R. E. (2000). Cultural psychology of surprise: Holistic theories and recognition of contradiction. *Journal of Personality and Social Psychology, 79*, 890–905.

Chomsky, N. (1968). *Language and mind*. New York: Harcourt, Brace and World.

Christensen-Szalanski, J. J., & Beach, L. R. (1984). The citation bias: Fad and fashion in the judgment and decision literature. *American Psychologist, 39*, 75–78.

Christensen-Szalanski, J. J., & Fobian Willham, C. (1991). The hindsight bias: A meta-analysis. *Organizational Behavior and Human Decision Processes, 48*, 147–168.

Cialdini, R. B. (2001a). *Influence: Science and practice* (4th ed.). Boston: Allyn and Bacon.

Cialdini, R. B. (2001b). The science of persuasion. *Scientific American, 284*, 76–81.

Cinner, J. (2018). How behavioral science can help conservation. *Science, 362*, 889–890.

Claidiére, N., Trouche, E., & Mercier, H. (Submitted). Argumentation and diffusion and counterintuitive beliefs.

Clark, H. H., & Chase, W. G. (1972). On the process of comparing sentences against pictures. *Cognitive Psychology*, *3*, 472–517.

Clarke, D. S., Jr. (1985). *Practical inferences*. London: Routledge & Kegan Paul.

Clarke, S. H., & Campbell, F. A. (1998). Can intervention early prevent crime later? The Abecedarian Project compared with other programs. *Early Childhood Research Quarterly*, *13*, 319–343.

Cleary, E. W. (1972). *McCormick's handbook of the law of evidence* (2nd ed.). St Paul, MN: West.

Cleckley, T. H. E. (1988). *The mask of sanity: An attempt to clarify some issues about the so-called psychopathic personality* (5th ed.). Guilford, VT: Echo Point Books and Media.

Clement, J. (1983, April). Analogical problem solving in science and mathematics. *Paper presented at the annual meeting of the American Educational Research Association*, Montreal, Canada.

Clement, J. (1991). Nonformal reasoning in experts and in science students: The use of analogies, extreme cases, and physical intuition. In J. F. Voss, D. N Perkins, & J. W. Segal (Eds.), *Informal reasoning and education* (pp. 345–362). Hillsdale, NJ: Erlbaum.

Clore, G. L., Schwarz, N., & Conway, M. (1994). Affective causes and consequences of social information processing. In R. S. Wyer & T. K. Srull (Eds.), *Handbook of social cognition* (Vol. 1, pp. 323–419). Hillsdale, NJ: Erlbaum.

Cohen, I. B. (1985). *Revolution in science*. Cambridge, MA: Harvard University Press.

Cohen, J. B., & Areni, C. S. (1991). Affect and consumer behavior. In T. S., Robertson & H. H. Kassarjian (Eds.), *Handbook of consumer behavior* (pp. 188–240). Englewood Cliffs, NJ: Prentice Hall.

Cohen, J. B., Pham, M. T., & Andrade, E. B. (2008). The nature and role of affect in consumer behavior. In C. Haugtvedt, F. Kardes, & P. Herr (Eds.), *Handbook of consumer psychology* (pp. 297–348). Mahwah, NJ: Erlbaum.

Cohen, L. J. (1979). Rescher's theory of plausible reasoning. In E. Sosa (Ed.), *The philosophy of Nicholas Rescher* (pp. 49–60). Dordrecht, Holland: Reidel.

Cohen, L. J. (1981). Can human irrationality be experimentally demonstrated? *The Behavioral and Brain Sciences*, *4*, 317–370.

Cohen, M. R., & Nagel, E. (1934). *An introduction to logic and scientific method*. London: Routledge and Kegan Paul.

College Board. (1976–1977). *Student descriptive questionnaire*. Princeton, NJ: Educational Testing Service.

Collins, A., & Michalski, R. (1989). The logic of plausible reasoning: A core theory. *Cognitive Science*, *13*, 1–49.

Collins, L. N., Graham, J. W., Hansen, W. B., & Johnson, C. A. (1985). Agreement between retrospective accounts of substance use and earlier reported substance use. *Applied Psychological Measurement*, *9*, 301–309.

Connell, L. (2004). Making the implausible plausible. *Proceedings of the annual meeting of the Cognitive Science Society* (pp. 244–249).

Connell, L., & Keane, M. T. (2003). PAM: A cognitive model of plausibility. *Proceedings of the annual meeting of the Cognitive Science Society* (pp. 264–269).

Connell, L., & Keane, M. T. (2006). A model of plausibility. *Cognitive Science, 30*, 95–120.

Conway, M. (1990). On bias in autobiographical recall: Retrospective adjustments following disconfirmed expectation. *Journal of Social Psychology, 130*, 183–189.

Conway, M., & Ross. M. (1984). Getting what you want by revising what you had. *Journal of Personality and Social Psychology, 47*, 738–748.

Cook, M., & Smallman, H. S. (2008). Human factors of the confirmation bias in intelligence analysis: Decision support from graphical evidence landscapes. *Human Factors, 50*, 745–754.

Cooper, A. C., & Dunkelberg, W. C., & Woo, C. Y. (1988). Entrepreneurs' perceived chances for success (1988). *Journal of Business Venturing, 3*, 97–108.

Copi, I. M., Cohen, C., & McMahon, K. (2010). *Introduction to logic* (14th ed.). Upper Saddle River, NJ: Pearson.

Cosmides, L. (1989). The logic of social exchange: Has natural selection shaped how humans reason? Studies with the Wason selection task. *Cognition, 31*, 187–276.

Costello, F., & Keane, M. T. (2000). Efficient creativity: Constraints on conceptual combination. *Cognitive Science, 24*, 299–349.

Costello, F., & Keane, M. T. (2001). Alignment versus diagnosticity in the comprehension and production of combined concepts. *Journal of Experimental Psychology: Learning, Memory, and Cognition, 27*, 255–271.

Court, N. A. (1961). *Mathematics in fun and in earnest*. Mineola, NY: Dover Publications. (Originally published in 1935.)

Creighton, J. E. (1922). *An introductory logic*. New York: Macmillan.

Crews-Anderson, T. A. (2007). *Critical thinking and informal logic*. ALCS Humanities-Ebook.

Crocker, J. (1981). Judgment of covariation by social perceivers. *Psychological Bulletin, 90*, 272–292.

Croskerry, P. (2003). The importance of cognitive errors in diagnosis and strategies to minimize them. *Academic Medicine, 78*, 775–780.

Crowley, A. E., & Hoyer, W. D. (1994). An integrative framework for understanding two-sided persuasion. *Journal of Consumer Research, 20*, 561–574.

Crowne, D. P., & Marlowe, D. (1964). *The approval motive*. New York: Wiley.

Crupi, V., Fitleson, B., & Tentori, K. (2008). Probability, confirmation, and the conjunction fallacy. *Thinking and Reasoning, 14*, 182–199.

Crutchfield, J. P., Farmer, J. D., Packard, N. H., Shaw, R. S. (1986). *Scientific American, 257*, 38–49.

Cummins, D. D. (1995). Naïve theories and causal deduction. *Memory and Cognition, 23*, 646–658.

Cummins, D. D., Lubart, T., Alksnis, O., & Rist, R. (1991). Conditional reasoning and causation. *Memory and Cognition, 19*, 274–282.

Cummings, N. A., & O'Donohue, W. T. (2005). Psychology's surrender to political correctness. In R. H. Wright, & N. A. Cummings (Eds.), *Destructive trends in mental health: The well-intentioned path to harm* (pp. 3–28). New York: Routledge.

Dale, D., Rudski, J., Schwarz, A., & Smith, E. (2007). Innumeracy and incentives: A ratio bias experiment. *Judgment and Decision Making, 2*, 243–250.

Damer, T. E. (1980). *Attacking faculty reasoning* (2nd ed.). Belmont, CA: Wadsworth.

Darley, J. M., & Berscheid, E. (1967). Increased liking as a result of anticipation of personal contact. *Human Relations, 20*, 29–40.

Davies, M. F. (1997). Belief persistence after discrediting: The impact of generated versus provided explanations on the likelihood of discredited outcomes. *Journal of Experimental Social Psychology, 33*, 561–578.

Davies, P. C. W. (1983). *God and the new physics*. New York: Simon & Schuster.

Davis, C. G., Lehman, D. R., Silver, R. C., Wortman, C. B., & Ellard, J. H. (1996). Self-blame following a traumatic life event: The role of perceived avoidability. *Personality and Social Psychology Bulletin, 22*, 557–567.

Dawes, R. M. (1976). Shallow psychology. In J. S. Carroll & J. W. Payne (Eds.), *Cognition and social behavior* (pp. 3–12). Hillsdale, NJ: Erlbaum.

Dawes, R. M. (1977). Case-by-case versus rule-generated procedures for the allocation of scarce resources. In M. F. Kaplan & S. Schwartz (Eds.), *Human judgment and decision processes in applied settings* (pp. 83–94). New York: Academic Press.

Dawes, R. M. (1988). *Rational choice in an uncertain world*. New York: Harcourt Brace Jovanovich.

Dawes, R. M. (1989). Statistical criteria for establishing a truly false consensus effect. *Journal of Experimental Social Psychology, 25*, 1–17.

Dawes, R. M., & Corrigan, B. (1974). Linear models in decision making, *Psychological Bulletin*, 81, 95–106.

Dawes, R. M., Faust, D., & Meehl, P. E. (1989). Clinical versus actuarial judgment. *Science, 243*, 1668–1674.

Dawes, R. M., McTavish, J., & Shacklee, H. (1977). Behavior, communication, and assumptions about other people's behavior in a commons dilemma situation. *Journal of Personality and Social Psychology, 35*, 1–11.

Dawes, R. M., Orbell, J. M., Simmons, R. T., & van de Kragt, A. J. C. (1986). Organizing groups for collective action. *American Political Science Review, 80*, 1171–1185.

Dawkins, R. (2009). *The god delusion*. New York: Random House.

Dawkins, R., & Carlisle, T. R. (1976). Parental investment, mate desertion, and a fallacy. *Nature, 262*, 131–133.

de Dombal, F. T., Leaper, D. J., Horrocks, J. C., Staniland, J. R., & McCann, A. P. (1974). Human and computer-aided diagnosis of abdominal pain: Further report with emphasis on performance of clinicians. *British Medical Journal, 1*, 376–380.

DeJoy, D. (1989). The optimism bias and traffic accident risk prevention. *Accident Analysis and Prevention, 21*, 333–340.

DeKay, W. T., Haselton, M. G., & Kirkpatrick, L. A. (2000). Reversing figure and ground in the rationality debate: An evolutionary perspective. *Behavioral and Brain Sciences, 23*, 670–671.

De Morgan, A. (1926). *Formal logic, or, the calculus of inference, necessary and probable* (2nd ed.) Edited by A. E. Taylor. London: Open Court. (Originally published in 1847.)

De Neys, W., Schaeken, W., & d'Ydewalle, G. (2003a). Causal conditional reasoning and strength of association: The disabling condition case. *European Journal of Cognitive Psychology, 42*, 177–190.

De Neys, W., Schaeken, W., & d'Ydewalle, G. (2003b). Inference suppression and semantic memory retrieval: Every counterexample counts. *Memory and Cognition, 31*, 581–595.

DePaulo, B. M., & Pfeifer, R. L. (1986). On-the-job experience and skill at detecting deception. *Journal of Applied Social Psychology, 16*, 249–267.

DePaulo, B. M., Charlton, K., Cooper, H., Lindsay, J. J., & Muhlenbruck, L. (1997). The accuracy-confidence correlation in the detection of deception. *Personality and Social Psychology Review, 1*, 346–357.

DePaulo, B. M., Kashy, D. A., Kirkendol, S. E., Wyer, M. M., & Epstein, J. A. (1996). Lying in everyday life. *Journal of Personality and Social Psychology, 70*, 979–995.

Detweiler, J. B., Bedell, B. T., Salovey, P., Pronin, E., & Rothman, A. J. (1999). Message framing and sunscreen use: Gain-framed messages motivate beach-goers. *Health Psychology, 18*, 189–196.

DeWall, C. N., Baumeister, R. F., Chester, D. S., & Bushman, B. J. (2016). How often does currently felt emotion predict social behavior and judgment? A meta-analytic test of two theories. *Emotion Review, 8*, 136–143.

Dewdney, A. K. (1993). *200 percent of nothing*. New York: Wiley.

Dholakia, R. R. & Sternthal, B. (1977). Highly credible sources: Persuasive facilitators or persuasive liabilities?, *Journal of Consumer Research, 3*, 223–232.

DiCarlo, C. (2011). *How to become a really good pain in the ass. A critical thinker's guide to asking the right questions*. Amherst, NY: Prometheus Books.

DiChristina, M., & Meyerson, B. S. (Eds.) (2018). Top 10 emerging technologies of 2018. *Scientific American, 321*, 26–37.

Dickstein, L. S. (1975). Effects of instructions and premise ordering errors in syllogistic reasoning. *Journal of Experimental Psychology: Human Learning and Memory, 104*, 376–384.

Dickstein, L. S. (1978a). The effect of figure on syllogistic reasoning. *Memory and Cognition, 6*, 76–83.

Dickstein, L. S. (1978b). Error processes in syllogistic reasoning. *Memory and Cognition, 6*, 537–543.

Dillard, J., & Shen, L. (2012). *The Sage handbook of persuasion: Developments in theory and practice*. Thousand Oaks, CA: Sage.

Dimnet, E. (1928). *The art of thinking*. New York: Simon & Schuster.

Ditto, P. H., & Lopez, D. F. (1992). Motivated skepticism: Use of differential decision criteria for preferred and nonpreferred conclusions. *Journal of Personality and Social Psychology, 63*, 568–584.

Ditto, P. H., Jemmott, J. B., & Darley, J. M. (1988). Appraising the threat of illness: A mental representational approach. *Health Psychology*, *7*, 183–201.

Dobrescu, B. A., & Lincoln, D. (2015). Mystery of the hidden cosmos. *Scientific American*, *313*, 32–39.

Drizin, S. A., & Leo, R. A. (2004). The problem of false confessions in the post-DNA world. *North Carolina Law Review*, *82*, 891–1007.

Druckman, J. N. (2001a). The implications of framing effects for citizen competence. *Political Behavior*, *23*, 225–256.

Druckman, J. N. (2001b). On the limits of framing effects: Who can frame? *The Journal of Politics*, *63*, 1041–1066.

Drummond, C., & Fischhoff, B. (2019). Does "putting on your thinking cap" reduce myside bias in evaluation of scientific information? *Thinking and Reasoning*, *25*, 477–505.

Dube, C., Rotello, C., & Heit, E. (2010). Assessing the belief bias effect with ROCs: It's a response bias effect. *Psychological Review*, *117*, 831–863.

Dube, C., Rotello, C., & Heit, E. (2011). The belief bias effect is aptly named: A reply to Klauer and Kellen (2011). *Psychological Review*, *118*, 155–163.

Dube-Rioux, L., & Russo, J. E. (1988). An availability bias in professional judgment. *Journal of Behavioral Decision Making*, *1*, 223–237.

Dubois, D., & Prade, H. (1990). An introduction to possibilistic and fuzzy logics. In G. Shafer & J. Pearle (Eds.), *Readings in uncertain reasoning* (pp. 742–761). Ithaca, NY: Morgan Kaufman.

Dubois, D., Rucker, D. D., & Galinsky, A. D. (2016). Dynamics of communicator and audience power: The persuasiveness of competence versus warmth. *The Journal of Consumer Research*, *43*, 68–85.

Dunning, D. (1993). Words to live by: The self and definitions of social concepts and categories. In J. Suls (Ed.), *Psychological perspectives on the self* (pp. 99–126). Hillsdale, NJ: Erlbaum.

Dunning, D., & Hayes, A. F. (1996). Evidence for egocentric comparison in social judgment. *Journal of Personality and Social Psychology*, *71*, 213–229.

Dunning, D., Heath, C., & Suls, J. M. (2004). Flawed self-assessment: Implications for health, education, and the workplace. *Psychological Science in the Public Interest*, *5*, 69–106.

Dunning, D., Perie, M., & Story, A. (1991). Self-serving prototypes of social categories. *Journal of Personality and Social Psychology*, *61*, 957–968.

Eagly, A. H., Wood, W., & Chaiken, S. (1978). Causal inferences about communicators and their effect on opinion change. *Journal of Personality and Social Psychology*, *36*, 424–435.

Easterbrook, P. J., Berlin, J. A., Gopalan, R., & Matthews, D. R. (1991). Publication bias in clinical research. *Lancet*, *337*, 867–872.

Ebbesen, E. B., & Konecni, V. J. (1980). On the external validity of decision-making research: What do we know about decisions in the real world? In T. S. Wallsten (Ed.), *Cognitive processes in choice and decision behavior* (pp. 21–45). Hillsdale, NJ: Erlbaum.

Edlow, D., & Kiesler, C. (1966). Ease of denial and defensive projection. *Journal of Experimental Social Psychology*, *2*, 56–69.

Edwards, A. L. (1957). *The social desirability variable in personality assessment and research*. New York: Dryden.

Edwards, K., & Smith, E. E. (1996). A disconfirmation bias in the evaluation of arguments. *Journal of Personality and Social Psychology*, *71*, 5–24.

Edwards, P. (1952). Bertrand Russell's doubts about induction. In A. G. N. Flew (Ed.), *Logic and language* (pp. 55–79). Oxford: Basil Blackwell.

Egglin, T. K., & Feinstein, A. R. (1996). Context bias. A problem in diagnostic radiology. *Journal of the American Medical Association. 276*, 1752–1755.

Ehninger, D. (1966). Validity as moral obligation. *Southern Speech Journal*, *21*, 215–222.

Ehninger, D., & Brockriede, W. (1963). *Decision by debate*. New York: International Debate Education Association.

Einhorn, H. J., & Hogarth, R. M. (1978). Confidence in judgment: Persistence of the illusion of validity. *Psychological Review*, *85*, 395–416.

Einstein, A. (1961). *Relativity: The special and the general theory*. New York: Bonanza books. (First published in 1916.)

Ekstrom, R. B., French, J. W., Harman, H., & Dermen, D. (1976). *Manuel for kit of factor-referenced cognitive tests*. Princeton, NJ: Educational Testing Service.

Eliades, M., Mansell, W., Stewart, A. J., & Blanchette, I. (2012). An investigation of belief-bias and logicality in reasoning with emotional contents. *Thinking and Reasoning*, *18*, 461–479.

Ellis, B. (1979). Hypothetical reasoning and conditionals. In E. Sosa (Ed.), *The philosophy of Nicholas Rescher: Discussion and replies* (pp. 33–45). Dordrecht, Holland: D. Reidel Publishing.

Ennis, R. H. (1985). Critical thinking and the curriculum. *National Forum*, *65*, 28–31.

Ennis, R. H. (2001). Argument appraisal strategy: A comprehensive approach. *Informal Logic*, *21*, 97–140.

Enos, R. D., Fowler, A., & Havasy, C. S. (2017). The negative effect fallacy: A case study of incorrect statistical reasoning by federal courts. *Journal of Experimental Legal Studies*, *14*, 618–647.

Epstude, K., & Jonas, K. J. (2015). Regret and counterfactual thinking in the face of inevitability: The case of HIV positive men. *Social Psychological and Personality Science*, *6*, 157–163.

Epstude, K., & Roese, N. J. (2008). The functional theory of counterfactual thinking. *Personality and Social Psychology Review*, *12*, 168–192.

Epstude, K., Scholl, A., & Roese, N, J. (2016). Prefactual thoughts: Mental simulations about what might happen. *Review of General Psychology*, *20*, 48–56.

Eraker, S. A., & Sox, H. C. (1981). Assessment of patients' preferences for therapeutic outcomes. *Medicinal Decision Making*, *1*, 29–39.

Erickson, J. R. (1974). A set analysis theory of behaviour in formal syllogistic reasoning tasks. In R. Solo (Ed.), *Loyola symposium on cognition* (Vol. 2). Hillsdale, NJ: Erlbaum.

Erickson, J. R. (1978). Research on syllogistic reasoning. In R. Revlin & R. E. Mayer (Eds.), *Human reasoning* (pp. 39–50). New York: Holt, Rinehart and Winston.

Erskine, H. (1973). The polls: Hopes, fears, and regrets. *Public Opinion Quarterly, 37*, 132–145.

Erstad, W. (2018). 6 critical thinking skills you need to master now. www.rasmussen.edu/student-life/blogs/college-life/critical-thinking-skills-to-master-now/

Evans, C. E. (1973). *Cults of unreason*. New York: Farrar, Straus, and Giroux.

Evans, J. St. B. T. (1977a). Linguistic factors in reasoning. *Quarterly Journal of Experimental Psychology, 29*, 297–306.

Evans, J. St. B. T. (1977b). Toward a statistical theory of reasoning. *Quarterly Journal of Experimental Psychology, 29*, 621–635.

Evans, J. St. B. T. (1982). *The psychology of deductive reasoning*. London: Routledge & Kegan Paul Ltd.

Evans, J. St. B. T. (1989). *Bias in human reasoning: Causes and consequences*. Hillsdale, NJ: Erlbaum.

Evans, J. St. B. T. (1993). Bias and rationality. In K. I. Manktelow & D. E. Over (Eds.), *Rationality: Psychological and philosophical perspectives* (pp. 6–30). London: Routledge.

Evans, J. St. B. T. (2012). Questions and challenges for the new psychology of reasoning. *Thinking and Reasoning, 18*, 5–31.

Evans, J. St. B. T., & Lynch, J. S. (1973). Matching bias in the selection task. *British Journal of Psychology, 64*, 391–397.

Evans, J. St. B. T., & Pollard, P. (1990). Belief bias and problem complexity in deductive reasoning. In J. P. Caverni, J. M. Fabre, & M. Gonzales (Eds.), *Cognitive biases* (pp. 131–154). Amsterdam: North Holland.

Evans, J. St. B. T., Barston, J. L., & Pollard, P. (1983). On the conflict between logic and belief in syllogistic reasoning. *Memory and Cognition, 11*, 295–306.

Evans, J. St. B. T., Newstead, S. E., & Byrne, R. M. J. (1993). *Human reasoning: The psychology of deduction*. Hove: Erlbaum.

Evans, J. St. B. T., Over, D. E., & Manktelow, K. I. (1993). Reasoning, decision making and rationality. *Cognition, 49*, 165–187.

Evans, J. St. B. T., Handley, S. J., Neilens, H., & Over, D. E. (2007). Thinking about conditionals: A study of individual differences. *Memory and Cognition, 35*, 1772–1784.

Evans, J. St. B. T., Newstead, E., Allen, J., & Pollard, P. (1994). Debiasing by instruction: The case of belief bias. *European Journal of Cognitive Psychology, 6*, 263–285.

Falchikov, N., & Boud, D. (1989). Student self-assessment in higher education: A meta-analysis. *Review of Educational Research, 59*, 395–430.

Falk, E. B., Rameson, L., Berkman, E. T. et al.(2010). The neural correlates of persuasion: A common network across cultures and media. *Journal of Cognitive Neuroscience, 22*, 2447–2459.

Falk, R. (1991). Randomness – an ill-defined but much needed concept (Commentary on Ayton, Hunt, & Wright's "Psychological conceptions of randomness"). *Journal of Behavioral Decision Making, 4*, 215–218.

Falk, R. (1993). *Understanding probability and statistics: A book of problems.* Wellsley, MA: A. K. Peters.

Falk, R. (2011). When truisms clash: Coping with a counterintuitive problem concerning the notorious two-child family. *Thinking and Reasoning, 17*, 353–366.

Falk, R. (2016). *Many faces of the gambler's fallacy: Subjective randomness and its diverse manifestations.* Charleston, SC: CreateSpace Independent Publishing Platform.

Falk, R., & Konold, C. (1992). The psychology of learning probability. In F. S. Gordon & S. P. Gordon (Eds.), *Statistics for the twenty-first century* (pp. 151–164). Washington, DC: Mathematical Association of America.

Falk, R., & Konold, C. (1997). Making sense of randomness: Implicit encoding as a basis for judgment. *Psychological Review, 104*, 301–318.

Falk, R., & Konold, C. (1998). Subjective randomness. In S. Kotz, C. B. Read, & D. L. Banks (Eds.), Encyclopedia of statistical sciences. Update Vol. 2 (pp. 653–659). New York: Wiley.

Falk, R., & Lavie Lann, A. (2015). Numbers defy the law of large numbers. *Teaching Statistics, 37*, 54–60.

Fawcett, H. P. (1938). *The nature of proof; a description and evaluation of certain procedures used in a senior high school to develop an understanding of the nature of proof.* Oxford, England: Teachers College, Columbia University.

Fearnside, W. W., & Holther, W. B. (1959). *Fallacy: The counterfeit of argument.* Englecliffs, NJ: Prentice-Hall.

Feeney, A., & Heit, E. (2011). Properties of the diversity effect in category-based inductive reasoning. *Thinking and Reasoning, 17*, 156–181.

Feldman, J. Miyamoto, J., & Loftus, E. F. (1999). Are actions regretted more than inactions? *Organizational Behavior and Human Decision Processes, 78*, 232–255.

Ferguson, K. (1994). *The fire in the equations: Science, religion, and the search for God.* London: Bantam Press.

Festinger, L., Schacter, S., & Back, K. (1950). *Social pressures in informal groups.* New York: Harper.

Fiedler, K. (2000). Beware of samples! A cognitive-ecological sampling approach to judgment biases. *Psychological Review, 107*, 659–676.

Fiedler, K., Armbruster, T., Nickel, S., Walther, E., & Asbeck, J. (1996). Constructive biases in social judgment: Experiments on the self-verification of question contents. *Journal of Personality and Social Psychology, 71*, 861–873.

Fields, J. M., & Schuman, H. (1976). Public beliefs about the beliefs of the public. *Public Opinion Quarterly, 40*, 427–448.

Fillenbaum, S. (1975). If: Some uses. *Psychological Research, 37*, 245–260.

Fillenbaum, S. (1976). Inducements: On phrasing and logic of conditional promises, threats and warnings. *Psychological Research, 38*, 231–250.

Fine, T. L. (1973). *Theories of probability.* New York: Academic Press.

Finocchiaro, M. A. (1980). *Galileo and the art of reasoning: Rhetorical foundations of logic and scientific method*. Dordrecht, Holland: Reidel.

Finocchiaro, M. A. (1981). Fallacies and the evaluation of reasoning. *American Philosophical Quarterly, 18*, 13–22.

Finocchiaro, M. A. (1986). An historical approach to the study of argumentation. In F. H. van Eemeren, R. Grootendorst, J. A. Blair, & C. A. Willard (Eds.), *Argumentation: Across the lines of discipline* (pp. 81–91). Dordrecht, Holland: Foris Publications.

Finocchiaro, M. A. (1995). Six types of fallaciousness: Toward a realistic theory of logical criticism. In H. V. Hansen & R. C. Pinto (Eds.), *Fallacies: Classical and contemporary readings* (pp. 120–129). University Park, PA: The Pennsylvania State University Press. (Originally published in 1987.

Fischhoff, B. (1975). Hindsight ≠ foresight: The effect of outcome knowledge on judgment under uncertainty. *Journal of Experimental Psychology: Human Perception and Performance, 1*, 288–299.

Fischhoff, B. (1977). Perceived informativeness of facts. *Journal of Experimental Psychology: Human Perception and Performance, 3*, 349–358.

Fischhoff, B. (1980). For those condemned to study the past: Reflective on historical judgment. In R. A. Schwede, & D. W. Fiske (Eds.), *New directions for methodology of behavioral science: Fallible judgments in behavioral research* (pp. 79–93). San Francisco, CA: Jossey-Bass.

Fischhoff, B. (1982). Debiasing. In D. Kahneman, P. Slovic, & A. Tversky (Eds.), *Judgment under uncertainty: Heuristics and biases* (pp. 422–444). Cambridge: Cambridge University Press.

Fischhoff, B., & Beyth-Marom, R. (1975). I knew it would happen: Remembered probabilities of once-future things. *Organizational Behavior and Human Performance, 13*, 1–16.

Fischhoff, B. A., & Chauvin, C. (Eds.) (2011). *Intelligence analysis: Behavioral and social scientific foundations*. Washington, DC: National Academy Press.

Fischhoff, B., Slovic, P., & Lichtenstein, S. (1977). Knowing with certainty: The appropriateness of extreme confidence. *Journal of Experimental Psychology: Human Perception and Performance, 3*, 552–564.

Fischhoff, B., Slovic, P., & Lichtenstein, S. (1978). Fault trees: Sensitivity of estimated failure probabilities to problem representations. *Journal of Experimental Psychology: Human Perception and Performance, 4*, 330–344.

Fisher, A. (1986). Using assertibility conditions to extract and evaluate arguments. In F. H. van Eemeren, R. Grootendorst, J. A. Blair, & C. A. Willard (Eds.), *Argumentation: Analysis and practices* (pp. 25–33). Dordrecht, Holland: Foris Publications.

Fisher, A. (1988). *The logic of real arguments*. New York: Cambridge University Press.

Fisher, A. (2004). *The logic of real arguments* (2nd ed.). Cambridge: Cambridge University Press. (First published in 1988.)

Flesch, R. (1951). *The art of clear thinking*. New York: Collier Books.

Flew, A. G. N. (1968). Introduction. In A. G. N. Flew (Ed.), *Logic and language* (pp. 1–10). Oxford: Blackwell.

Fohr, S. (1980). Deductive-inductive: Reply to criticisms. *Informal Logic Newsletter, 3*, 5–10.

Fong, G. T., Krantz, D. H., & Nisbett, R. E. (1986). The effects of statistical training on thinking about every-day problems. *Cognitive Psychology, 18*, 253–292.

Forgas, J. P. (1995). Mood and judgment: The affect infusion model (AIM). *Psychological Bulletin, 117*, 39–66.

Frances, A. et al. (1994). *Diagnostic and Statistical Manual of Mental Disorders IV.* Arlington, VA: American Psychiatric Association.

Franklin, B. (1907). A letter to Joseph Priestly, September 19, 1772. In A. H. Smyth (Ed.), *The writings of Benjamin Franklin* (pp. 437–438). New York: Macmillan.

Frase, L. T. (1966). Validity judgments of syllogisms in relation to two sets of terms. *Journal of Educational Psychology, 57*, 239–245.

Frase, L. T. (1968). Effects of semantic incompatibility upon deductive reasoning. *Psychonomic Science, 12*, 64.

Freeman, J. B. (1995). The appeal to popularity and presumption by common knowledge. In H. V. Hansen & R. C. Pinto (Eds.), *Fallacies: Classical and contemporary readings* (pp. 265–273). University Park, PA: The Pennsylvania State University Press.

Freeman, R. (August 6, 2006). *Was the atomic bombing of Japan necessary?* Common Dreams. www.commondreams.org

Freud, S. (1957). The ego and the id. In J. Rickman (Ed.), *A general selection from the works of Sigmund Freud.* Garden City, NJ: Doubleday. (Originally published in 1923.)

Friedman, N., & Halpern, J. Y. (1995). Plausibility measures: A user's guide. *Proceedings of UAI '95*, 175–184.

Friedrich, J. (1993). Primary error detection and minimization (PEDMIN) strategies in social cognition: A reintrerpretation of confirmation bias phenomena. *Psychological Review, 100*, 298–319.

Friestad, M., & Wright, P. (1994). The persuasion knowledge model: How people cope with persuasion attempts. *Journal of Consumer Research, 21*, 1–31.

Frisch, D. (1993). Reasons for framing effects. *Organizational Behavior and Human Decision Processes, 54*, 399–429.

Funder, D. C. (1980). On seeing ourselves as others see us: Self-other agreement and discrepancy in personality ratings. *Journal of Personality, 48*, 473–493.

Funder, D. C. (1987). Errors and mistakes: Evaluating the accuracy of social judgment. *Psychological Bulletin, 101*, 79–90.

Funder, D. C. (2001). The really, really fundamental attribution error. *Psychological Inquiry, 12*, 21–23.

Galinsky, A. D., & Ku, G. (2004). The effects of perspective taking on prejudice: The moderating role of self-evaluation. *Personality and Social Psychology Bulletin, 30*, 594–604.

Galinsky, A. D., & Moskowitz, G. (2000). Perspective-taking: Decreasing stereotype expression, stereotype accessibility, and in-group favoritism. *Journal of Personality and Social Psychology, 78*, 708–724.

Galinsky, A. D., Rucker, D. D., & Magee, J. C. (2015). Power, past findings, present considerations and future directions. In J. A. Simpson, J. F. Dovidio, M. Mikulincer, & P. A. Shaver (Eds.), *APA Handbook of Personality and Social Psychology, Vol. 3, Interpersonal relations* (pp. 421–460). Washington, DC: American Psychological Association.

Galotti, K. M. (1989). Approaches to studying formal and everyday reasoning. *Psychological Bulletin, 105*, 331–351.

Galotti, K. M., Baron, J., & Sabini, J. P. (1986). Individual differences in syllogistic reasoning: Deduction rules or mental models? *Journal of Experimental Psychology: General, 115*, 16–25.

Garland, H., & Newport, S. (1991). Effects of absolute and relative sunk costs on the decision to persist with a course of action. *Organizational Behavior and Human Decision Processes, 48*, 55–69.

Garner, R. (2005). Post-It note persuasion: A sticky influence. *Journal of Consumer Psychology, 15*, 230–237.

Garnham, A., & Oakhill, J. (1994). *Thinking and reasoning*. Oxford: Blackwell.

Garry, M., & Polaschek, D. L. L. (2000). Imagination and memory. *Psychological Science, 9*, 6–9.

Garry, M., Manning, C. G., Loftus, E. F., & Sherman, S. J. (1996). Imagination inflation: Imagining a childhood event inflates confidence that it occurred. *Psychonomic Bulletin and Review, 3*, 208–214.

Garssen, B. J. (1997). *Argumentatieschema's in pragma-dialectisch perspectief: Een theoretisch en empirisch onderzoek*. Amsterdam: IFOTT.

Gebauer, G., & Laming, D. (1997). Rational choices in Wason's selection task. *Psychological Research, 60*, 284–293.

Geis, M. C., & Zwicky, A. M. (1971). On invited inferences. *Linguistic Inquiry, 2*, 561–566.

Gelernter, D. (1994). *The muse in the machine: Computerizing the poetry of human thought*. New York: The Free Press.

Gentner, D., & Grudin, J. (1985). The evolution of mental metaphors in psychology: A ninety-year retrospective. *American Psychologist, 40*, 181–192.

Gerend, M. A., & Shepherd, J. E. (2007). Using message framing to promote acceptance of the human papillomavirus vaccine. *Health Psychology, 26*, 745–752.

Gertner, A., Zaromb, F., Schneider, R., Roberts, R. D., & Matthews, G. (2016). The assessment of biases in cognition: Development and evaluation of an assessment instrument for the measurement of cognitive bias. Mitre Technical Report (MTR) 160163. Westford, MA: The MITRE Corporation.

Gertner, A., Zaromb, F., Schneider, R. et al. (2013). Developing a standardized assessment of cognitive bias for the IARPA Sirius program: A review of the literature. Mitre Technical Report.

Gettys, C. F., Fisher, S. D., & Mehle, T. (1978). Hypothesis generation and plausibility assessment. Annual Report TR 15-10-78. Decision Processes Laboratory, University of Oklahoma.

Gigerenzer, G. (1984). External validity of laboratory experiments: The frequency-validity relationship. *American Journal of Psychology, 97*, 185–195.

Gigerenzer, G., & Brighton, H. (2009). Homo heuristicus: Why biased minds make better inferences. *Topics in Cognitive Science, 1*, 107–143.
Gilbert, D. T. (1991). How mental systems believe. *American Psychologist, 46*, 107–119.
Gilbert, D. T. (2006). *Stumbling on happiness*. New York: Random House.
Gilbert, D. T., & Malone, P. S. (1995). The correspondence bias. *Psychological Bulletin, 117*, 21–38.
Gilbert, D. T., & Wilson, T. D. (2007). Prospection: Experiencing the future. *Science, 317*, 1351–1354.
Gilbert, D. T., Krull, D. S., & Malone, P. S. (1990). Unbelieving the unbelievable: Some problems in the rejection of false information. *Journal of Personality and Social Psychology, 59*, 601–613.
Gilio, A., & Over, D. (2012). The psychology of inferring conditionals from disjunctions: A probabilistic study. *Journal of Mathematical Psychology, 56*, 118–131.
Gilovich, T. (1991). *How we know what isn't so: The fallibility of human reason in everyday life*. New York: The Free Press.
Gilovich, T., Savitsky, K., & Medvec, V. H. (1998). The illusion of transparency: Biased assessments of another's ability to read one's emotional states. *Journal of Personality and Social Psychology, 75*, 332–346.
Gilovich, T., Wang, R. F., Regan, D., & Nishina, S. (2003). Regrets of action and inaction across cultures. *Journal of Cross-Cultural Psychology, 34*, 61–71.
Gingerich, O. (1982). The Galileo affair. *Scientific American, 247*, 133–143.
Gino, F., Shang, J., & Croson, R. (2009). The impact of information from similar or different advisors on judgment. *Organizational Behavior and Human Decision Processes, 108*, 287–302.
Girotto, V., Legrenzi, P., & Rizzo, A. (1991). Event controllability in counterfactual thinking. *Acta Psychologica, 78*, 111–133.
Glance, N. S., & Huberman, B. A. (1994). The dynamics of social dilemmas. *Scientific American, 279*, 76–81.
Glenberg, A. M., & Epstein, W. (1985). Calibration of comprehension. *Journal of Experimental Psychology: Learning, Memory, and Cognition, 11*, 702–718.
Glenberg, A. M., & Epstein, W. (1987). Inexpert calibration of comprehension. *Memory and Cognition, 15*, 84–93.
Godden, D. M. (2003). Reconstruction and representation: Deductivism as an interpretative strategy (2003). OSSA Conference Archive, 26.
Goffman, E. (1967). *Interaction ritual*. Garden City, NY: Doubleday.
Goldings, H. J. (1954). On the avowal and projection of happiness. *Journal of Personality, 25*, 30–47.
Goldman, A. I. (1986). *Epistemology and cognition*. Cambridge, MA: Harvard University Press.
Golin, S., Sweeney, P. D., & Shaeffer, D. E. (1981). The causality of causal attributions in depression: A cross-lagged panel correlational analysis. *Journal of Abnormal Psychology, 90*, 14–22.
Good I. J. (1983). *Good thinking: The foundations of probability and its applications*. Minneapolis, MN: University of Minnesota Press.

Goodfield, J. (1996). *Reflections on science and the media.* New York: American Association for the Advancement of Science.

Goorden, D., & Fischer, T. (2011). Conductive arguments and 'inference to the best explanation.' OSSA Conference Archive 26.

Gopnik, A., & Astington, J. W. (1988). Children's understanding of representational change and its relation to the understanding of false belief and the appearance-reality distinction. *Child Development, 59*, 26–37.

Gordon, R. (1986). Folk psychology as simulation. *Mind and Language, 1*, 158–171.

Gorn, G. J., Goldberg, M. E., & Basu, K. (1993). Mood, awareness and product evaluation. *Journal of Consumer Evaluation, 2*, 237–256.

Gould, S. J. (1981). *The mismeasure of man*. New York: Norton.

Gould, S. J. (1994). The evolution of life on earth. *Scientific American, 271*, 84–91.

Govier, T. (1986). Beyond induction and deduction. In F. H. van Eemeren, R. Grootendorst, J. A. Blair, & C. A. Willard (Eds.), *Argumentation: Across the lines of discipline* (pp. 57–64). Dordrecht, Holland: Foris Publications.

Govier, T. (1987). *Problems in argument and evaluation*. Dordrecht, Holland: Foris Publications.

Govier, T. (1995). Reply to Massey. In H. V. Hansen & R. C. Pinto (Eds.), *Fallacies: Classical and contemporary readings* (pp. 172–180). University Park, PA: The Pennsylvania State University Press. (Originally published in 1987.)

Govier, T. (1999). *The philosophy of argument.* Newport News, VA: Vale Press.

Govier, T. (2011). Conductive arguments: Overview of the symposium. In J. A. Blair & R. H. Johnson (Eds.), *Conductive arguments: An overlooked type of defeasible reasoning* (pp. 262–276). London: College Publications.

Granberg, D., & Brent, E. (1983). When prophecy bends: The preference-expectation link in U.S. presidential elections, 1952–1980. *Journal of Personality and Social Psychology, 45*, 477–491.

Granberg, D., & King, M. (1980). Cross-lagged panel analysis of the relation between attraction and perceived similarity. *Journal of Experimental Social Psychology, 16*, 573–581.

Granberg, D., & Robertson, C. (1982). Contrast effects in estimating policies of the federal government. *The Public Opinion Quarterly, 46*, 43–53.

Grandy, R. (1973). Reference, meaning, and belief. *Journal of Philosophy, 70*, 439–452.

Gray, J. B. (2008). Framing: A communication strategy for the medical encounter. *Journal of Communication in Healthcare, 1*, 422–430.

Green, D. W. (2007). A mental model theory of informal argument. In W. Schaeken, A. Vandierendonck, W. Shroyens, & G. d'Ydewalle (Eds.), *The mental model theory of reasoning: Refinements and extensions* (pp. 189–208). Hove: Psychology Press.

Green, D. W. (2008). Persuasion and the contexts of dissuasion: Causal models and informal arguments. *Thinking and Reasoning, 14*, 28–59.

Green, D. W., & McCloy, R. (2003). Reaching a verdict. *Thinking and Reasoning, 9*, 307–333.

Green, D. W., Applebaum, R., & Tong, S. (2006). Mental simulation and argument. *Thinking and Reasoning, 12*, 31–61.

Green, M. C., & Brock, T. C. (2000). The role of transportation in the persuasiveness of public narratives. *Journal of Personality and Social Psychology, 79*, 701–721.

Greene, E., & Cahill, B. S. (2012). Effects of neuroimaging evidence on mock juror decision making. *Behavioral* Sciences and the Law, *30*, 280–296.

Greening, L., & Chandler, C. C. (1997). Why it can't happen to me: The base rate matters, but overestimating skill leads to underestimating risk. *Journal of Applied Psychology, 27*, 760–780.

Greenwald, A. G. (1980). The totalitarian ego: Fabrication and revision of personal history. *American Psychologist, 35*, 603–618.

Gregory, W. L., Cialdini, R. B., & Carpenter, K. M. (1982). Self-relevant scenarios as mediators of likelihood estimates and compliance: Does imagining make it so? *Journal of Personality and Social Psychology, 43*, 89–99.

Greifeneder, R., Bless, H., & Pham, M. T. (2011). When do people rely on affective and cognitive feelings in judgment? A review. *Personality and Social Psychology Review, 15*, 107–141.

Greitemeyer, T. (2014). Article retracted, but the message lives on. *Psychonomic Bulletin and Review, 21*, 557–561.

Grennan, W. (1986). A "logical audit" scheme for argument evaluation. In F. H. van Eemeren, R. Grootendorst, J. A. Blair, & C. A. Willard (Eds.), *Argumentation: Analysis and practices* (pp. 17–24). Dordrecht, Holland: Foris Publications.

Griffin, D. W., & Buehler, R. (1999). Frequency, probability, and prediction: Easy solutions to cognitive illusions? *Cognitive Psychology, 38*, 48–78.

Grootendorst, R. (1986). Some fallacies about fallacies. In F. H. van Eemeren, R. Grootendorst, J. A. Blair, & C. A. Willard (Eds.), *Argumentation: Across the lines of discipline* (pp. 331–342). Dordrecht, Holland: Foris Publications.

Grosset, N., & Barrouillet, P. (2003). On the nature of mental models of conditionals: The case of *If*, *If then*, and *Only* if. *Thinking and Reasoning, 9*, 289–306.

Gudjonsson, G. (2003). *The psychology of interrogations and confessions: A handbook*. New York: Wiley.

Guelzo, A. C. (2017). *America's founding fathers*. The Teaching Company. Recorded book produced in collaboration with The Smithsonian Museum.

Guilford, J. P. (1967). *The nature of human intelligence*. New York: McGraw-Hill.

Guinote, A., & Vescio, T. (2010). *The social psychology of power*. New York: Guilford Press.

Gula, R. (1979). *Nonsense: How to overcome it*. New York: Stein and Day.

Gutting, R., & Ferrell, J. (2004). Reality compared with its alternatives: Age differences in judgments of regret and relief. *Developmental Psychology, 40*, 764–775.

Haard, J., Slater, M. D., & Long, M. (2004). Scientese and ambiguous citations in the selling of unproven medical treatments. *Health Communications, 16*, 411–426.

Hacking, I. (1975). *The emergence of probability*. New York: Cambridge University Press.

Hadjichristidis, C., Sloman, S. A., & Over, D. E. (2014). Categorical induction from uncertain premises: Jeffrey's doesn't completely rule. *Thinking and Reasoning*, *20*, 405–431.

Hadley, J. E. (1936). Teaching poetry appreciation. *Studies in Higher Education, Bulletin of Purdue University*, *37*, 52–54.

Hafner, A., Ingels, S., Schneider, B., & Stevenson, D. (1990). *A profile of the American eighth grader: NELS, 88 student descriptive summary*. Washington, DC: National Center for Educational Statistics.

Hahn, U., & Hornikx, J. (2016). A normative framework for argument quality: Argumentation schemes with a Bayesian foundation. *Synthese*, *193*, 1833–1873.

Hahn, U., & Oaksford, M. (2006). A Bayesian approach to informal argument fallacies. *Synthese*, *152*, 207–236.

Hahn, U., & Oaksford, M. (2007). The rationality of informal argumentation: A Bayesian approach to reasoning fallacies. *Psychological Review*, *114*, 704–732.

Hahn, U., & Oaksford, M. (2012). Rational argument. In K. J. Holyoak & R. G. Morrison (Eds.), *The Oxford handbook of thinking and reasoning*. Oxford: Oxford university Press.

Hallihan, G. M., Cheong, H., & Shu, L. H. (2012). Confirmation and cognitive bias in design cognition. ASME 2012 International Design Engineering Technical Conferences and Computers and Information in Engineering Conference, American Society of Mechanical Engineers, Chicago (IL).

Halpern, J. Y. (2001). Plausibility measures: A general approach for representing uncertainty. *Proceedings of the seventeenth international joint conference on artificial intelligence* (pp. 1474–1483). Ithaca, NY: Morgan Kaufman.

Hamblin, C. L. (1970). *Fallacies*. London: Methuen.

Hamilton, D. L. (1979). A cognitive attributional analysis of stereotyping. In L. Berkowitz (Ed.), *Advances in experimental social psychology*, Vol. 12 (pp. 53–84). New York: Academic Press.

Hamilton, D. L. (1981). Illusory correlation as a basis for stereotyping. In D. L. Hamilton (Ed.), *Cognitive processes in stereotyping and intergroup behavior* (pp. 333–353). Hillsdale, NJ: Erlbaum.

Hamilton, D. L., & Gifford, R. (1976). Illusory correlation in interpersonal perception: A cognitive basis for stereotypic judgments. *Journal of Experimental Social Psychology*, *12*, 392–407.

Hample, D. J. (1979). Predicting belief and belief change using a cognitive theory of argument and evidence. *Communication Monographs*, *46*, 142–146.

Hample, D. J. (1981). What is a good argument? In G. Ziegelmueller & J. Rhodes (Eds.), *Dimensions of argument: Proceedings of the second summer conference on argument* (pp. 875–893). Annandale, VA: Speech Communication Association.

Han, B., & Fink, E. L. (2012). How do statistical and narrative evidence affect persuasion?: The role of evidentiary features. *Argumentation and Advocacy*, *49*, 39–58.

Hansen, H. V., & Pinto, R. C. (Eds.) (1995). *Fallacies: Classical and contemporary readings*. University Park, PA: The Pennsylvania State University Press.

Hardin, G. (1968). The tragedy of the commons. *Science, 162*, 1243–1248.

Hardin, G. (1985). *Filters against folly*. New York: Penguin.

Hardy, G. H. (1989). A mathematicians apology. Cambridge: Cambridge University Press. (Originally published in 1940.)

Harkness, A. R., DeBono, K. G., & Borgida, E. (1985). Personal involvement and strategies for making contingency judgments: A stake in the dating game makes a difference. *Journal of Personality and Social Psychology, 49*, 22–32.

Harman, G. (1986). *Change in view: Principles of reasoning*. Cambridge, MA: MIT Press (Bradford Books).

Harris, P. (1996). Sufficient grounds for optimism: The relationship between perceived controllability and optimistic bias. *Journal of Social and Clinical Psychology, 15*, 319–386.

Harris, D. M., & Guten, S. (1979). Health protective behavior: An exploratory study. *Journal of Health and Social Behavior, 20*, 17–29.

Harvey, N., & Fischer, I. (1997). Taking advice: Accepting help, improving judgment and sharing responsibility. *Organizational Behavior and Human Decision Processes, 70*, 117–133.

Hasegawa, T. (2007). *The end of the Pacific war: Reappraisals*. Stanford, CA: Stanford University Press

Hasher, L., Attig, M. S., & Alba, J. W. (1981). I knew it all along: Or, did I? *Journal of Verbal Learning and Verbal Behavior, 20*, 86–96.

Hasher, L., Goldstein, D., & Toppino, T. (1977). Frequency and the conference of referential validity. *Journal of Verbal Learning and Verbal Behavior, 16*, 107–112.

Hastie, R., & Kameda, T. (2005). The robust beauty of majority rules in group decisions. *Psychological Review, 112*, 494–508.

Hastings, A. C. (1962). *A reformulation of the modes of reasoning in argumentation*. Unpublished dissertation, Northwestern University, Evanston, IL.

Hastorf, A. H., & Cantril, H. (1954). They saw a game: A case study. *Journal of Abnormal and Social Psychology, 49*, 129–134.

Hatfield, E., & Rapson, R. L. (2000). Physical attractiveness. In W. E. Craighead & C. B. Nemeroff (Eds.), *The Corsini encyclopedia of psychology and behavioral science* (Vol. 3, pp. 1203–1205). New York: Wiley.

Hatfield, E., & Sprecher, S. (1986). *Mirror, mirror: The importance of looks in everyday life*. Albany, NY: State University of New York Press.

Hawkins, S. A., & Hastie, R. (1990). Hindsight: Biased judgments of past events after the outcomes are known. *Psychological Bulletin, 107*, 311–327.

Heider, F. (1944). Social perception and phenomenal causality. *Psychological Review, 51*, 358–374.

Heit, E., Hahn, U., & Feeney, A. (2005). Defending diversity. In W. Ahn, R. I. Golsdstone, B.C. Love, A. B. Markman, & P. Wolff (Eds.), *Categorization inside and outside the laboratory: Essays in honor of Douglas L. Medin* (pp. 87–99). Washington, DC: American Psychological Association.

Hempel, C. G. (1945). Studies in the logic of confirmation (I). *Mind, 54*, 1–26.

Henket, M. (1986). Ne bis in idem and related principles. In F. H. van Eemeren, R. Grootendorst, J. A. Blair, & C. A. Willard (Eds.), *Argumentation: Analysis and practices* (pp. 123–130). Dordrecht, Holland: Foris Publications.

Henle, M. (1962). On the relation between logic and thinking. *Psychological Review, 69*, 366–378.

Henle, M. (1981). Another vote for rationality. Commentary on Cohen, 1981. *The Behavioral and Brain Sciences, 4*, 339.

Henle, M., & Michael, M. (1956). The influence of attitudes on syllogistic reasoning. *Journal of Social Psychology, 44*, 115–127.

Herman, E. S., & Chomsky, N. (2008). *Manufacturing consent: The political economy of the mass media.* New York: Random House.

Herrnstein, R. J., Nickerson, R. S., Sanchez, M., & Swets, J. A. (1986). Teaching thinking skills. *American Psychologist, 41*, 1279–1289.

Hertwig, R., Gigerenzer, G., & Hoffrage, U. (1997). The reiteration effect in hindsight bias. *Psychological Review, 104*, 194–202.

Himsworth, H. (1986). *Scientific knowledge and philosophic thought.* Baltimore, MD: The Johns Hopkins University Press.

Hintikka, J. (2004). A fallacious fallacy? *Synthese, 140*, 35–45.

Hintikka, J., & Bachman, J. (1991). *What if?... Toward excellence in reasoning.* Mountain View, CA: Mayfield.

Hirt, E. R., & Markman, K. D. (1995). Multiple explanation: A consider-an-alternative strategy for debiasing judgments. *Journal of Personality and Social Psychology, 69*, 1069–1086.

Hirt, E. R., & Sherman, S. J. (1985). The role of prior knowledge in explaining hypothetical events. *Journal of Experimental Social Psychology, 21*, 519–543.

Hitchcock, D. (1986). Enthymematic arguments. In F. H. van Eemeren, R. Grootendorst, J. A. Blair, & C. A. Willard (Eds.), *Argumentation: Across the lines of discipline* (pp. 289–298). Dordrecht, Holland: Foris Publications.

Hitchcock, D. (1995). Do fallacies have a place in the teaching of reasoning skills or critical thinking? In H. V. Hansen & R. C. Pinto (Eds.), *Fallacies: Classical and contemporary readings* (pp. 319–327). University Park, PA: The Pennsylvania State University Press.

Hoagland, J. (1986). Arguments and explanations. In F. H. van Eemeren, R. Grootendorst, J. A. Blair, & C. A. Willard (Eds.), *Argumentation: Across the lines of discipline* (pp. 389–394). Dordrecht, Holland: Foris Publications.

Hobbes, T. (1919). *Leviathan.* London: J. M. Dent. (Originally published in 1651.)

Hoch, S. J. (1984). Availability and inference in predictive judgment. *Journal of Experimental Psychology: Learning, Memory, and Cognition, 10*, 649–662.

Hoch, S. J. (1987). Perceived consensus and predictive accuracy: The pros and cons of projection. *Journal of Personality and Social Psychology, 53*, 221–234.

Hoch, S. J., & Lowenstein, G. F. (1989). Outcome feedback: Hindsight and information. *Journal of Experimental Psychology: Learning, Memory, and Cognition, 15*, 605–619.

Hock, H. S. (1973). The effects of stimulus structure and familiarity on same-different comparison. *Perception and Psychophysics*, *14*, 413–420.

Hocking, M. B. (1991a). Paper versus polystyrene: A complex choice. Science, *251*, 504–505.

Hocking, M. B. (1991b). Relative merits of polystyrene foam and paper in hot drink cups: Implications for packaging. *Environmental Management*, 15, 731–747.

Hoeken, H., & Hustinx, L. (2009). When is statistical evidence superior to anecdotal evidence in supporting probability claims? The role of argument type. *Human Communication Research*, *35*, 491–510.

Hoeken, H., Šorm, E., & Schellens, P. J. (2014). Arguing about the likelihood of consequences: Laypeople's criteria to distinguish strong arguments from weak ones. *Thinking & Reasoning*, *20*, 77–98.

Hoeken, H., Timmers, R., & Schellens, P. J. (2012). Arguing about desirable consequences: What constitutes a convincing argument? *Thinking and Reasoning*, *18*, 394–416.

Hoffrage, U., & Hertwig, R. (1999). Hindsight bias: A price worth paying for fast and frugal memory. In G. Gigerenzer & P. M. Todd (Eds.), *Simple heuristics that make us smart* (pp. 191–208). New York: Oxford University Press.

Hofstadter, D. R. (2000). Analogy as the core of cognition. In J. Gleick (Ed.), *The best American scientific writing 2000* (pp. 116–144). New York: The ECCO Press.

Hogarth, R. M. (1981). Beyond discrete biases: Functional and dysfunctional aspects of judgmental heuristics. *Psychological Bulletin*, *90*, 197–217.

Holland, J. H., Holyoak, K. J., Nisbett, R. E., & Thagard, P. R. (1986). *Induction: Processes of inference, learning, and discovery*. Cambridge, MA: MIT Press.

Holmes, D. S. (1968). Dimensions of projection. *Psychological Bulletin*, *69*, 248–268.

Holzman, P. S., & Klein, G. S. (1954). Cognitive system principles of leveling and sharpening: Individual differences in assimilation effects in visual time-error. *Journal of Psychology*, *37*, 105–122.

Hoorens, V., & Buunk, B. P. (1993). Social comparison of health risks: Locus of control, the person-positivity bias, and unrealistic optimism. *Journal of Applied Social Psychology*, *18*, 291–302.

Hornikx, J. (2008). Comparing the actual and expected persuasiveness of evidence types: How good are lay people at selecting persuasive evidence? *Argumentation*, *22*, 555–569.

Hornikx, J., & Hahn, U. (2012). Reasoning and argumentation: Towards an integrated psychology of argumentation. *Thinking and Reasoning*, *18*, 225–243.

Hoskin, R. E. (1983). Opportunity cost and behavior. *Journal of Accounting Research*, *21*, 78–95.

Hovland, C. I., & Mandell, W. (1952). An experimental comparison of conclusion-drawing by the communicator and by the audience. *Journal of Abnormal Social Psychology*, *47*, 581–588.

Hovland, C. I., & Weiss, W. (1951/1952). The influence of source credibility on communication effectiveness. *Public Opinion Quarterly*, *15*, 635–650.

Hovland, C. I., Janis, I. L., & Kelley, H. H. (1953). *Communication and persuasion.* New Haven: Yale University Press.

Hovland, C. I., Lumsdaine, A. A., & Sheffield, F. D. (1949). *Experiments on mass communication.* Princeton, NJ: Princeton University Press.

Huelsen, R. (1988). Concrete accidental terms and the fallacy of figure of speech. In N. Kretzmann (Ed.), *Meaning and inference in medieval philosophy* (pp. 175–185). Dordrecht, Holland: Kluwer Academic.

Huff, D. (1954). *How to lie with statistics.* New York: W. W. Norton.

Hume, D. (1854). A treatise of human nature. In *The philosophical works of David Hume.* Book 2–3, Vol. 2. Boston: Little, Brown and Company. (Originally published in 1739.)

Hume, D. (1939). An enquiry concerning human understanding. In E. A. Burtt (Ed.), *The English philosophers from Bacon to Mill.* New York: Random House. (Originally published in 1748.)

Humphreys, P. W. (1978). (Review: Nicholas Rescher). *Plausible reasoning: An introduction to the theory and practice of plausibilistic inference. Journal of Symbolic Logic, 43,* 159–160.

Inbau, F. E., Reid, J. E., Buckley, J. P., & Jayne, B. C. (2001). *Criminal interrogation and confessions* (4th ed.). Gaithersburg, MD: Aspen Publishers.

Irwin, F. W. (1953). Stated expectations as functions of probability and desirability of outcomes. *Journal of Personality,* 21, 329–335.

Irwin, F. W., & Grace, C. N. (1968). Tests of the discontinuity hypothesis of the effects of independent outcome values upon bets. *Journal of Experimental Psychology, 76,* 444–449.

Irwin, F. W., & Metzger, M. J. (1966). Effects of probabilistic independent outcomes upon predictions. *Psychonomic Science, 5,* 79–80.

Irwin, F. W., & Snodgrass, J. G. (1966). Effects of independent and dependent outcome values upon bets. *Journal of Experimental Psychology, 71,* 282–285.

Isen, A. M., Shalker, T. E., Clark, M., & Karp, L. (1978). Affect accessibility of material in memory, and behavior: A cognitive loop. *Journal of Personality and Social Psychology, 36,* 1–2.

Jabr, F. (2017). Probiotics are no panacea. *Scientific American, 317,* 26–27.

Jackendoff, R. (1994). *Patterns in the mind: Language and human nature.* New York: Basic Books.

Jackson, S. (1983). The arguer in interpersonal argument: Pros and cons of individual-level analysis. In D. Zarefsky, M. O. Sillers, & J. Rhodes (Eds.), *Argument in transition: Proceedings of the third summer conference on argumentation* (pp. 631–637). Annandale, VA: Speech Communication Association.

Jackson, S. (1986). Rational and pragmatic aspects of argument. In F. H. van Eemeren, R. Grootendorst, J. A. Blair, & C. A. Willard (Eds.), *Argumentation: Across the lines of discipline* (pp. 217–277). Dordrecht, Holland: Foris Publications.

Jackson, S., & Allen, M. (1987). *Meta-analysis of the effectiveness of one-sided and two-sided argumentation. Paper presented at the annual meeting of the International Communication Association,* Montreal, Canada.

Jacobs, S. (1986). The management of disagreement in conversation. In F. H. van Eemeren, R. Grootendorst, J. A. Blair, & C. A. Willard (Eds.), *Argumentation: Across the lines of discipline* (pp. 229–239). Dordrecht, Holland: Foris Publications.

Jacoby, J. (2015). Shock and awe and Agrabah. *Boston Globe* (December 23, p. A11).

Jacoby, L. L., Bjork, R. A., & Kelley, C. M. (1994). Illusions of comprehension, competence, and remembering. In D. Druckman & R. A. Bjork (Eds.), *Learning, remembering, believing: Enhancing human performance* (pp. 57–80). Washington, DC: National Academy Press.

Jacquin, J. (2018). Argumentation in the workplace. In B. Vine (Ed.), *Handbook of language in the workplace* (pp. 284–294). London: Routledge.

James, W. (1979). *The will to believe and other essays.* Cambridge, MA: Harvard University Press. (Originally published in 1896.)

James, W. (1983). *The principles of psychology.* Cambridge, MA: Harvard University Press. (Work originally published in 1890.)

Janis, I. L. (1954). Personality correlates of susceptibility to persuasion. *Journal of Personality, 22*, 504–518.

Janis, I. L., & Frick, F. (1943). The relationship between attitudes toward conclusions and errors in judging logical validity of syllogisms. *Journal of Experimental Psychology, 33*, 73–77.

Janis, I. L., & King, B. T. (1949). The influence of role-playing on opinion-change. *Journal of Abnormal Social Psychology, 49*, 211–218.

Jaspers, K. (1952). *Reason and anti-reason in our time.* (Translated by S. Godman) New Haven: Yale University Press.

Jefferson, T. (2008). *Memoir, correspondence, and miscellanies from the papers of Thomas Jefferson* (Vol. IV). Frankfurt am Main, Germany: Outlook Verlag. (Second edition, edited by T. J. Randolph, originally published in 1830.)

Jeffrey, R. C. (1983). *The logic of decision* (2nd ed.). Chicago, IL: The University of Chicago Press.

Jemmott, J. B., Ditto, P. H., & Croyle, R. T. (1986). Judging health status: Effects of perceived prevalence and personal relevance. *Journal of Personality and Social Psychology, 50*, 899–905.

Jenkins, H. M., & Ward, W. C. (1965). Judgment of contingency between responses and outcomes. *Psychological Monographs: General and Applied, 79*, 1–17.

Johnson, M. K., & Sherman, S. J. (1990). Constructing and reconstructing the past and future in the present. In E. T. Higgins & R. M. Sorrentino (Eds.), *Handbook of motivation and cognition: Foundations of social behavior* (Vol. 2, pp. 482–526). New York: Guilford Press.

Johnson, R. H. (1986). Logic naturalized: Recovering a tradition. In F. H. van Eemeren, R. Grootendorst, J. A. Blair, & C. A. Willard (Eds.), *Argumentation: Across the lines of discipline* (pp. 47–56). Dordrecht, Holland: Foris Publications.

Johnson, R. H. (1995). The blaze of her splendors: Suggestions about revitalizing fallacy theory. In H. V. Hansen & R. C. Pinto (Eds.), *Fallacies: Classical and contemporary readings* (pp. 107–120). University Park, PA: The Pennsylvania State University Press. (Originally published in 1987.)

Johnson, R. H., & Blair, J. A. (1983). *Logical self-defense* (2nd ed.). Toronto: McGraw-Hill Ryerson.

Johnson, R. H., & Blair, J. A. (1993). *Logical self-defense* (3rd ed.). Toronto: McGraw-Hill Ryerson.

Johnson-Laird, P. N. (1975). Models of deduction. In R. J. Falmagne (Ed.), *Reasoning: Representation and process in children and adults* (pp. 7–54). Hillsdale, NJ: Erlbaum.

Johnson-Laird, P. N. (1983). *Mental models: Towards a cognitive science of language, inference and consciousness.* Cambridge, MA: Harvard University Press.

Johnson-Laird, P. N. (1993). *Human and machine thinking.* Hillsdale, NJ: Erlbaum.

Johnson-Laird, P. N., & Bara, B. G. (1984). Syllogistic inference. *Cognition, 16*, 1–62.

Johnson-Laird, P. N., & Byrne, R. M. J. (1989). *Only* reasoning. *Journal of Memory and Language, 28*, 313–330.

Johnson-Laird, P. N., & Byrne, R. M. J. (1991). *Deduction.* Hove: Erlbaum.

Johnson-Laird, P. N., & Byrne, R. M. J. (1993). Models and deductive rationality. In K. I. Manktelow & D. E. Over (Eds.), *Rationality: Psychological and philosophical perspectives* (pp. 177–210). London: Routledge.

Johnson-Laird, P. N., & Steedman, M. J. (1978). The psychology of syllogisms. *Cognitive Psychology, 10*, 64–99.

Johnston, W. A. (1967). An individual performance and self-evaluation in a simulated team. *Organizational Behavior and Human Performance, 2*, 309–328.

Jones, E. E. (1976). How do people perceive the causes of behavior? *American Scientist, 64*, 300–305.

Jones, E. E. (1979). The rocky road from acts to dispositions. *American Psychologist, 34*, 107–117.

Jones, E. E., & Davis, K. E. (1965). From acts to dispositions: The attribution process in person perception. In L. Berkowitz (Ed.), *Advances in experimental social psychology* (Vol. 2). New York: Academic Press.

Jones, E. E., & Harris, V. A. (1967). The attribution of attitudes. *Journal of Experimental Social Psychology, 3*, 1–24.

Joseph, H. W. B. (1906). *An introduction to logic.* Oxford: Clarendon Press.

Joseph, H. W. B. (1916). *An introduction to logic* (2nd rev. ed.). Oxford: Clarendon. (Originally published in 1906.

Jung, C. G. (1971). *Psychological types.* In G. Adler & R. F. C. Hull (Eds. & Trans), *The Collected works of C. G. Jung* (Vol. 6) Princeton, NJ: Princeton University Press. (Original published in German in 1921.)

Kahane, H. (1971). *Logic and contemporary rhetoric.* Belmont, CA: Wadsworth Publishing.

Kahane, H. (1984). *Logic and contemporary rhetoric: The use of reason in everyday life* (4th ed.). Belmont, CA: Wadsworth Publishing Company.

Kahneman, D. (2011). *Thinking, fast and slow.* New York: Farrar Straus & Giroux.

Kahneman, D., & Egan, P. (2011). *Thinking, fast and slow.* New York: Farrar, Straus and Giroux.

Kahneman, D., & Miller, D. T. (1986). Norm theory: Comparing reality by its alternatives. *Psychological Review, 93*, 136–153.

Kahneman, D., & Tversky, A. (1973). On the psychology of prediction. *Psychological Review, 80*, 237–251.

Kahneman, D., & Tversky, A. (1979). Intuitive prediction: Biases and corrective procedures. *TIMS Studies in Management Science, 12*, 313–327.

Kahneman, D., & Tversky, A. (1982a). On the study of statistical intuitions. *Cognition, 11*, 123–141.

Kahneman, D., & Tversky, A. (1982b). The simulation heuristic. In D. Kahneman, P. Slovic, & A. Tversky (Eds.), *Judgment under uncertainty: Heuristics and biases* (pp. 201–208). New York: Cambridge University Press.

Kahneman, D., & Tversky, A. (1984). Choices, values, and frames. *American Psychologist, 39*, 341–350.

Kahneman, D, Knetsch, J. L., & Thaler, R. H. (1990). Experimental tests of the endowment effect and the coase theorem. *Journal of Political Economy, 98*, 1325–1348.

Kahneman, D., Knetsch, J. L., & Thaler, R. H. (1991). The endowment effect, loss aversion, and status quo bias. *The Journal of Economic Perspectives, 5*, 193–206.

Kant, I. (2003). *Critique of pure reason.* Mineola, NY: Dover Publications. Translated by J. M. D. Meiklejohn. (Original published in 1781.)

Kappes, H. B., & Oettingen, G. (2011). Positive fantasies about idealized futures sap energy. *Journal of Experimental Social Psychology, 47*, 719–729.

Kappes, H. B., Oettingen, G., & Mayer, D. (2012). Positive fantasies predict low academic achievement in disadvantaged students. *European Journal of Social Psychology, 42*, 53–64.

Kappes, H. B., Schwörer, B., & Oettingen, G. (2012). Needs instigate positive fantasies of idealized futures. *European Journal of Social Psychology, 42*, 299–307.

Kareev, Y. (1995). Positive bias in the perception of covariation. *Psychological Review, 102*, 490–502.

Kassarjian, H. H., & Cohen, J. B. (1965). Cognitive dissonance and consumer behavior. *California Management Review, 8*, 55–64.

Kassin, S. M. (1997). The psychology of confession evidence. *American Psychologist, 52*, 221–233.

Kassin, S. M., & Fong, C. T. (1999). "I'm innocent": Effects of training on judgments of truth and deception in the interrogation room. *Law and Human Behavior, 23*, 499–516.

Kassin, S. M., & Gudjonsson, G. H. (2004). The Psychology of Confessions: A Review of the Literature and Issues. *Psychological Science in the Public Interest, 5*, 33–67.

Kassin, S. M., & Sukel, H. (1997). Coerced confessions and the jury: An experimental test of the "harmless error" rule. *Law and Human Behavior, 21*, 27–46.

Kassin, S. M., Goldstein, C. C., & Savitsky, K. (2003). Behavioral configuration in the interrogation room: On the dangers of presuming guilt. *Law and Human Behavior, 27*, 187–203.

Kassin, S. M., Drizin, S. A., Grisso, T. et al. (2010). Police induced confessions: Risk factors and recommendations. *Law and Human Behavior, 34*, 39–40.

Kates, R. W. (1962). Hazard and choice perception in flood plain management. Research paper 78. Chicago: University of Chicago, Department of Geography.

Katz, D., & Allport, F. (1931). *Students attitudes*. Syracuse, NY: Craftsman Press.

Keefe, C., Harte, T. B., & Norton, L. E. (Eds.) (1982). *Introduction to debate*. New York: Macmillan.

Kelley, C. M., & Jacoby, L. L. (1996). Adult egocentrism: Subjective experience versus analytic bases for judgment. *Journal of Memory and Language, 35*, 157–175.

Kelley, H. H. (1967). Attribution theory in social psychology. In D. Levine (Ed.), *Nebraska symposium on motivation* (Vol. 15) (pp. 192–241). Lincoln, NB: University of Nebraska Press.

Kelley, H. H. (1971). *Attribution in social interaction*. Morristown, NJ: General Learning Press.

Kelly, J. (2015). Types of thinking. *The Peak Performance Center*. http://thepeakperformancecenter.com/educational-learning/thinking/types-of-thinking-2/

Kelman, H. C., & Hovland, C. I. (1953). "Reinstatement" of the communicator in delayed measurement of opinion change. *Journal of Abnormal Social Psychology, 48*, 327–335.

Keysar, B., & Henly, A. S. (2002). Speakers' overestimation of their effectiveness. *Psychological Science, 13*, 207–212.

Keysar, B., Barr, D. J., Balin, J. A., & Brauner, J. S. (2000). Taking perspective in conversation: The role of mutual knowledge in comprehension. *Psychological Science, 11*, 32–38.

Keyser, C. J. (1926). *Thinking about thinking*. New York: Ditton and Company.

Kienpointner, M. (1986). Towards a typology of argumentation schemes. In F. H. van Eemeren, R. Grootendorst, J. A. Blair, & C. A. Willard (Eds.), *Argumentation: Across the lines of discipline* (pp. 275–287). Dordrecht, Holland: Foris Publications.

Kienpointner, M. (1992). *Alltagslogik: Struktur und Funktion von Argumentationsmustern*. Stuttgart-Bad Cannstatt: Friedrich Frommann.

Kinnier, R. T., & Metha, A. T. (1989). Regrets and priorities at three stages of life. *Counseling and Values, 33*, 182–193.

Kirkpatrick, L., & Epstein, S. (1992). Cognitive-Experiential Self-Theory and subjective probability: Further evidence for two conceptual systems. *Journal of Personality and Social Psychology, 63*, 534–544.

Klaczynski, P. A., & Lavallee, K. L. (2005). Domain-specific identity, epistemic regulation, and intellectual ability as predictors of belief-biased reasoning: A dual-process perspective. *Journal of Experimental Child Psychology, 92*, 1–24.

Klaczynski, P. A., & Robinson, B. (2000). Personal theories, intellectual ability and epistemological beliefs: Adult age differences in everyday reasoning biases. *Psychology and Aging, 15*, 400–416.

Klauer, K. C., & Kellen, D. (2011). Assessing the belief bias effect with ROCs: Reply to Dube, Rotello, and Heit (2010). *Psychological Review, 118*, 164–173.

Klauer, K. C., Musch, J., & Naumer, B. (2000). On belief bias in syllogistic reasoning. *Psychological Review, 107*, 852–884.

Klayman, J., & Ha, Y.-W. (1987). Confirmation, disconfirmation, and information hypothesis testing. *Psychological Review, 94*, 211–228.

Klayman, J., & Ha, Y.-W. (1989). Hypothesis testing in rule discovery: Strategy, structure, and content. *Journal of Experimental Psychology: Learning, Memory, and Cognition, 15*, 596–604.

Klein, W. M., & Kunda, Z. (1989). *Motivated person perception: Justifying desired conclusions.* Paper presented at the Eastern Psychological Association, Boston, MA.

Kleinmuntz, B. (1990). Why we still use our heads instead of formulas: Toward an integrative approach. *Psychological Bulletin, 107*, 296–310.

Kline, M. (1953). *Mathematics in western culture.* New York: Oxford University Press.

Kline, M. (1980). *Mathematics: The loss of certainty.* New York: Oxford University Press.

Kline, S. L. (1986). Identity management in argumentative discourse. In F. H. van Eemeren, R. Grootendorst, J. A. Blair, & C. A. Willard (Eds.), *Argumentation: Across the lines of discipline* (pp. 241–251). Dordrecht, Holland: Foris Publications.

Koehler, D. J. (1991). Explanation, imagination, and confidence in judgment. *Psychological Bulletin, 110*, 499–519.

Koger, S. M., & Winter, D. D. (2010). *The psychology of environmental problems: Psychology for sustainability* (3rd ed.). New York: Psychology Press.

Komorita, S. S., & Parks, C. D. (1996). *Social dilemmas*, Boulder, CO: Westview Press.

Kopperschmidt, J. (1986). The function of argumentation: A pragmatic approach. In F. H. van Eemeren, R. Grootendorst, J. A. Blair, & C. A. Willard (Eds.), *Argumentation: Across the lines of discipline* (pp. 179–188). Dordrecht, Holland: Foris Publications.

Koriat, A., Fiedler, K., & Bjork, R. A. (2006). Inflation of conditional predictions. *Journal of Experimental Psychology: General, 133*, 429–447.

Koriat, A., Lichtenstein, S., & Fischhoff, B. (1980). Reasons for confidence. *Journal of Experimental Psychology: Human Learning and Memory, 6*, 107–118.

Kornblith, H. (1993). *Inductive inference and its natural ground.* Cambridge, MA: MIT Press.

Krabbe, E. C. W. (1995). Appeal to ignorance. In H. V. Hansen & R. C. Pinto (Eds.), *Fallacies: Classical and contemporary readings* (pp. 251–264). University Park, PA: The Pennsylvania State University Press.

Krueger, J. (1998). On the perception of social consensus. In M. Zanna (Ed.), *Advances in experimental social psychology* (Vol. 30, pp. 163–240). San Diego, CA: Academic Press.

Krueger, J., & Zeiger, J. (1993). Social categorization and the truly false consensus effect. *Journal of Personality and Social Psychology, 65*, 670–680.

Kruglanski, A. W. (1989). *Lay epistemics and human knowledge*. New York: Plenum Press.

Kugler, T., Kausel, E. E., & Kocher, M. G. (2012). Are groups more rational than individuals? A review of interactive decision making in groups. (2012). *WIRES Cognitive Science, 3*, 471–482.

Kühberger, A. (1995). The framing of decisions: A new look at old problems. *Organizational Behavior and Human Decision Processes, 62*, 230–240.

Kühberger, A. (1998). The influence of framing on risky decisions. *Organizational Behavior and Human Decision Processes, 75*, 23–55.

Kühberger, A., Großbichler, C., & Wimmer, A. (2011). Counterfactual closeness and predicted affect. *Thinking and Reasoning, 17*, 137–155.

Kuhn, D. (1991). *The skills of argument*. Cambridge: Cambridge University Press.

Kuhn, D., & Crowell, A. (2011). Dialogic argumentation as a vehicle for developing young adolescents' thinking. *Psychological Science, 22*, 545–552.

Kuhn, D., Amsel, E., & O'Loughin, M. (1988). *The development of scientific thinking skills*. New York: Academic Press.

Kuhn, D., Shaw, V., & Felton, M. (1997). Effects of dyadic interaction on argumentative reasoning. *Cognition and Instruction, 15*, 287–315.

Kuhn, T. S. (1970). *The structure of scientific revolutions* (2nd ed.). Chicago, IL: University of Chicago Press. (Originally published in 1962.)

Kulp, D. H., II. (1934). Prestige, as measured by single-experience changes and their permanency. *Journal of Educational Research, 27*, 663–672.

Kunda, Z. (1987). Motivation and inference: Self-serving generation and evaluation of evidence. *Journal of Personality and Social Psychology, 53*, 636–647.

Kunda, Z. (1990). The case for motivated reasoning. *Psychological Bulletin, 108*, 480–498.

Kunda, Z., & Sanitioso, R. (1989). Motivated changes in the self-concept. *Journal of Experimental Social Psychology, 25*, 272–285.

Kusyszn, I. (1968). A comparison of judgmental methods with endorsements in the assessment of personality traits. *Journal of Applied Psychology, 52*, 227–253.

Ladha, K. K. (1992). The Condorcet jury theorem, free speech, and correlated votes. *American Journal of Political Science, 36*, 617–634.

Lakatos, I. (1970). Falsification and the methodology of scientific research programmes. In I. Lakatos & A. Musgrave (Eds.), *Criticism and the growth of scientific knowledge*. Cambridge: Cambridge University Press.

Lambert, K., & Ulrich, W. (1980). *The nature of argument*. New York: Macmillan.

Lann, A., & Falk, R. (2006). Tell me the method, I'll give you the mean. *The American Statistician, 60*, 322–327.

Laplace, P. S. (1951). *A philosophical essay on probabilities*. F. W. Truscott & F. L. Emory (Trans.) New York: Dover. (Originally published in 1814.)

Larrick, R. P. (2004). Debiasing. In D. J. Koehler & N. Harvey (Eds.), *Blackwell handbook of judgment and decision making* (pp. 316–337). Malden, MA: Blackwell Publishing.

Larrick, R. P., Morgan, J. N., & Nisbett, R. E. (1990). Teaching the use of cost-benefit reasoning in everyday life. *Psychological Science, 1*, 362–370.

Larsen, A., Hodge, J., & Perrin, C. (2003). *The art of argument: An introduction to the informal fallacies*. New York: Classical Academic Press.

Larson, E. D., Ross, M. H., & Williams. R. H. (1986). Beyond the era of materials. *Scientific American, 254*, 34–41.

Laughlin, P. R. (2011). *Group problem solving*. Princeton, NJ: Princeton University Press.

Lavner, J. A., Karney, B. R., & Bradley, T. N. (2013). Newlyweds' optimistic forecasts of their marriage: For better or for worse? *Journal of Family Psychology, 27*, 531–540.

Lazarsfeld, P. F., Berelson, B., & Gaudet, H. (1944). *The people's choice: How the voter makes up his mind in a presidential campaign*. New York: Duell, Sloan & Pearce.

Leary, M. R. (1982). Hindsight distortion and the 1980 presidential election. *Personality and Social Psychology Bulletin, 8*, 257–263.

Lefford, A. (1946). The influence of emotional subject matter on logical reasoning. *Journal of General Psychology, 34*, 127–151.

Leftow, B. (1994). From Jerusalem to Athens. In T. V. Morris (Ed.), *God and the philosophers: The reconciliation of faith and reason* (pp. 189–207). New York: Oxford University Press.

Legrenzi, P., Girotto, V., & Johnson-Laird, P. N. (1993). Focusing in reasoning and decision making. *Cognition, 49*, 37–66.

Legrenzi, P., Girotto, V., & Johnson-Laird, P. N. (2003). Models of consistency. *Psychological Science, 14*, 131–137.

Leippe, M. R., & Romanczyk, A. (1987). Children on the witness stand: A communication/persuasion analysis of jurors' reactions to child witnesses. In S. Ceci, M., & D. Ross (Eds.), *Children's eyewitness testimony* (pp. 155–177). New York: Springer-Verlag.

Leithy, S. E., Brown, G. P., & Robins, I. (2006). Counterfactual thinking and posttraumatic stress reactions. *Journal of Abnormal Psychology, 115*, 629–635.

Lemaire, P., & Fayol, M. (1995). When plausibility judgments supersede fact retrieval: The example of the odd-even effect on product verification. *Memory and Cognition, 23*, 34–48.

Lemay, E. P. Jr., & Venaglia, R. B. (2016). Relationship expectations and relationship quality. *Review of General Psychology, 20*, 57–70.

Lenz, J. W. (1974). Problems for the practicalist's justification of induction. In R. Swinburne (Ed.), *The justification of induction* (pp. 98–101). London: Oxford University Press. (Originally published in 1958.

Leo, R. A., & Ofshe, R. J. (1998). The consequences of false confessions: Deprivations of liberty and miscarriages of justice in the ager of psychological interrogation. *Journal of Criminal Law and Criminology, 88*, 429–496.

Lerner, J. S., & Tetlock, P. E. (1999). Accounting for the effects of accountability. *Psychological Bulletin, 125*, 225–275.

Lester, R. K. (1986). Rethinking nuclear power. *Scientific American, 254*, 31–39.

Levasseur, D. G., & Dean, K. W. (1996). The use of evidence in presidential debates: A study of evidence levels and types from 1960 to 1988. *Argumentation and Advocacy*, *32*, 129–142.

Levin, I. P., Chapman, D. P., & Johnson, R. D. (1988). Confidence in judgments based on incomplete information: An investigation using both hypothetical and real gambles. *Journal of Behavioral Decision Making*, *1*, 29–41.

Levin, I. P., Schneider, S. L., & Gaeth, G. J. (1998). All frames are not created equal: A typology and critical analysis of framing effects. *Organizational Behavior and Human Decision Processes*, *76*, 149–188.

Levin, I. P., Johnson, R. D., Russo, C. P., & Deldin, P. J. (1985). Framing effects in judgment tasks with varying amounts of information. *Organizational Behavior and Human Decision Processes*, *36*, 362–377.

Levin, I. P., Johnson, R. D., Deldin, P. J. et al. (1986). Framing effects in decisions with completely and incompletely described alternatives. *Organizational Behavior and Human Decision Processes*, *38*, 48–64.

Levine, T. R. (2014). Truth-default theory (TDT): A theory of human deception and deception detection. *Journal of Language and Social Psychology*, *33*, 378–392.

Lewandowsky, S., Oberauer, K., & Gignac, G. E. (2013). NASA faked the moon landing – therefore, (climate) science is a hoax: An anatomy of the motivated rejection of science. *Psychological Science*, *24*, 622–633.

Lewandowsky, S., Ecker, U. K. H., Seifert, C. M., Schwarz, N. J., & Cook, J. (2012). Misinformation and its correction: Continued influence and successful debiasing. *Psychological Science in the Public Interest*, *13*, 106–131.

Lewinsohn, P. M., Mischel, W., Chaplin, W., & Barton, R. (1980). Social competence and depression: The role of illusory self-perceptions. *Journal of Abnormal Psychology*, *89*, 203–212.

Lewis, H. B. (1941). Studies in the principles of judgment and attitude: IV, The operation of "prestige suggestion." *Journal of Social Psychology*, *14*, 229–236.

Lewis, H. B. (1990). *A question of values: Six ways we make the personal choices that shape our lives*. San Francisco, CA: Harper and Row.

Lichter, S. R., Rothman, S., & Lichter, L. (1986). *The media elite*. Washington, DC: Adler and Adler.

Liebrand, W. B. G., Messick, D. M., & Wolters, F. J. M. (1986). Why we are fairer than others: A cross-cultural replication and extension. *Journal of Experimental Social Psychology*, *22*, 590–604.

Lillis, J., O'Donohue, W. T., Cucciare, M., & Lillis, E. (2005). In R. H. Wright, & N. A. Cummings (Eds.), *Destructive trends in mental health: The well-intentioned path to harm* (pp. 283–302). New York: Routledge.

Linville, P. W., Fischer, G. W., & Fischhoff, B. (1993). AIDS risk perceptions and decision biases. In J. B. Pryor & G. D. Reeder (Eds.), *The social psychology of HIV infection* (pp. 5–38). Hillsdale, NJ: Erlbaum.

Lipman, M. (1991). *Thinking in education*. New York: Cambridge University Press.

Liu, Y., Su, Y., Xu, G., & Chan, R. C. K. (2007). Two dissociable aspects of feeling-of-knowing: Knowing that you know and knowing that you do not. *Quarterly Journal of Experimental Psychology, 60*, 627–680.

Locke, J. (1995). Four sorts of arguments. In H. V. Hansen & R. C. Pinto (Eds.), *Fallacies: Classical and contemporary readings* (pp. 55–56). University Park, PA: The Pennsylvania State University Press. (Originally published in 1690.)

Lockwood, B. (2016). Confirmation bias and electoral accountability. *Quarterly Journal of Political Science, 11*, 471–501.

Lopes, L. L. (1981). Decision making in the short run. *Journal of Experimental Psychology: Human Learning and Memory, 7*, 377–385.

Lord, C. G., Lepper, M. R., & Preston, E. (1984). Considering the opposite: A corrective strategy for social judgment. *Journal of Personality and Social Psychology, 47*, 1231–1243.

Lovallo, D., & Kahneman, D. (2003). Delusions of success: How optimism undermines executives' decisions. *Harvard Business Review, 81*, 56.

Lowe, E. J. (1993). Rationality, deduction and mental models. In K. I. Manktelow & D. E. Over (Eds.), *Rationality: Psychological and philosophical perspectives* (pp. 211–230). London: Routledge.

Lund, F. H. (1925). The psychology of belief: A study of its emotional and volitional determinants. *Journal of Abnormal and Social Psychology, 20*, 13–21.

Lycan, W. G. (1988). *Judgment and justification*. New York: Cambridge University Press.

Mackie, D. M., Gastardo-Conaco, M. C., & Skelly, J. J. (1992). Knowledge of the advocated position and the processing of in-group and out-group persuasive messages. *Personality and Social Psychology Bulletin, 18*, 145–151.

Mackie, D. M., Worth, L. T., & Asuncion, A. G. (1990). Processing of persuasive in-group messages. *Journal of Personality and Social Psychology, 58*, 812–822.

Macdonald, R. R. (1986). Credible conceptions and implausible probabilities. *British Journal of Mathematical and Statistical Psychology, 39*, 15–27.

MacGregor, D., Fischhoff, B., & Blackshaw, L. (1987). Search success and expectations with a computer interface. *Information Processing and Management, 23*, 419–432.

Mackworth, N. H. (1965). Originality. *The American Psychologist, 20*, 51–66.

Macrae, C. N., Milne, B. A., & Griffiths, R. J. (1993). Counterfactual thinking and the perception of criminal behavior. *British Journal of Psychology, 84*, 221–226.

Mahoney, M. J. (1977). Publication prejudices: An experimental study of confirmatory bias in the peer review system. *Cognitive Therapy and Research, 1*, 161–175.

Malka, A., Krosnick, J. A., & Langer, G. (2009). The association of knowledge with concern about global warming: Trusted information sources shape public thinking. *Risk Analysis, 29*, 633–647.

Malloy, L. C., Schulman, E., & Cauffman, E. (2014). Interrogations, confessions, and guilty pleas among serious adolescent offenders. *Law and Human Behavior, 38*, 181–193.

Mandel, D. R. (2001). Gain-loss framing and choice: Separating outcome formulations from descriptor formulations. *Organizational Behavior and Human Decision Processes, 85*, 56–76.

Manktelow, K. I. (2012). *Thinking and reasoning*. Hove: Psychology Press.

Manktelow, K. I., & Over, D. E. (1993). Rationality, utility and deontic reasoning. In K. I. Manktelow & D. E. Over (Eds.), *Rationality: Psychological and philosophical perspectives* (pp. 231–259). London: Routledge.

Manning, R. C. (1986). Beyond argumentation: The role of narrative in moral reasoning. In F. H. van Eemeren, R. Grootendorst, J. A. Blair, & C. A. Willard (Eds.), *Argumentation: Analysis and practices* (pp. 170–177). Dordrecht, Holland: Foris Publications.

Marcus, G. B. (1986). Stability and change in political attitudes: Observe, recall, and "explain." *Political Behavior, 8*, 21–44.

Marcus, S. L., & Rips, L. J. (1979). Conditional reasoning. *Journal of Verbal Learning and Verbal Behavior, 18*, 199–224.

Margalit, A., & Bar-Hillel, M. (1981). The irrational, the unreasonable, and the wrong. Commentary on Cohen, 1981. *The Behavioral and Brain Sciences, 4*, 346–349.

Margolis, H. (1987). *Patterns, thinking, and cognition: A theory of judgment*. Chicago, IL: University of Chicago Press.

Markman, K. D., & McMullen, M. N. (2003). A reflection and evaluation model of comparative thinking. *Personality and Social Psychology Review, 7*, 244–267.

Markman, K. D., & Tetlock, P. E. (2000). Accountability and close counterfactuals: The loser that nearly won and the winner that nearly lost. *Personality and Social Psychology Bulletin, 26*, 1213–1224.

Markman, K. D., Gavanski, I., Sherman, S. J., & McMullen, M. N. (1993). The mental simulation of better and worse possible worlds. *Journal of Experimental Social Psychology, 29*, 87–109.

Markman, K. D., Gavanski, I., Sherman, S. J., & McMullen, M. N. (1995). The impact of perceived control on the imagination of better and worse possible worlds. *Personality and Social Psychology Bulletin, 221*, 588–595.

Markovits, H. (1988). Conditional reasoning, representation, empirical evidence on a concrete task. *Quarterly Journal of Experimental Psychology, 40A*, 483–495.

Markovits, H., & Nantel, G. (1989). The belief-bias effect in the production and evaluation of logical conclusions. *Memory and Cognition, 17*, 11–17.

Markovits, H., & Potvin, F. (2001). Suppression of valid inferences and knowledge structures: The curious effect of producing alternative antecedents on reasoning with causal conditionals. *Memory and Cognition, 29*, 736–744.

Marks, G., & Miller, N. (1982). Target attractiveness as a mediator of assumed attitude similarity. *Personality and Social Psychology Bulletin, 8*, 728–735.

Marks, G., & Miller, N. (1987). Ten years of research on the false-consensus effect: An empirical and theoretical review. *Psychological Review, 102*, 72–90.

Marvin, C. (1988). *When old technologies were new: Thinking about electric communication in the late nineteenth century*. New York: Oxford University Press.

Massey, G. J. (1975a). Are there any good arguments that bad arguments are bad? *Philosophy in Context, 4*, 61–77.

Massey, G. J. (1975b). In defense of the asymmetry. *Philosophy in Context (Supplementary), 4*, 44–55.

Massey, G. J. (1991). The fallacy behind fallacies. In H. V. Hansen & R. C. Pinto (Eds.), *Fallacies: Classical and contemporary readings* (pp. 159–171). University Park, PA: The Pennsylvania State University Press. (Originally published in 1981.)

Massey, G. J. (1995). The fallacy behind fallacies. In H. V. Hansen & R. C. Pinto (Eds.), *Fallacies: Classical and contemporary readings* (pp. 159–171). University Park, PA: The Pennsylvania State University Press. (Originally published in 1981.)

Matlin, M. W., & Stang, D. J. (1978). The Pollyanna principle: Selectivity in language, memory and thought. Cambridge, MA: Shenkman.

Maxwell, J. C. (1873). Molecules. In W. D. Niven (Ed.), (1890). *Scientific papers, Vol. 2.* (pp. 361–377). Cambridge: Cambridge University Press.

Mayr, E. (1991). *One long argument: Charles Darwin and the Genesis of Modern Evolutionary Thought.* Cambridge, MA: Harvard University Press.

McCabe, D. P., & Castel, A. D. (2008). Seeing is believing: The effect of brain images on judgments of scientific reasoning. *Cognition, 107*, 343–352.

McConnell, A. R., Neidermeier, K. E., Leibold, J. M. et al. (2000). What if I find it cheaper someplace else? Role of prefactual thinking and anticipated regret in consumer behavior. *Psychology and Marketing, 17*, 281–298.

McCormick, M., & McElroy, T. (2009). Healthy choices in context: How contextual cues can influence the persuasiveness of framed health messages. *Judgment and Decision Making, 4*, 248–255.

McCracken, G. (1989). Who is the celebrity endorser? Cultural foundations of the endorsement process. *Journal of Consumer Research, 16*, 310–321.

McCrea, S. M., & Flamm, A. (2012). Dysfunctional anticipatory thoughts and the self-handicapping strategy. *European Journal of Social Psychology, 42*, 72–81.

McCroskey, J., Young, T., & Scott, M. (1972). The effects of messages sidedness and evidence on inoculation against counterpersuasion in small group communication. *Speech Monographs, 39*, 205–212.

McGauran, N., Wieseler, B., Kreis, J. et al. (2010). Reporting bias in medical research: A narrative review. *Trials, 11*, 37.

McGuire, W. J. (1960). A syllogistic analysis of cognitive relationships. In M. J. Rosenberg, C. I. Hovland, W. J. McGuire, R. P. Abelson, & J. W. Brehm (Eds.), *Attitude organization and change* (pp. 65–110). New Haven, CT: Yale University Press.

McGuire, W. J. (1964). Inducing resistance to persuasion. In L. Berkowitz (Ed.), *Experimental social psychology* (Vol. I) (pp. 191–229). New York: Academic press.

McKellar, P. (1957). *Imagination and thinking: A psychological analysis.* New York: Basic Books.

McKenna, F. P. (1993). It won't happen to me: Unrealistic optimism or illusion of control? *British Journal of Psychology, 84*, 39–50.

McKenna, F. P., Stanier, R. A., & Lewis, C. (1991). Factors underlying illusory self-assessment of driving skill in males and females. *Accident Analysis and Prevention, 23*, 45–52.

McKenzie, C. R. M., & Mikkelsen, L. A. (2000). The psychological side of Hempel's paradox of confirmation. *Psychonomic Bulletin and Review, 7*, 360–366.

McKeon, M. (undated). Argument. *Internet Encyclopedia of philosophy.*

McKerrow, R. E. (1987). Rescher's plausibility thesis and the justification of arguments: A critical analysis. In F. H. van Eemeren, R. Grootendorst, J. A. Blair, & C. A. Willard (Eds.), *Argumentation: Across the lines of discipline: Proceedings of the conference on argumentation* (pp. 317–322). Dordrecht, Holland: Foris Publications.

McMullen, M. N., & Markman, K. D. (2002). Affective impact of close counterfactuals: Implications of possible futures for possible pasts. *Journal of Experimental Social Psychology, 38*, 64–70.

McMullen, M. N., Markman, K. D., & Gavanski, I. (1995). Living in neither the best not the worst of all possible worlds: Antecedents and consequences of upward and downward counterfactual thinking. In N. J. Roese & J. M. Olson (Eds.), *What might have been: The social psychology of counterfactual thinking* (pp. 133–167). Mahwah, NJ: Erlbaum.

McNeil, B. J., Pauker, S. G., Sox, H. C., & Tversky, A. (1982). On the elicitation of preferences for alternative therapies. *New England Journal of Medicine, 306*, 1259–1262.

Medawar, P. B. (1979). A bouquet of fallacies from medicine and medical science with a sideways glance at mathematics and logic. In R. Duncan & M. Weston-Smith (Eds.), *The encyclopedia of delusions.* New York: Simon & Schuster.

Medvec, V. H., Madey, S. F., & Gilovich, T. (1995). When less is more: Counterfactual thinking and satisfaction among Olympic athletes. *Journal of Personality and Social Psychology, 69*, 603–610.

Mehle, T., Gettys, C. V., Manning, C., Baca, S., & Fisher, S. (1981). The availability explanation of excessive plausibility assessments. *Acta Psychologica, 49*, 127–140.

Meindl, J. D. (1987). Chips for advanced computing. *Scientific American, 257*, 78–88.

Meissner, C. A., & Kassin, S. M. (2002). "He's guilty!": Investigator bias in judgments of truth and deception. *Law and Human Behavior, 26*, 469–480.

Mellers, B., Ungar, L., Baron, J. et al. (2014). Psychological strategies for winning a geopolitical forecasting tournament. *Psychological Science, 25*, 1–10.

Mercier, H. (2011a). On the universality of argumentative reasoning. *Journal of Cognition and Culture, 11*, 85–113.

Mercier, H. (2011b). Reasoning serves argumentation in children. *Cognitive Development, 26*, 177–191.

Mercier, H. (2011c). When experts argue: Explaining the best and the worst of reasoning. *Argumentation, 25*, 313–327.

Mercier, H. (2016). The argumentative theory: Predictions and empirical evidence. *Trends in Cognitive Sciences, 20*, 689–700.

Mercier, H. (2017). How gullible are we? A review of the evidence from psychology and social science. *Review of General Psychology, 21*, 103–122.

Mercier, H., & Landemore, H. (2012). Reasoning is for arguing: Understanding the successes and failures of deliberation. *Political Psychology, 33*, 243–258.

Mercier, H., & Sperber, D. (2011). Why do humans reason? Arguments for an argumentative theory. *Behavioral and Brain Sciences, 34*, 57–111.

Mercier, H., & Sperber, D. (2017). *The enigma of reason.* Cambridge, MA: Harvard University Press.

Mercier, H., & Sperber, D. (2019). *The enigma of reason.* Cambridge, MA: Harvard University Press.

Mercier, H., Boudry, M., Paglieri, F., & Trouche, E. (2016). Natural-born arguers: Teaching how to make the best of our reasoning abilities. *Educational Psychologist, 52*, 1–16.

Mercier, H., Trouche, E., Yama, H., Heintz, C., & Girotto, V. (2015). Experts and laymen grossly underestimate the benefits of argumentation for reasoning. *Thinking and Reasoning, 21*, 341–355.

Merton, R. K. (1948). The self-fulfilling prophecy. *Antioch Review, 8*, 193–210.

Messer, R. (1997). *Does God's existence need proof?* New York: Oxford University Press.

Messick, D. M., Bloom, S., Boldizar, J. P., & Samuelson, C. D. (1985). Why we are fairer than others. *Journal of Experimental Social Psychology, 21*, 480–500.

Metcalfe, J. (1986a). Feeling of knowing in memory and problem solving. *Journal of Experimental Psychology: Learning, Memory, and Cognition, 12*, 288–294.

Metcalfe, J. (1986b). Premonitions of insight predict impending error. *Journal of Experimental Psychology: Learning, Memory, and Cognition, 12*, 623–634.

Metcalfe, J., & Weibe, D. (1987). Intuition in insight and non-insight problem solving. *Memory and Cognition, 15*, 238–246.

Meyerson, B. S. (2018). Bots that argue and instruct. *Scientific American, 319*, 35–36.

Michel, M., & Peters, M. A. (Submitted). Confirmation bias without rhyme or reason.

Milkman, K. L., Chugh, D., & Bazerman, M. H. (2009). How can decision making be improved? *Perspectives on Psychological Science, 4*, 379–383.

Mill, J. S. (1843). *A system of logic, ratiocinative, and inductive, being a connected view of the principles of evidence and the methods of scientific investigation.* London: Longmans.

Mill, J. S. (1874). *A system of logic* (8th ed.). New York: Harper & Brothers.

Mill, J. S. (1995). On fallacies. In H. V. Hansen & R. C. Pinto (Eds.), *Fallacies: Classical and contemporary readings* (pp. 85–94). University Park, PA: The Pennsylvania State University Press. (Originally published in 1892.)

Miller, D. T., & Ross, M. (1975). Self-serving biases in the attribution of causality: Fact or fiction? *Psychological Bulletin, 82*, 213–225.

Miller, G. A. (1986). *Assessing cognitive skills in mathematics and science.* Submitted to the National Assessment of Educational Progress (NAEP). Available from ERIC ED279690.

Mills, J., & Aronson, E. (1965). Opinion change as a function of the communicator's attractiveness and desire to influence. *Journal of Personality and Social Psychology, 1*, 173–177.

Minson, J. A., Liberman, V, & Ross, L. (2011). Two to tango: Effects of collaboration and disagreement on dyadic judgment. *Personality and Social Psychology Bulletin, 37*, 1325–1338.

Mintz, E. (1956). An example of assimilative projection. *Journal of Abnormal and Social Psychology, 52*, 270–280.

Mischel, W. (1968). *Personality and assessment.* New York: Wiley.

Mischel, W. (1979). On the interface of cognition and personality: Beyond the person-situation debate. *American Psychologist, 34*, 740–754.

Mischel, W. (2004). Toward an integrated science of the person. *Annual Review of Psychology, 55*, 1–22.

Mitchell, P., Robinson, E. J., Isaacs, J. E., & Nye, R. M. (1996). Contamination in reasoning about false belief: An instance of realist bias in adults but not children. *Cognition, 59*, 1–21.

Mitchell, T. R., & Kalb, L. S. (1981). Effects of outcome knowledge and outcome valence on supervisors' evaluations. *Journal of Applied Psychology, 66*, 604–612.

Miton, H., & Mercier, H. (2015). Cognitive obstacles to pro-vaccination beliefs. *Trends in Cognitive Sciences, 19*, 633–636.

Moore, B., & Parker, R. (1993). *Critical thinking.* Mountain View, CA: Mayfield.

Moore, D. A., & Healy, P. J. (2008). The trouble with overconfidence. *Psychological Review, 115*, 502–517.

Morewedge, C. K. (2015). How a video game helped people make better decisions. *Harvard Business Review*, October 13. https://hbr.org/2015/10/how-a-video-game-helped-people-make-better-decisions

Morewedge, C. K., Yoon, H., Scopelliti, I. et al. (2015). Debiasing decisions: Improved decision making with a single training intervention. *Policy Insights from the Behavioral and Brain Sciences, 2*, 129–140.

Morgan, J. J. B., & Morton, J. T. (1944). The distortion of syllogistic reasoning produced by personal convictions. *Journal of Social Psychology, 20*, 39–59.

Morley, N. J., Evans, J. St. B.T., & Handley, S. (2004). Belief bias and figural bias in syllogistic reasoning. *Quarterly Journal of Experimental Psychology: Section A, 57*, 666–692.

Moshman, D., & Geil, M. (1998). Collaborative reasoning: Evidence for collective rationality. *Thinking and Reasoning, 4*, 231–248.

Moutier, S., Angeard, N., & Houdé, O. (2002). Deductive reasoning and matching-bias inhibition training: Evidence from a debiasing paradigm. *Thinking and Reasoning, 8*, 205–224.

Mullen, B., Atkins, J. L., Champion, D. S. et al. (1985). The false consensus effect: A meta-analysis of 115 hypothesis test. *Journal of Experimental Social Psychology, 21*, 263–283.

Müller, F. M. (1887). *The science of thought.* Chicago, IL: Open Court.

Murphy, G. L., & Ross, B. H. (2010). Uncertainty in category-based induction: When do people integrate across categories? *Journal of Experimental Psychology: Learning, Memory, and Cognition, 36*, 263–276.

Murphy, G. L., Chen, S. Y., & Ross, B. H. (2012). Reasoning with uncertain categories. *Thinking and Reasoning, 18*, 81–117.

Murphy, G. L., Murphy, L. B., & Newcomb, T. M. (1937). *Experimental social psychology.* New York: Harper.

Murray, S. L., & Holmes, J. G. (1997). A leap of faith? Positive illusions in romantic relationships. *Personality and Social Psychology Bulletin, 132*, 586–604.

Mussweiler, T., Strack, F., & Pfeiffer, T. (2000). Overcoming the inevitable anchoring effect: Considering the opposite compensates for selective accessibility. *Personality and Social Psychology Bulletin, 26*, 1142–1150.

Myers, D. G. (2011). *Psychology.* New York: Worth.

Mynatt, C. R., Doherty, M. E., & Tweney, R. D. (1977). Confirmation bias in a simulated research environment: An experimental study of scientific inferences. *Quarterly Journal of Experimental Psychology, 29*, 85–95.

Naess, A. (1966). *Communication and argument: Elements of applied semantics.* London: Aiken & Unwin. (Translated from Norwegian by A. Hannay.)

Nagel, T. (1986). *The view from nowhere.* New York: Oxford University Press.

Nasby, W., Hayden, B., & DePaulo, B. M. (1980). Attributional bias among aggressive boys to interpret unambiguous social stimuli as displays of hostility. *Journal of Abnormal Psychology, 89*, 459–468.

Neilens, H., Handley, S., & Newstead, S. E. (2009). Effects of training and instruction on analytic and belief-based reasoning. *Thinking & Reasoning, 15*, 37–68.

Nelius, T., Eisenmann, M., Doeliken, M., Hergl, M., & Matthiesen, S. (2019). Improving decision making by teaching debiasing approaches: Motivating engineering students with reflection. *Human behavior in design.* Institute of product engineering, Karlsruhe Institute of Technology.

Nelson, T. O., Gerler, D., & Narens, L. (1984). Accuracy of feeling-of-knowing judgments for predicting perceptual identification and relearning. *Journal of Experimental Psychology: General, 113*, 282–300.

Nestler, S. (2010). Belief perseverance: The role of accessible content and accessibility experiences. *Social Psychology, 41*, 35–41.

Neumann, B. R., & Friedman, L. A. (1980). The effects of opportunity costs on project investment decisions: A replication and extension. *Journal of Accounting Research, 18*, 407–419.

Newstead, S. E. (1990). Conversion in syllogistic reasoning. In K. Gilhooly, M. Keane, R. Logie, & G. Erdos (Eds.), *Lines of thinking: Reflections on the psychology of thinking* (Vol. 1, pp. 73–84). Chichester: Wiley.

Newstead, S. E., & Evans, J. St. B. T. (1993). Mental models as an explanation of belief bias effects in syllogistic reasoning. *Cognition, 46*, 93–97.

Newstead, S. E., & Griggs, R. A. (1983). Drawing inferences from qualified statements: A study of the square of opposition. *Journal of Verbal Learning and Verbal Behavior, 22*, 535–546.

Newstead, S. E., Pollard, P., Evans, J. St. B. T., & Allen, J. (1992). The source of belief bias in syllogistic reasoning. *Cognition, 45*, 257–284.

Newstead, S. E., Handley, S. J., Harley, C., Wright, H., & Farrelly, D. (2004). Individual differences in deductive reasoning. *Quarterly Journal of Experimental Psychology, 57*, 33–60.

N'gbala, A., & Branscombe, N. R. (1997). When does action elicit more regret than inaction and is counterfactual mutation the mediator of this effect? *Journal of Experimental Social Psychology, 31*, 139–162.

Nickerson, R. S. (1986a). Reasoning as argument evaluation. ERIC ED279690.

Nickerson, R. S. (1986b). *Reflections on reasoning.* Hillsdale, NJ: Lawrence Erlbaum Associates.

Nickerson, R. S. (1986c). Why teach thinking? In J. Baron & R. J. Sternberg (Eds.), *Teaching thinking skills: Theory and practice* (pp. 27–37). New York: W. H. Freeman.

Nickerson, R. S. (1990). The teaching of thinking: Perspectives and approaches. In C. N. Hedley, J. Houtz, & A. Baratta (Eds.), *Cognition, curriculum and literacy* (pp. 21–33). Norwood, NJ: Ablex.

Nickerson, R. S. (1991). Some observations on the teaching of thinking. In R. F. Mulcahy, R. H. Short, & J. Andrews (Eds.), *Enhancing learning and thinking* (pp. 3–9). New York: Praeger.

Nickerson, R. S. (1994). The teaching of thinking and problem solving. In R. J. Sternberg (Ed.), *Thinking and problem solving*, Vol. 12 of E. C. Carterette & M. Friedman (Eds.), *Handbook of perception and cognition* (pp. 409–449). San Diego, CA: Academic Press.

Nickerson, R. S. (1996). Ambiguities and unstated assumptions in probabilistic reasoning. *Psychological Bulletin, 120*, 410–443.

Nickerson, R. S. (1998). Confirmation bias: A ubiquitous phenomenon in many guises. *Review of General Psychology, 2*, 175–220.

Nickerson, R. S. (1999). How we know—and sometimes misjudge—what others know: Imputing one's own knowledge to others. *Psychological Bulletin, 125*, 737–759.

Nickerson, R. S. (2001). The projective way of knowing: A useful heuristic that sometimes misleads. *Current Directions in Psychological Science, 10*, 168–172.

Nickerson, R. S. (2003). *Psychology and environmental change.* Mahwah, NJ: Erlbaum.

Nickerson, R. S. (2004). Teaching reasoning. In J. P. Leighton & R. J. Sternberg (Eds.), *The nature of reasoning* (pp. 410–442). New York: Cambridge University Press.

Nickerson, R. S. (2010). *Mathematical reasoning: Patterns, problems, conjectures and proofs.* New York: Psychology Press.

Nickerson, R. S. (2015). *Conditional reasoning: The unruly syntactics, semantics, thematics and pragmatics of "If."* New York: Oxford University Press.

Nickerson, R. S. (2020). Developing intelligence through instruction. In R. J. Sternberg (Ed.), *The Cambridge handbook of intelligence* (pp. 205–238). Cambridge: Cambridge University Press.

Nickerson, R. S., Baddeley, A., & Freeman, B. (1987). Are people's estimates of what other people know influenced by what they themselves know? *Acta Psychologica, 64*, 245–259.

Nickerson, R. S., Butler, S. F., & Barch, D. H. (in press). Validity and persuasiveness of conditional arguments. *American Journal of Psychology.*

Nickerson, R. S., Butler, S. F., & Carlin, M. (2009). Empathy and knowledge projection. In J. Decety & W. Ickes (Eds.), *Social neuroscience of empathy* (pp. 43–56). Cambridge, MA: MIT Press.

Nisbett, R. E., & Borgida, E. (1975). Attribution and the psychology of prediction. *Journal of Personality and Social Psychology, 32*, 932–943.

Nisbett, R. E., & Ross, L. (1980). *Human inference: Strategies and shortcomings of social judgment.* Englewood Cliffs, NJ: Prentice-Hall.

Nisbett, R. E., & Wilson, T. D. (1977a). Telling more than we know: Verbal reports on mental processes. *Psychological Review, 84*, 231–259.

Nisbett, R. E., & Wilson, T. D. (1977b). The halo effect: Evidence for unconscious alteration of judgments. *Journal of Personality and Social Psychology, 35*, 250–256.

Nisbett, R. E., Borgida, E., Crandall, R., & Reed, H. (1976). Popular induction: Information is not necessarily informative. In J. S. Carroll & J. W. Payne (Eds.), *Cognition and social behavior* (pp. 113–134). Hillsdale, NJ: Erlbaum.

Nisbett, R. E., Krantz, D. H., Jepson, D., & Kunda, Z. (1983). The use of statistical heuristics in everyday reasoning. *Psychological Review, 90*, 339–363.

Nogar, R. J. (1966). *The wisdom of evolution.* New York: New American Library.

Norman, W. T. (1969). "To see oursels as ithers see us!": Relations among self-perceptions, peer-perceptions, and expected peer-perceptions of personality attributes. *Multivariate Behavior Research, 4*, 417–433.

Norman, W. T., & Goldberg, L. R. (1966). Raters, ratees, and randomness in personality structure. *Journal of Personality and Social Psychology, 4*, 681–691.

Nozick, R. (1993). *The nature of rationality.* Princeton, NJ: Princeton University Press.

Nussbaum, E. M., & Kardash, C. M. (2005). The effects of goal instructions and text on the generation of counterarguments during writing. *Journal of Educational Psychology, 97*, 157–169.

Nyhan, B., & Reifler, J. (2010). When corrections fail: The persistence of political misperceptions. *Political Behavior, 32*, 303–330.

Oakhill, J., & Garnham, A. (1993). On theories of belief bias in syllogistic reasoning. *Cognition, 46*, 87–92.

Oakhill, J. V., & Johnson-Laird, P. N. (1985). The effects of belief on the spontaneous production of syllogistic conclusions. *Quarterly Journal of Experimental Psychology, 37A*, 553–569.

Oakhill, J., Garnham, A., & Johnson-Laird, P. N. (1990). Belief bias effects in syllogistic reasoning. In K. Gilhooly, M. Keane, R. Logie, & G. Erdos (Eds.), *Lines of thinking: Reflections on the psychology of thought* (Vol. 1) (pp. 125–138). Chichester: Wiley.

Oakhill, J. V., Johnson-Laird, P. N., & Garnham, A. (1989). Believability and syllogistic reasoning. *Cognition, 31*, 117–140.

Oaksford, M., & Chater, N. (1995). Theories of reasoning and the computational explanation of everyday inference. *Thinking and Cognition, 1*, 121–152.

Oaksford, M., Chater, N., & Larkin, J. (2000). Probabilities and polarity biases in conditional inference. *Journal of Experimental Psychology: Learning, Memory, and Cognition, 26*, 883–899.

O'Brien, T. C. (1972). Logical thinking in adolescents. *Educational Studies in Mathematics, 4*, 401.

O'Brien, T. C. (1973). Logical thinking in college students. *Educational Studies in Mathematics, 5*, 71–79.

Oesterle, J. A. (1952). *Logic: The art of defining and reasoning.* Englewood Cliffs, NJ: Prentice Hall.

Oettingen, G., & Mayer, D. (2002). The motivating function of thinking about the future: Expectations versus fantasies. *Journal of Personality and Social Psychology, 83*, 1198–1212.

O'Gorman, H. J., & Garry, S. L. (1976). Pluralistic ignorance – a replication and extension. *Public Opinion Quarterly, 40*, 449–458.

O'Keefe, D. J. (1997). Standpoint explicitness and persuasive effect: A meta-analytic review of the effects of varying conclusion articulation in persuasive messages. *Argumentation and Advocacy, 34*, 1–12.

O'Keefe, D. J. (1999). How to handle opposing arguments in persuasive messages: A meta-analytic review of the effects of one-sided and two-sided messages. *Annals of the International Communication Association, 22*, 209–249.

O'Keefe, D. J. (2013). The relative persuasiveness of different forms of arguments from consequences: a review and integration. In C. T. Salmon (Ed.), *Communication yearbook* (pp. 109–135, Vol. 36). New York: Routledge.

O'Keefe, D. J. (2017). *Persuasion: theory & research* (3rd ed.). Thousand Oaks, CA: Sage.

O'Keefe, D. J., & Jensen, J. D. (2007). The relative persuasiveness of gain-framed and loss-framed messages for encouraging disease prevention behaviors: A meta-analytic review. *Journal of Health Communication, 12*, 623–644.

Ormerod, T. C., Manktelow, K. I., & Jones, G. V. (1993). Reasoning with three types of conditional: Biases and mental models. *Quarterly Journal of Experimental Psychology, 30*, 705–716.

Osherson, D. (1995). Probability judgment. In E. E. Smith & D. N. Osherson (Eds.), *An invitation to cognitive science*, Vol. 3: Thinking (2nd ed., pp. 35–76). Cambridge, MA. MIT Press.

Osman, M., & Laming, D. (2001). Misinterpretation of conditional statements in Wason's selection task. *Psychological Research, 65*, 128–144.

Over, D. E. (2009). New paradigm psychology of reasoning: Review of "*Bayesian rationality: The probabilistic approach to human reasoning.*" *Thinking & Reasoning, 15*, 431–438.

Oxley, D. R., Vedlitz, A., & Wood, D. B. (2014). The effect of persuasive messages on policy problem recognition. *Policy Studies Journal, 42*, 252–268.

Pal, G. C. (2007). Is there a universal self-serving attribution bias? *Psychological Studies, 52*, 85–89.

Park, H. S., Levine, T. R., Kingsley, C. Y. et al. (2007). The effects of argument quality and involvement type on attitude formation and attitude change: A test of dual-process and social judgment predictions. *Human Communication Research, 33*, 81–102.

Pascal, B. (1947). Pensées. In S. Commins & R. N. Linscott (Eds.), *Man and spirit: The speculative philosophers* (pp. 199–230). New York: Random House. (Originally published in 1670.)

Paul, R. W. (1986). Critical thinking in the strong and the role of argumentation in everyday life. In F. H. van Eemeren, R. Grootendorst, J. A. Blair, & C. A. Willard (Eds.), *Argumentation: Across the lines of discipline* (pp. 379–382). Dordrecht, Holland: Foris Publications.

Paulos, J. A. (1995). *A mathematician reads the newspaper*. New York: Anchor Books.

Pechmann, C. (1990). How do consumer inferences moderate the effectiveness of two-sided messages? In M. E. Goldberg, G. Gorn, & R. W. Pollay (Eds.), *Advances in consumer research* (Vol. 17, pp. 337–341). Provo, UT: Association for Consumer Research.

Peirce, C. S. (1869). Preliminary sketch of logic. MS 154. *Writings, 2*, 294–297.

Peirce, C. S. (1956). The probability of induction. In J. R. Newman (Ed.), *The world of mathematics,* Vol. 2 (pp. 1341–1354). New York: Simon & Schuster. (Originally published in 1878.)

Pennington, D. C. (1981). Being wise after the event: An investigation of hindsight bias. *Current Psychology, 1*, 271–282.

Pennington, D. C., Rutter, D. R., McKenna, K., & Morley, I. E. (1980). Estimating the outcome of a pregnancy test: Women's judgments in foresight and hindsight. *British Journal of Social and Clinical Psychology, 19*, 317–324.

Penrose, R. (1989). *The emperor's new mind: Concerning computers, minds, and the laws of physics*. New York: Oxford University Press.

Penzias, A. (1992). Creation is supported by all the data so far. In H. Margenau & R. A. Varghese (Eds.), *Cosmos, bios, theos: Scientists reflect on science, God, and the origins of the universe, life and homo sapiens* (pp. 78–83). Chicago, IL: Open Court.

Perelman, C., & Olbrechts-Tyteca, L. (1969). *The new rhetoric: A treatise on argumentation.* Notre Dame, IN: Notre Dame Press. Translated by J. Wilkinson and P. Weaver.

Perkins, D. N. (1985). Post primary education has little impact on informal reasoning. *Journal of Educational Psychology, 77*, 562–571.

Perkins, D. N., Farady, M., & Bushey, B. (1991). Everyday reasoning and the roots of intelligence. In J. Voss, D. N. Perkins, & J. Segal (Eds.), *Informal reasoning* (pp. 83–105). Hillsdale, NJ: Erlbaum.

Perloff, L. S., & Fetzer, B. K. (1986). Self-other judgments and perceived vulnerability to victimization. *Journal of Personality and Social Psychology, 50*, 502–510.

Perner, J., Leekam, S., & Wimmer, H. (1987). Three-year-olds' difficulty understanding false belief: Cognitive limitation, lack of knowledge, or pragmatic misunderstanding. *British Journal of Developmental Psychology, 5*, 125–137.

Pessin, A., & Engel, S. M. (2015). *The study of philosophy* (7th ed.). Lanham, MD: Rowman and Littlefield.

Peterson, C. R., & Beach, L. R. (1967). Man as an intuitive statistician. *Psychological Bulletin, 68*, 29–46.

Petty, R. E., & Cacioppo, J. T. (1984). The effects of involvement on response to argument quantity and quality: Central and peripheral routes to persuasion. *Journal of Personality and Social Psychology, 46*, 69–81.

Petty, R. E., & Cacioppo, J. T. (1986). The elaboration likelihood model of persuasion. In L. Berkowitz (Ed.), *Advances in experimental social psychology* (Vol. 19, pp. 123–205), New York: Academic Press.

Petty, R. E., Cacioppo, J. T., & Goldman, R. (1981). Personal involvement as a determinant of argument-based persuasion. *Journal of Personality and Social Psychology, 41*, 847–855.

Pfeifer, N. (2013). The new psychology of reasoning: A mental probability logic perspective. *Thinking and Reasoning, 19*, 329–345.

Pfeiffer, B. E., Deval, H., Kardes, F. R. et al. (2014). No product is perfect: The positive influence of acknowledging the negative. *Thinking and Reasoning, 20*, 500–512.

Pham, M. T., (1998). Representativeness, relevance, and the use of feelings in decision making. *Journal of Consumer Research, 25*, 144–159.

Pham, M. T. (2009). The lexicon and grammar of affect-as-information in consumer decision making: The GAIM. In M. Wänke (Ed.), *Social psychology of consumer behavior* (pp. 167–200). New York: Psychology Press.

Pickering, M. J., & Traxler, M. J. (1998). Plausibility and recovery from garden paths: An eye-tracking study. *Journal of Experimental Psychology: Learning, Memory, and Cognition, 24*, 940–961.

Pighin, S., Byrne, R. M. J., Ferrante, D., Gonzalez, M., & Girotto, V. (2011). Counterfactual thoughts about experienced, observed, and narrated events. *Thinking and Reasoning, 17*, 197–211.

Pinto, R. C. (1995). *Post hoc ergo propter hoc.* In H. V. Hansen & R. C. Pinto (Eds.), *Fallacies: Classical and contemporary readings* (pp. 302–311). University Park, PA: The Pennsylvania State University Press.

Pinto-Prades, J. L., Martinez-Perez, J. E., & Abellán-Perpiñán, J. M. (2006). The influence of the ratio bias phenomenon on the elicitation of health states utilities. *Judgment and Decision Making, 1*, 118–133.

Platt, J. (1973). Social traps. *American Psychologist, 28*, 641–651.

Politzer, G. (2003). Premise interpretation in conditional reasoning. In D. Hardman & L. Macchi (Eds.), *Thinking: Psychological perspectives on reasoning, judgment, and decision making* (pp. 79–93). Chichester: Wiley.

Politzer, G. (2005). Uncertainty and the suppression of inferences. *Thinking and Reasoning, 11*, 5–33.

Politzer, G., & Carles, L. (2001). Belief revision and uncertain reasoning. *Thinking and Reasoning*, *7*, 217–234.

Polkinghorne, J. (1989). *Science and Creation: The search for understanding*. Boston, MA: New Science Library.

Pollard, P. (1979). *Human reasoning: Logical and non-logical explanations*. Unpublished PhD Thesis, Plymouth Polytechnic.

Pollard, P. (1982). Human reasoning: Some possible effects of availability. *Cognition*, *12*, 65–96.

Pollard, P., & Evans, J. St. B. T. (1980). The influence of logic on conditional reasoning performance. *The Quarterly Journal of Experimental Psychology*, *32*, 605–624.

Pollard, P., & Evans, J. St. B.T. (1981). The effect of prior beliefs in reasoning: An associational interpretation. *British Journal of Psychology*, *72*, 73–82.

Polya, G. (1954a). *Mathematics and plausible reasoning, Vol. 1: Induction and analogy in mathematics*. Princeton, NJ: Princeton University Press.

Polya, G. (1954b). *Mathematics and plausible reasoning, Vol. 2: Patterns of plausible inference*. Princeton, NJ: Princeton University Press.

Polya, G. (1957). *How to solve it: A new aspect of mathematical method*. Garden City, NY: Doubleday. (Originally published in 1945.)

Popper, K. R. (1965). *Conjectures and refutations* (2nd ed.). London: Routledge and Kegan Paul.

Popper, K. (1981). The myth of inductive hypothesis generation. In R. D. Tweney, M. E. Doherty, & C. R. Mynatt (Eds.), *On scientific thinking* (pp. 72–76). New York: Columbia University Press. (Originally published in 1962.

Porter, T. M. (1986). *The rise of statistical thinking 1820–1900*. Princeton, NJ: Princeton University Press.

Posner, E. (2014). Why does the court usually decide cases either 9–0 or 5–4? Supreme court breakfast table. https://slate.com/news-and-politics/2014/07/supreme-court-2014-why-are-most-cases-either-9-0-or-5-4.html

Possin, K. (2016). Conductive arguments: Why is this still a thing? *Informal Logic*, *36*, 563–593.

Postman, N. (1985). Critical thinking in the electronic era. *National Forum*, *65*, 4–8.

Poulton, E. C. (1982). Bias in quantitative judgments. *Applied Ergonomics*, *13*, 31–42.

Powers, L. H. (1995). Equivocation. In H. V. Hansen & R. C. Pinto (Eds.), *Fallacies: Classical and contemporary readings* (pp. 287–301). University Park, PA: The Pennsylvania State University Press.

Prado, J., & Noveck, I. (2006). How reaction time measures elucidate the matching bias and the way negations are processed. *Thinking and Reasoning*, *12*, 309–328.

Price, P. C. (2000). Wishful thinking in the prediction of competitive outcomes. *Thinking and Reasoning*, *6*, 161–172.

Price, P. C., & Stone, E. R. (2004). Intuitive evaluation of likelihood judgment producers: Evidence for a confidence heuristic. *Journal of Behavioral Decision Making*, *17*, 39–57.

Pronin, E., Lin, D. Y., & Ross, L. (2002). The bias blind spot: Perceptions of bias in self versus others. *Personality and Social Psychology Bulletin*, *28*, 369–381.

Puri, M., & Robinson, D. T. (2007). Optimism and economic choice. *Journal of Financial Economics*, *86*, 71–99.

Pyszczynski, T., & Greenberg, J. (1987). Toward an integration of cognitive and motivational perspectives on social inference: A biased hypothesis-testing model. In L. Berkowitz (Ed.), *Advances in experimental social psychology* (Vol. 20, pp. 297–340). New York: Academic Press.

Quayle, J., & Ball, L. (2000). Working memory, metacognitive uncertainty, and belief bias in syllogistic reasoning. *Quarterly Journal of Experimental Psychology*, *53*, 1202–1223.

Quine, W. V. (1960). *Word and object*. Cambridge, MA: MIT Press.

Radelet, M. L., Bedau, H. A., & Putnam, C. E. (1992). *In spite of innocence: Erroneous convictions in capital cases*. Boston, MA: Northeastern University Press.

Rafetseder, E., & Perner, J. (2010). Is reasoning from counterfactual antecedents evidence for counterfactual reasoning? *Thinking and Reasoning*, *16*, 131–155.

Rafetseder, E., & Perner, J. (2014). Counterfactual reasoning: Sharpening conceptual distinctions in developmental studies. *Child Developmental Perspectives*, *8*, 54–58.

Rahwan, I., & Simari, G. R. (Eds.) (2009). *Argumentation in artificial intelligence*. Dordrecht: Springer.

Rathje, W. L. (1989). "Rubbish!" *The Atlantic Monthly* (December), 99–109.

Rattner, A. (1988). Convicted but innocent: Wrongful conviction and the criminal justice system. *Law and Human Behavior*, *12*, 283–293.

Raymo, C. (1998). *Sceptics and true believers: The exhilarating connection between science and religion*. New York: Walker and Company.

Reder, L. M. (1982). Plausibility judgments vs. fact retrieval: Alternative strategies for sentence verification. *Psychological Review*, *89*, 250–280.

Reder, L. M., & Ross, B. H. (1983). Integrated knowledge in different tasks: The role of retrieval strategy on fan effects. *Journal of Experimental Psychology: Learning, Memory, and Cognition*, *9*, 55–72.

Reder, L. M., Wible, C., & Martin, J. (1986). Differential memory changes with age: Exact retrieval versus plausible inference. *Journal of Experimental Psychology: Learning, Memory, and Cognition*, *12*, 72–81.

Reed, B. C. (2018). The ongoing story of Hiroshima and Nagasaki. *American Scientist*, *106*, 88–94.

Reichenbach, H. (1938). *Experience and prediction*. Chicago, IL: University of Chicago Press.

Rescher, N. (1964a). *Hypothetical reasoning*. Amsterdam: North Holland.

Rescher, N. (1964b). *Introduction to logic*. New York: St. Martin's Press.

Rescher, N. (1976). *Plausible reasoning: An introduction to the theory and practice of plausible inference*. Amsterdam: Van Gorcum & Co.

Rescher, N. (1979). Reply to L. J. Cohen. In E. Sosa (Ed.), *The philosophy of Nicholas Rescher* (pp. 61–63). Dordrecht, Holland: Reidel.

Rescher, N. (2007). *Conditionals*. Cambridge, MA: MIT Press.

Resnick, L. B. (1986). *Education and learning to think*. Pittsburgh, PA: University of Pittsburgh, Learning Research and Development Center.

Resnick, L. B., Asterhan, C. S., & Clarke, S. N. (2013). *Socializing intelligence through academic talk and dialogue*. Washington, DC: American Educational Research Association.

Revlin, R., & Leirer, V. O. (1978). The effect of personal biases on syllogistic reasoning: Rational decisions from personalized representations. In R. Revlin & R. E. Mayer (Eds.), *Human reasoning* (pp. 51–81). Washington, DC: Winston.

Revlin, R., Leirer, V., Yopp, H., & Yopp, R. (1980). The belief bias effect in formal reasoning: The influence of knowledge on logic. *Memory and Cognition, 8*, 584–592.

Revlis, R. (1975a). Syllogistic reasoning: Logical decisions from a complex data base. In R. J. Falmagne (Ed.), *Reasoning: Representation and process* (pp. 93–133). New York: Wiley.

Revlis, R. (1975b). Two models of syllogistic inference: Feature selection and conversion. *Journal of Verbal Learning and Verbal Behavior, 14*, 180–195.

Reyna, V. F., & Brainerd, C. J. (2008). Numeracy, ratio bias, and denominator neglect in judgments of risk and probability. *Learning and Individual Differences, 18*, 89–107.

Rieke, R. D., & Sillars, M. O. (1975). *Argumentation and the decision-making process*. New York: Wiley.

Riggs, K. J., Peterson, D. M., Robinson, E. J., & Mitchell, P. (1998). Are errors in false belief tasks symptomatic of a broader difficulty with counterfactuality? *Cognitive Development, 13*, 73–90.

Rips, L. J. (1994). *The psychology of proof: Deductive reasoning in human thinking*. Cambridge, MA: MIT Press.

Rips, L. J. (1995). Deduction and cognition. In E. E. Smith & D. N. Osherson (Eds.), *Thinking: An invitation to cognitive science*, Vol. 3 (2nd ed.) (pp. 297–343). Cambridge, MA: MIT Press.

Rips, L. J., & Conrad, F. G. (1983). Individual differences in deduction. *Cognition and Brain Theory, 6*, 259–285.

Rips, L. J., & Marcus, S. L. (1977). Suppositions and the analysis of conditional sentences. In M. A. Just & P. A. Carpenter (Eds.), *Comprehension processes in comprehension* (pp. 185–219). Hillsdale, NJ: Lawrence Erlbaum Associates.

Rivers, S. E., Salovey, P., Pizarro, D. A., Pizzaro, J., & Schneider, T. R. (2005). Message framing and pap test utilization among women attending a community health clinic. *Journal of Health Psychology, 10*, 65–77.

Robbennolt, J. K. (2013). The effects of negotiated and delegated apologies in settlement negotiation. *Law and Human Behavior, 37*, 128–135.

Robbins, J. M., & Krueger, J. I. (2005). Social projection to ingroups and outgroups: A review and meta-analysis. *Personality and Social Psychology Review, 9*, 32–47.

Roberge, J. J. (1970). A study of children's abilities to reason with basic principles of deductive reasoning. *American Educational Research Journal, 7*, 583–596.

Roberge, J. J. (1978). Linguistic and psychometric factors in propositional reasoning. *Quarterly Journal of Experimental Psychology, 30*, 705–716.

Robertson, L. S. (1977). Car crashes: Perceived vulnerability and willingness to pay for crash protection. *Journal of Consumer Health, 3*, 136–141.

Robinson, E. J., & Beck, S. (2000). What is difficult about counterfactual reasoning. In P. Mitchell & K. J. Riggs (Eds.), *Children's reasoning and the mind* (pp. 101–119). Hove: Psychology Press.

Robinson, K. F. (1941). An experimental study of the effects of group discussion upon the social attitudes of college students. *Speech Monographs, 8*, 34–57.

Roese, N. J. (1993). *The functional basis of counterfactual thinking*. Doctoral dissertation. University of Western Ontario, Ontario Canada.

Roese, N. J. (1994). The functional basis of counterfactual thinking. *Journal of Personality and Social Psychology, 66*, 805–818.

Roese, N. J. (1997). Counterfactual thinking. *Psychological Bulletin, 121*, 133–148.

Roese, N. J., & Olson, J. M. (1995). Counterfactual thinking: A critical review. In N. J. Roese & J. M. Olson (Eds.), *What might have been: The social psychology of counterfactual thinking* (pp. 1–55). Mahwah, NJ: Erlbaum.

Rohatyn, D. (1986). When is a fallacy a fallacy? In F. H. van Eemeren, R. Grootendorst, J. A. Blair, & C. A. Willard (Eds.), *Argumentation: Analysis and practices* (pp. 102–109). Dordrecht, Holland: Foris Publications.

Rosemond, J., & Ravenal, B. (2008). *The diseasing of America's children: Exposing the ADHD fiasco and empowering parents to take back control.* Nashville, TN: Thomas Nelson.

Rosenbaum, M. E. (1986). The repulsion hypothesis: On the nondevelopment of relationships. *Journal of Personality and Social Psychology, 51*, 1156–1166.

Ross, L. D. (1977). The intuitive psychologist and his shortcomings: Distortions in the attribution process. In L. Berkowitz (Ed.), *Advances in experimental social psychology* (Vol. 10, pp. 174–221). New York: Academic Press.

Ross, L. (1978). Afterthoughts on the intuitive psychologist. In L. Berkowitz (Ed.), *Cognitive theories in social psychology* (pp. 385–400). New York: Academic Press.

Ross, L., & Anderson, C. A. (1982). Shortcomings in the attribution process: On the origins and maintenance of erroneous social assessments. In D. Kahneman, P. Slovic & A. Tversky (Eds.), *Judgment under uncertainty: Heuristics and biases* (pp. 129–152). New York: Cambridge University Press.

Ross, L., Amabile, T. M., & Steinmetz, J. L. (1977). Social roles, social control, and biases in social-perception processes. *Journal of Personality and Social Psychology, 35*, 485–494.

Ross, L. D., Green, D., & House, P. (1977). The "false consensus" effect: An egocentric bias in social perception and attribution processes. *Journal of Experimental Social Psychology, 13*, 279–301.

Ross, L. D., Lepper, M. R., Strack, F., & Steinmetz, J. L. (1977). Social explanation and social expectation: The effects of real and hypothetical explanations upon subjective likelihood. *Journal of Personality and Social Psychology, 35*, 817–829.

Ross, M., & Fletcher, G. J. O. (1985). Attribution and social perception. In G. Lindzey & E. Aronson (Eds.), *Handbook of social psychology* (3rd ed., Vol. 2, pp. 73–122). New York: Random House.

Ross, M., & Sicoly, F. (1979). Egocentric biases in availability and attribution. *Journal of Personality and Social Psychology, 37*, 322–336.

Ross, M., McFarland, C., & Fletcher, G. J. O. (1981). The effect of attitude on recall of past histories. *Journal of Personality and Social Psychology, 10*, 627–634.

Rothman, A. J., & Salovey, P. (1997). Shaping perceptions to motivate healthy behavior: The role of message framing. *Psychological Bulletin, 12*, 3–19.

Rothman, A. J., Bartels, R. D., Wlaschin, J., & Salovey, P. (2006). The strategic use of gain- and loss-framed messages to promote healthy behavior: How theory can inform practice. *Journal of Communication, 56*, 202–220.

Rothman, A. J., Salovey, P., Antone, C., Keough, K., & Martin, C. (1993). The influence of message framing on health behavior. *Journal of Experimental Social Psychology, 29*, 408–433.

Rothstein, H., Sutton, A. J., & Borenstein, M. (2005). *Publication bias in meta-analysis: Prevention, assessment and adjustments*. Chichester: Wiley.

Rotter, J. B. (1966). Generalized expectancies for internal versus external control of reinforcement. *Psychological Monographs, 80*, 1–28.

Rozeboom, W. W. (1997). Good science is abductive, not hypothetico-deductive. In L. L. Harlow, S. A. Mulaik, & J. H. Steiger (Eds.), *What if there were no significance tests?* (pp. 335–391). Mahwah, NJ: Erlbaum.

Rubin, J. Z., & Brockner, J. (1975). Factors affecting entrapment in waiting situations: The Rosencrantz and Guildenstern effect. *Journal of Personality and Social Psychology, 31*, 1054–1063.

Ruggiero, V. R. (1981). *The art of thinking: A guide to critical and creative thought*. New York: Harper & Row.

Ruggiero, V. R. (1984). *The art of critical thinking: A guide to critical and creative thought*. New York: Harper & Row.

Rumain, B., Connell, J., & Braine, M. D. S. (1983). Conversational comprehension processes are responsible for reasoning fallacies in children as well as adults. *If* is not the biconditional. *Developmental Psychology, 19*, 471–481.

Russell, B. (1961). A free man's worship. In R. Egner & L. Dennon (Eds.), *The basic writings of Bertrand Russell* (pp. 66–72). New York: Routledge. (Original published in 1923.)

Russell, B. (1967). *The problems of philosophy*. London: Oxford University Press. (Originally published in 1912.)

Russo, J. E., & Corbin, J. C. (2016). Not by desire alone: The role of cognitive consistency in the desirability bias. *Judgment and Decision Making, 11*, 449–459.

Russo, J. E., Carlson, K. A., Meloy, M. G., & Yong, K. (2008). The goal of consistency as a cause of information distortion. *Journal of Experimental Psychology: General, 137*, 456–470.

Sá, W., Kelley, C., Ho, C., & Stanovich, K. E. (2005). Thinking about personal theories: Individual differences in the coordination of theory and evidence. *Personality and Individual Differences, 38*, 1149–1161.

Sabini, J., Siepmann, M., & Stein, J. (2001). The really fundamental attribution error in social psychological research. *Psychological Inquiry, 12*, 1–15.

Salmon, W. C. (1963). *Logic*. Englewood Cliffs, NJ: Prentice-Hall.

Salmon, W. C. (1974). The pragmatic justification of induction. In R. Swinburne (Ed.), *The justification of induction* (pp. 85–97). London: Oxford University Press.

Samuelson, P. A. (1988). *Economics*. New York: McGraw-Hill.

Sanitioso, R. (1989). *Mechanisms for motivated changes in the self-concept*. Unpublished doctoral dissertation. Princeton University.

Sanitioso, R., Kunda, Z., & Fong, G. T. (1990). Motivated recruitment of autobiographical memory. *Journal of Personality and Social Psychology, 59*, 229–241.

Sanna, L. J. (1996). Defensive pessimism, optimism, and simulating alternatives: Some ups and downs of prefactual and counterfactual thinking. *Journal of Personality and Social Psychology, 71*, 1020–1036.

Sanna, L. J. (1998). Defensive pessimism and optimism: The bittersweet influence of mood on performance and prefactual and counterfactual thinking. *Cognition and Emotion, 12*, 635–665.

Savitsky, K., Medvec, V. H., & Gilovich, T. (1997). Remembering and regretting: The Zeigarnik effect and the cognitive availability of regrets for action and inaction. *Personality and Social Psychology Bulletin, 23*, 248–257.

Scheck, B., Neufeld, P., & Dwyer, J. (2000). *Actual innocence: Five days to execution and other dispatches from the wrongly convicted*. New York: Doubleday.

Scheffer, B. K., & Rubenfield, M. G. (2000). A consensus statement on critical thinking in nursing. *Journal of Nursing Education, 39*, 352–359.

Scheffer, B. K., & Rubenfeld, M. G. (2001). Critical thinking: What it is and how do we teach it? In J. M. Grace & H. K. Rubl (Eds.), *Current issues in nursing*. New York: Wiley.

Scheffler, I. (1965). *Conditions of knowledge: An introduction to epistemology and education*. Chicago, IL: Chicago University Press.

Scheier, M. F., & Carver, C. S. (1987). Dispositional optimism and physical well-being: Outcome expectances on health. *Journal of Personality, 55*, 169–210.

Schellens, P. J. (1985). *Redelijke argumenten: Een onderzoek naar normen voor kritische lezers*. Dordrecht, Holland: Foris Publications.

Schipper, E. W., & Schuh, W. W. (1960). *A first course in modern logic*. London: Routledge and Kegan Paul.

Schmidt, C. F. (1976). Understanding human action: Recognizing the plans and motives of other persons. In J. S. Carroll & J. W. Payne (Eds.), *Cognition and social behavior* (pp. 47–68). Hillsdale, NJ: Erlbaum.

Schmidt, R. A., & Bjork, R. A. (1992). New conceptualizations of practice: Common principles in three paradigms suggest new principles for training. *Psychological Science, 3*, 207–217.

Schopenhauer, A. (Undated). *The essays of Arthur Schopenhauer* (Translated by T. B. Saunders). New York: Willey Book Company. (Originally published in 1896.)

Schulze, C., & Newell, B. R. (2016). More heads choose better than one: Group decision making can eliminate probability matching. *Psychonomic Bulletin and Review, 23*, 907–914.

Schum, D. A. (1977). The behavioral richness of cascaded inference models: Examples in jurisprudence. In N. J. Castellan, Jr., D. B. Pisoni, & G. R. Potts (Eds.), *Cognitive theory* (Vol. 2) (pp. 149–173). Hillsdale, NJ: Erlbaum.

Schum, D. A., & Kelly, C. W. (1973). A problem in cascaded inference: Determining the inferential impact of confirming and conflicting reports from several unreliable sources. *Organizational Behavior and Human Performance, 10*, 404–423.

Schumacher, E. F. (1973). *Small is beautiful.* New York: Harper & Row.

Schuman, H., & Scott, J. (1987). Problems in the use of survey questions to measure public opinion. *Science, 236*, 957–959.

Schwartz, B. (1982). Reinforcement-induced behavioral stereotypy: How not to teach people to discover rules. *Journal of Experimental Psychology: General, 111*, 23–59.

Schwarz, N. (1995). Social cognition: Information accessibility and use in social judgment. In E. E. Smith & D. N. Osherson (Eds.), *Thinking: An Invitation to Cognitive Science,* Vol. 3 (2nd ed.) (pp. 345–376). Cambridge, MA: MIT Press.

Schwarz, N. (2007). Feeling and phenomenal experiences. In A. W. Kruglanski & E. T. Higgins (Eds.), *Social psychology: Handbook of basic principles* (2nd ed., pp. 385–407). New York: Guilford.

Schwarz, N., & Clore, G. L. (1983). Mood, misattribution, and judgments of well-being: Information and directive functions of affective states. *Journal of Personality and Social Psychology, 45*, 513–523.

Schwarz, N., & Clore, G. L. (2007). Feelings and phenomenal experiences. In A. W. Krugland & E. T. Higgins (Eds.), *Social psychology: Handbook of basic principles* (2nd ed., pp. 385–407). New York: Guilford.

Schweingruber, D., & Wohlstein, R. T. (2005). The madding crowd goes to school: Myths about crowds in introductory sociology textbooks. *Teaching Sociology, 33*, 136–153.

Scribner, S. (1986). Thinking in action: Some characteristics of practical thought. In R. J. Sternberg & R. K. Wagner (Eds.), *Practical intelligence* (pp. 13–20). Cambridge: Cambridge University Press.

Scriven, M. (1976). *Reasoning.* New York: McGraw-Hill.

Scriven, M. (1986). Probative logic. In F. H. van Eemeren, R. Grootendorst, J. A. Blair, & C. A. Willard (Eds.), *Argumentation: Across the lines of discipline* (pp. 7–32). Dordrecht, Holland: Foris Publications.

Scriven, M. (2009). Probative inference. In J. Ritola (Ed.), *Argument cultures: Proceedings of OSSA 09, CD-ROM* (pp. 1–10), Windsor, ON: OSSA.

Searles, H. L. (1948). *Logic and scientific methods.* New York: The Ronald Press Company.

Seifert, C. M. (2002). The continued influence of misinformation in memory: What makes a correction effective? *Psychology of Learning and Motivation; Advances in Research and Theory 41*, 265–292.

Sellier, A-L., Scopelliti, I., & Morewedge, C. K. (2019). Debiasing training transfers to improve decision making in the field. *Psychological Science, 30*, 1371–1379.

Sells, S. B. (1936). The atmosphere effect: An experimental study of reasoning. *Archives of Psychology, 29*, 3–72.

Sells, S. B., & Koob, H. F. (1937). A classroom demonstration of "atmosphere effect" in reasoning. *Journal of Educational Psychology, 28*, 514–518.

Servick, K. (2016). Sizing up the evidence. *Science, 351*, 1130–1132.

Settle, R. B., & Golden, L. L. (1974). Attribution theory and advertiser credibility. *Journal of Marketing Research, 11*, 181–185.

Shafer, G. (1976). *A mathematical theory of evidence.* Princeton, NJ: Princeton University Press.

Shapiro, S., & Kouri Kissel, T. (2018). Classical logic. In E. N. Zalta (Ed.), *The Stanford encyclopedia of philosophy* (Spring 2018 ed.) https://plato.stanford.edu/archives/spr2018/entries/logic-classical/

Sharot, T., Korn, C. W., & Dolan, R. J. (2010). How unrealistic optimism is maintained in the face of reality. *Nature Neuroscience, 14*, 1475–1479.

Shehryar, O., & Hunt, D. M. (2005). A terror management perspective on the persuasiveness of fear appeals. *Journal of Consumer Psychology, 15*, 275–287.

Shepperd, J. A., Klein, W. M. P., Waters, E. A., & Weinstein, N. D. (2013). Taking stock of unrealistic optimism. *Perspectives on Psychological Science, 8*, 395–411.

Sherman, S. J., Judd, C. M., & Park, B. (1989). Social cognition. *Annual Review of Psychology*, 40, 281–326.

Sherman, S. J., Skov, R. B., Hervits, E. F., & Stock, C. B. (1981). The effects of explaining hypothetical future events: From possibility to probability to actuality and beyond. *Journal of Experimental Social Psychology, 17*, 142–158.

Sherman, S. J., Zehner, K. S., Johnson, J., & Hirt, E. R. (1983). Social explanation: The role of timing, set and recall on subjective likelihood estimates. *Journal of Personality and Social Psychology, 44*, 1127–1143.

Shermer, M. (2015). Consilience and consensus. *Scientific American, 313*, 81.

Sidgwick, A. (1884). *Fallacies: A view of logic from the practical side.* New York: Appleton.

Silver, D. S. (2016). Mathematical induction and the nature of British miracles: A mathematical method of proof challenged traditional beliefs. *American Scientist, 104*, 296–303.

Simonson, I. (1992). The influence of anticipating regret and responsibility on purchase decisions. *Journal of Consumer Research, 19*, 105–118.

Skovgaard-Olsen, N., Singmann, H., & Klaur, K. C. (2016). The relevance effect and conditionals. *Cognition, 150*, 26–36.

Skyrms, B. (1975). *Choice and Chance: An introduction to inductive logic* (2nd ed.). Encino, CA: Dickenson.

Sloman, S. A., & Lagnado, D. (2005). Do we "do"? *Cognitive Science, 29*, 5–39.

Slovic, P. (1966). Value as a determiner of subjective probability. *Transactions of the Institute of Electronic Engineers: Human Factors Issue, HFE-7*, 22–28.

Slovic, P., & Lichtenstein, S. (1971). Comparison of Bayesian and regression approaches to the study of information processing in judgment. *Organizational Behavior and Human Performance, 6*, 649–744.

Slovic, P., Fischhoff, B., & Lichtenstein, S. (1976). Cognitive processes and societal risk taking. In J. S. Carroll & J. W. Payne (Eds.), *Cognition and social behavior* (pp. 165–184). Hillsdale, NJ: Erlbaum.

Smallman, R., & Roese, N. J. (2009). Counterfactual thinking facilitates behavioral intensions. *Journal of Experimental Social Psychology, 45*, 845–852.

Smith, E. E., Shafir, E., & Osherson, D. (1993). Similarity, plausibility, and judgments of probability. *Cognition, 49*, 67–96.

Snow, C. E., & Hoefnagel-Hohle, M. (1979). Individual differences in second language ability. *Language and Speech, 22*, 151–162.

Snyder, M., & Uranowitz, S. W. (1978). Reconstructing the past: Some cognitive consequences of person perception. *Journal of Personality and Social Psychology, 36*, 941–950.

Snyder, M. L., Stephan, W. G., & Rosenfield, D. (1976). Egotism and attribution. *Journal of Personality and Social Psychology, 33*, 435–441.

Soelberg, P. O. (1967). Unprogrammed decision making. *Industrial Management Review, 8*, 19–29.

Soeteman, A. (1986). Deduction in law. In F. H. van Eemeren, R. Grootendorst, J. A. Blair, & C. A. Willard (Eds.), *Argumentation: Analysis and practices* (pp. 102–109). Dordrecht, Holland: Foris Publications.

Sokal, A., & Bricmont, J. (1998). *Fashionable nonsense: Postmodern intellectuals' abuse of science*. New York: Picador USA.

Sosa, E. (Ed.) (1979). *The philosophy of Nicholas Rescher*. Dordrecht, Holland: Reidel.

Southwell, B. G., Thorson. E. A., & Sheble, L. (2017). The persistence and peril of misinformation. *American Scientist, 105*, 372–375.

Sowell, T. (1995). *The vision of the anointed: Self-congratulation as a basis for social policy*. New York: Basic Books.

Sowell, T. (2004). *Basic economics: A citizen's guide to the economy*. New York: Basic Books.

Sparks, P., & Shepherd, R. (1994). Public perceptions of the potential hazards associated with food production and food consumption: An empirical study. *Risk Analysis, 14*, 799–806.

Speer, S. R., & Clifton, C. (1998). Plausibility and argument structure in sentence comprehension. *Memory and Cognition, 26*, 965–978.

Sperber, D., & Wilson, D. (1986). *Relevance*. Oxford: Blackwell.

Stahl, C., Klauer, C., & Erdfelder, E. (2008). Matching bias in the selection task is not eliminated by explicit negations. *Thinking and Reasoning, 14*, 281–303.

Stalnaker, R. C. (1970). Probability and conditionals. *Philosophy of Science, 37*, 64–80.

Stanley, J. (2015). *How propaganda works*. New York: Princeton University Press.

Stanovich, K. E. (1999). *Who is rational? Studies of individual differences in reasoning*. Mahwah, NJ: Erlbaum.

Stanovich, K. E., & West, R. F. (1998a). Cognitive ability and variation in selection task performance. *Thinking and Reasoning, 4*, 193–230.

Stanovich, K. E., & West, R. F. (1998b). Individual differences in framing and conjunction effects. *Thinking and Reasoning, 4*, 289–317.

Stanovich, K. E., & West, R. F. (1998c). Individual differences in rational thought. *Journal of Experimental Psychology: General, 127*, 161–188.

Stanovich, K. E., & West, R. F. (2000a). Authors' response. *Behavioral and Brain Sciences, 23*, 701–726.

Stanovich, K. E., & West, R. F. (2000b). Individual differences in reasoning: Implications for the rationality debate? *Behavioral and Brain Sciences, 23*, 645–665.

Stanovich, K. E., & West, R. F. (2007). Natural myside bias is independent of cognitive ability. *Thinking and Reasoning, 13*, 225–247.

Stanovich, K. E., & West, R. F. (2008). On the failure of cognitive ability to predict myside and one-sided thinking biases. *Thinking and Reasoning, 14*, 129–167.

Starr, D. (2016). When DNA is lying. *Science, 351*, 1133–1136.

Staudenmayer, H. (1975). Understanding conditional reasoning with meaningful propositions. In R. J. Falmagne (Ed.), *Reasoning: Representation and process in children and adults* (pp. 55–79). Hillsdale, NJ: Lawrence Erlbaum Associates.

Staw, B. M. (1976). Knee-deep in the Big Muddy: A study of escalating commitment to a chosen course of action. *Organizational Behavior and Human Performance, 16*, 27–44.

Staw, B. M. (1981). The escalation of commitment to a course of action. *Academy of Management Review, 6*, 577–587.

Staw, B. M., & Huang, H. (1995). Sunk costs in the NBA: Why draft order affects playing time and survival in professional basketball. *Administrative Science Quarterly, 40*, 474–494.

Staw, B. M., & Ross, J. (1989). Understanding behavior in escalation situations. *Science, 246*, 216–220.

Steedman, M. J., & Johnson-Laird, P. N. (1980). The production of sentences, utterances and speech acts: Have computers anything to say? In B. Butterworth (Ed.), *Language production, Vol. 1: Speech and talk*. London: Academic Press.

Sternberg, R. J. (1981). Intelligence as thinking and learning skills. *Educational Leadership, 39*, 18–20.

Sternberg, R. J., & Wagner, R. K. (Eds.) (1986). *Practical intelligence*. Cambridge: Cambridge University Press.

Sterne, J., Egger, M., & Moher, D. (2008). Addressing reporting biases. In J. P. T. Higgins & S. Green (Eds.), *Cochrane handbook for systematic reviews of interventions* (pp. 297–334). Chichester: Wiley.

Stevens, S. S., & Greenbaum, H. B. (1966). Regression effect in psychophysical judgment. *Perception and Psychophysics, 1*, 439–446.

Stevenson, R. J. (1993). Rationality and reality. In K. I. Manktelow & D. E. Over (Eds.), *Rationality: Psychological and philosophical perspectives* (pp. 61–82). London: Routledge.

Stevenson, R. J., & Over, D. E. (1995). Deduction from uncertain premises. *Quarterly Journal of Experimental Psychology, 48A*, 613–643.

Stewart, I. (1989). Chaos: Does God play dice? *1990 yearbook of science and the future* (pp. 57–73). Chicago, IL: Encyclopedia Britannica.

Stich, S. P., & Nisbett, R. E. (1984). Expertise, justification, and the psychology of inductive reasoning. In T. L. Haskell (Ed.), *The authority of experts* (pp. 226–241). Bloomington, IN: Indiana University Press.

Stiff, J. B. (1986). Cognitive processing of persuasive message cues: A meta-analytic review of the effects of supporting information on attitudes. *Communication Monographs, 53*, 75–89.

Stove, D. C. (1982). *Popper and after: Four modern irrationalists.* Oxford: Pergamon Press.

Stove, D. C. (1986). *The rationality of induction.* Oxford: Clarendon Press.

Strack, F, Schwarz, N., & Gschneidinger, E. (1985). Happiness and reminiscing: The role of time perspective, mood, and mode of thinking. *Journal of Personality and Social Psychology, 49*, 1460–1469.

Strahilevitz, A., & Loewenstein, G. (1998). The effect of ownership history on the valuation of objects. *Journal of Consumer Research, 25*, 276–289.

Stupple, E. J. N., & Ball, L. L. (2008). Belief-logic conflict resolution in syllogistic reasoning: Inspection-time evidence for a parallel-process model. *Thinking and Reasoning, 14*, 168–181.

Surowiecki, J. (2005). *The wisdom of crowds.* New York: Anchor Books.

Svenson, O. (1981). Are we all less risky and more skillful than our fellow drivers? *Acta Psychologica, 47*, 143–148.

Svenson, O., Fischhoff, B., & MacGregor, D. (1985). Perceived driving safety and seatbelt usage. *Accident Analysis and Prevention, 17*, 119–133.

Swap. W. C. (1991). Psychological factors in environmental decision making: Social dilemmas. In R. A. Chechile & S. Carlisle (Eds.), *Environmental decision making: A multidisciplinary perspective* (pp. 14–37). New York: Van Nostrand Reinhold.

Swijtink, Z. G. (1987). The objectification of observation: Measurement and statistical methods in the nineteenth century. In L. Krüger, L. J. Daston, & M. Heidelberger (Eds.), *The probabilistic revolution, Vol. 1: Ideas in history* (pp. 261–285). Cambridge, MA: MIT Press.

Swinburne, R. (Ed.) (1974). *The justification of induction.* London: Oxford University Press.

Swinburne, R. (1981). *Faith and reason.* New York: Oxford University Press.

Synodinos, N. E. (1986). Hindsight distortion: I knew-it-all along and I was sure about it. *Journal of Applied Social Psychology, 16*, 107–117.

Tabachnik, N., Crocker, J., & Alloy, L. B. (1981). Depression, social comparison, and the false-consensus effect. *Journal of Personality and Social Psychology, 45*, 688–699.

Tajfel, H., & Wilkes, A. L. (1963). Classification and quantitative judgment. *British Journal of Psychology, 54*, 101–114.

Tajfel, H., Sheikh, A. A., & Gardner, R. C. (1964). Content of stereotypes and the inference of similarity between members of stereotyped groups. *Acta Psychologica, 22*, 191–201.

Tal, A. (2015). Looks like science, must be true! Graphs and the halo of scientific truth. *The Jury Expert: The Art and Science of Litigation Advocacy, 27*, 1–8.

Tal, A., & Wansink, B. (2014). Blinded with science: Trivial graphs and formulas increase ad persuasiveness and belief in product efficacy. *Public Understanding of Science*, October 15. doi:0963662514549688

Taleb, N. N. (2004). *Fooled by randomness: The hidden role of chance in life and in the markets* (2nd ed.). New York: Texere.

Taplin, J. E. (1971). Reasoning with conditional sentences. *Journal of Verbal Learning and Verbal Behaviour, 10*, 219–225.

Taplin, J. E., & Staudenmayer, H. (1973). Interpretation of abstract conditional sentences in deductive reasoning. *Journal of Verbal Learning & Verbal Behavior, 12*, 530–542.

Taylor, D., & Doria, J. R. (1981). Self-serving and group-serving bias in attribution. *Journal of Social Psychology, 113*, 201–211.

Taylor, S. E. (1989). *Positive illusions: Creative self-deception and the healthy mind.* New York: Basic Books.

Taylor, S. E., & Brown, J. D. (1988). Illusion and well-being: A social psychological perspective on mental health. *Psychological Bulletin, 103*, 193–210.

Taylor, S. E., & Brown, J. D. (1994). Positive illusions and well-being revisited: Separating fact from fiction. *Psychological Bulletin, 116*, 21–27.

Taylor, S. E., & Thompson, S. C. (1982). Stalking the elusive "vividness" effect. *Psychological Review, 89*, 155–181.

Taylor, S. E., Wood, J. V., & Lichtman, R. R. (1983). It could be worse: Selective evaluation as a response to victimization. *Journal of Social Issues, 39*, 19–40.

Tegar, A. I. (1979). *Too much invested to quit: The psychology of the escalation of conflict.* Elmsford, NY: Pergamon Press.

Teigen, K. H., & Nikolaisen, M. I. (2009). Incorrect estimates and false reports: How framing modifies truth. *Thinking and Reasoning, 15*, 268–293.

Teigen, K. H., Kanten, A. B., & Terum, J. A. (2011). Going to the other extreme: Counterfactual thinking leads to polarized judgments. *Thinking and Reasoning, 17*, 1–29.

Templin, O., & McCracken, A. (1927). *A guide to thinking.* Garden City, NY: Doubleday, Page & Company.

Tetlock, P. E. (1985). Accountability: A social check on the fundamental attribution error. *Social Psychology Quarterly, 48*, 227–236.

Tetlock, P. E., & Levi, A. (1982). Attribution bias: On the inconclusiveness of the cognition-motivation debate. *Journal of Experimental Social Psychology, 18*, 68–88.

Thagard, P., & Nisbett, R. E. (1982). Variability and confirmation. *Philosophical Studies, 50*, 250–267.

Thaler, R. (1980). Toward a positive theory of consumer choice. *Journal of Economic Behavior and Organization, 1*, 39–60.

Thomas, L. (1983). *The youngest science: Notes of a medicine-watcher*. New York: Bantam Books.

Thomas, R. C., & Jacoby, L. L. (2013). Diminishing adult egocentrism when estimating what others know. *Journal of Experimental Psychology: Learning, Memory, and Cognition*, *39*, 473–486.

Thomas, S. (1973). *Practical reasoning in natural language*. New York: Prentice Hall.

Thompson, V. A. (1996). Conditional reasoning: The necessary and sufficient conditions. *Canadian Journal of Experimental Psychology*, *49*, 315–319.

Thompson, V. A., & Evans, J. St. B. T. (2012). Belief bias in informal reasoning. *Thinking and Reasoning*, *18*, 278–310.

Thompson, V. A., Evans, J. St. B. T., & Handley, S. J. (2005). Persuading and dissuading by conditional argument. *Journal of Memory and Language*, *53*, 238–257.

Thompson, V. A., Newstead, S. E., & Morley, N. J. (2011). Methodological and theoretical issues in belief bias: Implications for dual-process theories. In K. I. Manktelow, D. E. Over, & S. Elqayam (Eds.), *The science of reason: A festschrift for Jonathan St. B. T. Evans* (pp. 309–338). Hove: Psychology Press.

Thompson, V. A., Striemer, C. L., Reikoff, R., Gunter, R. W., & Campbell, J. D. (2003). Syllogistic reasoning time: Disconfirmation disconfirmed. *Psychonomic Bulletin & Review*, *10*, 184–189.

Thompson, W. N. (1971). *Modern argumentation and debate: Principles and practices*. New York: Harper & Row.

Thorson, E. (2016). Belief echoes: The persistent effects of corrected misinformation. *Political Communication*, *33*, 460–480.

Thouless, R. H. (1931). Phenomenal regression to the real object, II. *British Journal of Psychology*, *22*, 1–30.

Thouless, R. H. (1947). *How to think straight*. New York: Simon & Schuster.

Thouless, R. H. (1950). *How to think straight*. New York: Simon & Schuster. (Published also in 1940.)

Thouless, R. H. (1953). *Straight and crooked thinking*. New York: Simon & Schuster. (Originally published in 1930.)

Toffoli, T. (1982). Physics and computation. *International Journal of Theoretical Physics*, *21*, 165–175.

Toplak, M. E., & Stanovich, K. E. (2003). Associations between myside bias on an informal reasoning task and amount of post-secondary education. *Applied Cognitive Psychology*, *17*, 851–860.

Torrens, D., Thompson, V. A., & Cramer, K. M. (1999). Individual differences and the belief bias effect: Mental models, logical necessity, and abstract reasoning. *Thinking and Reasoning*, *5*, 1–28.

Toulmin, S. (1958). *The uses of argument*. Cambridge: Cambridge University Press.

Toulmin, S., Rieke, R., & Janik, A. (1984). *Introduction to reasoning*, 2nd ed. New York: Macmillan. (Originally published in 1979.)

Touré-Tillery, M., & McGill, A. L. (2015). Who or what to believe: Trust and the differential persuasiveness of human and anthropomorphized messengers. *Journal of Marketing, 79*, 94–110.

Trabasso, T., Rollins, H., & Shaughnessy, E. (1971). Storage and verification stages in processing concepts. *Cognitive Psychology, 2*, 239–289.

Trapp, R., Yingling, J. M., & Wanner, J. (1986). Measuring argumentative competence. In F. H. van Eemeren, R. Grootendorst, J. A. Blair, & C. A. Willard (Eds.), *Argumentation: Across the lines of discipline* (pp. 253–261). Dordrecht, Holland: Foris Publications.

Traxler, M. J., & Pickering, M. J. (1996). Plausibility and the processing of unbounded dependencies: An eye-tracking study. *Journal of Memory and Language, 35*, 454–475.

Trippas, D., Verde, M. F., & Handley, S. (2014). Using forced choice to test belief bias in syllogistic reasoning. *Cognition, 133*, 586–600.

Trippas, D., Pennycook, G., Verde, M. F., & Handley, S. J. (2015). Better but still biased: Analytic cognitive style and belief bias. *Thinking and Reasoning, 21*, 431–445.

Trouche, E., Sander, E., & Mercier, H. (2014). Arguments, more than confidence, explain the good performance of reasoning groups. *Journal of Experimental Psychology: General, 143*, 1958–1971.

Turnbull, H. W. (1956). The great mathematicians. In J. R. Newman (Ed.), *The world of mathematics*, Vol. 1 (pp. 75–168). New York: Simon & Schuster. (Originally published in 1929.)

Turner, J. A. P., & Thompson, V. A. (2009). The role of training, alternative models, and logical necessity in determining confidence in syllogistic reasoning. *Thinking and Reasoning, 15*, 69–100.

Tversky, A., & Kahneman, D. (1973). Availability: A heuristic for judging frequency and probability. *Cognitive Psychology, 5*, 207–232.

Tversky, A., & Kahneman, D. (1981). The framing of decisions and the psychology of choice. *Science, 211*, 453–458.

Tversky, A., & Kahneman, D. (1983). Extension versus intuitive reasoning: The conjunction fallacy in probability judgment. *Psychological Review, 90*, 293–315.

Tversky, A., & Koehler, D. J. (1994). Support theory: A nonextensional representation of subjective probability. *Psychological Review, 101*, 547–567.

Tweney, R. D., & Doherty, M. E. (1983). Rationality and the psychology of inference. *Synthese, 57*, 139–161.

Ulrich, W. (1985). In defense of the fallacy. In J. R. Cox, M. O. Sillers, & G. B. Walker (Eds.), *Argument and social practice: Proceedings of the fourth SCA/AFA conference on argumentation* (pp. 110–126). Annandale, VA: Speech Communication Association.

Uttal, W. (2001). *The new phrenology: The limits of localizing cognitive processing in the brain*. Cambridge, MA: MIT Press.

Valins, S., & Nisbett, R. E. (1972). Attribution processes in the development and treatment of emotional disorders. In E. E. Jones, D. E. Kanouse, H. H. Kelley,

R. E. Nisbett, S. Valins, & B. Weiner (Eds.), *Attribution: Perceiving the causes of behavior* (pp. 137–150). Morristown, NJ: General Learning Press.

van Eemeren, F. H. (1986). For reason's sake: Maximal argumentative analysis of discourse. Recognizing enthymemes as such, and, in particular, distinguishing them from non-sequiturs can be difficult. In F. H. van Eemeren, R. Grootendorst, J. A. Blair, & C. A. Willard (Eds.), *Argumentation: Across the lines of discipline* (pp. 202–215). Dordrecht, Holland: Foris Publications.

van Eemeren, F. H., & Garssen, B. (Eds.) (2012). *Exploring argumentative contexts.* Amsterdam: John Benjamins.

van Eemeren, F. H., & Grootendorst, R. (1984). *Speech acts in argumentative discussions. A theoretical model for the analysis of discussions directed towards solving conflict of opinion.* Dordrecht, Holland: Foris Publications.

van Eemeren, F. H., & Grootendorst, R. (1992). *Argumentation, communication, and fallacies.* Hillsdale, NJ: Erlbaum.

van Eemeren, F. H., & Grootendorst, R. (1995a). *Argumentum ad hominem:* A pragma-dialectical case in point. In H. V. Hansen & R. C. Pinto (Eds.), *Fallacies: Classical and contemporary readings* (pp. 223–228). University Park, PA: The Pennsylvania State University Press.

van Eemeren, F. H., & Grootendorst, R. (1995b). The pragma-dialectical approach to fallacies. In H. V. Hansen & R. C. Pinto (Eds.), *Fallacies: Classical and contemporary readings* (pp. 130–144). University Park, PA: The Pennsylvania State University Press.

van Eemeren, F. H., & Grootendorst, R. (2004). *A systematic theory of argumentation: The pragma-dialectic approach.* Cambridge: Cambridge University Press.

van Eemeren, F. H., Grootendorst, R., Blair, A., & Willard, C. A. (1986). Argumentation: Across the lines of discipline, *Proceedings of the conference on Argumentation.*

van Eemeren, F. H., Garssen, B., Krabbe, E. C. W. et al. (2014). *Handbook of argumentation theory.* Dordrecht, Holland: Springer.

Vedung, E. (1986). Rational argumentation and political deception. In F. H. van Eemeren, R. Grootendorst, J. A. Blair, & C. A. Willard (Eds.), *Argumentation: Across the lines of discipline* (pp. 353–364). Dordrecht, Holland: Foris Publications.

Verplanken, B., & Pieters, R. G. (1988). Individual differences in reverse hindsight bias: I never thought something like Chernobyl would happen. Did I? *Journal of Behavioral Decision Making, 1*, 131–144.

Vinokur, A., & Burstein, E. (1974). Effects of partially shared persuasive arguments on group-induced shifts: A group-problem-solving approach. *Journal of Personality and Social Psychology, 29*, 305–315.

Visser, J., Lawrence, J., Wagemans, J. H. M., & Reed, C. (2018). An annotated corpus of argument schemes in U.S. election debates. *Proceedings of the 9th conference of the International Society for the Study of Argumentation (ISSA)* (pp. 1101–1111), Amsterdam.

Voigtländer, N., & Voth, H.-J. (2015). Nazi indoctrination and anti-Semitic beliefs in Germany. *Proceedings of the National Academy of Sciences of the United States of America, 112*, 7931–7936.

Vorobej, M. (1992). Defining deduction. *Informal logic, 14*, 105–118.

Wagemans, J. H. M. (2016). Constructing a periodic table of arguments. In P. Bondy & L. Benacquista (Eds.), *Argumentation, objectivity, and bias: Proceedings of the 11th international conference of the Ontario Society for the Study of Argumentation (OSSA), Windsor, ON: OSSA*, pp. 1–12.

Wagemans, J. H. M. (2019). Four basic argument forms. *Research in Language, 17*, 56–69.

Walker, G. B. (1986). Communicating across cultures: Argument and international negotiation. In F. H. van Eemeren, R. Grootendorst, J. A. Blair, & C. A. Willard (Eds.), *Argumentation: Analysis and practices* (pp. 238–252). Dordrecht, Holland: Foris Publications.

Wallace, D. B., & Kassin, S. M. (2012). Harmless error analysis: How do judges respond to confession errors? *Law and Human Behavior, 36*, 151–157.

Wallen, R. (1943). Individuals' estimates of group opinion. *Journal of Social Psychology*, 17, 269–274.

Wallsten, T. S., & González-Vallejo, C. (1994). Statement verification: A stochastic model of judgment and response. *Psychological Review, 101*, 490–504.

Walton, D. N. (1985). Are circular arguments necessarily vicious? *American Philosophical Quarterly, 22*, 263–274.

Walton, D. N. (1986). What is a fallacy? In F. H. van Eemeren, R. Grootendorst, J. A. Blair, & C. A. Willard (Eds.), *Argumentation: Across the lines of discipline* (pp. 323–330). Dordrecht, Holland: Foris Publications.

Walton, D. N. (1989). *Informal logic*. Cambridge: Cambridge University Press.

Walton, D. N. (1995). The essential ingredients of the fallacy of begging the question. In H. V. Hansen & R. C. Pinto (Eds.), *Fallacies: Classical and contemporary readings* (pp. 229–239). University Park, PA: The Pennsylvania State University Press.

Walton, D. N. (1997). *Appeal to pity*: Argumentum ad misericordiam. Albany, NY: State University of New York.

Walton, D. N., Reed, C., & Macagno, F. (2008). *Argumentation schemes*. Cambridge: Cambridge University Press.

Ward, A., & Brenner, L. (2006). Accentuate the negative: The positive effects of negative acknowledgment. *Psychological Science, 17*, 959–962.

Warren, R. J., II, King, J. R., Tarsa, C., Haas, B., & Henderson, J. (2017). A systematic review of context bias in invasion biology. *PLoS ONE, 12*, e0182502. https://doi.org/10.1371/journal.pone.0182502

Wason, P. C. (1966). *Reasoning*. In B. Foss (Ed.), *New horizons in psychology* (pp. 106–137). Harmondsworth: Penguin.

Wason, P. C., & Johnson-Laird, P. N. (1972). *Psychology of reasoning: Structure and content*. Cambridge, MA: Harvard University Press.

Wasserman, E. A., Dorner, W. W., & Kao, S. F. (1990). Contributions of specific cell information to judgments of interevent contingency. *Journal of Experimental Psychology: Learning, Memory, and Cognition, 16*, 509–521.

Watkins, R. (2002). *Cogito, ergo, sum: The life of René Descartes*. Boston, MA: David Godine.

Watts, I. (1995). Kinds of arguments and the doctrine of sophisms. In H. V. Hansen & R. C. Pinto (Eds.), *Fallacies: Classical and contemporary readings* (pp. 57–66). University Park, PA: The Pennsylvania State University Press. (Originally published in 1796.)

Weatherson, B. (2003). What good are counterexamples? *Philosophical Studies, 115*, 1–31.

Weddle, P. (1980). Good grief: More on induction/deduction. *Informal Logic Newsletter, 3*, 1–13.

Weddle, P. (1986). Informal logic and the deductive-inductive distinction. In F. H. van Eemeren, R. Grootendorst, J. A. Blair, & C. A. Willard (Eds.), *Argumentation: Across the lines of discipline* (pp. 383–388). Dordrecht, Holland: Foris Publications.

Wegrocki, H. J. (1934). The effect of prestige suggestibility on emotional attitude. *Journal of Social Psychology, 5*, 384–394.

Weiner, B., Frieze, I., Kukla, A. et al. (1972). Perceiving the causes of success and failure. In E. E. Jones, D. E. Kanouse, H. H. Kelley, R. E. Nisbett, S. Valins, & B. Weiner (Eds.), *Attribution: Perceiving the causes of behavior* (pp. 95–120). Morristown, NJ: General Learning Press.

Weinstein, N. D. (1980). Unrealistic optimism about future life events. *Journal of Personality and Social Psychology, 39*, 806–820.

Weinstein, N. D. (1989). Optimistic biases about personal risks. *Science, 246*, 1232–1233.

Weisberg, D. S., Keil, F. C., Goodstein, J., Rawson, E., & Gray, J. R. (2008). The seductive allure of neuroscience explanations. *Journal of Cognitive Neuroscience, 20*, 470–477.

Weiss, R. (2017). Nip misinformation in the bud. *Science, 358*, 427.

Wellman, C. (1971). *Challenge and response: Justification in ethics*. Carbondale & Edwardsville, IL: Southern Illinois University Press.

Wells, G. L., Taylor, B. R., & Turtle, J. W. (1987). The undoing of scenarios. *Journal of Personality and Social Psychology, 53*, 421–430.

Wertz, S. K. (1985). When affirming the consequent is valid. *International Logic Review, 31*, 17–18.

Wetherick, N. E. (1993). Human rationality. In K. I. Manktelow & D. E. Over (Eds.), *Rationality: Psychological and philosophical perspectives* (pp. 83–109). London: Routledge.

Wetherick, N. E., & Gilhooly, K. (1990). The figural effect in syllogistic reasoning. In K. Gilhooly, M. T. G. Keane, R. Logie, & G. Erdos (Eds.), *Lines of thought: Reflections on the psychology of thinking*, Vol. 1. London: Wiley.

Whately, R. (1995). Of fallacies. In H. V. Hansen & R. C. Pinto (Eds.), *Fallacies: Classical and contemporary readings* (pp. 67–94). University Park, PA: The Pennsylvania State University Press. (Originally published in 1853.)

Whitaker, J. O. (1965). Sex differences and susceptibility to interpersonal persuasion. *Journal of Social Psychology, 66*, 91–05.

Whitaker, J. O., & Meade, R. D. (1967). Sex of communicator as a variable in source credibility. *Journal of Social Psychology, 72*, 27–34.

White, W. S. (2003). *Miranda's waning protections: Police interrogation practices after Dickerson*. Ann Arbor, MI: University of Michigan Press.

Whitehead, A. N. (1956). Mathematics as an element in the history of thought. In J. R. Newman (Ed.), *The world of mathematics*, Vol. 1, (pp. 402–416). New York: Simon & Schuster. (Originally published in 1925.)

Whitehead, A. N. (1994). Religion and science. In M. Gardner (Ed.), *Great essays in science* (pp. 216–228). New York: Prometheus Books. (Originally published in 1967.)

Whewell, W. (1858). *The history of scientific ideas*. London: John Parker & Son.

Wildman, T. M., & Fletcher, H. J. (1977). Developmental increases and decreases in solutions of conditional syllogism problems. *Developmental Psychology, 13*, 630–636.

Wilkins, M. C. (1928). The effect of changed material on ability to do formal syllogistic reasoning. *Archives of Psychology, 16*, 83.

Willard, C. A. (1995). Failures of relevance: A rhetorical view. In H. V. Hansen & R. C. Pinto (Eds.), *Fallacies: Classical and contemporary readings* (pp. 145–158). University Park, PA: The Pennsylvania State University Press.

Williams, A. D. (1992). Bias and debiasing techniques in forensic psychology. *American Journal of Forensic Psychology, 103*, 19–26.

Wilson, E. O. (1978). *On human nature*. Cambridge, MA: Harvard University Press.

Wilson, E. O. (1999). *Consilience: The unity of knowledge*. New York: Vintage Books.

Wilson, T. D., Wheatley, T., Myers, J. M., Gilbert, D. T., & Axsom, D. (2000). Focalism: A source of durability bias in affective forecasting. *Journal of Personality and Social Psychology, 78*, 821–836.

Wisdom, J., & Barker, S. F. (1991). *Proof and explanation: The Virginia lectures by John Wisdom*. Lanham, MD: University Press of America. (Lectures given in 1957.)

Witkin, H. A., Lewis, A. B., Hertzman, M. et al. (1954). *Personality through perception: An experimental and clinical study*. New York: Harper.

Wittgenstein, L. (1972). *On certainty*. Edited by G. E. M. Anscombe & G. H. von Wright, translated by D. Paul & G. E. M. Anscombe. New York: Harper Torchbooks. (Originally published in 1950.)

Wixon, D. R., & Laird, J. D. (1976). Awareness and attitude change in the forced-compliance paradigm: The importance of when. *Journal of Personality and Social Psychology, 34*, 376–384.

Wolfe, C. R., & Britt, M. A. (2005). The use of other-side information: Explaining the myside bias in argumentation. *Paper presented at the 46th annual meeting of the Psychonomic Society*, Toronto, Canada.

Wolfe, C. R., & Britt, M. A. (2008). The locus of myside bias in written argumentation. *Thinking and Reasoning, 14*, 1–27.

Wood, G. (1978). The knew-it-all-along effect. *Journal of Experimental Psychology: Human Perception and Performance, 4*, 345–353.

Woods, J. (1995a). Appeal to force. In H. V. Hansen & R. C. Pinto (Eds.), *Fallacies: Classical and contemporary readings* (pp. 240–250). University Park, PA: The Pennsylvania State University Press.

Woods, J. (1995b). Fearful symmetry. In H. V. Hansen & R. C. Pinto (Eds.), *Fallacies: Classical and contemporary readings* (pp. 181–193). University Park, PA: The Pennsylvania State University Press.

Woods, J., & Walton, D. (1979). What type of argument is an ad verecundiam? *Informal Logic Newsletter*, *2*, 5–6.

Woodworth, R. S., & Sells, S. B. (1935). An atmosphere effect in formal syllogistic reasoning. *Journal of Experimental Psychology*, *18*, 451–460.

Wreen, M. (1986). When no reason is good reason. In F. H. van Eemeren, R. Grootendorst, J. A. Blair, & C. A. Willard (Eds.), *Argumentation: Analysis and practices* (pp. 56–64). Dordrecht, Holland: Foris Publications.

Wright, R. (April, 1988a). Did the universe just happen? *Atlantic Monthly*, *261*, 29–45.

Wright, R. (1988b). *Three scientists and their gods: Looking for meaning in an age of information*. New York: Times Books.

Wright, R. H., & Cummings, N. A. (Eds.) (2005). *Destructive trends in mental health: The well-intentioned path to harm*. New York: Routledge.

Wright, W. F., & Bower, G. H. (1992). Mood effects on subjective probability assessment. *Organizational Behavior and Human Decision Processes*, *52*, 276–291.

Wu, C., & Shaffer, D. R. (1987). Susceptibility to persuasive appeals as a function of source credibility and prior experience with the attitude object. *Journal of Personality and Social Psychology*, *52*, 677–688.

Wyer, R. S., & Frey, D. (1983). The effects about self and others on the recall and judgments of feedback-relevant information. *Journal of Experimental Social Psychology*, *19*, 540–559.

Wyer, R. S., & Srull, T. K. (1989). *Memory and cognition in its social context*. Hillsdale, NJ: Erlbaum.

Wylie, R. C. (1979). *The self-concept (Vol. 2): Theory and research on selected topics*. Lincoln, NE: University of Nebraska Press.

Xie, Y. (2017). Conductive argument as a mode of strategic maneuvering. *Informal Logic*, *37*, 2–22.

Xu, X., Arpan, L. M., & Chen, C-f. (2015). The moderating role of individual differences in responses to benefit and temporal framing of messages promoting residential energy saving. *Journal of Environmental Psychology*, *44*, 95–108.

Yama, H., Manktelow, K. I., Mercier, H. et al. (2010). A cross-cultural study of hindsight bias and conditional probabilistic reasoning. *Thinking and Reasoning*, *16*, 346–371.

Yamagishi, K. (1997). When a 12.86% mortality is more dangerous than 24.14%: Implications for risk communication. *Applied Cognitive Psychology*, *11*, 495–506.

Yaniv, I., & Kleinberger, E. (2000). Advice taking in decision making: Egocentric discounting and reputation formation. *Organizational Behavior and Human Decision Processes*, *83*, 260–281.

Yarmey, A. D. (1984). Age as a factor in eyewitness memory. In G. L. Wells & E. F. Loftus (Eds.), *Eyewitness testimony: Psychological perspectives* (pp. 142–154). New York: Cambridge University Press.

Yarmey, A. D., & Jones, H. P. T. (1983). Is the study of eyewitness identification a matter of common sense? In S. Lloyd-Bostock & B. R. Clifford (Eds.), *Evaluating witness evidence*. Chichester: Wiley.

Zabell, S. L. (1992). The quest for randomness and its statistical applications. In F. S. Gordon & S. P. Gordon (Eds.), *Statistics for the twenty-first century* (pp. 139–150). Washington, DC: Mathematical Association of America.

Zakay, D. (1983). The relationship between the probability assessor and the outcome of an event as a determiner of subjective probability. *Acta Psychologica, 53*, 271–280.

Zakay, D. (1984). The influence of perceived event's controllability on its subjective occurrence probability. *The Psychological Record, 34*, 233–240.

Zappel, K. (1986). Argumentation and literary text: Towards an operational model. In F. H. van Eemeren, R. Grootendorst, J. A. Blair, & C. A. Willard (Eds.), *Argumentation: Analysis and practices* (pp. 217–224). Dordrecht, Holland: Foris Publications.

Zeleny, L. D. (1940). Experimental appraisal of a group learning plan. *Journal of Educational Research, 34*, 37–42.

Zhao, J., & Osherson, D. (2010). Updating beliefs in light of uncertain evidence: Descriptive assessment of Jefferey's rule. *Thinking and Reasoning, 16*, 288–307.

Zimbardo, P. G., Johnson, R. L., & McCann, V. (2006). *Psychology: Core concepts*. Boston, MA: Pearson.

Zuckerman, M. (1979) Attribution of success and failure revisited, or: The motivational bias is alive and well in attribution theory. *Journal of Personality, 47*, 245–287.

Zur, O. (2005). The psychology of victimhood. In R. H. Wright, & N. A. Cummings (Eds.), *Destructive trends in mental health: The well-intentioned path to harm* (pp. 45–64). New York: Routledge.

Name Index

General Index

CPSIA information can be obtained
at www.ICGtesting.com
Printed in the USA
LVHW051722121220
674041LV00009B/188

9 781108 799874